NAVIGATING
GRIEF

NAVIGATING GRIEF

*finding strength for today
and hope for tomorrow*

Kirk H. Neely

© 2007 by Kirk H. Neely

Published by Revell
a division of Baker Publishing Group
PO Box 6287, Grand Rapids, MI 49516-6287
www.revellbooks.com

Spire edition published 2021
ISBN 978-0-8007-4046-7
eISBN 978-1-4934-3367-4

Previously published in 2007 under the title *When Grief Comes*

Printed in the United States of America

21 22 23 24 25 26 27   7 6 5 4 3 2 1

To Clare . . .

my wife,
the love of my life,
my best friend,
my companion in all things,
including joy and sorrow.

Contents

Acknowledgments

I am grateful

to the congregation of Morningside Baptist Church
for the privilege of being their pastor and for their
understanding that writing is a part of ministry,

to Kathy Green, who is simply the best secretary ever,

to Vicki Crumpton, Paul Brinkerhoff, and the excellent
staff at Baker Publishing Group whose skill has ushered this project along to completion,

to Janet Thoma, editor and agent, whose guidance and
collaboration made this book possible,

to Theron Price, who first saw the pastor in me,

to Carlyle Marney, mentor and role model, who helped
me see teaching, preaching, and writing as essen-
tially the same,

to Wayne E. Oates, teacher and mentor, who taught me
about grief and encouraged me to write,

to Mama and Dad, and

to Clare, more than anyone.

11

To the Reader

As much as I enjoy reading, I understand how difficult it is to read and cry at the same time. I found that when I wrote these pages, I had to give myself a break. Whether reading or writing, we can only dwell on grief and sorrow, death and dying, for a time, and then we need relief.

Please, be gentle with yourself. I want these pages to be a blessing to you, not a burden. You don't ever have to finish this book. It is written so that you can read a little, and stop, and then come back later. I have tried to write remembering how difficult it is to read when your heart is broken and your eyes are blurred with tears.

The book has several features that will help you take shortcuts through the deep forest of understanding your grief:

- The detailed table of contents will help you quickly find sections that are better suited to your grief at various points in your walk through bereavement.
- A list of comforting Scriptures is included to help you quickly access passages that may help.

- Though there are many books on grief, I have included a brief annotated list of a few that I have found especially helpful.

There are some things I cannot provide for you that will help. You will need to supply these things yourself as you read these pages:

- Something soothing to drink. Choose whatever is calming to you.
- A little comfort food. Chocolate seems to help many people.
- A sense of humor. If all you do is cry, this journey becomes very tedious.
- A box of tissues. If you need permission to cry, remember the shortest verse in the Bible, "Jesus wept."

Maybe you have heard the quip, "I was feeling despondent and someone said, 'Cheer up, things could be worse.' So, I cheered up, and sure enough, things got worse."

This is not intended to be a cheer-up book. Those usually make us feel worse, not better, when we are grieving.

Rather, this is a book of encouragement. I have been through deep sorrow. I have experienced the faithful, tender healing of God. I have every confidence that God will be with you as God has been with me.

I know that there are times when a grief-stricken soul is unable to pray. We may feel that God is absent, that he has abandoned us. I have learned that in those times, it is helpful if someone prays for us. My prayer for you is that the God of all comfort will bind up your broken heart and strengthen you with his grace.

Faithfully,
Kirk H. Neely

Acquainted with Grief

My grandfather died the year I graduated from high school. That summer, before I left for college, I had the opportunity to go on a mission trip to Southern Rhodesia, now known as Zimbabwe. My aunt and uncle were missionaries in this country. My trip lasted almost two months. While I was away, my grandfather, whom I called Pappy, suffered his second heart attack. My dad said, trying to soften the news, "He's got a bad ticker."

Pappy had always been my fishing companion, but there was no fishing that summer; only talk of fishing. There was no freshly caught fried fish with hush puppies; only broiled or baked store-bought fish. There was no fried chicken for Sunday dinner, and there were no sardines and pickled pigs' feet for Sunday supper; just a little sharp cheese, crackers, and buttermilk. Pappy's diet was severely restricted.

Mammy, my grandmother, suffered from asthma and arthritis. She took several pills every day for both ailments. She did everything she could to stave off an asthma attack, including keeping a tank of oxygen at her bedside.

One night after I was back from Africa, just before my eighteenth birthday, Mammy called me on the telephone. She thought a thunderstorm was coming, and she wanted me to lower the bedroom windows for her. I went to my grandparents' house immediately. The windows were already down. Pappy was breathing oxygen from Mammy's oxygen tank. I knew instantly that something was terribly wrong.

"Pappy, are you OK?" I asked.

"Kirk, every tooth in my head hurts."

I noticed his teeth, both upper and lower, were in the glass on the nightstand, as usual.

"Pappy, we need to call Dr. Burgess."

"No! Call Ed Brown."

"Pappy, Dr. Brown is a veterinarian."

"I know it. He doesn't have to ask his patients where it hurts."

I called Dr. Burgess, a heart specialist, anyway, and he sent an ambulance. Then I called my dad. Pappy was having his third heart attack. As well as I remember, my aunt Ann came to stay with Mammy.

The ambulance took Pappy to the emergency room. Dad and I rode together to the hospital. By the time we got there, four of my uncles were already at Pappy's side. Uncle Bill, the technical one in the family, was trying to regulate Pappy's oxygen. Pappy was gasping for air. He kept repeating, "Turn it up, Bill. I can't breathe." We could all hear the hiss of the oxygen now turned to maximum volume.

Finally, Uncle Wesley ducked under the bed to follow the oxygen tube. "No wonder!" he said. "The tube is not even connected!" Uncle Bill made the correction.

Pappy, now able to breathe better, muttered under his labored breath, "That's what they call a placebo."

Pappy was in the hospital for more than a month. His heart was severely damaged by the third attack. One of the uncles drove Mammy to the hospital each day. Another uncle would stay through the night. I was working at the lumberyard at the time. So, after the first few days, I volunteered to stay at night. In those last few weeks before entering college, I received an education in death and dying, life and the life beyond.

Pappy synchronized his internal clock to mine. Each day after I finished working at the lumberyard, I went home for supper, a nap, and a shower. I arrived at the hospital about ten o'clock at night. Pappy would sleep as much as a hospital allows during the day, and talk to me for several hours each night. Always a man of few words, he talked more those nights than usual. We reminisced about many things, especially fishing. We told stories back and forth as if volleying in a game of ping-pong.

Pappy knew he was dying. I was afraid he might be dying. We faced his death together.

In those long night hours, my grandfather told me about his own grief. When Pappy was only fourteen, his father died in a railroading accident. At the age of eighteen, Pappy lost his own grandfather who died after an extended illness.

Pappy said, "Kirk, we all come to this. Dying is just another part of life. We don't have to be afraid, because after the dying, there is a whole lot more living, better living than we've ever known."

"My time is short," Pappy said. "This part of life isn't so bad as long as you're ready for the next."

The night before I left home to enroll as a freshman at Furman University in Greenville, South Carolina, I stayed with Pappy. We both slept a little. He was a whole lot weaker. We told a few stories, and we prayed together. I prayed for him, and he prayed for me, reaching out and placing his strong, good hand on my hand, beseeching God to bless me. We hugged. "I love you, Pappy," I said, fighting back the tears. "And I love you," he said. I cried all the way home. It was the last time I saw him alive.

I had been at Furman only three weeks when the call came on a Monday night. Pappy had died. Mama and Dad were coming to get me. I cried a little. When we arrived at Mammy and Pappy's house, all of the family was there. The uncles told me the story.

After I left for Furman, Pappy insisted that Dr. Burgess let him go home from the hospital.

"I've got to get out of here," he said.

"What's your rush, Mr. Neely?" Dr. Burgess asked.

"More people die in the hospital than anywhere else. It's not a safe place to be. I'm going home."

Pappy was back at his home for only a few days. As the end drew near, the family was called in. Surrounded by his children, Pappy said, "Help me sit up." His sons lifted him. Pappy spoke the words of a favorite hymn, "Just as I Am." And he went home, home to heaven.

My grandfather, more than any other person, taught me that Christians need not be afraid of death. He taught me that death and dying are normal stages in human life. Discussing death with those you love is not to be avoided; it is to be welcomed. My grandfather taught me that grief is a part of the journey, an experience that sooner or later comes to us all.

Five years later, I entered divinity school. My teacher and mentor in the early days of my pastoral vocation was Dr. Wayne E. Oates, a professor of pastoral care and counseling at the Southern Baptist Theological Seminary in Louisville, Kentucky. I was attracted to him because he combined elements of Christian wisdom, a pastoral identity, a compassionate heart, and common sense. He was a witty and intelligent scholar whose teaching was rooted and grounded in real-life experience. He taught me not only to read the printed page but also to read the "tablets of human hearts," a phrase Dr. Oates adopted from the apostle Paul (2 Cor. 3:3). While I have learned much about bereavement from extensive reading, I have learned so much more from my personal encounters with grieving people during more than forty years of pastoral ministry.

Dr. Oates introduced me to the definitive research on the grief process in the work of Erich Lindemann, a psychiatrist. Dr. Lindemann coordinated the care of the relatives and friends of the 493 people, most of them young adults, who died in a fire at the Coconut Grove nightclub in Boston in 1942. These bereaved people came to Massachusetts General Hospital, which became a makeshift morgue, to identify their deceased loved ones. The hospital staff responded to the overwhelming sorrow by assigning a caring person— clergy, nurses, or social workers—to each of the families of the dead. Dr. Lindemann's personal conversations with these bereaved friends and relatives led to a paper that became a basis that furthered my understanding of grief: Erich Lindemann, "Symptomology and Management of Acute Grief," *American Journal of Psychiatry* (September 1944). Learning about the grief process was another step in my developing awareness that in grief we all share a common journey.

It has been many years since my grandfather died. Much of that time I have spent in pastoral ministry. I have served in a variety of positions as a hospital chaplain, a chaplain in an institution for juvenile delinquents, a pastoral counselor, and a parish pastor.

Through the years, I have remembered that grief is a part of the Christian pilgrimage. Sooner or later, our journey must go through the valley of the shadow of death. On this journey, we are fellow pilgrims. Often, we are able to share the load of sorrow with our fellow travelers, bearing one another's burdens as we go.

This book is written out of both pastoral and personal experience. The content has developed through teaching grief seminars, leading small support groups, and counseling individuals and families. The seven chapters of the book are arranged in three parts.

Part 1 will help us understand our journey through grief and how we come to terms with death. Sometimes death comes as a harsh intruder, sudden and shocking. At other times death is anticipated and comes as a gentle blessing following an extended illness. In both instances we share the common experience of grief that can be traced through predictable stages and expected phases.

Part 2 shows how we learn to grieve through a continuing series of attachments and separations. Events as diverse as the death of a pet, a broken courtship, and the death of a peer are grief experiences in childhood and adolescence. In adulthood the marriage of a child or the dependence of a parent are experiences of grief. This section concludes with the task of helping children with grief because adults in grief often must also help their children walk the same path. Part 3 points us to the gifts of grace and the symbols of hope that are ours through the faithfulness of God.

I am indebted to all of those who have walked this road with me—all of the families with whom I have waited for death to arrive and all those who have stood with me under a funeral tent, erected over an open grave as we said good-bye.

Many of the illustrations in these pages come out of my own family experiences. As the oldest of eight children and second oldest of thirty-six grandchildren, I have learned that people in large families attend a lot of funerals. I have conducted funerals for aunts and uncles, nieces and nephews, and several in-laws. In just a period of several months, I was a participating pastor in funeral services for my wife's mother, for our twenty-seven-year-old son, and for my mother. I write as a pastor who is also a fellow pilgrim in the journey through grief.

The prophet Isaiah writes of a Messiah who is to come. He was "a man of sorrows, and acquainted with grief." The prophet assures us that "surely he hath borne our griefs, and carried our sorrows" (Isa. 53:3–4 KJV). Jesus Christ is the fulfillment of Isaiah's prophecies. The Scriptures tell us that he wept over the city of Jerusalem. He wept at the grave of his friend Lazarus.

I have learned that we are never alone in our experiences of sorrow and loss. Not only are we in the company of fellow travelers through this valley of the shadow of death, but we are also accompanied by the Good Shepherd. Just as our Lord's companionship brings comfort to our grieving souls, so those of us who are acquainted with grief become comforters to those who are experiencing loss for the first time. It is my hope and prayer that when grief comes into your life, this book will bring to you strength for today and hope for tomorrow, and that you will be able to share those same gifts with others.

PART ONE

1

Our Journey through Sorrow

the grief process following sudden death

Our son Erik was a shoe-leather reporter. Rather than sitting at his desk, gathering details for his stories over the telephone, he preferred to go to the story. In his first newspaper job after college, he spent several weeks on the street, working especially at night, among homeless people. With his good friend and photographer Thomas, Erik published a series of stories that raised the consciousness of the community of Spartanburg, South Carolina, regarding the problem of homelessness.

When the Charleston *Post and Courier* hired Erik to cover the North Charleston area, Erik and his wife, June, moved to Charleston, South Carolina. The assignment—reporting on the Goose Creek City Council or the Berkley County School Board—was not appealing to a young reporter whose bent was to write human interest, feature stories. Erik viewed covering city council and school board meetings as paying the rent. "It gives me an office and a laptop so I can also do what I really enjoy," he said.

When he was hired, Erik asked if he could take Monday as his day off and work every Saturday. His editor was delighted to grant the request, since most reporters want the weekends off. Erik's willingness to work on Saturday gained him instant favor with most of the *Post and Courier* staff. There was one provision: He would have to drive into Charleston on Saturdays and work out of the main downtown office. It was like throwing Br'er Rabbit into the Briar Patch. Downtown Charleston was just where Erik wanted to be.

Right after this occurred, Erik telephoned me to share his excitement with his Saturday assignment. "Dad, I just need one big story, a story that will make the front page of Sunday's paper." It took only two weeks for him to find and write the big story. A ship with a Ukrainian crew was stranded in Charleston Harbor. They had been abandoned by the captain. The sailors had not been paid, and their supplies were dwindling. When Erik heard the story, he requested aid for the crew from Samaritan's Purse, a Christian relief organization. That Saturday afternoon the group sent a small boat with food, fresh water, and medical supplies out to the stranded ship. Erik rode on the boat. He interviewed the sailors, took photographs, and wrote the article. The story appeared on the front page of Sunday's newspaper. Erik had found his niche in his new community.

My wife, Clare, and I found special joy in our son's success. He had been diagnosed with epilepsy when he was six years old, about two weeks after he had chicken pox. As he entered adolescence his seizures had gotten progressively worse. Yet he had never allowed his disorder to hold him back. He had earned the Eagle Scout Award and attended three National Boy Scout Jamborees. In high school he played offensive lineman on the football team and was named scholar-athlete of the year in South Carolina. Erik also played football at Furman University for one year until he grew weary of too many leg and ankle injuries. When he left football, he took up journalism.

Clare and I avidly followed his career in Charleston. We subscribed to the Sunday edition of the *Post and Courier* and looked for Erik's byline. After a year or so in North Charleston, the newspaper moved him to the main office. He was assigned to the cop's beat, reporting on police activity in the greater Charleston area.

On the night of November 14, 2000, Erik called just before midnight. He had been working on the tragic story of a mother in the Charleston area who had killed two of her three children three days earlier. The woman said that God had told her to sacrifice her children. Erik had been to the school the children attended to interview teachers, counselors, and students. On the day of his call to me, he had spent several hours with the grandmother of the deceased children, the mother of the woman accused of the murders.

In our conversation that Tuesday evening, Erik said, "This is more than just a cop's story. This is a story about religion gone wrong." His empathy for the grandmother, the mother, the surviving child, and so many others involved in the tragedy struck me as uncommon. He wanted my input on the pathology of religious experience so he could write a story that would help the Charleston community try to make sense out of the nonsense. We talked for nearly forty-five minutes, concluding our conversation with our usual "I love you."

This was my final conversation with our son.

Early on Wednesday morning, his wife, June, called. "Please come as soon as you can. We have a bad problem.

EMS is here working with Erik. He is not breathing. I'll meet you at the hospital."

I made sure that June had our cell phone number and that we had hers. I called my brother-in-law Terry Wilson, who is chaplain at the Medical Center in Charleston. Then Clare and I left immediately for the two-hundred-mile drive from our home in Spartanburg, South Carolina, to Charleston.

For the next two or three hours, Clare and I prayed for Erik, for June, for the paramedics, for the physicians, for Terry. We talked of Erik and June. They had met at Furman. He graduated two years ahead of her. Their wedding following her graduation was a joyful celebration. Their love and their marriage was Erik's greatest joy.

Halfway through our drive to Charleston, June called my cell phone. She was with Terry in his office at the hospital. Erik was pronounced dead on arrival at the emergency room. Cause of death: an apparent seizure. It would be weeks before the autopsy report would confirm the coroner's initial report.

For the remainder of our trip, Clare and I prayed for June, for our other four children, for our extended family, for the church we serve, and for ourselves. We took turns crying, though I continued to drive. Clare remembered the Scripture verse that became our watchword: "The eternal God is your refuge, and underneath are the everlasting arms" (Deut. 33:27).

The Grief Process

With Erik's death came my time to walk a lonesome valley. I had been through valleys of grief before, but this one was deeper, longer, and darker than any other. It is a lonesome valley. As the Southern spiritual phrases it:

> You got to walk that lonesome valley.
> You got to walk it by yourself.
> Nobody else can walk it for you.
> You got to walk it by yourself.

In his book *Anxiety in Christian Experience*, Wayne Oates included a chapter entitled "The Anxiety of Grief," which outlined six stages of the grief process. I have used the knowledge of this process for over forty years of pastoral ministry. And as I moved through the six stages of grief after Erik's death, I learned that I was never alone.

Stage 1: Initial Shock

Blindsided. Slapped in the face. Doused with ice water. Hit by a train. Run over by an 18-wheeler. These are all ways that people have described the initial shock following news of a sudden death.

The night following Erik's death, Clare and I stayed with her brother and sister-in-law, Ben and Patricia. I will never forget Ben's first word to his grieving sister. As he hugged her, he simply said, "Bummer." Like my grandfather, Ben has always been a man of few words. At a time when others offered far too many words, Ben's one word was enduring comfort to his sister, Clare.

A minimum of words is best following the death of a loved one, particularly sudden death. Job's friends came to him in his sorrow. For seven days they sat with him in silence, just what Job needed. Then his friends started trying to explain the reason for his loss. In doing so they aggravated an already wounded soul.

People grieve in different ways. The disciple Thomas is often criticized for not being with the other disciples when the resurrected Jesus appeared to them in the Upper Room. Doubting Thomas, as he is labeled, was perhaps a man who preferred to grieve alone. As a twin, he had struggled to establish his individuality most of his life. In his bereavement following the death of Jesus, Thomas needed some time away from the crowd. I needed some time away as well.

At the time of Erik's death, Ben and Patricia lived on the Isle of Palms near Charleston. Early in the morning, long before daylight, I bundled up against the November chill and walked on the beach. The stars were bright in the morning sky. The lights of Charleston glowed in the distance. The silent rhythm of the Charleston Harbor lighthouse drew my attention, and I walked down the island toward the sweeping beam. The sound of the waves and the salt air invited me to weep. I sobbed as I have never sobbed before. I had mourned the loss of grandparents, aunts, uncles, in-laws, and our unborn children lost in miscarriage. Grief following those losses was like a tidal surge in a tropical storm compared to the tsunami of sorrow that swept over me the morning after Erik's death. David's words in Psalm 69 gave expression to my feelings:

> Save me, O God,
> > for the waters have come up to my neck.
> I sink in the miry depths,
> > where there is no foothold. . . .

Rescue me from the mire,
    do not let me sink; . . .
Do not let the floodwaters engulf me
    or the depths swallow me up.

                  verses 1–2, 14–15

People in shock need practical help. Our family and friends rallied around us. The evening before Erik's death was my dad's eightieth birthday. Clare and I had hosted a party for twenty-five people. As our guests left, I suggested that we leave the dirty dishes soaking in the sink overnight. Clare declined. She washed the dishes while I talked with Erik on the phone about the story he was working on. We continued talking while Clare vacuumed the carpet and tidied the house.

The next day, after June's call telling us of Erik's death, Clare commented through her tears, "Well, at least the house is clean."

Following the death of a loved one, particularly sudden death, the smallest blessings are welcomed. For the next three days, we were busy with arrangements in Charleston. Our home in Spartanburg was a hub of activity as our dear friends received food, flowers, phone calls, and visitors in our absence, carefully recording each act of kindness and maintaining order in the midst of chaos.

I found that soon after the initial shock of the death of a loved one, particularly a sudden death, we become numb.

Stage 2: Numbness

I have come to believe that numbness is one of the small tender mercies of God, an unexpected grace. To weep and to feel immobilized by the pain of sudden death is completely normal. We quite naturally recoil from the hurt, but the harsh truth is that difficult decisions must be made and unpleasant tasks have to be completed. In order to function, we need the anesthesia provided by God. This is God's way of allowing us to take the pain in small doses.

Once we are numb, others may marvel at our composure. "Isn't she taking it well?" or "He's just the rock of Gibraltar" are among the things people might say of us. The numbness is not our strength. It is God's gift. But this anesthesia is not complete. We still have episodes of uncontrolled emotion. When the tears flood our eyes, we need to let them flow. Struggling to hold ourselves together is not wise. The stress of grief can cause emotional and physical illness. Crying during grief is a tension outlet similar to the safety valve on a pressure cooker. Tears reduce the stress. We may be able to choose our times and a place to weep, but we need to allow ourselves the opportunity to cry in order to provide relief.

Once numbness sets in, some people have difficulty weeping at all. "I feel as if I have been wrapped in insulation," one woman said to me. "I can't feel what I should be feeling." In the same way that we do not need to force composure, we do not need to force our grieving.

Grief is an individual experience; every grieving person's emotions are different. Yet for all of us the process of grieving is like a river. We cannot push our grief and make it go faster. Attempts to dam our emotions up and hold them back are unwise. Eventually the dam will break, and the force of delayed grief may cause harm. Like a river, it is best to let our grief flow at its own pace.

Family members will find themselves taking turns breaking down. This, too, is helpful. We found it important to set aside one room in our home that was off-limits to all visitors during those days of heavy traffic from loving friends and caring church members. Providing a safe, private haven during those periods of intense grief allowed us to be genuine when we did meet and greet others.

Stage 3: The Struggle between Fantasy and Reality

About two weeks after Erik's death, I called the Charleston *Post and Courier*, the newspaper for which he wrote. I needed to make arrangements to pick up the personal belongings that were in his desk. Erik was a pack rat, so I knew there would be several boxes of accumulated items. I dialed the newspaper's telephone number, a fixture on our bulletin board for two years. The call was answered by voice mail, and the prerecorded message was Erik's voice.

I was stunned as I listened. "Hello. You have reached the desk of Erik Neely. I am either away from my desk or on another call. If you will leave your name, number, and a brief message, I'll get right back to you. If you need immediate assistance, dial zero for the operator. Thank you for calling."

I hung up the phone and wept. I thought, *Erik, you are away from your desk, but you are not going to get right back to me.*

It was a moment of truth, a moment of harsh reality.

A moment of fantasy occurred in the early spring following Erik's death when I spent one morning cleaning flower beds, preparing them for new plantings. The March sky was clear; the breeze was brisk. As I worked on my hands and knees clearing debris and pulling weeds, I thought I heard Erik's voice behind me calling, "Dad! Dad!"

I straightened quickly and turned around to see no one. I listened closely and again heard the sound, this time less distinct, less clear. Above my head the wind moved through the branches of a large, wild cherry tree. As I heard the sound a third time, I noticed two huge limbs of the tree rubbing against each other. The sound was no longer the voice of my son, but a naturally occurring sound of nature.

The process of grief involves a lengthy struggle between the fantasy that our loved one is still with us and the reality that he or she is gone. The experiences that I have described are not uncommon. Yet I have found bereaved people reluctant to talk about these episodes. They even wonder, *Am I going crazy?*

In grief following the death of a loved one, these experiences are simply a part of our recovery from loss. Newly bereaved marriage partners often sense the presence of their deceased spouses. Occasionally they will have conversations with them. Conscientious Christians may feel apologetic or ashamed of these occurrences, fearing that these experiences may border on the occult, as though they were communicating with the deceased.

Through my own grief and through the privilege of being a pastor to grieving people, I have come to understand these events as quite similar to the phantom pain suffered by amputees. Recovery from the loss of a limb includes the sensation of burning or itching in limbs that are no longer present. Amputees who have lost a leg will sometimes attempt to walk, forgetting that the leg is gone. In the same way, grief requires coming to grips with the reality of our loss. The circumstances of some grief experiences prolong the struggle between fantasy and reality.

A U.S. Marine fighter jet crashed in a wooded area in our county in the early 1980s. A worker at the Red Cross asked if I would conduct an early Sunday morning worship service at the crash site for the marines who had come to investigate the accident. I arrived to find a team of twenty young men and a seasoned colonel. Most of the marines had known the pilot personally and had volunteered for the assignment. Though they attempted to be stoic, they were clearly grieving.

Following the worship service, the colonel asked if I could return midweek to conduct a memorial service at the site. At the Thursday morning service, soldiers silently wept as we shared the comfort of Scripture together. "They that wait upon the LORD shall renew their strength; they shall mount up with wings as eagles" (Isa. 40:31 KJV).

As I was leaving, the colonel said, "Let me show you something." From a small canvas bag, he took a scrap of cloth that had been ripped from the pilot's flight suit by the force of the crash. It was the young marine's name strip. "This is the reason we came," the colonel said.

Then he explained: "In a crash like this there are almost never any physical remains. We search these craters for evidence about what caused the crash, but we also look for anything that will confirm the pilot's identity. It is difficult to estimate how important that is to the family in their sorrow. Just knowing beyond any doubt that it was their son, their husband, or their father helps them accept the loss."

The struggle between fantasy and reality is complicated when there are no physical remains. My wife, Clare, lost her grandfather in a house fire. You know the agony that is added to grief if you have lost a loved one in a similar way. Following the attack on the World Trade Center on September 11, 2001, firemen, policemen, and other officials searched the rubble and ashes to find any trace of those who had died. Though it was a grim duty, it was a way to help the bereaved.

Early in my ministry, a young man told me that he and his mother were having a very difficult time getting over his father's death. When I inquired about the way his father died, he said, "My dad was a steel worker in Pittsburgh. He fell into a vat of molten steel. Every time I drive under an overpass on the interstate, I look up at those big beams and wonder if that is where my dad's body is."

I remembered the Old Testament story of Abraham in the land of Canaan. He owned no land until Sarah died. Then, the aged patriarch insisted on buying a cave near Hebron as a place to bury his wife's body.

I learned that the young man's father had purchased two cemetery plots just a year before his death. I suggested that the young man and his mother have a private committal service at the cemetery, burying some of his dad's personal items in the plot. They did exactly that and marked the grave. Simply having a designated place gave them an opportunity to better face the reality of death.

Humor is sometimes a part of this struggle between fantasy and reality. One woman told me that early morning was one of the most difficult times of the day for her following the loss of her husband of fifty-two years. Her husband woke up early each morning, started the coffeemaker, and took his shower. She missed the aroma of coffee and the sound of the shower when she woke up each day.

One morning, several months after her husband's sudden death, she awoke to the pleasant fragrance of coffee, and she heard the shower running. She even thought she heard her husband whistling in the shower, as he so often did. She ran to the guest bathroom, which was filled with steam, and pulled back the shower curtain—much to the chagrin of her startled son. She had forgotten that her adult son had telephoned the day before to say that he was coming to town but would arrive late. He had let himself in without disturbing his mom. Over the years, he had developed the same morning routine as his dad. The moment of surprise was a moment of reality for both of them, one they would laugh about many times over.

I am convinced that God's grace allows us to come to terms with our loss in small doses. The struggle between fantasy and reality is the most extended stage of the grief process following the sudden death of a loved one. It takes time for us to fully accept our loss. Birthdays, anniversaries, Father's Day, Mother's Day, and other holidays may be encounters with reality.

Be gentle with yourself. Remember, grief is like a river. Let it flow at its own pace. The first year is especially difficult, but do not expect grief to end simply because you pass the one-year milestone. Every time you absorb more of the truth of your loss you come closer to recovery from grief.

But you must remember that a flood of grief can happen at unexpected moments, sometimes months or even years after the loved one's death.

Stage 4: The Flood of Grief

Erik was a large young man. He stood six feet two inches tall and weighed 250 pounds. Erik's widow wanted his clothes to be put to good use. In the months after his death, she gradually dispersed items from his closet in various ways. But she kept for herself the clothes he wore the day before he died.

Erik enjoyed wearing brightly colored neckties, a trait that was well known to family and friends. For Christmas, just six weeks following his death, June gave his ties to those who could enjoy them with fond memories.

My mother asked for two of his shirts and two pairs of pants. We all thought the request odd. When Christmas came, at our family celebration, she presented Erik's wife, mother, and sister—June, Clare, and Betsy—teddy bears wearing overalls. Erik's cousin Casey had made the bears from Erik's khaki pants and fashioned the overalls from his shirts.

After living in Charleston for seven months following Erik's death, June decided to move back to her hometown, Nashville, Tennessee. Saying good-bye to Charleston was an important part of June's grief process. She returned to live in the place where her mother and grandmother were close by. These women, both single, were, and continue to be, strong, loving role models of comfort for June.

Shortly before June left for Nashville, she brought the last of Erik's clothes to our home. I carried the two large boxes into our living room, and we all looked through them together. On top was a very nice black cashmere overcoat that June had given Erik for their last Christmas together. She wanted me to have it. I wear it on cold days and especially on winter days when I have a funeral to conduct. The warmth of the coat is comforting, not only against the cold. Wearing the coat feels a little like a bear hug from Erik.

As we went through the other clothes, the item in the bottom of the box startled me: Erik's high school letter jacket.

When I saw it, I burst into tears. The depth of grief I felt in that moment was overwhelming. I thought I had moved beyond that level of intense sorrow. Yet the sight of the letter jacket and a sudden avalanche of memories triggered a surprising flood of grief.

A flood of grief almost always marks grief following the death of a loved one, particularly a sudden death. Some months after the death of our loved ones, we sense that we are doing better. We have faced the shock and numbness and have struggled with the reality of death. Surely, we think, we are beyond the worst of the pain and sorrow. Yet months, even years later, a moment or series of events may cause a resurgence of grief.

For those who are grieving a death following an extended illness, the flood of grief may actually occur at the time of the funeral. As we will see in the next chapter, the grief process is initiated even before death when the death is anticipated.

My friends, Jan and Jack Byrd, the parents of three daughters, all named for birds, have also experienced such a flood of grief. Wren, the oldest, actually was given her mother's maiden name. The two youngest, Robyn and Lark, were named as children born in the sixties were often named: their names came out of the air. (Pun intended.) I once asked Jan and Jack what they would have named a son. Jay was the male name in reserve.

The second daughter, Robyn, was a senior at a college in Florida. She called home to Kentucky the first weekend in November to announce to her parents that she had received an engagement ring for her birthday. Robyn and her fiancé, whom she had been dating for more than a year, planned to visit his family in Georgia on their way to Kentucky for Thanksgiving.

It was an exciting time for Jan and Jack as they made preparations for Thanksgiving Day and a party on the following Saturday to announce the engagement to family and friends.

On Wednesday night before Thanksgiving, a phone call came. Robyn was having dinner at the home of her future in-laws when she collapsed. She was rushed to the local hospital by ambulance. She died of a massive cerebral hemorrhage. The Byrd family was devastated. The festive mood of Thanksgiving evaporated into profound sorrow. Instead of an engagement party, the family had to plan a funeral for the Sunday afternoon after Thanksgiving.

As Jan and Jack struggled with their grief, their already stressed marriage fell apart. About two-thirds of the couples who suffer the loss of a child later dissolve their marriages. Though it is unwise to generalize, men and women do seem to grieve differently, which can lead to misunderstandings. Sometimes one partner will blame another for the death of the child. For the Byrds, Jack's attempt to drown his sorrow in alcohol was their undoing.

Jack and I lost touch with each other. As his attempt to escape with alcohol grew more desperate, he no longer wanted contact with me either as a friend or as a pastor. I continued to minister to Jan through a complicated and tragic time.

Though every day had its moments, Jan had several very difficult episodes: Mother's Day, the day Robyn would have graduated from college, the day the wedding was to have been, Robyn's birthday, and the Thanksgiving holiday one year after the death and the funeral. All in all, Jan moved through a difficult year rather well.

On Mother's Day, a year and a half after Robyn's death, Jan celebrated with Wren; Jeff, Wren's husband; a newly born grandchild; and Lark. She talked about the day and reported that she felt she was finally on the way to recovery.

Then, on a Saturday morning in late May, I answered the telephone. It was Jan. She was so distraught that she could hardly speak. Immediately Clare and I went to her home. Jan told her story. She and Lark had been watching a mother robin build a nest in a hedge near their driveway. The bird had laid three eggs. Jan and Lark watched as the fledglings hatched. On Saturday morning, Jan was going grocery shopping when she noticed that one of the little birds had fallen from the nest and was on the pavement. She carefully returned the bird to the nest, lifting it gently with a piece of cardboard. When she returned from the grocery store, the tiny fledgling was lying dead in the driveway. Jan started weeping uncontrollably.

"I feel so stupid!" she said. "Why am I crying over a silly bird?"

"Jan," I asked, "how many eggs did the mother bird lay?"

"Three."

"And how many babies does the mother bird have now?"

"Oh, I see!" she said, wiping her tears. "And the birds are robins."

The flood of grief almost always takes us by surprise. We are under the impression that our grief is just about over. We may even think that we have few tears left to be shed. Months, even years, after our loss there comes a moment or a series of events when the reality of our loss sinks in, and we pour out our hearts in a flood of grief.

Take courage! It is part of the process, and you are on your way to recovery.

Stage 5: Stabbing Memories

Sometimes memories stab like a knife to the heart. Even as we recover from grief, there are times when memories hurt. We may come across a photograph or an old letter that we had forgotten. Suddenly we feel the pain again. We may have moments of remorse, wishing we had said or not said something to the person before his or her death. Special places, special events, special songs may be the source of bittersweet memories. Even now, when I watch a football game on television or in person, I find myself paying close attention to the players on both teams who are wearing the number 67. Those players are almost always offensive line- men, and I usually have a tear in my eye.

Three years after Erik died, I met up with a couple I had not seen in several years. They have a daughter who had been in high school with Erik. As we talked the mother asked, "Tell me about Erik. How is he doing?"

"Erik is doing fine," I said. "He's the only child I have that I don't worry about. He went to heaven about three years ago."

The couple was taken aback. I reassured them. "Thank you for asking. We do not expect everyone to know about his death, and we are always glad to talk about our children." Then I asked about their children.

One of the most serious mistakes grieving people make is to refuse to speak about their loss. While the silence of would-be comforters is appropriate early in the grief process, as this river of bereavement flows those who are mourners need to be able to talk to close friends and relatives.

To assume that the mention of a deceased person's name is off-limits is usually incorrect. Some friends and family members may believe that talking about the loss will be too painful. The truth is that nothing in grief is unspeakable, though there will certainly be pain and tears.

Silence is never more deafening than it is in grief following suicide. When a person takes his or her own life, neither the mourners nor the comforters have words adequate to make sense out of death that seems so senseless. Bereavement following suicide is often called the grief that never ends. It is complicated by a multitude of questions without answers, as well as by remorse, regret, and anger.

If you are grieving the loss of a loved one by suicide, you will find several helpful books that will guide you through the particular difficulties of your sorrow. David Cox and Candy Arrington's book, *Aftershock* (Nashville: Broadman & Holman, 2003), is an excellent resource.

Another source of help following suicide can be a support group. For example, our church sponsors a Survivors of Suicide ministry. Led by a well-trained pastoral counselor, it is a group for those who have experienced the death of a loved one by suicide.

At Erik's funeral our good friend and colleague Bob Morgan encouraged us to have an old-fashioned Irish wake. An integral part of the grieving process for family and friends, Irish wakes are occasions that combine joy and sadness. The life of the deceased is celebrated. Good food, music, and storytelling make the wake feel somewhat like a party. Though it is a time of sadness, the presence of friends and family makes it more bearable. There is laughter as well as tears as the deceased loved one is fondly remembered.

Though the apostle Paul was not Irish, his words set a pattern for remembering the deceased: "Whatever is true, whatever is noble, whatever is right, whatever is pure, whatever is lovely, whatever is admirable—if anything is excellent or praiseworthy—think about such things" (Phil. 4:8). I have learned that people enjoy remembering the good, the noble, and the humorous things about the person they loved. The more that bereaved people are able to talk, the less saintly the deceased becomes. This is a way of facing the reality of life, as well as the loss.

I have learned from Clare that joy and sorrow are not mutually exclusive. We have found a way to celebrate Erik's birthday and the anniversary of his death that is helpful to us. We do some of the things we know Erik would have enjoyed doing. We usually enjoy a meal together. We choose foods that Erik would have relished. We try to include as many of our dear ones as can be with us. We take a little time for Bob Morgan's recommended Irish wake.

Stage 6: Recovery

Recovery from grief does not mean that life goes on as if we never experienced the loss. In this final stage of the grief process, we find what many have termed "the new normal" for our lives. Recovery means that we learn to live life with the loss, just as Wayne Hyatt did.

Wayne is an inspiration to all who know him. When Wayne was a freshman in college, a boating accident mangled his right leg. Surgeons had no choice but to amputate his damaged leg at the hip. As a friend and pastor, I followed closely his long journey to recovery following his loss. Several years following the difficult process of physical therapy, Wayne met Diane, a physical therapist, who became his wife and the mother of their three beautiful daughters. His disability has never interfered with his ability. Since he lost his leg, Wayne has played first base on a church softball team, played in a volleyball league, and competed in a downhill skiing event. He is an avid outdoorsman. Wayne completed his undergraduate degree and responded to God's call to pastoral ministry, earning a master of divinity degree prior to his ordination. He later completed a doctor of ministry degree. Wayne has done well. His right leg is still missing. He still experiences occasional phantom pain. He still uses crutches, but he has found "the new normal" in his life.

People who have suffered orthopedic injuries can experience complete healing. But on cold, rainy days the injured joint or bone may still hurt. Healing from bereavement is much the same. Our life is reoriented. The loss is no longer central. We are able to resume life without the intense focus on our loss, which is so much a part of the grief process. For people who have lost a marriage partner, remarriage becomes a possibility.

The story of Naomi, Ruth, and Orpah is an account of three bereaved women. This mother-in-law and her two daughters-in-law experienced profound grief when the men of their lives died. Naomi lost her husband and both of her sons. Ruth and Orpah each lost their husband and their father-in-law. We can hardly fault Orpah for her quite natural decision to return to her family. Yet the remarkable story of Ruth and Naomi illustrates the importance of maintaining supportive relationships following shared grief. These two women not only survived their loss together, but they also experienced the joy of recovery together.

Clare and I cherish the relationship we continue to enjoy with our daughter-in-law June. Though she returned to her hometown of Nashville seven months after Erik's death, we have appreciated regular visits, letters, and phone calls. One of the things June and I share is our love for gardening. We have worked together on her flower beds in front of her beautiful Tennessee home.

One spring day as we planted lilies together she asked, "Papa Kirk, if I ever get married again and have children, will you be like a grandfather to them? Will you tell them stories and teach them to fish?" Nothing could please me more. June is not just our daughter-in-law; she is our daughter-in-love. For us, that will never change.

Maintaining personal relationships with family and friends is vital to healthy recovery from grief. Unfortunately some people choose a different path. They withdraw or avoid relationships during this difficult time. Yes, some of us need more private space than others, but we all need relationships to sustain us.

When the people we love choose isolation, there is little we can do but to wait, hope, and pray. Sometimes a low level of initiative is helpful. A card or a letter that does not require a response gives the same message every time a person reads it. This is one way of reaching out to those in isolation that allows them to decide when and if they want a closer relationship.

Here is a wise old saying I made up: Don't ever waste a good experience of suffering. An important aspect of our healing from grief is the discovery that we have the ability to help others. Job's friends did not know how to help, perhaps because they had not been stricken with grief such as Job suffered. His friends were most comforting when they said nothing. Sitting in silence for seven days was good, but trying to explain away Job's grief did not help.

You will notice that there are many well-meaning people who do not know what to do or say. Grieving people hear all of the tired clichés: "We just have to accept God's will." "We don't understand, but we must not question." "We all have a time to go." "At least we know where he is."

Those of us who are acquainted with grief can help those who do not know what to do or say. After Erik's death, I missed two Sundays in the pulpit of my church. After I returned I preached a series of sermons entitled "Can These Holidays Be Holy Days?" during the first three Sundays of Advent. I was as open as I knew how to be. I spoke about gentle touches, grace notes, and tender mercies.

On the first Sunday back, I noticed some members of the church avoiding me. I realized that I needed to help them. In the second sermon I said, "Please know that you don't have to say anything to us. Just give us a hug and pray for us." After the service it was as if we were receiving friends just as we had done before the funeral. Dear friends would say things like, "Thank you for telling me I don't have to say anything. I really didn't know what to say." Often grieving people have to help others know how to help.

Several years before Erik died, I did a funeral for a young man, a high school senior, who drowned. I did my best to minister to his parents, Randy and Susan, and their family. When we returned to our home from Charleston, the day before Erik's funeral, Randy came to see me. His visit was most helpful, not because of anything he said or did. I just knew he understood. There is a fellowship of suffering. The apostle Paul writes, "We can comfort those in any trouble with the same comfort we ourselves have received from God" (2 Cor. 1:4). Randy and I occasionally meet for breakfast and often invite other grieving dads to join us.

The New Testament asserts, "We do not . . . grieve as others do who have no hope" (1 Thess. 4:13 NRSV). Hope is difficult to define since, as the Scriptures put it, "hope that is seen is not hope" (Rom. 8:24). Nevertheless, hope is a first cousin to faith and love (1 Cor. 13:13).

Hope is certainly an important factor in our recovery from grief. The pages of the Bible teach us that hope is revealed to us symbolically. Symbols of hope are usually simple wonders of creation, gifts of grace from the Creator. For Elijah, signs of God's presence were a small cloud shaped like a hand and a still, small voice, a quiet whisper, a gentle breeze. For the early church, the waters of baptism, a cup, and bread were symbols of a new covenant with God. The final chapter in this book will consider more thoroughly symbols of hope that minister to our spirits. But one personal example may help here.

November in South Carolina is usually a mild month. Not until after Thanksgiving does the weather begin to really feel like winter. Erik died on November 15. The temperature in Charleston was warm. The day we returned from Charleston to our home in the upstate, the sky was bright and sunny. Sunday morning, the day of the funeral, dawned gray, cold, and damp. Temperatures continued to fall through the day. By the time we arrived at the church for the funeral, light snow was falling. When we went to the cemetery for the committal service, the ground was covered with snow.

Some of our friends expressed regret that the weather was inclement on the day of our son's service. In our imagination, we thought that Erik had put in a request to the Almighty. Something like, "Lord, you know this will be a hard day for my family. Could you do something to surprise them?"

We viewed the snow as a symbol of hope.

In my first sermon after Erik's death, I interpreted the snow as a gentle touch from God, a gift of grace in our grief, and a symbol of hope. Many of the Christmas cards and Christmas presents we received that year included a snow theme. As Christmas approached, we decided to decorate our Christmas tree only with snowflakes and snow orna- ments. Hand-cut snowflakes adorned our windows.

As spring approached the following year, Clare and I knew we needed a symbol of hope for the warmer months. God provided a sign of hope. In late February, I conducted a funeral for a church member in the same cemetery where Erik's grave is located. At the conclusion of the service, I stopped beside our son's newly placed tombstone. From a distance, I could see an Eastern bluebird perched atop Erik's gravestone. I called Clare on the cell phone just as the bird flew away. "I think I have found a new symbol for spring and summer," I said when she answered. "It's a bluebird that has just flown away."

"Just wait a minute or two. Maybe he will come back," Clare said.

Sure enough, the bluebird returned. He perched on Erik's marker and was joined by his bluebird mate. Two bluebirds on the marker gave us our new symbol of hope. Bluebird nesting boxes in our yard invite these lovely creatures to make their home near ours. Every spring since then we have enjoyed as many as three bluebird families as visitors to our yard.

Symbols of hope carry us through the grief process. They are reminders of God's promise, "I will never leave you nor forsake you" (Josh. 1:5; cf. Heb. 13:5).

Sometimes people will say, "I'm sorry you lost your son." More often than not, my answer is, "Erik is not lost. I know exactly where he is."

2

Anticipating Death

the phases of grief during extended illness

Sometimes death is sudden, entering our lives as a harsh intruder. Sometimes the end of life is anticipated, especially when it is accompanied by painful suffering. Then death may be a gentle blessing, and a welcomed visitor. Either way, the grief process is a predictable path we all follow on our journey through the valley of death's shadow. There are differences, to be sure, between grief following sudden death and anticipatory grief accompanying expected death. One difference is that in bereavement when death is anticipated, several stages of the grief process are completed before death occurs. Another is that anticipatory grief moves through six predictable phases that usually occur prior to the death. Both the dying person and his or her loved ones can experience these phases.

A helpful distinction is to remember that the stages of the grief process occur in sequential order. Imagine hiking on a mountain trail. When death comes, we descend into a dark valley. After death, particularly sudden death, we begin a long uphill climb. Eventually, we realize that we have reached a plateau, the path has become more level, walking is a little easier. More strenuous climbing is ahead, but for now we are able to breathe fresh air and have our strength renewed.

In anticipatory grief, the path is constantly uneven. While the phases are predictable, it is difficult to know what each day will bring. For example, a cancer patient receiving chemotherapy will have good days and bad days. With the good and bad, the emotions of the patient and the family ebb and flow. One day they are discouraged, the next they may be more hopeful, even denying the reality of impending death. The following day, they may return again to what John Bunyan called the Slough of Despond. The husband of a long-term cancer patient described the valley of despair this way: "I've been through this gully a hundred times in the last fourteen months. I know every stump and rock. I also know this is not the place to camp. There is no water and no rest. It's just a dry red-dirt hole."

This arduous journey is exhausting. When death comes, it often brings a welcomed relief. At that point much grieving has been completed, and finally the path reaches a plateau where weary souls find temporary rest.

Alzheimer's is a mean disease. In its early stages, Alzheimer's is sneaky and deceptive. It comes creeping along, stalking almost unnoticed into the life of a person we love. Like a giant constrictor, Alzheimer's coils around a beautiful and vibrant person, gradually tightening, squeezing, and crushing until all life is gone. The deadly grip of this disease does its damage before death actually occurs. As one grieving husband said to me, "I lost my wife three years ago. She just has not died yet."

Miz Lib was my mother-in-law. At her funeral I remarked, "It is a good thing I fell in love with Clare before I met her mom and dad, because if I had met her parents first, she might have thought I married her just to be near them." Miz Lib was a master gardener and an avid bird-watcher. She was a voracious reader and a connoisseur of the arts. Her biscuits and double fudge brownies would put Betty Crocker to shame.

When her husband, Mr. Jack as I called him, died of congestive heart failure, Miz Lib responded with her usual spunk. She became involved in a grief support group known as New Roads. She was elected to the board of the Methodist church where she was a member. She became a member of the beautification committee in the arts partnership in her town. She traded two older cars for one new car because, as she said, "I have a lot of traveling to do." Her traveling was mostly in the direction of her grandchildren. She stood on the sidelines, cheering at soccer games. She went to music recitals, school plays, and assorted church activities, sharing her life with our family. She walked three miles a day and created a walking club in her neighborhood. Miz Lib went to the beach each summer. She built sand castles and looked for seashells, thoroughly enjoying all of it.

When Miz Lib's health starting failing, we were saddened. At first, there were little things that eventually escalated into more severe problems. When her memory started failing, she was able to cover it well for a time. "I just have too much to remember," she said.

Then came the outbursts of anger. After one especially dramatic episode in which this sweet Methodist lady turned the air blue with profanity we had never heard before from her lips, I said to Clare, "Your mother had a secret life. She must have been a sailor, and we did not know it." There was just no good explanation for her deteriorating condition.

Miz Lib had a wonderful physician who went above and beyond the call of duty. He told us how difficult it is to diagnose these problems in elderly people. Perhaps there were ministrokes or some sort of general dementia, perhaps Alzheimer's. He was the one who told her she could no longer drive her car. A tantrum ensued. He was the one who told her she could no longer live alone. Again, she had a fit. This loving physician took as much of the heat as he could, sparing the family.

We were determined to keep Miz Lib in her own home as long as we could, and we were able to do that through the assistance of two loving women who cared for her around the clock. While this was quite expensive, we felt it would be best to keep things as stable as we could for the woman we loved so much. Finally, the day came when we knew Miz Lib would have to go to a nursing home.

The day we brought her the seventy-eight miles from her home to a nursing facility in our town, she was calm. We simply told her we were following doctor's orders. Her compliance was appreciated. We also realized much of her spunk was gone. Her health continued to deteriorate. Within a matter of months, she died. Sometimes, death comes as a harsh intruder. Sometimes, the end of life is a gentle blessing, and death is a welcomed visitor.

When death is anticipated, the end of life is frequently viewed as a blessing. Anticipatory grief moves through predictable phases. In her groundbreaking book *On Death and*

Dying (New York: Macmillan, 1969), Dr. Elisabeth Kübler-Ross identified five transition stages experienced by both a dying person and grieving family members. I prefer to think of these as phases because they do not necessarily occur in a predictable order. While the stages in the grief process (discussed in the previous chapter) follow one after another, bereaved people tend to move in and out of these phases as the grief of anticipated death progresses. I have added a sixth phase that usually concludes the process. In anticipatory grief, these phases usually occur prior to the death.

Phase 1: Denial

When people begin to have symptoms that might indicate a serious illness, they often put off going for medical attention. They will delay having prescribed tests. It is as if they do not want to know the truth. Sometimes, family members will discount their symptoms. They might say, "You must be tired," or "You have been working too hard." Multivitamins and homemade remedies are often suggested. When my mother's mother, Granny, was dying of renal failure, an uncle fixed her a milkshake and spiked it with bourbon. He was convinced that Granny just needed "a little stimulant," as he put it. Granny, who had been a teetotaler throughout her life, spewed the concoction back in his face.

Such denial is seen when a person is diagnosed with cancer.

A physician was looking at a chest X-ray with his patient. "This dark spot on your right lung looks suspicious," he said.

"It is okay, Doc," replied the patient. "I am a photographer. Let me take the X-ray to my darkroom, and I'll just touch it up."

Denial is our first reaction. If a physician orders a biopsy, our tendency is to avoid the *C* word. Rather than say the word *cancer*, we may ask for a second opinion. Second opinions are a good idea, but even when another physician confirms a life-threatening disease, our reaction may be denial. "Tell me it is not so."

Denial is helpful in two ways. It buffers the initial pain and prepares us to begin the long process of accepting the truth in small doses. People in denial express dismay at their circumstance. "I feel like I am in a bad dream. Surely I will wake up, and this will all be over." Once we start coming to terms with the reality of the illness, we are able to move beyond denial.

Phase 2: Anger

Family members who have experienced the early stages of a serious illness in a loved one may feel angry because medical help was refused, or they may feel guilty because they were not more insistent on medical examinations and care.

When death is anticipated, anger is a common and normal part of the process. Sometimes people have trouble identifying their emotion as anger. They may express a feeling of injustice. "This is not the way it is supposed to be." They may feel that life or God is being unfair to them and to the people they love.

This sense of anger and injustice occurs frequently in families of young people who are stricken with a terminal disease. Parents of a child with leukemia may express these strong emotions with questions such as, "Why my child? Why couldn't this disease strike somebody who is old and decrepit?"

Many a fist has been shaken at heaven for felt injustice. Dylan Thomas wrote, "Do not go gentle into that good night. / Rage, rage, against the dying of the light." Facing the reality of an impending death may bring about rage.

For devout Christians, these feelings of anger can be difficult. I often listen to people express their anger prefaced by words such as, "I know I should not question God but . . ." As our loving heavenly Father, God is big enough to handle our questions and accept our anger. Do not forget what Jesus said from the cross. He quoted from Psalm 22: "My God, my God, why have you forsaken me?" This is a vivid example of our Lord himself asking the kind of question many of us ask in the midst of suffering.

The soul of the psalmist overflows with questions and complaints like a clogged gutter spilling debris:

> I cried out to God for help;
>> I cried out to God to hear me.
> When I was in distress, I sought the Lord;
>> at night I stretched out untiring hands
>> and my soul refused to be comforted.
> I remembered you, O God, and I groaned;
>> I mused, and my spirit grew faint.
> You kept my eyes from closing;
>> I was too troubled to speak.
> I thought about the former days,
>> the years of long ago;
> I remembered my songs in the night.
>> My heart mused and my spirit inquired:
> "Will the Lord reject forever?
>> Will he never show his favor again?

> Has his unfailing love vanished forever?
>> Has his promise failed for all time?
> Has God forgotten to be merciful?
>> Has he in anger withheld his compassion?"
>
> Psalm 77:1–9

I count six questions in the last three verses. The biblical evidence is that when we are hurting, it is perfectly permissible to ask why. It is also quite probable that we will receive few, if any, satisfactory answers. The challenge for all of us is to move beyond the questions and seek the meaning in our grief.

Our anger may diminish, or it may persist for a long time. Some people are reluctant to relinquish their rage. They nurture it until it becomes bitterness. This reaction, while quite understandable, is somewhat like a pouting child who will not accept the truth that things are not always going to go his or her way. To hold on to anger until it becomes bitterness does not help. It only deepens our hurt and the hurt of others.

A person who is suffering a serious illness may also become enraged. In retrospect, I have been able to see the outburst of temper on the part of our Miz Lib in this light. I believe that she knew something was wrong. Her displays of anger, expressed to the people she loved most, were her attempts to keep from giving in to the illness she sensed but did not understand. When loved ones become angry, we respond to them the way we respond to a great white shark. We do not want to get too close because we do not want to get our heads bitten off. Avoidance on our part only compounds the problem. The sense of being abandoned creates a more desperate feeling of losing control and therefore more anger.

When anger subsides, we then enter a period of bargaining.

Phase 3: Bargaining

Christians usually believe in miracles. We know that God answers prayer. We remember stories from the Bible that assure us that Jesus can heal the sick and even restore life to those who have died. Our questions become, "Why should others be healed and not my loved one?" "How can Jesus, to whom I have been so faithful, fail me at a time like this?" It is important to remember that miracles do happen. God does do miraculous things, but not always. By definition, a miracle is something that happens out of the ordinary. Miracles are more unusual than they are usual.

An elegant woman, the wife of a prominent attorney, was diagnosed with leukemia. As her disease advanced, her husband commented on his prayers for her. Speaking as a lawyer would speak about a case he was about to lose, he said, "My prayers now are at the point of plea bargaining."

We have been taught that prayer changes things. It does. However, prayer most often changes us. Prayer is more likely to change our mind than to change God's mind. We might regard the prayer of Jesus in the Garden of Gethsemane as bargaining: "If it be possible, may this cup pass from me." That plea from our Lord is immediately followed by the prayer of surrender: "Yet not as I will, but as you will." Jesus's prayer on the Mount of Olives did not change God's mind. Instead, this was a prayer of confirmation insuring that the will of Jesus was conformed to the will of his Father.

As we read the New Testament, we see that Jesus routinely refused to perform miracles on demand. During his temptations in the wilderness, he decided that he would not be a spectacular Messiah, intent on pleasing the crowd. Instead, the examples we have of his healing ministry are always connected to spiritual growth in others, such as the encounter by the Sheep Gate in Jerusalem, recorded in John 5.

A man had been paralyzed for thirty-eight years. The Scripture records that as Jesus entered the city, he saw crowds of people gathered around the pool of Bethesda. All of them were sick, and all were waiting for a miracle. When an angel stirred the water in the pool, the first person into the water would be healed. Jesus went to the paralyzed man, who was one among many, and asked, "Do you want to get well?" Even though the man made excuses and there was no expression of faith on his part, Jesus healed him.

I can imagine others in the crowd of people shouting, "Hey, how about me? I want to be healed!" Only one was healed. When we have suffered or our loved one has suffered, and we know that others have been healed, we wonder, *Why them? Why not me or my loved one?* Christians who have grown to maturity in the life of prayer understand that prayer is far more than just making requests. Prayer is a relationship, our heart's desire for closeness with our heavenly Father. When we pray, we do not always get what we want. However, I believe we always receive what we need.

Yet the temptation to bargain with God is very real. I ministered to a woman who had recurring cancer and was perhaps the best bargainer I have yet encountered. She got through her denial and her anger. Then she entered the bargaining stage. She said, "Lord, I just want to live to see my daughter graduate from high school." Her cancer went into remission, and her daughter graduated from high school.

I saw her about a month or two after her daughter graduated. I said, "You got what you prayed for. You have been praying that God would let you see your daughter graduate from high school."

"Yes, but now I told him I want to see her graduate from college."

"That is four more years."

"I know. He can handle that, though. I just want to see her graduate from college."

During her daughter's college years, this woman had another round of cancer. She went through chemotherapy and radiation. She lived another four years, and her daughter graduated from college.

Right after her daughter graduated, I was talking with her. I said, "You know, you moved the goalpost and God came through, didn't he?"

"Yes, now I asked him to let me just see her married."

"Is she even engaged?"

"No, she is not engaged, but I know the time will come."

This woman did live to see her daughter engaged, but she died before the wedding.

I conducted the wedding ceremony for this daughter. During the course of the service, I said to the bride, "You know, your mother always wanted to be at your wedding. I am sure she is celebrating from the balcony of heaven."

Perhaps the remission ends, and the battle with terminal illness intensifies. Body systems start shutting down. Now we enter a period of passive resignation as death draws closer.

Phase 4: Despair

A despondent person is difficult to console. A dying person experiencing a deep depression may consider taking his or her own life. Family members may have similar thoughts. Job's wife said to her beleaguered husband, "Curse God, and die!"

One of the mistakes that well-meaning Christians often make with suffering people is to offer easy answers. These are often presented in clichés such as "It is God's will," or "Everything works for the best." We can all learn an important lesson from the example of Job's friends. For seven days, they sat next to their suffering friend without speaking a word. That was good. They should have left after that, but they did not. Instead they tried to explain Job's suffering. Their explanations were like salt in his wounds. Well-meaning comforters became relentless tormentors.

When loved ones are in despair, it is important to stand with them. They may spend more time in silence or in weeping. This period of despair is a time when dying people may evaluate their lives. Those of us who are with them need to be as positive and as affirming as we can. Casseroles are more comforting than contrived explanations.

In the fall of 2003, I conducted a funeral for a very dear lady. She was a wonderful member of our church and one of the most devout women of prayer I have ever known. The last time I visited in her home, my wife went with me.

We were standing by her bed when she said, "You know, I pray for you every day."

I thanked her and said, "Ruth, that is your ministry."

"I know it is. It took me a while to see that even as I am bedridden, even as I approach death, I still have a ministry."

Hers was a ministry of intercession and encouragement. She did it well right up until the end of her life.

Sometimes the thing that helps a person come through the period of despair is the recognition that life has not been wasted. So often, people worry about being a problem to others. You may have heard a loved one say, "I am such a burden to everybody." Of course, it is true that caring for a dying person can be demanding and difficult. It is equally true that a person approaching death can be a joyous blessing to those around.

Beyond despair is acceptance of the reality of death.

Phase 5: Acceptance

When people enter the time of acceptance, they are in a position to make good decisions, provided their minds are still keen, undulled by medication or diminished by disease. Once we accept the reality of death, we begin to develop a new perspective of the end of this life. We affirm our Christian faith that death is a defeated enemy. Death is viewed through the eyes of faith as a transition from this life into life eternal.

Through the years I have learned that people need to talk, especially as they face their own death. I spoke with a man in his hospital room about his impending death.

"Tell me what this is like for you."

"Well, I have been thinking about it. It is funny you should ask."

I knew he had been thinking about it.

"If somebody had given me the choice as to whether or not I wanted to be born, I would have said, 'No thanks.' I was comfortable. I was warm. All my needs were met in my mother's womb. There was not a reason in the world why I would want to be pushed out into a cold world and greeted with a spank on the bottom. As I look back on it, I am glad I was born.

"Ask me if I want to die, and I will say, 'No thanks. I like it here. I have enjoyed my life.' I do not want to die, but I do not get to choose. I have the notion that when I get to the other side, I am going to look back and say, 'Boy, I am glad that happened.' I believe that life keeps getting better and better. Just as I am glad that I was born, I think the time will come when I will be glad that I have been through the experience of death."

Once death has been accepted, we are ready to go.

Phase 6: Release

Ronald Wells, a talented musician and gifted worship leader, was a devout man of prayer whose life was a blessing to many people. It was my privilege to serve in ministry with him for sixteen years. After a brutal battle with cancer over the span of several years, Ronald came to the end of his life. His death had been anticipated for months. His acceptance of death was complete. In the last weeks of his life, he did an unusual thing. Every visitor to his bedside received a blessing, a literal blessing. At the conclusion of visits that were necessarily brief, Ronald would ask if he could pray for his visitor. Those who had gone to minister to him instead received his ministry. "I want to give you a blessing," he would say. He would invite the person to kneel beside his bed. He would place his hand on that person's head and pray a prayer of blessing.

As Jesus came to the end of his life at the hands of Roman executioners, he blessed others: a dying thief, his own mother, the beloved disciple John, and even those who put him to death. His word of forgiveness from the cross is a word of blessing for all people in all times. This is grace offered in love to the whole world. And so Jesus could say, "It is finished." This sense of completion leads to release: "Into your hands I commit my spirit."

It has been my privilege to walk with many Christians to the doors of death. They no longer pray for a miracle. They know that resurrection is the greatest miracle of all. As one woman said, "Resurrection is the complete makeover. I am going to get a brand-new body. It is a total transplant." The apostle Paul writes, "Even though our outer nature is wasting away, our inner nature is being renewed day by day" (2 Cor. 4:16 NRSV).

The point of release can be a beautiful experience and a sacred moment. Those present with the dying person often feel that they are standing on holy ground. My grandfather, who taught me so much about death, asked his children to help him sit up in bed. He said with his dying breath, "Just as I am."

Nine years later, just before her death, my grandmother exclaimed, "Isn't that beautiful? Oh, how beautiful!" I do not know what she saw or what she heard, but I know that for her the final moments in this life were filled with beauty.

Release requires courage, both for the dying person and for those who love them. That courage comes from the faith "that the sufferings of this present time are not worth comparing to the glory that is to be revealed to us" (Rom. 8:18 RSV). That is a remarkable attitude. That is Christian hope.

The last few months of Miz Lib's life were difficult. It was heartrending for Clare and her brother, Ben, to see their mother in so much misery. Our goal in medical treatment at that time was to do everything possible to make Miz Lib comfortable. The last month of her life, when she was awake and able to speak, she moaned over and over, "I want to go home.

I want to go home. I want to go home." Her mother's crying caused Clare to second-guess the decision to move Miz Lib to the nursing home. A caring geriatric psychiatrist reassured Clare, "The home your mother longs for is not on this earth."

We had first believed that Miz Lib was crying out for the home she had lived in for the last twenty-six years. Then it became clear to us that she was not talking about that home at all. Next we thought she was thinking about the home that she lived in when she was a little girl. Clare remembered stories about Miz Lib's childhood. Her mother, Mother D, would put her five children to bed at night. Then she would go down the stairs of the large Victorian home, sit at the grand piano, and play the music of Rachmaninoff.

Clare had an idea. We bought a simple CD player that had a repeat button. We purchased several recordings of Rachmaninoff's piano music. We placed the CD player in Miz Lib's room at the nursing home so that the familiar music would be a constant lullaby. Miz Lib became more calm and peaceful. Miz Lib's younger brother, Clare's uncle Jimmy, commented, "Oh, that's a wonderful idea. Momma always played the piano until we went to sleep." The music played. Miz Lib went to sleep, and eventually she went home, to her new home in heaven.

Just hours before Miz Lib died, my wife and I stood outside her room at the nursing home. I asked my wife, "Clare, are you ready to let her go?"

"Yes, I feel like she has already been gone for a long time."

I prayed with my wife a prayer that I have prayed with many families. It is a prayer of release, a simple prayer: "Lord, this is our loved one. She belongs to you. We commit her to you and to your care."

Even after the death of your loved one, you can pray that prayer of release. You can say, "Lord, this person is yours. I commit him or her to your care." If you can do that, you can have peace of heart and peace of mind beyond human understanding. You will be on your way to recovery from the grief of anticipated death. This will not happen instantaneously. This is a process like so many other things in life. It flows like a river. You cannot get behind a river and push it. You cannot make it go faster. You have to let it flow. At the end of anticipatory grief, you can have peace like a river in your soul.

No two people mourn in exactly the same way. Some become bogged down in an extended state of denial. Others seethe in anger for months, harboring a sense of injustice for their loss. Many are able to move quickly to acceptance. Even with our differences, we have much in common as bereaved people.

Whether grief hits us suddenly like a head-on collision with an immediate and unexpected death or whether grief blindsides us following the diagnosis of a terminal illness and death is anticipated, we all share a similar reaction. No matter how grief comes, a deep, persistent yearning for our loved one seems to be the common denominator.

Recent research validates what many have learned through their suffering. In their article "An Empirical Examination of the Stage Theory of Grief" (*Journal of the American Medical Association*, February 21, 2007), Paul Maciejewski, Baohui Zhang, Susan D. Block, and Holly G. Prigerson identify *yearning* as the dominant grief symptom following the loss of a loved one.

Even after we have recovered from our grief and have moved on with our lives, we continue to long for the person who has died. Deep yearning is an enduring emotion. I still miss Miz Lib's fried chicken and homemade biscuits. I still miss Pappy's stories and the aroma of his cigars. I still miss my mother's hugs and the fragrance of her perfume. I still miss Erik. I think I always will.

In our grief, peace comes through our resurrection faith. The yearning of our souls never ends this side of heaven. For Christians, that deep longing is soothed by a calm assurance. We can look forward in hope to an eternity when we will be reunited with those for whom we grieve. Our deep yearning will be satisfied in a grand family reunion in glory.

PART TWO

3

Attachments and Separations

learning to grieve

The umbilical cord is cut, and a newborn is separated from the mother. The baby cries in its first expression of grief. The mother draws her child close to her breast to comfort and to nurture. A new bonding is initiated; a new attachment begins. In the days ahead some mothers may experience baby blues or postpartum depression, which are both grief reactions following childbirth.

From birth to death, life is a long series of attachments and separations. Every attachment puts us at risk for a grief experience when inevitable separation occurs. An infant, bonded to her mother, awakens, crying in the night because her mother is not near. Each experience of loss teaches us how to grieve.

Grief in Early Childhood

Any witness to the leave-taking between mothers and their little ones has seen the grief of little children. Young children left in the care of another person do not want their mother to leave. Young mothers, too, have difficulty turning to walk away from their crying child. The dear souls who keep the nursery or day care will advise parents not to linger and not to look back. Make the departure short and sweet with as little drama as possible. For very young children, out of sight means out of mind. Once the parents have departed, the child's attention can usually be diverted.

This is one practical reason why children who begin nursery at an early age adjust more easily to the temporary separation at the Sunday school door. When they grow beyond the out-of-sight, out-of-mind stage of development, they have learned to trust that the parents will return. Learning to say good-bye is an early step in learning to grieve.

As we grow, we learn that many of the things we enjoy are only temporary. Chocolate ice cream cones on a hot summer day will not last very long, especially when tilted sideways. Snowmen in the winter are a delight to create, but their days are numbered. Helium-filled balloons have a very short life expectancy. When one of these childhood treasures is taken away, children experience grief.

We enjoyed a pleasant afternoon at the Kentucky State Fair with our two-year-old son. The sights, smells, and sounds were a feast of sensory stimulation for him. He was especially fascinated with a treat he had never before experienced, cotton candy. I held him in my arms as he watched a woman twirl the spun sugar onto a paper roll. I allowed a taste before the cotton candy was encased in a plastic bag for the trip home.

As we walked to the parking lot, he asked for one more taste. I removed the treat from the plastic wrap and let him hold it. As he took a taste, it dropped on the ground right beside the car. The cotton candy was covered with dirt, grass, and grit. I explained that we would have to throw it away when we got home. I thought it wise to give him a little more time with his now-spoiled treat before abruptly tossing it.

When we arrived at our home, he ran to the bathroom sink, turned on the water all by himself, and attempted to wash the debris from the spun sugar. Instantly, the cotton candy disappeared before his eyes. He looked at me in dismay.

Holding his empty hands toward the sky, he cried in astonishment, "All gone!" From a two-year-old, it was the ultimate expression of shock following sudden loss.

Grief during the Elementary Years

When I was nearly seven, the oldest of five children, our family moved to a larger house surrounded by open fields on three sides and deep woods in back. Though Mama had her hands full caring for our family, Dad knew that it was time for me to have a dog. My birthday gift was a beagle pup. I named her Katie. She was an outside dog because that was the only kind Mama would allow. Katie's favorite pastime was chasing rabbits. Many a morning I was awakened by her hound dog howl as she ran a rabbit through a field and into the woods.

Just down the road from our place was a dairy farm. The farmer depended on contented cows to give sweet milk. When Katie could not scare up a rabbit for her early morning run, she was always able to find a cow or two to pester. Early one spring morning, I heard her baying, followed by a rifle shot, then silence. Worried, I quickly dressed and hurried downstairs. Dad already had Katie settled in a cardboard box. She was injured and bleeding.

We carried her to Dr. Ed Brown, a family friend and veterinarian. Dr. Brown, whose son Tommy was my age, took my dad aside and told him that my beagle's back legs were paralyzed and that she would have to be euthanized. He assured us that Katie was not in pain. His advice was that I take my dog home for a few days so I could pet her and have a little time to say good-bye. She never left the cardboard box. Her beagle eyes were sad; her tail could no longer wag.

A day or two later, Dad said, "Kirk, you know Katie is not going to get well."

I knew, and I cried. Once I pulled myself together, I said, "We need to let Dr. Brown put her to sleep." Together my dad and I took Katie in her cardboard box to the vet, and I said good-bye one more time. The reality and mystery of death confronted me for the first time. Saying good-bye to Katie was the first of many good-byes to follow.

The Death of a Pet

The death of a pet is often the first deeply felt grief in childhood. It also gives children the opportunity to role-play the funeral experience. When our children were young, we often had pets, several at a time and usually a variety. One Saturday morning, we discovered that one of the fish swimming in the aquarium in our den had died. Together the children and I removed the dearly departed swordtail from the tank, carefully placed him in a matchbox lined with tissue, and ceremoniously took the contrived casket to the flower bed. We dug a hole, sang "Shall We Gather at the River?" and had a prayer, and then buried the box.

Back inside, we discovered another fish had gone belly-up. This time, there was less ceremony. We wrapped the second swordtail in a tissue, with none of the reverence afforded the first, and deposited him in a shallow grave.

Upon our return to the den, we found yet another dead fish. It seemed one of our sons had discovered that pecans would float in the fish tank. No doubt, the pecan shells had been treated with a pesticide. We were suffering a fish kill in our aquarium.

This third death called for even less ritual. Our seven-year-old reasoned, "Dad, this fish has lived in water all of his life. I think we should bury him at sea." We flushed the third swordtail down the toilet.

The Death of a Grandparent

The death of a grandparent is a common childhood loss, though with increased longevity of senior adults, some people are able to enjoy relationships with grandparents well into adulthood. For children, the death of a grandparent may be their first significant loss of a loved one, as was the death of my own grandfather. Our first encounter with grief for a person we love prepares us for similar experiences throughout life.

Grief during the Teen Years

Teenagers tend to have an intensity about life experiences that seems over-the-top, even melodramatic, to many adults. This, simply put, is due to a lack of experience.

Early in my ministry, I served as a chaplain in Louisville, Kentucky, at Ormsby Village Treatment Center, an institution for juvenile delinquents. A seminary student working as a chaplain-in-training under my supervision was called to minister to a fifteen-year-old girl. The teenager's mother had died in an automobile accident. The girl and her mother had been separated from each other for several years because the mother had abandoned her children. Still, the teenager had often expressed her hope that they would be reunited.

The student chaplain was asked by a social worker to tell the girl about her mother's death. He made sure of the details in preparation for his difficult task. The chaplain was clear, concise, and compassionate. The girl reacted to the news the way she typically reacted to other threatening and painful situations—with her fist! She attacked the startled chaplain, pounding his chest with clinched fists, screaming, "Do something! Do something! Do something!"

The chaplain grabbed her arms and earnestly asked, "What do you want *me* to do?"

The surprised teenager was brought up short by his question and cried out, "You're new at this, aren't you?"

The chaplain responded, "Yes, and you are too. Let's see if we can figure this out together."

With that calm assurance, the student chaplain became the girl's pastor. Along with the social worker, they attended the mother's funeral. Over the following months, both learned about the process of grief.

Broken Dreams

Broken dreams are a unique form of adolescent grief. High school basketball is a part of March Madness in the commonwealth of Kentucky. The Sweet Sixteen Tournament regularly draws crowds of more than sixteen thousand fans, and some-times the arena named for the legendary Adolph Rupp reaches its capacity of twenty-three thousand. Each year, sixteen teams gather in Lexington for fifteen games over five frenetic days to decide the state championship. Some say the high school tournament is the most important sporting event in Kentucky, more important than the Kentucky Derby or University of Kentucky basketball.

Almost every year, one or two teams from small towns un-expectedly win their division and make it to the state tourna-ment. High school students from farms in western Kentucky and coal miners' kids from eastern Kentucky travel to the Mecca of Bluegrass Basketball to join a crowd of fans larger than the population of some of their hometowns. Teenagers come with the grand dream that their team will be crowned state champions. The same scenario, played out in neighbor-ing Indiana, is depicted in the movie *Hoosiers*. As in the film, sometimes the Cinderella team wins the championship, but that is rare. In the first two days of the Sweet Sixteen, there are eight games and eight losing teams. Much weeping and wailing, an abundance of tears, and many broken dreams accompany the losses.

Fallen Heroes

Fallen heroes are another source of bereavement during the teen years. The most anticipated heavyweight title fight since Joe Louis defeated Max Schmeling in 1938 was the first contest between Muhammad Ali and Joe Frazier in March 1971. It was simply called "The Fight of the Century." The fight was unique in that for the first time in history it matched an unbeaten former heavyweight champion against the unbeaten current champ.

At the time of this first fight between Muhammad Ali and "Smokin'" Joe Frazier, I was still serving as a chaplain at Ormsby Village Treatment Center. Most of the young men incarcerated in the institution were from the inner city of Louisville, the home of Muhammad Ali.

After refusing induction into the army in 1967, Ali was stripped of his title. Since he had not lost the crown in the ring, he proclaimed himself the people's champion. As he entered the ring against Frazier, his record stood at 31-0 with 25 knockouts.

In Ali's absence, Frazier won recognition as heavyweight champion in 1970 after defeating champion Jimmy Ellis. As he climbed into the ring, his record was 26-0 with 23 knockouts.

Ali was still held in contempt by much of the country. He was viewed as a brash, draft-dodging Muslim who represented the defiance of the antiwar movement. Frazier, who read the Bible and liked to sing hymns, was held up as the conscientious, blue-collar champion. For the teenagers at Ormsby Village, Ali was a hero. The Champ, as they referred to him, grew up in their neighborhood and had literally fought his way out. He embodied the hopes of every ghetto kid in Louisville. He was unbeaten, and the teenagers thought there was no way Frazier could defeat him.

Though Muhammad Ali would win the next two fights in his classic struggle with Joe Frazier, he lost the first. He was knocked down twice by Frazier's vicious left hook. It is estimated that three hundred million people watched the fight on television that night.

I watched the boxing match in a room filled with street-hardened boys. I had seen these young men respond to their own personal tragedies with a stoic attitude. Two weeks before, upon learning that his father had committed suicide, one of the boys shed not a single tear. But on the night that Ali lost to Frazier, he wept, as did all of the others. Their hero had fallen.

Celebrity heroes are not the only ones who are a cause of sorrow in the lives of teenagers. To adolescents, changes in the lives of people they admire may represent a fall. A special coach takes a job at a rival school, a youth pastor accepts a call to another church, a favorite teacher announces her plans to be married, or a scoutmaster resigns because his company has transferred him. These all are occasions for adolescent grief.

A Broken Courtship

A broken courtship is a third kind of teenage loss that causes significant grief. Adults tend to regard adolescent love as puppy love and to dismiss breakups with a glib comment like, "You'll find somebody new by the weekend."

It is true that teenage romance is often mere infatuation, lacking the depth of adult relationships. It is also true that adolescents can move to another interest rather quickly. Even so, the pain of a broken courtship is real.

Love stories sometimes turn tragic because families decide that young love cannot be true love. *Romeo and Juliet* and *West Side Story* are but two such examples. A wise family physician often prescribes tincture of time as a remedy for common ailments. A little time may also be the best cure for lovesickness.

I shall never forget the day Clare and I drove to the Atlanta airport to meet our daughter, then eighteen years old, upon her return from a mission trip to Romania. She had traveled with a group from our church. All of our contact with the group during their time of ministry indicated that the young people on the trip had meaningful experiences and that all had gone well. This was prior to the events of September 11, 2001, when families were still allowed to meet passengers at the arrival gate. Betsy emerged from the airplane, walked to us, and gave us a perfunctory kiss and hug. I could tell that she had been crying. She hurried straight to a public pay telephone and, using my long-distance phone card, placed a call to Romania.

"Who are you calling?" I dared to ask.

"I am calling the man I am going to marry!" she said.

Puzzled, I turned to Clare, who said, "We'll find out more on the drive home. For now, just be glad he's still in Romania. At least she did come back, and he was not on the plane with her."

During the four-hour drive back home, we learned that the man in question had been the interpreter for the mission group. He was twenty-eight. He played the guitar. Betsy had met his parents at a church in Romania. They loved her. She was sure that we would love him. Meanwhile, she considered it imperative that she learn the Romanian language so they could communicate by email.

On the way home, we stopped at a large bookstore. There, at Clare's suggestion, Betsy selected and I paid for a book and an accompanying cassette tape to help her learn to speak and write Romanian. The long-distance romance continued for several weeks.

My mother and my dad long ago modified a wise old saying: "Absence makes the heart grow fonder—for somebody else." That's exactly what happened with Betsy and her Romanian boyfriend. When the breakup came, there were a few tears.

School started in the fall, and with it came a new boyfriend. I was glad for Clare's wisdom and glad that I had listened to her instead of overreacting to my eighteen-year-old daughter's twenty-eight-year-old boyfriend. My only regret was that her new boyfriend didn't also live somewhere far away. By the way, we still have the book and the tape on learning Romanian. We saved them as a reminder to exercise patience in all things.

The Death of a Peer

The death of a peer is frequently the most difficult loss for a teenager. Sandy and I were good friends in high school. He and I both enjoyed biology and were planning on entering medical school following college. Sandy's father, Dr. Black, was a surgeon and suggested that, since both Sandy and I were thinking of going to medical school, we might like to stand in on an operation. We arranged to be at the hospital on a Friday morning. Dr. Black had scheduled three surgeries. All three patients were men, and all had consented to our presence in the operating room. While I doubt such a thing as this opportunity could happen now, it proved to be a good experience for both of us.

After high school graduation, I went to Furman University and Sandy went to Davidson College. We agreed that we would see each other at Christmas break of our freshman year. I did not see him again. He was killed in an automobile accident coming home for Christmas. Perhaps you will recall that I had lost my grandfather in September that same year, a very difficult loss for me. Now at nineteen I experienced the death of someone my age.

Teenagers tend to believe that they are immortal. A World War II veteran, decorated for valor, said, "When you're eighteen, you're not afraid of anything. The reason the army wants teenagers is because kids don't think anything can happen to them. But that doesn't last long. Once you see one of your buddies hit, then you know that war is a life-or-death situation."

The way adolescents walk across a street, the way they drive an automobile, and the way they volunteer for military service are all indicative of a mistaken attitude of immortality. The death of a peer is a startling wake-up call to our own frailty.

I spent several hours one night in a living room filled with teenagers. They were grieving the loss of two of their friends who died in an automobile accident the previous night. Their grief was profound, but equally significant was the emerging sense of their own mortality. As one young woman put it, "If something this awful could happen to our friends, it could happen to any of us."

The Death of a Sibling

The death of a sibling is even more profound than the death of a peer. It is a wrenching grief experience. To an adolescent, the loss of a brother or a sister feels like the Grim Reaper has breached the security of the family. As our Betsy put it after her brother Erik's death, "It was hard enough to see my older brothers go off to college, get married, and move somewhere else. At least I still could see them every now and then. Now, Erik is just gone, and I won't see him again until heaven! Who wants to wait for that?"

Betsy has always enjoyed her brothers. Being the youngest child and the only daughter might have some drawbacks, but Betsy and her brothers have loved and respected each other deeply. On one occasion, when we were gathered together as a family, Betsy reflected, "Being the youngest has its advantages, but the truth is that I am probably going to have to go to a funeral for every one of you. That thought makes me very sad."

Scottish writer Sir James Barrie was the seventh of eight children. When he was six years old, his older brother died in a skating accident. His mother fell into a deep depression. James tried to make her feel better by wearing his older brother's clothes and doing the things his brother used to do. At some point, it occurred to young Barrie that his dead brother would never grow up. That idea led to his story of Peter Pan.

After I experienced three significant losses over the course of fourteen months, a pastor friend helped me debrief and sort through my grief. He spoke with me about the wisdom of sorrow, the learning that is gleaned from grief. The grief experiences of childhood and adolescence serve a dual purpose. They provide basic training for the difficult experiences of loss in adulthood. As we become acquainted with our own grief, we develop a memory bank that enables us to pass along our hard-earned wisdom of sorrow to those who follow in our footsteps.

4

Grief in Adulthood

learning through the losses of life

After years of alcohol and drug abuse, a forty-one-year-old woman died of pneumonia. I visited with the mother and the twenty-year-old daughter of the deceased woman. Though neither the older woman nor her young grand-daughter had been surprised by the death, both grieved at the tragic life and death of a person they loved deeply. For the mother, also a widow, this was the second child she had lost. Five years earlier, a jealous boyfriend had murdered her younger daughter.

As I listened to the twenty-year-old speak openly about her bereavement, she affirmed the strength of her grand-mother, the person with whom she had lived since infancy. "I don't know what I would do without my grandmother. I've had a lot of loss in my life, but she has had so much more. I have learned from her how to deal with these things."

Some, like this young woman, make the transition to their adult years having had multiple grief experiences. But, no matter how much we have learned about bereavement in childhood and adolescence, there is always more to learn about grief. Other people enter their adult years never having lost a loved one. Still, they have experienced the ebb and flow of attachment and separation that is common to all of our lives.

Marriage and Grief

Marriage and grief may seem like strange bedfellows, but a wedding is another link in life's chain of attachments and separations. In the first pages of the Bible, we read words that are later quoted by both Jesus and Paul in reference to marriage: "Therefore a man leaves his father and his mother and clings to his wife, and they become one flesh" (Gen. 2:24 NRSV). This leaving-and-cleaving transition applies to both husband and wife and to their families. The way a bride and groom and their new in-laws make the initial transition will determine the degree of friction and conflict they will experience in the future.

The time-honored adage "Don't think of it as losing a daughter; think of it as gaining a son" is really not very helpful. As joyful as a wedding can be, when the newlyweds leave for their honeymoon, both they and their parents are aware that relationships have changed.

After he met his college-aged daughter's steady boyfriend for the first time, an insightful father said to the young man, "You're planning to take her away from me, aren't you?" It was an expression of anticipated grief.

The Childless Couple

The childless couple may be a grieving couple. The weeping of Hannah in the temple at Shiloh expressed what the Scripture refers to as "the bitterness of her soul" (1 Sam. 1:10). Her lament echoes in the heart of every woman who longs for a child but is unable to conceive and give birth.

In the early years of our marriage, Clare and I wanted very much to start a family. After nearly two years of unsuccessfully attempting to conceive, we sought medical advice. After a series of tests, we were told that it was unlikely that Clare would ever become pregnant. If she did, she probably could not carry a child to full term. We felt the shock and numbness that accompany sudden loss.

As we grieved, we began slowly to rethink our expectations. We started exploring our options, including adoption. As we tried to decide, we were delighted that Clare became pregnant. She carried the baby for about three months, but the pregnancy ended in miscarriage. We, of course, were saddened, but we were also encouraged that she had been able to conceive.

About six months later, Clare became pregnant again. This time she carried the child longer, and we even felt the baby move. Then came the second miscarriage. Clare was devastated, almost inconsolable. I will never forget her crying, apologizing to me, and belittling herself.

I became angry at the injustice of it all. Several days later, while a good friend was visiting Clare, I took a long walk in the woods. In frustration, I shook my fist toward heaven and spoke out loud to God, "I do not understand! People around the world who don't even want children can have babies like rabbits! Why can't we have a child?"

My outburst was met with silence. I heard nothing except the wind in the trees. I saw nothing but fluttering leaves. I cried, and I prayed. And then, inaudibly, a question came from somewhere deep within my spirit. "Kirk, how do you expect to be a father until you learn how to hurt?" The question surprised me and led me to a startling realization. God, our divine parent, suffers the pain of parenting. That insight has had a far-reaching impact in my life and in my personal theology. My understanding of the crucifixion deepened. My awareness of my relationship to God expanded. How often have I, as a child of God, been responsible for God's suffering?

Clare and I actively pursued adoption. We completed all of the paperwork and went through the home visits. Six weeks before we were to receive our adopted child, we confirmed that Clare was pregnant a third time. After much prayer and deliberation, we made the decision to terminate adoption procedures. We did not think it wise to have two infants only a few months apart in age. That decision precipitated additional grief and fear. Then, on Christmas Day 1970, our first child was born!

The Attachment-Detachment Continuum in Parenting

The attachment-detachment continuum in parenting is a long process. Infants are almost totally dependent upon parents. Healthy young adults struggle to become independent. The years between are marked with developmental mileposts, each one indicating progressive growth and each one accompanied by an experience of grief.

A crawling child reaches for the edge of the coffee table and pulls upright, testing gimbaled legs and discovering an entirely new world at eye level. Parents become aware that knickknacks must be relocated. It was at that stage in my life that I ate a colorful arrangement of pansies floating in a bowl of water. I have enjoyed flowers ever since.

Learning to walk and learning to ride a bicycle are accomplishments that require the parents to literally let go. Each warrants a sense of pride, but each is also accompanied by apprehension.

On the first day of school, a mother leaves her child in the care of another person for more hours in the day than the mother will have with the child. Each Monday morning during the school year, immediately after dropping their children off at school, mothers gather at our church to pray together for their children and their schoolteachers and administrators. In many ways, it is a grief support group.

More independence means less control for the parent and more danger for the child. Walking and riding a bicycle as a child is the prelude to driving an automobile as a teenager. Leave-taking at elementary school is preparation for leaving home for college or career. For the past ten years Wofford College in Spartanburg, South Carolina, has invited me to address the parents of entering freshmen at the close of orientation week. The purpose of our session is to help them make the difficult transition of leaving their children. It is a grief experience.

Military Service

Military service involves difficult grief. I recently officiated at a large formal wedding for a wonderful young couple. At the beginning of the service I announced what many in the congregation did not know, that the couple had already been married for fifteen months. I explained that the ceremony was conducted by a justice of the peace in a small county seat town in southern Georgia the day before the groom was deployed to Iraq. While both wanted a wedding with their families and friends, they also wanted to be married before he left on an uncertain mission. I reminded the congregation that this kind of thing happened frequently during World War II, the Korean War, and the Vietnam War. I interpreted the church wedding service as a continuation and completion of their civil ceremony; a time to celebrate what God had already done in their lives and to give them our support, our love, and our blessing.

When parents say good-bye to a son or daughter entering military service, they experience a sense of loss, but in wartime their emotions are heightened and are akin to anticipatory grief.

Clare and I live in the house built by my grandfather in 1937, at the end of the Great Depression. In our home is a small room that my grandmother called her prayer parlor. Each night Mammy and Pappy went to the parlor to read the Bible and pray before bedtime. During the Second World War, they had a son who was aboard a landing vessel in the Normandy invasion, another who was shot down while flying bombing raids over Berlin, a third son in the Pacific, and a son-in-law who was captured by the Germans and became a prisoner of war. At the same time, they had one son on the mission field in South America. Our family knows that the walls of the small room are saturated with prayer.

The Empty Nest

The empty nest is another time of transition. Clare and I were told that when our time for the empty nest came, we would be filled with emotion, and we were—exhilaration! Launching young adults into their own orbit is like launching a space shuttle. It is expensive and there are risks. It is important to keep communication open in case there is trouble in orbit, but overall it is good to know they are flying on their own. There are moments of grief when the basketball court in the backyard is silent and there is no music booming from a bedroom, but the relative peace and quiet of life resumed as a couple is delightful.

As one father of three daughters said, "Our nest didn't stay empty very long. For some reason, the girls keep coming back, looking for a soft place to land. And when they return, they bring a husband and children with them." The empty nest, whenever it is empty, is a symbol that an important mission has been accomplished. It is one of those life experiences that includes both a sense of loss and a feeling of satisfaction.

The Death of a Child

The death of a child has a profound effect on a wide circle of people. I will always remember December 1984 as one of the most difficult times in my ministry. Within three weeks, I stood with three families by the graves of their children, one of them my niece. The sight of a tiny casket is heartrending for parents, grandparents, aunts, uncles, brothers, sisters, cousins, and a large group of friends.

The death of a child is sometimes referred to as untimely death. Whether sudden or anticipated, the death of a child precipitates an enduring grief. When a child dies, family members have the sense that they have lost not just a beloved son or daughter but also a part of their future. It is easy for bereaved parents to get caught up in what might have been.

Marriages become vulnerable to the point of breaking following the death of a child. Men and women grieve differently, and misunderstanding often results. A man who, in his bereavement, sinks himself into his work may be perceived by his wife as not grieving enough over the loss of their child. Sometimes the damage to marriage results from blame and guilt focused on one partner or the other. Neither blame nor self-blame is helpful following a painful loss. The divorce rate for parents following the death of a child is significant.

After our son Erik died, Clare and I agreed that we wanted to guard our marriage. We have made a strong commitment to be companions in our shared grief. We have always been best friends to each other. I encourage other couples to make the same commitment rather than becoming wounded, alienated strangers to each other. Three key components can provide the stability and safe mooring needed to insure the survival and strengthening of marriage in the maelstrom following the death of a child. Those components are (1) clear communication that believes nothing is unspeakable; (2) a firm, unwavering commitment; and (3) a marriage that is centered on God through the life of prayer.

Separation and Divorce

Separation and divorce must be included among those life experiences from which we learn about grief. Nearly every family has been touched in some way by what has become a common crisis in American life. To put it simply, the breakup of a marriage hurts. No matter how amiable or vengeful, whether by mutual agreement or not, whether the marriage was long-term or short, separation and divorce are painful. The grief that follows marital dissolution can last for years. When death occurs there is a finality and a funeral. Not so in divorce. One woman commented, "If there were a corpse, I would eventually get over this, but my ex is still walking around haunting my life."

In cases of infidelity, the losses go far beyond that of a marriage partner. The loss of integrity, self-esteem, trust of someone thought to be trustworthy, financial security, and home are all on the list of casualties.

The divorce of parents creates a difficult grief experience for children and teenagers. They may feel as if it is their fault. Parents sometimes treat children like spies in the enemy's camp. Children can feel pulled and stressed like the rope in a tug-of-war. Except in cases of abusive relationships, the myth that divorce is better for the children is almost always just that—a myth.

Several years ago just before Thanksgiving, I had a passing conversation at the post office with a longtime acquaintance.

I offered, "I hope you have a good Thanksgiving."

He responded, "I won't have a good Thanksgiving until my mom and dad are back together."

I was startled by his reply. I knew that he was in his midforties and that his parents had been divorced for more than twenty years. I recalled that the divorce was final while this man was still in college. I knew, too, that his father had moved to another state and had remarried. His mother had a long-term illness that required the constant use of oxygen. "How can your parents get back together?" I asked.

"I really don't think they ever will, but I'll never have a good Thanksgiving until they do."

The pain of divorce lasts a long time.

The Loss of a Job

The loss of a job also deserves mention here. One study indicates that job loss is among the most difficult experiences for a breadwinner. A sense of self-worth as a provider is wrapped up in having a job. To be unemployed, for whatever reason, is to be unwanted. In that regard, the loss of a job is a first cousin to divorce. There is hardly any joy greater than being selected, and hardly any pain greater than being deselected.

When a large textile manufacturing plant shut down in a North Carolina town, hundreds of people were without jobs. A pastor had the opportunity to observe the variety of ways people reacted to their loss. He established support groups not only for church members who had lost their jobs but also for any unemployed workers in the town. The groups helped the unemployed deal with their grief and encouraged them to develop an action plan.

The pastor noticed that those who focused on the injustice of life were passive and became bitter and sullen. They felt despondent and out of control and remained unemployed longer. On the other hand, those who grieved but also decided that improving their plight was up to them were active in trying to find work and tended to feel that they had more control over their future.

The Death of a Parent

The death of a parent can be a difficult turning point for adult children. If mom and dad have been active and vibrant, living life to the fullest and enjoying every minute of it, losing them is especially hard. A woman grieved deeply when her eighty-seven-year-old father died unexpectedly in his sleep. "I feel like a strong wall has tumbled down. I could still count on Dad for good advice. When we were together, we always had a good laugh about something. He was so witty, so full of life. He couldn't get around like he used to and had to depend on his cane. But in conversation, he was as sharp as ever. I'm really going to miss him."

Someone has said that when an elderly person with a keen mind dies, it is like a library burning to the ground. The loss of knowledge and wisdom is beyond comprehension. Native Americans refer to such elders as wisdom keepers. They are a repository of common sense and uncommon insight. Grieving for them is like standing before a tumbled down wall or a burned library and coming to the realization that now we have to be the strong source of security and the repository of wisdom for those who follow us. In this bereavement a torch of responsibility is passed to us.

The death of a parent can be a blessed relief if the parent has been afflicted with a long and debilitating illness such as Alzheimer's disease. We feel a quiet sense of gratitude when the agony and the misery of prolonged life give way to the peaceful rest of death and the hope of heaven. This reality is often felt and thought but seldom spoken by adult children as their parent approaches death.

When her mother suffered a stroke, an adult daughter, who was married and had three teenagers, took her bedridden mom in to live with her. Family financial constraints gave her no other choice. After several years of exhausting caregiving during which her mother became almost totally unresponsive, the daughter said, "I suppose it is wrong to wish for your own mother's death, but, truthfully, I do."

I responded, "Heaven is next, and that will be so much better for her."

"Yes," said the daughter. "And when she goes to heaven that will be better for all of us too."

We had a prayer of release together and, less than a month later, the mother died of renal failure.

As a parent becomes more and more feeble, it is important for adult siblings to speak openly about their feelings. When we are free to express our deeper thoughts, we move more easily to acceptance and release.

The Grief of Older Adults

Grief is a frequent visitor in the lives of older adults. Members of a senior adult men's Sunday school class were asked to serve as honorary pallbearers for three funerals in two weeks. As we left the cemetery following the third service, one of the men said to me, "Pastor, we've got to stop meeting like this!"

When I was an associate pastor, a ninety-three-year-old woman telephoned me at the church office to request a visit. "I want you to help me plan my funeral," she explained. I did not know the elderly woman well and was curious as to why she chose me to speak with about her plans. When I arrived, her home was filled with antique furniture and musty old books. I could tell immediately that she had a social visit in mind. Her silver service was polished, and she offered hot tea and homemade cookies.

We talked for some time about a variety of topics. She had some books she wanted to pass on to me, volumes that were out of print that had been part of her father's library. She told me that she had particularly appreciated the times when she had heard me preach and especially enjoyed the stories I told. They reminded her, she explained, of her father and his preaching style.

When we finally came to the subject of her funeral, she explained, "I want you to conduct my funeral. Your manner reminds me so much of my father, I know the service will be comforting to my children and grandchildren. Besides, you are younger than the other ministers on the staff; they may all be gone by the time I die."

We laughed together at her wit as she added, "When you do my funeral, you can say that all of my family and friends in heaven will be surprised to see me when I arrive. I have lived so much longer than all of them; they will think that I went somewhere else instead. They'll be shocked to see me when I finally get to heaven."

Thinking of all the people who had preceded her in death, I asked, "You have attended a lot of funerals, haven't you?"

"Yes, I have. The longer you live, the more grieving you have to do."

Retirement

Retirement can be a significant grief experience. A popular myth is that retirement means quitting work and doing nothing. Very few people experience retirement in that way. One man said, "I have been so busy since I retired that I don't know when I found the time to work before I retired!"

For many, retiring from one job is an opportunity to assume other responsibilities. For many others, it means a second career. A dear friend and colleague recently announced her retirement. She was somewhat ambivalent as she made the decision. "This is my second time to retire," she explained. "I retired as a schoolteacher and immediately started working in the church. This will be the first time in a long time that I will not have a job." I know her to be a people person with a high energy level. I have no doubt that she will be busy. Both she and her family are looking forward to having more time together.

In the Greek language, there are two words for time. *Chronos* is time that is measured, as with a clock or a calendar. Wristwatches are sometimes called chronometers. Perhaps *chronos* is the concept of time that prompts the giving of a watch to people who retire.

Kairos is a second Greek word for time. It conveys the idea that there is a right time for certain things in life, as in the expression "the time is ripe." Ecclesiastes observes, "For everything there is a season, and a time for every matter under heaven" (Eccles. 3:1 NRSV). The proper time for retirement is not so much determined by the calendar as it is by our awareness that the time is right.

Though retirement is rarely mentioned in the Bible, the concept is embedded in our understanding of keeping the Sabbath holy. In the same way that the Creator rested and reflected on the act of creation, retirement is a time to take delight in a life's work that has been well done.

Being the Last Remaining Sibling

Being the last remaining sibling is good reason for sorrow. Elderly adults have an especially difficult time when a brother or sister dies. Many times I have heard a person say something like, "Well, there were four of us, and I'm the last one left." My father was one of nine children. At this point, four of the nine are deceased. I have been honored to conduct the funerals for these aunts and uncles. The ninth in the family, the youngest brother, said at the last funeral, "This is when being the youngest is no fun. I really don't want to be the last one left."

I am the oldest of eight children. My sister Kitty is the youngest of us eight. Our daughter, Betsy, has four older brothers. While Kitty and Betsy have enjoyed the benefits of being the youngest child in their families, both have expressed the dread of being the last one left. The younger children, especially in large families, frequently express their sense of foreboding: "I just don't want to go to everybody's funeral!" or "I don't even want to think about it!"

Of course, death does not always follow birth order. A ninety-year-old who was the second oldest of six and who had outlived the other five said, "I never would have guessed that I would have to say good-bye so many times."

The Loss of Health

Losing one's health is part of the process of aging. As we grow older, time and gravity take their toll. Degenerative disease begins to affect mind and body. The Scriptures say of Moses just before his death that "his eye was not dim, nor his natural force abated" (Deut. 34:7 KJV). For most of us, that will not be the case. Canes, walkers, and wheelchairs, along with hearing aids and trifocals, bear witness to the widespread effects of aging and declining health. The apostle Paul writes, "Even though our outer nature is wasting away, our inner nature is being renewed day by day" (2 Cor. 4:16 NRSV).

One of the most unforgettable people I have ever known is a woman who has been a widow for nearly twenty years. She is afflicted with rheumatoid arthritis and has endured multiple surgeries, including the amputation of one leg. Confined to a wheelchair, she lives alone in an apartment in a retirement center. Though she does have a helper who assists with her daily routine, she manages much of her life quite well from her wheelchair. The most remarkable characteristic about this woman is her attitude. In spite of her constant pain and more suffering than most of us could ever imagine, her spirit is contagiously cheerful. Those who know her are unanimous in their opinion that a visit with her is a blessing for the visitor.

Paul, who suffered with his own thorn in the flesh, writes, "Suffering produces perseverance; perseverance character; and character hope. And hope does not disappoint us" (Rom. 5:3–5). When we view declining health and the suffering that accompanies it as a beginning point on the path to hope, our attitude is positive and a blessing to others.

The Loss of Place

The loss of place is an experience of grief. The grandmother I called Granny lived in a large, two-story home near the center of our town. The house had a wraparound porch with large rocking chairs where I listened to uncles tell stories about family history, especially the Civil War. I remember catching lightning bugs in the yard on summer nights and playing Mother, May I with my cousins on the front steps. When I was in junior high school, I used to walk to Granny's house after school.

When Granny died, her house was vacant and soon fell into disrepair. The city condemned the house as a part of an urban renewal project. My dad and I saw bulldozers demolish the old home. Though we salvaged some of the lumber, watching Granny's house turned to rubble was a painful experience. The loss of place is difficult.

Thirty years ago, I was asked by a psychiatrist to visit a woman suffering from depression in a nursing home. She had been unwilling to speak to anyone about her despair. Following several long periods of silence, I posed a question: "What have you lost?"

After another long silence, she asked, "Do you know where they are building that new shopping mall? The one out by the new interstate, where they've poured all that concrete? That used to be my grandpa's dairy farm. I used to pick wildflowers and swing on a tire swing hanging from a big oak tree where all that concrete is now. They have paved my grandpa's farm."

Several years ago, a land developer purchased E. P. Todd Elementary School in our town. The school was the one my dad and his brothers and sisters attended during the Great Depression. It was the school where all of my brothers and sisters and I were students when Mr. E. P. Todd was the principal. Later, after the school was named for Mr. Todd, all of our children went to elementary school in the same building.

Then the school building was bulldozed and the land cleared for a shopping center. When the building was demolished, three generations of our family grieved. My dad and two of our sons went with me to gather a few of the bricks from the old building. They occupy a spot in our garden as a memorial to a place that was important to us all but is now gone.

The Loss of a Mate

The loss of a mate after many years of marriage is such a profound bereavement that many senior adults never stop mourning. Whether sudden or anticipated, the death of a marriage partner has been described as losing a part of oneself. Grief following the loss of a mate can be compounded in several ways. Multiple deaths or a series of losses in close proximity to each other can confuse the process of grieving. When an elderly loved one in poor health loses a lifetime mate and is no longer able to live at home as a result, that person experiences a triple grief—loss of mate, loss of health, and loss of place.

My mother and father were married for nearly fifty-eight years. Though earlier she had been diagnosed with congestive heart failure, Mama died rather unexpectedly from a stroke. Dad mourned deeply. Even at the age of eighty, he continued his usual custom of going to the lumberyard to work at 5:30 every morning.

After Mama died, he had no difficulty going to sleep at night, but when he woke up, he could not go back to sleep. "That bed is mighty empty without her," he lamented.

Several months after Mama's death, Dad, Clare, and I were having a late supper together. At the end of the meal, I said,

"Clare and I are going to Wal-Mart. Is there anything we can get for you?"

"No, thank you. I'll probably go early in the morning."

"Before you go to the lumberyard?" I asked.

"Yep. Wal-Mart stays open all night."

"Have you been going to Wal-Mart in the middle of the night?"

"When I wake up in the night, I still reach for your mama. She's not there, so I get up, get a shower, and drive to Wal-Mart. That's when I do my shopping. I usually wake up about 3:00 in the morning. I can shop at Wal-Mart, eat breakfast at The Waffle House, and still get to work by 5:30."

When my mother died, Dad expressed his surprise and sorrow that she died before he did. "We always talked about this as if I would go first. I just didn't expect her to die before me."

A major help in Dad's grief was his awareness that because he had lived longer than Mama, she did not have to go through the grief of losing him.

Though he had often declared that he would never be married again, I was not at all surprised when he fell in love. Ruth is a dear woman he had known for years. She lost her husband after his long battle with cancer. Three years after Mama died, Dad and Ruth were married.

At their wedding, with family and friends in attendance, Dad and Ruth promised their love " 'til death do us part." They understood very well what they were pledging in their vows. Both had known the sorrow of bereavement after losing a marriage partner. Both knew full well that one of them would know that grief again. Dad explained, "I loved your mama for a long time, and I still do. Ruth had a good marriage to her husband, Ray, for fifty-one years, and she still loves him. A second marriage is different, but we sure do love each other. We want to be married for whatever time the good Lord has in mind for us."

Both Dad and Ruth have so much love to give that their marriage has been a joyful relationship to witness. Recently, a woman who did not know them saw Dad and Ruth holding hands. They were saying the blessing before a meal at a local restaurant. The woman asked, "How long have you two been married?"

With a twinkle in his eye Dad quipped, "We've been married for a hundred and twelve years."

The startled woman was speechless.

Then Dad added, "I was married fifty-eight years to my first wife; Ruth was married fifty-one years to her first husband; and we've been married to each other for three years. That makes one hundred and twelve years of marriage."

Learning What It Means to Grieve

What does learning to grieve mean? A major step in learning to grieve is to give up the expectation that things will always be the same. There is no vaccination against loss. It will come to all of us sooner or later. Sorrow will be a part of every life. A part of learning to grieve is to understand that we will not be exempt. Once we accept that reality, we can make decisions that will move us along through grief to resolution.

I have some experience canoeing and rafting in white-water rivers. Think of life as a journey down a river. The river confronts us with a series of rapids and stretches of flat, calm water. As we begin the journey, the rapids are generally less difficult, the turbulence less threatening.

As we successfully negotiate those initial rapids, we learn to handle our paddle and our canoe or raft. Experience teaches us that in calm water we can drift and let the flow of the river carry us along. In white water, to avoid boulders and other dangers, we must paddle with more effort and precision.

Occasionally the river of life shocks us with thundering rapids so turbulent that we have little control. Only by paddling our craft with practiced skill do we have any control at all. While these severe rapids sap our energy and threaten to sink us, we have more confidence in our ability and greater assurance that calm water is ahead. As we negotiate the swirling rapids of loss and sorrow, we continue our lifelong journey of learning how to grieve.

Horatio Spafford was a Chicago businessman in the late nineteenth century. A senior partner in a prosperous law firm and devout elder in the Presbyterian church, Spafford and his wife, Anna, lived comfortably with their four young daughters. In 1871, when the Great Fire of Chicago reduced the city to ashes, it also destroyed Spafford's sizable investments.

Two years later, the family planned a trip to Europe. At the last moment Spafford was detained by business. Anna and the girls went ahead, sailing on the ocean liner SS *Ville de Havre*. On November 21, 1873, the liner was accidentally rammed by a British vessel and sank within twelve minutes. Anna was rescued clinging to a floating board. The four children drowned. A fellow survivor recalled Anna saying, "God gave me four daughters. Now they have been taken from me. Someday I will understand why." Nine days after the shipwreck Anna landed in Cardiff, Wales, and cabled her husband, "Saved alone. What shall I do?"

After receiving Anna's telegram, Spafford immediately left Chicago to bring his wife home. On the Atlantic crossing, the captain of his ship called Horatio to his cabin to tell him that they were passing over the spot where his four daughters had perished. Horatio wrote the words to the hymn "It Is Well with My Soul" as he passed over their watery grave.

> When peace, like a river, attendeth my way,
> When sorrows like sea billows roll;
> Whatever my lot, Thou hast taught me to say,
> It is well, it is well, with my soul.

When we have learned to grieve, we, too, can affirm in any grief experience, "It is well with my soul."

5

Helping Children with Grief

Grief is rarely a solo experience. We almost always have companions in our sorrow. Among those companions are children. If you are a bereaved parent or grandparent, the children in your life are grieving along with you. Even if you are a single person, you may have nieces or nephews who mourn the loss of the loved one for whom you also grieve. Understanding the grief of children is an important component in our own journey through sorrow.

In my experiences of grief, I have been keenly aware of the bereavement of my children. When Clare's mother died and when my mother died, our children had lost their grandmother. When Erik died, our children had lost a brother. In these experiences, our grief mingled and merged with theirs. When my mother died, all forty-two of her living grandchildren grieved. I felt a responsibility to help my brothers and sisters and my nieces and nephews through that experience.

A single woman who taught five-year-olds in Sunday school for more than thirty years made a practice of visiting the children in her class whenever they had a loss. She always took some simple remembrance to the grieving child, usually a piece of candy or a coupon for an ice cream cone. She told me, "Even though these children may not understand death the way adults do, they have feelings that are important." When this dear lady died, it was not surprising that the sanctuary was filled for her funeral. Many of those in attendance had been in her Sunday school class.

A grandfather and his six-year-old grandson had a very close, loving relationship. When the grandfather died suddenly, the family wanted to be as gentle as possible as they told the boy about the death. His mother, father, and grandmother tearfully told him that his grandfather had gone to heaven to be with Jesus. The next day the family gathered at the funeral home to view the body. The six-year-old saw his grandfather's body in the casket. The boy looked around the funeral home and asked, "Is this heaven?"

"No," he was told. "This is a mortuary."

When the family returned to the grandparents' home, the boy announced to gathered friends, "Grandpapa is not in heaven. He is down the road in a motel, dressed up in a coat and a tie, sound asleep."

Children think in concrete terms. Little children, especially children under the age of five or six, usually experience death in a matter-of-fact way. Their childish perspective and their honesty can be refreshing, helpful, insightful, and even humorous to the grieving adults around them.

When our oldest son, Mike, was three years old, I took him to visit my eighty-six-year-old grandmother. We walked into her home and sat down in her living room. Mike's first words to his great-grandmother on that occasion were, "Mammy, you are going to die."

"Well, yes, I am," she said. "Why do you say that?"

"Because, Mammy, you are very old."

Mammy, who had nine children and thirty-six grand-children, laughed and asked her three-year-old great-grandson, "Mike, when I die, are you going to come to my funeral?"

"If you invite me, I will."

"You are invited. You tell your daddy to bring you to my funeral."

When Mammy did die about six months later, Mike re-membered that he was invited to her funeral.

The family had a graveside service for my grandmother. She had always said that she did not like riding in cars when she was alive, and she certainly did not want to be driven around town after her death. We took Mike to this service. The casket was in place.

"Where is Mammy?" Mike asked.

"Do you see that big box over there?" I asked. "That is called a casket. Her body is inside that box. Her spirit is in heaven."

He said, "I just want to take a little peek."

"We are not going to do that. Mammy wanted her casket to stay closed."

"How do you know she is in there?"

"I just know that her body is in there. Her spirit is in heaven."

After the service was over, Mike wanted to see the workers close the grave. Beginning what has become a time-honored family tradition, we stayed to watch. The casket was lowered into the vault, and the lid was put in place. Mike watched the men with the shovels throw the dirt on top of the vault. Then he wanted to jump up and down on the dirt. With tears in my eyes, I let him experience this event in his usual exuberant way. I thought nothing would please my grandmother any more than to have a great-grandchild jumping up and down on her grave.

After Mammy's freshly closed grave was covered with flowers, we got into our station wagon to drive away from the cemetery. I looked in the rearview mirror; Mike was looking out the back window. He said, "Hey, Dad. How is Mammy going to get out of that box?"

That is concretized thinking. It is very difficult for young children to understand the way we conceptualize death, especially the concept of bodily death and bodily resurrection.

How then are parents and family members to tell children about death? In more than forty years of pastoral ministry, I have learned some guiding principles that I have found helpful. While each situation and every family is unique, these six principles are helpful to almost all of us.

Principle 1: Tell the Truth

Nothing is more confusing to a child than deception, even when well-intentioned. Like most of us, children have built-in radar. They can sense when something is troubling the adults in their world. The advice of the apostle Paul to Christians is "speaking the truth in love" (Eph. 4:15). To speak the truth in love, as simply and with as few words as possible, is the best way to tell children about death.

One Monday afternoon, I waited with a mother and grandparents for a five-year-old to return home from kindergarten. This intelligent child's parents were divorced. He had spent the previous weekend with his daddy. Early on Monday morning, after the boy had returned to his mother, the boy's father committed suicide. The child's mother and grandparents asked that I be there when the boy came home from school to help them tell him about the death. Yet I knew it was important for them, not me, to actually speak the truth.

The little boy bounded out of his aunt's minivan, clutching a crayon-drawn picture in his hand. When he entered the room, he went straight to his mother. He crawled into her lap and put his hand on her cheek. "Mama," he asked, "why are you crying?"

She hugged him close to her and said, "Your daddy died this morning, and I am very sad."

For a while there were quiet tears and no words. Then the grandmother brought milk and chocolate chip cookies from the kitchen. Surprised, the boy asked if he could really have a snack in the den, something usually not allowed. He took a few bites of a cookie and a sip of milk. Then he broke the silence. "I drew a picture today," he said. "It is Daddy and me fishing." He explained that over the weekend he and his dad had been fishing, and he had caught his first fish. After a while longer, the boy put his head on his mother's shoulder and asked, "Mama, what killed my daddy?"

The young mother mustered her courage and said, "He did." It was enough to say.

Telling the truth is important, but it does not have to be told with many words. Often children will set the pace, asking questions when they are ready for more information. Remember, grief is a process for children as well as for adults. Recovery from some grief experiences, as in the case of the one I have described here, will take years.

Principle 2: Use Clear, Simple Words

We have developed a euphemistic language for our descriptions of death. Phrases like "passed away," "went to meet his Maker," or "gone to be with Jesus" are not the best ways to talk with children about the reality of death. Unfortunately, conscientious parents and caring adults become concerned that they need to communicate Christian doctrine to their little ones when death occurs. There is a time in a child's life to teach about resurrection and eternal life, but it may not be in the intensity of bereavement. Wise parents and teachers will wait for the teachable moment when these abstract concepts can be better taught.

A fellow pastor and good friend shared an experience that he had while serving a rural church in North Carolina early in his ministry. An eight-year-old boy had a pet beagle, Barney. Each morning Barney followed the boy to the bus stop and met the school bus every afternoon. The boy and his dog played together every day after school. One cold winter morning, after the school bus drove away, the beagle was hit and killed by a dump truck. The boy's mother asked the young pastor if he could be at the home when her son returned.

Eager to help, the pastor was at the farmhouse and did all of the talking, far too much talking. The gist of his fifteen-minute explanation was "Barney was in the road. A dump truck ran over him." Then compromising and confusing his own beliefs, the inexperienced minister added, "Jesus has taken your dog to heaven."

Finally, the pastor paused and asked, "Son, do you have any questions?"

The boy thought for a moment and inquired, "Preacher, what does Jesus want with a dead dog?"

When euphemistic language is used to tell children about death, it is usually more confusing than clarifying. I realize that Paul wrote to the Thessalonians about the resurrection of "those who have fallen asleep" in Jesus (1 Thess. 4:14). But I encourage you not to make the mistake of telling a child that a deceased loved one has fallen asleep in Jesus. With some children, associating sleep with death will cause trouble at bedtime for weeks to come.

Principle 3: Children Are People Too

Though children may express their feelings differently, their grief is just as deep as that of the adults around them. We help them when we enable them to express their sorrow in childlike ways.

The Neelys are a large family. I am the oldest of my parents' eight children. Mom and Dad have forty-five grandchildren, four deceased. One grandchild, William, was stillborn. Another grandson, Kres, William's twin, was hydrocephalic and profoundly retarded. Kres died at age twelve. Still another, Katherine, was brain-damaged before birth in an automobile accident when my sister was eight months pregnant. After an emergency Caesarean birth, Katherine lived for only six months. The fourth, our son Erik, was twenty-seven when he died following an epileptic seizure. Large families experience a lot of grief.

Among Mom and Dad's children are six ordained pastors. When we have a family funeral or a family wedding, the question is not who will conduct the service, but how many. When the funeral service for a grandchild has been planned, our custom has been to ask the boy cousins to be pallbearers. When my mother died, her eighteen grandsons carried her coffin. These young men have had multiple grief experiences and have served as pallbearers more times than many adults ever will.

In New Testament times, children were considered less than fully human—"half people" as it were. Perhaps the old adage "Children should be seen and not heard" had a very early beginning. Jesus, however, treated children differently. Jesus welcomed children just as he did all people (see Mark 9:36–37; 10:13–16).

My wife, Clare, has often reminded me of the importance of responding to children in their time of grief. Little children live life in a world of kneecaps. If we are to respond to them effectively, we must bend to their eye level. We must speak their language, but most of all we must pay attention to their feelings. Listening is better than talking. However, there is a sensitivity that goes beyond even listening.

My son Erik loved his cousins. He enjoyed playing football, softball, and basketball with them. He tussled with the boys and teased the girls. Because he was so big, his cousins thought of him as a large teddy bear. He was a gentle giant. On the day of Erik's funeral in mid-November, we were surprised by a snowfall. November snow in South Carolina is quite rare. We regarded it as a gentle mercy from a loving Lord.

At the grave, snow had accumulated enough on the grass to allow for making snowballs. After the committal service, while older cousins gathered around Erik's grave and sang Native American songs they had learned together in Boy Scouts with Erik, Taylor, who was one of the younger nephews, did what ten-year-old boys do. He made a snowball. He and Erik had enjoyed a happy relationship. No doubt they had thrown snowballs at each other in winters past.

When Taylor's mother saw the snowball in his hand, she corrected him. Clare, ever the caring aunt, intervened. "Please let him make a snowball," she pled, adding, "Taylor, throw it at Erik."

As the singing continued, Taylor walked to the edge of the grave, snowball in hand. Much to the dismay of the stunned funeral director, Taylor flung the snowball against the closed vault holding the body of his older cousin. Then, bursting into tears, he ran into the arms of his mother. Finally, catching his breath, he sobbed, "I wish he could throw one back at me."

Always remember: children are people too.

Principle 4: Take Age into Consideration

The age of a child can give clues as to what his or her reaction to death and grief might be and what adult responses might be most helpful. Frances Ilg and Louise Bates Ames's book *Child Behavior*, revised edition (1955; New York: Harper & Row, 1981) is a valuable guide to understanding how children develop. Preschoolers up to about age five might be expected to react to the death of a loved one in a matter-of-fact way. As we have seen, younger children think in concrete terms.

While predicting behavior for any child at any age is subject to error, eight-year-olds consistently seem to present unique problems. There is a time in the developmental process when the finality of death becomes a reality. This point of awareness of reality generally corresponds to age eight, sometimes a little earlier, sometimes a little later. Until this time, death seems reversible to a child. Once they can comprehend the finality of death, the time is ripe to teach the Christian hope of resurrection. The death of Jesus and his sacrifice become more meaningful, and the power of his victory over death becomes more significant.

When the finality of death becomes a reality, children enter a period in which they are especially susceptible to fear. Eight-year-olds cognitively can understand the finality of death, so we need to be especially careful about what we tell them.

An eight-year-old boy who has previously enjoyed weekend visits with his grandparents no longer wants to spend the night in their home. He begins to realize that they could die, and he is afraid he will wake up one morning with two corpses in the house. An eight-year-old girl is afraid for her parents to go away together for an out-of-town trip. Her fear is that they will both die in an accident, and she will be left alone.

As a pastoral counselor, I learned early to ask the age of the child when parents made an appointment to discuss concerns regarding a child. Many times the child in question was an eight-year-old. A fearful child makes for fearful parents. They worry that something is wrong with their child. Sometimes parents and other adults insist that the child face his or her fears at the time of a death. I have known relatives who forced frightened children to reach into an open casket to touch Grandpa's hand or who lifted them up to kiss Grandma's cheek one last time. Believe me, these forced tactics do not reduce fear. They more likely increase fear and cause continuing problems for the child and the parents.

The role of caring adults is to be the calm amidst the storm of fear in a child's life. Letting children decide if they want to view the body of a loved one is best. Speak tenderly to them with respect for their feelings and understanding of their fears. Reassure them of your love. Extend to them the same courtesy you would to any other person who preferred not to view the body or even attend the funeral.

Principle 5: Children Learn from Grieving Adults

Funeral customs in any culture can be quite strange to any person who witnesses them for the first time. One specialist in the religious education of children, who was also a close friend of our family, recommended that parents take their children to a funeral before the age of six. She suggested that the funeral might be for a person that neither the parents nor the child knew in a close, personal way, someone who was a casual acquaintance. Our friend felt this would give children an opportunity to experience cultural traditions regarding death before the highly emotional loss of a beloved family member.

Sometimes, well-meaning adults protect children from hurt by omitting them from the family visitation and the funeral. Remember that the death of a loved one and the subsequent bereavement provides an opportunity for children to learn how adults, especially people of faith, deal with their own grief. Children will learn best if adults around them are open to them. To say "I am sad because Granddaddy died" is appropriate. It is also accurate for Christians to affirm "I am also glad because Granddaddy has gone to heaven."

For many families, a funeral provides the occasion for a family reunion. For several years, Clare's family had funerals so frequently that cousins joked with each other, "We've got to stop meeting like this." Upon taking their leave from each other, they might comment, "See you at the next funeral, if it is not mine." Such banter would perhaps bother some, but for Clare's family this added a little lightheartedness to the sadness.

The death of a loved one becomes the occasion for time together for many families. Some families spend this time in a variation of an Irish wake, sharing food, fellowship, and treasured stories about the deceased. Other families have a New Orleans–style celebration with a band and dancing. I have been with bereaved families in the mountains of Kentucky as they gathered in grief, singing hymns to the accompaniment of guitars, banjos, and mandolins. Whatever the family custom, this is a rich opportunity for children to be with their larger family and to learn from the adults who serve as role models.

On a recent visit to a bereaved family that had experienced several deaths in a few years, I heard an older teenager explaining things to her younger siblings and cousins. "When somebody in this family dies, Aunt Judy plays the piano and cries a lot, Dad acts like he's in charge and tells corny jokes to try to cheer everybody up, Aunt Jill takes over the kitchen and makes sure everyone eats well, and Uncle Joe sits on the back porch and doesn't say anything." Then she added, "I've decided I'm going to do this Mom's way. She laughs a little, cries a little, prays a lot, and loves a lot." Children learn by observing the adults around them. Faith, hope, and love are contagious.

Principle 6: Adults Can Learn from Children Too

Children learn from adults, and adults can also learn from children. The Gospel of Mark records two occasions when Jesus taught important lessons with the assistance of children.

In the first, following an argument among the disciples about who was the greatest, "[Jesus] took a little child and had him stand among them. Taking him in his arms, he said to them, 'Whoever welcomes one of these little children in my name welcomes me'" (Mark 9:36–37).

When I visit a family following a death, I invite the entire family to sit together, including the children. On one such visit, I began by speaking to a grandson: "Tell me about your granddad. What was he like?"

To the amazement of the adults in the room, the twelve-year-old said, "He taught me how to fish and how to throw a football. The best thing he ever did for me was after I was caught shoplifting. He made me pay for the candy bar I stole, and then he told me how to give my heart to Jesus." No one else in the family previously knew what the grandfather had done for his grandson.

Sometimes the children will speak immediately; sometimes they are more reserved. I make sure they have the opportunity to share their opinions. If we will pay attention, children have much to teach us.

The second occasion in which Jesus taught a lesson to the disciples with the assistance of a child was when they forbade children access to him. "When Jesus saw this, he was indignant. He said to them, 'Let the little children come to me, and do not hinder them, for the kingdom of God belongs to such as these. I tell you the truth, anyone who will not receive the kingdom of God like a little child will never enter it'" (Mark 10:14–15).

Many of the principles discussed in this chapter apply to adults as well as to children. Becoming as little children, as Jesus instructed, may mean to trust as a child, to have a childlike sense of wonder, to cultivate playfulness, or to acknowledge our dependence. In times of grief, becoming as little children may mean to "rejoice with those who rejoice; [and to] mourn with those who mourn" (Rom. 12:15).

My mother hated funerals. At an early age, she was held over the casket of a person she did not like even when he was alive. She was forced to hug the cadaver; she never got over it.

When a friend or family member died, my mother would find refuge in the company of her eight children and her many grandchildren, often offering to keep the children while others went to the visitation and the funeral. Consequently, my dad used to say, "If I die before your mama does, please don't make her go to my funeral."

My mother's birthday was the Fourth of July. Because it was also a national holiday, it was a perfect time for all of us to gather at her home. Each year a part of her birthday celebration was a parade around their spacious yard. With flags and hats, horns and kazoos, we marched in a crazy, hilarious, fun-filled procession. The parade included two physician sons-in-law, six ordained pastors, a nurse, a pharmacist, and several schoolteachers—all distinguished professional people on any other occasion. On Mama's birthday, eight children, eight in-laws, and forty-four grandchildren marched in her parade! A year or two before she died, she announced in no uncertain terms, "I want you to have a parade at my funeral."

Though she was not in the best of health, Mama's death came suddenly. She died in Dad's arms, at home in her bedroom, covered by one of her favorite quilts. It was exactly the way she would have wanted to die.

At her funeral, Mama's four sons spoke. We remembered her life and celebrated her new life in heaven. I suggested that perhaps God had reserved a rocking chair for her in heaven and that God had asked her to take care of the little children. My mother loved children; she had taught the three-year-old children in her church for fifty-four years. She taught a backyard Bible club at our home in the early days of the Child Evangelism Fellowship. She was responsible for leading many children to the Lord.

As we left the sanctuary to go to the cemetery, the organist played "The Battle Hymn of the Republic," another of her requests.

At the grave, one of my brothers and his wife surprised some of us by passing out kazoos. I am sure that colleagues, friends, and community leaders were astonished. I am also sure that nothing could have pleased Mama more than a joyful, tearful kazoo rendition of "When the Saints Go Marching In." At this unforgettable moment, children and adults alike became as little children. In that moment, I believe we were all a little closer to the kingdom of God.

Adults can learn from children.

A pastoral colleague brought his three elementary-age daughters to my mother's funeral. It was their first funeral and an opportunity for them to learn customs regarding death.

Following the service, my friend said his children had benefited from the experience. "The problem," he said, "is that the next time they go to a funeral, they will ask, 'Where are the kazoos?'"

Jesus told a brief parable about children in the market-place calling out to each other. "We played the flute for you, and you did not dance; we sang a dirge and you did not cry" (Luke 7:32). Through this simple parable our Lord implicitly encouraged his adult listeners to be responsive to both the joys and sorrows of life. Children seem to intuitively know how to respond to sorrow. After my mother's death, our family gathered at the home with my dad. I watched as one of Dad's granddaughters made her way through a room crowded with adults. She crawled up on my dad's lap, tenderly touched his face, and said, "I'm sorry, Bebop." Responding to others in their grief is at least part of what it means to become as little children.

PART THREE

6

Gifts of Grace

the tender mercies of god

Late one afternoon in the fall of the year, a fifteen-year-old girl stood in the church office sobbing and waiting to see me. We sat down together as I handed her a box of tissues.

"Tell me about your tears," I urged.

Barely able to speak, she explained that she had not been selected to be a cheerleader at her high school. Many were not selected, many more than selected, but her plight was different. Her mother had been a cheerleader. All three of her older sisters had been cheerleaders at the same high school she attended. From the time she was a little girl, she had gone to football games with her parents and watched her older sisters lead cheers. She had looked forward to the day when she would follow in their footsteps. Alas, it was not to be. They were all outgoing and popular. Though she was a beautiful young woman, she was more retiring and shy. She considered herself a failure because she was not selected as a cheerleader.

Over the next few weeks, we talked together several times. I encouraged her to go to the high school football games and suggested to her parents that they go with her. As I ministered to her, a concept came to mind that had never occurred to me before. The world has plenty of cheerleaders and precious few grief leaders. I suggested that she befriend the others who had not been selected as cheerleaders. Soon she discovered that out of her own disappointment, she could make a difference in the lives of other students who felt left out.

Over the years I watched as this young woman grew into maturity. God has blessed her with a ministry of encouragement in which she brings comfort and strength to others.

The kingdom of God needs grief leaders, people of compassion and sensitivity who can lead grieving people through the process of recovery. Grief leaders are those who are not afraid of tears, neither those of others nor their own. They understand that tears are a gift of grace.

The Gift of Tears

Following Erik's death, Clare gave a necklace to June, our daughter-in-law. A small antique bottle called a lachrymatory, a bottle for tears, was fastened as a pendant on a chain. This was a reminder of a verse from the psalmist David. Psalm 56 says God keeps track of our sorrows. He collects all our tears in a bottle (v. 8 NLT). Clare and June thought that the only problem with the tiny bottle was that it was just not large enough.

A further explanation of a lachrymatory is found in Rebecca Wells's book *The Divine Secrets of the Ya-Ya Sisterhood* (New York: HarperCollins, 1996). "In olden days it was one of the greatest gifts you could give someone. It meant you loved them, that you shared a grief that brought you together" (348).

I had coffee with two doctors on the medical staff at a local hospital. One physician who had suffered a deep loss said, "I know now why we are equipped with tear ducts. They are intended to be used." There is psychosomatic evidence that links chronic sinus problems in some people with an inability to cry adequately when it is appropriate to do so. The other physician explained, "Sinus problems are sometimes caused by weeping backwards. The tears flow internally rather than externally." This rather clinical discussion over coffee points to the truth that we all need to cry. There are no exemptions, even for caring professional people.

The Scriptures do not conceal the tears of Jesus. He wept at the tomb of Lazarus, and he wept over the city of Jerusalem. He wept in the Garden of Gethsemane and on the cross of Golgotha. Tears were a part of the humanity of Jesus. His weeping becomes an example for his first disciples and for us. As Jesus had predicted, after denying his Lord a third time Simon Peter was convicted by the crowing of a rooster in downtown Jerusalem, and he ran away weeping bitterly. The women who followed the grim procession along the Via Dolorosa, the way of sorrow, wept in grief. I continue to be astonished when well-meaning Christians instruct grieving people not to cry. If we cannot cry at the time of deep sorrow, then when should we cry?

Tears are gifts from God. Psalm 6 speaks to those who are grieving:

> I am worn out from groaning;
>> all night long I flood my bed with weeping
>> and drench my couch with tears.
> My eyes grow weak with sorrow.

> *verses 6–7*

In the same way that a loving parent understands and interprets the crying of a child, so our heavenly Father hears and understands our tears. Our tears become prayers without words. David recognized this when he said:

> The LORD has heard my weeping.
> The LORD has heard my cry for mercy;
>> The LORD accepts my prayer.

> *verses 8–9*

In the early stages of grief, there are times when tears flow uncontrollably. At other times, we are better able to monitor our crying and can even choose our own time and place to weep. This is not to say that our tears should be postponed indefinitely. The truth is that sometimes it is just inconvenient to cry.

My wife, Clare, has been my companion in both joy and sorrow. As best friends we have experienced that marital intimacy that allows us to learn from each other. Her clear insight and honest wit put things in a perspective that I appreciate. On the issue of choosing a time and place to weep, Clare said to friends, "I cry in the shower. Somehow being in the flow of warm water gives me permission to cry. It is the best place to really cry. It is just not as messy as crying any other time."

If all we do is cry, grieving becomes very boring. Laughter brings a balance to the grief process that can be found in no other way.

The Gift of Laughter

Some may find the notion that laughter can be a part of grief rather odd, even irreverent. The truth is that laughter can be a vital part of our grieving and can bring much-needed relief. Surprisingly, laughter is mentioned more times in the book of Job than in any other book of the Bible except the Psalms. There are seven references to laughter in both Job and Psalms. Though the references to laughter in Job are mostly mocking, the wisdom of Hebrew Scripture nonetheless offers a profound insight: "Even in laughter the heart may ache" (Prov. 14:13).

One of the neglected beatitudes of Jesus connects the experiences of weeping and laughter: "Blessed are you who weep now, for you will laugh" (Luke 6:21). The beatitude restates the Old Testament promise that God will grant his people "gladness instead of mourning" (Isa. 61:3).

Bill suffered a brain injury when he was an infant. His mother dropped him when she slipped on an icy sidewalk. The severe head injury resulted in lifelong cerebral palsy. As he grew older his body grew more and more contorted. His speech was slurred almost beyond understanding. His hand-eye coordination was nonexistent.

With all of his physical limitations, Bill had feelings, hopes, and aspirations that were normal. He wrote a weekly newspaper column and radio program on a typewriter, laboriously pressing the keys one at a time with a pencil held in his mouth. President Gerald Ford honored Bill as Handicapped American of the Year at a ceremony in the White House Rose Garden. Bill was a remarkable man despite his many problems. But Bill was prone to severe bouts of depression, plus he had made several attempts to take his own life. He often became angry because of a deeply held sense of injustice.

I received a telephone call informing me that Bill had been admitted to the hospital. When I entered his room he was laughing almost uncontrollably. In the many hours I had spent with Bill, I had only occasionally seen him laugh. His laughter became contagious as I tried to understand what was so funny. Finally, after more than an hour of laughter, Bill helped me understand. With his slurred speech, he said, "I fooled everybody. I always thought I would die of cerebral palsy complications or suicide. But I have colon cancer, and I am going to die like a normal person."

Bill's laughter may seem odd until we understand that his fervent prayer for years had been for normality in his life. His ability to laugh at the diagnosis of cancer reveals the kinship between humor and prayer. Genuine humor is a first cousin to prayer. We pray and laugh about the things that are most important to us. Honest humor is neither sarcastic nor biting. It is, rather, the ability to laugh at the very things we pray about, those things that are most important to us. Real humor is the ability to laugh at ourselves.

Throughout this book, I have tried to season the lessons I have learned about grief with humor. I take the same approach with bereaved families. Immediately before a funeral service, I usually gather the family for prayer. I tell them that we are going to worship. I ask that they have tissues at hand because they probably will cry some. I also tell them not to be afraid to laugh if something strikes them as funny. This is a pastoral way of granting permission to the family to experience the full range of emotions that accompany grief.

Mr. Jack was my father-in-law. He was a storyteller, with a quick wit and a wry smile that endeared him to almost everyone. His speech was as colorful as my grandfather's, salted with Southern witticisms and profanity. Shortly before his death from congestive heart failure, Mr. Jack and I had a private conversation. His acceptance of his impending death was evident. "This path that I'm on is getting mighty narrow. I don't believe I'm going to be able to turn around this time."

He went on to assure me that his relationship to God was in order. He asked me to conduct his funeral. He said, "Kirk, you're going to have to look out for Lib. She's going to need help, and I know I can count on you." I felt the burden of that responsibility, but I would not have had it any other way. He told me that he had written two letters to the family. One was to be read immediately after his death, before arrangements were made for his funeral. The other letter was to be read immediately after his funeral. I would find both letters inside a ledger in the top right-hand drawer of his rolltop desk.

Two weeks later Mr. Jack died. The family gathered the morning after his death, and I read the first letter aloud. He had included so much of himself, so much humor, that we laughed together for nearly an hour. His directions on finding pallbearers were especially funny. "Now that I'm gone," he wrote, "they may all refuse to attend. But they all owe me in one way or another." He explained that one lost a bet to him and had never paid him. Another, he said, should make a good pallbearer but only if he could have a little bourbon before the funeral. With that first letter, Mr. Jack had established an attitude of joy for his own funeral.

Then we went to the local mortuary in the small town where Clare's parents lived in order to make the funeral arrangements for Mr. Jack. We selected a polished pine casket because he had enjoyed woodworking. The funeral director then showed us a selection of vaults.

"We have three to choose from," he said in a somber tone.

"What is the difference?" I inquired.

Pointing to the top one, he said, "This is our top-of-the-line model." He paused and added, "It comes with a lifetime guarantee."

I stared at him in amazement. "Whose lifetime?"

He stammered, "I don't really know."

"How can a vault have a lifetime guarantee?"

"No one has ever asked that. That's just what they told me to say."

We purchased the bottom-of-the-line model.

You can imagine the laughter in Mr. Jack's service when I told the story of the vault selection. You may also be able to imagine the chagrin of the funeral director.

Mr. Jack's body was to be laid to rest in the churchyard of Emory United Methodist Church. The plots for the members of his large family had been designated for years. There had even been a family feud over who was to be buried in which plot. One brother and one sister had refused to be buried next to each other. For some, sibling rivalry continues all the way to the grave.

Thankfully, Mr. Jack's grave was undisputed territory, but when the mortuary sent a crew to open the grave, they encountered a problem. About two feet down, they found an underground granite slab. They solved the problem by partially opening the grave designated for Miz Lib, excavating under the slab deeper than the usual six feet, and sliding Mr. Jack's bottom-of-the-line vault containing the pine casket sideways under the slab. I, of course, explained this at his funeral and speculated about what he would have said about it all. Laughter was the congregational hymn at his memorial service. Family members enjoy remembering it to this day with comments like, "Jack would have loved every minute of it."

Following the drive back from the country churchyard, I again gathered the family to read the second letter. We could hardly wait. It was a sweet, touching letter about his love for each of us. He included a section on how he had tried to provide for his wife and his children. Then this line: "Lib, I believe there will be enough for you to live out your days in contentment and comfort. You will not be able to live in the lap of luxury, and there is certainly not enough for you to have a live-in boyfriend. If you take up with somebody, I may have to come back and straighten things out." There was no word on how he expected to get past that granite slab on top of his inexpensive vault.

The wisdom of the Bible says, "A cheerful heart is good medicine" (Prov. 17:22). Laughter is a natural tranquilizer, and, as far as I can tell, it has no adverse side effects. There is, as Scripture affirms, "a time to weep and a time to laugh" (Eccles. 3:4). In my experience, grief is a time for both.

To be together and remember our loved one will almost certainly prompt tears and laughter. Paul counsels Christians, "Rejoice with those who rejoice, mourn with those who mourn" (Rom. 12:15). The ability to do both in times of bereavement is a healing blessing.

The Gift of Helping Hands

For several months following my son's death, I had been reading Eugene Peterson's book *Living the Message* as a part of my daily devotions. On May 24, Erik's birthday, I read a selection entitled "Christian Hope Alerts Us." It was a reminder that hope spurs us to action.

The response that others make to bereaved people is active. The ministry of casseroles is only one of the many ways people respond. After Erik died, our daughter-in-law wanted to wear Erik's wedding band on a chain as a pendant. She visited a local jewelry shop owned and operated by longtime family friends. They helped her select a nice chain and gave it to her as a gift. When June returned to our home wearing the ring on the new chain, she coined a phrase: "I've heard you talk about the ministry of casseroles, but this is a ministry of jewelry!"

Immediately following death, either sudden or anticipated, there is much to be done. Friends gather to say, "What can I do?" Many practical tasks are best done by nonfamily members. Grab a legal pad and start a list of those who phone or come by to visit. Write down who brings which dish to the home. Get a roll of masking tape to put names on the bottom of dishes that will need to be returned. Write down who sent which flower arrangement. A grieving family can be helped greatly by friends who organize the kitchen and coordinate the meals. Sometimes those who are grieving have to be reminded to eat and sleep.

Clare and I experienced three major losses: Miz Lib's death, Erik's death, and my mother's death, all within fourteen months. One of the most thoughtful acts of kindness to us came from a friend who offered to help address thank-you notes. The good friend received one of the first notes of appreciation.

In the church that I serve, we have a group of men who are skilled carpenters. When a person has suffered a stroke or another debilitating illness that requires assistance, these men volunteer to make the modifications that make the home wheelchair accessible. They have constructed many a wheelchair ramp. They have widened doorways and changed kitchen appliances to facilitate the adjustment to life for the wheelchair dependent.

In an extended illness the wheelchair ramp is a visible reminder of those who care. Following the death of a wheelchair-dependent person, the ramp is a reminder that the loved one is no longer limited by physical infirmity. When the family is ready, the same men who built the ramp return to remove it.

Another expression of love was given to Christie, who wanted a porch, a place to park in her wheelchair and enjoy the breeze and the sunshine. Christie was a remarkable woman, a physical education teacher for multiple handicapped children at the South Carolina School for the Deaf and Blind. For many of her fifty-three years, she tried to help children overcome their physical limitations.

Christie was in our church choir and also played handbells. Because she knew sign language, she often interpreted for the deaf in our worship services. Frequently, she put on an apron and worked in the church kitchen. Christie had a servant's heart.

Then Christie was diagnosed with cancer. For five years she fought a valiant battle. "I wish I had a porch," she said one day near the end of her life, "a place where I can sit in the sun and enjoy the breeze." A member of her Sunday school class took her comment to heart and rallied a group of church members. Some donated money; others gave hours of skilled labor to construct a porch on Christie's house. The project was a labor of love.

On a visit to the cancer unit at the hospital, I spoke with Christie about the mystery of life and death. "The angels may come to take me to heaven before I get to see the porch," she said.

"If that happens," I suggested, "ask them to give you a flyover."

Christie was able to sit in the breeze on her porch, just one time.

The Gift of Redemptive Grief

Grief is an exhausting, depleting experience. Luke, the physician, gives a compassionate interpretation as to why the disciples fell asleep in the Garden of Gethsemane. When Jesus rose from prayer and returned to the disciples, "he found them asleep, exhausted from sorrow" (Luke 22:45).

The sheer fatigue of grief can be debilitating. Early in the grief process, we may feel immobilized, unable to do the routine tasks of life. Immediately after the death of his daughter, a despairing father told me, "It takes me half an hour to put on my socks." One reason that our bodies seem to be moving in slow motion is that our minds are working overtime trying to make sense out of what seems to be nonsense.

In the first days and weeks of a long bereavement, our meaning and purpose may focus on setting an example for others in our family. A woman who lost her husband wondered, "He was in every part of my life. What am I going to do without him?" My answer was, "This is your opportunity to teach your children and grandchildren how a Christian faces such deep sorrow and continues to live life to the fullest." As difficult as it is to put one foot in front of the other, Christians in grief learn that "they that wait upon the LORD shall renew their strength; . . . they shall walk, and not faint" (Isa. 40:31 KJV).

In his book *Man's Search for Meaning*, Viktor Frankl describes how he found meaning in the horror of the Nazi death camps during World War II. As a physician without medicine or other medical supplies, he could do little to alleviate the suffering of his fellow Jewish prisoners. He would sit by their beds, picking lice from their bodies or mopping their fevered brows with a cold rag. Out of his own suffering, he found meaning in giving comfort to others.

Any person who has had a loved one in a hospital intensive care unit knows that there are actually two intensive care units. There is that area with limited visiting hours behind the double doors where the medical staff cares for those who are seriously ill. The second intensive care unit is the intensive care waiting room where family members spend long hours hoping and praying for their sick loved ones on the other side of those double doors. When I visit a family in the intensive care waiting area, I am often asked to include other patients and other families in prayer. People who suffer together before the uncertainty and the fragility of life quickly find a common bond, a fellowship of suffering.

Over the years, I have made up a wise old saying: "Don't ever waste a good experience of suffering." It is not just my idea. Scripture enjoins us to redeem the time (see Eph. 5:16 KJV), which simply means to make the most of our time, even our times of mourning. Those of us who are bereaved come to a point in the grief process when our joy and our energy begin to return. As that occurs, we are better able to discover our own area of ministry.

Organizations such as MADD (Mothers Against Drunk Driving) or programs such as the Amber Alert System each had their beginnings in a decision made by grieving persons to take action to prevent others from being hurt by the same suffering they have endured. The church that I pastor has a Survivors of Suicide group started by two men, a mortician and a pastoral counselor, who both know the agonizing grief following the suicide of a family member. Another group that meets at our church, Healing Hearts, is a ministry for parents who have suffered the death of a child. A mother who lost a child in a drowning accident started the group.

The apostle Paul expresses this concept of taking action when he writes, "Praise be to the God and Father of our Lord Jesus Christ, the Father of all compassion and the God of all comfort, who comforts us in all of our troubles, so that we can comfort those in any trouble with the comfort we ourselves have received from God. . . . And our hope for you is firm, because we know that just as you share in our sufferings, so also you share in our comfort" (2 Cor. 1:3–4, 7).

In the Bible's love chapter (1 Corinthians 13), Paul ends his discourse on the nature of love with the affirmation, "These three remain: faith, hope and love" (1 Cor. 13:13). As mentioned earlier, I have often referred to the Christian's response to bereavement as a ministry of casseroles. When caring people don't know what to say, they bring food. The more difficult the loss, the more covered dishes come through the kitchen door! One man told me that after the sudden death of his mother, his family received fourteen macaroni-and-cheese casseroles. (Those inclined toward bringing covered dishes might try a little variety!)

Combining hope, which we will talk about in the next chapter, with love creates a blend of spiritual ingredients that becomes comfort food for those who are grieving. A simple casserole is an outward expression of an inner concern that provides physical nourishment for the body and spiritual sustenance for the soul. The ministry of casseroles is a ministry of grace, symbolizing the faith, hope, and love that surround us in our mourning.

7

Hope in the Midst of Grief

symbols of God's presence and peace

My teacher Dr. Wayne Oates often said, "Trying to define hope is like trying to nail Jell-O to the wall." The apostle Paul attempts a definition of hope in his marvelous treatise on suffering: "Hope that is seen is no hope at all. Who hopes for what he already has? But if we hope for what we do not yet have, we wait for it patiently" (Rom. 8:24–25).

Anyone who knows grief personally can appreciate the difficulty an apostle as great as Paul had in defining a longing that is not seen and not fully available until the waiting has ended. A man grieving deeply for his wife of fifty-three years asked honestly, "I know as a Christian I am supposed to have hope, but is there really any hope this side of heaven?" Paul asserts, "We do not . . . grieve as others do who have no hope" (1 Thess. 4:13 NRSV). Likewise, the writer of Hebrews says, "We have this hope as an anchor for the soul, firm and secure" (Heb. 6:19). The assurance of hope in the midst of bereavement is a welcomed comfort.

The Colors of Grief and Hope

The sorrow of grief is depicted as colorless. A photographer whose wife died with a brain tumor said, "I am living in a black-and-white world. There is no color, only shades of gray." From 1901 to 1904 the artist Pablo Picasso painted all of his pictures in shades of blue. His subjects during this "Blue Period" were the lonely, suffering, poverty-stricken outcasts from society. At the time, Picasso was despondent, nearly penniless, perhaps unable to afford a variety of colors. Certainly the Blue Period in his work corresponds to a blue period in his life. When people are despairing, they are often described as feeling blue. An entire genre of music, the blues, puts the life of sorrow into song.

Try to imagine Noah standing on the deck of the ark. The rains have ended, but the sky is as heavy and overcast as it has been for the five months since it stopped raining. The noise and the stench within the ark are almost unbearable. The waterlogged world before him is desolate. Thoughts of unspeakable death flood Noah's mind. He is looking for some sign of hope.

As he searches the barren horizon, Noah spies a small bird flying toward him. The same dove he had released earlier, returning as it had seven days before. On that occasion, the dove returned with no sign of hope. Now, as the dove wings its way closer, Noah can see that the bird carries something in its beak. He reaches out his hand to receive the bird and sees the fresh green tip of an olive branch. Not much of a gift, to be sure, but it is a sprig of hope, just enough green in a gray world to make the eyes of a six-hundred-year-old man brim with tears.

When the ark finally finds a resting place and the animals return to nature, Noah worships God. As he does, the gray skies break with a shaft of sunlight. For the first time, Noah witnesses the colors of hope: the resplendent colors of the rainbow.

On more than one occasion, I have stood with a family at a graveside under a gray sky. As if choreographed by the Divine Director himself, sunlight breaks through the clouds, creating a multicolored rainbow. In another setting, these rainbows would be of momentary interest, briefly enjoyed and then forgotten. For a bereaved family, the rainbow becomes an enduring, colorful symbol of hope.

Symbols of Hope

Because hope is difficult to define, I have learned that symbols of hope can be meaningful to those who are grieving. As I discussed in the first chapter of this book, snowflakes became a comforting symbol for our family in that first winter following Erik's death. At our home in South Carolina, an occasional snowfall is regarded differently than in areas where snow becomes wearisome.

In the spring and summer following our son's untimely death, the bluebird became our warm weather sign of hope.

Feathered Hope

Birds are an oft-claimed symbol of hope. Emily Dickinson wrote,

> Hope is the thing with feathers
> That perches in the soul,

And sings the tune without the words,
And never stops at all.

No. 254 (composed ca.1861;
first published 1891)

Dickinson's analogy between hope and birds is not un-common. Sally Middleton is a North Carolina artist who specializes in wildlife paintings. When I first became familiar with her work, I noticed a single blue jay feather in almost all of her paintings. I knew there must be a story behind this pattern in her work. Yet blue jays do not enjoy the best reputation in the world of ornithology. Legend has it that on Fridays this raucous bird carries sticks to the devil to keep the fires of hell stoked. Why, I wondered, was Sally Middleton so consistent in including a blue jay feather in her paintings?

I later learned the story. One gray day, burdened with fam-ily problems and financial concerns, Sally Middleton took a walk in the woods near Asheville, North Carolina. As she walked, a blue jay feather floated down in front of her. She caught the feather in her hand and took it as a gift of grace. From that day on, the blue jay feather was her personal sym-bol of hope.

A while back, I was asked to participate in a funeral service for a young man who died in a drowning accident during the first month of his senior year in high school. His death, of course, was very difficult for his family, especially for his parents. Their grief was compounded by the fact that their son was an excellent swimmer.

The funeral service was at a Methodist church filled to overflowing by teenagers, parents, teachers, and family friends. The body was cremated so that the committal could be at a camp where this young man had spent several happy summers.

I was invited to travel to the camp to lead the committal service for family and a few close friends at a beautiful spot beside the lake. Throughout the day I had been trying to think of a symbol of hope for the parents and siblings of the young man. As I walked along a path through the woods, I found one blue jay feather and then another. Picking up both feathers, I put them in my Bible. When we arrived at the burial site, a shovel with a stirrup handle had been pushed into the ground behind the simple wood and brass urn containing the ashes. The shovel stood as a marker above the place of interment.

I began the committal service by reading the verses from Romans 8 that I mentioned earlier—"Hope that is seen is no hope at all. Who hopes for what he already has? But if we hope for what we do not yet have, we wait for it patiently"— and I shared the story of Sally Middleton. Then I gave both the father and the mother one of the blue jay feathers, suggesting that these feathers might become a sign of hope for them. We had a closing prayer, which included the words of committal. Just as I concluded the prayer, a blue jay squawked, flew through the circle of those gathered, and perched on the handle of the shovel just behind the urn.

The audible gasp of the assembled mourners gave way to a holy silence. No one made a sound, not even the blue jay.

It was a singular moment of quiet reverence.

Later in the week the young man's mother returned to the camp to place flowers on her son's grave. As she stood weeping with a friend, she was astonished when a blue jay landed on her shoulder. After a moment or two, the bird flew away.

Later a camp ranger gave a logical explanation for the blue jay's behavior. During the summer, the camp staff had fed peanuts to the blue jay, training him to perch on their shoulders. When the camping season ended, the blue jay, unafraid of humans, continued to beg for peanuts whenever they visited his domain. Even so, for those parents the reasonable explanation did nothing to diminish the blue jay and his feathers as symbols of hope.

Other birds can also be a symbol of hope. The state bird of Tennessee is the mockingbird. With its repertoire of thirty or more songs, it was my grandfather's favorite bird. I never see or hear one without thinking of him.

The sight of a bright red cardinal reminds me of my mother and my grandmother. A perky Carolina wren brings to mind my mother-in-law, Miz Lib. A simple birdfeeder will bring these signs of hope flocking to your backyard.

Other symbols of hope abound in nature.

Flowering Hope

In the Sermon on the Mount, Jesus taught his disciples how to manage anxiety. The Master instructed them to pay attention to the birds of the air and the flowers of the field (Matt. 6:25–26, 28–29). Like birds, flowers can also become symbols of hope for those who mourn.

Gene was a dear friend who grew up on a farm in Cherokee County, South Carolina. His success with the family business enabled him to build a home on the family farm within a stone's throw of the old home place. The beautiful new house had a wraparound porch, graced with big rocking chairs. Visitors to the home entered a long driveway flanked on the left by a horse pasture and a weathered barn. Up a hill to the right was the foundation of the former farmhouse. In the early spring, this hill was covered with bright yellow daffodils, originally planted by Gene's mother around the old home's fieldstone foundation. The daffodils had naturalized, spreading helter-skelter down the hillside. Each year the flowers bloomed from late February through March.

After several months of health concerns, Gene became quite ill. The diagnosis was a rapidly growing, rare form of cancer. His death came quickly, far sooner than most of us had expected. While his death was anticipated, it was also sudden, making the grief experience jagged and confused.

In mid-March, on a bright, warm Sunday afternoon, just before he died, Gene asked if he could see the daffodils. Surrounded by his loving wife, four children, and several grandchildren, Gene was transported by wheelchair down the driveway near the barn. He sat quietly for a few moments, taking in the sight of the hillside covered in delicate yellow blooms dancing in the breeze.

Three days later, on Wednesday, Gene died. At the graveside in a country churchyard, the children and grandchildren each placed a daffodil, picked from the hillside, on the wooden casket. Yellow daffodils will be a perennial symbol of hope for Gene's family.

Flowers can be as surprising as the unexpected appearance of a rainbow or the unusual timing of a brightly colored bird. A young wife and mother died suddenly while in routine surgery. The bright October day of her funeral began early for the young husband. As he walked the family dog early in the morning, he noticed a tall blue iris blooming in the flower bed planted and cared for by his wife. The iris had bloomed, as expected, the previous spring. The October bloom came as a complete surprise. He cut the single flower and had a woman in his church arrange it with greenery in a vase to be placed at the front of the church for his wife's funeral. The iris was a symbol of resurrection hope for him and for his family.

In the late afternoon following Erik's funeral, I walked alone in my garden. The mid-November day was cold. We had been pleasantly surprised by an inch of snow. Though the snow was melting, a patch remained in a shady spot beneath a large oak tree in our yard. I could hardly believe my eyes when I saw the bloom of a purple violet nodding in the snow. The violet was blooming entirely out of season, but it was exactly the right season for my sorrowing heart. I knew this was a touch of God's grace, a tender mercy.

Symbols of hope are all around us for those with eyes to see and ears to hear.

All Things Bright and Beautiful

Only the divine imagination of the Creator God limits the possibilities for these external symbols of hope. Throughout the pages of the Bible, the stars in the night sky, the grains of sand on the desert floor, a burning bush, and a cloud shaped like a hand all become signs of God's presence in the lives of his people. In both the Bible and in contemporary life, the evidence of angels brings hope and comfort.

In forty years of ministry, I have learned that the bereaved can find hope in the small things of life, in "all things bright and beautiful." A line from the familiar hymn by that title affirms, "He made their glowing colors, / He made their tiny wings." Many times over the years I have stood with families at a grave surrounded by flowers. I have seen a ladybug perch on my own lapel as if it were pinned in place. I paused in midsentence to watch a hummingbird dart under a funeral home tent for a sip of nectar from a spray of flowers on a casket. Bumblebees and honeybees are frequent summer visitors among mourners where blossoms abound.

One of my most memorable funeral experiences was the service for a woman whose home in North Carolina was decorated with a butterfly theme. She tended a special butterfly garden in her backyard designed to attract what she referred to as "flying flowers."

When she died after an extended illness, it was only natural to emphasize her love of butterflies at her memorial service. Flower arrangements sent by friends and family members included silk butterflies. We sang the congregational hymns "For the Beauty of the Earth" and "All Things Bright and Beautiful." The solo by a family member was "How Great Thou Art." In the eulogy, I pointed out that the butterfly was a Christian symbol for the resurrection.

At the interment in a cemetery on a mountainside, the crowning touch to her service came as a complete surprise. As I finished reading the Scripture and just before I offered the prayer of committal, a monarch butterfly fluttered into the funeral tent and alighted on the Bible I held in my hands. The tiny creature perched like a bookmark between the opened pages. For a few silent seconds all of us marveled at the amazing timing of divine choreography. After the orange-winged visitor departed, I suggested that we sing "Amazing Grace," which was also unplanned. You can imagine what that spontaneous moment meant to the woman's bereaved family.

These external symbols of hope bring with them encouragement and comfort. Like baptism and communion, they are outward signs of an inner grace. These outward symbols point to a sacred reality: All things created by God can become instruments of his grace and peace for those who are suffering.

However, the ultimate hope for Christians is eternal life.

Eternal Life Then and Now

Two young seminarians had summer employment with an evangelistic organization in South Carolina. They went door-to-door throughout a rural county. One sweltering August afternoon they visited an unpainted farmhouse. The dirt yard was teeming with children, chickens, and dogs. Stepping up on the porch, the young men could see through the patched screen door. A woman was on her hands and knees scrubbing the floor.

They knocked on the door. The woman rose from her work to greet them. The tired soul pulled her hair back out of her face and said wearily, "What can I do for you?"

One seminarian answered, "We've come to tell you how you can obtain everlasting life."

The woman wiped the sweat from her brow. "No, thank you," she said. "I've had about all of this I can stand."

If everlasting life is just more of the same, it is not very good news. Yet the biblical concept of eternal life is not only more life, it is also better life. Neither is eternal life limited to life after death. Eternal life begins with our relationship to Christ this side of death. Jesus taught, "I have come that they may have life, and that they may have it more abundantly"

(John 10:10 NKJV). The Christian hope of eternal life has to do with the quality of life as well as the quantity of life. Christian hope for those who are grieving is not only the hope of heaven, though it is certainly that. Our hope is also found in living life here and now with this eternal quality even before death. And yet our ultimate hope is found in heaven.

The Hope of Heaven

We actually know precious little about heaven. I recently asked the congregation at the church I serve to point to heaven. Almost all of them pointed up toward the sanctuary ceiling. I suggested that if we considered the rotation of the earth and repeated the exercise in exactly twelve hours, we would be pointing in the opposite direction. When we try to imagine what heaven is like, we are limited by our perception of time and space.

I encourage grieving people to use their imagination when thinking of heaven. When I conduct a funeral, I try to make the service as personal as possible. For an avid golfer, I imagine entering heaven as walking up the eighteenth fairway at Augusta National Golf Course during the Masters Tournament. The azaleas are blooming, the sky is clear, and a great gallery of witnesses is cheering. For an avid fisherman, heaven includes a pristine trout stream. Paradise must certainly be a place where "a river runs through it," as a novel and a movie by that title suggest. For the diabetic, long prohibited from enjoying good desserts, the table of heaven surely must include strawberry shortcake and banana pudding.

As I shared in an earlier chapter, when we saw the snow falling on the day of Erik's funeral, Clare said, "I imagined

Erik saying to God, 'Lord, this is going to be a hard day for my family. Could you please surprise them?' "

Some object to this way of thinking about the heavenly kingdom of God. Imagination is too much fantasy and too little solid theology. Please remember that the entire book of Revelation recorded by John is a vision. On a Sunday morning, exiled on the island of Patmos, gazing at the waves with the wind in his face, an elderly John received his divinely inspired vision of heaven. It is also important to keep in mind that the book of Revelation is ultimately a book of hope.

I enjoy the story about an old shoeshine man who kept a Bible close at hand. A college professor took the chair to have his shoes polished. He noticed that the Bible was opened to the book of Revelation.

"I see you are reading the book of Revelation," the professor commented to the old man bent to the task of shining his shoes.

"Yes, sir!"

"Do you understand what you are reading?"

"Oh, yes, sir. I understand!"

The professor paused. "That is impossible. Biblical scholars have debated the meaning of the book of Revelation for centuries. How can you, a simple shoeshine man, possibly understand it?"

"Professor, I understand it!"

"Tell me, then. What does it mean?"

"It means that the Lord is going to win!"

The gift of imagination is a path to hope exactly because it makes clear the central reality of heaven affirmed throughout Christian history: *Christus Victor*!

When Jesus gathered his disciples in the Upper Room to celebrate Passover on the eve of his death, he offered words of comfort and hope: "I am going to prepare a place for you. And if I go and prepare a place for you, I will come back and take you to be with me that you may be where I am" (John 14:2–3). Jesus identifies heaven as a particular place, made ready for our arrival. More importantly, we will be with him.

The hope of heaven is more than looking forward to a peaceful, beautiful place. This ultimate hope involves anticipating an intimate relationship with our Lord and Savior. The apostle Paul writes that in heaven we will know fully, even as we are fully known. Our understanding of heaven now is like seeing "through a glass, darkly," or gazing into a badly silvered mirror. We see only a dim reflection. In heaven, we will know our Savior "face to face" (1 Cor. 13:12 KJV).

The promise of a face-to-face, intimate relationship with Christ gives rise to the hope of the renewal of other close relationships. Though there are many unanswered questions about the nature of our heavenly relationships, we can imagine a joyful reunion with those we love.

Frank and Martha had a good marriage for nearly forty years. As an airline pilot, his work required frequent international travel, a part of his job he found appealing. She, too, enjoyed traveling. After their only child became an adult, Frank and Martha adjusted their life together to make the most of his need to travel and her desire to travel. They arranged their schedules so that four or five times a year they would meet in a foreign city and spend about a week together. Airfare was always a bargain for them, making each rendezvous quite affordable. When Martha was diagnosed with ovarian cancer, Frank took early retirement. After a long illness, Martha died.

Several weeks after her funeral, Frank and I had breakfast together. He told me how he was coping with her death. "At her funeral, it was as if I had taken her to the airport. She has flown on to a beautiful city, and she is waiting, as she so often did, for me to arrive. When I get there, we are going to have the best time of our lives."

I also anticipate a great family reunion in heaven. My mother was one of eleven children. My father was one of nine. I am the oldest of eight children. Clare also has a large extended family. People in large families have to say good-bye often. Gathering for funerals and grieving becomes a regular part of life.

As these sad occasions occur, I try to imagine what it must be like for those family members who have gone before us. In my mind's eye, I can see a family reunion. As another member of the family arrives, the person is greeted with gladness and love. In my imagination my grandfather, Mr. Jack, and Erik are swapping stories. My mother, Miz Lib, and my grandmothers are seated in rocking chairs with babies in their laps. My three uncles, all in the construction industry in this life, were not issued harps, but hammers, upon their arrival. They are at work helping to prepare those places that are being readied for the arrivals of the rest of us. All of this, of course, is just my imagination, but it is based on the firm belief that heaven is where relationships are renewed. Our relationship to Christ is central, but others are important as well.

Last year I conducted one of the most beautiful and unusual funerals in my ministry. Joy was the oldest child in a family of six. She had a teaching certificate and worked as a school psychologist. She wanted to be a wife and a mother. Joy loved the Lord, her family, contemporary Christian music, her dogs, and her flip-flops—her preferred foot attire. Flip-flops would become a symbol of hope for her friends and family.

Joy had frequent conversations with her mother. The two women were best friends and prayer partners. After several conversations about Joy's desire to find a husband, mother and daughter began praying that God would bring a husband into her life. For more than six months, they prayed specifically about this request.

Joy died suddenly. When I met with her parents, her mother told me how they had been praying for a husband for Joy. Her mother said, "I was praying for a groom for Joy, never realizing that God was preparing her for the Bridegroom. This funeral needs to be like a wedding, a real celebration of her life."

A florist who frequently prepares for weddings at our church prepared the sanctuary for Joy's funeral. White flowers, candles, and delicate tulle decorated the church. Visitors to the church who knew nothing of my conversation with the parents commented that it looked like a wedding. In the eulogy, I used Jesus's parable in Matthew 25 about the five wise virgins who were ready when the bridegroom arrived. At the funeral, one solo was sung, Joy's favorite song, a song about heaven by MercyMe called "I Can Only Imagine."

The hope of heaven is based on a personal relationship to God in Christ. Imagination gives shape to that hope as it did for John, writing his inspired vision from Patmos. Near the end of his recorded revelation, John wrote of heaven:

> I saw the Holy City, the new Jerusalem, coming down out of heaven from God, prepared as a bride beautifully

dressed for her husband. And I heard a loud voice from the throne saying, "Now the dwelling of God is with men, and he will live with them. They will be his people, and God himself will be with them and be their God. He will wipe every tear from their eyes. There will be no more death or mourning or crying or pain, for the old order of things has passed away."

He who was seated on the throne said, "I am making everything new!"

Revelation 21:2–5

No more tears? No more death? No more mourning? No more grief?

I can only imagine!

Comforting Scriptures

Let the beloved of the LORD rest secure in him,
    for he shields him all day long,
      and the one the LORD loves rests between his
      shoulders.

                            Deuteronomy 33:12

The eternal God is your refuge,
    and underneath are the everlasting arms.

                            Deuteronomy 33:27

Have I not commanded you? Be strong and courageous.
Do not be terrified; do not be discouraged, for the LORD
your God will be with you wherever you go.

                                   Joshua 1:9

Be merciful to me, LORD, for I am faint;
    O LORD, heal me, for my bones are in agony.
My soul is in anguish.
    How long, O LORD, how long? . . .
I am worn out from groaning;
    all night long I flood my bed with weeping
    and drench my couch with tears.

My eyes grow weak with sorrow;
>they fail because of all my foes. . . .
The LORD has heard my cry for mercy;
>the LORD accepts my prayer.

>>>Psalm 6:2–3, 6–7, 9

The LORD is my shepherd, I shall not be in want.
>He makes me lie down in green pastures,
he leads me beside quiet waters,
>he restores my soul.
He guides me in paths of righteousness
>for his name's sake.
Even though I walk
>through the valley of the shadow of death,
I will fear no evil,
>for you are with me;
your rod and your staff,
>they comfort me.

You prepare a table before me
>in the presence of my enemies.
You anoint my head with oil;
>my cup overflows.
Surely goodness and love will follow me
>all the days of my life,
and I will dwell in the house of the LORD
>forever.

>>>Psalm 23

As the deer pants for streams of water,
>so my soul pants for you, O God.
My soul thirsts for God, for the living God.
>When can I go and meet with God?

My tears have been my food
    day and night,
while men say to me all day long,
    "Where is your God?"
These things I remember
    as I pour out my soul:
how I used to go with the multitude,
    leading the procession to the house of God,
with shouts of joy and thanksgiving
    among the festive throng.

Why are you downcast, O my soul?
    Why so disturbed within me?
Put your hope in God,
    for I will yet praise him,
    my Savior and my God.

My soul is downcast within me;
    therefore I will remember you
from the land of the Jordan,
    the heights of Hermon—from Mount Mizar.
Deep calls to deep
    in the roar of your waterfalls;
all your waves and breakers
    have swept over me.

By day the LORD directs his love,
    at night his song is with me—
    a prayer to the God of my life.

I say to God my Rock,
    "Why have you forgotten me?
Why must I go about mourning,
    oppressed by the enemy?"

My bones suffer mortal agony
   as my foes taunt me,
saying to me all day long,
   "Where is your God?"

Why are you downcast, O my soul?
   Why so disturbed within me?
Put your hope in God,
   for I will yet praise him,
   my Savior and my God.

Psalm 42

Hear my prayer, O Lord;
   let my cry for help come to you.
Do not hide your face from me
   when I am in distress.
Turn your ear to me;
   when I call, answer me quickly.

For my days vanish like smoke;
   my bones burn like glowing embers.
My heart is blighted and withered like grass;
   I forget to eat my food.
Because of my loud groaning
   I am reduced to skin and bones.
I am like a desert owl,
   like an owl among the ruins.
I lie awake; I have become
   like a bird alone on a roof.
All day long my enemies taunt me;
   those who rail against me use my name as a
      curse.
For I eat ashes as my food
   and mingle my drink with tears.

Psalm 102:1–9

Praise the LORD, O my soul;
    all my inmost being, praise his holy name.
Praise the LORD, O my soul,
    and forget not all his benefits—
who forgives all your sins
    and heals all your diseases,
who redeems your life from the pit
    and crowns you with love and compassion,
who satisfies your desires with good things
    so that your youth is renewed like the
        eagle's. . . .
For as high as the heavens are above the earth,
    so great is his love for those who fear him;
as far as the east is from the west,
    so far has he removed our transgressions from
        us.
As a father has compassion on his children,
    so the LORD has compassion on those who fear
        him;
for he knows how we are formed,
    he remembers that we are dust.
As for man, his days are like grass,
    he flourishes like a flower of the field;
the wind blows over it and it is gone,
    and its place remembers it no more.
But from everlasting to everlasting
    the LORD's love is with those who fear him,
    and his righteousness with their children's
    children.

Psalm 103:1–5, 11–17

I love the LORD, for he heard my voice;
    he heard my cry for mercy.

Because he turned his ear to me,
    I will call on him as long as I live.

The cords of death entangled me,
    the anguish of the grave came upon me;
    I was overcome by trouble and sorrow.
Then I called on the name of the LORD:
    "O LORD, save me!"

The LORD is gracious and righteous;
    our God is full of compassion.
The LORD protects the simplehearted;
    when I was in great need, he saved me.

Be at rest once more, O my soul,
    for the LORD has been good to you.

For you, O LORD, have delivered my soul from
      death,
    my eyes from tears,
    my feet from stumbling,
that I may walk before the LORD
    in the land of the living.
I believed; therefore I said,
    "I am greatly afflicted." . . .
Precious in the sight of the LORD
    is the death of his saints.

                    Psalm 116:1–10, 15

Out of the depths I cry to you, O LORD;
    O Lord, hear my voice.
Let your ears be attentive
    to my cry for mercy.

If you, O LORD, kept a record of sins,
    O Lord, who could stand?

But with you there is forgiveness;
    therefore you are feared.

I wait for the LORD, my soul waits,
    and in his word I put my hope.
My soul waits for the Lord
    more than watchmen wait for the morning,
    more than watchmen wait for the morning.

O Israel, put your hope in the LORD,
    for with the LORD is unfailing love
    and with him is full redemption.
He himself will redeem Israel
    from all their sins.

Psalm 130

Do you not know?
    Have you not heard?
The LORD is the everlasting God,
    the Creator of the ends of the earth.
He will not grow tired or weary,
    and his understanding no one can fathom.
He gives strength to the weary
    and increases the power of the weak.
Even youths grow tired and weary,
    and young men stumble and fall;
but those who hope in the LORD
    will renew their strength.
They will soar on wings like eagles;
    they will run and not grow weary,
    they will walk and not be faint.

Isaiah 40:28–31

Who has believed our message
    and to whom has the arm of the Lord been
        revealed?
He grew up before him like a tender shoot,
    and like a root out of dry ground.
He had no beauty or majesty to attract us to him,
    nothing in his appearance that we should
        desire him.
He was despised and rejected by men,
    a man of sorrows, and familiar with suffering.
Like one from whom men hide their faces
    he was despised, and we esteemed him not.

Surely he took up our infirmities
    and carried our sorrows,
yet we considered him stricken by God,
    smitten by him, and afflicted.
But he was pierced for our transgressions,
    he was crushed for our iniquities;
the punishment that brought us peace was upon
        him,
    and by his wounds we are healed.

                        Isaiah 53:1–5

Come to me, all you who are weary and burdened, and I
will give you rest. Take my yoke upon you and learn from
me, for I am gentle and humble in heart, and you will find
rest for your souls. For my yoke is easy and my burden is
light.

                      Matthew 11:28–30

Jesus said to her, "I am the resurrection and the life. He who
believes in me will live, even though he dies; and whoever

lives and believes in me will never die. Do you believe this?"

John 11:25–26

Do not let your hearts be troubled. Trust in God; trust also in me. In my Father's house are many rooms; if it were not so, I would have told you. I am going there to prepare a place for you. And if I go and prepare a place for you, I will come back and take you to be with me that you also may be where I am. . . .

Peace I leave with you; my peace I give you. I do not give to you as the world gives. Do not let your hearts be troubled and do not be afraid.

John 14:1–3, 27

I consider that our present sufferings are not worth comparing with the glory that will be revealed in us. The creation waits in eager expectation for the sons of God to be revealed. For the creation was subjected to frustration, not by its own choice, but by the will of the one who subjected it, in hope that the creation itself will be liberated from its bondage to decay and brought into the glorious freedom of the children of God.

We know that the whole creation has been groaning as in the pains of childbirth right up to the present time. Not only so, but we ourselves, who have the firstfruits of the Spirit, groan inwardly as we wait eagerly for our adoption as sons, the redemption of our bodies. For in this hope we were saved. But hope that is seen is no hope at all. Who hopes for what he already has? But if we hope for what we do not yet have, we wait for it patiently.

In the same way, the Spirit helps us in our weakness. We do not know what we ought to pray for, but the Spirit himself intercedes for us with groans that words cannot express. And he who searches our hearts knows the mind of the Spirit, because the Spirit intercedes for the saints in accordance with God's will.

And we know that in all things God works for the good of those who love him, who have been called according to his purpose. For those God foreknew he also predestined to be conformed to the likeness of his Son, that he might be the firstborn among many brothers. And those he predestined, he also called; those he called, he also justified; those he justified, he also glorified.

What, then, shall we say in response to this? If God is for us, who can be against us?

Romans 8:18–31

When the perishable has been clothed with the imperishable, and the mortal with immortality, then the saying that is written will come true: "Death has been swallowed up in victory."

"Where, O death, is your victory?
Where, O death, is your sting?"

The sting of death is sin, and the power of sin is the law. But thanks be to God! He gives us the victory through our Lord Jesus Christ.

1 Corinthians 15:54–57

Praise be to the God and Father of our Lord Jesus Christ, the Father of compassion and the God of all comfort, who comforts us in all our troubles, so that we can comfort those in any trouble with the comfort we ourselves have received from God. For just as the sufferings of Christ flow over into our lives, so also through Christ our comfort overflows.

2 Corinthians 1:3–5

For our light and momentary troubles are achieving for us an eternal glory that far outweighs them all. So we fix our eyes not on what is seen, but on what is unseen. For what is seen is temporary, but what is unseen is eternal.

2 Corinthians 4:17–18

Brothers, we do not want you to be ignorant about those who fall asleep, or to grieve like the rest of men, who have no hope. We believe that Jesus died and rose again and so we believe that God will bring with Jesus those who have fallen asleep in him. According to the Lord's own word, we tell you that we who are still alive, who are left till the coming of the Lord, will certainly not precede those who have fallen asleep. For the Lord himself will come down from heaven, with a loud command, with the voice of the archangel and with the trumpet call of God, and the dead in Christ will rise first. After that, we who are still alive and are left will be caught up together with them in the clouds to meet the Lord in the air. And so we will be with the Lord forever. Therefore encourage each other with these words.

1 Thessalonians 4:13–18

And I heard a loud voice from the throne saying, "Now the dwelling of God is with men, and he will live with them. They will be his people, and God himself will be with them and be their God. He will wipe every tear from their eyes. There will be no more death or mourning or crying or pain, for the old order of things has passed away."

Revelation 21:3–4

Helpful Books

Many helpful books on grief are available. These are some that have helped me.

John Claypool, *Tracks of a Fellow Struggler: How to Handle Grief*, rev. ed. (1974; New Orleans: Insight Press, 1995). A collection of sermons from the heart of an exceptional preacher delivered during the terminal illness and following the death of his daughter, Laura Lou.

David Cox and Candy Arrington, *Aftershock: Help, Hope, and Healing in the Wake of Suicide* (Nashville: Broadman & Holman, 2003). I recommend this book for those suffering grief following suicide. David is a seasoned pastoral counselor whose father committed suicide. Candy is a gifted Christian writer who enabled those grieving the loss of a loved one by suicide to tell their story.

C. S. Lewis, *A Grief Observed* (1961; repr., New York: Harper-Collins, 1996). The world's foremost Christian apologist writes about the challenge to his own faith in his grief following the death of his wife, Joy.

Harold Ivan Smith, *A Decembered Grief: Living with Loss while Others Are Celebrating* (Kansas City: Beacon Hill, 1999). The author is a grief counselor who understands the difficulties that holidays can present to those who are bereaved.

Granger E. Westberg, *Good Grief* (1962; repr., Minneapolis: Fortress, 1971). This is the tried-and-true classic for the grief-stricken and is still in print after forty-five years.

Nicholas Wolterstorff, *Lament for a Son* (Grand Rapids: Eerdmans, 1987). The author is a professor of philosophical theology at Yale Divinity School. The book is a devotional collection of brief reflections following the death of his son Eric in a mountain-climbing accident.

Kirk H. Neely is senior pastor of Morningside Baptist Church in Spartanburg, South Carolina. He holds a doctor of ministry degree in pastoral counseling and psychology of religion from The Southern Baptist Theological Seminary. Neely has been a pastor and counselor for over forty years.

"Just sayi[ng] you've don[e]

Misty handed him a box of red velvet cupcakes. "These are just a token of my appreciation."

"You didn't have to go to all this trouble, but thank you." Leon was touched beyond words by her thoughtfulness. Misty wasn't the first woman to bring him baked goods, but unlike some of the others, she didn't have a hidden agenda.

"I am forever grateful, Leon."

He took a bite, then another. "Aunt Eleanor's right. You definitely know your way around a kitchen."

She laughed. "It's just a cupcake."

The look Misty gave him was so galvanizing it sent a tremor through him. The pounding of his heart quieted only once she disappeared outside.

Dear Reader,

I'm so excited to introduce my new series set on the fictional island of Polk Island, South Carolina, a small coastal town founded by Polk Rothchild in 1870. The lush green foliage, sandy beaches and well-maintained homes attract tourists from all over the world.

An unfortunate circumstance brings new resident Misty Brightwater into Leon Rothchild's life unexpectedly. Their initial meeting is tense, but eventually Leon and Misty discover they are destined to be a part of one another's lives.

This is a story of a love that was always meant to be, of new beginnings and finding the courage to take a second chance in love despite past experiences. I hope you will enjoy Leon and Misty's journey to their happily-ever-after. Thank you for your support, and I look forward to hearing from you.

Best,

Jacquelin Thomas

Facebook: Facebook.com/JacquelinWrites

Twitter: Twitter.com/JacquelinThomas

HEARTWARMING

A Family for the Firefighter

—

Jacquelin Thomas

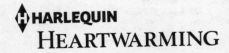

HARLEQUIN
HEARTWARMING

HARLEQUIN®
HEARTWARMING™

Recycling programs
for this product may
not exist in your area.

ISBN-13: 978-1-335-17988-3

A Family for the Firefighter

Copyright © 2021 by Jacquelin Thomas

All rights reserved. No part of this book may be used or reproduced in
any manner whatsoever without written permission except in the case of
brief quotations embodied in critical articles and reviews.

This is a work of fiction. Names, characters, places and incidents
are either the product of the author's imagination or are used fictitiously.
Any resemblance to actual persons, living or dead, businesses,
companies, events or locales is entirely coincidental.

This edition published by arrangement with Harlequin Books S.A.

For questions and comments about the quality of this book,
please contact us at CustomerService@Harlequin.com.

Harlequin Enterprises ULC
22 Adelaide St. West, 40th Floor
Toronto, Ontario M5H 4E3, Canada
www.Harlequin.com

Printed in U.S.A.

Jacquelin Thomas is an award-winning, bestselling author with more than fifty-five books in print. When not writing, she is busy catching up on her reading, attending sporting events and spoiling her grandchildren. Jacquelin and her family live in North Carolina.

Books by Jacquelin Thomas

Harlequin Kimani Romance

Five Star Attraction
Five Star Temptation
Legal Attraction
Five Star Romance
Five Star Seduction
Styles of Seduction
Wrangling Wes
Five Star Desire
Forever My Baby
Only for You
Return to Me
Another Chance with You

Visit the Author Profile page
at Harlequin.com for more titles.

CHAPTER ONE

TIRED AND HUNGRY, Leon Rothchild parked in the driveway of his aunt's home in the Victorian district of Polk Island a few minutes past 8:00 a.m. He'd just finished a twenty-four-hour shift at the local fire department. Whistling softly, he got out of the truck and walked past neatly trimmed rosebushes in pink, red and white to the steps of the wraparound porch. Perched on each side of the front door were Eleanor Rothchild Pittman's beloved Boston ferns. He paused in his tracks when he spied her keys still in the lock.

Aunt Eleanor forgot to take her keys inside... They'd probably been out here all night. He grabbed them and entered the house that he had grown up in.

"Hey... It's just me, Auntie." Leon always felt a sense of security whenever he visited his childhood home.

"C'mon to the kitchen, son," she called out in response. "You're just in time for breakfast."

He'd been fighting hunger pangs all morning, so her words were music to his ears.

The sound of bacon sizzling in the pan on the stove, the smell of fresh coffee and the stack of pancakes made Leon's mouth water.

Eleanor assessed him as he strolled into the kitchen. "Son, you look like you're losing weight. I don't know what they feed you at that station, but you need to come by here or the café every day to pick up a plate of food."

Laughter spilled from his lips as Leon embraced her. "Aunt Eleanor, I'm fine. You don't have to worry about me." Dangling her keys, he said, "But you're going to have me worrying about you. You really need to be more careful. We get a lot of strangers on the island."

"Oh, my goodness," she murmured. "I would've been running myself ragged looking for them." Eleanor took the keys and hung them on a hook beside the refrigerator.

When his parents died in a car accident twenty years ago, Eleanor and her husband, Walter, stepped up to care for Leon and his younger brother. He was ten years old at the time and Trey was eight. Four years later, Walter passed away. Bonded by blood and their grief, Eleanor and the boys clung tight to one another.

Leon picked up a plate and placed two slices of bacon and a small stack of pancakes on it.

"I'm glad you finally hired somebody for the bakery. You've been working some pretty long hours for the past couple of months." Leon poured himself a cup of coffee, then strode over to the table in the breakfast nook and sat down.

"Me, too," Eleanor stated. "She started earlier this week. She moved to Polk Island from Charleston. She's very dependable and the girl can *bake*..."

"Sounds like she's perfect for the job, then."

Eleanor pressed both hands over her eyes as if they burned with weariness. "It's perfect timing too with June right around the corner. I already have five contracts for wedding cakes. This month and the next are gwine be busy months. Polk Island, South Carolina, is becoming a popular spot for weddings. There was even a nice article in one of the bridal magazines about our little island."

The ringing of the telephone cut into their conversation.

"Hey, sugar... Your ears must've been burning. I was just talking about you..." Eleanor's left eyebrow rose a fraction. "Whoa... Slow down... I'm having trouble understanding you."

Leon blessed his food, but before he could take a bite, the change in Eleanor's tone caught his attention. When she hung up, he asked, "Everything okay?"

Worry colored her expression. "I'm not sure. I need to go to the shop, son. My new employee has a family emergency. Silas isn't coming in until noon. Josh can't handle the morning rush alone. Finish eating your breakfast." Eleanor picked up her purse and keys. "Just put everything in the dishwasher when you're done."

"You're finally using it?" Leon asked in amazement. She'd put up a fuss when he first purchased it for her nearly two years ago. His aunt had insisted it could never clean her dishes as well as she could.

Eleanor broke into a grin. "I've seen the light."

He chuckled.

She planted a kiss on his cheek. "Love you, son."

"I love you too, Auntie."

Leon returned his attention to the food on his plate.

TEARS BLINDING HER eyes and choking her voice, Misty Brightwater rushed into the day care. "How could you just let my ex-husband walk in here and take my daughter? I should've been notified the moment he arrived." She struggled to keep her voice at a normal volume to avoid upsetting any of the children.

The woman working the front desk uttered, "I had no idea… I'm so sorry."

"I made it clear to the director that John didn't have permission to ever take Talei from here. He has *supervised* visitation only." Misty put a hand to her mouth to keep from screaming as her heart pounded rapidly. After a moment, she said, "I've called the police. They should be here any minute."

"I'm so sorry, Miss Brightwater. I didn't know."

"Where's Mrs. Washington?" Misty asked. She grappled to keep the panic she felt from her voice. She was working at Polk Island Bakery & Café when John called to let her know he had their daughter and was going to disappear. "I wouldn't have known a thing if my ex-husband hadn't called me."

"Mrs. Washington left to pick up some supplies, but she should be back soon. I really am sorry. There wasn't a note in the system."

"Well, there should've been," Misty stated.

The thought of Talei being with John terrified Misty. His actions of late had caused her to take certain precautions to avoid exactly what just happened.

Twenty-six years old, Misty had moved to Polk Island three weeks ago to build a new life for her and her three-year-old daughter, Talei.

When she and John were first married, Misty used to ride with him in his delivery truck to different towns, including Polk Island. She fell in love with the small-town charm of the place. After their divorce was final, she decided to put down roots here. It was the perfect place to raise Talei.

At least she thought so at the time.

LEON LOCKED UP his aunt's house and climbed into his car. He was so tired his nerves throbbed. The May air blowing hot through the open windows of his truck did nothing to stop the sweat dampening his neck and chest. Leon made a mental note to take his truck to the shop to have the air conditioner checked out before the hot weather took over. He considered stopping by his mechanic right now, but he really wasn't up for it.

Leon was exhausted. He never slept well whenever he had to stay at the station. At the moment, he was looking forward to a shower and his bed. A couple of hours of sleep would do him a world of good.

A cow darted out into the middle of the road just as a car was speeding up the road. Stomach churning, Leon watched the events unfold as if in slow motion.

The Mercedes Benz GLS 580 connected full

force with the animal before it careened off the road and smashed into a huge oak tree, stopping the car.

Leon quickly pulled off the road and parked. His heart fluttered hard against his ribs. He took a deep breath, then exhaled to calm himself. Certified as an EMT, he called 9-1-1 as he rushed over to the vehicle to check on the occupants inside.

"There's been an accident on Highway 171," Leon said when someone answered. "I have a male unconscious. Massive head trauma, extrication necessary… John…" he uttered, recognizing his friend. For a moment, he forgot to breathe. "Thirty-year-old male."

The sound of a child screaming hysterically commandeered his attention.

Leon's gaze swept to the back seat. A little girl strapped in a car seat sobbed and trembled with fear. He worked swiftly to get to her. "It's gonna be okay, little one," he murmured. Faced with the choice of whom to care for first, Leon chose to remove the child. John's injuries were life-threatening, which made performing triage in the field impossible.

Talei… John's daughter…

"There's a toddler in the vehicle, as well," he told the operator who was on speaker.

He laid the phone on top of the vehicle to free

the little girl from the restraints of the car seat and checked for visible injuries. "She's scared but looks okay otherwise."

Leon's emotions were all over the place when she stopped crying and clung to him for dear life. "We're gonna get your daddy some help," he whispered while keeping John out of his daughter's view.

"Daddee…" she said, her eyes bright with unshed tears. "I w-want Da… Daddy. I…s-scared."

Leon's heart broke at the stark fear he saw in her eyes. "You're safe, Talei. I promise."

Teary-eyed, she looked up at him.

"My name is Leon. I'm a friend of your daddy."

"Eon," she said in a trembling voice. "I scared."

He took her tiny hand in his. "You don't have to be afraid."

Leon glanced over his shoulder at his friend and prayed help would arrive soon. He released a short sigh when he heard sirens. "Hang in there, buddy. Paramedics are coming. I have your little girl and she's fine. Hang in there." He could see the fire engine moving swiftly toward them. He knew an ambulance would be close behind.

The paramedics arrived seconds later, followed by a police car.

Leon gestured for a female coworker to come over. He was more than a little relieved to hand over the little girl to someone else. Had his own daughter lived, she would've been the same age. It was too much of a painful reminder.

"This is my friend Lizzie. She's going to stay with you so I can help your daddy."

"Help D-Daddy."

"Hey, sweetie. I have this little guy for you." Lizzie gave Talei a teddy bear wearing a T-shirt with the fire station logo emblazoned on it. "He's gonna be right here with you, and so am I."

His coworker Charles asked, "You know the driver?"

"Yep. He's the friend I told you about. His name is John Hayes."

Leon and John had been roommates in college until John was forced to withdraw from school to help his father with the family trucking business in Orangeburg, South Carolina. He was shocked seeing John and wondered when he'd arrived on the island. Normally, his friend would notify him whenever he was coming to the area.

Leon walked with Charles to the damaged vehicle, where they were in the process of extricating John.

"This doesn't look good," he mouthed under his breath.

Charles placed a comforting hand on his shoulder. While he stood there, random thoughts circulated in his mind. Leon recalled the moment when John asked him to be Talei's godfather. He couldn't accept at the time because it was too soon after the death of his own wife and child. Leon wasn't able to attend John's wedding because he'd just started training with the fire department, so he never had the opportunity to meet his ex-wife.

In recent months, John often confided his struggles and frustration in wanting to get his family back together. He'd shared with Leon that his marriage had been a tumultuous one. He blamed his ex-wife for being selfish and thinking only of herself.

Once John was extricated, paramedics transported both him and his little girl to the hospital. Talei put up a fuss when they put her in the ambulance, but she calmed eventually when Lizzie promised to ride to the hospital with her. They decided it was best to transport John in a separate ambulance.

Leon gave the police an overview of what happened, then he was free to leave.

Exhausted and emotionally drained, Leon headed in the direction of his home but turned around abruptly and drove to the hospital instead. There was no point in going home when his thoughts were of John and Talei.

A notification came across his phone. It was an Amber Alert for Talei Hayes.

"John, what did you do?" Leon whispered, bewildered. "They're acting like you kidnapped your daughter."

At the hospital, he spoke briefly with a nurse who informed him that his friend was taken to the trauma center.

His stomach in knots, Leon dialed the number to Hayes Trucking. "Hello... I need to speak with Elroy regarding his son. Tell him it's Leon Rothchild calling."

Elroy came on the phone a minute later. "Hey, it's good to hear from you..."

"John's been in an accident," Leon quickly interjected. "He's at Polk Island Hospital."

"What happened?"

"A cow ran into the middle of the road... His daughter was with him."

"Is Talei..." Elroy's voice broke.

"No... She's fine," Leon quickly assured Elroy. "She's scared, as you can imagine, but no injuries. But John's in serious condition."

"Clara and I will be heading your way within the hour. Keep me posted on my son, Leon, until we arrive."

"I will."

Leon hung up and placed another call. "Aunt Eleanor, I'm at the hospital. John was in an accident. He's in bad shape."

"Oh, honey, I'm gonna pray for him."

"They're saying he kidnapped his daughter. I need to speak with the sheriff. It has to be a misunderstanding."

"Lawd, noo," Eleanor moaned.

"What's wrong?" Leon inquired.

"Misty's little girl was taken by her daddy. That's why I rushed over here to the shop."

He was stunned. "Is her name Talei?"

"Yes."

Leon couldn't believe it. There had to be an explanation. "John wouldn't do something like this, Auntie. I've known him a long time."

"The man Misty described sure doesn't sound like the one I got to know and love," Eleanor said. "I had no idea that she was even married to John Hayes. She never mentioned his name."

"I called his parents. He's in surgery right now, but I thought they should know what happened."

"Of course they should," Eleanor agreed. "Sugar, how are you doing?"

"I don't know what to do with all this," Leon confessed. "When I last saw John, he mentioned taking his daughter on a trip. I knew he and his ex were fighting for custody, but he led me to believe that they had worked everything out."

"I can't believe he'd just take his daughter like that," Eleanor said. "John must've felt pretty desperate."

"There are two sides to this story—that's for sure," Leon stated.

"When Silas comes to work, I'll come to the hospital to sit with you."

"Thanks, Auntie."

Leon heard Talei crying for her mother. He walked in quick strides toward her room.

As soon as the little girl saw him, she reached for him.

Leon hesitated a moment, unsure whether he should pick her up, but the fear on her face propelled him into action. He took her into his arms. "Talei, hey. It's alright. You're safe. This nurse just wants to make sure you're okay. Her name is Amy."

Sniffling, Talei eyed him as a lone tear rolled down her cheek.

"Leon, how does she know you?"

"Her father is my friend. Were you able to make contact with her mother?"

"She's on the way," Amy responded. "Do you think you can stay with this little princess while I check her out?"

He nodded.

"I want M—Mommy," Talei whimpered.

"She will be here soon," Leon said. Stark fear glimmered in Talei's eyes. He just wanted to make her feel safe.

"Daddy...c-car..."

"The doctor's taking good care of him," Amy told her. "Can you tell me who this is on your dress?"

"Minty M—Mouse."

"I love Minnie Mouse." Smiling, Amy continued to check Talei's vitals. "I love Mickey Mouse, too."

"Mickey and Minty on TV."

"Yes, they are. Would you like to watch some television?"

Talei nodded.

Amy turned to the Disney Channel. "Here you go, cutie."

"Wado," she whispered when the nurse left the room.

Wado. Leon recalled a conversation he'd had with John. His friend had boasted about his daughter learning the Cherokee language and traditions. He'd also confided that his father was against it—Elroy Hayes thought it disgraceful that his daughter-in-law had dismissed her Black heritage by choosing to live as a Native.

Leon sat on the bed with Talei on his lap. Mickey and Minnie Mouse danced across the screen, but the little girl remained strangely quiet. Every now and then she would jump at the sound of a loud noise.

"I scared," she mumbled.

"I'm not gonna let anything hurt you," Leon assured her. "Your mom will be here soon, but until she gets here, I'm not gonna leave you, little one."

She turned to look at him. "Eon... I want Daddy."

"He would be here with you, but he got hurt, so the doctor has to take care of him."

"Doctor make him better?"

"Yes. The doctor's going to take care of him."

Amy entered the room.

"Leon..." She placed her hand on his shoulder. "I'm sorry."

He felt the familiar stirrings of sadness. He knew John's condition was serious, but still he'd hoped and prayed for a positive outcome.

"He didn't make it," Amy said softly.

Leon fought back tears. "Thanks for letting me know." A raw and primitive grief overwhelmed him.

He glanced down at Talei, who looked to be falling asleep. When Leon tried to lay her down in the hospital bed, she began crying again.

"I'm here, sweetie. I'm not going anywhere.

I just wanted to make you comfortable. You look sleepy."

Talei clung to him, her dark curly puffs of hair tickling his neck.

"Okay, little one." Leon held her close to his heart.

Talei's eyelids grew heavy. She fought her exhaustion, but eventually drifted off to sleep.

Leon swallowed hard as he rocked gently back and forth.

John was dead. His friend was gone.

Anguish threatened to overwhelm him. His heart hadn't fully healed from the deaths of Vera and his own child. It was still broken into so many fragments, he wasn't sure it could handle another loss.

CHAPTER TWO

FEAR AND ANGER knotting inside her, Misty parked in the first available spot she could find near the emergency room. She nearly lost her footing when rushing out of the car, but she didn't let that stop her from running.

At the main registration desk, she demanded, *"Where's my daughter?* Her name is Talei Hayes."

The woman directed her to room 230.

When she neared the nurses' station, a doctor approached. "Are you John Hayes's next of kin?"

"Yes."

They found a quiet place to talk. "We did all we could, but John passed away while we were performing surgery. I'm very sorry."

"Where's my daughter?" Misty asked a second time, her voice rising an octave. "I want to see my little girl."

"Mrs. Hayes…"

"My last name is Brightwater. John and I are divorced." Misty eyed the doctor, shifting indignantly from foot to foot. "Look, I can't deal with his death right now. I just need to be with my child. She's probably terrified, and I need to be with her."

At the moment, she didn't care what anyone thought of her actions. Her focus was only on reuniting with Talei. Misty was devastated at the news of John's death, but she couldn't think about that now. He'd made her life miserable.

SHE WALKED BRISKLY toward the room, resisting the urge to break into a run. She burst in without knocking and was shocked to see a man holding and comforting her daughter. "Hello," she greeted. "Who are you?"

"I'm Leon Rothchild. I witnessed the accident."

She gave him a wry appraisal. "You're John's friend. You went to college together."

"Yeah, I am," he confirmed. "I just found out that you work with my aunt at the bakery. I called her earlier to tell her about John."

"Miss Eleanor was kind enough to give me a job when I needed one." Misty took her sleeping child out of his arms without preamble.

"She fell asleep about ten minutes ago."

They stared at each other.

His face was bronzed by long hours in the sun. Dark compelling eyes framed his handsome square face—Leon held his head high with pride. Misty noted how his long, muscled legs filled out the dark jeans, and the navy T-shirt with the fire department logo emblazoned across it pulled taut over his broad torso. His profile spoke of power and strength, but she was drawn by the sadness of his face.

As the silence stretched out, Misty grew more and more uncomfortable. She chewed on her bottom lip, while Leon stood so still, she could barely make out the slight rise and fall of his chest as he breathed.

After a moment, Misty said, "You said that you were there when the accident happened."

"Yeah. A cow ran out into the road. All John could do was swerve to keep from hitting the animal. I didn't know it was him at the time. I was the first person on the scene."

"It's fortunate that you of all people were there." Misty gestured to his shirt. "Being a firefighter and all."

"Yeah," Leon responded. "I just wish I could've done more."

"They told me when I got here that John died on the operating table." Holding her daughter close, she said, "I wanted to see Talei. I needed to be sure she was okay."

He leaned forward in his chair, and in a controlled voice, stated, "The police are saying he kidnapped her."

Misty eyed him as if trying to read his expression. "It's true. John took her from day care without my permission."

His eyes flickered a little. "I don't understand."

"John was upset over the judge's decision. I was given sole physical custody and he had supervised visitation."

Leon shook his head in dismay. "I know that John never would've hurt that little girl," he responded. "He loved his daughter."

"You don't really know the kind of man he was…"

Leon rose in one fluid motion. "I'll leave you to spend time with your daughter."

The tense lines on her face relaxed. "Thank you for everything."

"I'm just sorry things didn't turn out better for John. His parents are on the way here. I don't know whether to call and tell them that he's gone or just wait until they get here."

"It won't matter," Misty said. "It's not going to go well at all. They just lost their son."

LEON HADN'T EXPECTED to be struck by Misty's beauty or her generous mouth, which he found incredibly inviting. She had a curvy build, and her black hair flowed past her shoulders in soft waves. Her coppery-brown skin glowed from the sheen of perspiration. She wore a pair of faded jeans and a loose, floral-printed top.

That awareness of Misty; even the unfamiliar compulsion Leon had to stare at her was unlike him. It unsettled him in her presence. "I guess I'll go make that call."

He walked briskly out of the room just as his aunt was fast approaching.

"I came as quickly as I could," Eleanor said. She took a moment to catch her breath before asking, "How is Talei?"

"The doctor says she's fine physically. She fell asleep when I was holding her." Leon glanced over his shoulder toward the room. "Her mother's in there with Talei now."

Eleanor looked visibly relieved by the news. "How's John?"

"He didn't make it, Auntie. I'm about to call his parents now." Leon's stomach clenched tight. This was not a call he ever wanted to make, but he had to be the one to do it—he owed John that much.

Tears welled in Eleanor's eyes. "Nooo…" she moaned softly.

"Talei and her mom are in room 230. I'll be right back after I make this call."

Leon found a quiet area near the waiting

room where he could inform John's parents of the sad news.

After the difficult call, he walked back to the hospital room and peeked inside.

Eleanor and Misty appeared to be in deep conversation, so he decided to give them some privacy.

He wandered to the waiting room and sat down to wait for John's parents to arrive. The muscles of his forearm hardened as he clenched his hand so fiercely that his nails dug into his palm.

Leon sat there silently for a long time. He hated hospitals. He had been in this one too many times, and all of the memories were tragic. He became a firefighter to save people. It pained him that when it came to those he loved, he wasn't able to help any of them.

"HIS PARENTS NEVER thought I was good enough for John," Misty told Eleanor as they sat in the room waiting for Talei to wake up. They were careful to keep their voices down. "I'm not sure why. I've never done anything to them."

"From all you've told me, it seems like it's more your father-in-law who has something against you. Not Clara," Eleanor responded.

"Elroy is a mean-spirited, controlling jerk who thinks the best way to deal with people is by being abusive. I once asked John if his father was abused growing up because that would explain why he acted the way he did... Miss Eleanor, he got so angry with me."

"I can't believe John could do something like this."

Misty nodded as she tried to sheath her inner feelings. "That's why I divorced him. I grew up in an abusive home, and there's no way I was going to allow my daughter to go through that." She paused a moment before confessing, "I'm so angry with John right now for taking Talei, but I never wanted him to die."

"Sugar, I'm so sorry."

"I was so in love with John—from the moment I met him. I thought he was the perfect man for me, Miss Eleanor. But then I realized John wasn't happy," Misty said. "I used to tell him that he needed to get some professional help, but John would become furious with me. I really wanted our marriage to work. However, the verbal abuse was nonnegotiable for me."

"I'd have to say I would've done the same thing."

Misty gently stroked her daughter's cheek. "I'm so grateful to your nephew for being there when the accident happened."

"Leon is a good man and he's always been the type of person to help others," Eleanor said.

"As a child he would recue animals, assist the elderly. His degree is in criminal justice, so I thought he'd be in law enforcement, but I wasn't surprised when he decided to become a firefighter."

"John told me that Leon lost his wife and a child."

"Yeah, losing Vera and baby Selena nearly took him out of this world. Leon shut down, and even now he's still not the man he used to be. He works hard. That's all he does. *Work.* I think he does it to keep from thinking about all he's lost."

An image of Leon's handsome face swam before Misty anew, along with the unexpected impact of his sad, dark eyes. Despite everything she'd gone through, she was still a woman who appreciated a gorgeous man.

He was a grieving widower, she reminded herself. Definitely not her type.

Two HOURS LATER, Elroy Hayes burst through the doors of the emergency room pulling his wife, Clara, along behind him.

Leon approached, walking swiftly. He gestured for the doctor to join him.

"Where's my son?" Elroy asked. "I want to see him now."

The physician standing beside Leon went on

to explain, "We did everything we could to save your son... "

Leon had to put some distance between him and the doctor's words. He couldn't bear to hear it a second time. He waited near the nurses' station for John's parents.

Her slender frame seemed fragile as Clara walked over to him with shoulders slumped, arms folded across her chest and tears glistening on her heart-shaped face. "Where's my granddaughter?"

"She's sleeping right now," Leon stated. "Her mother is with her."

When Elroy joined them, he led them toward Talei's room.

"Misty is the reason John is dead," Elroy uttered as they stood in the hallway. His angry eyes were wet with unshed tears.

"I had nothing to do with your son's death," Misty said, her voice thick. She strode up to them with Eleanor. "John took my daughter without permission and had an accident. Elroy, whether you believe me or not, I hate that he's gone. I was hoping we'd find a way to co-parent Talei."

"I don't believe that for a minute," Elroy shot back, sending Misty a sharp glare. He stood in front of her, his stance intended to be intimidating. "You wanted John out of that child's life—that's why you took him to court and took away his rights. I warned him about marrying you in the first place. John should've just listened to me."

Misty didn't flinch. She boldly met his gaze, saying, "I'm sorry for the pain you're going through, but I'm not going to stand here while you badmouth me. When you can control your anger, then you're more than welcome to see your granddaughter." Not wanting to cause a scene, she turned to walk away, but paused long enough to say to Clara, "I'm really sorry for your loss."

Misty went back into Talei's hospital room.

Shocked by Elroy's behavior, Leon placed a hand on his shoulder. "I know you're hurting right now, but she's not responsible for what happened to John. It was a tragic accident." He knew grief was causing Elroy to strike out like that. Unfortunately, Misty was the closest target.

"If she'd just let John have his daughter, none of this would've happened. I told him to let the attorney handle everything."

Eleanor eyed Leon but remained silent. He could tell by the expression on her face that she was struggling to keep silent. She had a low tolerance for people like Elroy. After a moment of tense silence, she uttered, "I'm gwine check on Misty."

She walked with purpose into room 230.

Leon had known John's parents for a long time. Elroy was always belligerent and controlling, but he was stunned by the man's treatment of Misty.

Looking about ready to explode, Elroy stalked off to speak with someone at the nurses' station.

"Leon, my husband's in a lot of pain," Clara said. She gulped hard, hot tears slipping down her cheeks. "We're both in such agony. Our son is gone."

"I understand that, but it doesn't give him the right to talk to Misty that way. John was the one in the wrong here."

Leon caught a flash of hurt in her eyes.

"She gave my son no choice. You understand? I don't know how well you know Misty, but she's just as stubborn as John. Sure, he made mistakes as a husband, but I know for a fact that she wouldn't let him forget his shortcomings."

"She's the mother of your granddaughter," Leon said. "You don't want to alienate Misty."

Clara shrugged. "I know, but Elroy can't stand the girl. It won't be easy to change his mind about Misty after all that's happened." Swiping at a lone tear, she said, "I love Talei and I'm not gonna let anyone stop me from being in my granddaughter's life, even if it means going against my husband."

CHAPTER THREE

LEON CHECKED ON Talei while Elroy and Clara went to say a final goodbye to John. He had to escape the heart-wrenching sobs coming from the grieving mother.

He knocked on the door of Talei's room.

"Come in."

Misty was sitting beside the bed where her daughter lay sleeping. Eleanor sat in the chair near the window.

"How are you holding up?" Leon inquired.

"I'm numb right now," Misty responded. "I feel terrible for Clara, but Elroy—that hateful man makes it so hard for me to feel anything but disdain for him."

"This is a sad situation all around…"

"One that I'd rather not talk about." Misty picked up the teddy bear. "Tell me, Leon. What made you become a firefighter?" Although Eleanor had given her some insight, she wanted to hear directly from him.

"My dad," Leon responded. "I'm second generation. I used to love going to the station with my father, but it wasn't until I was in college that I realized I wanted to be a firefighter."

"My dad was a volunteer firefighter," Eleanor said. "I don't know if I ever told you that, Leon. I just remember him helping when that fire nearly destroyed the house two doors down from the old church."

"Are you talking about the Praise House?" Misty inquired. "I've heard a couple of people mention it."

Eleanor nodded.

Just then Talei woke up and saw her mother. "Mommy..."

"Hey, baby..."

Talei's gaze slid to where Leon stood. She smiled, then reached for him.

Leon felt a warm glow flow through him at her response to him and picked her up.

"I told you I'd keep you safe, little one."

She held up the teddy bear for him to see. "Eon."

Rising to her feet, Eleanor said, "I'm gwine to the cafeteria to get something to drink. Y'all want anything?"

"I'm fine," Misty responded.

"*Fench* fries," Talei interjected before reaching for her mother.

Leon chuckled as he put her down and pulled out his wallet. "Would you get the little one some French fries, Auntie?"

Misty opened her purse, but he stopped her. "I got it. It's my treat."

"Thank you."

"I'll be right back, sweetie." Eleanor walked out into the hall.

"John enjoyed being a dad," said Leon when they were alone in the room.

"Did he tell you that?" Misty inquired.

"He didn't have to tell me," Leon stated, "I could hear it in his voice whenever he talked about Talei."

"You look a lot like your father," Misty said, changing the subject. She didn't want to become emotional while talking about John. His death was beginning to have an effect on her. "Miss Eleanor has a picture of your parents in her office."

"She and my dad were very close. I know she misses him as much as I do. My whole family is pretty close-knit." Leon met her gaze. "What's it like to be the new star of the Polk Island Bakery & Café?"

She smiled. "I don't know about all that, but I do love my job."

They continued their small talk until Eleanor returned with a drink, French fries and a juice box.

Talei clapped her hands in glee. "*Wado*, Miss Ellie."

"It's Tsalagi... Cherokee for *thank you*," Misty explained. Her expression suddenly became tense when she heard Elroy's voice outside the room.

Seconds later, Clara stuck her head inside. "Is it okay if we come in to see Talei?"

"Yes, of course," Misty responded.

Talei seemed thrilled to see her grandparents. "Granma... Paw Paw..."

"I'm going to head on home," Leon told Misty. "I'm glad Talei is fine and I'm sorry for your loss."

"I really appreciate everything you did today."

He smiled. "It's nice to finally meet you, Misty. I'm sorry it was under these conditions."

"Same here. I'm sure it won't be the last time I see you. The island's not that big."

Leon smiled. "No, it's not."

He hugged Eleanor, then Clara, before leaving the room.

Leon strode toward the hospital exit with purpose. His body ached with weariness; he just wanted to go home, shower and relax. He needed to process everything that had happened today.

MISTY AND ELEANOR sat in a small waiting area to give Elroy and Clara some time with Talei.

"I hope the doctor releases her soon. I'm so ready to take my baby home and get her settled." Misty sighed. "To be honest, I'd like to go back to bed and start this day all over again."

Eleanor chuckled. "If only it was that easy."

"Thank you for coming to support me. I'm not sure I would've gotten through all this without you."

"It's my pleasure, Misty." Eleanor stood up. "I'm gwine go relieve Josh at the shop. You take tomorrow off and spend it with Talei. Make sure she's okay."

The two women embraced.

Just as Eleanor was about to leave, Elroy and his wife walked out of Talei's hospital room. "Maybe I'll hang around a lil longer," she told Misty.

"Talei was asking for her daddy. Isn't that right, Clara?"

His wife nodded. "I didn't know what to say to her."

"She's too young to really understand," Misty said. John's parents were heartbroken and grieving, so, she was careful with her words. "Talei knows about heaven, so I guess we can just say he's up there."

"We wouldn't have to have this discussion at

all," Elroy said, "if you hadn't run away with Talei."

"I didn't run away. I moved here to start a new life in peace," Misty stated. "*Something I didn't have in Orangeburg.* Miss Eleanor offered me a chance to do what I've always loved doing and I accepted the job."

"You knew taking Talei from John would destroy my son," Elroy hissed. "You're selfish and you never cared about what he wanted. You humiliated my son."

"That was *you*," Misty responded, struggling to keep her temper in check. "It was your controlling ways that destroyed your son."

"Emotions are running high right now," Eleanor interjected. "Misty, I think I hear Talei calling for you. Why don't you go check on your daughter?"

She gave Eleanor a grateful nod, then walked into her daughter's room.

"Did I hear correctly that she works for you?" Elroy asked, his brow pulled into an affronted frown.

"She does."

A muscle flickered angrily at his jaw. "You might want to watch her—she can't be trusted."

Eleanor eyed Clara and asked, "Is there anything I can do for you?"

Elroy wasn't going to be ignored. "Can you bring John back?"

"You shouldn't talk to Eleanor this way," Clara said. "None of this is her fault."

He sent his wife a sharp glare.

"It's fine," Eleanor stated. "I understand grief and the many ways it can affect a person. We're all sad about losing John, but right now we need to try to come together for Talei. The last thing she needs is to see what's left of her family fussing and carryin' on like this. That little girl needs every one of y'all. Try to remember that."

Elroy eyed her.

She stared back until he looked away.

"Please tell me they're gone," Misty said when Eleanor returned to the room. "The doctor released Talei and I just want to take her home."

"They left." Eleanor shook her head in dismay. "That man... He started to get on my last nerve. I don't know how Clara puts up with him. I've never seen anyone so embittered and angry with the world."

"He's always like that, which makes everyone uneasy around him," Misty said. "The strangest thing is that he's a completely different man with Talei. He adores his granddaughter—that's about the only good thing I can say about him."

Misty picked up her purse. "C'mon, sweetie...

Let's get you home. We've both had a very long day."

In the parking lot, she said, "Thanks so much for being here for me."

Eleanor embraced her. "It's my pleasure. You sure you're okay?"

She nodded. "I called my mother and she's coming to the island to spend a couple of days with us. I'll be fine."

Deep down, Misty wasn't as confident as she wanted Eleanor to believe. She was faced with having to raise her daughter alone. Although she and John had been at odds, she never thought he wouldn't be around to be a father to Talei.

AT HOME, LEON wandered from room to room. He felt restless, unsettled and his mood heavy.

He recalled the day he and Vera moved into this house. John had come up with his truck to help with the move. Leon leaned in the doorway of the master bedroom.

"This is the room where the Rothchild legacy will continue," John had proclaimed that day. "Make lots of beautiful babies."

Shaking his head sadly, Leon walked down the stairs to the first level.

He spent the rest of the evening going through his college photo album. It was still difficult for him to believe that John had gone as far as to kidnap his daughter. He sat down on the sofa, his thoughts traveling back to one of the many conversations he'd had with his friend.

"It was thoughtless of me to ask you to be my daughter's godfather in light of all you had to deal with. I should've realized that you were still grieving the passing of Vera and little Selena, but I want you to know my offer still stands. Whenever you're ready. If something ever happens to me, I want you to be there for Talei."

"I'll do what I can, John."

"Is it getting any better for you?"

"I still wake up expecting to see Vee." Leon picked up the napkin and wiped his mouth. *"I still haven't packed up her stuff or the baby's room."*

"I can come over to help you," John offered.

Leon shook his head. "You need to spend every moment you have working on your relationship with your wife and being a father to that little girl of yours. Life is fleeting."

"Sometimes I think that getting married was a mistake, Leon," John blurted. *"I don't think either of us was ready."*

"Why do you say that?"

"I proposed three months after we started dating and we got married eight weeks later. We should've spent more time getting to know

one another. We rushed into this whole marriage thing."

"Marriage is hard work, John. Now that you're divorced, I think it's an even bigger challenge to have a positive relationship with your ex-wife."

The sound of the telephone ringing cut into his thoughts.

"Hello."

"Hey, sugar. I'm just leaving the hospital."

"Is Talei okay?"

"Yes," Eleanor said. "They released her, so Misty's taking her home right now."

He settled back against the cushions, trying to get comfortable. "And John's parents? Are they still there?"

"They left," Eleanor said. "Son, that Elroy..."

"He's not an easy man by any means, but he loves his family." Leon had no idea why he kept making excuses for Elroy's behavior. Maybe it was because he felt bad for the man.

"I have to tell you. I can't stand the way he treats Misty. It ain't right by no means."

Still trying to stay neutral, Leon said, "We don't know their history. Maybe there's a reason he responds to her like that."

"You and I see things very different on this situation."

"I don't agree with his actions, Auntie. I'm

just taking into consideration that Elroy lost his son. I think we should give him some slack."

"I would agree with you, but the same should go for Misty. She lost the father of her child."

"There are no winning sides," Leon stated. "If I could've talked to John, I'm sure I could've gotten him to return Talei to her mother. If only that cow hadn't run out into the road, things would be different right now."

"We can't change what happened, son. No matter how much we may want to, we just can't."

Leon released a long sigh. "Auntie, I know that from personal experience. Like I said, nobody wins."

CHAPTER FOUR

AFTER A BUBBLE BATH, Talei climbed into her mother's bed and was asleep within minutes. Misty decided to let her stay there in case she had a bad dream. She knew her daughter would experience some depth of trauma after such a frightening experience.

Now that she was in a quiet place of peace, Misty could take a moment to allow her emotions free rein.

She sat down on the padded window seat in her bedroom and stared outside. Stars were carefully sprinkled across the sky so as not to upstage the moon as it shone brightly against the blanket of darkness.

Pen in hand, Misty reached for the journal that lay open. There was so much she wanted to say, but she didn't know where to start.

Her stomach churned with nervous energy. Talei was safe, but John was gone. Misty thought about the way she'd responded to his death at the hospital and felt a thread of guilt snake down her spine.

Teary-eyed, she began to write:

Today I lost the man I once thought I'd spend the rest of my life with. John had a lot of problems, but I always hoped he'd overcome them. All we ever really wanted to do was love each other—instead we ended up hurting one another. My heart is sad that John is no longer here; that he won't get to see his little girl grow up. He won't see her graduate high school or college; he won't be here to walk her down the aisle on her wedding day.

I was so angry with him for taking our daughter—I didn't want to care that he'd gotten hurt in the accident. In a way, I felt justified, but it lasted not even a minute. It was more of a passing thought. What lingered in my mind is whether or not John would be able to rest eternally knowing what he'd done.

John acted out of desperation, and in part I feel responsible. My intentions were to protect my daughter at all costs, giving no thought as to how it would affect him. Now I have to live with the question of whether I made the right choice in seeking supervised visitation. I know he didn't want me to leave Orangeburg, but that place gave me no peace—the environment was too toxic. I wanted to be away from his parents, more so that father of his. I wanted to get away from John because I got tired of him just show-

ing up whenever he wanted to my home. I also
wanted to be closer to my mother because she
made me feel safe.

Was this a selfish decision?
Is John's death my fault?

MISTY THOUGHT ABOUT her father and how he
never once tried to reach out to her or her
mother, Oma, after they left Atlanta. He didn't
contest the divorce. It was as if he had washed
his hands of the two of them.

She was glad he was no longer a part of their
lives, but she felt the sting of his abandonment.
It was clear he didn't love her enough to try to
change for the better. He didn't love her mother
enough to fight for the marriage.

There were times when she heard her mom
crying over the breakup of her marriage. Misty
had even overheard Oma confiding her heartache to her own mother. She'd loved Michael
Taylor and once believed he was the love of
her life.

After the divorce, Oma had both her and
Misty's surname changed legally to her maiden
name. She was done with Michael and wanted
a fresh start.

Over the years, there were no interactions
with his family. When Oma called her former mother-in-law, she was told that Michael

didn't want his family communicating with her. Misty's grandmother thought it was best to appease her son by forsaking her granddaughter.

She shrugged, trying to shake off the hurtful jabs of rejection piercing her heart.

"Talei and I are fine," she whispered.

We don't need them. I have my mom and my daughter, and they have me. This is enough.

The doorbell sounded.

Misty rushed down the staircase to open the door for her mother.

"I'm so glad you're here," she said, falling into Oma's embrace.

"Why didn't you call me earlier? I would've come straight away."

"So much was happening at the time, Mama."

Oma sat down her tote. "I'm going to make you some tea to help you relax. Where's Talei?"

"She's in my bed sleeping."

They walked to the kitchen.

Oma washed her hands. "I'm sorry about John."

"Mama, he's gone, and I don't know how to explain to my daughter that he's never coming back." Tears fell from her eyes.

Her mother embraced her a second time. "I'm so sorry."

Misty gave in to the sobs that had been threatening to consume her.

TWO DAYS LATER, Leon walked into the Polk Island Bakery & Café for breakfast, where he was greeted by the aroma of coffee, baked goods and an assortment of meats. He was always assaulted with a sense of nostalgia whenever he came here—the shop that had been in his family for a couple of generations. He'd spent a lot of time in this place over the years with friends and family, eating, talking and laughing. He'd brought past girlfriends here on date nights. He and Vera used to come here often.

The shop was the setting for people looking to find ways to make their lives better. It was a place where solutions to problems were discovered; a place to enjoy company. For Leon, it was a fragment of heaven.

A line had already formed to order coffee and herbal tea drinks. He sat at an empty table in the center facing the door on the right and the kitchen on the left.

He glanced around looking for his aunt. He glimpsed Misty in the kitchen and waved in greeting. The plastic cap on her head, no makeup and the apron she was wearing did nothing to diminish her natural beauty. He could tell that she wasn't a slave to fashion, but he had no doubt Misty cleaned up well. Her job required comfortable, functional clothing and shoes.

Waving back, Misty rewarded him a tentative smile.

"I didn't expect to see you here today," he said when Misty came to his table a few minutes later.

"I couldn't just sit home another day. I need to keep busy," she responded. "It takes my mind off things."

"I've been there for sure." Leon glanced around. "Is my aunt here?"

"Not yet. Miss Eleanor called five minutes ago to say she was on the way. She should be here at any moment."

"How is your daughter doing? I know the accident was very traumatic for her."

"Talei isn't sleeping well. She wakes up screaming and she's been a bit clingy," Misty said. "There's a part of me that's so angry with John for doing this to my baby. He never should've taken her from day care."

Leon's face went grim. "It's not as if John intended to have an accident."

Arms folded across her chest; Misty frowned with cold fury. "You're actually defending his actions?"

"He made an error in judgment," Leon said. "All he wanted was his family back."

"Then he should've been a much better husband," Misty said sharply. She tossed her hair and eyed him with cold triumph.

"What are you talking about?"

"There was a side of John that you didn't know about. He had a temper and like his father was verbally abusive. The one time it almost turned physical, I ended the marriage."

Leon shook his head in disbelief. "I know John had his issues, but he wouldn't harm a woman."

She glared at Leon. "I don't have any reason to lie about his treatment of me."

Her words had taken him by complete surprise.

"Leon, I should've figured you'd be here," Eleanor said, interrupting his conversation with Misty.

He smiled. "I'm not about to miss the fish and grits."

Eleanor chuckled. "You can always count on Leon to show up bright and early on Friday for the breakfast special. Leon loves seafood." Her gaze traveled from him to Misty. "What's going on?"

"Your nephew seems to think I'm a liar." Misty's lips thinned with irritation. She lifted her chin, meeting his gaze straight on.

"That's not what I said," Leon stated.

"Oh, the implication was clear," she countered. "The fact of the matter is I don't really care what you think of me. Nothing will change the truth. John kidnapped our daughter and threatened to do it earlier. That was the reason his visits had to be supervised."

He didn't respond.

When Misty walked away, Eleanor sat down across from her nephew. "She's been through a lot, Leon."

"I'm sure it wasn't a cake walk for John either. All he ever talked about was trying to get his family back."

"I know how much you love your friend, but John was abusive."

Leon shook his head in disbelief. "I guess that's why John didn't fight the divorce," Leon said almost to himself. "That's what he meant when he said Misty didn't give him any choice but to sign off on the petition."

"She did what she had to do—I would've done the same thing," Eleanor said. "I don't blame her at all."

Leon studied Misty as she moved about the restaurant. She seemed nice enough. Misty was fiercely protective of Talei—as any mother would be under the circumstances. He thought back to his last conversation with John.

"I love Misty and I'm working hard to get her back, Leon."

"Does she still love you?"

John finished his drink. "I think so, but she wants me to leave the company. As much as I want to quit, I can't do that. My dad needs me. We've been having a lot of employee turnover."

"I thought you wanted to leave, as well."

"It's not about what I want, Leon. It's what I have to do. I keep trying to get Misty to understand this, but she's only focused on what she wants."

"How is the co-parenting going?"

John shrugged. "Fine, I guess. Only I don't get enough time with my daughter. My ex is doing a good job teaching Talei about Native American culture and traditions. My dad is against it, of course."

"Why?"

"He feels that it will complicate Talei's life and he doesn't want her confused. He wants her to identify as Black—not Native. He thinks that Misty denies her Black side." John shrugged. "It doesn't make sense to me. I want my daughter to experience both cultures."

"Did you tell Elroy that?"

John signaled for another drink. "Leon, you know my dad. You can't tell him anything. I just let him talk. It doesn't matter, though. I'm doing what I can to get along with Misty, and it's working out great. She's finally agreed to let

*me spend more time with Talei. I've been think-
ing of taking her on a trip somewhere out of
the country. I could definitely use a vacation."*

"Is Misty okay with this?"

*John nodded. "Yeah, things are so much bet-
ter between us right now."*

Silas brought Leon's meal.

"Thanks," he said.

While he ate, Leon replayed his final conversation with John repeatedly in his head. Each
time brought him back to the same troubling
conclusion.

When Eleanor came to check on him, he said,
"Auntie, I was just at Rusty's store and he mentioned that you'd made a couple of pies for him.
I told him I'd pick them up. I have to go back
by there to pick up my order."

"He installed a couple of ceiling fans for me.
He wouldn't accept payment, so I told him I'd
make him a key lime and his favorite, a chocolate peanut butter pie." Smiling, Eleanor said,
"I knew he wouldn't turn them down."

Leon laughed. "You know Rusty is in love
with you."

"Rusty Stanley and I have been friends since
we were in middle school. He took me to my
junior prom and when it was over, he didn't
even attempt to kiss me. He's never even flirted
with me."

"He also never married."

"That's probably because he hadn't met the right person or maybe he enjoys being one of the island's eligible bachelors," Eleanor suggested. "Regardless, I consider him one of my dearest friends, but that's all we have between us."

Leon shook his head. "I don't know about that, Auntie. Whenever you talk about him, I see something in your eyes."

Eleanor laughed. "Boy, you need to worry about your own love life. Speaking of which... Don't you think it's time for you to get back out there?"

Leon regarded her with amusement. "I'm fine."

"You're too young to live life alone."

"I'm not alone. I have you, Auntie."

MISTY WALKED OUT of the kitchen carrying a tray of fudge. She was keenly aware of Leon's scrutiny. It bothered her that he thought so little of her. He didn't even give her the benefit of the doubt—just believed everything John had told him about her.

"Try not to be so hard on my nephew, Misty," Eleanor said as she wiped down the counter.

"Maybe he shouldn't be so judgmental."

"Leon considered John a friend. I know they kept in contact."

She wiped her hands on her apron. "Oh, I had no idea."

"John came to the funeral when Leon's wife and child died. He definitely helped Leon get through that day."

"Really? He never told me." Misty was surprised to hear how her ex-husband could be so supportive to Leon, but extremely selfish when it came to his own family.

"Yes. They were closer than you know. I know that Leon encouraged John to fight for his marriage." She poured herself a cup of tea. "When my brother and his wife died, Leon and his brother…" Eleanor paused for a moment, then continued. "Oh, Misty, they were so heartbroken. I never thought they'd ever get over losing their parents. Then Leon met Vera in college. I hadn't seen him that happy since they were children. Just when he'd found happiness with his wife and the impending birth of their little girl, tragedy struck a second time. Vera developed what they said was an amniotic fluid embolism. Somehow the fluid entered Vera's bloodstream. Losing both Vera and Selena—it was almost too much to bear for all of us."

Her gaze traveled to Leon. "I can't imagine going through something like that."

"I was terribly worried about him during that time. He shut completely down—it was John who was finally able to get through to Leon and get him out of his shell."

"Miss Eleanor, excuse the interruption, but we're almost out of eggs and sugar," Silas said.

She frowned. "Silas, we should have plenty. A delivery came yesterday."

"There were no deliveries, Miss Eleanor."

Her eyes widened in alarm. "They come every Wednesday."

"Yes ma'am, I know. I just checked with Josh and he said we didn't have one yesterday."

Misty made a quick phone call. She hung up a few minutes later, saying, "They had no record of an order, but don't worry—I placed it and they're rushing it through. They should be here in about fifteen to twenty minutes."

Eleanor released an audible sigh of relief. "I can't believe I forgot to order supplies. I need to do a quick inventory to make sure we have everything we need."

"There was a lot going on," Misty said. "If you hadn't been there for me and Talei, you probably wouldn't have forgotten."

"It was a busy day." Eleanor shrugged. "I thought for sure I'd placed that order."

"It was an easy fix," she reassured her.

Leon pushed away from the table, stepping in Misty's path. "I need to ask you something."

"What is it?"

He captured her eyes with his. "During my last conversation with John, he told me that you'd agreed to let him spend more time with Talei," Leon said. "He mentioned that he was planning to go on vacation out of the country and take her with him. Is any of that true?"

"No, it's not. There's no way I'd let Talei go without me."

He took a deep breath. "He was planning to run away with her. Misty, I want to apologize to you," Leon said. "I know there are two sides to every story and I only know John's side. I should've kept my mouth shut."

"Leon, I appreciate the apology. I get that John was your friend, but he was troubled more than you knew."

"I see that now." Distracted, Leon glanced over at his aunt.

"Is Aunt Eleanor okay? She looks upset about something."

"Yes," Misty said. "She forgot to place an order, but it's been taken care of—no worries."

"I keep telling her that she needs to slow down. She feels like she has to be here every day."

"Miss Eleanor loves this place."

Leon smiled. "Yeah, she does. I can't even think of this shop without my aunt's presence. Aunt Eleanor did all of the baking back then."

He glanced around the room. "I have a lot of wonderful memories in this place."

"I'm sure," Misty murmured. "I hear that a lot from the locals. A few of them have told me that their families have been coming to the shop for generations. The other half say they're related to your family. One of the things I love about Polk Island is the history."

He smiled. "I'll have to give you the five-dollar tour one day."

"I'd like that," she responded.

She cautioned herself not to get too involved with Leon. The last thing the handsome widower needed in his life was someone who was more broken than him.

CHAPTER FIVE

THE NEXT MORNING, Leon reported to the station house for work.

Charles greeted him when he entered the day room. "Hey, Leon, how you doin'? I know you have to be pretty broken up about your friend."

"It doesn't really seem real to me yet." He walked with Charles to the dorm area. "I have to tell you... I don't know what or how to feel. Grief seems to be a permanent fixture in my life."

There they were joined by another coworker. "I heard that it was your friend who died in the accident. The truck driver."

"Yeah," Leon responded, ignoring the stab of pain in his heart. He stuffed his backpack into one of the metal lockers.

"Did he really kidnap his daughter?" one of the other coworkers questioned.

"Hey, don't ask the man something stupid like that," Charles interjected. "He just lost his friend."

"I honestly didn't mean anything by it, Leon."

"Joe, I know you didn't. Look, John just wanted to spend time with his little girl. He wasn't a bad person, but he handled this situation wrong and it cost him his life."

"I'm sorry for your loss."

"If I were married to Misty Brightwater, I'd do everything I could to get my family back, too," Leon overheard another one of the guys say. "She's stunning."

His coworker was right. Misty was a beautiful young woman, but there was a side to her that Leon perceived as unsympathetic. When she first learned of John's death, she wasn't overcome with emotion. He knew she was more concerned about Talei, yet it bothered him that she hadn't displayed any outward signs that John's passing upset her.

John had once told him that she could be cold. He said she had the ability to just turn her emotions on and off. Leon had witnessed this himself.

Misty was the type of woman he would never give a second thought. She could break a heart with just the flick of a switch.

IT WAS THE hottest day in May so far this year. A perfect day for spending time at the Sterling Village community pool. Misty laughed in pure delight as a giggling Talei dipped her tiny toes in the wading pool while enjoying the momentary cool breeze swirling around them.

"Mommy…"

"Yes, baby?" she prompted.

Pointing to the Olympic-sized pool on the other side of the gate, she said, "I wanna get in wata…"

"We have to stay on this side, sweetie. It's too many people over there." Misty led her toward the middle of the children's pool. She sat down with Talei beside her. "This feels good, doesn't it?"

Her daughter nodded. "Daddy love wata."

"Yes, he does." She ran her fingers through Talei's curly puffs. "He did love the water."

Looking up at Misty, the little girl asked, "Daddy coming?"

She shook her head regretfully. "No, sweetie. He can't come."

"He hurt," Talei said softly.

"Yes, your daddy was really hurt from the car accident." She released a short sigh. "Do you remember where heaven is?"

Talei pointed upward. "Daddy go to heaven?"

Fighting back tears, Misty said, "Yes."

"Daddy get better in heaven."

She planted a kiss on her daughter's forehead. "Yes, my beautiful little girl. Your daddy is in a much better place. He is going to watch over you always."

Talei chuckled when she put her duck in the water. She watched it float, then went after it.

Misty loved the sound of her daughter's laughter. It signaled that she was feeling safe and secure, but she missed her father.

The best thing she had done was move here, Misty thought. She loved living on picturesque Polk Island. The beaches, the oaks draped in Spanish moss and the awesome beauty of the island were the main reason she'd come to the area. Historical landmarks citing the rich Rothchild history were prevalent around the island. This was the perfect place to raise Talei, especially now.

She left work early to spend quality time with Talei, and also to note if her daughter might be experiencing any trauma. Her mother left for Charleston when Misty arrived home earlier. It had been wonderful having her with them.

Misty glanced down at her as she played in the water. "Five more minutes, then we're going home."

"Okaay."

When time was up, Misty said, "We have to leave now."

Batting her long eyelashes, Talei responded, "Five minutes, pleeze."

Misty eyed her daughter in amusement. "Okay, but after that we have to go home so I can make dinner."

Talei continued splashing around in the pool, happily.

Misty checked her phone, then stood. "Time's up. We have to get out of the pool."

Talei didn't protest, provoking a soft sigh of relief from Misty.

She wrapped a towel around her daughter, then placed one around herself, as well. Misty picked up her tote. "So, what are we gonna cook?" She held Talei's hand as they walked along the tree-lined sidewalk to her condo.

"Hot dawg and *fench* fries."

She bit back a smile, then offered a suggestion. "How about grilled chicken nuggets, broccoli and—"

"Macarooni," Talei interjected.

"We can do that." Misty stifled her chuckle.

Five minutes later, they walked inside their home, a two-bedroom condominium with a picturesque view of the ocean from the patio and the balcony. It was this stunning view that sold her on the property. Her condo wasn't a large place, but it provided just enough space for her and Talei, and her alimony payments covered the rent and utilities. Now that John was gone, Misty considered that she might have to take on a second job. It didn't matter. She would do whatever was necessary to make ends meet.

"Let's get our baths out of the way."

Talei patted her damp swimsuit. "Mommy, I don't need bath. I clean."

Misty chuckled. "We still need to bathe after we get in the pool, sweetie."

Talei sighed. "Okay, Mommy."

They entered Talei's bedroom, a yellow-and-white haven stocked with stuffed animals, dolls and a closet filled with everything from everyday clothing to Native American fringed dresses, and a feather headdress designed by Misty's mother, Oma.

She opened a drawer to retrieve a pair of pajamas.

In the bathroom across the hall, Misty gave Talei a bath, dried her off and then dressed her in pink-and-white-polka-dotted pajamas.

Talei followed her into the master bedroom. "Sweetie, you can watch television in my room while I take my shower."

Misty left the bathroom door ajar.

She came out dressed in a pair of black yoga pants and an oversize black-and-white T-shirt. Talei was sitting cross-legged in the middle of the king-size bed playing with Pooh Bear and the one she called Eon. She looked up and said, "I hungry."

"Dinner will be ready soon, sweetie."

Thirty minutes later, they sat down to a quiet dinner.

"Mommy, we call Daddy?" Talei asked.

Misty wiped her mouth with a napkin. "I'm afraid we can't, sweetie. Daddy's not able to talk to us."

Talei nodded, and then turned her attention to the bear she'd brought to the table. Normally, Misty wouldn't allow it, but this bear was a gift from John and her daughter kept it close.

"How is Pooh Bear feeling today?" Misty inquired.

"Sad," Talei responded. "Her miss Daddy."

She got up and went around the table to her daughter. "I know you miss your daddy. I want you to know that he loves you. He will always love you, sweetie." She knew that Talei was too young to fully comprehend the reason for John's absence.

Misty cleaned the kitchen afterward while her daughter watched television.

With Talei settled in for the evening, Misty retrieved a box of photos from her closet—photos of her with bruises on her arms, neck and face. Leon had no idea the chameleon John was; he could be charming and loving one minute, and then transform into a malicious, abusive tyrant in another. She decided there was no need to keep the pictures any longer, so she ripped them up and threw them in the trash. She didn't want Talei to ever see them. Misty didn't want to taint her daughter's memory of her father.

LEON LEFT WORK and met up with John's parents at the funeral home. They were making the arrangements to transport his body home to Orangeburg. The magnitude of their despair was almost overwhelming.

"Thank you so much for coming," Elroy said, shaking Leon's hand. "I don't know how we're going to get through this. I never thought I'd outlive my own son."

"I understand."

They were seated in the lobby area when Misty walked in, surprising them all.

"What are you doing here?" Elroy demanded, rushing to his feet. "You're not John's wife anymore. You have no right to be here. This is family business."

"I'm still the mother of his daughter," Misty responded. "I came to be a source of support. Not to fight with you."

It was clear to Leon that she refused to let herself be intimidated by this brute. He watched her in amazement.

Pulling on his sleeve, Clara pleaded, "Elroy, please don't make a scene."

"Just go home, Misty. We don't want you here or at the funeral."

Leon glimpsed the hurt in her eyes. They were all in pain and it bothered him that John's death still couldn't bring them together as a family. This was not the time for fighting.

She swallowed hard before saying, "So, you will deny your granddaughter a chance to say goodbye to her father?"

"No," Clara quickly interjected. "Misty, you must attend the service. John would want you there." She met her husband's enraged gaze. "He would want her at his funeral, and you know it."

"Your wife is right," Leon said.

"Y'all think you know *my* son better than I did. I'm telling you that woman over there ruined his life."

Leon decided not to remain silent. "This has gotten way out of hand, Elroy. I know you're grieving, but I'm not going to let you attack Misty like this—she was the love of John's life."

"You don't have to protect me, Leon," Misty stated. "I'm leaving."

"Elroy, you're making a scene."

He glared at his wife. "Stay out of this." Turning his attention back to Misty, he said, "We're gonna sue for custody of Talei."

Misty kept her voice low. "Give it your best shot. Once my attorney sees the police report, you'll be lucky if you get visitation because trust me, I intend to let the judge know about your history of physical abuse, as well."

Her words rendered Elroy speechless.

She glanced at Leon before leaving.

"You see what a hateful woman she is," Elroy stated. "Misty is nothing but a selfish woman looking to take advantage of the kindness of others. She tried to get my son to leave the family business."

Leon knew that John was not happy as a truck driver but didn't have the courage to stand up to his father. "Misty was John's wife," he stated. "She is the mother of his child. I'll say it again. She should be allowed to attend the funeral."

"I don't agree."

"I want my granddaughter there to say goodbye to her father," Clara said. If Misty can't come, she won't allow Talei to attend. Let's just keep the peace for John's homecoming service." Tears slipped from her eyes. "I'm tired of all this fighting. That poor girl hadn't done nothing to you. She and John had their issues, but none of that matters now."

Leon embraced her. "Everything is going to work out, Clara."

"I've lost my son, Elroy. Isn't that *enough*?" She broke down into sobs.

Having witnessed Elroy's venom, Leon had

a much better understanding of what Misty and John had to deal with through the course of their relationship and marriage.

A wave of disappointment flowed through him. Elroy had verbally attacked Misty and it was unwarranted. If he didn't work through his anger, he would end up missing out on a relationship with his granddaughter.

Leon knew Misty would fight them with her all—even if it meant keeping Talei away from Elroy and Clara. She was determined to protect her daughter from a toxic environment.

He prayed it wouldn't come to that.

"I DIDN'T EXPECT you back here so soon," Eleanor said when Misty walked into the shop.

"Elroy started acting a fool when I showed up," she responded. "He didn't want me there, so I left."

Disgusted, Eleanor shook her head. "That man needs to be ashamed of himself."

Misty shrugged in nonchalance. "It's fine. He's probably right. I have no right to be there. I'm no longer married to John."

"You're still the mother of his child," Eleanor countered.

"Your nephew was there, and he stepped up to defend me. I felt bad for him. He was so uncomfortable." She pasted on a smile. "Leon is the nicest man I've ever met."

"He's one of the good ones for sure," Eleanor said. "He and Trey never gave me an ounce of trouble. Don't get me wrong. They did the normal kid stuff, but that's about it."

"It's a testament to you."

"I did my best to give them what they needed."

Misty nodded in understanding. "That's all I want to do for Talei."

"Don't trouble your mind, sugar. You're doing a good job with that little girl." Eleanor frowned. "I can't remember if I ordered the meat for the box lunches. They have to be ready by Friday."

Misty slipped on her apron. "I can do a quick check."

"Thank you. If not, we need to do it right away."

This was the second time Eleanor had forgotten to restock the kitchen. Misty knew she had a lot on her mind these days. Maybe it was becoming more of a challenge to run both the bakery and the café.

"We're good on meat," Misty told Eleanor. "The only thing we need is more condiments. We have enough to put in the boxes, but we're going to be wiped out pretty much after that."

"Thank the Lawd."

"Miss Eleanor, would it be easier if I focused

on working the bakery? This would leave you to manage the café."

"I like that idea."

"Really? Please don't think I'm trying to tell you how to run your business."

"This is why I hired you, Misty. It made good business sense."

"Thank you for your faith in me, Miss Eleanor."

Misty spent most of her day in the kitchen, preparing baked goods for the next day.

"We just got an order for your key lime layer cake," Eleanor said. "They want to pick it up by noon tomorrow."

"I can do that." Misty stirred the ingredients in the bowl to make frosting for the carrot cake baking in the oven.

At three o'clock, she left to pick up Talei from day care. From there, they drove home.

Their daily routine was pretty low-key, Misty thought. Home, dinner, bath, bedtime story, sleep, then do it all over again the next day. However, she wouldn't trade the simplistic and peaceful life they led for anything in the world.

She made spaghetti for dinner, a choice that thrilled Talei.

Misty quietly observed her daughter as they ate their meals. Her heart was saddened at not being able to say a final goodbye to John. She wanted a sense of closure.

Later that night as she prepared for bed, the telephone rang. She looked at the caller ID and debated whether or not to answer. She didn't want to deal with any more drama.

"Hello."

"This is Clara…"

"What can I do for you?" Misty worked to keep her tone neutral and devoid of any emotion.

"I would like for you and Talei to attend John's funeral and sit with the family."

"Elroy made it clear that he doesn't want me there. I really don't want to be humiliated in front of your family and friends."

"This is my decision. Elroy's not thrilled about it, but he won't make a scene, Misty."

"I know how he feels about me, Clara," she responded. "I'm sorry but this feels like a setup."

"It's not. I give you my word."

"You and I both know that you can't control your husband."

"I promise you Elroy will be on his best behavior. My family will be here. *All* my brothers are coming. Trust me… With my family present, my husband will be on his best behavior."

CHAPTER SIX

ON THE DAY of John's funeral, Leon got up early to drive to Orangeburg. He was not particularly looking forward to saying goodbye to yet another person he cared about. In truth, he was tired of grieving, having lived with it for so long. Despite his feelings, Leon felt it was his duty to attend.

When he arrived at the church, Leon was surrounded by somber-faced mourners dressed in black. He accepted a program one of the ushers handed him.

Leon was standing near the door to the sanctuary when he spied Misty and Talei entering the church. He had never seen a simple black dress look so stunning on a woman. Her hair was pulled back into a sleek ponytail. Talei's white dress was trimmed with a black-and-white-striped ribbon around the collar and the waist.

The little girl saw him, smiled and waved.

Grinning, he waved back.

Leon bent down to speak to her as they approached him. "Do you remember my name?"

Talei looked up at her mother.

"This is Leon, remember? He was your daddy's friend," Misty said.

"Eon."

He glanced up at Misty. "I'm glad to see you."

"I had no intentions of coming, but Clara called me last night and insisted that we attend the service."

Leon responded. "You have as much right to be here as any of these other folks."

"I don't know about that." She glanced over her shoulder, then back at Leon. "Elroy has done a pretty good job of poisoning almost everyone's thoughts about me. You see how people are staring and whispering."

Leon shrugged with nonchalance. "Don't let it bother you."

"I'm not. I'm just here for my daughter." Misty pulled gingerly at the collar of her dress. I'm also here out of respect for John."

"Eon," Talei patted his hand.

He kneeled down so he could better hear her.

"Daddy in heaven. He get better."

Leon didn't know how to respond so he remained silent. She was so young and seemingly unaffected by her father's death.

"I didn't know what else to tell her," Misty said.

Standing up, he nodded in understanding. "I can imagine it's difficult."

"She thinks he can come back. Talei keeps looking for him, Leon."

The funeral director signaled for the family to line up for the processional.

Inside the sanctuary, Misty sat beside Clara in the front row while he sat on the opposite side of the sanctuary on the second row.

Leon could tell by Elroy's body language that he wasn't happy about Misty being there, but he didn't make a scene.

When it was time for him to speak, Leon walked up to the podium. His gaze traveled and settled briefly on Misty.

"I met John when we attended Clemson University. He was my roommate. It didn't take us long to realize that we had a lot in common. We were instant friends. One of my memories of John was his boundless enthusiasm. He and I had a lot of fun and laughed a lot. When his daughter, Talei, was born, it was clear that she had stolen his heart. John was beside himself with happiness."

His eyes watered. Leon inhaled deeply and released the breath slowly before he continued. "I had dinner with John the day after Mother's

Day. Ten days later, he was gone, and to be honest, I'm still trying to wrap my mind around it. Instead of celebrating his birthday with him at his favorite restaurant in Charleston like we planned, I'm here to say a final farewell. There are no words to explain the hole he's left in my life—in all of our lives." Looking upward, he said, "We're going to really miss you. Rest in heaven, John."

He could feel Misty's eyes on him. Leon felt uncomfortable showing his vulnerability in her presence. He preferred to be seen as a pillar of strength.

CLARA EMBRACED HER during the repast. "Thank you so much for coming, Misty."

"I wanted to be here…to say goodbye to John."

"I hope he can finally have peace," Clara murmured. "Losing you and Talei broke his heart, Misty. He truly loved you. I hope you know that."

She gave a slight nod. "I believe that he loved me. He just didn't know how to show it."

Careful to keep her voice low, Clara said, "You should know that you're the sole beneficiary on John's life insurance."

She handed Misty a business card. "You need to call and give them your information."

Misty was stunned. "I had no idea about this."

"He wanted to make sure you and Talei were taken care of in case…"

"Clara, we need to speak with Pastor Reynolds before he leaves," Elroy muttered, taking her by the arm and whisking her away.

Misty saw Leon standing by a window. She walked up to him saying, "What you said about John—it was really nice. He would've loved it."

"Thank you."

They joined the buffet line to get something to eat.

"Talei seems to be having a great time with Elroy," Leon observed. It thrilled him to see the little girl in such a happy mood despite the somber surroundings.

"He's always been very good with her."

They got their plates and found a table with empty chairs.

Misty discovered she didn't have much of an appetite.

"Are you okay?" Leon inquired; his expression filled with concern.

"I'm not really hungry right now."

"I always thought John and I would grow to be two old men…" Leon's voice trailed off momentarily. "He was looking forward to scaring the boys away from Talei. He always said she was going to be stunning like you."

Misty's eyes became bright. "We shouldn't be here in this place. John should be alive and well."

Leon nodded in agreement.

She scanned the room, her gaze landing briefly on Elroy. He was seated across the room glaring at her.

When Leon prepared to leave, Misty asked, "Do you mind if I follow you back to the island?"

"Are you ready to go?"

"Yes," Misty responded. "I'll get Talei and meet you outside."

She stayed behind Leon's truck the whole way back to Polk Island. He'd called her a couple of times to make sure she was fine.

"Do you want to grab a bite to eat before we cross the bridge?" he asked. "You didn't touch your food earlier."

"I'd like that." Misty was grateful Leon couldn't hear her stomach growling.

They stopped at a fast-food restaurant and sat in a corner booth.

"You love French fries, don't you, Talei?" Leon chuckled when their food arrived. "I love them, too."

Turning up her smile a notch, Talei nodded. "Fench fries and hot dawg." She pointed to his plate. "Shilli dawg."

Misty and Leon laughed.

"She's a sweetheart."

Misty placed an arm around her daughter. "I love her more than my own life. She's such a beautiful blessing."

She looked at him, noting the pain etched in his expression. "I'm sorry. It must be so hard for you."

"It's not as bad as it was," Leon responded. "I couldn't be around children for a while. To be honest, Talei is the first child I've held since my daughter died."

"Oh, wow... I had no idea."

"I want to be here for you and Talei as her godfather," Leon stated. "It's what John would have wanted. I hope it's fine with you."

"It's definitely okay with me," Misty said.

Pointing to Leon, she stated, "Talei, this is your godfather."

"Gawfather..."

He burst into laughter when Talei scrunched up her face at him. "Is that a happy face or a sad face?"

"Funny face," she said before bursting into giggles.

Misty and Leon cracked up laughing.

"She can be a little silly at times."

"I love it," he responded. It was nice to be

able to laugh after such an emotional day that started in sadness.

Encouraged, Talei continued to make faces and Leon responded in laughter and light banter.

When they finished eating, Leon walked them to their car. "I'm sure it's been a long day for you both. I'll check in with you tomorrow."

"I'll talk to you then." Misty unlocked her car door and helped Talei into her seat. Once her daughter was all buckled in, she climbed into the driver's seat. "As soon as we cross the bridge, we'll be back on the island, sweetie. Almost home."

"Almost home," Talei repeated. "Eon in car."

"Yes, he's in his car. He's in front of us."

Two hours after they arrived home, Misty put Talei to bed, then went down to the kitchen to work on a new recipe that had been floating around in her mind for days.

She opened the refrigerator and retrieved the carton of eggs. Next, she went to the pantry and took out a bag of flour. Minutes later, Misty had all the ingredients she needed to make what she called a buttery cinnamon cake. Baking was a way to relieve her stress. At the moment, she was feeling very stressed. By midnight, she had baked a cake, a dozen cupcakes and peanut butter cookies.

THE NEXT DAY, Leon woke up with his brother, Trey, weighing heavy on his mind. They texted often but he hadn't had a real conversation in over a month.

He picked up his phone and punched in a number.

"Hey, big brother."

Leon exhaled a long sigh of contentment. "Trey, it's so good to hear your voice. I miss you, man."

"Same here," Trey responded. "How's Aunt Eleanor?"

Leon sat up in bed, propped against a stack of pillows. "She's fine. Hey, you remember John Hayes?"

"Yeah. How is he?"

"We buried him yesterday."

"What?" Trey gasped in surprise. "What happened?"

"He had a bad car accident here on the island." Leon decided not to tell his brother about Misty and Talei over the phone. There would be time for that later.

"Man, I'm sorry to hear that," Trey said.

"How are things with you?" Leon inquired.

"Things are actually good for me. I have leave coming up, so I'll be home the twenty-second of June until the day after the Fourth of July. I can't wait to see everyone."

Leon couldn't be happier at the news. "That's great. Can I tell Aunt Eleanor?"

Trey laughed. "Yeah. That's fine. The last time I tried to surprise her, she almost had a heart attack."

"Man, I can't wait to see you."

"Same here," Trey said. "Well... Duty calls, big brother. I'll call you and Aunt Eleanor sometime next week."

When he arrived at work, Leon phoned his aunt while still in the car. "Guess who's coming home in a couple of weeks."

"Trey," she responded. "Is my baby boy coming back to the island?"

He laughed. "Yes, ma'am."

Leon talked to his aunt a few minutes more, then said, "I'm at work. It's time to get my day started."

He ended the call and got out of his truck.

Leon saw Lizzie as she was leaving the station house and threw up his hand in greeting.

He navigated to the dorms, put his backpack away, then headed to the bay where the fire engines were stored.

"Leon... Where are you?" Charles called out.

"Over here. I'm washing engine two."

"You have visitors. They're waiting for you in the lobby."

"Me?" Leon walked from the back of the truck. "Who is it?"

"Go up there and see for yourself."

He washed and dried his hands, then walked into the station. Leon's heart turned over when he saw Misty and Talei. He felt a ripple of excitement.

"*Oseeyo*, Eon," the little girl said and rushed over to him. She gave him the bag containing peanut butter cookies.

"*Osiyo,*" Misty clarified. "It means *hello*."

"I figured it was something like that."

"Just saying thank you for everything you've done didn't seem quite enough." Misty handed him a box of red velvet cupcakes. "These are just a token of my appreciation."

"You didn't have to go to all this trouble but thank you." Leon was touched beyond words by her thoughtfulness. Misty wasn't the first woman to bring him baked goods, but unlike some of the others, she didn't have a hidden agenda.

"I am forever grateful, Leon. I'm also glad you want to be her godfather."

Leon picked up the toddler. "We already have a bond, don't we?"

Talei nodded, then pointed to a stuffed Dalmatian puppy on the desk behind him.

"Dawggie."

Misty laughed. "My child can spot a stuffed animal anywhere. It's like she has a sixth sense or something."

"Here you go," Leon said. "It's my gift to you, little one."

"What do you say, Talei?"

"Wado."

"Is it okay if she shares a cupcake with me?"

Misty nodded. "Sure."

Leon escorted them to the dining area. He sliced a cupcake in two and gave a half to Talei while he kept the other.

He took a bite, then another. "Aunt Eleanor's right. You definitely know your way around a kitchen." Misty's nearness made his senses spin.

She laughed. "It's just a cupcake."

"You should've met the guy you replaced. I don't know if he started having issues with his vision but even on his best day, not one of his baked goods were as good as this cupcake."

Misty smiled and took Talei out of his arms and set her on the floor. "We need to let Leon get back to work, sweetie."

"Bye, Eon," Talei said, wrapping her arms around his legs.

"Thank you again for the goodies," Leon said.

The look Misty gave him was so galvanizing it sent a tremor through him. The pounding of his heart quieted only once they disappeared outside.

CHAPTER SEVEN

AFTER MISTY AND Talei left, Leon's coworkers tossed a bunch of questions at him.

"Hey, you're gonna share those, right? Those cupcakes look pretty delicious."

"You and Miss Brightwater sure seem pretty close."

"We're friends," Leon said. "That's all y'all need to know." He felt an unfamiliar shiver of awareness. There was something more than a mild interest where Misty was concerned. An undeniable magnetism was building between them. He had to wrench himself away from his ridiculous preoccupation. He and Misty could only be friends.

Nothing more.

"So, what about those cupcakes and cookies?" Charles interjected. "You sharing your bounty?"

Amused, Leon nodded. "Sure."

He placed the snacks on the table just as the alarm sounded, prompting the team to rush and gather equipment.

"Engine one," Charles called out.

Leon grabbed his gear and jumped into the truck.

"It sure is good to see you smile again," Charles told him. "That little girl seems to have taken a strong liking to you."

"John asked me to be her godfather, but I couldn't accept it until now. I'm going to be there for her since her dad can't."

"Your friend will be able to rest easy," Charles said.

Leon leaned back against the seat. They were on their way to the site of a car accident.

"You okay?" Charles asked.

"Yeah, I'm good," Leon said as he stared out the window and tried to keep his mind focused on the job.

They arrived at the accident location.

It was quickly determined that they weren't needed, much to Leon's relief.

"Now we can pick up where we left off," Charles said with a chuckle once they'd returned to the station. "I can't wait to get my hands on one of those red velvet cupcakes."

Leon laughed, then headed to his bunk. Now that he had some downtime, he couldn't escape the thoughts of Misty that plagued him. Fate had ushered her into his life, blindsiding him plain and simple. The chemistry between them shook Leon down to his bones. Misty and Talei had stormed into his life like a tornado, turning his world inside out. He was unprepared for the emotions that were suddenly running rampant and rattling him to the core.

Leon lay down on his bunk and closed his eyes. *What do I do now?*

MISTY DROVE TO the shop so that Talei could spend some time with Eleanor.

"She's been asking to see you."

Smiling, Eleanor hugged Talei. "Hey, sugar. I'm so glad you came to visit me."

"Where Mr. Josh?" the little girl asked.

"He's in the kitchen. I'll let him know you're here."

Misty guided her daughter into a booth, then sat down beside her. Leon was at the forefront of her mind. She had no ulterior motives in taking the cupcakes and cookies to the station, but there was something different in her interaction with him—something new. She'd felt an eager affection coming from him earlier. It was as if something intense flared between them, not to mention the tingling in the pit of her stomach—the way her heart lurched, and her pulse pounded whenever she was around Leon.

Eleanor walked to the entrance of the kitchen and said, "Talei wants to say hello to you."

Josh appeared, wiping his hands on his apron. "Hey, little Princess."

Grinning, Talei waved, then said, "You got fench fries?"

"I sure do," Josh said. "Would you like a grilled cheese sandwich to go with them?"

"Yes, pleeze."

Misty kissed the top of her daughter's head. "I love you so much, munchkin."

"Love you, Mommy."

Eleanor walked over a few minutes later carrying Talei's lunch. She sat down across from Misty and watched as the little girl dived into her food.

Gesturing to the stuffed animal on the table, she said, "Did you go by the station?"

"I did," Misty responded. "I dropped off some cupcakes and peanut butter cookies to Leon. I wanted to thank him for what he did—from the accident to the funeral. He's really been a great help to me."

"I'm sure he appreciated the treats. My nephew has a sweet tooth."

"He even offered to be Talei's godfather. It's what John always wanted."

"I'm so glad to hear this," Eleanor said. "It means that he's finally ready to move past his own pain and grief. I actually think you have something to do with this change in him."

"I have a meeting with Brittany in an hour, so we'd better head home," she announced, checking her watch. "I'll see you in the morning."

"Thanks for bringing this little lady to see me," Eleanor said. "She really made my day."

One thing Misty hadn't counted on—her emotions where Leon was concerned. Unnerved by the intensity of her response to Eleanor's comment, she forced herself to shut out all thoughts of him.

MISTY WAS ON the planning committee for the upcoming Children's Festival taking place the first weekend in August. She'd missed the last meeting because of John's funeral, so her friend Brittany had graciously offered to come by the house to update her and had also emailed her the notes.

She designated the dining room table as a workspace for them.

Talei was in her bedroom watching a Disney movie when Brittany arrived.

Opening her tote, Brittany said, "I brought the pictures from the festival last year. We had people come from the mainland attend—it was great. Ours is a smaller version of the one they have every year in Charleston."

"I'm super excited to be a part of this event," Misty responded. "I read the notes from the last meeting. Looks like it was a very productive one."

"It was," Brittany said. "I wanted to stop by because I have more great news. Annie Bell Watts contacted me about doing a workshop on quilting. She's even supplying all of the materials."

"That's wonderful," Misty murmured as she made some notes of her own. "The island is known for the beautiful quilts sold in the boutiques. I think the craft should appeal to the teens."

Misty updated Brittany on the tasks she'd completed. "All of the sponsorship packets have been sent out and we've gotten some great responses. I've just emailed you an updated list of the donors for this year."

They spent forty-five minutes going over more details. Misty made a couple of phone calls regarding the venue.

"Everything's confirmed," she said after the last call.

"That's everything on the festival," Brittany stated. "How did things go in Orangeburg?"

"John's father was his usually angry self. I'm so glad Leon was there—I didn't want to deal with that man alone."

"I take it things are going well with Leon, then."

"He's really nice, Britt. I'm hopeful that we're going to be great friends." Misty was careful to keep any emotion out of her voice.

Brittany gave her a sidelong glance. "Friends... That's all you want with that gorgeous man? A *friendship*?"

"Yeah. After John, I realized I make terrible choices with men. I think I'm better alone."

"Do you really believe that?"

"Britt, you have no idea the emotional abuse I endured with my father. I had a string of bad relationships, and when I met John, I thought all that changed, but it was more of the same. Trust me, Britt... I'm better off alone."

Shaking her head, Brittany said, "You just haven't met the right man. *Until now*."

LEON EXITED THROUGH the gym doors, wiping his brow with a towel as he made his way to his car.

"I'm beginning to see you everywhere."

His heart jolted at the sound of her voice. "It's bound to happen every now and then," Leon said smoothly. "We live on an island."

Pointing to his gym bag, Misty inquired, "On your way to a workout?"

"Actually, I finished up not too long ago." Misty's nearness made his senses spin, and he couldn't ignore the smoldering flame in her eyes. Without thinking about the consequences, he said, "I was about to grab some lunch. Would you like to join me?"

"You're stepping out on your aunt," Misty said when they walked through the door of Tony's Italian Bistro. "Shame."

"Every now and then I come over here for the Italian sandwich."

"I have to confess that I love Tony's sandwiches, as well."

Leon swallowed tightly as he dropped down next to her. It made him feel good to be around Misty.

"What's on your agenda for the weekend?" Leon inquired once their food arrived.

"My mom's here," Misty said. "We're going to enjoy some girl time with Talei."

"I hope y'all have a great visit."

"What are your plans?" Misty asked. She took a bite of her sandwich.

"I'm working."

She gave him a tiny smile. "I hope that it will be a quiet weekend for you, then."

"Thank you. I'm taking vacation for a week. I need to do some much-needed work and repairs around my house. My brother is coming toward the end of June for a visit."

"How wonderful for you and Miss Eleanor. She misses him a great deal."

"I know." Leon bit into his sandwich. He

swallowed, then said, "I'm really glad you decided to attend John's service."

"He was my ex-husband. I wanted to say goodbye," Misty responded. "I debated whether to bring Talei. My mom didn't think it was a good idea, but in the end, I felt like she needed to be there."

"How is Talei doing?"

"She still talks about her dad. She woke up a couple of times saying he was hurt in the car. This morning she picked up my tablet and said she wanted to see him. John used to FaceTime with her."

"I know this isn't easy for either of you."

"It's not," Misty said. "It's heartbreaking to watch my little girl yearn for her daddy and there's nothing I can do to help her."

"You're doing all the right things," Leon assured her. "I'm curious. What does her name mean?"

"*Talei* means *Precious One*," she responded.

"It fits her." He finished the last of his sandwich and considered a moment before speaking. "For the record, I never knew about John's treatment of you."

"I'm not surprised," Misty said. "He didn't want that getting out to anyone. Growing up with a man like his father, John didn't know how to stand up to him. Drinking was the way he dealt with it; only it made him just like the man he despised."

Leon took a sip of his water. "John could never really handle his alcohol. After a couple of drinks, I'd have to practically carry him back to our dorm room."

Misty smiled. "He told me how you always looked out for him."

Leon agreed. "Yeah."

"I love your aunt," Misty said, changing the subject.

"Everybody loves her. Aunt Eleanor used to tell me that she was called to be of service to others. If you didn't have any money you could still eat in the café. She just asked that you come talk to her first. Each year, elementary school students tour the bakery. Aunt Eleanor always makes sure there are cookies, even gluten-free options, for the children."

"I saw all the thank-you cards in her office from the different schools," Misty said.

"John never mentioned that you were a baker," Leon stated.

"He didn't want me to work while we were married. This is my first real job in a while. I came to Polk Island to see some property and had lunch at the café. Miss Eleanor and I got to talking. I went back to Charleston with a condo and a job. It seemed like the perfect choice."

CHAPTER EIGHT

"I'M BACK, MAMA," Misty said when she arrived home. "I ran into a friend. We had lunch together." She laid her purse on the counter. "Where's Talei?"

Oma came out of the kitchen carrying a bottle of water. "She's taking a nap. She's been down for about fifteen minutes. I made some fried squash bread and Cherokee casserole for dinner."

"Thanks, Mama. You know how much I love your squash bread."

They sat down in the living room.

Misty freed her hair from its ponytail. "Was she still asking for John? She had a tantrum this morning because she couldn't FaceTime him."

"A couple of times. What's an *eon*?"

"She means Leon. He was the first person there when the accident happened and again at the hospital. He's the person I had lunch with earlier."

"Is he a firefighter?"

"Yes, he is. Why?"

"Talei has a bear with a Polk Island Fire Department T-shirt in bed with her. She would give it to me and say *eon*. I didn't know what the child was talking about."

"I think he gave it to her the day of the accident. Leon and John were friends. He's known him since college."

Oma looked surprised. "Really?"

Misty nodded. "I didn't know they still kept in touch."

"What do you think of this man?"

"He's nice," she said. "Leon is a caring person—he looks out for his aunt and all the people he cares about. He's been here for me and Talei. He's friendly and funny. A little old-fashioned in some of his ways, but I like it."

"Is he married?"

"He lost his wife and child three years ago."

"How tragic," Oma murmured.

"Very much so," Misty said. "He would've made a great father. You should see him with Talei."

"She was talking to that bear as if it were him. Now, when did he become her godfather? I never heard mention of it before."

"John named Leon her godfather. He couldn't accept initially because of what he was dealing with, but he wants to be there for Talei now."

"That's nice of him."

Misty agreed.

Her eyes strayed to a bag containing a colorful quilt. "Who is that for?"

Oma smiled. "It's for you. I thought it might look nice on your bed."

Misty pulled the quilt from the bag. "Mama, it's gorgeous. I love it."

"I also bought some new moccasins for Talei. The others look like they're too small for her feet."

"*Wado*, Mama."

"*Hawa.*"

"Have you heard from Aunt Lois?"

"I haven't spoken to her in years. Your father doesn't want any members of his family communicating with me, so they don't. They never wanted to be in the middle."

Misty's eyes grew wet. "I guess he divorced me when you divorced him."

"I'm so sorry," Oma said.

"It's not your fault, Mama. There's no way we could've stayed with him. He was an alcoholic and a cheater. You deserved better than that."

"When I found out he had a baby on the way, I knew the marriage was forever broken."

"It's just really sad that he cut his whole family off from me. I would love to have gotten to know them. I have siblings I've never met. I don't even know their names. There was a time when I didn't care to meet them, but I feel differently now."

"Misty, you can reach out to your family—you don't have to wait for them to contact you."

"I know that, Mama. You've never tried to keep me from them. When I was younger, I felt like they should be the one to contact me since I was a child. The truth is that my grandmother has been on my mind a lot lately. She's the one I'd like to see."

"Then you should give her a call, Misty. I don't know if the number I have for her is still good, but it's a start."

Misty embraced her mother. "I'll try to contact her tomorrow."

She could purposely ignore the feeling of abandonment that flowed through her, but it was always there, taunting her. Misty hadn't forgiven her dad for disrespecting her mother by parading his girlfriend around their friends and even bringing her to one of Misty's school events. He was intent on embarrassing Oma. When her mother left him, he never attempted to reach out to her. He simply moved on with his new family.

Misty blamed him for all the dysfunctional relationships in her life. She blamed him for the hole that was left in her heart because of his absence. She faulted him for not loving her enough to at least try to be a better father.

THE NEXT DAY, Misty did what she'd told Oma she would—she keyed in the phone number, hoping her grandmother would answer on the other end.

"Hello."

"Is this Waverly Taylor?" she asked.

"Yeah. Who is this?"

"This is Misty…your granddaughter."

"Misty? Mike's daughter?"

"Yes, ma'am. Oma is my mother."

"I haven't heard from your mama in years. I didn't know if y'all was dead or alive. If you lookin' for your daddy, he ain't here. He lives in New York now."

"No, ma'am, I'm not calling about him. You've been on my mind a lot," Misty said. "That's why I called."

"Baby, I'm so glad to hear from you. I know Mike didn't do right by you and your mama. I want you to know I didn't raise him to be that way."

"I don't need a father," Misty said. "I have a beautiful little girl and we're fine. My mother is good. Like I said, you've been on my mind for a while and I decided to just reach out. There's no need to live in the past."

"Sounds like you're a right smart young woman. Are y'all still in South Carolina?"

"Yes. My mom is in Charleston, but I live on Polk Island."

"I would certainly love to see you and my great-granddaughter before I go home to glory."

Misty smiled. "I would love to see you, too."

"I'm gonna tell you this. I'm sorry for letting Mike keep you away from us. I hope you and Oma can forgive me. I was trying to keep the peace in my family back then, but it was wrong. I should've spoke up."

"It's okay, Grandmother. I know how my dad can get. Besides, I allowed him to keep me away as well, but I won't let him do it again."

"I won't either," Waverly promised. "I'm gonna do better by you, Misty."

When they hung up, Misty found her mother and gave her a quick recap.

"Sounds like you and your grandmother had a good conversation."

"We did, Mama. She wants to see me and Talei."

"That's wonderful news. The creator will work things out and his timing is always perfect."

"I'm glad I called her. I won't have to spend any more time wondering what would happen or if she ever thought about me."

"I'm happy for you."

Misty scanned her mother's face. "Are you really happy, Mama? You don't feel like I'm betraying you or anything? I want you to tell me."

"You should know me better than that," Oma responded. "I've always wished for you to have a relationship with Michael's family."

"I'm so lucky to have you as a mother."

"And I've been blessed to have you as my daughter. I want you to have the life you've always dreamed of—it's still possible."

Misty settled back against the cushions. "I thought I had it with John, but I was never so wrong."

"That's all in the past now."

"You're right. Time to live in the present."

LEON DROVE TO Charleston to pick Trey up from the airport. "I'm so glad you're home."

The two men embraced.

"Big brother, I'm so happy to be here. You know the first place I want to go is to the café. I need some of Aunt Eleanor's chocolate cake in my life."

"She has a new employee named Misty helping her with the baking. Man… She truly has a gift. She's been at the bakery since May and business has increased, according to Aunt Eleanor. They had several wedding cakes for this month already and more for July."

"Really?"

Leon nodded. "In fact, she was married to John."

Trey's eyes grew wide in his surprise. *"John Hayes?"*

"Yeah. It's a small world..."

"How did John's wife end up working for Aunt Eleanor?"

"When Misty came to the island to find a place to live, they connected."

"Wow, it really is a small world," Trey said. "I can't wait to meet her."

Grinning, Leon glanced at his brother. "Auntie is gonna be beside herself when she sees you. She really misses you."

"I miss her, too."

"We're here," Leon said as he pulled into a vacant parking space in front of the café.

Eleanor was standing in the doorway. "Trey, I'm so glad to see you," she said, embracing her nephew.

Trey kissed her cheek. "It's great being back on the island."

Misty walked out of the kitchen. When she spotted Leon, she gave a tiny wave.

He gestured for her to join them. "Trey, this is the lady I was telling you about."

Trey shook her hand. "Leon was actually talking about your cakes."

She smiled. "Okay…"

Eleanor made the introductions. "This is Misty. Leon's right. Her cakes sell out fast. We've had wedding cake orders every weekend this month. Birthday cakes, too."

Rubbing his hands together, Trey said, "I have to try this chocolate cake right here."

"I'll cut you a slice." Smiling, Misty glanced over at Leon. "You want anything?"

"No, I'm good."

Leon and Trey sat down with Eleanor at one of the tables near the kitchen.

"How have you been?" Trey grabbed the menu and perused it. He glanced up at Eleanor.

"I'm doing fine. I've been a lil forgetful from time to time. I guess it comes with getting old."

"Auntie, I've told you that you're not old," Leon interjected. "You need to stop saying that."

"Leon's right. You're nowhere near old."

"In my mind I feel twenty-five years old, but my body constantly reminds me that I'm fifty-five."

One of the servers brought a plate laden with a huge slice of chocolate cake. She placed it in front of Trey.

Leon's eyes kept traveling to the kitchen for glimpses of Misty. As much as he tried to fight the emotions threatening to escape from behind the wall, he'd carefully erected to protect what was left of his heart, she was still able to infiltrate somehow. Leon found himself looking forward just to seeing that beautiful smile of hers.

He tried to deny the pulsing knot that had formed in his stomach when Misty walked out of the kitchen.

"She's beautiful," Trey said.

Leon nodded in argument. "Yes, she is."

"Well, if I were in your shoes, I'd do something about it."

His words gave Leon something to consider.

MISTY STOLE A peek into the café area. Leon and Eleanor looked to be having a wonderful reunion with Trey. She enjoyed seeing him so happy. A visit from his brother was like medicine for him.

She gave herself a mental shake, then went back to decorating the cake she'd been working on before Leon and his brother showed up.

Eleanor appeared in the doorway. "Sugar, when you get a free minute, come join us."

"I will," Misty said. "Give me five minutes."

She did a quick check in the mirror to make sure she didn't have any flour on her face. Eying her reflection, Misty removed the cap and freed her curly tresses.

Leon moved over to make room for her. She could feel the heat emanating from his body and drank in the comfort of his nearness.

"Looks like they're keeping you pretty busy today," he said.

Misty nodded. "I have to have a birthday cake done for pickup later today. I spent most of my morning helping out in the café."

"Trey, this lady here is a godsend," Eleanor stated. "She can practically run this shop all by herself."

"I wouldn't say that," Misty responded. "I just do what I can to help out around here."

"Hey, Aunt Eleanor isn't one to give meaningless compliments." Trey picked up his water glass. "She's really needed someone new. The last time I was home that other guy wasn't that good."

Eleanor chuckled. "He was fine, but after his heart attack, nothing was the same."

"I'm with Trey on this one," Leon said. "Aunt Eleanor had to make all of the specialty cakes."

"Y'all leave Augustus alone. He done retired."

"Thank goodness," Trey said.

"Why don't we have a cookout or something for the Fourth of July?" Eleanor suggested.

"Sounds good to me," Trey responded.

"That's the perfect way to end my vacation. I love the day after."

Leon agreed, then looked over at Misty. "You're invited, too."

Smiling, she said, "I'd love to come. Can I bring anything?"

"Cake," Leon and Trey said in unison, sparking laughter all around the table.

CHAPTER NINE

"I CAN TELL that you really like Misty," Trey stated when they walked out of the shop. "I saw the way you were looking at her."

Leon gave his brother a sidelong glance. "What are you talking about?" He wasn't ready to admit his attraction to anyone—not even himself.

"Man… You know you like that woman. Hey, I can't blame you. She's gorgeous."

"She was married to my friend."

"From the sound of it, John wasn't the man we thought he was," Trey responded. "Sounds like he didn't deserve a woman like her. I think she'd be good for you, Leon."

"I haven't gotten over losing Vera. It wouldn't be fair to her when I still have feelings for my late wife."

"A part of you never will never stop loving Vee, but life isn't over for you, big brother. It's time for you to get back out there, Leon."

"That's what everybody keeps telling me, but

it's just not that easy. I can't erase my feelings for Vee. I miss her more and more every day."

"Leon, I get that."

"I don't want to meet someone and mislead them. I'm not ready to date."

"Okay," Trey murmured. "I'm not gonna push you."

"I wish I could get Aunt Eleanor to stop."

"You know she means well."

"Yeah."

"I think I'd like to walk around the town for a bit," Trey said. "It's been a while and I miss the island."

"Is that your way of making sure the ladies know you're back?" Leon teased.

Trey burst into laughter. "Hey, I just want to say hello to a few people. What are you about to get into?"

"I'm going home," Leon said. "I think it's time I redecorated my room."

"Why don't you ask Misty to help you?"

"I'm sure I can manage," Leon responded. "I'm just getting new bedding. Something to match that new quilt Aunt Eleanor made for me last Christmas."

He unlocked the door to his truck. "You want me to drop you off anywhere?"

"I'm good," Trey responded.

"Think you'll be around for dinner?"

"Yeah. I'll be there."

Five hours later, the doorbell rang just as Leon was about to make dinner. He left the pack of hamburger sitting on the kitchen counter and went to answer the door.

He opened it quickly, expecting a package delivery or one of his neighbors bringing mis-delivered mail, but instead he found Trey standing there, holding two boxes of pizza.

"No offense, brother, but you're not a cook, so I thought I'd spare you by getting dinner to-night."

Leon took the pizza boxes from him. "Nothing like a night of pizza, beer and brotherly conversation."

They sat down at the dining room table, eating and talking.

"I'm really glad you're here," Leon said. "I know Auntie feels the same way."

"Have you noticed that she's starting to re-peat some things? She mentioned being forget-ful. Anything we should be worried about?"

"I don't think so, Trey. I can be forgetful at times."

After several slices of pepperoni and sau-sage pizza, they watched a movie before Leon marched upstairs, calling it a night. "Come by the station if you run out of things to do or peo-ple to see."

Carrying the paper plates to the trash, Trey laughed. "I'll do that."

Leon showered, then slipped on a pair of pajama pants and a T-shirt.

He climbed into a king-size bed. Most times, he slept in the guest room, which had a full-size bed. It didn't make him feel quite as lonely as he did in the one he'd shared with Vera. With Trey there, he had no choice but to sleep in the master bedroom. The third bedroom had been converted into a home office.

Three hours later, Leon punched his pillow with his fist. Plagued with thoughts of Misty, he was having a tough time sleeping. His mind warred between his attraction for a woman who wasn't his late wife and his guilt for feeling that way. Although he no longer wore his wedding ring, Leon was still bound by his vow to Vera.

She's gone, he told himself. The promises made on their wedding day remained in force only until the day she died. However, Leon chose to continue to remain faithful as a way to honor Vera. She'd meant the world to him and he wasn't going to dismiss her so easily.

He had not expected to develop feelings for Misty beyond friendship. After all, she was John's ex-wife.

Although Misty tried to keep her expression neutral, Leon knew that their attraction was mutual. He was rusty when it came to this sort of thing, but he was sure that he'd caught glimpses of interest in her eyes whenever they were in the same room.

Groaning, Leon turned from his left side to the right. He was scheduled to be at the station at 8:00 a.m. to start his shift.

Why was it so hard to get this woman out of his head?

Why couldn't he stay away from her?

THE NEXT MORNING, Misty followed her usual routine of dropping Talei off to day care at 6:00 a.m., then heading down Main Street to the shop to start the morning baking.

As she waited for the lemon blueberry muffins to come out of the oven, she worked on carrot cake muffins next, all the while trying to keep her mind off Leon.

She was failing miserably.

If Leon hadn't been so blatant in his attraction to her, Misty could've easily dismissed his actions as simply the thoughtful gestures of a nice guy.

Initially, Misty had been certain he kept his distance because she was John's ex-wife. But now she felt his reservations were less about whom she'd been married to and more about his grief. In his present state of mind, Misty represented a risk to his broken heart. His daughter would be around Talei's age now—how often did being around her remind him how much he missed her? If her daughter got too attached to Leon… It worked both ways. Misty ran the same risk.

She was so conflicted. It seemed wrong to feel any sort of attraction or desire for a man grieving his late wife and child.

She had worked hard so far to keep a polite distance, but the truth was the damage had already been done.

Leon accepted the cup of coffee from Trey. "Thanks, man. You don't know how much I need this." He wasn't really a coffee drinker, but after a night with no sleep, he needed the caffeine.

"Actually, I do. I heard you moving around in your room. I knew you had trouble sleeping."

"I suffer from a little insomnia," Leon said. "Since Vee died. I thought changing the bedcovers and stuff would help, but it didn't."

"Maybe you need to say goodbye," Trey suggested. "A real goodbye."

Leon looked at his brother. "I know."

"You can't move forward until you stop being Vee's husband. She's gone and she's not coming back."

Leon didn't respond.

"I made breakfast," Trey announced. "Nothing special. Just scrambled eggs, bacon and toast."

"That's probably all you can cook," Leon said with a chuckle.

"Neither one of us inherited Aunt Eleanor's cooking skills." Trey handed a plate to his brother.

"You're right about that."

They sat down to eat.

"Thanks for this," Leon said. "I appreciate it."

After they finished eating, Leon cleaned the kitchen before heading out to work.

Leon's day at the firehouse started with an exchange of information from the previous day. When the meeting ended, he spent the latter half of the morning checking his fire apparatus and protective gear.

He helped his team clean up around the property before leaving to do fire hydrant maintenance.

The tasks complete, Leon returned to the station house. It was his turn to make dinner for the crew.

Leon made spaghetti for the evening meal while Charles prepared a large bowl of salad to go with the entrée.

An image of Misty formed in his mind as he

stirred the pasta in the hot boiling water. There was a part of him that wanted to be with her and Talei. In fact, it took everything in him to not pick up the phone and call her.

The timer on the oven went off.

With a sigh, Leon tried to forget the woman who stayed on his mind night and day.

CHAPTER TEN

MISTY WAS LOOKING forward to spending the holiday with Eleanor and Leon. Otherwise, she and Talei would've spent it on the beach or at home. Her mother had gone to visit her sister in Florida, and her friend Brittany was vacationing with her fiancé.

"Happy Fourth of July," Trey greeted when he opened the front door. "Leon's out back with Aunt Eleanor."

Bending down, he said, "This pretty girl must be Talei. Hey, cutie."

"*Oseeyo,*" she said, grinning.

"My name is Trey. Leon is my brother."

"Trey," she repeated, then peeked around him. "Where Eon?"

"He's back here." Trey led Talei and Misty to the patio.

"Eon... *Oseeyo.*" Talei ran up to him. "Gawfather."

Trey looked at Leon. "Did she just call you godfather?"

He nodded.

"Cool."

Trey moved on to greet other guests.

Leon sat down beside Misty. "I know we told you to bring cake, but I heard about your shrimp and crab deviled eggs from Eleanor and hope you brought some."

"I did," she confirmed. Lowering her voice, she whispered, "And I bought an extra tray just for you."

"And a cake?"

Smiling, she nodded. "Yes, I brought cake, too."

Leon broke into a grin. "You know you just made my day, right?"

Misty laughed.

There was something in Leon's manner that soothed her, making her feel safe and secure.

Misty wasn't able to shut out any awareness of him, so she embraced it instead. He wasn't like the other men she'd dated, and he had no hidden motives. She could call him *friend* and it was true by any definition of the word. Misty had never believed in the label "perfect gentleman," but that's exactly what Leon was—a perfect gentleman.

THE FOURTH OF July cookout was in full swing.

Misty heard a giggle near the rosebushes in

the backyard. She crept through the grass to find Talei hiding near them.

"What are you doing, sweetie? Remember, don't touch Miss Eleanor's roses."

"I hiding from Trey. He tickle monster. He wanna get me."

She felt the presence of someone behind her and glanced over her shoulder.

"Where is the little princess?" Trey questioned. "When I find her, I'm gonna tickle her."

Talei burst into giggles, leading him straight to her hiding place.

Trey swooped past Misty to pick up Talei.

"Who's gonna save the princess now?" he asked.

"Eon," Talei called out.

"I'm coming to the rescue, little one," Leon responded.

Eleanor was standing beside Misty. "Both my boys are gwine make great daddies."

Misty nodded. "I believe you're right."

Talei was a bubble of pure joy being the center of attention. When she wasn't following behind Leon, she was with Trey. However, when other children began arriving, Talei abandoned them both. It didn't last long. One of the boys found a worm, which sent her running back to Leon.

Misty and Eleanor shared a look of amusement.

"She's definitely my daughter. I hate bugs and worms—all forms of insects."

"I'd better go tell them kids to stop scaring her," Eleanor said.

Misty coaxed Talei into playing with another little girl who was about the same age.

"I need to finish the pasta salad," she told Leon. "Do you mind keeping an eye on her? I shouldn't be gone long."

"Take your time," he responded. "She'll be fine."

Fifteen minutes later, the food was ready to be served.

Misty and Eleanor made plates for the children first.

She was one of the last people to eat. Misty sat down beside Leon, who seemed to be enjoying his burger.

"Thanks for fixing a plate for me," she said.

He responded, "You were so busy looking out for everybody else. I didn't want you to miss out." Lowering his voice to a whisper, he added, "Aunt Eleanor's friend Rusty is nice, but his relatives like to pack up food to take home."

"Oh, I see."

Misty loved the way Leon's lips parted when he laughed that deep, throaty laugh. Being this close to him made her very aware that it had been a long time since a man had made her feel special. She was not a woman who needed a man in her life, but that didn't mean she wanted to be alone either. She had always wanted to share her life with someone—a man who was family-oriented, had a strong work ethic, great sense of humor—a man who would love her and value her with his whole heart.

Misty just wasn't sure a man like that existed.

After they finished eating, Trey hooked up a speaker to his iPhone to play an old-school music playlist.

She swayed to the music. Talei ran up to her and began dancing with her.

"That's right, baby, I like your moves," Misty told her daughter.

Trey swooped in, picking up Talei and swinging her around. "Dance with me, Princess."

"Having fun?" Leon asked when she joined him by the chest containing the drinks. He handed a soda to her.

"I am," Misty said. "I'm going to have to run ten miles to lose the extra pounds I gained from eating all this food. Everything was delicious. In fact, I might have to have one more hamburger."

"I've never seen you eat this much," Leon said. "You normally eat like a bird."

"Really? That's what you think?"

"Maybe I shouldn't have said it like that. All

I'm saying is that I've never seen you finish a meal—you normally take half of it home."

Misty smiled. "That's intentional, Leon. A girl has to watch her figure."

A group of people started a line dance.

She grabbed Leon by the hand and led him to join in.

"I'm not good with this," he said.

"Just follow me," Misty encouraged. She was having the time of her life.

At six thirty, everyone walked down to the park to watch the fireworks.

Misty noted the set of earphones in Leon's hand. "Who are those for?"

"For Talei," he responded. "Some children don't like the noise. It scares them."

She gave him a gentle nudge. "You're so sweet and thoughtful."

When it was time for the fireworks to begin, Leon found a great area for them to sit to watch the display.

The fiery sparks burst through the night like brilliant colors on a canvas of stars. The explosive sounds startled Talei, but she was fine once he placed the headphones over her ears.

Misty thought the soaring golden yellow, red, green and blue flares resembled flowers exploding in the air.

"Pretty…" Talei murmured, pointing upward. "Look, Mommy."

Leon reached over and took Misty's hand in his own.

Misty felt the electricity of his touch. It made her feel good, and she was glad to be with him.

IN SPITE OF the dreary weather, and Trey's leaving to return to Camp Pendleton, Leon was in a great mood as he drove his brother to the airport. He had thoroughly enjoyed their time together.

Leon was sad to see Trey go but grateful for the time they'd had. This brief visit was exactly what he'd needed—to reconnect with his brother.

"I hope you're finally gonna go after Misty," Trey said. "You're good together."

He stole a glance at his brother. "You really think so?"

"Yeah," Trey responded. "So does Aunt Eleanor and probably the whole town."

Leon burst into laughter.

Trey pointed to the console. "I've been meaning to ask… You have this state-of-the-art satellite-navigation system in your truck. Have you ever used it? Do you even leave the island?"

"I'm not a hermit, Trey. I get out," he said as

they drove across the bridge to Charleston. "In fact, I plan on getting out a lot more."

"I'm happy to hear this. Hopefully you'll be taking Misty with you. It's time for you to jump back into the dating pool. You deserve to have that family you always wanted."

Leon grinned. "I hear you, little brother, and I'll consider your advice."

He pulled curbside to the airport. "Here we are…"

Trey nodded. "Back to California. Next time, you gotta come out to see me. You'd love Oceanside."

"I'll do that."

Leon got out to embrace his brother. "Stay safe and thank you for your service."

CHAPTER ELEVEN

"So, I met Trey," Misty told Brittany when they got together for dinner and a movie. "He's such a sweetheart."

"Yeah…he is… I had fun with him when we dated. I hate I missed seeing him while he was in town."

"Well, you were vacationing with your bae," Misty said. "Did you have a good time?"

Brittany held up her left hand to display an engagement ring. "I had a wonderful time."

Misty gasped. "Congratulations, Britt. Oh, my goodness! You're getting married."

"Girl, it's about time," Brittany uttered. "Rick and I have been together for five years. We've been talking about marriage forever. Even though I was already saying he was my fiance… it's official now."

"You spoke it into existence."

"I sure did."

Misty laughed. "I'm happy for you, Britt."

The waitress arrived with their meals.

"How are things between you and Leon?" Brittany inquired while they ate.

Misty wiped her mouth on a napkin. "What do you mean? There's nothing going on with us."

Brittany picked up her wineglass. "Girl, pleeze…"

"You're wrong about this. Leon is a nice guy but it's obvious that he's still grieving the loss of his wife."

"I saw you two at the barbecue. Y'all are good together. I think you're just what Leon needs to move on with living. *You and Talei.*"

"My daughter loves him, Britt. She lights up every time she sees Leon. He's her godfather so I don't want to mess things up between us. But… I can't stop thinking about him."

"Take it one day at a time," Brittany advised. "And enjoy the journey."

They finished dinner, paid the bill and walked across the street to the movie theater.

Two and a half hours later, they exited through the glass doors and headed to their cars.

"I was hesitant initially about taking Talei to meet my dad's mother," Misty announced, "but after seeing this movie, I'm going to do it."

"*Really?* You talked to her?"

Misty nodded. "We've had a couple of conversations and they've been very positive. I'm looking forward to seeing her again. It's been a long time."

"What about your father?"

"I've made it clear that I'm not ready to see him. He's moved on with his new family—that doesn't have to change."

The two women embraced.

"I'm really happy for you," Brittany said before getting into her car.

Misty climbed into her vehicle and locked the door. She followed her friend out of the parking lot and then turned in the opposite direction. She had to pick up Talei from Eleanor's house.

"GOOD MORNING, MISS ELEANOR," Misty greeted. "Thanks again for watching Talei for me."

"Great morning to you. It was my pleasure." Eleanor slipped on an apron. "What are you working on?"

"Pastries and doughnuts," Misty replied. "We had a pretty busy morning. The raspberry cream cheese muffins sold out quick."

"Really? I think we should add them to the regular menu."

Eleanor washed her hands, then began working across the table from Misty. "I need to make some more grits." She placed a towel next to the burner as she talked. "How are you feeling now that things are settling down?"

"I hate that John's gone...that he won't get to see Talei grow up. Our marriage ended before it really began. His father had a lot to do with that."

"That Elroy is a piece of work."

"That he is," Misty responded as she kneaded the dough. "When I put these in the oven, I'll change the daily specials on the sign outside."

"Okay. Josh just left to pick up some napkins and other stuff. I'm going to get everything ready for lunchtime."

Misty grabbed the signs once the pastries were baking and headed outside.

Humming softly, Eleanor moved about the kitchen retrieving ingredients for items on the lunch menu. Next, she seized the broom and walked out of the shop.

"Hello, Eleanor," someone greeted.

"Mamie, I haven't seen you in a while."

"I was in Philadelphia taking care of my mother. I'm so glad to be back here on the island. I've missed my morning ritual of your fresh-baked muffins."

"This is Misty Brightwater," Eleanor said. "She's the new baker. Wait until you taste her baked goods."

They stood there with Mamie in deep conversation for the next twenty minutes.

"Eleanor, I think there's a fire in your kitchen," Mamie cried suddenly.

They rushed inside the shop to see timbers charring and blackening, a smoke haze coating the room and paint bubbling as the full blaze threatened to get out of hand quickly.

Misty tried but couldn't get to the fire extinguisher through the billowing flames.

Eleanor called the fire department.

The cackle of the fire had Misty's attention, but it was the woof and hissing sounds that concerned her. "We need to get out of here," Misty said. "C'mon, Miss Eleanor."

Outside a crowd was gathering.

Josh ran over to them. "I was worried when I didn't see y'all. What happened?"

"I think I left my towel on the stove," Eleanor said and shuddered.

Misty embraced her. "Here comes the fire truck."

Eleanor's eyes teared up and she started to cough from the thick smoke and ash.

Leon rushed to her side. "Auntie, are you okay?"

"I'm fine. We all got out. The s-shop…"

"I need to get in there."

Eleanor wiped away her tears. "Be careful, Leon."

"Don't worry. They're going to do what they

can to save the shop," Misty said. "Looks like most of the damage will be in the kitchen."

Rusty walked up. "I heard about the fire and wanted to make sure everyone was safe."

"We're fine," Eleanor said. "Devastated and heartbroken, but fine."

LEON AND THE other firefighters worked furiously as the blaze moved quickly, leaving behind a trail of damage. They were able to contain it there, but the rest of the shop couldn't escape the flood of water that was everywhere.

Eleanor placed a call to her insurance company. "I need to file a claim for fire and water damage." She gave them the policy number.

"Mrs. Pittman, I'm afraid that policy lapsed a month ago for nonpayment."

"That can't be right," Eleanor said indignantly. "I paid the premium and y'all gwine do your part. I'ma check my records and give you a call back with the proof."

She covered her face with trembling hands and gave vent to the agony of her loss.

What if she'd messed up? She had been so forgetful lately.

Leon and Charles walked over to discuss the damage in full. She gave them her full attention.

When everyone left, she sat down in the café area with her laptop.

"What in the world…" Stunned, Eleanor stared at her bank account. She had no memory of some of the transactions or the cash withdrawals. Worse, she couldn't find proof of payments that were made to the insurance company. Eleanor had been told that her policy had lapsed, but as far as she was concerned, they were wrong.

"Why didn't I make the payments?" she whispered.

Eleanor knew that she'd been a little forgetful, but mostly small things. Thankfully there was no mortgage on the bakery or on her house. However, if her insurance had truly lapsed, how was she going to pay for the repairs on the bakery?

She looked back at the computer monitor. Could someone be stealing from her? Eleanor wasn't ready to accept that her memory issues were greater than she had assumed.

"Miss Eleanor…"

She glanced up to find Misty standing there. "C'mon in, sugar."

"Are you okay? Is there anything I can do for you?"

Eleanor checked her watch, then glanced around. "We need to get moving. The lunch crowd will be arriving within the hour."

Misty eyed her. "I put a sign on the door."

"Why?"

"The fire... Miss Eleanor, the kitchen is a disaster."

She looked confused. "It is?"

"Yes, ma'am."

Eleanor stood up and went to the kitchen. "Oh, Lawd, there's so much damage..." she uttered. Tears sprang into her eyes once more. "Noooo."

Misty embraced her. "There's damage but Leon feels like it can easily be repaired. He said it looks worse than it really is—it's going to be okay."

Eleanor nodded. "You're right. I just need to call the insurance company."

"Josh and I will start cleaning up the debris. Silas said he'd come by when he returned from Charleston."

"I guess there's nothing for me to do but go home, but I might need your help, Misty. I need to find the insurance paperwork."

"Let me finish here and make sure Josh is okay. I'll be there shortly."

"Thanks, sugar." Right now, Eleanor was filled with nothing more than nervous energy.

Polk Island Bakery & Café was her baby—her lifeblood. The thought that it had nearly been destroyed by fire brought tears to her eyes.

CHAPTER TWELVE

MISTY RANG THE doorbell and waited for Eleanor to open the door. Her eyes landed on the large Boston ferns framing the entry. They were a vivid green, luscious and full. Eleanor's yard was a beautiful landscape of rosebushes in red, pink and white blooms. Misty wished she possessed a green thumb. She didn't have a gift for taking care of plants or flowers, which was why all the arrangements in her house were artificial.

Eleanor opened the door and released a sigh of relief. "I'm so glad you're here. I need to find my insurance documents. Maybe you can help me."

"Sure." Misty noted how Eleanor was repeating herself. Maybe it was because she was still upset over the fire. That was enough to stress anyone.

She found the insurance cancellation notice amid the stack of paperwork on Eleanor's desk. Bewildered, Misty knew Eleanor was too responsible to just let the policy lapse for nonpayment. Something was definitely going on with her.

"Did you find anything?" Eleanor asked.

"Just a letter of cancellation."

The spark of hope in the older woman's gaze was quickly extinguished. "I've really made a mess of things."

"Miss Eleanor, you don't need to blame yourself," Misty said. "It was just an accident."

Tears filled her eyes. "I can't understand how I let things get so out of control. I've always been good about paying my bills. I'm never late on them."

"I know that."

"I really can't figure out how I missed paying the insurance company, but they're telling me that's what happened. I know I've been forgetful..."

"Miss Eleanor, I'd like to help with the repairs," Misty offered. "We were both outside talking and weren't paying attention to what was going on in the kitchen. I feel just as responsible."

"Sugar, you don't have to worry about this. I'll figure something out."

"Have you considered seeing a doctor?" Misty asked. "I've noticed that you seem a bit more forgetful lately, but it's not just that. A couple of times you had some confusion at the cash register. I know you've had a lot on your mind, so it might just be that, but it won't hurt to get checked out by a doctor."

"I'm just getting older," Eleanor stated. "Just wait and see... It will happen to you eventually."

"I'm not trying to upset you. You've been so good to me and my daughter. I'm just worried about you."

"There are times when I do feel confused," Eleanor confessed. "I forget to take my keys out of the door... One time, I even left my car door open after I got out. Someone could've stolen it. The more I talk about this... Misty, you might be right. This isn't me and I'm scared."

"You don't have to be afraid, Miss Eleanor. I'm here for you and so is Leon."

"I don't want Leon to know anything about this. He doesn't need to worry about me." Eleanor paused a moment, then said, "Please don't tell him about the insurance."

"Let me help you," she insisted.

"I can't take your money, Misty. I have some money saved. This is all my fault, so I'll have to deal with the fallout."

"Miss Eleanor," she pleaded, "when I needed help, you came to my aid. We will keep this between us. No one has to know."

"You are such a dear. Thank you, Misty, but it'll be fine. I'll take care of everything somehow."

"IS MY AUNT HERE?" Leon asked the next morning. He left the station and went straight to the shop to check on her. He knew Eleanor was upset. He also wanted to make sure that an insurance claim had been filed. The sooner they received payment, the sooner the bakery and café would be back up and running.

Misty shook her head. "She's at home. I told her I'd come in and help Josh and Silas with moving some stuff around."

A timeless moment stretched while she stared at him, absorbing the warmth of his gaze above smooth high cheekbones, appreciating the fullness of his mouth. A pulse of uneasy heat flickered in the pit of her stomach. Misty cleared her throat noisily.

Leon pointed to the mop in the corner. "You need some help?"

Misty snatched in a quick breath to regain her flustered wits.

"Oh, no… We got it covered, Leon. Thank you, but I think it's best you go check on your aunt. Miss Eleanor tried to hide it, but I could tell she was really shaken by the fire. It took a lot for me to convince her to go home."

Leon was instantly concerned. "I'll head over there now."

"Call me if she needs anything."

He smiled. "I will."

Misty stood at the window watching Leon as he strode to his truck. He climbed inside, turned the ignition and drove away.

She found it strange that she already missed him.

LEON BROKE INTO a grin when Eleanor opened the front door. "I see you finally took some time off."

"I was actually ordered to stay home by my staff," she responded. "They told me they would take care of everything. I decided to let them."

"It was a good call," Leon said. "I went by there. They have everything under control. Now all we need to do is let the insurance company do their part. I came by to see if you need any help with filling out the claims paperwork."

"Oh, you don't have to worry about that," Eleanor stated. "Everything's done."

The doorbell sounded.

Leon followed Eleanor to the foyer.

She broke into a smile when she opened the door. "Rusty, hello. C'mon in. I guess everybody's checking on me today. I'm a lucky woman."

"That's because we love you," he said, closing the door behind him.

"Rusty's right," Leon interjected. "You're loved by this community."

"I feel it and I'm grateful." Making her way into the living room, she said, "We might as well make ourselves comfortable."

Leon chose the love seat while Rusty sat down beside Eleanor on the floral-printed sofa.

"How long do you think the shop will have to be closed?"

"I stopped by there before I came here," Rusty said. "I'd say you're going to be closed two weeks to a month. Shouldn't be any longer than that. Josh and Silas can work at my store in the meantime. I doubt Misty will have any interest in building supplies."

Eleanor smiled. "That's so sweet of you, Rusty. Josh and Silas will appreciate that. Misty, I think, will be all right."

"Don't worry, Auntie. We're going to have the shop back up and running as quickly as we can. We have the whole community behind us." Leon rose to his feet. "I need to leave but I'll give you a call later."

"Thanks for coming by, son," Eleanor stated. She waited until Leon walked out of the house and said, "Rusty, thank you for coming by. I was planning to call you. I need to talk to you about something."

"Sounds important."

"Hopefully, it's nothing." Eleanor didn't know quite how to begin, so she opened up with, "We've been friends for a long time, Rusty."

He nodded. "We have."

"I've always been able to count on you. Right now, I need to unburden myself." Eleanor got up and stood in front of the fireplace.

"What's wrong, Ladybug?"

"I let my insurance lapse. It was not intentional. I just don't know what happened. I've been forgetting a lot of stuff lately. I'm getting scared because I'm missing important things like locking my car, leaving the keys in the front door and not paying my insurance premium."

Rusty stood up, walked over and embraced her. "I think that comes with age. I walk into a room, then forget why I went in there the first place."

"That's what I thought at first, but now... I think something might be wrong with me."

"One way to find out for sure," he responded. "If you want, I'll go with you to see your doctor. I think you should get a professional opinion."

Eleanor smiled. "I knew I could count on you. But I need you to keep this just between you and me, Rusty. I don't want to worry Leon."

"I'll do whatever you want."

"Thank you, Rusty." Eleanor picked up her phone. "I'd better call the doctor now while it's on my mind."

CHAPTER THIRTEEN

RUSTY DROVE ELEANOR to her doctor's appointment.

While seated in the waiting area, she confided, "I have to admit that I'm scared. What if I have a tumor on my brain or cancer?"

He reached over and gave her hand a light squeeze. "Don't be afraid, Ladybug. It's gonna be alright. I feel it in my spirit."

She smiled. "You're just saying that."

"Is it working?" Rusty teased.

His words had the desired effect. Eleanor chuckled. "You're right. I have to remain positive."

"That's my girl."

"Thank you so much for coming with me."

Eleanor was called to the back where the examination rooms were located while Rusty stayed in the waiting room.

After seeing the doctor, she walked out and said, "Dr. Brown wants me to have an MRI done. They took some blood work. He mentioned Alzheimer's disease." Eleanor glanced at Rusty. "What if he's right and I have that disease? What will happen to the café? Or to me if I lose my memory?"

"Whoa… Let's not worry until we have a reason to do so, Ladybug."

She couldn't stop herself from pondering aloud, "But what if that's what is wrong with me, Rusty?"

"You won't be alone. I'll be here to take care of you, and you have your family."

"I don't want to be a burden."

"You won't be—none of us would ever consider you a burden."

Eleanor met his gaze. "There's something I want to know. Why didn't you ever get married?"

"Because the only woman I ever loved chose someone else to spend her life with."

"You're talking about me," Eleanor said with complete clarity.

"I am," he confirmed. "You have owned my heart since I saw you walk into the classroom when we were in first grade in the red-and-black polka-dot dress. You reminded me of a ladybug."

"Rusty, you never said anything in all these years. Why are you telling me now?"

"This is the first time I ever thought you'd

take me seriously." He took her hand in his own. "Eleanor, I love you and I want to marry you."

She gasped in surprise.

"We've known each other a long time. We have no idea what the future holds, but we can face it together."

"I used to have the biggest crush on you, Rusty, but I never thought you were interested."

"I didn't think I was good enough for you," he confessed. "You're a Rothchild. I don't feel that way anymore. I need to know how you feel about me."

Eleanor placed a hand to his face. "I've always cared for you—you know that. You're a very dear friend and if I were to marry again, you would be the man I'd choose."

"So, you're turning down my proposal?"

"No, I'm not. I'd just like to take some time to think about it," Eleanor responded. "Until this moment, I honestly never considered marrying anyone. To be honest, I thought that part of my life was over."

"I'm tired of being alone. Aren't you?" Rusty asked. "I want to share whatever life I have left with the only woman I've ever loved."

She nodded. "I get lonely."

"Then consider spending the rest of your life with me as my wife, my best friend and my ladybug."

"I will," Eleanor said. "I'm going to give it a lot of serious thought."

"I hope you do," Rusty responded. "Because I want you to marry me."

MISTY HELPED TALEI out of the vehicle. She stood there surveying the charming one-level brick house. They had come to Atlanta for a visit with Waverly Taylor, the grandmother she hadn't seen in years. A wave of apprehension washed over her, but she pushed through it. She had come too far. There was no turning back now.

Talei grabbed her hand. "Mommy, I scared."

"Sweetie, there's no reason to be afraid," Misty assured her. "We're just visiting my grandmother."

"Ganmother."

"That's right." Misty rang the doorbell.

She swallowed her nervousness as she waited for someone to answer the door. She took Talei's hand with her right. In her left, Misty carried a box.

Her grandmother suddenly appeared in the doorway. Misty's gaze swept over the woman's sturdy frame, her hair a stunning platinum-gray color and pulled back into a bun at the nape of her neck. Her beautiful cocoa-tinted complexion bore few wrinkles—it was as if time had stood still for Waverly Taylor. She looked just as Misty remembered.

"Oh, my goodness, I'm so happy to see y'all." Waverly glimpsed Talei and exclaimed, "Look at this little angel right here. She's downright gorgeous, Misty."

She ushered them inside.

The inside looked nothing like Misty remembered. The main living area boasted high ceilings with a skylight. A crystal chandelier in the living room doubled as a fan.

"Grandmother, the house is beautiful."

"Thank you. Mike had it completely renovated last year for my birthday. He put this luxury tile in the kitchen. I got granite countertops, stainless-steel appliances and all new carpet in the bedrooms."

"That was really nice of him." Misty swallowed the sour taste of bitterness that threatened to rise up. She remembered the huge argument her parents had when her mother wanted a new washing machine. Misty reminded herself that he was supposed to be a different man now. And Waverly was his mother and not his wife.

"How was the drive?"

"Not too bad," Misty responded. "Talei slept most of the trip."

"I'm so glad you decided to come. I really wanted to see you and the baby." Waverly paused a moment, then said, "I have to confess that I told your daddy about our phone conversation."

Misty shrugged in nonchalance. "It's fine, Grandmother. I don't care if he knows."

"I'm glad to hear you say that. I don't want no secrets. I just want my family to come together. I don't know how many more days I have on this earth—we're blood, and we need to start acting like it."

She led them to the family room at the back of the house. Waverly eased down in an olive-green recliner while Misty and Talei sat down on a matching sofa.

"I'm not ready for a conversation with Mike. I hope you'll respect my decision."

Waverly nodded. "I hope one day you'll change your mind about that."

Misty didn't respond.

Waverly didn't push her. "How is your mother doing, Misty?"

"She's good. Mama's always on the go—she travels, volunteers…anything to keep busy."

"Good for her," Waverly said. "Does she still sew? She used to make the most beautiful blankets and quilts."

"She still does," Misty responded. "She designs clothing, as well."

Waverly settled back in her chair. "I've always liked your mother."

"She says the same thing about you."

"I feel terrible over everything that happened. I surely do."

"Grandmother, it's okay," Misty told her. "I'm just glad to have you in my life now."

"I keep looking at the box you brought in here. What's in it?"

"I made you some banana bread. I remembered that it was your favorite, only this one is gluten-free."

Waverly broke into a wide grin. "You did? I haven't had no banana bread in such a long time. Well, since they told me I had a gluten allergy. I can't tell you how much I've missed it. I bought a gluten-free one and it tasted horrible."

Misty chuckled. "Well, I hope you'll find this one to your liking."

Waverly sampled a piece. "Oh, this is delicious, Misty. You have to tell me how you made it."

"I just replaced all-purpose flour with wheat-free, gluten-free, dairy-free, one-to-one baking flour. You can turn any recipe into a gluten-free one easily."

"I'ma have to get me some of that."

They exchanged recipes for the next thirty minutes.

"I think you might have inherited your love for baking from me," Waverly said. "I hadn't done much of it lately because of this gluten-free diet the doctor put me on."

"I'm so happy we've reconnected, Grandmother. There's so much I want to know about this side of my family."

"Your aunt Lois and your cousins are coming to the house around lunch. They're all very excited to meet you. Boo Boo—her name is Christina but we call her Boo Boo—has a little girl the same age as Talei. Your aunt Marsha will be here in a few."

"I can't wait to meet them."

"Mike and his family live in New York. I made it clear no one was to say anything to him about your visit just yet."

"Thank you, Grandmother. I know that I have to have a conversation with him—I just want do it on my terms."

"I respect that, but I have to tell you that I don't like keeping secrets."

"I understand."

By the end of the day, Misty had met two aunts, three first cousins and five second cousins. She'd also met a great-aunt Lucy, who was Waverly's sister. Her dad's brother lived in Virginia, but she was able to speak with him via FaceTime.

Mike's youngest sister, Marsha, offered to call Mike, but Misty politely declined the offer.

"I only want to enjoy this day with all of you," she explained.

Talei rushed over to her from the back of the house. "Mommy, I have fun."

"Me, too."

"Where's her dad?" Marsha inquired.

"He passed away in May," Misty stated.

"Oh, I had no idea. I heard her mention him when the kids were eating lunch."

"Oh, if you hear her say anything about an Eon, she's talking about her godfather. His name is Leon."

"I did hear her say that a few times. I didn't know what she meant. I thought it might be Cherokee or something. She must be pretty close to him."

"He's been a great comfort for her since losing her father."

Marsha embraced her. "I hope life has been good to you, Misty."

"It's been *life*. Some good some bad, but I'm grateful for all of it. I've learned a lot about me."

"Well, you look beautiful and very well-adjusted. I'm really glad you reached out to Mama. We wanted so much to contact you, but…"

"I'm sure Mike didn't want that. It's okay."

"No, it really isn't," Marsha stated. "I'm sure you know my brother wasn't no joke back in the day. He did some terrible things, but now he's a different man. He's really turned his life around."

"He truly has," Lois said. She sat down beside Misty on the sofa. "My brother is a different man."

"I'm glad to hear that," Misty said. "All I can remember about him is that he was really mean."

The room was enveloped in silence.

After a moment, Marsha changed the subject. They three women discussed the adventures of motherhood.

That evening, Waverly showed Misty to the room she and Talei would sleep in.

Talei was out by the time her head hit the pillow.

Misty went back to the front of the house to help her grandmother straighten up.

"I know you got to be tired. Go on to bed," Waverly said.

"I'm good," Misty responded. "Grandmother, thank you for today."

"Thank you for giving us another chance. You didn't have to because of your father."

"You're not Mike," she stated. "He is solely responsible for his actions."

"I been praying for the day he'll come to you and make things right," Waverly said.

Misty bagged up the trash. "I'll put this outside."

When she returned, Waverly said, "Now you go on to bed. I know you plan on leaving early to get back home. I'm very happy you came."

The two women embraced.

"Grandmother, I love you. I'm beyond thrilled to have you back in my life."

"Don't hold on to that anger and unforgiveness forever."

"I hear you, Grandmother. It's just going to take time. I didn't just get here overnight."

SHOES IN HAND, Leon walked along the sandy beach, enjoying the solitude of his late afternoon stroll and watching the squadrons of brown pelicans fly into an endless horizon. The sand dunes held stories and secrets of those who had lived on the island and were long buried.

He found a spot on a grassy knoll and sat down to reflect on his life. Three years had passed since the death of Vera and his daughter. There was a moment in time when Leon didn't think he would survive a day without them. His throat still tightened at the thought that she was truly gone from his life forever.

Leon heard laughter and turned his attention

to a woman and small child walking along the beach. As they neared, he recognized them.

Misty looked beautiful dressed in a pair of denim shorts and tank top, her black hair tumbling down past her shoulders. She seemed free from any worries and her smile flashed frequently as she and Talei walked to the water's edge. He was by no means blind to her attractiveness, as much as he tried to ignore it.

Leon had always wanted a beautiful wife and children—he wanted a family. And this sweet, loving pair seemed to fit right into his heart. He had to remind himself that this wasn't his life and never would be. The only thing he could offer Misty was friendship.

He stood up and made his way down to the beach.

Talei saw him first and waved animatedly. "Eon… Eon… Mommy, look."

"Hey, little one," Leon greeted as he picked her up and swung her around.

Her laughter filled the air.

Leon smiled at Misty. "I see we had the same idea this Sunday afternoon."

"Yeah, we did. I wanted to come and enjoy this beautiful view."

Still in his arms, Talei touched Leon's cheek. "I like ocean."

"So do I," he told her.

"I wanna play in ocean."

"Not today, sweetie," Misty said. "I'll take you to the pool when I get off work tomorrow."

Talei pursed her lips into a pout.

"You're going to have so much fun at the pool," Leon said. "I'm jealous. I'll be at the station working."

"I gonna have fun."

"Have some fun for me, too."

Talei nodded.

"I drove back from Atlanta this morning. We went to meet my dad's side of the family."

"Did you enjoy your visit?"

Smiling, Misty said, "Very much. I hadn't seen my grandmother since I was a child. My grandmother is a hoot. It was nice meeting my aunts and their children, too. Talei has quite a few little cousins."

"I love family get-togethers, too."

"How are the repairs going at the shop?" Misty inquired. "How is Miss Eleanor holding up?"

"Some of the men in the community have agreed to help with the repairs of the café," Leon announced. "Hopefully, we can have everything done in a month or two at the latest. My aunt's doing okay when she's not beating herself up over this."

"I told her it could've happened to any of us," Misty said.

"That place means everything to my aunt. Actually, to the community as a whole. It's been a part of my family's history for many years."

"I read somewhere that it was your great-great-great-grandfather who founded the island."

"In 1870, Polk Rothchild left Darien, Georgia, with his family to start a new life in New York. His wife, Agnes, became ill and died during the journey. She always loved the water, so he buried her here. Polk couldn't bear to leave his beloved wife behind, so instead of continuing on to New York, he settled on this island to raise his family. His brother Hoss soon joined him. They decided to carve the uninhabited patch of swampy land into suburban plots. Hoss had a passion for farming, so he planted indigo, cotton and rice."

"I've heard that indigo was a valuable export back then."

Leon nodded. "It was pretty profitable for Polk and Hoss because of the demands for the dye product in the textile industry. Hoss eventually opened a fabric store. He wasn't just a farmer. He could sew. I'm told he designed several suits for the Rockefeller and other wealthy families. They would stop here whenever they journeyed to Sea Island, Georgia. Hoss's shop was where the café stands now. My grandparents converted it after he died. His sons worked with him, but they left the island for New York after his death."

"I know this island is known for the beautiful quilts made by residents. There are some very talented quilters on this island," Misty said.

"If you're not in a rush to get home, I can give you a quick tour of my family's land and our history.

"I'll get Talei a snack and we're good to go."

Misty followed him in her car to a property on the other side of the island.

When they got out of their cars, Leon said, "There was a time when Polk Island was only accessible by ferry. The original houses were built from a mixture of lime, shells and water. This is the house that Polk built for his family. Next door is the church. That's our family cemetery in the back. Polk, his wife and all but one of their children are buried there. His son Abraham is buried in Savannah. Hoss and his wife are buried back there, but the rest of the family is buried in Forest Lawn across town."

Misty read the sign over the door. "Polk Island Praise House... Wow, what a wonderful remnant of history. So, Polk was also a minister?"

Leon nodded. "Yeah. So was his son Ezra. He's my great-great-great-grandfather." Pointing, he said, "This is what's left of the house where Ezra and my great-great-grandfather Eli were born," Leon said. "It was destroyed when a tropical cyclone touched down on the island in 1893. It struck this island, Hilton Head, Daufuskie, Parris, with some of the smaller islands getting the worst of it. The storm killed more than two thousand people along the coast—it was one of the worst storms to hit until Hurricane Hugo in 1989."

"The Praise House doesn't appear to have suffered any damage," Misty said.

"I know," Leon responded. "My family considered it a miracle that practically everything on this street was destroyed, but the church wasn't touched."

"I'm curious… Why didn't they rebuild?" Misty inquired.

"They did. Just not on this side of the island. Aunt Eleanor said they always intended to rebuild this area—it just never happened. They built a house on the land where my aunt lives. Her grandfather built the house she's in now when the one before that was damaged by fire."

Leon had a captive audience in Misty. She loved hearing about his family and the history of the island.

"Did Polk ever leave the island?" she asked.

"Only once and that was to find a mother

for his ten children," Leon said. "His new wife brought her family with her. When Polk died in 1940, at the age of one hundred, the island had grown to a population of nine hundred. Seven generations of the Rothchild family has lived here."

"And now it's one of South Carolina's most popular areas."

"I know," Leon replied. "It's a good thing, but there are times when I wish we didn't have so many tourists coming here. Especially during spring break. That's when we have problems with crime—nothing big, but it's still a nuisance."

"I can imagine it gets pretty wild."

"Yes, it does," Leon agreed.

He bent down and plucked a handful of leaves from a prickly ash tree. "Put one in your mouth and chew it."

Misty did as he instructed. Within a few seconds she experienced a numbing sensation.

"We call this the toothache tree."

"I'll have to remember this whenever Talei has one."

Leon pointed to the Spanish moss. "Stuffing some of that in your shoes will relieve you of aches and pains. People here had to come up with their own first aid treatments at that time."

"Wow."

He chuckled. "They don't do that anymore—we simply call 9-1-1."

"I do know about this one," Misty said as fingered a yellowed flowered plant. "Life everlasting. My mother uses it as a tea and an essential oil for inflammation and stomach issues. She says that it has anti-aging properties."

"I have peppermint, aloe and life everlasting plants in my yard," Leon announced. "Vera never liked taking medicine—she would always seek out alternative solutions."

"She and I have that in common."

Talei began jumping up and down on a piece of wood.

Leon figured she was getting bored, so he said, "This ends this part of our tour. I'll take y'all around the island on another day."

Smiling, Misty responded, "Looking forward to it. Thank you for sharing your family history with me."

CHAPTER FOURTEEN

TALEI CLIMBED OUT of the car asking, "Mommy… where Eon?"

"He had to go home, sweetie. We'll see him again another day."

Inside the house, Talei ran over to the couch to get her teddy bears.

Misty noticed that her daughter kept Pooh Bear and the teddy in the fire department shirt with her most of the time. She would've taken them to the beach with her, but Misty had her leave them home.

While Talei played on the carpet with her bears, Misty stretched out on the couch with a novel she was determined to finish before going to bed.

She was able to read through five chapters before her daughter commanded her attention.

"I want Eon."

Misty swung her legs off the couch and sat up. "Sweetie, he's at his house."

Talei pointed to the tablet on the coffee table.

Misty sat up. "You want to FaceTime Leon?"

"Yes, Mommy."

"Let me see if he's busy." Misty sent him a quick text.

Seconds later, he called her via FaceTime.

Talei lit up when she saw Leon on camera. *"Oseeyo..."*

"I heard you wanted to talk to me, little one."

"Yes," she responded.

"I was happy to see you today."

"I happy, too." Talei proceeded to tell him about her stuffed animals and what was on the television.

Leon was an animated listener as he engaged her daughter in conversation.

"You can call me anytime you want to talk, okay?" Leon said.

"What you doing?" Talei inquired.

"I'm just sitting over here watching some television."

"You want talk to Mommy?"

"Sure."

Talei handed the tablet to Misty.

"Clearly she's done with me," Leon said with a chuckle.

"I think whatever is on television just caught her attention," Misty responded. "Thank you for doing this."

"Anytime. I'm always here for you both."

There was something in Leon's manner that soothed her. He made her feel safe.

Misty knew their attraction was mutual, but she resolved to keep her emotions grounded and in check. She wasn't really looking for a relationship. Her most important priority right now was to make sure Talei was adjusting well to their move to the island and the sudden loss of her father.

"HAS THE ADJUSTER come by here yet?" Leon asked. "It's been about a week and a half."

Eleanor picked up some papers off her desk and pretended to be reading them. She was still trying to figure out what to tell her nephew.

"Do you want me to give the insurance company a call? It shouldn't take this long to have someone come out for an inspection."

"Uh gwine gone dey tomorruh," she uttered as she turned her back to him.

Leon eyed her. His aunt spoke the Gullah language only whenever she was nervous or troubled about something. "What's going on, Auntie? What aren't you telling me?"

"Actually, I'm not gwine file a claim," she stated, turning to face him. "I'm just gwine pay out of pocket for the repairs."

Frowning, Leon inquired, "Why would you do that?"

"I don't want to go through the fuss of all that."

"But that's the reason you're paying for insurance, Auntie."

"And I decided not to use it."

Shaking his head, Leon said, "This doesn't make sense to me."

"Son, don't worry. I have everything taken care of. Rusty told me he's gonna come by with you on Saturday to get started on the repairs. I really appreciate y'all helping me."

"You know we don't mind, Auntie." Leon paused a moment, then said, "You really should file the claim."

Eleanor sighed heavily. "Seeing that you ain't gwine let this go… I might as well tell you the truth."

"The truth about what?"

"The insurance company ain't gwine pay nothing. I let it lapse. I didn't do it on purpose. Somehow I missed a payment."

"How?"

Shrugging, Eleanor replied, "I don't know."

"I showed you how to put everything in Bill Pay."

"I know, but I must have forgotten about it, Leon. I'm just devastated. I have so much going on in my head all the time… I feel like I'm running around in a million different directions."

"You probably just need to slow down, Auntie." Leon poured himself a cup of coffee. "We need to go over your finances just to make sure everything is good."

Eleanor agreed. "Yeah, we need to do that. The older I get, the more forgetful I become."

"I'll get the materials we need for the repairs."

"Son, I don't want you to go through all that expense. Besides, Rusty already said he'd donate the materials we need."

Rusty's family owned Stanley Building Materials & Construction. The Stanley and Rothchild families had been friends for generations. Leon believed that Rusty had feelings for Eleanor, but she would dismiss his claim with a chuckle and a wave of her hand.

Leon took a sip of coffee. "If you need help with *anything*, I want you to come to me."

"You have your own life."

"Don't do this, Auntie. You were there when Trey and I needed you most. I'm here for you, as well. Never doubt that."

"I know and I love you for it."

"Some of my coworkers and others in the community have offered to help with the repairs," Leon announced.

"That's so sweet," Eleanor said. "I love the way we all come together to help one another. This is what Polk and Hoss envisioned all those years ago."

MISTY LAID DOWN her cell phone. "Brittany, I'm sorry. I needed to check on Talei. She wasn't feeling well this morning. Now, where were we?" She picked up her iPad. They were in Brittany's office going over the final notes for the festival.

"I was saying that the fire department will be sending a couple of guys to man a booth *and* they're even bringing one of the fire trucks for the children to tour."

"They're gonna love that," Misty murmured, while wondering if Leon would be in attendance.

"I heard that Leon is going to be there," Brittany stated as if she'd read her mind.

"Misty, how are you doing with everything?"

"I'm fine," she responded. "John not being here still doesn't seem quite real. Even though we were divorced, he was still the father of my child and it hurts me when I see her sad. She misses him a lot."

Brittany nodded in understanding.

"Leon has been great by stepping up as her godfather. I reconnected with my grandmother, so now Talei has her Nana, aunts and a host of cousins. But the reality is that none of them can replace her father."

"She's adjusting well. At least from what I

can tell," Brittany said. "She's a very happy and secure little girl."

Misty smiled. "Thank you for saying that."

Brittany's phone rang.

"Girl, I'm sorry. I need to take this."

When she finished her call, she stated, "Now back to business. This year's festival is going to be huge. We are expecting twice the attendance of last year."

Misty broke into a grin. "That's great news. I've really enjoyed working on this event."

"I'm glad because I'd really like for you to stay on the board." Brittany broke into a grin. "And not just for the tasty snacks you always bring."

"Miss Eleanor told me that you're the reason the Polk Island Children's Festival exists in the first place," Misty said. "You never told me."

"I worked the one they have in Charleston and thought it would be nice to have an annual one here on the island. Now we're in our second year." Brittany took a sip of her smoothie. "I hope I'm not being too nosy, but I just have to ask. Are you interested in Leon?"

"Why would you ask me that?"

"Because you get this certain look in your eyes whenever his name is mentioned."

"I like him," she confessed. "I feel like we're building a friendship." Misty was fine with this as she had to fight her own battle of personal restraint. She was unable to give herself completely to any man at this time, so friendship was good. She was pretty sure Leon felt the same way.

Changing the subject, she asked, "Did you ever hear back from Robert with the petting zoo?"

"Yeah, I did," Brittany answered. "We're good on that. He will be bringing his animals."

"Talei is going to be thrilled. She loves animals."

"Petting zoos seem to be a popular attraction for children."

An hour later, Misty and Brittany ended their meeting.

Brittany slipped her purse over her left shoulder. "We'll have one final meeting the day before the festival with the rest of the staff."

"Great," Misty murmured. "I'll finalize the list of vendors and send that to you later this evening."

"Your mom is one, right?"

"Yes. She's going to sell some of the fringe dresses and ribbon skirts she's made. They will be in both children and adult sizes. She may have some blankets, as well."

"I'm so excited."

Misty smiled. "Me, too."

She walked out of Brittany's office. "I'll talk to you later."

The July weather was nice and sunny, which had prompted Misty to walk from the café to her friend's place of business.

She strolled along the sidewalk on Main Street, enjoying the feel of the sun on her face and arms. As much as she wanted to stop and peruse some of the boutiques along the way, Misty needed to get back to the shop. Some of the men were coming to work on the repairs.

She heard the blaring sound of a siren blasting. It was coming from the fire station located a couple of streets over. Her immediate thought was of Leon, and she hoped he would be safe.

One of their customers came in not long after Misty got back to the café. "There's a fire over on Oak Street. The fire department got there just in time."

"Was it a big one?" Misty inquired.

"No, I think it was pretty much contained to one room, but the owner of that house is in her nineties. She was able to get out with the help of her neighbor."

"That's great," she said.

"First the bakery and now poor Mrs. Warren's house. Hopefully, this doesn't become a trend. I hate fires."

Misty walked outside in time to see the fire

truck on its way back to the station. Leon stuck his head out of the window on the passenger side and waved.

Smiling, Misty waved back.

CHAPTER FIFTEEN

TRUE TO HER WORD, Eleanor had given Rusty's proposal a lot of thought. She'd called him earlier, inviting him to dinner.

Eleanor eyed her reflection in the full-length mirror. The emerald-green color complemented her complexion. She ran her fingers through her short salt-and-pepper curls.

The answer to his proposal had come easily. She and Rusty had been friends most of their life. Eleanor had always felt an eager affection coming from him. The night he took her to their junior prom, she assumed he would declare his feelings for her, but Rusty said nothing, leading Eleanor to believe that she had been wrong.

In recent years, every time Rusty's gaze met hers, Eleanor's heart turned over in response. Whenever she thought of him, she felt a tingling in the pit of her stomach, although she tried to dismiss it as something else.

"I'm thrilled you could join me for dinner, Rusty," Eleanor said when he arrived thirty minutes later. Her heart jolted and her pulse pounded.

"I was glad to receive your invite." Rusty's stare was bold as he assessed her. "Ladybug, you look beautiful."

His words sent her spirit soaring. "You look pretty sharp yourself," Eleanor responded. "Why don't we sit down in the family room and talk while we wait for dinner to be ready. It shouldn't be much longer."

Rusty sniffed the air. "You made my favorite meal," he said with a grin. "I love your home-made chicken potpie."

Eleanor smiled. "I had to look up the recipe. I couldn't remember all the ingredients. It's so frustrating at times."

Rusty took her hand in his. "I know but we're going to find out what's going on and then we can put together a plan of action."

"I'm really grateful to you for going to see the neurologist last week. I'm tired of all these tests but I know they're necessary. I just need answers."

"We will get them," Rusty assured her.

Eleanor rose to her feet. "It's time for the food to come out of the oven."

"Let me help you," Rusty said, following her into the kitchen.

They took their plates to the dining room table and kept the conversation light while they ate.

"I made enough for you to take the leftovers home," Eleanor said.

"Thanks, Ladybug."

After dinner and dessert, they settled down into the family room to talk.

"I've done a lot of thinking about your proposal. Rusty, do you really want to be tied down to a woman who may have Alzheimer's or dementia?"

"I want you to be my wife for better or worse. In sickness and in health, but even if you refuse to marry me, I intend on being by your side no matter what." Rusty kissed her. "The real question is do you think you can wake up to my ugly mug every day?"

"You're nowhere near ugly," she murmured. "You were handsome all those years ago and, in my opinion, you've improved with age. I don't have a problem waking up next to you for the next fifty or sixty years. I plan on living a very long time. You know Polk lived to be over a hundred years old and Hoss was almost ninety-six when he died."

Rusty looked hopeful. "Does this mean…"

Eleanor nodded. "I want to marry you, Rusty. I don't want to face whatever this is alone, and I don't want to be a burden to Leon. But let me be clear. It's not the only reason I want to be married to you. You're my best friend and I care deeply for you."

He couldn't stop grinning. "You have no idea how happy you've made me."

Her eyes clung to his, analyzing his reaction. "I'm very happy about this, too."

"How do you think Leon and Trey are going to take the news of our getting married?"

"Trust me, they will be surprised for sure, but no doubt pleased. They think the world of you, Rusty."

Rusty's large hand took Eleanor's face and held it gently. "I can't wait for you to be my wife." He kissed her slowly and thoughtfully.

The kiss sent the pit of her stomach into a wild swirl. Eleanor hadn't felt this way since she was in high school. It was a feeling she never thought she'd experience a second time.

ELEANOR AND RUSTY invited Leon and Misty to join them for dinner the next day.

When they arrived, she stated, "Rusty and I have some news we'd like to share." Eleanor could barely contain her excitement over her engagement. She didn't want to hold off telling the people she cared most about.

Leon looked from one person to the other. "What's going on?"

"We're getting married."

Misty gasped in surprise while Leon's mouth dropped open in his shock.

When he found his voice, he asked, "When did this happen? Don't get me wrong—I'm happy about it. I just didn't think you wanted to remarry, Auntie."

"I'd been thinking about it for a while," Eleanor responded. "I just didn't know if I'd meet someone special enough, but Rusty has been here all along. He finally spoke up."

Leon laughed. "Took you long enough."

Seated side by side, Eleanor said, "We're thinking of something small and intimate at the church and a dinner at the café. Rusty called Pastor Nelson and we can get married August 8."

"That's the Saturday after the children's festival," Misty stated.

"Wow," Leon uttered. "You're not wasting any time."

"We've already done a lot of that," Rusty said as he took Eleanor's hand in his.

She agreed.

"This is wonderful news," Misty said. "I'm thrilled for you both."

Leon got up and walked over to his aunt. "Congratulations. You know I want you to be happy."

Shaking Rusty's hand, he said, "I'm happy for you both. Man, it's about time…"

They laughed.

THE NEXT DAY, Eleanor and Rusty announced their engagement at the shop to the staff. She wanted to tell them before the rest of the locals found out. Her employees were her extended family. Leon stopped in that morning for the announcement.

Misty walked him out to his truck afterward. "I had no idea your aunt was dating Rusty," she said. "Did you know?" They didn't have much time to talk after the dinner because she had to leave to pick up Talei.

"No clue. I'm thinking they've known each other forever that they're just heading straight to matrimony with no stops along the way," Leon responded. "He's her best friend and I know he's been in love with her for years. I suspected Aunt Eleanor had feelings for him as well, but she kept denying it."

"Well, I'm really excited for them both."

"So am I."

"It was sweet of Miss Eleanor to ask me to design the wedding cake."

"I'm not surprised. You know that she's your biggest fan."

"I feel the same way about her," Misty said.

"I need to call Trey. Hopefully, he'll be able to come home for the ceremony," Eleanor interjected when she walked out of the shop to join them. She gave a short chuckle, then said, "Lawd my sister is going to faint when I tell her Rusty and I are getting married. I'll call her and Estelle after I talk to Trey."

"Don't forget Howard," Leon said.

"I won't," she responded. "It's going to be nice having the family together. So much to do in a short amount of time."

Misty gave her a reassuring hug. "I'm here to help in any way I can, Miss Eleanor. Your wedding is going to be the talk of the island."

Leon turned the ignition in his truck. "Ladies, I need to get out of here. Love you Auntie. Misty, I'll call you later."

They watched him drive down Main.

"Before too long, I suspect there's going to be another wedding we'll be planning." Eleanor met Misty's gaze. "Mark my words."

CHAPTER SIXTEEN

"LEON AND I are working the first shift at the Fire and Safety Booth," Charles announced after they finished their meal. "Al and Rob have the second shift…"

"If anyone wants to take my place, they can," Leon said. He wasn't comfortable with the idea of having to interact with a lot of children. Until he met Talei, he didn't think he could ever spend more than a minute around a child, especially one close to the age that his own daughter would've been.

"Kids love you," one of his coworkers commented. "You're a natural."

Leaning over, Leon whispered, "Charles, I'm not sure I'm really ready for this."

"You are," his friend reassured him. "Look how you are with Misty's little girl. Besides, the kids will be more interested in the truck than two boring firemen."

Leon chuckled. "You're probably right."

He strode into the kitchen, preparing to clean up. He tackled the dishes first, then the pots and pans. Suds and soapy water up to his elbows, Leon found his thoughts turning to Misty and his growing affection for her.

Everyone seemed to think he and Misty were a perfect match, and he liked her a lot. In truth, he was developing strong feelings for her. But Leon felt they were building a great friendship, and no way would he risk ruining that.

As soon as his shift ended, Leon left the station and went home to take care of some tasks around the house. He wanted to get them out of the way before going to his aunt's shop. He hoped to be able to start painting the kitchen today. The new appliances were scheduled to be delivered at the end of the week.

Rusty was inside sweeping up debris when he arrived shortly after two o'clock. "The construction crew just left not too long ago."

Leon surveyed the area. "It looks good in here."

"Your aunt keeps wanting to come see the place," Rusty said. "I don't know how long I can keep her away. I told her to focus on the wedding planning and let me take care of the shop."

Leon sighed. "I keep telling her that we want to surprise her. Don't worry—I'll talk to Aunt Eleanor."

Rusty pointed to the two paint cans in the corner. "They're ready for you."

"I brought a jumpsuit to change into," Leon said. "The last time I messed up a good pair of jeans."

"If you want, I can stay a while longer to help."

"Rusty if you don't mind putting down some tape on that side—that'll help me a lot."

"I got you."

An hour later, Leon was ready to paint. He was glad that Rusty had been able to match the original color, which was what his aunt wanted. She wanted the appliances updated but the style to reflect the way the kitchen looked before the fire.

Sweat poured off him as he worked to finish the painting in a few hours. Leon glanced at the clock. It was close to four o'clock.

He slid the roller upward, then down, leaving a trail of dove-gray paint on the wall.

Leon heard the front door open and close.

"Hey, you," Misty greeted as she walked cautiously around a ladder. "Wow… The kitchen is really coming together."

"We've been working hard at it."

She discreetly admired his physique as he pulled off the jumpsuit to reveal his T-shirt and jeans. "I'm sure your aunt truly appreciates all you've done. I know that I'm looking forward to getting back to work."

Misty walked out of the kitchen and sat down in one of the booths.

Leon washed his hands before joining her. "How is Talei?"

"She's doing great. Every now and then she mentions John, but she's adjusted well."

"That's good to hear," he responded.

"I don't think I've asked, but how are you dealing with John's death?"

"I miss my friend," he admitted.

"Despite everything John and I went through, I miss him, too."

Leon studied Misty. He could see the truth of her words in her eyes. "Hopefully, he's at peace now."

"I certainly hope so," she said. "That's all I ever wanted for both of us. Just not together."

"Do you have any plans for tomorrow evening?" Leon asked. "There's a new Disney movie playing. I thought we could take Talei."

Misty broke into a smile. "She would love that."

"So, what do you say?"

"I say let's do it," she responded. "It's a date."

LEON PICKED UP Misty and Talei a few minutes before 6:00 p.m. the next day. They had pizza for dinner, then walked across the street to the theater.

He carried a sleeping Talei to the car when they emerged two hours later. "She'd held on as long as she could."

Misty chuckled. "My baby put up a good fight. She stayed awake for most of the movie, though."

Leon was able to put Talei in her car seat without disturbing her sleep. "She's such a beautiful little girl. She's funny, too."

"She's learning the art of manipulation," Misty said.

He laughed as he opened the door to the passenger side for her. "I'm sure. I think that's one of the first lessons all children learn. How to manipulate their parents."

"You're probably right. I'm going to have to ask my mom if I did that. I know I tried in my teens."

On the drive to her place, Misty said, "We had a wonderful time, Leon."

He glanced at her. "So did I."

"You did a great job painting. You think I can convince you to paint my bathroom?"

"When would you like me to start?"

Misty gave him a sidelong glance. "Are you being serious right now?"

"Yeah. I enjoy painting. I'd do it for you."

Leon parked in front of her building. "Do you want me to carry her inside for you?"

"If you don't mind," Misty responded. "Thank you."

He carried Talei into the condo and laid her on the sofa. "We'll have to do this again some-time."

Smiling, Misty said, "I'd like that."

At home, Leon showered and prepared for bed. He was scheduled to work the next morning.

Although he'd enjoyed seeing the movie with Misty and Talei, he was left feeling conflicted. His emotions were all over the place where she was concerned. Leon didn't want to tamper with their friendship—it meant too much to him. But he was extremely attracted to Misty; he couldn't deny it.

Just let go and enjoy the journey.

Leon had heard this on more than one occasion. Time for him to really act on it. He was tired of living with loneliness. If he wanted to have a fragment of happiness back in his life, then he had to reclaim it.

CHAPTER SEVENTEEN

WHAT IF A relationship with Misty doesn't work out? How will this affect Talei?

It was a question that haunted Leon. The little girl lost her father—he didn't want her to lose someone else in her life. It was the main reason why he was constantly debating whether to pursue a relationship with Misty. His feelings for her were growing, but deep down he feared becoming too attached to Talei. Leon also didn't want to cost Misty or her daughter any heartache; he also wanted to spare himself more pain and loss.

He left the firehouse, grateful that he was off work for the next two days. Instead of going home, he drove to the cemetery.

Leon stopped by his parents' graves and then headed over to Vera's. Before taking a seat on the bench, he placed the dozen roses he'd bought at Vera's headstone.

"Hey, Vee. You know I had to come out here to wish you a happy birthday in heaven. I brought you your favorite roses—the pink ones.

I can't tell you how much I miss you. Vee, you deserve to be here, enjoying life and raising our daughter… I will never understand why you had to leave me," Leon said. "I know you don't want me mourning you forever. I'm doing my best to move on. I even met someone. The thing is that she was married to John. Her name is Misty. You'd like her, Vee."

Leon pulled a weed from the grass and tossed it. "John's gone now, too. I can't remember if I told you when I was here the last time. I've lost too many people and I'm tired of it." He shook his head. "I know all about the circle of life and that this is a journey that we all have to take, but Vee… Dying's not the hard part. It's surviving the death of the people you love—it's not easy.

"Spending time with Misty and her daughter has helped me through some pretty tough days. I've developed feelings for Misty and I'm crazy about her daughter. But I do worry what might happen if it doesn't work out. I know what you'd say. You'd tell me to just take it one day at a time."

His eyes traveled to the flowers. "Here I am talking about my issues when it's your special day. I came here to tell you that I'm so happy to have been your husband, even for the short time we were married. There's not a day that I don't think about you, Vee. You were the love of my life."

Leon rose to his full height. "That will never change."

He could see himself spending the rest of his life with Misty. While Vera was his first love, he now realized that there was room in his heart to love another. He just had to have the courage to walk the journey.

THE FIRST SATURDAY in August brought with it lots of sunny weather for the second annual children's festival. Misty and Brittany did one final walk through the area secured for the event.

"All the vendors are set up and ready. The authors are in the VIP area near the stage," Misty said as she went through her checklist.

"This is gonna be huge," Brittany said. "People are already lining up to get into the festival."

"Talei was very excited this morning. She wants to see the pink dinosaur from that TV show and the petting zoo. My mother is bringing her. They should be here shortly."

"Look who's here all nice and early," Brittany said, gesturing toward the fire truck.

"Leon Rothchild."

"He told me that he'd be working the festival today, but only until noon."

"I'm really glad we were able to get the fire department to come out here today."

Misty eyed Leon as he arranged stuffed Dalmatians and teddy bears on a table behind the booth. She had known there was something special about him from the very beginning. Quickly, she banished the thought. They were friends. Nothing more.

"There's that look again," Brittany said. "You like him more than you'd care to admit."

"Can we talk about something else?" Misty asked.

Her friend chuckled. "Sure. Why don't we go check out the petting zoo?"

Misty held up the map of the festival. "Sounds good to me."

She glanced over her shoulder. Leon was so preoccupied with his tasks that he hadn't even seen her. Misty wasn't concerned because she'd stop by the booth at some point during the festival to say hello.

"Looks like everything is in order," Brittany said. "We're ready to get this event started."

LEON ARRIVED AN hour early to set up the booth for the children's festival. They hadn't allowed anyone entry yet, so the area was quiet, yet very colorful. There were balloons and cartoon characters everywhere.

He poured a large bag of assorted candies in a bowl, an easy way to summon the children.

Leon looked around at the different vendors. He caught a glimpse of Misty with Brittany, but they looked deep in conversation. He'd heard that they were part of the committee who coordinated the event.

Charles arrived. "Everything looks great. The truck is on its way."

"They're starting to let people in," Leon observed aloud. A wave of apprehension flowed through him at the sight of two small children running toward their booth.

"Can I have a fire hat?" the little boy asked.

Wearing a smile, Leon responded, "You sure can. Do you want to be a fireman when you grow up?"

"Yeah."

"What would you like, young lady?" Charles inquired.

In a sudden bout of shyness, the little girl covered her face with her hands.

A woman walked up, gently scolding them. "I told you two not to run off."

Charles held up a stuffed Dalmatian. "Would you like one of these?"

She nodded.

"Here you go…"

The fire engine arrived and parked beside the booth.

Within thirty minutes, there was a host of children lined up to tour the truck. Leon liked that they were busy. It helped to pass the time.

If Vera and his daughter had lived, the three of them would have attended this festival as a family. Every time Leon saw a father with his wife and daughter, he felt a stabbing pain in his chest. He would never understand why his parents died when he was only ten or why he had to lose his uncle five years after that, but he'd refused to lose hope. Leon always believed his life would get better. For the most past, it did, especially when he met Vera.

His life with her was perfect.

When Vera told him that she was pregnant, Leon doubted life could get any better, but then tragedy struck, and his life came to a crashing halt. Where hope once resided, there was none.

It was hard to picture life without his beloved Vera. During that first year, there were days when Leon felt each crushing breath would be his last. Somehow, he managed to make it to the second anniversary of her death. He'd spent most of it angry and bitter. It wasn't until the third year that Leon found acceptance.

CHAPTER EIGHTEEN

LEON ROTHCHILD.

Courageous, handsome and of high moral character. Misty watched him navigate coolly through the growing sea of children wanting a tour of the fire truck to the booth. When his dazzling gaze latched onto hers, the bustle and noise of the kids running ahead of their parents all faded into the background.

"How's it going?" Misty inquired as she glanced around the booth. "Looks like it's been busy over here."

"It's the fire engine," Leon said. "They love getting inside and climbing to the top. We practically have to beg them to take one of the stuffed dogs. We're already out of the toy engines and fire hats."

Misty chuckled.

"You've been one busy lady," Leon said. "Every time I looked up; I saw you running from one place to another. You did a nice job with this festival."

"This is my first year on the board. I've really enjoyed working on this event."

"We've got a great turnout. Congrats to you and the staff."

Misty was touched by the compliment. "Brittany would love to hear that."

"I'll make sure to tell her," he responded.

"Did you go by the bakery booth?" Misty asked. "Your aunt is there with an assortment of cupcakes and slices of cake. She has that lemon one you love so much."

"I'd better run over there right now," Leon responded. "I'm done here for the day."

"I'm actually on my way there. Want to join me?"

He smiled. "Sure."

Leon and Misty made their way through the crowd to get to the food area.

"Her booth is over there."

His eyes scanned the table. "Aunt Eleanor, I came to get some lemon cake, but looks like it's all gone."

She smiled. "Now, you know I saved you a couple of slices."

"Thanks, Auntie."

A volunteer walked over to Eleanor saying, *"De chillun full' up wid baa'becue."*

Misty glanced up at Leon, who said, "You'll

hear the Gullah language spoken from time to time from some of the older people."

"Sounds like she was saying that the children were full of barbecue."

"Close enough," Leon replied. "She said the children filled their stomachs with barbecue."

"You speak the language?"

He gave a slight nod. "Some."

"I don't know much about it," Misty said. "Just that Gullah refers to the people and culture along the coastal landscape of South Carolina, Georgia and the Sea Islands."

"Only a handful of old-timers still speak Gullah. They spoke it really heavy when my parents were growing up," Leon said. "Now, it's fading. We attended school on the mainland and the teachers would make us speak proper English."

"I find that fascinating. My mom has always wanted me to learn the Tsalagi language. She had the same experience when she was in school. That's why she believes it's important to keep our Cherokee language and traditions alive."

"I agree," Leon said. "The love for our history is something we have in common."

"It's important that we know where we come from," Misty responded. "That's the one regret I have about my father. I don't really know his side of my family."

"You can always change that."

"You're right."

"Where's Talei?" Leon inquired. "I saw her for a few minutes when she came to see the engine."

"I'm pretty sure we'll find her and my mother at the petting zoo," Misty said. "We weren't sure we'd be able to get the animals this year, but we were lucky. They had a cancellation."

Just as Misty said, Talei and Oma were at the petting zoo, which included twenty rare and exotic animals from around the world.

Talei pointed at the potbellied pig named Jake. "Mommy, look…pig."

"Yes, I see him."

"Eon, I like pig," she said happily.

He grinned. "He's as big as you are, little one."

"I like him."

"His name is Jake," Misty said.

"Jay…" Talei repeated as she waved. "Hey, Jay."

The pig was ushered over so that she could pet him. Talei touched him, then burst into giggles.

After she spent some time with Jake, Oma convinced her to visit with Rascal, the fox in the next stall.

"She seems to love animals," Leon said.

"She does," Misty responded. "Especially rabbits."

Misty watched Talei reach tiny fingers in to touch the baby rabbits. For the moment, the little girl was laughing and happy.

"You're doing so well with that rabbit."

"Her so cute," Talei said.

Smiling, Oma patted her back. "Be careful with her."

They went to the stall where the camels were kept.

"Mommy, I wanna ride horse."

"That's a camel, baby girl. That's Bubba. He's not a horse."

"I wanna ride cammer," Talei stated. "Eon, I wanna ride."

Leon read the sign. "It says here that Bubba drinks Diet Coke."

"Really?"

He nodded.

Misty chuckled. "Okay, then. I have to say that's new to me. A camel drinking Diet Coke."

They stood in the line for rides, and when it was Talei's turn, Leon helped lift her onto the back of the camel.

Misty and her mother both took pictures of the little girl riding with Leon and the owner on either side of her.

Oma took Talei home around four o'clock,

leaving Misty to finish her day working the festival.

"I'm here if you need any help with the cleanup," Leon said.

"That's really sweet of you, but I wouldn't ask this of you."

"You didn't ask," Leon responded. "I offered."

"Then you'll have to let me buy you dinner."

He smiled. "That's an offer I can't pass up."

Two hours later, they sat in a seafood restaurant enjoying their meal.

"You're very good with children," Misty said.

"It's hard sometimes being around them," he confessed. "It's a reminder of what I'm missing. I've always wanted my own family."

"I'm sorry."

Leon shrugged, then finished off a glass of ice water. "Life goes on. At least that's what I've been told."

"It does," Misty said. "You just have to take it one day at a time."

Leon gazed at her. "That's exactly what Vera would've said."

Misty wiped her mouth on the edge of her napkin. "They say great minds think alike."

Leon ordered dessert. "I hope you're going to help me with this walnut blondie brownie."

"You really have a sweet tooth." Misty took a sip of her tea. "I called to check on John's parents the other day. Clara's still a bit emotional and Elroy was just rude as always."

"It's kind of you to even call them after everything that's happened."

Misty shrugged. "Clara's always been pretty decent to me. It's her husband who has always been the issue. I've done everything I could to be nice to him, so I just gave up. As long as he's good to my daughter, I'm good."

"I have to say that I admire you, Misty. You've been a pillar of strength through everything. I find strength in a woman a very attractive quality."

The waiter arrived with the dessert and two spoons.

"Did you know that John made me a beneficiary of an insurance policy?" Misty inquired. "I didn't expect that at all."

"All he ever told me was that he intended to make sure you and Talei were taken care of if anything happened to him."

"Do you think he's at peace now?"

He nodded. "I choose to think so—otherwise his death wouldn't make sense to me."

They finished off the brownie and ice cream.

Oma was in the kitchen when Misty arrived home an hour later.

"Hey, Mama. Where's Talei?"

"She's in her room watching a movie. I just came down to make her some warm milk."

Oma retrieved a carton from the refrigerator. "How was your dinner with Leon?"

"Nice," Misty murmured. "It was great being able to have a meal and conversation with a man with no expectations. Leon doesn't drink. That was kind of nice, too. For the first time, I was able to see what it feels like to have a normal relationship with a man. Leon's still grieving some, but he has such a kind heart."

"Don't judge him for what others have done to you in the past."

"I'm not, Mama," Misty said. "I'm not rushing into anything with Leon. We're just building a friendship. If it goes further than that, then it does. I'm focusing on the present."

She went to check on Talei.

"Mama, why didn't you ever remarry?" Misty asked when she walked into the dining room.

"My focus was making sure you were going to be okay. I didn't have time to meet men and determine if they were worthy of being in our life."

"What about now?"

"I'm happy with my life the way it is, Misty. Your father was a good man, but then the alcohol changed him. It became his god. He chose it over his family. Then he started running around with other women. When I got the phone call from that woman bragging how she was pregnant with his child. I was done for good."

"All I remember of my dad is that he was mean-spirited. I remember the way he used to treat you."

"You have to forgive him, Misty."

"I'm trying, Mama. I'm really trying to forgive him and John."

When she was upstairs in her room, her cell phone rang.

Misty grinned when she saw the ID of the caller.

Picking up, she said, "Leon, hello."

"Thanks again for having dinner with me."

"I enjoyed myself," Misty responded.

"Look, I'm not really good at this—more like out of practice—but I'd like to get to know you better," Leon said. "I'm really not good at this at all."

She smiled. "You're doing fine. I want to get to know you better, as well."

He released an audible sigh. "Now that we got that out of the way, I can relax some."

Misty chuckled. "I know the feeling. It's not like it's been all that long, but it feels like it's been a while since I've been on a date."

"Maybe it's because we're both anxious about what could come of our dating."

"I'm hoping for something good," she confessed.

"I don't intend to do anything to hurt you or Talei," Leon stated. "I want a relationship of substance—something real."

"We're definitely on the same page, then."

They talked for the next hour, discussing books, the island history and the things they had in common.

Misty fell asleep with thoughts of Leon dancing through her mind.

MONDAY AFTERNOON, MISTY met Brittany at a shop downtown for some retail therapy.

"Let me just get this out of the way by telling you that Leon and I have a date tomorrow," she announced. "We're leaving early and spending the day in Savannah. He's going to be busy the rest of the week with Miss Eleanor and Rusty."

"That's right. The wedding is Saturday," Brittany exclaimed as they wandered around the clothing boutique. "I'm not surprised that you're going on a date with Leon. Girl, I knew you had a thing for him."

"Okay you're right. I really, *really* like him but I'm so nervous," Misty confessed. "It's actually been a while since I've been on a date. I know this is last minute, but do you mind watching Talei?"

"I don't mind at all. That's my little princess."

"What should I wear?" Misty picked up a red sundress. "You like this one?"

"I like this better." Brittany help up a strapless dress in yellow.

"It's nice, but not appropriate for a day trip to Savannah."

"Make sure you wear comfortable walking shoes with something cute. Those cobblestone streets are agony on your feet."

"I remember. That's why I need to find something to go with my walking shoes. I'm looking for something in red or navy." Misty walked over to the next clothing rack. "Congratulations again on making partner. It's well deserved."

Brittany held up a shirt against her body and eyed her reflection in the full-length mirror. "Girl, thank you. I'm excited about it. We're actually planning to expand our office to Charleston."

"Oh, wow. That's wonderful."

"Mary's boyfriend lives there, and he's asked her to marry him."

"So, she plans on running that office while you manage the one on the island?"

Brittany nodded. "Exactly."

"Thank you for babysitting Talei. You know how much I appreciate you."

"Talei and I are gonna have a good time.

Enjoy your day with Leon. Don't worry about rushing back. She can just stay the night and I'll drop her off at school. She and I will be fine. Talei loves her auntie Britt."

Misty smiled. "Yes, she does. That's because you spoil her."

They left the store and walked across the street.

"Let's try this place here," Misty said. "I need to find something in the next ten minutes. I have to get back to work."

Later that evening, Misty tried on the two different outfits she'd purchased earlier. She was having a difficult time trying to find the perfect one for her date with Leon.

It was past eleven o'clock by the time she chose the sundress in a hot pink color with white sneakers. Misty also retrieved a light white cardigan to take with her.

She climbed into bed and exhaled a long sigh of contentment. Misty propped herself up against her pillows and relaxed for a few minutes, then she slid out of bed.

Misty went downstairs to the kitchen. She'd made a decision to bake lemon cupcakes for Leon.

Misty wanted to do something special for him.

ELEANOR HANDED HER nephew a cup of coffee to go with his dessert. "So, you're going out with Misty."

"We've been spending time together," Leon told his aunt. "We took Talei to see a movie, and we were together at the children's festival... I'd like to get to know her better."

"I had a feeling you two would be getting together," Eleanor said.

Holding up his hand, Leon uttered, "Whoa, Auntie... We're just learning more about each other. We're not a couple or anything like that."

"I have an instinct about stuff like this. You two gwine be a couple before long. Mark my words."

Leon chuckled. "Do me a favor and don't tell Misty any of this—I don't want you to scare her off."

"It's good to see you going out. It's about time."

"Aunt Eleanor, I'm not going to rush into anything with Misty. I'm not even sure if I'm really ready for this, but I'm going to give it a shot. I can't get her out of my head. I think about her all the time."

"Vera never wanted you to become a hermit. You're not the type of man meant to be single. You're a family man, Leon."

"I know, but Vee was the love of my life. Maybe that's all we get—that one great love."

"Sometimes that's all we get," Eleanor said.

"But there are times when life surprises you with a new love...a new beginning."

"I miss Uncle Walter."

"I do, too," Eleanor said with a soft sigh. "We used to close the shop, turn on our favorite songs and we'd just dance... Those were some good times."

Leon chuckled. "I remember this one time when Trey and I were in the office—we heard y'all talking and laughing. We crept out and saw Uncle chasing you around the room. He caught you, then you two started kissing. Back then, Trey and I thought it was gross, but now I realize it was a really romantic moment between the two of you."

"Your uncle was a very romantic man," Eleanor murmured as she sat down at the table facing Leon. "I'm very lucky to have another good man to spend my life with. All those happy memories I have with Walter—they're in my heart."

"I know what you mean, Auntie. I keep all the memories I have of Vee close to mine."

Eleanor reached over and took Leon's hand. "She was a wonderful person."

"Yes, she was," he agreed. "We had so many plans for our life and our family. I never once thought Vee wouldn't be here."

"So, what do you really think of Misty?"

"I think she's a nice person," Leon said. "She's attractive and appears to be a wonderful mother. I just want to get to know her better. I have no other expectations."

"But are you open to the possibility?"

"Aunt Eleanor, I have to admit that I'm dealing with some guilt about seeing Misty. I feel like I'm cheating on Vera."

"You loved being married, son. I don't think I'd ever seen you so happy. You were meant to share your life with someone special."

"I don't know if I ever want to love that much again," Leon confessed. "Losing Vera and Selena... My heart is still in pieces."

"I have a feeling Misty may be the one to help put those pieces back together, sugar."

"You are forever the matchmaker, Auntie."

Eleanor broke into a grin. "It's a gift. I have a real instinct about two people who belong together."

He didn't look convinced.

"Leon, just give yourself a chance to find love again. Be open to it."

"I'll try, Auntie."

Eleanor pushed away from the breakfast table and rose to her feet, then frowned. "I was just about to do something but for the life of me, I can't remember what it was. Rosemary told me

I need to take fish oil, I think. She said it would help keep your memory sharp."

"You should try it, Auntie," Leon said. "But I don't think you have anything to worry about. There's nothing wrong with you."

CHAPTER NINETEEN

Misty curled her hair with a curling wand and applied her makeup with a light hand. She looked forward to spending this day with Leon. Misty decided not to look too much into the swirling emotions she felt—she had to take things slow. She couldn't afford to make another relationship mistake.

Leon picked her up at 8:00 a.m. for the drive to Savannah.

They began their day in Forsythe Park.

Misty ran over to the nineteenth-century cast-iron fountain that was designed to resemble the grand fountain in Paris. She found it breathtaking. Camera in hand, she snapped several photographs.

They were surrounded by other couples lounging on colorful blankets beneath green shade trees.

"So, you're a photographer, as well?" Leon asked.

"I guess an amateur one. I enjoy taking pictures," Misty said. "I took a course online and watched YouTube. I mostly take pictures of nature—mostly flowers. I still have a lot to learn."

"I'm sure you do a much better job than I can," Leon said. "You're the official picture taker on this trip."

Misty chuckled. "Okay."

When they sat down at a picnic table to have lunch, Leon said, "I noticed the white box you brought to the car."

"I made lemon cupcakes for dessert."

Leon smiled. "I could kiss you right now."

"What's stopping you?"

His kiss was sweet, surprisingly gentle and a delicious sensation.

After lunch, they strolled along the tree-lined pathways of Chippewa Square. Did you know that the north side was one of the locations in the film *Forrest Gump*?"

"I have a confession to make," Misty said. "I have never seen that movie."

Leon looked completely shocked. "We have to remedy that. You *have* to see *Forrest Gump*."

"Why?" Misty inquired. "What makes this particular film so special?"

"*Forrest Gump* is one of those inspirational movies that show us how to turn our greatest weaknesses into our greatest strength. Forrest accomplished a great many things while facing adversities."

"I'm willing to give it a shot, Leon. We'll have a movie night one-night next week when you're off."

"Make sure you have a box of tissues on hand. You're gonna need them."

At dusk, they took a private carriage ride along the cobblestone streets to view some of the historic mansions.

"I have to say that you did a great job planning out this day," Misty said. "I've really enjoyed myself."

"I'm glad," Leon responded. "This city is one of my favorite places to visit."

"You showed me a side of Savannah I hadn't really noticed before."

"We're going to have dinner at Elizabeth on 37th," he announced. "It's off the beaten path, but I'm sure you'll appreciate the atmosphere and the cuisine."

The moment they arrived; Misty instantly fell in love with the twentieth-century mansion that housed the restaurant.

Leon ordered the half-moon river clams with roasted Vidalia onions, country ham and truffle oil for the appetizer.

For her entrée, Misty ordered the spicy Savannah red rice with shrimp while Leon chose the roasted chicken with wild mushrooms.

When their appetizers arrived, Leon offered a quick prayer of thanksgiving.

"This is sooo delicious," Misty said.

Leon nodded his agreement.

The entrées looked equally wonderful. Leon sampled the braised collards and corn bread dressing before cutting into the chicken breast. He glanced at her. "How is your food?"

Smiling, Misty responded, "I can't complain about a thing."

MISTY HAD A wonderful sense of humor. Leon couldn't remember the last time he'd laughed so much. He was truly enjoying himself.

"I'm stuffed," she murmured.

"You only ate half of your food."

"I eat until I feel full. Don't worry, it's not going to waste. I'm eating the rest of it tomorrow for lunch."

Misty's smile warmed him. Leon had no idea why she affected him the way she did, but instead of dwelling on the thought, he pushed it to the back of his mind and focused on enjoying the rest of his evening with her.

Misty fell asleep in the car during the drive back to Polk Island.

She woke up just as they were about to turn on her street. "Oh, Leon… I'm sorry for falling asleep on you like that."

"You're fine. It's been a long day."

"Thank you for making today so special and memorable."

Leon got out and walked around his car to open the door for Misty. "Don't forget about planning movie night for next week."

"Oh, I won't," she promised. "I'm actually looking forward to seeing *Forrest Gump*." She kissed his cheek, then gave his hand a little squeeze. His flesh prickled at her touch, and his heart hammered in his chest at a steadfast rate. *Focus.*

It's what Leon kept telling himself, but it wasn't that simple. Misty made him feel things he'd never experienced before. Or maybe it was because he was so out of touch with these particular emotions.

RUSTY HOSTED A family dinner the night before the wedding at his home. Maggie, Eleanor's sister and her cousin Estelle arrived earlier in the day. Rusty also had a couple of relatives coming to the island from out of town. Many of his family members were local residents.

Leon received a text stating that his second cousin Howard had gotten in late the night before and was staying at the hotel on Main. He texted that he'd come to Eleanor's house after his son and daughter's flight landed. Trey's flight was scheduled to land a couple of hours after the dinner.

He stopped by the church because he knew that Eleanor would be there with the florist going over the decorations.

Leon was surprised to see Misty with Eleanor, but it really wasn't that surprising. She was always willing to help his aunt. She had such a warm, loving spirit and was always smiling. He loved her sometimes-quirky sense of humor, and the sense of freedom she seemed to have in her life. Not only was Misty beautiful, but she was intelligent and caring, as well. The more Leon got to know her, the more he wanted to know about her.

I have real feelings for this woman.

The silent declaration shocked him, but Leon didn't bother to deny the truth.

He'd come to offer his assistance, but it looked like the women had everything under control. Leon decided to check on Rusty before meeting Howard at the hotel. He would see Misty tonight at the dinner. The next day, they were planning to help with last-minute wedding arrangements, which included moving Eleanor's things into Rusty's house. She'd decided to close up her house for now. They would decide later what to do with it.

CHAPTER TWENTY

ELEANOR WOKE UP feeling what she could describe only as a bit fuzzy in the brain. She stared at the simple lavender-and-silver dress hanging on the door of her closet.

It was her wedding day.

She sat up with a start at the sound of the knock on her bedroom door.

Leon stuck his head inside the room. "You up, Auntie?"

"C'mon in, sugar." Eleanor glanced at the clock on her nightstand. "How long have you been here?"

"Long enough to make you some breakfast," he announced, entering with a tray.

"Thank you, son."

"How did you sleep?"

"I think I was out almost immediately. I slept pretty good considering I was up well past midnight talking with Maggie and Estelle."

"I'm still surprised that Aunt Maggie drove all the way from Raleigh," Leon said.

"Although cousin Estelle said she slept the whole way down."

Leon positioned the tray on the bed so she could eat comfortably.

Eleanor chuckled. "Must've been some good sleep 'cause she tried to keep us up all night. I kept trying to tell them I don't need any more luggage under these eyes."

Trey knocked before walking inside the bedroom. "Good morning, beautiful." He planted a kiss on her cheek. "I need to know something before Leon and I walk you down the aisle."

She picked up her fork. "What is it you want to know?"

"Do you love Rusty?"

"I do," Eleanor responded. She met his gaze straight on. "Trey, I've always loved him. Not in the same way that I loved your uncle, but I have deep feelings for him. I'm always telling Leon that he should move on. Well, I realized that I needed to do the same."

"I'm glad to see you're taking your own advice."

Eleanor swatted at Leon. "Alright, smartypants." She smiled at her nephews.

"I want y'all to know this day couldn't be more perfect. I have my two boys here to share in this special moment of my life."

Trey kissed her cheek. "I have to fly out tomorrow morning, but there was no way I was going to miss your wedding, Auntie. I'm glad you've found a good man to share your life with. I've always liked Rusty except when he was my football coach in middle school."

Eleanor laughed. "I'm so happy you're here."

"Me, too," Trey stated. "Especially since I'm going to deploy to Afghanistan in a couple of weeks."

Eleanor gasped and her eyes filled with tears.

He sat down on the edge of her bed. "Auntie, don't cry. Everything's gonna be fine. I wouldn't have told you if I'd known it would upset you."

"I'm just gwine miss you so much. I know that's your job, but I hate you have to go over there."

"I'm gonna be careful and I know you'll keep me covered with your prayers. Today is your wedding day. Let's focus on all of us being here together—family."

"Finish your breakfast," Leon said. "We leave for the church in less than two hours. Aunt Maggie needs to hem Trey's pants. They're too long."

Trey stood up. "That's right. I need to see if she can get started on that right after breakfast." He walked briskly out of the room.

"Auntie, Trey is gonna be fine. Don't get yourself worked up over his deployment. Not today."

Eleanor smiled. "I won't. I just won't think about it today."

Leon made his way to the door. "Good."

He went downstairs.

Eleanor finished off her food, then climbed out of bed.

After a quick shower, she slipped on a flowy caftan and went downstairs. Leon jumped up from his seat to take the tray from her.

She sat down beside her sister, who asked, "Did you get any sleep?"

"Some. I wouldn't have gotten any if I'd left it up to you and Estelle."

ELEANOR AND RUSTY had both decided to keep their wedding a simple affair. However, the sophistication of the event would be carried throughout the ceremony and old-fashioned champagne and cake reception. Eleanor felt the intimate setting would emphasize what was important to her and Rusty as a mature couple versus the frills that most young couples often preferred.

She and Rusty both owned homes so they politely asked invited guests to opt out of bringing gifts. While planning the wedding, Eleanor chose not to have any bridesmaids.

She decided on a lavender-colored gown because it was the same color of the dress she wore to her junior prom with Rusty—the one and only time they ever went out.

It was time to leave for the church.

Eleanor headed to the dressing room with Leon in tow, carrying her gown and tote packed with other essentials.

Ten minutes later, Misty arrived to help with hair and makeup.

"If I'd had a wedding party, Talei would've been a gorgeous little flower girl."

"She's at home with my mama. They're going to Charleston to buy fabric and some other materials. By the way, I ran into Rusty when I stopped by the café. He looks so handsome in his charcoal-gray suit. His shirt is the exact shade of your dress. Great job on the coordination."

"We didn't coordinate what we were wearing—he has no idea the color of my gown."

Misty's eyebrow rose in surprise. "Really?"

Eleanor broke into a smile. "These are the colors we wore to our junior prom."

"This is so incredibly romantic, Miss Eleanor. It's a sign that you two are meant to be together."

She laughed. "It means we're two old sentimental fools."

Misty shook her head in denial. "This shows

that you both put a lot of thought into the start of a new life together. *I love it.*"

Eleanor wanted her hair pulled back into a bun. Misty stuck pearl-tipped hairpins around it to match her earrings and necklace.

Surveying Eleanor's face, Misty said, "You don't need much more than a little powder, some mascara and lipstick."

She handed Eleanor a mirror. "What do you think?"

"I love it. Thank you, sugar."

Misty glanced around the room. "Where's your bouquet?"

"I'm not carrying one," Eleanor responded. "I don't need all that." She had also decided against walking down the aisle. As soon as she was dressed and ready, Eleanor left the dressing area with the photographer to take a few pictures outside the church.

"You look so beautiful and happy," her friend Rose said. "You certainly made poor Rusty wait long enough. That man has loved you forever."

"Everybody seems to have been aware of his feelings but me."

"Well, you know he's always been shy and then when you met Walter, Rusty didn't stand a chance."

"I think this is the perfect time for us to start our lives together," Eleanor said. "I'm not sure

I would've really appreciated him or been able to give him what he needed before."

Rose smiled. "Better late than live a life alone with nothing but memories."

Leon joined them, saying, "Pastor Nelson just arrived. Rusty's on his way inside. The photographer took some photos of him outside the church."

MISTY SPIED TREY standing near the door with an arrangement of orchids and lilies. She walked up to him, saying, "Your aunt just told me that she wasn't carrying a bouquet."

The florist made this for her."

Smiling, Misty said, "I'm glad. Make sure Miss Eleanor carries it."

"Have you met my aunt?" Trey asked with a chuckle.

"All you have to do is give her one of your winning smiles."

"Okay, I see how you wrapped my brother around your little finger. You bat those long lashes of yours and stroke his ego…"

"Trey, I have no idea what you're talking about." Amused, Misty walked away in search of Leon.

She found him standing outside while Eleanor was being photographed in her gown.

He glanced over his shoulder at her, smiling.

"She looks beautiful," Misty said.

Leon nodded in agreement. "She sure does."

"The florist sent over a bouquet for her to carry. Trey has it—I told him to make sure she carries it down the aisle."

Leon gave her a sidelong glance. "You've worked with my aunt long enough to know she's gonna do what she wants."

"I'm telling you the same thing I told your brother—flash one of those charming smiles of yours."

Leon pulled her into his embrace.

She settled there, loving the feel of his arms—she felt safe and secure. In this moment there was no other place she wanted to be.

CHAPTER TWENTY-ONE

RUSTY'S NEPHEW PLAYED several selections on the violin while guests took their seats to wait for the ceremony to begin. A Rothchild cousin to Leon and Trey would perform a sax solo near the end of the service.

It was time for the ceremony to begin, Eleanor realized.

When the music started, Leon and Trey stood on either side of her.

"My brother and I are going to walk you down this aisle," Leon stated. "We insist on it."

"And the florist made you this bouquet, Auntie," Trey said. "I really think you should carry it."

Eleanor looked at the flowers. "It *is* pretty."

"It looks really nice with your dress," Leon contributed.

"Since she went through all this trouble, I'll carry it."

The doors to the sanctuary opened.

Escorted by her nephews, Eleanor teared up

when she glimpsed Rusty up front with the minister.

Misty was right. He looked handsome in the dark gray suit. His silver cuff links complemented the silver studs on her gown.

He met her as she neared the altar. Taking her hand, Rusty said, "I've always loved that color on you."

"Same here," Eleanor murmured.

They had both agreed to forgo writing their own vows, sticking to tradition.

Eleanor blinked back tears of joy as she and Rusty repeated their vows. She forced away all thoughts of her medical condition and what it meant for her future. She just wanted to revel in this shared moment of pure happiness. The love she saw reflected in Rusty's eyes was burned into her memory. It was a look she never wanted to forget.

After the ceremony, Eleanor and Rusty took more photographs before heading to the café for the reception.

"Mrs. Joshua Henry Sanford... Since everybody calls you Rusty... maybe I should just introduce myself as Mrs. Rusty Sanford."

"I love them both," he said, beaming with pride.

Placing a hand to his cheek, Eleanor said, "I

adore everything about you—especially that sandy-red hair and your freckles."

He kissed her. "You've made me the happiest man alive."

"I pray we have a long life together."

"We will, Ladybug. I believe this with my whole soul." Taking her arm, he said, "It's time for us to head to the shop for the reception."

They walked over to the waiting car. Trey sat behind the wheel grinning. "Alright, you two lovebirds. Time to party."

There was no evidence of the fire that had ravaged the kitchen a few weeks ago. Shiny new appliances, new cookware, plates and silverware...all purchased by Leon and Trey. She'd tried to talk them out of spending so much money, but her boys wouldn't take no for an answer. Rusty had been generous with his donation of the supplies necessary to repair the shop. A group of men from the community volunteered long hours during the week to make sure the repairs were completed in time for the wedding.

I'm so blessed to be surrounded by loving family, friends and a caring community.

When they arrived at the café, Eleanor smiled and murmured, "All of you did a beautiful job in here."

"We left the decorating up to Misty," Rusty said with a chuckle.

In the center of the room, round tables were covered in white tablecloths with gardenia and orchid centerpieces. Place settings included dessert plates and champagne glasses. The tables in booths had been covered as well with elaborate candle displays in the center. Balloons and streamers hung from the ceiling. Soft music flowed throughout, a combination of jazz and R&B that could be enjoyed by guests of all ages.

Rusty and Eleanor navigated around the room, greeting and thanking their guests for coming. They made their way over to the booth where Leon sat with Misty.

"You did a fabulous job with the decorations." Eleanor gestured toward the small table in the center holding the wedding cake. "It's beautiful. I appreciate everything you've done."

Rusty agreed. "Thank you for everything, Misty."

"I didn't do it by myself. Leon and Brittany helped."

Eleanor smiled. "I love y'all so much."

Rusty took her hand. "We need to speak with the pastor before he leaves, Ladybug." He pulled an envelope from a pocket inside his jacket.

"This is one of the happiest days of my life," she whispered.

Rusty kissed her cheek. "I feel the same way. I've waited most of my life for this day. I love you, Ladybug."

"Never let me forget it."

"THE CEREMONY WAS so sweet and romantic," Misty said. She reached up and grabbed the string of a floating balloon.

Leon took a sip of punch. "Aunt Eleanor looks very happy. So does Rusty for that matter. I've always believed that those two belonged together." He hadn't realized how much he'd wanted to see his aunt sharing her life with someone who truly adored her.

"Look."

He followed Misty's gaze. Rusty and Eleanor were in the middle of the room dancing. As he watched them, Leon felt a bottomless sense of peace.

"I've enjoyed meeting other members of your family," Misty said. "They really know how to have a good time."

"It's great seeing Aunt Maggie and everyone. We've always been a close family." Leon stepped over a pair of shoes on the floor where someone had kicked them off. "I used to wish that they'd all move back to the island when I was younger, but now I realize we all have to walk our own paths even if they take us away from Polk Island."

"I can tell family's very important to you."

He nodded. "You feel the same way."

"I do," Misty said. "I don't know my relatives on my father's side very well. They live in and around Atlanta. I've spent most of my time with my mother's family. Most of my summers were spent in North Carolina with my grandparents."

"Do you miss your dad?" Leon inquired.

"Not really. I've been so angry with him for so many years for the way he mistreated my mom. I used to adore him when I was younger, but my feelings changed when I was able to understand what was happening."

"Understandable."

After a slice of wedding cake and the champagne toast, Leon asked, "Would you like to dance?"

"Sure." Misty slipped off her shoes.

He got up and led her to the dance floor. They danced until she needed to get some air.

They walked outside and sat down on a bench near the shop.

Fanning herself, Misty said, "Whew... I needed this little break. My feet were begging for it. I can't hang like I used to—I could stay on the dance floor for a couple of hours straight."

"I know what you mean," Leon said. "I'm starting to feel old."

She laughed. "Well, I'm not claiming that. You're by yourself with that."

"I love hearing you laugh. It's like you're free and just at peace."

"I haven't felt like this in such a long time," Misty said. "This is what life should feel like, Leon. It's liberating."

"I used to feel like that, but then tragedy struck, and things changed for me. Since I've met you, my life has gotten better. You're a great example of moving past adversity. You inspire me."

Misty was touched by his words. "That's really sweet of you to say that."

Rusty and Eleanor left the shop an hour later.

Leon hung behind to help with the cleanup, which thrilled Misty. She wasn't ready to part company with him just yet.

"I'm meeting Howard, Junior and Renee for breakfast tomorrow morning. If you're free, I'd like you to join us," Leon said when they walked out of the shop.

"I'd love to join you," Misty said. "And the timing is perfect. I don't have to work until noon."

"Who watches Talei for you when you work late?" Leon inquired.

"My friend Brittany."

"She used to date my brother, you know."

"She told me."

Once the café was restored back to its normal look, Misty had no reason to keep Leon with her. She consoled herself with the fact that she'd see him in the morning. "I'd better get home. My mom has been dealing with Talei all day. I'm sure she's ready for a break."

Leon kissed her on the lips. "I'll see you tomorrow for breakfast."

THE NEXT MORNING, Leon and Misty met Howard and his children at the hotel for breakfast. They were seated in a booth near the window.

"Trey had an early flight, so he wanted me to pass on his farewells."

"It's wonderful being back on the island," Howard said. "I hadn't realized how much I missed being here."

"Maybe you'll consider moving back," Leon suggested.

Howard laid down his menu. "To be honest, I've been thinking about it."

"I've been thinking about it, too," Renee interjected. "I'd like to open a clothing boutique on the island—it would be my designs, though."

"My daughter is a fashion designer," Howard said. "You should see some of her work."

"I'd love to see them," Misty responded.

"I have some on my phone." Renee passed her cell to Leon, who gave it to Misty.

She scanned through the photographs. "Oh, wow, these are all beautiful. I think you'd do well on the island."

Leon agreed. "We could use a high-end boutique around here. All the locals end up going to Charleston or Savannah to shop. It would be good to keep that revenue on the island."

"The space next to the bakery is available," Misty said.

Renee's eyes widened in surprise. "Really?"

Misty took a sip of her juice. "If you have time, I can take you to check it out."

"I'd love that. My flight isn't until noon. I can just take an Uber later to the mainland."

"I can drop you off," Leon offered. "I'll take you to the airport."

CHAPTER TWENTY-TWO

"So, HOW LONG have you and Leon been seeing each other?" Renee inquired. "I couldn't help but notice how close you two seem to be at the wedding."

"For a few weeks," Misty responded.

"It's really nice seeing him happy again."

She smiled. "Leon definitely makes me happy."

Misty parked curbside. "Are you seriously considering moving to the island?"

"I am," Renee said. "I want to start over some place fresh. Polk Island is my home—it's the best place for a new beginning."

"I called the owner and had him unlock the door for us."

Once they were inside, Renee's gaze bounced around the empty space. "This is perfect for what I envisioned."

Misty hung back, allowing her to wander about the shop. A boutique next door to the bakery and café would bring in more business for them both. It would also make Leon happy. She was a witness to the joy being around family brought him.

"I really like this spot."

"Do you want the owner's information?" Misty asked.

"Yes."

They walked out of the vacant space and headed back to the car. "I'd like to show you one other place that might fit your needs. I don't think we'll be able to get in with this being Sunday, but I can try to see it tomorrow and get some photos for you."

Renee smiled. "Great. I'm getting excited. You have no idea how bad I want to move back here."

AFTER SEVERAL DIAGNOSTIC tests and multiple visits to her doctor, and a neurologist, Eleanor and Rusty were back at the doctor's office for the results. They had just returned from a week in Hawaii for their honeymoon.

"No matter what, we're gonna be just fine," Rusty assured his wife.

She nodded in agreement, but deep down she was scared.

Her doctor entered the room and didn't waste any time with the diagnosis. "What we suspected has been confirmed..."

"I have early onset Alzheimer's," Eleanor stated as calmly as she could manage.

"Yes," her doctor said. He then lapsed into the treatment plan.

Eleanor sat there listening and numb.

Holding her hand in his, Rusty did the talking. He asked questions; lots of them.

She sat there thinking about all the plans she had for her golden years; plans for the shop. Her condition was going to change everything. She now had to attend to practical matters such as putting a plan in place to protect her financial assets.

When they were back at the house, Eleanor said, "I want to keep this just between us for now. Trey is deploying soon and Leon—with the jobs they have, they have to stay focused."

"Ladybug, you know your nephews are gonna want to know what's going on with you. They're gonna be mighty upset when they find out. This is not something we can keep to ourselves for too long. Besides, friends and family are some of the best medicine that any of us will have, in a journey such as this one."

"I hear what you're saying, Rusty, but I stand by what I said. It's not the right time." She paused a moment. "I'm going to turn my house over to Trey. He can decide if he wants to keep it or sell it. As for the shop, I'm thinking of talking to Misty about buying it. She told me when she began working for me that she wanted to own her own bakery one day. She has a great head for business and Lawd knows, the girl has a gift when it comes to baking. She's a good cook period."

"Are you sure you want to sell your shop? It's been in your family for years."

"Nobody in my family is interested in running it. Maybe if my brother had lived... Maggie loves her life in Raleigh." Eleanor took Rusty's hand in her own. "I know Misty will take care of the shop. I can see that she loves it as much as I do. Besides, she and Leon seem to be getting close. Perhaps it will stay in the family after all."

She suddenly grew quiet. Eleanor put her hands to her face and groaned.

Rusty was instantly concerned. "What's wrong, Ladybug?"

Placing her hands on her lap, she said, "I was about to do something, but I can't remember what it was."

"Close your eyes and quiet your mind. Think of someplace peaceful," he suggested.

Eleanor did as he said. She thought about their time in Hawaii. It was like they were in their own little paradise. She and Rusty enjoyed the different fruit stands and boutiques.

A smile tugged at her lips as she thought about the tiny roadside shack on the side of one of the roads that sold the best banana bread—it even rivaled Misty's delicious banana bread.

"I bet you're thinking about Hawaii."

Eleanor opened her eyes. "How did you know?"

"Because you had the same expression on your face just now that you had the whole time we were there."

Smiling, she said, "Maybe we should go back."

"We will," Rusty said. "But right now, why don't you lie down for a bit while I go pick up your medicine."

"I think I will. I was going to check in on the shop, but it's probably best if I don't. I don't quite feel like myself."

While Rusty was gone, Eleanor sat in bed contemplating her situation. Although she hadn't wanted to admit it before, she had begun to recognize changes in her own behavior, like her ability to manage multiple projects. There were a couple of instances when she found herself veering off course when she was supposed to be headed to a specific location.

Early onset Alzheimer's.

Eleanor wondered how long it would take before the reality of her fate really sunk in. She had zero control and this feeling of helplessness scared her. Her doctor mentioned an Alzheimer's Association chapter in Charleston. At this point, Eleanor wasn't sure she'd reach out—the thought was overwhelming.

There is no known cure, so I might as well accept what I can't change. I just worry about my family, especially Leon and Trey. Rusty... dear sweet Rusty. He was her rock. He had always been a man of strong faith, but she was afraid that this test would prove to be too much for even him.

Her eyes filled with tears. *Maybe I shouldn't have married him. It isn't fair for Rusty to have to witness my decline. I know he loves me, but he deserves a wife who is healthy.*

Eleanor knew what Rusty would say if he could hear her thoughts. They'd talked about this at length before the wedding. He assured her that he wanted to spend the rest of his life with her. She believed him—it was just a lot to ask of anybody. Yet, if it was the other way around, she would never abandon Rusty.

She heard him enter the house and make his way up the stairs. A smile tugged at her lips.

Rusty made her feel safe and she was glad he was home.

"I thought you'd be sleeping."

"I couldn't," Eleanor said. "I had a lot on my

mind. This is just so much to take in and I have a lot to do before my condition gets worse."

"Do you have plans for this weekend?" Leon inquired. His gaze traveled over her face and searched her eyes. They had just gotten back to her place after seeing a movie.

"I'm going to a powwow in Charleston. Talei and I are competing."

"Really?"

Misty nodded. "Yeah, it's something I've done since I was five years old."

"I've never been to one, but they seem to be pretty popular. Tell me... What exactly is a powwow?"

"It's a traditional gathering. A time for nations to come together to share songs and dances," Misty explained. "It's fun, it's sacred and it's social. If you're not busy, Talei and I would love to have you there."

"I'll be there."

"Since this is your first time, there are some things you should know. If you're asked to dance by an elder, do so. It's considered rude and disrespectful if you don't."

"I'm sure I don't know how to do any of the dances."

Misty met his gaze. "How can you learn if you turn the elders down? Our dances are more of a ceremony and a prayer… Some dances are old, and some are brand-new."

Leon grinned. "I guess you have a point."

"When the master of ceremonies calls an intertribal dance, it's expected that all visitors get out on the dance ring. The reason for this is that it's not considered polite to just watch as others perform. It's about honoring the circle." She smiled. "You still interested in coming?"

"Yeah, I'm actually intrigued. I know John loved to dance," Leon said. "I'm surprised he didn't try to steal the show."

"He never wanted to come," Misty said. "Talei and I always went with my mother."

"Oh."

"He was never into learning anything about this part of my culture, but it was more because he knew Elroy would've pitched a fit. His dad was always quick to remind me that my father is Black. I guess he thought that outweighed my Native heritage."

Leon frowned. "I don't understand that."

"I didn't either."

"We've been told that Polk's grandmother was Seminole, but there's nothing to back up the claim. Aunt Eleanor said Polk and Hoss wanted to make sure they documented our history going forward, so that we would at least know as much of it as possible. We can go all the way back to 1830."

"That's huge," Misty said. "Some people can't get past the 1900s."

"Aunt Eleanor has some quilts with pictures showing the history of Polk Island. She keeps them under lock and key. The director of the cultural center here has asked to display them, but she refuses."

"I'm sure she worries that they might end up damaged or, worse, stolen."

"Probably. I've been thinking of turning the church into some type of museum—one run by the Rothchild family."

"Leon, I think that's a fabulous idea. You should do it."

"I'll have to talk to the rest of the family first. I think we need to be all in if we want this to work."

Leon settled back against the couch cushions. "So, do you want to give me a preview of what I'm going to see at the powwow?"

"I think it's best to just let you experience it firsthand. No preview."

"Chicken," Leon said with a chuckle.

Misty's mouth dropped open in shock. "I can't believe you just said that. No more lemon cupcakes for you. When you attend the powwow, you'll understand why I'm not performing it for you right now."

"Since I can't get you to dance for me, can we just sit here and cuddle?"

She grinned. "Yes, yes and *yes*."

CHAPTER TWENTY-THREE

MISTY AND OMA picked herbs from her mother's indoor aero garden. She sniffed the basil. "I might have to try my hand at this, but I can't deal with bugs."

"You're bigger than the bugs."

"Doesn't matter, Mama. They gross me out."

"You've passed your fear on to your daughter," Oma said. "The last time she was here, that poor child worked herself into a frenzy over a fly."

Misty burst into laughter.

She carried the bowl of herbs to the sink to rinse them off. "Leon's coming to Charleston for the powwow tomorrow."

"Eon…" Talei said with a smile as she played with her two favorite bears.

Scanning her face, Oma asked, "I know you've been seeing quite a bit of Leon. Is this getting serious?"

Misty shrugged. "I don't know. Both of us have been through a lot, so we're just taking things slow. I want to really take time to get to know him. I've always rushed into my past relationships."

"Are you interested in something more with him?"

"I enjoy his company, Mama. I'm good with the way things are between us. I don't want any drama—I just want to have a good time."

"I can tell you like him, though."

Misty chuckled. "It's true. I like Leon a lot."

"One thing you have to learn to do is trust your heart and your gut instincts. There were red flags with the other guys you dated, but you ignored them."

"You're right," Misty mumbled. "I wanted to believe in the good I saw in them, but I found out that it was mostly an act. Thankfully, there haven't been any red flags with Leon. He seems pretty normal and well-adjusted. It's such a relief, Mama."

"Enjoy the journey."

"But I have to remember that he's not perfect. Leon has to have flaws. We all have them."

"True. Just make sure you're not waiting for something bad to happen. That's no way to enjoy a relationship."

"I'm very optimistic about dating Leon, Mama. But I'm also being realistic."

Misty helped Oma prepare a light meal for

the three of them, ate and then settled in her mother's sewing room.

She watched her mother sew ribbons on the bottom of a blue skirt and said, "It's beautiful."

Misty fingered one of the ribbons that represented prayers. "Are you wearing that tomorrow?"

"Yes," Oma responded. "Prayer is needed more than ever in this world."

"Are you going to have some for sale?"

Her mother pointed to a stack of clothing on a nearby chair. "I'm also selling the other ones I made along with some of the fringe dresses."

"Do you have any more of the quilts you made? I'd like to buy one for Miss Eleanor. She gave me one of hers—it's so pretty. I'll have to send you a picture of it."

"Take the one with the indigo blue flowers. I think she'll like that one."

Misty opened her purse, but Oma stopped her by saying, "It's a gift for your employer."

She gave her mother a hug. "*Wado*, Mama."

DRESSED IN NATIVE regalia in vibrant rich colors, Misty and Talei met Leon at the entrance of the grounds where the powwow took place. Talei's hair was in two braids with ribbons entwined while Misty's hair was pulled back into a bun with an eagle feather sticking up.

Leon picked up Talei. "Hello, pretty girl."

"*Oseeyo*, Eon." She pointed down to her moccasins. "Cute."

"Yes, they are. I see they match your mom's. You think they have some to fit my feet?"

"Yes." Talei pointed toward the area where the vendors were set up.

Leon met Misty's gaze and laughed. "She should get commission. You look beautiful, by the way."

She smiled. "Thank you. My mother wore this dress when she used to perform the healing dance."

"That sounds spiritual. Is that why you wouldn't dance for me the other night?"

"Yeah," she responded. "It's a sacred dance."

Leon glanced around the grounds. "This is amazing. I'm looking forward to this event. I especially can't wait to see this little one out there dancing."

Talei giggled.

"C'mon. I want to take you to see Mama. She wants to say hello."

Oma was with a customer when they walked up.

While they waited for her to complete the sale, Leon and Misty strolled around the tent, looking at the clothing, blankets and quilts.

"These are beautiful," he told Oma when she joined them.

"Mama, this is Leon Rothchild."

"It's nice to finally meet you," Oma stated.

He smiled. "Same here."

The powwow began with a grand entry. Leon watched as all the dancers entered the circle led by the veterans and head dancers. He stood up along with everyone in attendance when the opening prayer was said.

When it was time for the intertribal dance, Oma took Leon by the hand and led him into the arena. Talei joined him and Oma as the music began.

"I have no clue what I'm doing," he said in a low voice.

"Just walk with the beat," Oma advised.

He studied the man in front of him and mimicked what he did. Out of the corner of his eye, he saw Oma give a slight nod of approval.

When they left the arena, Leon said, "I probably looked crazy out there."

"You did great," Oma said. "I have to go back to my tent, but I'll be back when Talei dances."

He never knew that powwows were so sacred and spiritual. He'd just assumed they were nothing more than entertainment.

Leon felt a surge of fatherly pride as he watched Talei in the arena with the other children doing the candy dance. She looked like she was having a wonderful time. He had been so intent on watching her that he didn't notice Oma sitting beside him.

"Talei did a fantastic job," he said. "How long has she been dancing?"

"This is her second year competing, but she's been dancing since she was big enough to walk. She would watch Misty and try to imitate her."

Leon watched Talei line up a second time with the other children. She was the smallest, so she was right behind the head dancer holding eagle fans.

"This is called the Eagle Dance," Oma responded.

Leon grinned, watching Talei mimic the leader's movements, extending her arms to soar and spiral, before bringing them closer to her body and crouching on the ground. The line of children winded their way around the circle, surrounding the head dancer when he kneeled.

Talei waited until she exited the arena before running over to Oma and Leon. Misty was on the other side of the arena with a group of female dancers.

Oma planted a kiss on Talei's forehead, then returned to her tent.

Talei sat in the chair beside Leon. "Mommy dance."

"I can't wait to see that." He turned to face the little girl. "You did a great job out there. I'm so proud of you."

She grinned. "I not scared."

"I could tell," he said. "You're such a brave little girl, Talei."

"Hot dawg and fench fries, pleeze."

Leon burst into laughter. "C'mon, little one."

They returned to their seats in time to watch Misty perform the Dance of Life.

He was mesmerized by her graceful movements.

When she joined him and Talei after the dance, Leon said, "Wow... You were amazing."

"Amazing," her daughter repeated.

"I'm glad I came out here today. I've learned a lot."

"This is a huge part of who I am—I wanted you to experience it with me," Misty stated.

Talei got up and crawled onto Leon's lap so her mother could sit down.

The male dancers in fancy regalia entered the arena to perform.

Misty pointed to the dancer closest to where they were sitting. "My mom made his clothing."

"She's very talented."

By the end of the event, Leon found all of the dancers awe-inspiring. "When is the next pow-wow?" he asked.

"There's going to be one in Savannah next month," Misty said. "Interested in joining us?"

"I'm there," he responded with a grin.

TODAY THE STATION house was a busy one.

Leon and his coworkers started off washing engines one and two, then inspected their personal protective equipment. They had to be ready for any calls for assistance.

"Don't forget we have training in thirty minutes," Lizzie reminded him as she poured out the pail of dirty water. "Today is on special operations."

"Yeah," Leon uttered. They trained three days a week at the station. "I hope I can stay awake."

"Late night?" she asked as they strolled into the dorm.

Leon sat down on his bunk. "I went to a pow-wow in Charleston. I was there all day long."

"I haven't been to one of those in a long time."

"It was my first. I really enjoyed it. Misty and Talei performed."

Lizzie smiled. "I bet Talei was adorable."

Leon swept the kitchen area before heading to the training room.

When the session ended, he and the other firemen returned to dusting, sweeping and mopping the station. Charles did the laundry before leaving to talk to students at a community center about fire prevention and how to use a fire extinguisher as part of the station's public outreach program.

Leon spent the next hour working out with Lizzie and another member of the unit. They were required to exercise for one hour each shift.

"So, have you said those three little words to Misty?" Lizzie inquired.

He pretended not to know what she was talking about. "Huh?"

She laughed.

"I don't know what you're waiting for. We can see how much you care about Misty."

"Lizzie, have you told Rob how you feel?" Leon countered.

She stepped off the treadmill and wiped her face with a towel. "It's not the same."

He reached for his water bottle and took a long drink before putting it back down. "When the time is right, I'll tell Misty how I feel about her," Leon stated. He picked up a couple of hand weights. "Things are great between us, but we've only been together a short while. Neither one of us wants to rush the relationship."

CHAPTER TWENTY-FOUR

"MISTY, WHEN YOU get a minute, I'd like to talk to you."

"I have some time now, Miss Eleanor."

"Great, let's talk in my office."

Eleanor closed the door behind them, then sat down at her desk.

"Is everything okay?"

"Now that Rusty and I are married, I've been thinking about the future. One thing I want to do is to spend more time with him."

Misty smiled. "Ah…the honeymoon phase."

"It's more than that, sugar," Eleanor said. "There are some things that have come up in my life and it's changed my focus. I'm actually thinking of selling the shop to you…that is if you're interested."

A soft gasp escaped Misty. "You're not serious. This place has been in your family for years."

"I know that you will take care of it."

"Miss Eleanor, what's really going on?"

Misty inquired. "I know how much this place means to you."

"I'm gwine retire and spend time enjoying life with Rusty."

Misty shook her head in denial. "I'm not really buying that story. There's something more going on. I'm not trying to get in your business, Miss Eleanor, but I know you wouldn't just up and sell the shop like this. Don't get me wrong. I would love to buy this place from you. John left me and Talei well taken care of, so the money isn't an issue."

"Misty, I owe you the truth. What I'm about to tell you, I need you to keep to yourself. Rusty and I are the only ones who know this information."

"I won't say a word," Misty said.

"This means you're going to have to keep a secret from Leon," Eleanor clarified.

"He would want to know what's going on with you. You know that he adores you."

"I know but he can't know about this just yet. I have early onset Alzheimer's," Eleanor announced. "We just found out a couple of days ago and I need some time to process the news myself before I start telling everybody."

Misty's body stiffened in shock. "Miss Eleanor... I don't know what to say..."

Eleanor gave a slight shrug. "It's fine, sugar.

But I hope you can understand why I want to sell. There's no way I can keep up with the demands of the shop. I would take great comfort in knowing that I've left it in good hands with you, Misty. I know you want your own business. What do you think?"

"I never expected this," she responded. "Are you sure you want to do this, Miss Eleanor?"

She nodded. "Rusty and I discussed it at length. You have a brilliant mind for business and you also have a passion for what you do."

"But what about your other family members?"

"None of them are interested in this shop. I couldn't get not a one of them to work when I needed extra help."

"Not even Leon?"

"He has enough on his plate, Misty. So does Trey. He's committed to the marines and looking to make a career of the military."

"Please give this some serious thought and let me know, Misty. I don't want to sell to strangers."

"I don't have to think about it," she said. "I'll take over the shop, Miss Eleanor. I love it here."

MISTY LOOKED DOWN at the baggy sweatpants and T-shirt she was wearing. Leon was due to

arrive at any moment. They were staying in tonight and she wanted to be comfortable.

Maybe I should change clothes.

She dismissed the thought as quickly as it
had come. *Why am I worried about what he's
going to think?* This was part of her normal routine. "Might as well let him see the real me,"
she whispered.

The doorbell sounded.

Misty opened the door and threw herself into
his arms. Leon gave the best hugs.

Once they were seated in the living room,
Misty stated, "I was thinking we could make
homemade pizza."

"Works for me."

Talei walked into the room. "Mommy...
Eon..." She climbed into his lap with her stuffed
bears. "I playing with Pooh Bear and Eon," she
said, pointing to the bear in the fire department
T-shirt.

"You named him after me?" Leon asked.

"Yes," Talei responded.

"I'm honored."

Talei grinned, then laid her head on his chest.

Misty's heart warmed as she watched her
daughter with Leon. The two had really bonded
over the past few months.

"Who's ready to make pizza?" she asked.

"Me," Leon and Talei responded in unison.

Laughing, they made their way to the kitchen.

Leon set Talei on a stool while Misty gathered the ingredients.

"Pepperooni."

"You want pepperoni pizza, Talei?"

"Yes. Mommy like pepperooni, too." Talei picked up the packet from the counter and tried to open it.

"Let me help you," Leon said.

She gave him the bag of pepperoni slices. Pointing to a blue container, Talei inquired, "What that?"

"Mushrooms," he responded. "I like them on my pizza."

She made a face, prompting laughter from Leon. "Do you like olives, little one?"

Frowning, Talei shook her head no.

"She's a plain pepperoni-and-cheese kind of girl," Misty said.

When it was time to put the toppings on her pizza, Talei placed one mushroom and one olive on hers.

"Look at my brave girl," Misty said. "I'm so proud of you for trying new things."

"When Daddy come home from heaven?" Talei blurted when they gathered at the dining room table. "Daddy got hurt in car."

Misty glanced over at Leon, then said, "Sweetie, your dad isn't here."

"Your daddy's in heaven watching over you," Leon stated.

After they finished eating, Misty turned on a Disney movie for Talei to watch.

Keeping her voice low, she said, "I think I made a mistake."

"What do you mean?" Leon asked.

"I told Talei that John went to heaven. She thinks he's coming back."

"If you'd like, we can try to explain it to her together."

"Come here, honey," Misty said. "We want to talk to you about Daddy."

"Okay." Talei climbed down from the sofa. She skipped back to the table where they were sitting.

"You remember the car accident?"

Talei nodded. "Daddy got hurt. Eon help Daddy."

"That's right. He was taken to the hospital. The doctors tried to make Daddy better, but they couldn't. He was too hurt." Misty paused a moment, then said, "Daddy *died*. He didn't want to die, but he was too hurt."

"Your mom's right," Leon said. "Your daddy never wanted to leave you. I know that he misses you very much because he can't see you or your mom again."

Talei's eyes filled with tears. "He not coming back."

"When you die, you can't come back. You go to live in heaven. It's okay for you to miss him."

"Your dad's up there watching over you," Leon said. "He will always live in your heart, little one. His love for you will never stop."

"We still have pictures and memories of Daddy," Misty stated. "You will always remember how much he loved you."

"I want Daddy." Talei began to cry.

Leon embraced her. "He loved you so much. Your daddy was crazy about you. He made me promise to look after you when he was gone. I'm going to keep my word to your daddy. I will always be here for you." He wiped away her tears. "It may not seem like it now, but it's going to be okay, little one."

Talei eased out of his lap and ran off to her room.

Misty shook her head. "This is so hard."

After a while, Talei returned with her bears Pooh and Eon. Without a word, she climbed into Misty's lap. "I wanna watch Minty Mouse."

"Me, too," Leon said with a grin.

Misty planted a kiss on Talei's cheek.

"Do I get one of those?" he asked.

She kissed his cheek in response. "Thank you."

Misty felt guilty about the secret she was keeping from Leon. He deserved to know about his aunt's condition, but Eleanor wasn't ready to tell him. Misty had no choice but to respect her decision.

Inside, she felt terrible about it.

Misty also worried that she could lose Leon once he knew the truth about the shop and Eleanor's condition. She prayed he would understand that she was only honoring his aunt's wishes.

"What's on your mind?" Leon asked, cutting into her thoughts.

"It's nothing," she replied with a smile.

He scanned her face. "You sure you're okay? You look a little troubled.

"I am. Everything is fine. I'm just tired."

"I've been meaning to ask how my aunt's been doing at the shop. I know she's been a bit forgetful."

Misty chewed on her bottom lip and pretended to be interested in watching television. "I've been forgetting stuff myself. That's why I have to write everything down."

"I know she runs herself ragged at times."

"I've been trying to get Miss Eleanor to slow down. Now that she's married, I think she will."

"I hope so," Leon said. "I offered to help out on days when I don't have to work."

"You're such a sweetheart."

"Aunt Eleanor took care of me and Trey when we lost our parents. When Vee and my daughter died, my aunt wouldn't let me quit on life." Leon eyed her. "Misty, I was in so much pain." His voice broke.

Misty hugged him. "I'm so sorry for all you've been through."

"Aunt Eleanor moved in with me because she was so worried about me. My coworkers checked on me to the point they were getting on my nerves. I owe them so much."

"I understand what you mean," Misty said. "The good thing is that you had so many people rallying around you."

"I had a lot of people. The whole community was here for me."

"Hearing this lets me know that I chose the perfect place to raise my daughter. This is the way it should be."

LEON COULDN'T ESCAPE the feeling that Misty was hiding something from him. He didn't know if it had to do with her feelings or something else. She seemed troubled or uneasy, but he couldn't get her to open up to him.

He decided to give it one more shot. "Misty, how are you feeling about us?"

She looked perplexed by his question for a brief moment, then responded, "I love the way things are between us. We have a great time together. We have a lot in common and there's no drama." Misty scanned his face. "Why do you ask?"

"I just wanted to make sure we're on the same page," Leon said. "I really like you and I need to know that you're as invested in this relationship as I am."

Smiling, Misty said, "You don't have anything to worry about. I'm very invested."

Leon believed her, but still couldn't shake the feeling that there was something more going on. He intended to find out what Misty was hiding. He didn't like secrets.

"So, WHAT ARE you gonna do about the shop?" Brittany asked. "It would be a great investment for you."

"I don't know," Misty said with a shrug. "I want to buy it, but I just feel that Miss Eleanor's going through a lot right now. I'm not sure she's thinking clearly about everything. This is not a decision to make while emotions are high."

"I hope it's nothing serious."

"She's starting a new life with Rusty. Miss Eleanor deserves to spend every moment making new memories, but the shop has been in her family a few generations."

"Apparently, she's fine with selling it, Misty.

I just wonder how Leon's gonna feel about all this. He's big on family. So is Trey for that matter."

Misty shrugged. "Miss Eleanor made it clear that it's *her* decision."

"Okay, then. There you have it."

After she left her best friend, Misty decided to pay Leon a visit.

She found him working in the yard. "Hey, you."

"Hello," he responded.

"Want some help?"

"Sure."

She started weeding across the garden from him.

He hunched over, his hands resting on his thighs. "You're not working today?"

"No. I'm taking Talei to the doctor later this afternoon and I ran some errands this morning." She couldn't tell him that she spent her morning working out the financing for the shop.

"When you're done, you wanna come do mine?"

The voice, from a passerby, prompted Leon to look up and see who was talking to him. "Hey, Pete."

Leon pushed to his feet and walked down the driveway, leaving Misty to continue her task. She didn't pay much attention to them.

"How could you take advantage of my aunt like that?" Leon demanded when he returned. He glared at Misty with burning, reproachful eyes.

She shielded her eyes from the sun as she looked up at him. "What are you talking about?"

"My great-great-grandparents opened that shop. Aunt Eleanor loves that place. She wouldn't sell it to *anyone* unless she was manipulated." A sudden thin chill hung on the edge of his words.

Misty seethed with disappointment and anger. She stood up to him. "Do you really think that I'm the type of person who would do something like that?"

"All I know is that she would want the shop to stay in the family."

"It's clearly time for me to leave," Misty said. She wasn't about to stand there and argue with him. "For the record I didn't steal your aunt's business." She felt weak and vulnerable in the face of Leon's anger. "You will have to ask her about why she wants to sell."

"I never said you were stealing anything."

"You're an idiot," Misty uttered. "You don't have to worry, Leon. I don't need to buy it—I can open my own somewhere else."

"Aunt Eleanor loves that place. It doesn't make sense that she would want to sell it. That's all I know."

"Miss Eleanor knows that she's not able to keep running it, Leon."

"Why not?" he asked.

Misty hadn't meant to say that much. "You'll have to ask your aunt."

"I'm asking *you*. Why would my aunt suddenly decide to up and sell her business? I know that there's something you're not telling me."

"Miss Eleanor came to me, Leon. If you want to know more, ask her." Misty wiped her hands with a nearby towel. "Goodbye... Oh and lose my number."

CHAPTER TWENTY-FIVE

Upset, Misty left Leon's house and drove to see Eleanor. The last thing she wanted was to cause friction in their family. It was better to take herself out of the equation.

Eleanor opened the door and stepped back to let Misty enter the foyer. "What a pleasant surprise. C'mon in, sugar."

They sat down in the living room. "Miss Eleanor, I thought about it and I don't think it's a good idea for me to buy the shop."

Eleanor looked disappointed and near tears. "Why not? You seemed pretty excited about it when we had our discussion."

"I was… I am… The truth is that Leon's not really happy about the idea. In fact, he accused me of manipulating you to get you to sell to me."

"*What?* How in the world did he find out?"

"One of his neighbors mentioned it. I think his name is Pete."

"He works at the law firm. My lawyer must have mentioned it to him, but you don't have to worry about my nephew. I'll set him straight."

"Leon's right about how much you love the shop, Miss Eleanor. Maybe there's another way…"

"Misty, the only person I'd trust with the shop is you. I know that you love it as much as I do."

"I do love this place, but I don't want to cause friction between you and Leon. In fact, I'm thinking about moving back to Charleston."

"Misty, I hope it doesn't come to that."

"Miss Eleanor, you didn't see the way Leon reacted. He really hurt my feelings."

"Don't make any decisions just yet. I'll straighten everything out, Misty. The bakery and café are mine to do what I will with it. I don't need my nephew's permission to sell."

"Regardless, the damage is already done. Leon and I won't be seeing each other anymore."

"I know that you care for Leon. Don't give up on him."

"I can't make any promises, Miss Eleanor. I refuse to date a man who thinks so little of me. I don't know what John told him about me, but apparently he believes it."

"I'm so sorry, sugar."

"Miss Eleanor, it's not your fault. I'm actually glad it happened. I needed to know who I was dealing with."

Eleanor took Misty's hand in her own. "I

want to sell my shop to *you*. I will only have peace if I know it's in your hands."

"I'll think about it and give you a call tomorrow."

"Even if you decide not to buy the shop, I know you love this island. Don't let what happened run you off."

"Miss Eleanor, I can't imagine living so close to Leon and not being with him. It would hurt too much to see him around town... My feelings for him are strong." She paused a moment, then said, "I'm in love with him."

"I can see that clear as day."

"That's why his actions today hurt so much." Misty stood up. "I need to get home, but I'll give you a call tomorrow to let you know what I decide."

LEON WAS IN search of answers.

"Rusty, do you know anything about my aunt selling the shop?" Leon asked. "Pete told me that she met with her lawyer about it."

"Have you spoken to Eleanor?"

"Not yet," Leon responded. "Is this because the two of you got married?"

"Eleanor will be home soon," Rusty said. "You should talk to *her*."

"What's with all the secrecy?" Shaking his

head in frustration, Leon stated, "I just hope this wasn't Misty's plan all along."

"You don't really believe that, do you?"

Leon shrugged. "I don't know what to believe. John used to tell me that she used manipulation to get whatever she wanted from him."

"John also took his own daughter without Misty's permission," Rusty said. "I would say his credibility was questionable at best. He was your friend, but clearly there was a side to him that you didn't know about."

"All the more reason to wonder if there's a side to Misty that I have no knowledge of—don't you think?"

"Has she ever lied to you?"

"I don't think so," Leon responded. "Rusty, I know where you're going with this. Believe me, I want to give Misty the benefit of the doubt."

"Join us for dinner tonight," Rusty suggested. "You can talk to your aunt and get all of your questions answered."

Leon nodded. "I'll definitely be back."

None of this made sense to him. He would never believe that his aunt would just up and sell a business that had been in his family for generations. She wouldn't do something like that unless she was somehow forced into it.

He would find out the truth in a few hours.

WHEN LEON ARRIVED, Eleanor had the food prepared and was ready to serve. He washed his hands, then joined them at the dining room table.

Rusty said the blessing.

Leon sampled his food. "Auntie, everything is delicious."

He tried to keep the discussion light while they ate, but questions hammered at him.

Halfway through the meal, Eleanor glanced over at Rusty, then said, "I hear Pete opened his big mouth before I had a chance to talk to you. There's something you should know."

Leon wiped his mouth with his napkin. "Is this about the shop?"

"Yes," she responded. "First off... You were wrong for blaming Misty for anything. It was my idea to sell the shop to her. She's the perfect person to take ownership because I know she'll take care of it. Rusty and I talked about this at length. It's what I want to do, and you have no say-so in the matter."

"But why do you suddenly want to sell the shop?" Leon inquired. "This didn't come up after the fire. I don't understand."

"There's something I need to tell you, son."

The expression on her face made him ask, "What's going on, Auntie?"

"I have early onset Alzheimer's," Eleanor announced. "I thought I was just getting forget-ful…that it was because of my age… I never considered that it would be something more. I wake up in the morning sometimes and I don't feel rested. But mostly, I don't know what day of the week it is…the date or even the month. There are times when I don't remember what I planned for the day."

"Sometimes I have days like that, Auntie. I think everyone goes through times like this."

"I didn't realize until today that I get up and wear one of three outfits all the time, Leon. I have a closet full of clothes. This morning at the café, I couldn't remember where the coffee was, and I couldn't remember where I keep the flour. I found myself reading the same article over and over again this afternoon."

"I'm so sorry, Auntie."

"I'm sure you've noticed I ask you the same questions over and over again. This is my life."

"Why didn't you tell me you were going through this?" He gazed at Rusty. "Did you know?"

"Yes," Rusty answered.

"Leon, I didn't want to worry you, son," Eleanor stated. "I didn't want you worrying about me. And don't be upset with my husband—he wanted to tell you but respected my decision to tell you when I was ready."

"That's not your call, Auntie. I love you so I'm always gonna worry about you."

"Now I need you to not say anything to Trey. I want to tell him in my own time, Leon. He's over in Afghanistan. I need your brother to keep his head straight so he can be safe."

"I won't say anything," Leon provided. "I was just thinking how I made a fool of myself with Misty. I owe her a huge apology."

"Well, you better do it soon. Misty's thinking about leaving the island," Eleanor announced.

Leon's eyebrows shot up in surprise. "What are you talking about?"

"She told me that she might be moving back to Charleston. I don't know what happened between you two, but she was really hurt by it."

Leon laid down his fork. "I never meant to hurt Misty. I accused her of manipulating you into selling the shop."

"Boy, you done lost your mind. Yeah, you need to make it right or you stand to lose her forever. *Mark my word.*"

"I will," he said. "I'll go by her place when I leave here."

Leon's heart was in a panic at the thought of losing Misty. He had to talk to her—to make things right.

CHAPTER TWENTY-SIX

LEON SAT OUTSIDE her condo for ten minutes, trying to figure out the best approach. He had been a complete jerk to her. He prayed he could repair the damage done.

"I apologize for just showing up, but I really wanted to talk to you," Leon said when Misty opened the front door. "May I come in?"

"I'm not sure we have anything to discuss."

She was still clearly upset with him. "I want to apologize for the things I said earlier."

They settled in the living room.

"I just left my aunt's house," Leon began. "She told me everything. Misty, I'm very sorry for the way I treated you."

"You should've known better," she said. "The fact that you think I'd do something like that—it really bothers me."

"Misty, I honestly don't know why I said that to you—it just didn't make sense that my aunt would even think of selling her shop. I'm so sorry."

After a moment, she said, "I accept your apology."

"I assume my aunt told you why she wants to sell you the shop."

Misty nodded. "I know she has Alzheimer's. For the record, she wanted me to keep her secret until she was ready to tell you. She didn't want you to worry about her."

"She told me the same thing, but it doesn't matter. She's my aunt and I care what happens to her."

"Miss Eleanor knows that," Misty said. "I have to be honest, Leon. You really hurt my feelings. I have always wanted my own business, but there's no way I'd swindle Miss Eleanor out of her shop. Or anyone else for that matter. I'm not that type of person."

"I know that," he responded. "For the record, I never thought you cheated her."

"Maybe not, but you did accuse me of manipulating your aunt. That sounds just as bad, Leon. Just so you know, I backed out of buying the shop."

"Aunt Eleanor made it clear that she wanted you to take over the bakery. Now that I know everything, I agree with her. You should buy it."

"I don't know."

"Misty, can we get past this?"

She met Leon's gaze. "What happened has made me realize that you don't really know me."

"I want to get to know you more. I admit that I messed up, but I'm hoping you'll give me another chance. I should say give *us* another chance."

"I need some time to think about it, Leon."

He gave a slight nod. "I understand. I'll give you some space."

Leon rose to his feet.

"Don't leave," Misty said when he reached for the doorknob. "I don't want you to go."

He came and sat back down beside her.

"If we're going to see each other, I need you to trust me unless I prove to be untrustworthy. I don't know what John told you about me, but whatever he said must have colored your opinion of me."

"I agree," Leon said. "You deserve that and more. As for John—he had nothing to do with what happened. I jumped to conclusions without all the information. I won't make that mistake again. I give you my word."

"Thank you for coming here to make things right. I appreciate that."

"Were you seriously thinking about moving back to Charleston?" Leon asked.

"I was," she responded.

"And now?"

"I thought about moving, but the truth is that Talei and I love it here. I'm not leaving. Polk Island has become our home."

"I'm happy to hear you say this," Leon said. "I don't want to lose you or Talei. You've both come to mean a lot to me."

"I need to know something. If I buy the bakery and café, how will you feel about it? I want you to be honest."

"I'll be okay. I know you'll be great."

"You really mean that?" Misty asked.

"I do."

Misty picked up the television remote. "I was just about to watch a movie. Would you like to stay?"

"Sure. I can't think of a better way to spend the evening."

They watched in companionable silence until a commercial break.

"How was your day?" Leon asked.

"It was great," Misty responded. "The shop was busy nonstop. I picked Talei up from day care, we got ice cream, then walked the beach."

She turned down the volume to the TV while they talked.

"Leon, how are you feeling about your aunt's diagnosis?"

"I need to learn more about the disease," he responded. "I'm worried for her. I know Rusty's there for her, but I can't abandon her either. I just don't know what I can do to help my aunt."

Misty took his hand in her own. "I read somewhere that they are making great strides in slowing down the progression of Alzheimer's. You can't lose hope."

"One thing I've noticed is that whenever we watch the news, I can tell my aunt gets bothered—she doesn't like hearing about all the bad things happening in the world. Minutes later, Aunt Eleanor didn't even remember what it was that bothered her. She asks the same question over and over again. She can remember things she did as a child..."

"Her short-term memory is affected by the disease," Misty said. "What can I do to help?"

"I don't know," Leon responded. "I'm glad she has Rusty because I'm not sure how much longer she could've lived alone." He released a long sigh. "I wish I knew what to do to help her. She's always been there for me."

"You have to allow her to live as normal a life as possible, Leon. My grandmother had dementia and my mother was her caregiver. As her disease progressed, there were days she didn't recognize her own daughter. It was hard on my mom because of Granny's inability to communicate her thoughts or remember faces and names." Misty pasted on a smile. "Your aunt is one strong-willed lady. She is going to fight back with her entire being."

"She's tough," Leon agreed.

"Make sure she takes her medicine. My granny hated taking hers. There were times when she'd get violent with my mom." Misty took Leon's hand in her own. "I'm here to help in any way I can. I know Rusty has to run his business and you're working at the station."

"You're going to be running the shop and you have Talei. I can't intrude in your life any more than that."

"You're not," Misty responded. "I'm offering."

"I guess we'll both just have to wait and see how this disease progresses. Aunt Eleanor was herself when I went to see her earlier. She made dinner and it was delicious. She looked good. Misty, she looked really happy."

"That's good to hear, but you may notice her asking you the same questions repeatedly or she may be confused or forgetful—those are the things you have to be on the watch for with Miss Eleanor."

"I'm scared of losing her, Misty."

"Don't think that way. Just take it one day at a time. Learn about the disease. You might want to join a support group if that will help."

"I'm glad that I have you, Misty."

"I'll always be here for you, Leon. Don't ever forget that."

He pulled her into his embrace, holding her close. No words were necessary.

RUSTY COULDN'T LEAVE work so Leon picked up Eleanor for her doctor appointment. During the fifteen-minute drive, she asked the same question four times. "Where are we going?"

"To see your doctor, Auntie."

"Is it time for my physical?" She frowned. "Seems like I already did that. I saw Dr. Allen last month."

"We're going to see Dr. Grady," Leon announced.

"Ooh…" she responded. "I like Dr. Grady. I need to talk to her about getting my license back."

"Auntie, you don't need to worry about driving. I'll take you anywhere you need to go."

"Sugar, you have to work. I don't need you running me around. I can drive myself."

Her determination filled Leon with angst. He didn't want to upset her, but there was no way he'd let her get behind the wheel of a car in her condition. However, he couldn't tell her—she would be angry and devastated.

After the appointment, Eleanor asked, "Where are we going?"

"Home. We just left your doctor's appointment," he responded patiently.

"We did?" Eleanor appeared confused.

"Yes, ma'am."

"I just saw Dr. Allen. I think it was last month."

"We saw Dr. Grady, Aunt Eleanor."

"What did she say? Did she give me my license back? I don't know why she took it in the first place."

Rusty had prepared him that his aunt would have moments like this. Still, Leon found it heartbreaking to see her going through this.

"How about I make you some lunch?" Leon suggested when they arrived back at the house.

"Sure," Eleanor responded.

He found some chili in the refrigerator and heated it up.

She ate only half of what was in the bowl.

"You're not hungry?"

"It didn't have a lot of flavor," Eleanor responded.

"I've never been the cook that you are." Leon didn't have the heart to tell her that she'd made it. She was right, of course. It wasn't the same recipe she often used in the past—it was missing something.

"Sugar, I'm sorry. I wasn't trying to hurt your feelings."

"You didn't, Auntie."

"Where's Rusty? I thought he'd be home by now."

"He should be here soon," Leon said. "I'm gonna hang around until he gets here to keep you company."

"Great," Eleanor murmured. "Sometimes I don't like being here alone."

She finished off her water, then asked, "How are things going with Misty?"

"Fine," Leon responded. "We're in a good place."

"You two make such a lovely couple. It's good to see you smile again. Misty is perfect for you, but then you know this already. She's been through so much in her lifetime. She's a survivor...that one."

THE NEXT DAY after Rusty left for work, Eleanor began to have dark, negative thoughts. She had no idea why. She checked the locks on the doors and the windows. She was safe.

Her emotions ranged from feeling depressed, angry, even crying. Oftentimes music lifted her spirits. Eleanor didn't venture to the café as much now because she wasn't able to drive, and she didn't want to burden anyone with chauffeuring her around.

She spent the rest of her afternoon figuring out word games in a puzzle magazine Leon purchased for her. When she grew bored with that, she attempted to read a book but lost the narrative after a few pages.

Eleanor picked up her phone and tapped on a number.

"Ladybug, I was just about to call you. I was going to pick up lunch from the café. You know how much I love Josh's brisket sandwich."

"That's fine," she responded. "Just get me whatever you're having."

"Did you need something?"

"No, I was just checking to see when you'd be home. I miss you."

"I'll be there shortly."

"Tell Josh to make sure he checks behind Silas. I don't want any of my customers ever complaining about dirty silverware."

"I'll let him know."

"Ladybug, you sold the shop to Misty, remember?"

"Oh, yeah. That's right."

When she hung up, Eleanor burst into tears.

CHAPTER TWENTY-SEVEN

OMA WAS VISITING for the weekend.

"I'm so glad you're here, Mama."

"Misty, how are you doing really? I know how much you internalize things."

"I'm fine," she responded. "Moving here was a good choice for me. This is probably the first time in a long while that I've felt safe and at peace."

"How do you feel about John's death now?"

"I hate that he's not here, Mama. This isn't the way I wanted Talei to grow up, without her father. I just hoped he'd get it together." She paused a moment, then said, "There's something I've been wanting to ask you."

"Go ahead. You know you can ask me anything."

"Mama, did daddy ever hit you during your marriage?"

"No. Your father always had a temper and sometimes he was verbally abusive, but he never laid a hand on me."

"I promised myself that I would never marry

someone like him. I was so sure I knew the man I'd fallen in love with. John was such a sweetheart when we dated. Like Daddy, he had a bit of a temper, but he seemed to manage it well until we got married." Misty shook her head. "I was such a fool."

"John's father was a trigger for him. Y'all were fine until that man started interfering in your marriage."

"He never thought I was good enough for his son."

"He was wrong," Oma uttered. "You were too good for John Hayes."

"I dread the thought of having to deal with his parents, although his mother has been pretty nice since John's death."

"She doesn't want you to keep her grandchild away. You see John's sister doesn't have anything to do with them."

"Sherry didn't come to the funeral, but she did call me. She refuses to have her children anywhere near her father."

"He's nothing but a bully."

"I don't mind Talei spending time with her grandmother, but Elroy... I'm not so comfortable with him."

Later when Misty climbed into bed, she retrieved her journal from the nightstand and began to write.

Everybody keeps asking me how I'm dealing with John's death. I tell them I'm fine, but is that really the truth?

I haven't told anyone, but I feel like John's death is on me. It's my fault that he felt desperate enough to kidnap Talei. If I hadn't pushed for supervised visitation, he would probably still be alive.

When Talei asks about her daddy, there are days it's hard for me to look her in the face.

She misses him so much. How can I ever make this up to her?

How can I ever forgive myself for John's death?

I can't talk about this to anyone because they just won't understand. I didn't want anything bad to happen to John. I didn't want to fight with him over custody. I wanted our marriage to work, but I couldn't live with the man he had become. All I wanted was for John to get the help he needed so he could be a good father to Talei.

Elroy blames me for John's death. I refuse to give him the satisfaction of knowing that I blame myself, as well. I will never get the chance to tell you this, so I'll write it here:

John, I'm so sorry. I didn't want to hurt you, but I couldn't live with you hurting me. I feared that you would one day hurt our daughter. If

*you hadn't threatened to take Talei from me...
if you hadn't threatened my life... We wouldn't
have been in this space. You made me afraid
of you. I'm tired of being afraid. I don't want
to be a victim anymore. I want to live in peace
and without drama.*

*I hope that you have finally found the peace
that escaped you in life, John. I'm so sorry for
everything. I promise Talei will never forget
you. Leon has stepped up to be her godfather.
I can clearly see why you chose him. He's good
to us.*

THE NEXT MORNING, Eleanor woke up early. It
took a minute or so to recognize her surroundings. She eased out of bed and went to the bathroom. She heard the lawn mower and stole a
peek outside.

She watched Rusty as he mowed the grass, a
smile on her lips.

Fifteen minutes later, she strolled into the
kitchen to prepare breakfast. She hit a wrinkle
in her preparations because Eleanor was unsure of whether she'd already put in the right
amount of baking soda. She was making Belgian waffles for Rusty with fresh berries and a
homemade strawberry glaze.

"Why can't I remember something so simple?" Eleanor whispered. The feeling of frustration left a lingering effect.

"Good morning, Ladybug."

She pasted on a smile. "Rusty... What time did you wake up?"

"I got up around five thirty. I wanted to get that grass cut before it got real hot out there."

"For all your hard work, I was going to make you some Belgian waffles, but I'm having trouble remembering all the ingredients." Tears filled her eyes. "Rusty, I hate being this way."

He embraced her. "Honey, it's gonna be okay. The meds they're giving you will help slow down the progression. As for breakfast, I can help you with that."

"But you shouldn't have to, Rusty. I'm your wife. I'm not helpless," Eleanor stated. "I've made Belgian waffles for as long as I can remember."

"The truth is that I've always wanted to learn how to make them." Rusty placed his arms around her, whispering, "You know I love *cooking* with you."

"I don't know if I put in all the right ingredients," Eleanor said.

"It's fine. We can start over," Rusty responded. He pulled out his phone. "I'll find a recipe that's close to yours and we'll use that one. If it's not right, you can change it." He kissed her cheek. "Now stop crying, Ladybug. *We got this.*"

"I'm very lucky to have you in my life. I've always known that. I want to go to the café today," Eleanor announced. "I feel like I need to stay busy today."

"If you're sure you're up to it," Rusty responded. "Don't forget to take your medicine."

"I better get it now." She rose to her feet and left the dining room.

Eleanor returned a few minutes later with medication in hand. "If I don't take it now, I'll forget." She paused to look at him. "Rusty, I'm scared."

"I know, Ladybug. Just remember that you're not alone. You have me."

LEON WATCHED MISTY as she held the ball straight, her arms fully extended. Her right hand supported the ball underneath. She looked as if she knew what she was doing. He, on the other hand, hadn't played in a while but used to be on the bowling team with some of his co-workers.

Aware that his gaze had traveled from the back of her head downward to the curve of her hips, Leon forced his attention back to the game.

Misty released the ball, rolling a perfect strike. "Yes. Let's see if you can match that."

It was his turn.

His ball left three pins standing. "I guess not."

"It's okay, Leon," Misty murmured. "You can knock them down."

"I appreciate the encouragement."

She kissed him on the cheek. "I heard you were on a bowling team."

"Aunt Eleanor talks too much."

Misty chuckled.

Leon placed the bowling ball on the rack before drawing Misty into an embrace. He pressed his lips against hers, and then gently covered her mouth. Leon kissed the top of her nose, then her eyes, and finally, he returned his attention to her lips.

After they left the bowling alley, they went to Misty's condo.

She quickly prepared a simple fare of shrimp alfredo over pasta, a garden salad and garlic bread.

Misty watched him as he took a bite. "How is it?"

"Delicious," Leon responded.

She felt a warm glow go through her, prompting her to take several sips of her iced tea. Misty couldn't keep from peering at him throughout dinner. She'd never felt this way about any other man.

Swallowing hard, she forced those thoughts out of her mind.

Misty breathed a sigh of relief when Brittany brought Talei home.

CHAPTER TWENTY-EIGHT

ELEANOR WALKED OVER to the French doors leading to the patio and stared out. Rusty was at the grill making burgers and chicken. "Leon just arrived with Misty and Talei."

She was looking forward to spending the day with family and friends. It was something Eleanor hadn't done in a while. Before her symptoms appeared, she would often have gatherings on Sunday afternoons.

She gave the patio one last glance, then joined Leon in the kitchen. He was putting a bowl of potato salad in the refrigerator.

"Don't worry, Misty made it."

Eleanor chuckled. "Thank the Lawd…"

"Is there anything I can do to help?" Misty inquired.

"Rusty will probably need more burgers."

"I'll make them," Misty said. She quickly washed her hands, then reached into the bowl containing ground beef. She and Leon made small talk while forming the meat into patties.

"Thanks for having us over, Auntie."

"I'm so glad y'all could come," Eleanor said.

Talei skipped into the kitchen. "I want juice."

Misty smiled at her daughter. "Is that how you're supposed to ask?"

"May I have juice?"

"That's better."

Eleanor picked up a paper cup. "I have some apple juice, Talei."

"*Wado*, Miss Ellie."

Rusty's nephew and his family were the next to arrive.

Eleanor felt blissfully happy in this moment. She felt like herself before the memory loss. Before the diagnosis.

Rusty entered through the patio doors. He gave her a huge smile. "You look like you're having a good time."

"I am," she responded. "There's no confusion. I feel fine, Rusty. Maybe the medication is working." Eleanor gloried in this shared moment. "This is a perfect day."

LEON HADN'T HAD this much fun in a long time.

He played a couple of rounds of basketball with the guys while Misty and the other women sat around the pool chatting.

Eleanor strolled outside carrying a plate stacked with corn on the cob. She handed it to her husband.

Leon glanced around the yard, looking for Talei. He found her with the other kids kicking around a ball.

His heart sang with delight at the sound of her laughter.

Thirty minutes later, the game ended and the men, with T-shirts drenched in perspiration, dispersed.

"I'm going to take a quick shower," Leon told Misty. "I'll be back in a few."

When he returned, he found her and Talei seated at one of the picnic tables eating.

"We couldn't wait for you," Misty said. "Sorry."

"That's fine."

Leon fixed a plate, then walked over to join Misty and Talei. "I think my basketball days are over. My body feels like it's on fire."

"Did you stretch beforehand?"

"I did," Leon said. "I don't think it helped."

"I want chicken, Eon." She pointed to the drumstick on his plate.

He stuck his fork into the meat and put it on hers.

"Wado."

"This is such a beautiful day," Misty said. "We'd better enjoy it while we can before the weather starts to change."

Leon took a sip of his iced tea. "The fall weather is usually pretty mild."

He embraced her. "I don't care where we are as long as we're together."

Rusty found two decks of cards, prompting a discussion of who was good when it came to playing spades.

"You don't want none of this over here," Leon said with a grin. "Misty and I play well together. We don't lose."

"That's because you haven't played me and Sarah," Luke countered.

Rusty laughed. "Nephew, I don't know. When was the last time you played?"

"It doesn't matter," Misty said. "We got this."

Leon's features became more animated. "Yeah, I'm definitely the right man for this woman."

THE FOLLOWING WEEKEND, they decided to dine at a local Italian restaurant. Afterward, they were going to the park for the last outdoor concert of the year.

"I really like this side of you," Misty commented as she scanned her menu. She took a sip of her iced water.

He laughed. "I take it that you thought I was pretty boring."

"Not really," she replied. "No, I didn't think that. I felt like you were still grieving."

"Do you still feel that way?"

She met his gaze. "I feel like you're at the stage where you've accepted your wife's and child's deaths."

"I have," Leon confirmed. "They're gone, but it isn't the end of the world. When they died, it sure felt like it. I'm at the point where I know it's okay to move on with my life."

He picked up his menu and looked it over. "I think I'm having the chicken Marsala," he said. "Do you know what you want?"

"I'm in the mood for the shrimp scampi."

They gave the waiter their orders when he returned to the table.

"Misty, you don't have to worry about me. I did right by Vera and our child. I feel good about moving on with you."

"That's very sweet of you to say," Misty stated with a tender smile. "I was a little afraid of getting involved with someone else. I was concerned how Talei would be affected if things didn't work out for us."

"I will always be her godfather, Misty. However, I intend to make sure on my end that we work."

The waiter returned with their food on a tray.

Leon blessed the food.

Misty sampled her food. "This is delicious. I love it when I can taste the garlic and other spices in the scampi sauce."

"Mine is really good," he responded. "I love chicken Marsala."

She smiled. "Is that a hint?"

"Yes, it is," Leon answered. "This is like my favorite meal of all time."

Misty looked around the dining area. "It feels good being out on such a beautiful night. I'm excited about the concert. I can't wait to see Kem perform. I love all his music."

After signaling for the check a short time later, Leon inquired, "Are you ready to party?"

She awarded him a smile. "Definitely."

They left the restaurant and drove down the street to the park. There were cars everywhere, but Leon found an empty space a block away from the location.

He held Misty's hand as they walked.

"You were lucky to find that parking space. I thought we'd end up having to walk at least three or four blocks."

"I'm glad we left the restaurant when we did," Leon said. "Great timing."

At the park, Leon set up their chairs.

Misty settled in her seat. She closed her eyes, savoring the feel of the night air on her face while enjoying the music on the deejay's playlist. The concert wasn't due to start for another forty minutes.

Leon brought her hand up to his lips and placed a gentle kiss on it. "I can't believe that I found someone as wonderful as you."

She felt a warmth wash over her like waves.

Turning her to face him, Leon leaned over and kissed her softly on the lips. "I have been wanting to do this from the moment I arrived at your place to pick you up."

In response, Misty pulled his head down to hers. Their lips met and she felt buffeted by the winds of a gentle harmony.

Breaking their kiss, Leon said, "I love you."

His words caught Misty by surprise. Tears glittered in her eyes as she responded, "I love you, too."

CHAPTER TWENTY-NINE

MISTY FELT LIKE she was floating on a cloud. Her evening with Leon couldn't have been more perfect. Sharing delicious food and great music with the man she loved equaled the making of wonderful memories.

She checked on Talei when she got home, then had a glass of wine with Brittany.

"Thank you so much for watching her."

"We had a good time. She was showing me how to do the candy dance. At least I think that's what it was called."

Misty laughed. "She performs it at the pow-wows."

"We also did some shark dance, too." Brittany sat her glass down on the counter. "Girl, I'm tired."

They broke into laughter.

After Brittany left, Misty went upstairs to her room and showered.

She came out of the bathroom ten minutes later and checked her phone. Misty smiled when she read the sweet good-night text from Leon.

Tonight was perfect!

LEON WENT TO the cemetery to clean up around the graves of his parents and Vera. He also wanted to put out some fresh flowers. After pulling all the weeds and tossing them in a garbage bag, he took a seat on the cement bench at the foot of his wife's grave.

"I can't put into words how much I miss you, Vee. Not a day goes by that I don't think of you and our daughter. I wanted to let you know that I finally have the strength to move on. I told you about Misty... Well, we've been seeing each other, and things are good between us. I love her, Vee, and I'm happy."

He sat there, taking in the warmth of the sunlight. "I feel like you're looking down on me and smiling. Probably giving me your *I told you so* look."

"I had a feeling I'd find you here."

Leon glanced over his shoulder. "Auntie, you had a mind to come to visit the family, too?"

"I did," she responded. "The weather's nice today. I figured I'd come put some fresh flowers on Walter's and my parents' graves, then I saw you sitting over here."

Eleanor sat down beside him. "It gets a little easier with each passing day."

"Yes, it does," Leon said. "Spending time with Misty has helped. I still grieve, but it's not as intense as it was before."

"Do you still feel like you're cheating on Vee?"

He nodded. "A little. I know she's gone and it's okay for me to date in my heart—I just need my mind to fully catch up."

"Why don't we get out of this cemetery," she suggested. "Let's go grab some lunch."

Leon stood up, then assisted Eleanor to her feet. "I think we should hire a groundskeeper. I'd like to have flowers on all the graves. Maybe we can plant a garden over there near Polk's grave."

"I agree," Eleanor said. "That's a good idea."

"Where would you like to eat?" Leon asked.

"I'm in the mood for seafood."

He chuckled. "You always want seafood. That's not surprising."

The only vehicle parked on the street was Leon's truck. "You walked here?"

"Yeah," Eleanor answered. "It's so nice out."

He unlocked his truck and opened the passenger side door.

Eleanor climbed inside.

They drove to an oceanfront restaurant.

"Thank you, son" she murmured, taking a seat in the chair Leon pulled out for her.

He walked around the table with the vibrant red tablecloth and eased into a chair facing her. Leon picked up his menu. "I always have a hard time deciding what I want to eat whenever I come here. Everything is delicious."

"I can tell you and Misty are becoming close," Eleanor said. "You're falling in love with her."

He gave a slight nod. "Not falling, Auntie. I'm in love with her."

"I'm relieved to hear this. I had hoped this was the case and not because you want to take care of her and Talei out of loyalty to John."

"I think it may have started that way," Leon confessed. "I really have strong feelings for Misty. It's crazy, but whenever I'm with her, the world feels different. I'm sure that makes no sense at all."

Eleanor smiled. "Actually, it makes a lot of sense. That's what happens when you fall in love."

Leon laid down his menu. "Misty told me that she loves me, too."

"You seem surprised."

"I guess I shouldn't be," he said. "I know she cared something for me, but I wasn't a hundred percent sure that it was love."

MISTY SHOWED BRITTANY the cake she'd designed for the historical society gala taking place tomorrow night. "What do you think?"

"It's beautiful. Meredith is gonna love it."

She closed the box back up. "Thanks for the

referral. Miss Eleanor said this is the first year that we were asked to do the cake."

Lowering her voice, Brittany said, "Meredith broke up with the guy who provided the cakes in previous years."

"Oh, wow."

They sat down at an empty table in the bakery area.

Brittany chuckled. "I take it that things are still good between you and Leon?"

"They are," Misty stated. "Our relationship has hit another level."

"Another level...meaning?"

"We love each other."

"So, you've said the actual words?"

She nodded. "Yes."

"Leon is one of the good ones."

"That's the biggest relief," Misty said. "After all the bad choices I've made in my past relationships... It's great to have someone so nice in my life."

"He's got you glowing, that's for sure."

"I feel really good about us. Life is so drama-free and I love it."

"Well, all the bad stuff is over now," Brittany said. "Enjoy."

Misty smiled. "I intend to do so. Now we're supposed to be talking about your wedding cake. Do you know what you want?"

"Nothing too fancy," Brittany said. "Rick and I both want carrot cake—it's our favorite. I was thinking that we could have cupcakes for the guests that may want something different."

"I like that," Misty said. "Do you want the frosting to match your wedding cake?"

"Yes. And can we have flowers instead of the bride-and-groom topper?"

"Sure. You can have whatever you choose. I can create them, or you can have your florist create a topper with the wedding flowers. I'll need it the day before the ceremony." Misty quickly typed in notes on her iPad.

"I'll see her when I leave here, so I'll get back to you on that," Brittany responded. "You know I want you to be in the wedding. I'd like you to be a bridesmaid. My sister is my maid of honor."

Misty was genuinely touched by her offer. "I'd be honored to be a part of your wedding. Thank you."

"Girl, thank *you*. We're not having a big wedding. I want to keep it small and intimate with three in my wedding party only because Rick has three brothers. Some of my friends are seriously tripping and arguing about who should be in *my* wedding. I told them to be happy that they're getting an invite." Brittany shook her head sadly. "Unnecessary drama."

Misty chuckled. "Wow."

"Oh, and I want Talei to be my flower girl."

"Oh, my goodness! She is gonna love that, Britt. We won't be able to convince her that she's not a princess."

"March can't come quick enough for me. I'm so ready to become a wife."

Smiling, Misty nodded in understanding. "I loved being married—it just wasn't to the right man. I haven't given up on love everlasting though. Even if it turns out that Leon and I aren't meant to be, he's given me a peek into what it looks like. I'll always be grateful to him because of that."

CHAPTER THIRTY

When Leon and Misty entered the ballroom, they were immediately enveloped in a warm haze of music and happy voices. A harpist played something slow and lovely in the background beneath a strong undercurrent of conversation that rose and fell like waves crashing against the shore.

There was a sea of people dressed in tuxes and bright, colorful dresses roaming around talking and taking photographs. Leon saw it all, yet the woman on his arm kept his full attention. Misty stood out. Each time he looked at her, he felt a strange mixture of calm and excitement churning through his bloodstream.

Misty, dressed in a deep purple gown, did one final check on the cake. She wanted it to be perfect for the gala. Her hair was a tumble of soft curly tendrils that called out to him to run his fingers through their silkiness. Leon inhaled the light floral perfume Misty wore, flavoring his very breath with her scent.

Fresh flowers in vases and small plants graced every tabletop, and the soft lighting reflecting off the mauve wallpaper created a magical glow.

"You need to relax," Leon said. "The cake is beautiful, and it looks delicious. Half the people in here have tasted your baked goods. You have nothing to worry about."

"Thank you for saying that," Misty responded. "I'm just nervous because this is the first time they commissioned us to do the cake." Her gaze traveled from his head to his shoes. "Oh, my… You look so handsome."

"And you're stunning in that dress." In truth, Misty was electrifying.

Smiling, she lifted her chin, tossed her hair away from her face and placed her hand in his. "We should find our table."

Leon looked down into Misty's sparkling brown eyes.

He was in deep trouble. His feelings for her were intensifying so much that the very air around him seemed electrified.

She picked up her wineglass and took a sip. "You do realize that you're staring at me."

"I'm sorry," Leon responded. "I don't mean to stare but I can't help it. You're a beautiful woman." Everything took on a clean brightness when she was with him. Each time Misty smiled at him, the pull was stronger.

They made small talk with the other guests at the table while dining on filet mignon, baby asparagus and large, fluffy baked potatoes.

"Now you're the one staring," he said, feeling the heat of her gaze on him.

"Guilty," Misty murmured.

"Would you like to dance?" Leon asked when the deejay put on a popular R&B song.

"I'd love to," she responded as she rose to her feet.

Swaying to the music, Misty took his hand and led him to the dance floor. "I love dancing."

Leon smiled. "I know."

They danced through two songs, then returned to their table.

All around them, people were enjoying themselves, leaning toward each other, smiling, laughing, talking. The clink of glassware and the waves of conversation became a white noise pulsating in the background, but Leon had eyes and ears only for Misty.

He stared into her eyes and resisted the urge to reach out and touch her face. There was so much Leon wanted to say to Misty, but it would have to wait until later when they were alone.

The music called out to them once more, prompting their return to the dance floor.

AT THE END of the night, Leon parked at the curb outside her condo.

Even in the moonlight, he could see the colorful flower beds nestled around the grounds.

Leon's gaze stayed on Misty as they made their way to her home and she unlocked the door.

He walked in behind her, taking in the eclectic decor and artistic pieces of Native American art displayed around the living room.

When Misty hit a switch, pools of golden light fell across the hardwood floors.

Leon removed his tuxedo jacket and draped it across one of the dining room chairs before joining her on the dark green leather couch.

"You really mean the world to me, Misty," he murmured without thought. "I wasn't expecting this. I never thought I'd feel this way again. I didn't think it was possible."

Leon pulled her in close and kissed her, then said, "You and Talei are an important part of my life. Misty, I'm not looking for something recreational. I loved being a husband and I wanted to be a father. I want all that again." Leon paused a moment. "I hope I'm not scaring you. I'm not real good at this, but I want to make sure we're on the same page."

Misty smiled. "We're definitely on the same page, Leon. I'd never really given much thought to the idea of getting married again...until I met you." She leaned into his embrace, enjoying the feel of his arms around her.

"Do you have any plans for tomorrow?" Misty inquired.

"Nothing concrete. What's up?"

"Clara called me earlier and asked if I'd bring Talei for a visit tomorrow. I told her I'd come, but I would like you to join us."

"What time do you want to leave?" Leon asked.

"I was thinking around nine in the morning."

"I'll be here."

She smiled. "*Wado*, my sweet Leon."

"*Hawa*."

LEON GLANCED OVER at Misty and asked, "Ready?"

"I'm as ready as I'll ever be," she responded. Biting her lip, Misty looked away. She wasn't worried about Clara, but Elroy... Misty would've preferred to have avoided him at all costs.

"I ready," Talei interjected from her seat.

"Let's hit the road, then."

They weren't down the road a good thirty minutes before Talei was sleeping.

Amused, Leon glanced up at the rearview mirror. "That didn't take long."

"Thank you for coming with me," Misty said. "I didn't want to deal with Elroy alone."

"I understand," Leon said. "When I first met Elroy, I felt like he couldn't stand me. It took a minute, but he eventually warmed up."

"Well, he hates me," Misty stated. "From the moment John introduced me to his family, that man never had a kind word to say about me. I'm to the point that I don't care how he feels about me personally—this is about my daughter."

He wasn't going to let Elroy attack Misty any longer. Leon fully intended to speak up on her behalf. He hoped it wouldn't come to that, but he was prepared if it did.

They talked, sang along with the radio, then talked some more, but the closer they got to Orangeburg, the quieter Misty became.

"You okay?" Leon inquired.

"I'm just bracing myself mentally for whatever Elroy has to say. I haven't spoken to him since that day at the funeral home. Clara and I communicate regarding Talei. But since I'm going to be at his house, I'm sure Elroy won't hold his tongue."

Leon parked in front of the Hayes' ranch-style house.

Misty got out of the vehicle, saying, "Here goes…"

She gently woke Talei. "Hey, sweetie. We're at Paw Paw's house. You ready to see Grandma and Paw Paw?"

Talei nodded, then stretched and yawned.

Clara opened the front door. "Leon, hello. We didn't expect to see you."

She stepped aside to let them enter.

"I asked him to come with me," Misty interjected. "I hope that's okay."

"Of course," she responded. "C'mon in. He is always welcome here."

Clara led them to the den. "Make yourselves at home."

"Looks like you two have gotten mighty close," Elroy stated when he walked into the room.

Misty stirred uneasily in the chair. Before she could respond, Leon said, "We're dating."

Talei ran over to him. "Paw Paw."

"Hey there, baby girl. I've missed you something fierce."

"Would y'all like something to drink?" Clara inquired, breaking the tense silence that enveloped the room.

"I'm fine," Misty and Leon said in unison.

"I just want to make sure I understand what's going on. Are you two involved?"

"Why is that important, Clara?" Misty asked. She and Leon weren't doing anything wrong and she refused to allow her ex-in-laws to make her feel otherwise.

"I'm sorry if I'm being intrusive."

"Don't you apologize," Elroy uttered. "It's our right to know who's hanging around our grandchild."

Leon opened his mouth to speak, but Misty gave a quick shake of her head. It wasn't worth the drama. "Clara, the answer is yes as Leon already told you. The two of us are dating."

Elroy muttered something under his breath, then abruptly left the room.

Misty sighed, clasped her hands together, and stared at Clara.

"He's not been feeling well lately," Clara offered as an excuse. "That's why I asked you to bring Talei for a visit. I thought seeing her would cheer him up."

Elroy returned, cold fury in his eyes. "How can you do this to John? He was your friend."

"Do what?" Leon asked, keeping his voice low.

"Is that why you moved to that island? Elroy accused Misty. "To be with *him*? I told my son you were no good."

Clara pulled Talei close to her. "Don't do this in front of this child."

"She's right," Leon stated, rising to his full height. "You and I can have this conversation outside." He'd had enough of Elroy's rudeness.

"Leon, it's okay," Misty said. Her anxiety level increased with each passing moment.

"Sweetheart, it's not okay and it stops today."

CHAPTER THIRTY-ONE

WHEN THEY WERE OUTSIDE, Leon said, "Tell me something. Elroy, how can you treat the mother of your grandchild like that? What did she do to you?"

He looked indignant. "You may have been John's friend, but you have no right to talk to me like this."

"I'm making it my right. Look around you. Look at what your anger has cost you. Your daughter left and never looked back. She won't even bring her family around you. John wanted to leave but he didn't want to break your heart."

Elroy frowned. "What are you talking about?"

"John never wanted to leave school, but he felt like you'd given him no choice—you threatened to cut him off financially." Leon paused a moment before saying, "You know he hated being a truck driver."

"He was weak."

"John was loyal to you," Leon countered. "But you never appreciated him. All he ever wanted was your approval."

"If that's true, then he should've listened to me when I told him to stay away from that girl. Because of Misty, my son is dead."

"What is your problem with her?"

"She just wasn't right for John. Now she's running after you. I guess you turned out to be the *best man* after all."

Leon clenched his lips together and struggled to maintain his calm.

"You know I always thought you were smart—"

"I'm not going to let you finish that thought," Leon interjected. "One thing you need to remember right now—I'm not John. What I do is my business and you have nothing to say about it. Elroy, I've done my best to remain neutral in this situation and I've tried to see both sides... You're blowing your chance to have a relationship with your granddaughter. Instead of bashing her mother to me, you should be inside that house enjoying time with Talei."

After a moment, Elroy said, "I'm not going to be disrespected on my property."

"And I'm not going to stay here and allow you to disrespect Misty. We're leaving." Leon headed back inside the house.

He entered and looked at Clara. "I'm afraid we need to head back to the island."

Tears sprang into Clara's eyes. "Noo... Please don't leave."

"Let 'em go," Elroy yelled from the outside.

"I'm sorry, Clara. This is for the best." Misty sighed, picked up Talei and followed Leon to the front door.

Leon wrapped an arm around her.

Standing a few feet away, Elroy suddenly collapsed to the ground.

Leon sprang into action. "Call the paramedics." He glanced over his shoulder at Misty, who was buckling Talei in her seat.

Clara came running out of the house. "What's wrong with him?"

Elroy looked as if he wanted to say something, but he couldn't get the words out.

Leon glanced over at Clara. "I think he's had a stroke. The paramedics are on the way."

Elroy was transported to the hospital with Clara by his side.

"He may have had a stroke," Leon said, following behind the ambulance.

When Misty didn't respond, he glanced over at her. "Did you hear me?"

"Yeah, I heard you. I'm just trying to remove the image of Elroy on the ground like that. I had to shield Talei from seeing him."

"He was getting so worked up over nothing."

"It was a mistake coming here," Misty said. "I should've known better."

"This isn't your fault. You know that, right?"

Misty didn't respond.

"Where Paw Paw?" Talei asked when they arrived at the hospital.

"He's with the doctor," Clara said.

"He sick?"

"He's just getting a checkup, sweetie," Misty interjected. "Your Paw Paw is fine."

"Why would you tell her that?" Clara asked in a loud whisper. "We have no idea what's wrong and if he'll come out of it okay."

"I don't want to traumatize my daughter. The last time she was in a hospital, John died."

Clara walked over to a nearby window and stared out.

Leon took Talei and sat down in the waiting area.

Misty stood beside Clara. "I'm sorry about all this. I don't think it was a good idea for us to come."

"I invited *you*. I thought seeing Talei would make Elroy feel better. Since John's death, the business has suffered. We keep losing drivers and contracts... He's been under a tremendous amount of stress," Clara wiped away a tear. "I tried to get him to let me help. I grew up around trucks. I did all my daddy's paperwork for him until I married Elroy." She glanced over her shoulder at Leon, then said, "I don't think he should've come with you. This was the last thing my husband needed."

"Leon and I have nothing to hide, Clara."

After a moment, she responded, "You're right. Of course, Misty. Leon is a good man and after what my son put you through... Well, you deserve to be happy. It's just that Leon was John's friend."

"You're entitled to feel how you feel, but it has nothing to do with me," Misty stated.

Clara glared at her. "John always said you were selfish. He said that you only think of yourself and what *you* want. I've tried to give you the benefit of the doubt, but I'm beginning to see just how right he was about you."

Misty wasn't about to make a scene, so she walked away with uttering a response.

"Leon, I think we should just head home."

He stood up. "Is everything okay between you two?"

"I just need to get out of here."

Misty was quiet most of the ride back to Polk Island.

"Are you okay?" Leon asked.

"I'm... I've just been thinking."

"About?" he prompted.

"I can't do this—any of it," Misty said. "All I want is to live a peaceful life, Leon. *That's it*. I'm not going to have it as long as I have to deal with Elroy and Clara. As long as we're together, they are not going to let me live in peace. I need to be completely free of my past and the hell that came with it. Unfortunately, this means that you and I can't see each other either."

"Because of my relationship with your ex-husband, we can't be together—that's what you're saying. Right?"

Misty ached with an inner pain. "I think it's b-best." Her voice broke miserably. Clara's words had wounded her deeply. Maybe she was being selfish. She hadn't contemplated how being with Leon would disturb them. Misty hadn't considered how taking Talei and moving away would affect John.

She wiped away her tears. "I'm sorry but I just can't do this, Leon."

"I'm at a loss here."

"I have to get Talei in the house," Misty said. "I'm sorry."

MISTY PUT TALEI to bed.

Inside her room, she removed her clothes and padded barefoot into the bathroom to take a shower.

Warm tears streamed down her face, merging with the water from the showerhead.

Run?
Panic?

Escape?

Why was that always her first instinct?

Misty shook off the questions. *I did the right thing. I can't live with that type of turmoil in my life. Clara was right about my being selfish. I have to consider everyone in this situation. As much as I care for Leon, he's an innocent partner in my turbulent relationship with the Hayeses. I just hope one day we can get past this—maybe even be friends.*

One thing was abundantly clear. Shadows still clung to her heart. The ones Misty thought she'd banished with counseling, determination and the new life she'd built.

She picked up her phone and saw that she had a text from Clara informing her that Leon was right. Elroy had a stroke but fortunately it left little effect to his body.

Misty sent a response saying she was relieved to hear that he would recover. She couldn't think of anything else to say so she left it at that.

Sleep did not come easy for her. Every time she closed her eyes, she saw the hurt and disappointment registered on Leon's face. The last thing she ever wanted was to break his heart. Her selfishness taunted her.

"THANK YOU FOR letting me know, Clara." Leon's throat ached with defeat.

Leon laid his phone on the wireless charger, then got up to remove his clothes.

He had chosen to love again. To hope again.

Then the waves of heartbreak came crashing all around him. He'd allowed Misty into his life and now she was gone.

Frustrated, Leon tossed a pillow across the room.

He had no idea what Clara had said to Misty at the house, but it clearly upset her, and he couldn't get her to tell him anything. Before today, they could talk about any and everything. This time she just shut down completely.

Her rejection hurt, wounding him to the core of his soul. Misty wanted out of their relationship and there was nothing he could do about it.

He told himself that it was best that it happened now rather than later.

Leon's heart ached as it yearned for the woman he thought he'd one day marry. He'd allowed himself to believe that he could have a second chance at love.

He thought about Talei and felt another throbbing ache. Leon wasn't going to abandon his goddaughter—he just had to find a way to erect a wall around his heart where Misty was concerned.

He vowed to never give her a chance to hurt him again.

MISTY HIRED TWO part-time employees to help out in the shop. She had three weddings on the schedule, an anniversary celebration and several other events requiring cakes and other baked goods. She planned to expand their catering menu to include sandwiches and other specialties.

At two o'clock, Misty left the shop to pick up Talei. They were going to visit with Eleanor. Although she was the new owner of the Polk Island Bakery & Café, Misty continued to seek guidance from her.

Eleanor embraced Talei, then Misty. "I'm so glad to see y'all. I made some lunch for us."

Lunch turned out to be parmesan chicken, wild rice and mixed greens. She'd even made a cheesecake for dessert.

Misty said, "You didn't have to go through all this trouble but thank you."

"It wasn't no trouble. I try to keep busy, but I can't stand being in this house all day long."

They sat down at the table to eat.

"Miss Eleanor, you're supposed to be a lady of leisure."

She chuckled. "That just sounds boring to me." Eleanor paused a moment, then asked, "Have you seen Rusty? I thought he was in the yard working. I want him to eat while the food's hot."

"I think he's at work, Miss Eleanor. I saw his car there when we were driving here."

"Oh, that's right. I can be so forgetful at times."

Misty smiled. "I have days like that, too."

"Rusty has me working on puzzles. He says it helps improve your memory."

"I'm going to have to give it a try."

"How's the shop?"

"It's going well," Misty said. "I just hired two part-time employees, but to be honest, we all miss you not being there."

"Maybe I could come in a couple days a week to help out. Just to get me out of the house. I hate being here alone all the time."

Misty smiled. "That would be great."

The doorbell sounded.

"Would you like me to get it?" Misty asked.

Eleanor nodded. "I'm not expecting anyone."

Misty opened the front door to find Leon standing there.

He seemed just as surprised to see her.

"Hello, Leon."

When he looked at her, she could see the pain reflected in his gaze. "I didn't expect to see you. I came to see my aunt."

"Talei and I stopped by for a visit." Misty stepped back so he could enter.

"I'll just come back later." He spoke calmly, with no light in his eyes, no smile of tenderness.

"Leon, you don't have to leave. It doesn't have to be this distance between us. We're still friends, I hope."

"I can't have this conversation right now."

"Can we talk later?"

Leon eyed her. "You made a decision about us without talking it through with me, Misty. This was *your* decision. We both have to live with it." He glanced down at his watch. "Tell my aunt I'll be back in an hour."

Her throat closed as she watched him walk away, shoulders squared, back straight—a picture of strength.

Added to her disappointment was a feeling of guilt.

When Misty returned to the table, Eleanor said, "I take it things are a little bumpy between you two."

"It's worse than that," she said. "We're not seeing each other anymore. I ended it because I thought it was the best thing to do."

Eleanor eyed her. "You're not looking like you really believe that. You love him, and I know he loves you, Misty. Don't make the same mistake I did for years. Work it out."

Her eyes filled with tears. "It's too late for that."

Smiling, Eleanor said, "It's never too late for love."

CHAPTER THIRTY-TWO

"A few of us are going out tonight," Charles announced when their shift ended. "Care to join us?"

"Not tonight," Leon responded. "Next time, though. Right now, I'm not in the mood to be around people." All pleasure left him the night Misty ended their relationship. He needed more time for his raw emotions to heal from the shock.

"Trouble in paradise?"

"I don't know what to call it, truthfully." He shrugged. "But it is what it is…" His attempts to figure out how he and Misty had come to be in this space left his thoughts painful and jagged.

"Leon, I don't know what happened between you and Misty, but don't give up on the relationship. You two are good for each other. And that little girl… She adores you."

"That's the hard part," Leon confessed. "I miss Talei."

"What about her mom?" Charles asked. "Do you miss her, too?"

"I miss them both."

"Maybe Misty got scared."

"She wanted out and it was after she had a conversation with John's mother."

"I'm sure they're not happy about her moving on with their son's best friend," Charles stated.

"You're right about that, but I can't understand why Misty would suddenly start caring about what they think."

"Leon, I have a feeling she's going to have a change of heart once she has a chance to think things through."

His life was once again a bitter battle and his sense of loss went beyond the hurt he felt. "I opened myself up once to her, Charles. I'm not going to make that mistake a second time."

"Are you really going to give up so easily on her?"

"Look how easy it was for her to give up on me," Leon replied in sinking tones.

THE NEXT DAY, Eleanor spent most of the morning observing Misty. She'd never seen her look so sad.

She called Leon and invited him to have lunch with her. "I'm at the shop."

"What are you doing there?"

"I'm not one for being home all the time," Eleanor said. "I come here three days a week just to get out of the house."

"I'll be there at noon."

"See you then, son."

When Leon arrived, Eleanor gestured for him to join her in a booth near the huge window in the front of the shop. "I know I have trouble with my memory, but one thing I'm pretty clear on right now is that something's going on between you and Misty. You want to tell me what happened?"

"I wish I could, Auntie. I don't fully understand it myself."

"Is it fixable?"

"Both people in a relationship have to want it to work."

"You love her?"

"I do," Leon said. "I never thought I'd ever feel this way again. To be honest, I wasn't sure I wanted to love another woman like this. I took the leap and now it's bitten me in the behind."

"Son, I can't believe you're giving up so easily. Misty loves you, too. Y'all have something worth fighting for. You're letting your fears get in the way."

Eleanor rose to her feet. "I almost forgot. I need to make another lemon pound cake. We sold the last one earlier."

"Auntie, you don't have to worry about that,"

Leon said gently. "You sold the shop to Misty, remember?"

She wore a confused look on her face. "I did?"

"Yes, ma'am. You wanted to spend more time with Rusty. I hear you're going to Hawaii in a couple of weeks. Let's order some lunch. They have some new items on the menu."

"That's right," she murmured. "We're going on a cruise to Hawaii."

"Have you started packing yet?"

Eleanor chuckled. "No. I have to make a list of everything we're gonna need. It's been a while since I was on a cruise ship."

"If you'd like, we can get started on that list right now," Leon suggested. "I can tell you right now that you need to make sure you pack your medications."

"You sound like Rusty." Eleanor pulled out a small notebook and a pen.

MISTY TOOK TALEI to Atlanta for the Labor Day weekend to see her grandmother. She needed some time away from the island.

"Honey, there's something I need to tell you," Waverly said when they arrived.

Concerned, Misty asked, "What is it? Are you okay?"

"My mother's fine," a voice said from behind her.

Shocked, she turned around to face her father.

"Hello, Misty."

Waverly took Talei by the hand and led her into the house, saying, "Nana's got some lunch for you."

"You gonna say something to your daddy?"

"No, I'm not. I don't have anything to say to you." The disdain in her voice was ill-concealed.

She heard his quick intake of breath before he said, "You owe me a measure of respect."

Misty burst into a short laugh. "*Respect?* Mike, I don't *owe* you anything. I lived in fear because of you. You talked to my mother like she was nothing and you disrespected her with other women until she finally had the good sense to leave you. You were nothing more than an alcoholic and cheater. What is there to respect?"

He flinched at her words but recovered quickly. "I'm not that person anymore."

"You kept your family away from me," Misty uttered, her breath burning in her throat. "You cut me out of your life."

"No, your mother did that," Mike stated. "She didn't want any part of us."

Misty eyed him. "That's not true and you know it. What we're not going to do is lie about what happened. If you have truly changed, tell the truth."

He looked taken aback by her response.

"You wanted to hurt my mom—that's why you shut us out." Shrugging, Misty said, "It doesn't matter anymore because we survived, Mike. We made it in spite of *you*."

"Why are you coming around now?" he asked. "What do you want from my mother?"

"I don't want anything other than a relationship with my grandmother."

"Misty, I admit I had some problems in the past, but I'm not that man anymore."

"I'm sure your family's very happy about that," she countered icily.

"I came here to make amends. I've missed you, Misty."

She waved off his declaration. "I don't believe that."

"Please hear me out."

"Mike, what else is there really to say? I'm a grown woman with a child of my own. I don't need a daddy now."

"Let me start with the admission that I was a terrible husband and father. I drank too much. I hurt your mom—"

Misty interrupted him by interjecting, "You humiliated my mother."

"Yes, I was wrong. I need you to understand

that I've changed. I've been sober for over twenty years."

"Congratulations," she said tersely.

"I'm sorry for what I did to you and your mom. It is my hope that one day you'll find it in your heart to forgive me."

Misty didn't respond.

"My family is here with me. I want you to meet Jennifer and your siblings. Maybe talking to them will convince you that I'm no longer the monster you believe I am."

Arms folded across her chest, Misty responded, "I can't make any promises, Mike." She wasn't going to allow him to manipulate her into just believing his words. It was about action—she'd learned that from her marriage to John.

"Fair enough."

"I know it's hard to believe, but your daddy is telling the truth," Waverly said in a low whisper. "He is a changed man."

Misty glanced over her shoulder to find Waverly standing in the doorway.

"Grandmother, it remains to be seen. I don't just want to hear about it."

"I can't prove it to you if you won't give me a chance," Mike stated.

A girl who appeared to be in her late teens walked out of the house.

"Misty, I'm Sierra…your sister. I've been wanting to meet you for a while."

Mike and his mother left them alone on the porch to talk.

They sat down on the swing. "He told you about me?"

"Yeah, he did, but last night was the first time he told us about all the horrible things he did to you and your mother."

"I have to be honest with you, Sierra. I don't trust Mike and I'm not sure I ever will."

"I can understand why. It may take some time."

Misty eyed her sibling. "How was he as a father?"

"He's good to me and Michael. For me, it's really hard to reconcile the father I have to the man he used to be."

"As you know it's the reverse for me. I will just have to see what happens from this point forward."

"I'm hoping you and I will be able to have a relationship regardless. I've always wanted a sister."

"Of course. I want to get to know you better, Sierra."

"Talei is adorable," she said. "I can't believe I have a little niece."

"How old are you?" Misty inquired.

"I'm twenty," she responded. "Michael is eighteen."

"Are you in college?"

Sierra nodded. "I'm in school at UNC Greensboro."

"What are you studying?"

"Psychology. I want to be a psychiatrist."

Misty chuckled. "Sign me up for the friends and family rate."

Sierra laughed. "From the way you handled our dad, you're good."

Mike returned with a woman and a teenage boy.

"This is my mom, Jennifer," Sierra said, making the introduction. "And our brother, Michael."

Smiling, Misty responded, "It's nice to meet you both."

Michael gave her a hug. "*Osiyo*. I read that was the way to say hello in Cherokee. Did I pronounce it correctly?"

"It was perfect," she murmured.

"It's such a pleasure to finally meet you, as well," Jennifer said. "You're very beautiful, Misty. I saw pictures of you when you were little. You were a beauty even then."

"How long have you known about me?"

"About a year after I met your father."

"So, you were okay with the way he just disappeared from my life?"

"Misty…" Mike began.

"No," Jennifer interjected. "It's a fair question. Misty, I've been on Mike for years to reconnect with you. It was the one thing we've always disagreed on."

"I was afraid you'd reject me," Mike confessed. "I was ashamed to face you, Misty. That's the truth."

In that instance, she believed him. His eyes were glittering ovals of shame and regret.

"I'd like to speak to my dad in private, please."

When they were alone, she said, "Mike, you have a beautiful family."

"They're your family, too."

"True and because of you, I've missed out on so much with them. However, I'm really grateful to finally have the chance to get to know all of them. Thank you for coming here today."

"I hope you mean that, Misty. I can't change the past, but I really would like a second chance with you. I'd like to be a part of my granddaughter's life. She's so beautiful."

"Talei lost her father a few months ago."

"My mom told me. I'm so sorry."

"I want to have a life of peace," Misty stated. "I'll give you that second chance, but I'm telling you now—any sign of the old you… I'm gone. I'm not that little scared girl anymore."

"I know it doesn't matter but I'm very proud of the woman that you've become."

Talei ran out of the house. "Mommy…"

"Hey, sweetie, I'm right here." Misty picked her up. "I want you to meet my daddy. This is…"

"Grandpa if that's alright with you."

"This is Grandpa."

"Gandpaw," she repeated.

"So, what do you say to him?" Misty asked.

Grinning, Talei said, "*Oseeyo*, Gandpaw."

He smiled. "*Osiyo*, my beautiful granddaughter." A lone tear slid down his face. "I am truly sorry for everything I've done, Misty."

"We're not going to live in the past. We have this chance to start over and I'd like to do that. But I have to be honest. I'm gonna have to work hard on forgiving you. I'm just not there yet."

"I understand completely." He kissed Talei on the cheek. "I'm warning you now. I'm gonna spoil this little girl."

She gave a short laugh. "She's already spoiled."

CHAPTER THIRTY-THREE

"I SAW MY DAD, Miss Eleanor," Misty announced when she returned to work on Tuesday. "We spent the weekend getting to know one another."

"I guess it was bound to happen with that being his mama's house and all. How do you feel about him now?"

"He's not the same man I grew up fearing," Misty said. "He seemed truly repentant. I told him I'd give him a second chance."

"Good for you," Eleanor responded. "It was the right thing to do."

"I'm cautiously optimistic."

"I would be too, sugar. We have to forgive, but we don't have to be blind to reality."

"I also met my siblings," Misty announced. "I have a brother and a sister."

Eleanor grinned. "You seem happy about it."

"I am. I never wanted to be an only child. And I'm glad Talei has an aunt and uncle on my side of the family. John's sister has nothing to do with his family."

"I'm glad to see things working out for you, Misty."

"Everything is great except with Leon. Miss Eleanor, I messed up big-time with him and I don't know if I can fix it. I thought we could at least try to be friends."

"Give him some space, sugar. Leon will come around."

"I hope so," Misty responded. "I really miss him."

Eleanor slipped out of the booth. "Time sure flies. It's almost time for the lunch crowd to come rushing in."

"Everything's ready, Miss Eleanor. Just sit and relax."

"The shop won't run itself."

"Miss Eleanor... Remember you sold the shop to me," Misty said. "You don't have to worry about anything. The staff here is great."

Eleanor looked confused. "What are you talking about? I sold my shop?"

"Yes, ma'am."

Rusty walked in, humming softly.

Misty gestured for him to join them.

He greeted his wife with a kiss. "Hey, Ladybug."

"Rusty, did I sell the shop?"

He sat down at the table. "Yes, you did. With

your health, you thought it best to turn it over to Misty. She's done a great job, too."

Eleanor smiled. "I remember now… I'm sorry, Misty."

"No need to apologize."

"You're really doing a fine job. I was right to sell this place to you."

When Rusty excused himself to go to the restroom, Eleanor said, "I'm scared this disease is progressing."

"Why do you say that?"

"I've been having some difficulty writing a simple check. I have to have Rusty review it to make sure it's the right amount and date. Some days I can't even plan a meal. I didn't even remember that it was Labor Day weekend, Misty."

"Have you shared any of this with Rusty?"

Eleanor nodded. "He's such a sweet and patient man. He makes time to go grocery shopping with me or he'll do it alone. He always offers to help with the cooking. It just makes me sad that I'm not the wife I want to be for him. I feel so useless." Her eyes teared up.

Misty reached over and took her hand. "Miss Eleanor, you're anything but useless. You're still that amazing woman I met when I came here looking to relocate and find a job. You're not going to let this disease take over your life— fight back."

"What if I get to the point where I can't fight anymore?"

"Then we will all fight for you."

"THANKS FOR COMING to my birthday celebration," Lizzie said. "My family enjoyed meeting you. I talk about you all the time—they were beginning to think I'd made you up."

"I appreciate you inviting me," Leon said. "Otherwise, I would've spent the day on my couch binge-watching Netflix."

"I heard that you and Misty broke up. I don't get it. You're a good man. Any woman would be lucky to have you."

Leon smiled through his confusion. He and Lizzie had worked together for two years and he considered her a friend, but from the way she was looking at him right now, he wondered if she was interested in something more.

"I've always liked you, Leon. I never said anything because I didn't think you were ready to start dating..."

"Lizzie, you're my friend and we work together."

"You don't date your coworkers."

"I don't," Leon confirmed. "Besides, I still have feelings for Misty."

Smiling, Lizzie responded, "I hope things won't be weird between us now."

"They won't. I take it as a compliment."

"If Misty is as smart as I think she is, she'll be back, Leon."

MISTY DROVE TO Charleston to see her mother the following weekend.

They sat down on the patio. "You were right, Mama. You said Mike was going to show up one day. He was in Georgia last weekend."

"What did he say?" Oma asked.

"First he tried to put the blame on you, but I nixed that immediately," Misty said. "Then he admitted fault, apologized and asked for forgiveness."

"Really?"

She nodded. "I couldn't believe it myself, and I thought it was all a lie, but now I really think he was telling the truth."

Oma looked skeptical.

"Mama, you didn't see his face. I talked to his wife and his children—Mike's been a great husband and father to them. They adore him. Oh, he's been sober for twenty years."

"That's good to hear."

"I'm tired of holding on to all the anger, the fear and the hurt," Misty said. "If I really want to move on with my life, I have to find a way to forgive Mike."

"You're right," Oma responded. "I forgave

him a long time ago, but I know it's been hard for you."

"I'm not going to let my past interfere with my future anymore. Leon was wonderful to me and Talei. Breaking up with him was the biggest mistake I've ever made, Mama. I love him. I can't see my life without him in it."

"So, what are you going to do about it?" Oma asked.

"I've got to find a way to fix this."

"Just tell him what you've just told me."

"First I have to find a way to get him to talk to me," Misty responded. "The last time I saw Leon, he made it clear he wanted nothing to do with me."

"I'm sure he's hurt and confused by the abrupt way you ended things with him."

What in the world was I thinking? Things were perfect between us and I ruined it.

"At the time I thought it was best. I was wrong."

MISTY STRODE INTO the kitchen dressed in a pair of jeans and carrying a bag of groceries. Josh greeted her before turning his attention back to stacking plates on the counter. "We needed more tomatoes, onions and mushrooms," she said. "I also bought some other stuff that was on sale."

"We have a delivery scheduled on Wednesday," Josh stated.

"I know, but it's not like we can't use this stuff. We've had a really busy past few days."

The to-go order sitting on the counter caught her attention. "Who is this for?"

Josh responded, "It's for Leon. He should be here any minute."

Misty yearned to see him. She missed the sound of his voice, his laughter and the feel of his arms around her.

She pasted on a smile when he burst through the door of the shop a few minutes later. "Hey."

"I came to pick up an order," Leon said.

"It's ready," Misty said.

Josh strolled out of the kitchen. "Here you go, Leon."

Misty stepped out of the way so that one of the servers could ring up his ticket.

She moved from behind the counter to try to talk to Leon, but he brushed past her. Misty wasn't about to let him walk away a second time.

Warm air fanned over her as she followed him outside the restaurant. "Leon, I know things are tense between us right now, and that's on me, but I'd like the chance to explain myself."

"You made yourself pretty clear, Misty."

"Please hear me out."

A look of tired sadness passed over Leon's features as he unlocked his truck. "You want to do this now?"

She shook her head no. "Not here. Can you come by my place tonight?"

After a moment of tense silence, he asked, "What time?"

"Six thirtyish."

"I'll see you then."

Misty released a short sigh of relief. At least Leon had agreed to meet with her. Now all she had to do was convince him to give her another chance.

CHAPTER THIRTY-FOUR

MISTY SPENT THE late afternoon planning the menu for dinner. She flicked through several cookbooks, trying to work out what she could pull together given the limited supplies in her refrigerator. Talei wanted to go to the pool when they got home, so Misty didn't have time to go grocery shopping. She settled for a pasta dish—tortellini with salami, goat cheese and Kalamata olives, and fresh bread.

She began prepping for dinner at five o'clock so she could take her time and enjoy the process. Misty was both excited and nervous about seeing Leon tonight. She forced herself to remain hopeful that they could work things out and start over.

Misty had everything ready by six o'clock, the table set by a quarter past.

In her bedroom, she decided to slip on a flowy sundress that was comfortable and made her feel elegant. She paired it with a pair of sandals.

Misty ran nervous fingers through her hair as she eyed her reflection in the full-length mirror.

Leon arrived promptly at six thirty.

Misty stepped aside to allow him to enter her condo. "Thank you for coming."

They sat down in the living room.

"I made dinner. I figured we could eat first, then talk after."

"Where's Talei?" Leon asked as he rose to his feet.

"She's having dinner with Rusty and Eleanor." Misty smiled. "She has quite the social life."

Leon pulled out a chair for Misty at the dining room table, then sat down across from her.

They made small talk while eating.

"I made a key lime pie for dessert," she announced.

"Maybe later," Leon said.

He helped her clear the table.

"I'll put everything in the dishwasher later," Misty said. "We can sit in the living room to talk."

When they settled on the sofa, she was the first to speak. "Leon, I first want apologize to you for the way I handled this situation. You deserved better and I'm so sorry."

"I understand that John and his father put you through a lot—I get it. What I don't get is how I was thrown in with them. I've never done anything to intentionally hurt you."

"I was overwhelmed by all the drama in that moment. Leon, I grew up with an alcoholic and verbally abusive father. After that, it was a string of toxic relationships—the very thing I wanted to avoid. I started to feel like a magnet for the worst choices of men." Tears filled her eyes. "I was relieved when she finally chose to leave him, but deep down I wanted him to change and come after us. I wanted him to love us enough to become a better man. Leon, I wasn't going to allow Talei to grow up in that type of environment."

"My aunt mentioned in passing that you'd been through a lot."

"I had no real idea of how toxic his relationship with his father was until a few months before our wedding. I wanted to call off the engagement. John promised me that we'd be okay, but things only got worse. He started drinking and that's when the abusive behavior began."

"John loved you and when you divorced him, he felt betrayed."

"He said I was selfish. Clara said the same thing at the hospital, and it made me question all of the decisions I'd made, including wanting to be with you," Misty said. "It was not my intention to keep my daughter away from her father. I wanted to push John to get some help.

"Leon, I spent two years in therapy, learning to move past all this stuff. I saw my father a week ago for the first time in twenty years. We talked and I'm finally able to work toward forgiving him. All I ever wanted was a better life for me and Talei. I wanted to feel a sense of normalcy." Misty met his gaze. "I wasn't being selfish. I was trying to survive."

"Misty, we can't help who we fall in love with—I never thought I'd feel this way about anybody after Vera. I never want to bring chaos into your life."

"You haven't," she said. "Things just got out of control when we went to see Elroy and Clara. I was overwhelmed, confused and I panicked. But I want you to know that I'm clear on what I want regardless of what they think."

"What are you telling me?"

She hesitated a moment, measuring Leon for a moment. "I love you. Being apart from you showed me a few things. I always felt so safe with you and peaceful—everything I've always wanted in a relationship. I regret not realizing it sooner."

He didn't respond.

Misty chewed on her lip and stole a look at him.

"It was a lot for me to open my heart to loving someone again." Leon's voice was carefully colored in neutral shades.

"I know," she murmured. "I'm hoping you will trust me with your heart again. I'm asking for a second chance."

He was staring as if assessing her.

"Please say something, Leon." Misty tried to sheath her inner feelings.

He reached over and took her hand in his own. "When you broke up with me—I told myself that was it. I was done."

Her eyes filled with tears.

"But the more I tried to forget about you, the more I realized that what we have between us is worth fighting for," Leon said. "I'm not ready to give up on love."

Tears streaming down her face, she said, "I love you so much and I want to be with you."

"I need you to be sure of what you want, Misty. No more flip-flopping."

She wiped away her tears with the back of her hands. "I am very clear on this. I want you and me. *I want us*."

Leon leaned over and planted a kiss on her lips. "You take my breath away every time I see you."

"I missed you so much," she whispered against his mouth.

"I really missed you, too."

He captured her mouth with his own a second time.

When they parted, he said, "I love you, Misty, and it's very real."

She placed a hand to his cheek. "I know. I feel it even when we're not together."

During dessert, Misty said, "Your aunt's birthday is coming up at the end of October. Rusty came to see me earlier. He wants to surprise Miss Eleanor with a party at the shop. She's been so good to me—I told him I'd be happy to plan it. What do you think?"

"I think it's a good idea."

"Great," she said. "Once I have a solid plan, I'll go over everything with Rusty."

"I've been trying to figure out what to get her for her birthday."

"You have all those family pictures and Miss Eleanor has a bunch. What about putting together a memory book for her?" Misty suggested. "We can have the photos scanned. We can organize them online and put names, dates—anything you want."

"Will they put it in book form?" Leon asked.

"Yeah. They can do it anyway you want."

"I'd love to do that for Aunt Eleanor. Maybe it'll help if she starts to lose some of those memories."

"WHERE ARE YOU off to in such a hurry?" Charles inquired, blocking Leon's path. "You're running outta here like you have a hot date or something."

Leon broke into a grin. "I have to be somewhere. I'm actually on my way to the jewelry store."

"Really?"

"Yeah. I love Misty and I want to spend the rest of my life with her and Talei."

"My man…"

"I'm going to propose after my aunt's surprise party."

"Congratulations, Leon. I'm happy for you."

"I hope she's ready for this next step."

"Misty loves you. She's gonna say yes. I'm sure of it. I bet Vera's smiling down from heaven seeing you happy. She would've wanted you to keep living. For a while there, you had me worried."

"I couldn't imagine loving anyone other than Vee," Leon responded. "We'd made so many plans for the future—it was supposed to be the two of us against the world." He chuckled. "That sounded so cliché."

"Yeah, but it's true. It's the same with me and Betty. I never thought I'd come home one day to her wanting a divorce."

"I see she's been coming around a lot," Leon said. "Are you two getting back together?"

"We've been going to counseling," Charles

said. "I want my marriage. Betty says she does, too. I guess we'll see."

"I hope it works out for you both."

Leon left the station and headed to the mainland. He was going to see the jeweler who'd designed Eleanor's wedding ring in Savannah.

He hadn't been this happy in a long time. Leon was actually looking forward to the future now that he'd found the person who gave his life new meaning. He even toyed with the idea that it was fate that had kept him from meeting Misty while she was married to John. Otherwise, they would be in a different space.

Leon didn't question whether John would approve of their relationship—he knew that John would understand. That was all that mattered.

"JOSH, DO WE have everything we need for the party tomorrow?" Misty asked, checking her watch. "I'm meeting Leon at noon for lunch. I can pick up the stuff we need after that."

"As far as I can tell, we're good," he responded. "I'll text you if we're missing anything."

She removed her apron, then went to the bathroom to take off her plastic cap and fluff her hair.

Misty walked out saying, "I have to get out of here."

She walked the two blocks to the restaurant. Leon was already seated when she arrived.

"How long have you been here?" Misty asked.

"Just a couple of minutes," Leon said. "I actually just got off the phone with Clara."

"How is Elroy?" Misty asked.

"He's coming along. Clara is running the business and even Elroy had to admit she's doing a great job. She's hired more staff and they are busier than ever. I had no idea that she used to drive for her father's trucking company whenever he needed an extra driver."

Misty's eyes widened in surprise. "Really? I had no idea that she drove a truck or that she worked for her father. I know she's always wanted to help with the business."

"Elroy apologized and he wants to talk to you. He asked me to bring you and Talei for a visit. He realizes now that he'd allowed his frustrations to take over his life. He says the stroke humbled him. He wants to make amends if possible. He understands that it may take some time for you to feel comfortable around him."

"If he's willing to make peace, then I'm all for it. He is Talei's grandfather and I want them to have a relationship."

A server came over with glasses of water. While she was there, they gave her their order.

"Is everything ready for the party?" Leon asked when the server left the table.

Misty nodded. "Yes. I've already prepared the trays of lasagna. They're in the freezer. I'll have the cake ready by tomorrow morning."

"When will your mother arrive?"

"She got here this morning," Misty responded. "She and Talei were putting together a puzzle when I checked on them a few minutes ago."

"Are you sure you want to cook dinner tonight? I don't mind picking up something for us."

"Mama actually made dinner for us," she said. "Wait until you taste her brisket and garlic mashed potatoes... I'm telling you, Oma Brightwater is a fantastic cook."

"Apparently you inherited her skills."

"Thank you." Misty looked at the clock on the wall. "I have to go back to work, but I'm looking forward to seeing you later."

Leon kissed her. "I should be there no later than seven...seven fifteen."

"See you then."

Misty walked back to the shop grinning from ear to ear.

Her life had changed for the better since moving to Polk Island and she was determined to live for the moment. And each day with Leon brought wonderful moments and memories. They had spent the past few months exploring different festivals, dancing all night at social events, touring historic cities like Savannah and Charleston. Misty and Leon had eaten in tiny boutique restaurants and bistros. They spent a lot of time at the beach or the pool with Talei.

Occasionally, Misty had fallen asleep in his arms on the sofa in the living room. He was always the perfect gentleman. He gave her flowers and was generous with his compliments, but most important to her was the quality time spent with her and Talei.

She was grateful Leon had given their relationship a second chance. She finally had the type of man she'd always dreamed about. As far as Misty was concerned, life couldn't get any better than this.

CHAPTER THIRTY-FIVE

IT WAS THE evening before Halloween. Misty did one final check to make sure everything was perfect for the party. Leon was helping one of the employees set up two more tables. She broke into a smile. He just couldn't seem to keep himself from pitching in to help. Misty couldn't deny that it was one of the qualities she loved about him.

"I hope she likes everything," she said when Leon walked over to her.

"She's going to love it," he assured her. "Misty, I want you to relax."

"I will once the party is over," she said, "and Miss Eleanor's had the time of her life."

Leon checked his phone. "Rusty just texted me. They're on the way."

Misty announced, "Everyone, Miss Eleanor should be here in a few minutes."

She reached over and took Leon's hand, squeezing it. She was bubbling over with excitement. When Rusty came to her about the party, Misty promised she would create a well-planned memorable event to honor Eleanor. She wanted both Rusty and Eleanor to be pleased.

"Here they come," someone said.

"Oooh, the shop looks beautiful," Eleanor murmured, her eyes traveling the room. "What's the occasion?"

"We're celebrating you," Misty responded with a smile. "Happy Birthday, Miss Eleanor."

Leon embraced Eleanor. "Happy Birthday, Auntie."

She glanced over at Rusty. "Did you know about this?"

"It was my idea," he confessed. "I came to Misty with it and she graciously agreed to help me with the planning."

Eleanor kissed him. "Thank you, my sweet husband. I am truly blessed."

Rusty took her hand. "Let's greet your guests. A lot of people came to celebrate with us."

"I love seeing them together," Misty told Leon. "Such a beautiful couple."

He agreed. "They say the same thing about us."

Misty grinned. "I know."

Leon placed his arms around her. "I can't see my life without you and Talei in it. These past few months have been better than I could ever hope to be."

"I feel the same way despite the bumps along the way."

The open buffet was spectacular, Misty thought to herself. Fried chicken, macaroni and cheese, turkey, stuffing and a host of vegetables—all of Eleanor's favorites.

The laughter of the patrons, lively conversations and the music playing softly in the background pleased Misty. Rusty had entrusted her with planning the event and she worked hard to ensure that he felt his money was well spent.

"Come sit," Leon said, pulling out a chair for her at the table. "You did all this work—it's now time for you to enjoy this delicious food you prepared."

Misty couldn't remember the last time she had felt this way or had so much fun. Her senses were heightened in Leon's presence.

A server brought tall drinks to the table for them, left then returned with plates laden with food.

While Misty ate, she swayed to the music blaring through the speakers. "I love the O'Jays."

"No wonder you and Aunt Eleanor get along so well," Leon said with a chuckle. "You're both into old-school R&B."

Misty smiled. "I see you over there dancing in your chair."

"I love all types of music, but I love some

jazz. I have some friends I'd like you to meet," Leon said when a couple walked up to the table. "This is Landon and Jadin Trent. They live in Charleston. Actually, Jadin and I are related. Our great-grandmothers were cousins."

Misty smiled. "It's really nice meeting you both." Eyeing Jadin, she asked, "You look familiar. You work with the DuGrandpre Law Firm, right?"

"Yes, I do."

"My wife is a DuGrandpre," Landon stated.

"How's the family?" Leon asked. "I haven't seen Ryker in months."

"Everyone is fine," Jadin responded. "Jordin sends her love. She couldn't come because she's due any day now. My dad had knee replacement, so Mom stayed home with him."

Leon said, "Please extend my congratulations to your sister."

"We're going to have to head back to Charleston," Jadin said. "Our son is with Ryker and Garland. I'm sure with their four children, he's probably running them ragged."

Leon stood up and embraced her. "Thank you for coming."

"I wouldn't dare miss out on celebrating Eleanor's birthday. Whenever we came to the island for vacation, she always sent my parents an apple pie and she'd bake chocolate raspberry brownies for me and Jordin."

"The DuGrandpres still have a home here on the island," Leon explained.

Jadin nodded. "It belonged to my great-great-grandparents. Landon and I have been thinking about renovating it. I want to bring my son here for vacation. I have so many great memories on this island."

When they left, Misty said, "They're a cute couple."

Leon agreed. "They said the same thing about us."

When the guests began to disperse an hour later, Misty said, "I need to help the staff clean up."

"Do you want an extra set of hands?"

"No, we can take care of it."

"Any plans for later?" Leon asked. "I'd like to come by your place. There's something I want to discuss with you."

She smiled. "Meet me there in about an hour."

"See you then."

Misty rushed home to change clothes. She chose a comfortable loose maxi dress with spaghetti straps to wear. She heard a car pull up into the driveway and broke into a smile. *He's here.*

She opened the door to let him enter.

When Leon embraced her, Misty swore she could feel the heat of his light touch clear down to her toes.

He looked her in her eyes. "I love you, and I know that you love me, too. We are so much a part of one another that separate we're nothing. You're the other half of my soul and I need you in my life, Misty."

It was true. She loved him with her whole heart.

Misty felt the sting of tears.

Still holding her hands within his own, Leon placed them against his broad chest. "I want you to marry me."

Looking up into his handsome face, Misty couldn't speak for a few seconds. She thought she was dreaming, but as his words began to permeate every portion of her mind and soul, she took a step back from him. "Leon, do you really want to get married?"

He smiled, then held up a ring box. "I can't live without you. Please say that you'll be my wife." Leon opened it to reveal a stunning sapphire engagement ring. He knew it was her favorite gemstone.

Misty's heart swelled with happiness and she covered his face with kisses. "Yes, Leon. Yes, I'll marry you."

Leon's arms encircled her, one hand in the small of her back. She buried her face against his throat.

Misty relaxed, sinking into his cushioning embrace.

They reluctantly stepped apart.

"It's a nice evening," Leon said. "How about a moonlight stroll on the beach?"

"Let me grab a shawl," Misty responded.

They took a walk on the shoreline to the sounds of powerful waves crashing in the ocean.

Misty snuggled into Leon's shoulder as they walked and admired the moon reflecting on the water and the backdrop of stars sprinkled against the sky. The moonlit view was spectacular but so was the view of Leon's physique every time she stole glances at him. It was nice to be with someone who respected her choices and loved her for who she was. Leon made her feel appreciated.

Stifling a yawn, Misty reached over and took his hand in her own. "Why don't we head back to the condo," she suggested.

"You're tired," Leon said. "I know it's been a long day for you."

When they got back to her place, he suggested, "Why don't you go soak in a nice hot bath."

"You're not leaving yet?" she asked.

"I'll be here when you come out."

Leon sat down on the sofa to watch television while Misty went to her bedroom.

While the water was running, she undressed. Humming softly, she sank down in a tub of bubbly water, scented with lavender bath salts. It had been a long day and she was exhausted. Misty trailed her fingers in the hot liquid, playing with the bubbles. Picking up the bar of soap that sat in a dish beside the tub, she bathed.

Misty got out and dried her body with a soft fluffy towel. She picked up a bottle of scented body lotion and slathered it on her skin. She slipped on a pair of lightweight sweatpants and a tank top. She pulled her hair into a high ponytail, then went to join Leon.

"You look relaxed." His gaze roved to the creamy expanse of her neck and traveled downward, then back to her face. "Did you enjoy your bath?"

Smiling, Misty nodded. "I did." She walked up to him. "I love you."

"I love you, too. More than you could possibly know."

THE NEXT MORNING, Misty woke up to the sound of clanging coming from the kitchen. She got out of bed, then padded barefoot in the bathroom to wash her face and brush her teeth.

She strolled into her kitchen to find Leon staring at the carton of eggs, sliced mushrooms and spinach. Misty burst into laughter at the expression on his face.

"I love you but I'm the better cook in this relationship, so you sit down and relax. I'll make us some breakfast." She kissed his cheek. "I do appreciate the thought, though."

"Okay, I'll stay in my lane."

Misty quickly and adeptly prepared spinach and mushroom omelets and home fries and even had time to slice up some fresh fruit.

"What time are we picking up Talei?" Leon asked, accepting the plate of food she handed him.

"I told my mom that we'd be there at two o'clock."

"You're going to have to teach me how to make an omelet."

Misty opened a cabinet door and pulled out a black pan. "This is an omelet maker. Use this and it's super easy."

"We need one of these at the firehouse. Somebody's always trying to make an omelet, but it ends up just being a scrambled mess."

They laughed.

"I know we just got engaged," Leon began,

"but any thoughts on when you'd like to get married."

"I know that I don't want a long engagement," Misty responded. "And I don't want a huge wedding."

He released an audible sigh of relief, prompting laughter from her. "I can't tell you how happy I am to hear you say this."

"Tomorrow is the first of November, so when would you like to get married?"

"In the summer," Leon said. "I've always wanted a beach wedding at sunset. Vera and I had a church ceremony. It's what her parents wanted."

"John and I got married in a church, too. I'd prefer to do something different this time around. The beach is the perfect location."

"I can hardly wait to start my life with you."

"We can always go the same route as Miss Eleanor and Rusty," Misty suggested. "We can just have an intimate ceremony and not worry about a big fancy wedding."

"The idea is tempting," Leon said. "But I really want to say our vows at sunset against the backdrop of the ocean." He paused a moment, then asked, "How do you think Talei will take the news of us getting married?"

"She loves you, Leon. Everything will be fine."

"How do you think Elroy and Clara are going to react?" he inquired.

Misty shrugged. "Clara might eventually be okay with it, but Elroy… It's hard to call. The thing is that it really doesn't matter. This isn't about them. This is *my* life and I intend to live it *my* way."

"What do you think about hosting a huge Thanksgiving dinner?" Leon asked. "We can bring our families together and make the announcement then."

"I like that idea," Misty said with a grin. "Although it means I won't be able to wear my beautiful ring just yet."

"We don't have to wait."

"No, I really like making the announcement on Thanksgiving."

Leon pulled Misty into his embrace. "I can't wait to make you my wife."

THE MID-NOVEMBER weather was nice. The temperature was still warm and the day nice and clear. The leaves were dressed in red, yellow and burgundy hues.

"Rusty, what do you think?" Leon asked, pointing to the turkey.

"Looks good to me. I don't know if you remember, but your daddy was a beast when it comes to roasting a turkey."

"That's what everybody tells me. I wanted to make some barbecue chicken, but I'm still trying to get my barbecue sauce to taste like his. Aunt Eleanor said he guarded that recipe like it was gold."

Rusty laughed. "He added honey."

"Really? How do you know?"

"He told me," Rusty responded, slipping him a piece of paper. "He swore me to secrecy, but you're his son—this recipe belongs in your family."

Leon smiled. "Thank you."

Eleanor stepped out onto the patio. "What are you two whispering about?" She set a bowl of corn on the cob on the counter.

"Just two men bonding, Ladybug."

"Uh-huh…" Eleanor uttered. "I better check on the potatoes. I can't mess up Leon's potato salad."

"That's right, Auntie."

Leon heard the sound of tiny footsteps.

"*Oseeyo*, Eon… *Oseeyo*, Mr. Russy," Talei greeted from behind them. "You have hot dawg, pleeze?"

"It's almost ready, little one." Leon glanced over his shoulder just as Talei sat down at a nearby table.

"She sure does love herself some hot dogs," Rusty said, keeping his voice low. "I tried to give her some pizza the last time she was at the house—she wanted nothing to do with it. She just wanted a hot dog and French fries."

Leon chuckled. "One smile from her brightens my entire day. I think she stole my heart the day I took her out of that car. I love Talei as if she were my own blood."

Misty walked to the door. "Are you ready to slice the ham?"

Leon took the platter from her.

"I hungry," Talei said. "I want hot dawg and fench fries."

"The hot dog should be ready," he said. "It's in that pot over there. The fries are in the air fryer."

Misty winked at Leon before saying, "Go wash your hands, sweetie, while I fix your plate."

"Oh, yeah... I know that look very well," Rusty said. "You got that big-dog love going on. Ain't no puppy love here."

Leon shrugged. "Guilty."

He watched Misty brush a curly strand of dark hair back from the soft curve of her cheek. She was intelligent, beautiful and exquisite, Leon acknowledged.

Misty caught him staring at her. Grinning, she gave him a tiny wave.

Leon found himself looking forward to

spending time with her when the dinner was long over. In truth, he was excited about sharing the rest of his life with Misty. There was nothing he wanted more than to be her husband and a father to Talei.

CHAPTER THIRTY-SIX

MISTY BURST INTO the kitchen. "Mama, he's here," she announced. "My dad and his family just arrived."

Oma wiped her hands on her apron. "Don't worry. I'm fine."

"I just don't want this to be awkward between y'all."

"Everything is going to work out. Now go out there and greet your guests."

"Mike, thank you for coming." Misty gave him a tentative hug.

"Thank you for inviting us," he responded.

She embraced her grandmother, Jennifer and her siblings, then led them around the room as she made the introductions.

Misty held her breath when Oma walked out of the kitchen to greet Mike and his family. Her father looked uncomfortable initially, but as they talked, he visibly relaxed.

She bit back a smile. Her mother had boldly and graciously confronted the man who'd tormented her for years—a man who promised to love and cherish her. Oma was able to forgive and truly move on with no regrets. It was a beautiful scene to witness.

Leon was polite and chatted briefly with her father before moving around to greet their other guests.

Misty smiled when Jadin Trent arrived with her parents and her sister. She hadn't realized that Jadin and Jordin were twins—this was her first time seeing them together.

"Wow, you two are identical."

Jadin smiled and made the introductions. "Jordin, this is Leon's girlfriend, Misty."

"It's very nice to meet you, and congratulations. Miss Eleanor mentioned you'd had your baby three weeks ago. I have to say you look great."

"I like her," Jordin said with a smile. "Thank you, Misty. I still have some baby weight to lose. This is my third and last one, so I'm trying to get this body back in shape."

"Don't let her fool you," Jadin stated. "Her husband owns a chain of gyms. Trust me... My sister will have no problem getting her body back to pre-pregnancy size."

"She looks great for three pregnancies."

"Two," Jadin corrected. "She has a set of twins."

"I hear you have the most adorable little girl

and that she has Leon wrapped around her little finger. I can't wait to meet her."

Misty smiled. "Jordin, she can be sweet and then there are those days when she's just intent on having her own way." She glanced over her shoulder. "I'm pretty sure you'll find Talei somewhere near Leon."

The three women were talking about motherhood when another woman joined them.

"This is Garland. She's married to our cousin Ryker."

Misty embraced her.

"It's nice to meet you. I've heard great things about you, Misty. Eleanor raves about your baking skills. She also says you're a great cook, but that baking is your gift."

"You're the chair for the Children's Festival in Charleston. I remember Brittany mentioning your name. I was on the planning committee for the one we had here in August."

"I've worked with Brittany—lovely girl. I read that the festival was very successful."

"It was," Misty responded. "I really enjoyed being a part of the event."

Jadin introduced Misty to her parents.

Misty enjoyed meeting members of Leon's extended family. She was curious how Leon felt about meeting her father. She was working toward forgiving Mike and hoped that he and

Leon would be able to forge some type of relationship.

She shook off all negative thoughts. She and Leon would soon start a new life together—everything was going to work out.

When Leon gestured for her to join him, Misty slipped on her engagement ring.

"Misty and I love family and we wanted to bring all of you together," he said after everyone had gotten their plates and had settled down to eat.

He pulled Misty into his embrace, and then continued. "We wanted to share the news that we're getting married."

Everyone around them cheered and applauded.

Eleanor hugged Leon, then Misty. "I'm so happy for you both. This is what I've been praying for—that you both would find real love—one that would last a lifetime."

Talei ran up to them. "I getting married, too."

Leon bent down to her level. "Who are you marrying?"

"You."

He kissed her cheek, picked her up and said, "I have been doubly blessed. This little lady just agreed to marry me, as well."

Jordin walked over to where they were standing. "Talei, you're absolutely adorable."

"I'm so happy you, Jadin and your parents

were all able to come," Misty said. "We appreciate it."

Leon agreed.

Jadin joined them. "I spoke with my parents and they agreed to renovating the house and making it a summer retreat once again. Looks like you'll be seeing us more, especially me and Jordin. We love the beach. I've been spending time on Jekyll, but this is a family home."

"And we have so many wonderful memories on this island," Jordin interjected.

"That's great news." Leon glanced across the room. "You have to tell Aunt Eleanor. She's going to be ecstatic."

"She told me about her diagnosis. My mom took it pretty bad."

"Her mother was named after my aunt," Leon explained to Misty. "So, they're pretty close."

"Today was a great day," Misty said after everyone left and they were cleaning up. The last person had gone home an hour ago.

"It really was," Leon agreed.

"I noticed that you were a bit distant with my dad."

He looked at her. "After hearing how badly he treated you, Misty, it's going to take some time for me to warm up to him. I enjoyed your grandmother, though. She doesn't bite her tongue at all."

"No, she doesn't," Misty said. "As for my dad, we'll both take it one day at a time."

Leon kissed her cheek. "I'm willing to give him a chance. I believe everyone deserves a second chance, but I don't like the way he treated you and your mother."

"That's one of the reasons I love you so much."

EPILOGUE

Eighteen months later

LEON STARED IN awe at the two-day-old infant in his arms.

"He's beautiful, isn't he?" Misty touched her husband's arm.

He was speechless, too overcome with emotion to offer a response.

"Leon…" she prompted.

"We have a son. A very healthy little boy."

Smiling, she responded, "Yes, we do."

"I never thought I'd have another child," Leon said, fighting back tears. "I love Talei like my own—you know that. When Selena died… I just didn't think I'd ever have a family. I couldn't see it at the time. This is the one thing I've always wanted—a wife and children."

Oma entered the room with Talei. "She wanted to visit with Leo."

Leon waited until the little girl was seated in the armchair before placing the baby in her arms.

"He's so cute," Talei murmured. "I love him." She scrunched up her face, then grinned. "I love you, Dad."

Leon's heart warmed at her declaration. "I love you, too."

He enjoyed watching Talei with her baby brother. His heart was full beyond measure.

"I'm going to finish preparing dinner," Oma stated.

"Thank you," Leon said.

"Dad, it's *wado*," Talei told him.

Amused, Leon responded, "Yes, ma'am, little one."

Leon took Talei to the park to play while Misty and the baby were napping. He enjoyed being a father and looked forward to raising his children to adulthood. However, he didn't want them growing up too fast. He and Misty wanted their kids to enjoy being children—something they both missed out on.

"I have two daddies," Talei announced. "Daddy in heaven and you."

"You're a very lucky girl," Leon said. "Because we both love you dearly."

"We have a baby."

He chuckled. "Yes, we do."

"I wanna hold my brother when we get home. I won't hurt him."

"I'm not worried about that. You're a big girl and I know how much you love Leo. If he's awake, you can spend some time with him. Okay?"

Talei smiled. "Okay."

They left the park and stopped to visit with Eleanor before heading home.

"*Osiyo*, Auntie," Talei greeted. "Uncle home?"

"He's at work, sugar. How's my big girl doing?" Eleanor asked. "You just had a birthday. You're growing up on me."

"I'm four."

Leon smiled. Talei's birthday was last month, but for Eleanor, time passed differently. A touch of sadness rose up in him, but he brushed it away as quickly as it had come. She was still so full of life—he cherished every moment he had with her.

OMA HAD DINNER ready when they returned to the house.

They gathered at the dining room table to eat as a family. Leon hadn't expected Misty to join them. He'd had her mother prepare a plate and was in the process of placing it on a tray when she strolled into the kitchen.

"Sweetheart, why don't you go back to bed. You just had a baby."

"Leon, I'm a little sore, but I'm not sick. It won't hurt me to sit and have dinner with my family. I can't just lie around in bed. I need to move around."

"I wanna say the grace," Talei stated.

"Go for it, little one."

Her head bowed down, she said, "Our Father, thank you for our food we eat. Thank you for your love. We love you, too. Amen."

"Good job, sweetie."

Grinning, Talei picked up her fork and dived into the macaroni and cheese.

Leon glanced at Misty and smiled. The day that little girl had come into his life, he was forever changed.

As promised, Talei was allowed to not only hold Leo, but she was also able to feed him after her mother pumped breast milk in a bottle.

When it was time for bed, Leon tucked Talei in for the night. His eyes traveled to the framed photo of him and John on the nightstand. The other photo was of Misty.

"That's you and Daddy."

"Yes, it is," Leon said, picking up the picture. "He was a good friend."

"Do you miss him?"

He nodded. "I do. I miss John a lot."

"Me, too." Talei sat up in bed. "Sometimes

he visits me in my dreams. He told me that he was happy that you're my dad now."

Leon believed that if there was a way possible for John to visit with his daughter, he would do it. "I promised him that I'd take care of you."

Talei sat up and took his hand. "I like my baby brother, Dad. Can I have a baby sister, too? I want her for Christmas."

Leon chuckled. "I think we have to ask Mommy about that."

Oma entered the bedroom. "I promised Talei a glass of warm milk and a bedtime story."

"I'll leave you to it," he said after planting a kiss on her forehead. "Good night, little one."

Leon returned to the bedroom just as Misty had finished changing the baby. "You need anything?" he asked.

"We're fine," she responded. "Especially this little sleepyhead. He fell asleep in the middle of my changing him."

Misty repositioned the pillows behind her. "Did Talei go down without a fuss?"

"Pretty much. You mom brought her some warm milk to help her sleep," Leon said. "Oh, Talei just told me that she wants a baby sister for Christmas." He took the sleeping baby from Misty and placed him in the bassinet at the foot of their bed.

"As in seven months from now?"

He nodded. "Yes."

"Our little girl is about to experience her first Christmas disappointment," Misty said. "There's no way we can accomplish that. I'm not even willing to try."

"Maybe we can consider it in a year," Leon suggested.

Misty nodded. "I'm good with that. She'll be in school."

Leon sat down on the chaise to remove his shoes. He padded barefoot to the bathroom and took a shower.

Ten minutes later, he climbed into bed beside his wife.

"*Wado, adali'i.* You've given me such a beautiful gift."

Misty broke into a smile. "Have you been taking lessons from Mama?"

"I wanted to know how to say *wife* in Cherokee."

"What else did you learn?"

"*Gvgeyu'i.*"

Misty kissed him, then whispered, "I love you, too."

Leon was still awake long after she had fallen asleep. He slipped out of bed and went to check on Talei, who was sleeping soundly. The light in the guest room was still on, so he assumed Oma was still up, but he didn't disturb her.

He returned to his bedroom and eased back into bed, careful not to disturb Misty.

Leon had everything he wanted—a job he loved, a beautiful wife and two adorable children. The shadows across his heart were completely gone. He no longer feared losing those he loved so fiercely. Having experienced so much loss, Leon recognized how fleeting life could be, so he vowed to live and love each day as if it were his last.

"You can't sleep?"

"What are you doing awake?" Leon asked. "Leo will be wanting to nurse soon."

Misty sat up in bed. "What's going on? Why can't you sleep?"

"I think I'm just excited about what the future holds for us. We've both weathered terrible storms—we've walked through the fire and we're better for it. I was afraid to love someone again, but you and Talei changed that—you changed me."

"Your love saved me, Leon," Misty said. "I never thought I'd meet a man like you. You came into my life during a difficult time. You didn't try to rush things between us. You allowed me to grow."

Leon pulled her close to him. "From this moment forward, our life will be a blaze of love, laughter and memories to last a lifetime."

Snuggling against him, Misty whispered, "And the firefighter and his lady lived happily ever after."

* * * * *

Get 4 FREE REWARDS!

We'll send you 2 FREE Books plus 2 FREE Mystery Gifts.

Love Inspired books feature uplifting stories where faith helps guide you through life's challenges and discover the promise of a new beginning.

FREE
Value Over
$20

YES! Please send me 2 FREE Love Inspired Romance novels and my 2 FREE mystery gifts (gifts are worth about $10 retail). After receiving them, if I don't wish to receive any more books, I can return the shipping statement marked "cancel." If I don't cancel, I will receive 6 brand-new novels every month and be billed just $5.24 each for the regular-print edition or $5.99 each for the larger-print edition in the U.S., or $5.74 each for the regular-print edition or $6.24 each for the larger-print edition in Canada. That's a savings of at least 13% off the cover price. It's quite a bargain! Shipping and handling is just 50¢ per book in the U.S. and $1.25 per book in Canada.* I understand that accepting the 2 free books and gifts places me under no obligation to buy anything. I can always return a shipment and cancel at any time. The free books and gifts are mine to keep no matter what I decide.

Choose one: ☐ **Love Inspired Romance Regular-Print** (105/305 IDN GNWC)   ☐ **Love Inspired Romance Larger-Print** (122/322 IDN GNWC)

Name (please print)

Address   Apt. #

City   State/Province   Zip/Postal Code

Email: Please check this box ☐ if you would like to receive newsletters and promotional emails from Harlequin Enterprises ULC and its affiliates. You can unsubscribe anytime.

Mail to the Harlequin Reader Service:
IN U.S.A.: P.O. Box 1341, Buffalo, NY 14240-8531
IN CANADA: P.O. Box 603, Fort Erie, Ontario L2A 5X3

Want to try 2 free books from another series! Call 1-800-873-8635 or visit www.ReaderService.com.

HARLEQUIN SELECTS COLLECTION

19 FREE BOOKS IN ALL!

From Robyn Carr to RaeAnne Thayne to Linda Lael Miller and Sherryl Woods we promise (actually, GUARANTEE!) each author in the Harlequin Selects collection has seen their name on the *New York Times* or *USA TODAY* bestseller lists!

#379 CAUGHT BY THE COWBOY DAD
The Mountain Monroes • by Melinda Curtis

Holden Monroe and Bea Carlisle are hoping a road trip will give them time alone for a second chance—but it's a special Old West town they happen upon that helps them rediscover their spark!

#380 THE TEXAN'S SECRET SON
Truly Texas • by Kit Hawthorne

Single mom Nina Walker is shocked to see Marcos Ramirez again. Especially since her ex-husband has no idea he's a father to a son! Will the Texas rancher forgive her and finally claim his family?

#381 A FOURTH OF JULY PROPOSAL
Cupid's Crossing • by Kim Findlay

Former bad boy Ryker Slade came home to sell his father's house, then he'll leave. Instead he finds a connection with the pastor's daughter, Rachel Lowther. But Rachel also plans to leave town—unless Ryker gives her a reason to stay...

#382 THE MAN FROM MONTANA
Hearts of Big Sky • by Julianna Morris

Tessa Alderman has questions about her twin sister's death in a white water rafting accident, at the same time she's drawn to the man who may have the answers...Clay Carson.

Visit ReaderService.com Today!

As a valued member of the Harlequin Reader Service, you'll find these benefits and more at ReaderService.com:

- Try 2 free books from any series
- Access risk-free special offers
- View your account history & manage payments
- Browse the latest Bonus Bucks catalog

Don't miss out!

If you want to stay up-to-date on the latest at the Harlequin Reader Service and enjoy more content, make sure you've signed up for our monthly News & Notes email newsletter. Sign up online at ReaderService.com or by calling Customer Service at 1-800-873-8635.

EXILE FROM REALITY

The great djinn waited in the hearth fire, ready to carry them across the void, but Kestrel hesitated.

Then there was a sudden commotion. Four wizards in sweat-dampened robes burst into the room. "There they are!" one shouted. "The ones who conspired against the august council. We've caught them at last!"

Kestrel saw them rushing toward Phoebe and made up his mind. Closing his eyes, he pushed her forward toward the great djinn's chest, moving to join her. He felt the wings close around them and Astron's demon elbow pressed painfully into his side. Reality vanished. The last thing he remembered was hearing the archimage's words:

"If they escape, broadcast the word across land and sea. There is to be no place safe for them in all the realm of man!"

By Lyndon Hardy
Published by Ballantine Books:

MASTER OF THE FIVE MAGICS

SECRET OF THE SIXTH MAGIC

RIDDLE OF THE SEVEN REALMS

Riddle of the Seven Realms

LYNDON HARDY

A Del Rey Book

BALLANTINE BOOKS • NEW YORK

To my daughters, Melinda and Jennifer

CONTENTS

PART FOUR: *The Two Realms of Symmetry*

PART FIVE: *The Realm of the Aleators*

PART SIX: *The Ultimate Precept*

THAUMATURGY

The Principle of Sympathy —— like produces like
The Principle of Contagion —— once together, always
together

ALCHEMY

The Doctrine of Signatures —— the attributes without mirror
the powers within

MAGIC

The Maxim of Persistence —— perfection is eternal

SORCERY

The Rule of Three —— thrice spoken, once fulfilled

WIZARDRY

The Law of Ubiquity —— flame permeates all
The Law of Dichotomy —— dominance or submission

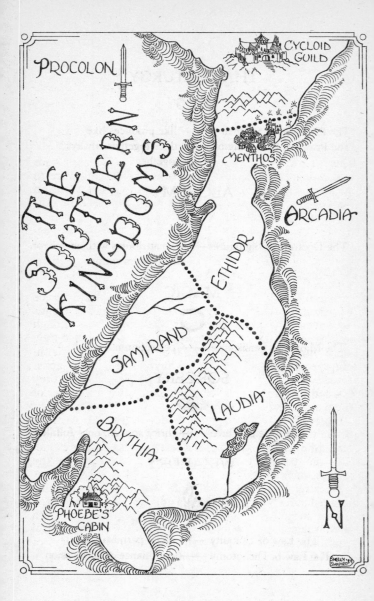

Prologue

KESTREL looked past the flame toward the cabin door and estimated his chance of escape if something were to go awry. Like the lairs of most wizards, there were no windows in any of the walls; the distractions of the outside could well be done without.

He glanced back to the center of the room at the figure standing in the chalk-drawn pentagram that surrounded the firepit. Phoebe was not reputed to be a wizard of prowess and it was no simple devil that she was trying to summon.

If only she had been as greedy as the rest! The price he asked for an entire wagonload just like the branches he waved in front of their faces was usually low enough to hurry all of their thoughts away from testing what they were to receive. Some stored it all in their larders without even bothering to examine any of the leather sacks. Usually he was well into the next kingdom before they learned that a simple woodsman had gotten the better of the bargain rather than they.

But this one chose even to doubt that the sack he brought inside contained only anvilwood and nothing else. She had insisted upon a test to see that more than just the merest of imps was contacted through the realms, once the fire was lit.

Kestrel looked around the cabin. Thick beams bridged stout walls of white plastered mud. On the left, a bed of straw with room for only one stood underneath a shelf sagging with rolls of parchment. Behind Kestrel and extending along the wall on the right were tiers of wood-framed cubbyholes rising to the high ceiling, a scrambled collection of nailed-together boxes and wide-mouthed bins.

In most of the openings Kestrel could see the contents stuffed nearly to overflowing and spilling onto the wood-planked floor with goat-bladder sacks, vials of deeply colored powders, dried lizard tongue, sunflower seeds, licorice, and aromatic woods; this was as well stocked a wizard's larder as Kestrel had ever seen.

Kestrel looked again at the wizard staring intently into the flame. He had sought her out because of the tales of her wealth. All the practitioners in the Brythian hills, though they thought little of her skill, admitted that she was the richest. But if not for that, his interest might have been piqued anyway. Rather than in ratted tangles, her well-groomed hair fell in a cascade of shiny black down the back of her robe. The broad and youthful face was clear and unwrinkled. It carried the open simplicity of an unspoiled peasant girl, rather than the somber broodings of one who dared to thrust her will through the fire. The sash of the robe, adorned with the logo of flame, attempted to pull tight a waist a bit thicker than the current fashion. But at the same time, it accentuated curves that would otherwise be hidden. Despite her caution, her manner had been quite warm. She did not display the disdain that vindicated in part what he did.

Kestrel ran his hand down the back of his head, feeling how well the thinning hair still covered the beginning of a bald spot. He imagined how he must have appeared to the wizard when he had knocked on her door barely an hour ago—brown curls on top, what there was of them, deep-set eyes about a long slash of a nose, and wide lips in a sincere-appearing smile. His clothing was plain but still fairly new. The road dust on tunic, leggings, and boots had just been applied around the bend from the cabin, rather than being the result of a three-day journey, as he had said.

How much had his ease in gaining entrance, Kestrel wondered, been because of other thoughts in Phoebe's mind, rather than the possibility of acquiring some of the rare anvilwood that peeked from the rucksack on his back. He savored the mental image which suddenly sprang into his mind. What would it be like to offer a wagonload of true potency instead of the disguised snags and rotten branches and to ask a fair price, rather than display an apparent ignorance of the value of what he possessed, or not to hurry away before his deception was discovered?

No. He shook his head sadly. He could not take the risk. He had to take advantage of the base impulses of others. It was his only defense. Long ago, he had trusted—and the scars still remained.

Phoebe suddenly stiffened. "I am yours to command, master," she said.

Kestrel immediately sensed that something was wrong. The air above the flame shimmered and danced. A hand emerged from nowhere, and then a head with features more plain than bizarre. The demon was no towering giant with menacing fangs and crackles of lightning, but Phoebe's jaws went slack and her hands fell to her sides all the same. She had not won the contest of wills; the demon had done so, instead.

Kestrel made a step to the left and then hesitated. The demon might be content with domination of the wizard and pay no attention to him as he slowly glided past. It was still morning. He could be well away before nightfall and anyone else suspected. On the other hand, he would be abandoning what little anvilwood he had remaining with nothing to show for it.

In mixed fascination and fear, he watched as the demon continued to tear apart the fabric of reality and emerge into the realm of men.

PART ONE

The Realm of Daemon

CHAPTER ONE

Astron's Trek

ASTRON ran his tongue over the stubs of fangs he had filed away. In the palm of his fist, now clinched with tension, he felt nails ground short in the manner of men. Only two small knobs protruded from his back where one would expect the powerful wings of a splendorous djinn. Unlike his clutch brothers, Astron had no real weapons with which to fight.

The broodmothers' talk was that Elezar's mood was most foul. Only the foolish or those consumed by the great monotony would elect to be near a prince of demons when his disposition was less than ideal. Far more pleasing were the thoughts of the cozy contours of Astron's own den where he could spend eons rearranging the small collection of artifacts he had managed to keep for his own. If hints of boredom did begin to grow, he could catalogue more of the names that the skyskirr gave to their lithons or even start his investigation of what men called love. The summons of his prince easily could have waited until the next scheduled time.

Astron looked about the outer perimeter of Elezar's domain. He was standing on a thin plane of matter which hung suspended in the black expanse that constituted the realm of the demons. On the flatness were massed the splendid domes of his prince, mighty structures that soared into the blackness and blazed with color. In the distance other pinpoints of light shone against the background of ebony, some steady and pure, beacons of the princes who did not choose to hide. Others flickered at the edge of visibility, lures for the unwary or perhaps evidence of the enormous weavings of warring djinns.

7

Astron glanced down at his feet and the smooth surface of the plane. It glowed with a soft iridescence, pleasing to the eye. Pathways to the various domes were subtly marked for those who knew the signs. Behind him, the plane ended abruptly not far from where he stood, the edge sculpted in a graceful pattern that encircled the entire periphery. If he peered over the side, Astron knew, he would see a scene very similar to the one above—glimmering lights in a pitch-black sky.

Astron picked out a trail and followed it into the midst of the domes. The ones near the periphery were squat and ornate, no more than simple hemispheres encrusted with arabesques and intricate designs, lairs for broodmothers and little more. Behind them towered the true marvels of Elezar's domain, stiletto spires that soared to heights far beyond what their delicate walls would seem to support. In clusters and splendid isolation, they sat atop broad vaults and fluted ellipsoids; over a sea of juxtaposed and intersecting bubbles they pierced the emptiness of the void. Fierce lights of lavender and orange upwelled from ports cut into the roofs of the domes. Intense beams ricocheted from shiny mirrors on the spires and scattered from curves and planes glittering with twinkling jewels. Elezar did not hide his domain from others who hoarded their meager store of matter in the blackness of the realm.

Astron quickly threaded his way between the outer domes and then entered an archway that opened into one of the larger central vaults. He paid no attention to the small devils huddled around the lump of rock in the first chamber, nor to the manner in which the stone jerked and bobbed above their craned necks. Levitating a boulder was beyond his abilities, even if aided by the will of others.

He passed sleeping lairs resonating with deep snores, treasure vaults crammed with artifacts from dozens of realms, quiet rooms of dark contemplation, and weaving alcoves shimmering with half-finished constructions. Finally he entered the grand rotunda itself at the very center of the domain.

Astron saw that the great hall was nearly empty. Except for Elezar, in the pit at the very center, sitting on a pillow of silk and down, and a swarm of imps buzzing about his head, no other demons were present. The prince was clothed in a glittering robe of deep sea-green, covering all of his slender body, except for his fingertips. Delicate features, an upturned nose, thin lips, and ears that were barely pointed sculpted a narrow face. Straw-pale hair ran over a brow flecked with gold, and half-closed eyes glowered under long curving lashes. No great scales or hair-pierced warts marred the smooth skin. Like Astron himself, Elezar could pass unnoticed in the realm of men if he were not too closely regarded.

Astron saw the discontent smouldering behind Elezar's eyes and felt his limbs begin to tighten. Slowly he started down tile-covered steps toward the prince, barely bothering to notice if any weavings had altered the shape of the rotunda since his last visit. As before, the ceiling was a large inverted bowl with a span greater than the outstretched wings of a hundred djinns. Sprays of soft colors caressed its glassy-smooth surface and glowing crystals throbbed with light all around the periphery.

A dozen entrances pierced the circular wall which supported the dome, each framed with fluted columns and interspersed with sculptures of heavy metal or artifacts wrested from other realms. The flooring was a series of concentric circles, each one a step lower than the last and converging on the pit in the very center.

"You are late, cataloguer." Elezar's soft voice floated upward from the hub. "Surely even one whose only concern is the making of lists must know the folly of displeasing a prince."

Astron's arms and legs tightened further. Even his stembrain stirred from its slumber. The broodmothers had been right; the prince was troubled and did not care if his irritation showed. With eyes discreetly averted, Astron descended the remaining distance to the pit and squatted uncomfortably on a small cushion at Elezar's feet.

The prince waited a long moment before he spoke

9

again, eyeing Astron with a cruel smile. "If I had not watched the hatchings myself, I would not believe that the demon that huddles before me is no less than a splendorous djinn," he said.

Astron kept his head down and said nothing.

"And what of the broodmothers, mighty cataloguer?" Elezar stepped forward and thrust his toe into Astron's ribs. "What of the carriers of our seed? Do they tremble with anticipation in your presence? Does their skin grow moist at your touch?"

The prince paused and then kicked forward a second time. Astron felt a stab of pain in his side, but did not move. It was but a mere token of what Elezar could do if he unleashed his great power.

"Or perhaps, instead, they merely confide their whispers, as if you were one of their own," Elezar continued. "Yes, as if you served no more purpose than they. Why should you not retire to their dens and prove your worth by becoming a warmer of eggs?"

Despite the iron-tight bands of his will, Astron felt his stembrain stir. Eggwarmer indeed. Only the deformed and slow of wit were charged with such a task. His value to the prince was far greater, as he had demonstrated dozens of times before. Who else had deduced the meaning of the cakes of congealed fats that mortals called soap, the purpose of the forged metal they thrust into the mouths of horses, or, the most perplexing of all, why their warriors grasped right hands in greeting?

He opened his mouth to speak, feeling the words rush upward sharp and cutting, but at the last moment he slammed his teeth together, biting off the sound. Deliberately he pushed the hot thoughts away and concentrated instead on visualizing the safe and comfortable contours of his own lair. Let the prince say what he would, Astron would not be provoked like some minor devil.

For a long moment nothing more happened. Then Astron saw Elezar's shadow retreat and heard the swish of silk as the prince sat back down on his cushion. Cautiously Astron raised his head upward and judged that finally he must speak.

"I have been of use to my prince in the past," he said. "Perhaps there is some additional service that is to be performed as a result of this summons."

Elezar took another moment before answering. "Any of your brothers would have replied with bolts of power, even though it would have surely meant their death," he said. "How could even one such as you retain clear thoughts after what has been spoken?"

"I am not like my brothers," Astron said quietly. "I am different in more ways than those that you have chosen to notice."

Elezar grunted. "And it is those very differences upon which I am now forced to depend," he said.

Before Astron could reply, the prince looked up into the cloud of imps above his head and gestured rapidly with his left hand. Instantly the swarm began to twinkle rapidly with a kaleidoscope of color, each sprite brightly glowing in a vivid hue. Their lazy hovering changed into a complex tangle of loops and dives. Astron saw a pattern suddenly emerge from the random motion. Arcs of fiery red imps, like droplets of molten lava, soared upward in a central column and then cascaded over onto waves of emerald-green that seemed to dance in empty air. Blues and yellows threaded through the rest, knitting complex tapestries that pulsated and changed in subtle ways that one could not quite follow.

Then, as suddenly as it had begun, the synchronized display winked out. The cloud of imps returned to their aimless hovering above the prince's head. The membranes retracted and Elezar's eyes refocused. His brow wrinkled with a scowl.

"More than three eons it took to train them all." Elezar waved at the swarm. "Three eons for that one clutch alone." The arc of his arm continued around the expanse of the rotunda. "I will not give them up, cataloguer. Not them or a single dram of hard matter in my domain."

"You are among the mightiest of princes," Astron said. "And the djinns who obey your commands number more than those of any other. What demon could possibly challenge you for possession of—?"

"Your skill is supposed to be one of making lists," Elezar interrupted. "Your knowledge of the other realms is the most profound of any in my retinue. Tell me quickly then, what are the seven laws that govern the affairs of men?"

Astron wrinkled his nose, puzzled. Such knowledge was widespread throughout the realm. Even the prince himself would have at least a casual acquaintance with the seven laws. Why would Elezar choose to exercise him through a memory drill like a broodmother instructing her scion? Astron started to ask the reason for the question but then saw the frown deepen in Elezar's face.

"The first two laws are the concern of wizardry," he said quickly, "the law of ubiquity—flame permeates all, and the law of dichotomy—dominance or submission. It is through fire that the barriers between our realm and the others are broken. And when, through it, we contact a dweller on the other side, one must end up the controller of the other; there is no middle ground.

"Of all the realms, ours is unique. The fires of the other universes connect them only to us and never to each other. If ever men, the skyskirr, the fey and all those who exist elsewhere interact it is because we have brought them together.

"And although these others can coexist side by side with no threat from one to another, our own involvements are much more tightly bound. Whenever one of us leaves our realm to sojourn elsewhere, it must be as the master of the one who has summoned or else as his slave.

"But you know all of this quite well, my prince. None less than you organized the great plan to conquer the entire realm of men and bend it to your will but a tick in time ago. Had it not been for the one that the mortals call the archimage—"

Elezar's hands clutched spasmodically and Astron veered back to his original course. The prince did not like to be reminded of his defeat by a mere human. "The next is the rule of three," Astron rushed. "Or as it is commonly cast—thrice spoken, once fulfilled. The

12

proper chants intoned three times over give men the power of sorcery and illusion to cloud the minds of one another.

"The maxim of persistence is the fourth. As the magicians in the guilds like to state it—perfection is eternal. If certain precise rituals are enacted flawlessly, then items can be produced that will last as long as the life of any demon.

"The fifth is the doctrine of signatures—the attributes without mirror the powers within. Based upon closely guarded secret formulas, those that men call alchemists brew strange concoctions that sometimes produce remarkable results. Far more powerful would be the craft if chance did not play a role in every successful brewing."

Astron again glanced at Elezar's hands but saw no change. Somehow the listing of the laws of magic was bound up in whatever was vexing the prince.

"The last two are the principles of sympathy and contagion," Astron hurried to finish. "The thaumaturges who use them speak of 'like producing like' and 'once together, always together,' but sympathy and contagion are what they mean. By taking a small part of a whole and exercising it in a simulation, the rest of the bulk is forced to act correspondingly. It is the craft by which men build their walls and transport heavy burdens."

"My prince," a deep voice suddenly rumbled from one of the rotunda entrances, "the signal lights have been blinking. Gaspar with his retinue is now on his way. There are twenty-two djinns of lightning and lesser devils as well."

On the rim of the rotunda, the entrance was darkened by the massive form of a colossal djinn, his folded wingtips scraping the archway as he entered. Powerful black muscles rippled across his chest as he moved. Slitted eyes of piercing yellow glowed in a face of darkest jet.

"What is your command, my prince?" the djinn asked. "Though we are fewer, my clutch brothers and I can make his landing one that will cost."

Elezar turned to answer, "No, no, Delithan. To

13

meet Gaspar on his own terms is surely a strategy of defeat. Invite him in unchallenged. We will use the time to our advantage."

"A djinn lives to fight, my prince," Delithan rumbled. "He exists only to rip matter asunder and drink deeply of its dying shrieks. If that is denied, there is little that restrains surrender to the great monotony."

"There will be many more battles in the epochs to come, Delithan," Elezar said. "Do not deny yourself the opportunity to engage in them by a miscalculation now. Push aside thoughts of the brooding doom. As you have in the past, trust in your prince."

"An epoch ago, none could call himself master of my lord," Delithan said. "But now there is indeed one who can so claim and he is only a man. Perhaps Gaspar too is mightier and the coming struggle is the last."

With a sharp crack, a spark of blue light suddenly arched from Elezar's left thumb to his forefinger. His arm swung out from his body in the direction of Delithan, a mask of anger etching the fine lines of his face. The huge djinn brought an arm up over his eyes. The pale outline of a shield began to materialize in front of his chest.

For a moment the two demons stood frozen, the crackle of ionization covering any words that they might have spoken. Then, as quickly as it had sprouted, the arc of energy in Elezar's hand winked out of existence. His face softened. He rotated his palms upward in Delithan's direction.

"Gaspar has grown so bold as to attack me in what all the princes acknowledge as my strength," Elezar said softly, his sudden outburst back under control. "It is a foolish boldness for him to do so and I will not reply in kind. There may yet be the thrill of battle for you against his djinns of lightning, Delithan, but as long as I am your prince, it will be a time of my own choosing. Now take your clutch brethren into the void as I have commanded and escort him here without incident."

Delithan's shield disappeared before it completely formed. He hesitated a moment and then dipped his head

14

in acquiescence. Stooping to clear the archway, he turned back the way he had come. "A djinn lives to fight," he rumbled as he left.

"Gaspar," Astron blurted as Elezar turned back to face him. "Gaspar of the lightning djinns. Though his numbers are large and mighty, he would not dare to challenge you without due cause. None of the other princes would permit it. They would rally to your aid and against all he has no chance."

"His attack is not one of djinn against djinn," Elezar said. "Instead it was something quite unexpected, although, of course, I showed no surprise." Elezar paused. His eyes flared. "He has posed a riddle, cataloguer, a riddle to test the prince most noted for cunning of all those who rule.

"The stakes are familiar, the ones I have accepted from demons with far keener minds. If I answer correctly, then Gaspar and all who follow him are mine to do with what I will. If not, then I and my domain are his."

"A riddle?" Astron said. "Then surely there is no threat at all. The likes of Gaspar could not formulate a puzzle that would long give pause to one such as you, my prince. And if you were—were too busy to answer yourself, then many in your domain would have sufficient wit to formulate the solution."

Elezar ignored Astron's words. "You were telling me of the laws that govern the realm of men. What of the metalaws which lie behind them?"

"Of the three of them I know far less," Astron said. He felt his stembrain again begin to stir. Elezar was moving on to things with which he was far less familiar.

"Three of them," Elezar repeated. "So you state that there are ten laws rather than seven?"

"No, the three metalaws are quite different from the rest," Astron said. "Each of the other realms, that of men, the skyskirr, the fey, and the others, is governed by seven laws of magic out of infinitely many. The metalaws govern which ones are active and how they are changed."

Elezar looked over Astron's head to the far side of the rotunda. Translucent membranes flicked down over his eyes to remove external distractions as he defocused in thought. "The metalaws were known by some of the most ancient princes," he said. "Even if we could not use them ourselves, we understood their manipulations well. And in the realm of the skyskirr, they are all-important; compared to them, the laws themselves pale into insignificance."

Elezar stared back at Astron. "But in the realm of men, for epochs none realized that such things as metalaws existed. For the mortals, there were only the seven laws of magic as you have stated them, constant and unfailing. Humankind spent their brief lives entirely ignorant of the greater powers that slumbered all about them."

The prince paused. "So you see, it is indeed possible. Gaspar's riddle might be a valid question, one with a definite answer. Ah, for the answer." Elezar looked away. "The answer that would give me victory over yet another who thinks his power greater than mine."

The prince ran his slender tongue over his lower lip, apparently savoring an imagined victory. He smiled and waved to the hovering imps for another display. But as the complex pattern formed. Elezar shook his head and motioned them to return to stillness. He looked back at Astron. "But I have no ready reply, cataloguer," he said. The words were forced and came with difficulty. "I stall for more time and Gaspar guesses at my weakness. He even taunts me with clues, so sure is he that I will fail."

Astron felt his thoughts suddenly boil and tumble. Elezar, Elezar the one who was golden—of all the princes, he was the one with the keenest mind. The others might wage their games of power by mustering great arrays of djinns into eye-blinding battles, but Elezar time after time bested them all with deft strokes of high strategy or bound up the outcome in riddles for which only he could unravel the answer in the end.

And if this time Elezar could not provide the solution, then there was great peril for all that he commanded as

16

well. The barely controlled rages of Gaspar were well known throughout the realm. None without an equal appetite for ripping things asunder could hope to survive for long under the rule of a prince of lightning. Astron looked down at his short nails and flexed the wings on his back that were never there.

But mixed with all of that, the surprise and the fear, there was something else that churned with the rest—a riddle, a riddle that even Elezar himself could not solve, a mystery that led perhaps even to the realm of men. What new and wonderful things might then be learned by one sent to observe or by one tasked to record the labors of those questing to find the answer? What increase in power could come to one who catalogued rather than fought?

Elezar apparently did not notice Astron's momentary inattention. The prince stood up and waved his arms in the air. "As you have stated, cataloguer, for every realm that we can contact, fire is the medium that breaks down the barrier between us. And for each of those connections, we are at the mercy of those who dwell on the other realm to build the flame and send their thoughts through it. We must wait for the call, the tugging at our own being, before we can begin the struggle that matches our wills against theirs.

"How much more powerful we would be if we could initiate the interaction, to go forth into the other realms at our own choosing rather than await events of chance. That is the essence of Gaspar's riddle, cataloguer. He states that the power of the laws and metalaws pale for the one who has the answer. It is the ultimate precept, he says, the underlying principle upon which all else is built."

Elezar brought his arms back to his chest. "The riddle is quite simply stated: In the realm of daemon, how does one build a fire?"

Astron saw the eyes of the prince again widen. He felt a rush of questions but knew better than to speak.

"We have great control over the little matter that has been brought back through the barriers to our realm,"

17

Elezar continued. "We can weave and transform it into exotic shapes that please the eye for eons. But somehow, in all the epochs that I can remember, no one in our realm, whether mighty prince or lowly sprite, has ever created a flame. None have been able to form the dance of ions that signify the combination of air with other things. The answer indeed must be the ultimate precept, cataloguer, and Gaspar's riddle or no, I, among all the princes who rule, will be the first to find out how it is done."

"But how will you learn?" Astron asked cautiously. "Is it perhaps in the realm of men that the answer would lie?"

"None in my personal domain have any hint to the solution, cataloguer," Elezar said. "I have decided that it is elsewhere I must look." The prince paused and intensified his stare. "But there is little time for undirected and random search. First, I must ask the one who might have a greater chance of knowing the answer to the riddle than even I."

Astron's interest suddenly vanished. Cataloguing in the relative safety of the realm of men was one thing. Dealing with others of his own kind was quite another. And if it was the one he suspected that the prince had in mind—

"Not old Palodad," he said. "The broodmothers say that even mighty djinns cannot return from his domain unscathed." He looked in Elezar's eyes and saw the prince nod slightly.

"Yes, Palodad," Elezar said, "the one who reckons."

Astron felt his stembrain begin to struggle harder to free itself from his rational control. Knowledge was power, it was true, but the risk must be commensurate with the reward. Even with a well-disciplined phalanx of splendorous djinns, Astron would not care to enter the domain of the demon reputed to be maddest of all. Besides, his specialty was in the other realms. It would not make sense to send to the domain of another prince one without the ability to weave or fly. Surely it must have been for something else that Elezar had summoned him before the scheduled time.

"Which of your phalanx have you selected to dispatch?" Astron managed to say through jaws drawing suddenly tight. "How have you balanced between the need for strength in a far domain as well as here to impress Gaspar when he arrives?"

"You are the emissary, Astron, you alone, the one I have selected above all others in my domain."

"But I am a mere cataloguer." The protest rushed from Astron's lips. "Far more do I know of the workings of men than the traps in our own realm. I serve better helping to unravel what information another might bring back from such a trek than braving the perils myself.

"Look at my fangs," Astron said as he spun quickly around. "See again the stubs on my back. My role is to observe and record. It is the calling of the devils and djinns who can weave to perform actions for their prince."

Elezar shook his head slowly. "The broodmothers are most likely correct; Palodad's lair will be dissimilar to any other in the realm. But it is because you cannot fight that I have chosen you, cataloguer. The unfamiliar will not provoke you to rage. You above all else will keep your stembrain under control, because you must."

Astron looked beyond the prince to the cool serene walls of the rotunda, familiar sights that he had viewed many times before. He thought of the comforts of his own lair with the artifacts whose purposes were yet to be discovered. Even the realm of men with the strange customs and exotic structures was to be preferred to the dangers that lurked for the unwary in his own realm. He felt the tug and pull of his stembrain straining to be free, to run amok and control his limbs in a frenzy of chaos and self-destruction.

"There is more at stake than the rule of my domain," Elezar said. "Gaspar will treat my own djinns with dignity, grant them a final battle that would satisfy even their lusts for destruction." He paused and bored his sight into Astron. "But as for you, my wingless one, a

19

nimble wit and knowledge of arcane lists will have little value for him. At best, your torture would serve as a moment's distraction. You might hope that the process would not be a lingering one."

Astron looked into Elezar's eyes, searching for even a hint of indecision, but saw only the resolve of a prince. His shoulders slumped. The last thoughts of his den faded away. For a moment, he did not speak, but finally he willed his tongue to move. "Arrange for the djinn who will transport me," he said softly. "I will perform my duty as the prince commands."

CHAPTER TWO

The One Who Reckons

As the dimly flickering light grew brighter, the over-whelming emptiness of the realm began to fade. Astron craned his head upward at the djinn who carried him, each shoulder tight in a unflinching grip. The demon showed no change in expression as they closed on their destination, the boredom of flight just another indication of the encroachment of the great monotony into its mind.

Looking over his shoulder, Astron could no longer distinguish the shine of Elezar's domain. It was lost in the sparse scatter of glowing dots that gave a feeble hint of pattern in an otherwise featureless expanse. Despite countless eons of slowly wresting matter through the flame from the other universes, the great vastness was still the true character of the realm. Only in the small confines of one's own lair or in the everchanging patterns of the domain of a prince could one temporarily forget the meagerness that enshrouded imp and djinn alike.

Endowed with the power to cover great distances almost without effort and the ability to transform whatever one saw into unlimited other shapes, the cruel jest of it all was that there was so very little on which those powers could be exercised. It did not take long before the farthest corners of the realm had been explored, all the interesting weavings formed and destroyed, and the bizarre mysteries of men and those of the other realms sampled and discarded. Ultimately all that was left was to sit and wait, contemplating the curse of an immortal lifetime—sit and wait until the great monotony drove one to surrender to the stembrain and self-destruction in a new and interesting way.

Astron shook his head free of the brooding thoughts as the features of Palodad's lair became more clear in the darkness. Just as the other domains, the domain of the one who reckoned hung in space. Unlike Elezar's, however, it cast forth no shafts of brilliant light. Only the glow of a single imp marked the entrance to a long, sloping tunnel that led to Astron knew not what.

After he was deposited at the entrance, Astron bade the djinn to wait and cautiously entered. He felt the smooth surface of time-worn stone beneath his feet— true stone of condensed matter, rather than a web of fleeting energy that merely hinted at substance. Around his head and shoulders, the gnarled tunnel walls squeezed downward in the total darkness. The solidness of the steps was a surprise and the darkness too much a reminder of the cold and depressing emptiness of the realm. But there was no other choice. Astron clasped his fingers into fists and began descending as rapidly as he could, each step less than a heart beat.

Images of what could come to pass if indeed he did not succeed flitted through Astron's mind—Gaspar's rasping laugh, the small mites that crawled in the greasy stubble on the prince's chin, his minions ripping asunder the delicate columns and domes that Elezar had taken eons to weave, demigorgons crushing the skulls of the imps in their massive hands and degutting the larger devils with searing bolts of flame.

Astron tightened the coils of his fists. He for one was not ready for such a fate. His hatching had been less than an era ago. The great monotony did not yet dampen his will to live as it did for some of the others, who had sampled a dozen times over all that Elezar had to offer, others who would have to be goaded out of a jaded lethargy even to die. No, if and when they came for him, surrounding his slight body with stares and gloats, it would be far too soon.

Astron grimaced. If and when they came, he hoped that for once he would have the strength of his clutch brothers, strength to deny to Gaspar any satisfaction, strength to be able to look back with unblinking eyes and stand silent, even though they pulled away his fingers and toes one by one.

It was all because of arrogance, Astron thought. His prince had been too proud not to accept Gaspar's challenge on the terms with which it was given. Elezar should have denied the fairness of the riddle. But he was too concerned about what the other princes would think if he refused a test in which, after all, he was supposed to be the strongest of all.

The tunnel turned sharply to the left without warning, and Astron banged his head against a jutting overhang. His thoughts jangled back to his immediate concern. "More than a million steps in total darkness," he muttered. "This Palodad constructs an approach of more than a million when a few hundred easily would do. Even a sublime devil guards his lair with only fifty. Fifty steps, though he might weave the essence of a rose."

Astron rubbed the throb in his temple with one hand while he cautiously extended his other forward. "There must be some truth to the accounts," he said to himself. "What sane demon would dare to be so wasteful? To squander his wealth on stride after stride of featureless rock when he could occupy himself for epochs building intricate sculptures instead."

His question echoed unanswered down the dark tunnel and Astron paused a moment more, trying to will himself into placid composure. To approach in a state of visible apprehension would place him at an immediate disadvantage. He was, after all, the emissary of a prince.

He squeezed his fists all the tighter and set a grim mask on his face. In silence, he trod the last ten thousand steps, not even bothering to count.

Finally he reached the entrance barrier and pulled it aside. The tunnel suddenly blazed with light. Translucent membranes flicked over his eyes as he stared into the brilliance. The drone of tiny wings mixed with the slur of countless curses, creating a din that assaulted even the most insensitive ears.

He saw the walls expand outward from where he stood to form a giant sphere, dotted with smaller globes of incandescence that banished all shadows from its interior. He stood on a ledge that circumnavigated this globe, a small pathway that gently curved and finally disappeared out of sight on both sides behind the massive constructions that filled the enclosed volume.

Directly in front, a causeway arched from the ledge to link with the nearest of the structures. The edifice looked like some gigantic gameboard, a collection of tightly packed cubical cells built of rusty iron spars with row upon row of repeated patterns forming an immense vertical plane. Thousands of cells were stacked into a single column, and thousands of columns ranked together from left to right.

Each cell was occupied by an imp, mostly rock gremlins with pale green skin, warted eyelids, and thick leathery wings. But here and there, Astron saw other types, waterwisps, smouldering fifenella, and pigmy afreets almost as tall as the span of his forearm.

Every imp, regardless of type, was collared with iron and linked with short pieces of chain to the lattice. The inhabitants of each row were joined together by lengths of rope that draped from cell to cell and looped around right wrists outstretched rigidly above slumbering heads. The end of each rope terminated on a separate shaft of steel at the edge of the lattice that ran to other constructions farther back in the sphere.

More cords dangled from shafts above each column, connecting the left wrists of the demons positioned in the same vertical line. Although all seemingly were asleep,

23

about half had their mouths open and long dangling tongues oozed a drool onto those confined below.

As Astron watched, a shaft on the side suddenly twitched away from the lattice, joggling the arms of the row of gremlins to which it was connected. They all sprang alert. An instant later one of the rods on the top also lurched from its resting place, waking a column as well. Another moment passed with the aroused demons tensed and eyes open wide. Then, almost as quickly as they had wakened, they returned to their rest, facial expressions the same as they had been before. They all returned, that is, except for one, the one who had been common to both row and column, the one who had had both arms tugged.

The selected imp waited restlessly until another gremlin, free-flying and unfettered, buzzed into view to position itself in front of the lattice.

"Bad news, mintbreath. It's a tongueout," the newcomer squeaked. "And from the way things are cycling, I doubt another change will come for an eon or so."

"Gimme a break," the awakened imp answered. "I'm way ahead on tongueouts. I had to drool for over an eon just a few cycles ago. My jaw still aches from the effort. And I can remember my state in my head just as well as you. Wake me in an era and I will still recall whether I had been set to be in or out."

"Tongueout," the hovering gremlin insisted. "Or do you want me to report you stuck? If the upkeep crew replaces you, then you will be sent to the register pit. At least here you get to sleep most of the time."

The imp in the lattice grimaced and then finally spat out its tongue at the messenger. With a growl he pitched his head forward on his chest, letting his body dangle from its fetters. The fluttering gremlin then flew away just before another tug on the rods aroused a fifenella and the cycle started again.

Astron shifted his attention to other lattices nearby the first. Some were identical in construction, giant arrays of sleeping imps. In others, tall columns of sprites were bound spread-eagled with a limb stretched tight toward each corner of its cell and the fetters running from the leg of one to the arm of another. In spasmodic waves the demons twitched and shuddered, jiggling the left leg if only one arm were tugged and the right if both were stretched instead.

In yet other cages, mighty djinns flipped from being erect to standing on their heads in response to the jabs and pokes of their neighbors next in line. Back into the recesses of the cavern the jumble of imprisoned demons filled the span of the eye, islands of symmetry joined in a chaotic web of lines, shafts, and darting imps. All of it was alive with jerk and tug, great rolling waves of activity that coursed and pulsed in patterns that could not quite be followed.

Astron's mind whirled. He had been prepared for strangeness. If nothing else, his many trips into the worlds of men had accustomed him to the unusual. But the expanse was too great. Never before in his own realm had he seen so much matter concentrated in one place. Countless numbers of fetters and chains, cell placed upon cell, lattice after lattice, receding into the distance. Elezar was reputed to be among the richest of the princes, but all his fanciful domes would be lost among the massive constructs in the sphere.

"With no matter for payment? One dares to come with no matter?" A raspy voice sounded over the noise.

Astron looked upward and saw a platform that jutted from the wall of the sphere some hundred spans above where he stood. Descending from it in a rope-hung bucket was a demon of about his size although certainly not his shape and form.

The posture stooped; a long curved neck cantilevered from the deep valley between bony shoulders. The scales of the face were cracked and peeling. Near the gnarled ears, some scales were missing altogether, revealing a pulsing underlayer that quivered like freshly flayed flesh. Eyes squinted out from grimy hollows, one rheumy with phlegm and the other jerking in erratic directions, independent of its mate. Emaciated arms terminated in three-clawed hands, one wrapped permanently

25

about a crystal of some polished metal, the webbing between the fingers spread like a threadbare cape over the gleaming surface.

"And no wings as well, I see," the voice continued as the basket descended to eye level. "Quite presumptuous to come without wings to get you from here to there."

Astron stared at the demon as it slowly swung a spar from the basket over to the ledge and hobbled across. "I am unfamiliar with the tradition of this domain," he said slowly to the advancing figure. "This is the first time I have come. I act upon the request and demand of my—"

"What did you say?" The demon cupped his free hand behind his ear. "This is the first what?"

"The first time," Astron repeated. "The first time that—"

The rest of his words were drowned in sudden laughter. The approaching demon tilted back his head and boomed with a repetitious grate, each rasp more dissonant than the last. Astron opened his mouth to speak again, but then thought better of it, waiting instead for the other finally to lapse back into silence.

"Time," the demon repeated with his last rasp. "Not only time but the first time. Here, hatchling, look at this."

The good hand reached into a small pouch hung over a pointy hip and produced a curiously shaped glass, two bulbs, one above the other with a small constricted passage between and grains of sand slowly draining from top to bottom.

"This is time, hatchling. See it flow incessantly. In a continuous stream. Eons, eras, epochs, one after the other without seam, without division, apparently without start and finish. There is no first time, there is no last. There is only time and it is one."

Astron retracted his membranes and stared at the figure before him. The awe for the surroundings gnawed at his resolve. "Palodad?" he asked cautiously. "Are you the devil, Palodad, the one who reckons?"

"I am indeed he." The demon straightened his back slightly, his demeanor suddenly sober. "And you no doubt are the messenger of some prince who cannot see his way out of a problem. This may be your first visit, but across the eons it is but one of countless others."

"I come by the command of Prince Elezar," Astron said. "He strives against Gaspar of the lightning djinns for the right of supremacy."

Palodad's good eye brightened. He put away the sandglass and looked over Astron far more carefully than he had before. "Ah, Elezar, Elezar, the one who is golden," he said slowly.

"Yes, and as you say, I come with a riddle that is in need of its key."

"If Elezar cannot answer, then it must be a puzzle indeed," Palodad said. "I have advised him once before on matters of great weight. If this is of like proportion, then a mere fistful of iron will not suffice for payment."

"Nevertheless, the answers the prince must know."

Palodad grunted. For a long moment he stared unblinkingly at Astron. Then he put away his glass and turned to hobble slowly back onto the spar. "Come," he called over his shoulder. "Come and tell me what exactly perplexes the great Elezar so. I will elect to be flattered by his attention, even though it has been slow in coming. It certainly is about time he again has decided to ask for my aid."

Palodad suddenly jerked to a halt and smiled. "Yes, it is about time," he repeated with a rasp. "About time. It could be for nothing less." He tilted his head back and opened his mouth into a great circle. His laugh filled the air and echoed from the wall. For a dozen cycles of the nearest lattice, the demon clutched his arms to his sides, rocking back and forth, oblivious to everything around him.

Then, as abruptly as he began, Palodad stopped and resumed his shuffle toward the bucket. "I had instructed you to follow," he called back as he entered the basket. "Or did your prince send just an imp still afraid of its broodmother?"

Astron looked again into the interior of the sphere, at the bound and jerking sprites. He heard again the howls of pain and maledictions. The scene troubled him greatly, far more than any mystery in the realm of men. A reluctance coursed through his stembrain, putting stiffness into his limbs when he commanded them to move.

"I will remain untouched," he muttered to himself. "I need only stay until I have information for the prince." With a pace no swifter than Palodad's he moved toward the waiting bucket.

CHAPTER THREE

Lore of the Listmaker

ASTRON lost track of the number of pulley baskets he rode before he finally reached Palodad's destination, deep in the interior of the sphere. As the last bucket whisked from view, he found himself in an open-top box of stone as solid as the steps that had led to the entrance of the old demon's lair.

To his immediate left, in front of one of the four confining walls, a continuous belt moved on rollers and creaked off through a dark recess into the sphere beyond.

Directly in front stood a collection of glass jars, densely packed with swarms of swirling mites. Behind them were stacks of what looked like shallow baking sheets, some piled in precarious columns and others only two or three deep littering the floor. Through an archway in the distance, Astron saw a small devil brushing a sticky glue onto the surface of one of the sheets and adding it to another stack. A cloyingly sweet odor drifted from the glue and hung heavy in the air.

On the right, the wall was covered with tiny glowsprites, each one crammed between the limbs of his neighbors, but somehow arrayed in precise lines. The small demons winked on and off with random bursts of light across the spectrum. All the colors of the rainbow stirred in motley patterns, each imp no larger than a thumbnail, but with thousands of neighbors producing a pulsating and almost hypnotic glitter.

"It is here that questions are composed," Palodad said behind Astron. "Here I affix the mites to the matrix and send the instructions to my minions who await beyond."

"But to what purpose?" Astron turned and shook his head, unable to contain himself any longer. "Why the million steps? How can so many submit to such an existence?"

"These are the questions of your prince?" Palodad asked.

"No, no, not these. His is much more profound." Astron regretted the words as soon as they had left his lips. They revealed that Elezar's messenger was not totally unimpressed by what he saw and hinted therefore that Palodad's power might be the greater. The prince would not be pleased.

"But nevertheless I am a cataloguer," Astron added quickly. "It is my nature to ask so that I can observe and record."

"A cataloguer. Indeed." Palodad paused and squinted. "No doubt the lack of wings and protruding fangs gives you greater satisfaction with your amusement."

Astron turned away his eyes. Things were not starting well at all. "I am, in fact, a splendorous djinn," he said softly. "At least my clutch brethren were. But I was hatched without wings and grew in stature no greater than you see me now."

He hesitated a moment and looked back at Palodad. "But no matter that I cannot weave great cataclysms or burst assunder condensed rock with the wave of my hand. I am a cataloguer and a good one. I filed my fangs myself so that the effect would be complete. With hood and cape I have passed among men, raising not a modicum of suspicion. And yes, I even managed the domination of a strong-willed one or two."

"No doubt," Palodad said. "Even the smallest imp declares he has a few wizards under his spell."

"What I say is true. I have no need to speak otherwise."

"It does not matter." Palodad waved the words aside. "I have little use for the boasts of others in any case. The workings of my domain tell me far more of what has happened and what yet will come to pass." He paused and stared at Astron. "Perhaps, as a cataloguer, you might appreciate that more than the others. Tell me your name. We will see what I know of the followers of Elezar the prince."

"It is Astron—Astron the one who walks."

"Ah, Astron. It will be easy enough," Palodad said, turning to pick up one of the metal sheets from the floor. "Not thousands of syllables that record all of your exploits like some who have come."

He placed the sheet on the belt and pulled a lever to stop it moving. Then he turned the lid on one of the jars at his feet, releasing a cloud of mites. Moving with a quickness that surprised Astron, the old demon began plucking the tiny imps from the air one by one and affixing them to the sticky surface of the sheet. With the metal ball in his other hand he smashed them flat so that they would stay. In what seemed like an instant he had immobilized several precise rows of mites, some with their heads aligned along the lines and others perpendicular to it.

Palodad surveyed his handiwork for a moment and then kicked the empty jar aside, waving the unused mites away. He hobbled back into the stacks behind them and returned a moment after with several more sheets, these already filled with imprisoned imps. He formed a chain of the trays on the belt. With one final grunt, he pulled the lever to start them moving toward the slit in the wall.

"Pay attention to the glowsprites," Palodad said. "It will take awhile for the framing instructions to be obeyed. After that the images will unfold quickly enough."

Astron looked at the random dance of lights on the far

wall. For a moment nothing happened; then suddenly the pattern changed. The glowsprites began pulsing in unison, creating bands of color that seemed to move across the wall. Kaleidoscopic shapes formed and dissolved; scenes of other parts of Palodad's lair exploded into sharp focus and then faded away. Faces of great djinns snapped into view, one after another, faster than Astron could follow. Then the flickering stopped. A single image remained for him to view.

Astron stared at what he saw. A slight demon somehow familiar seemed to frown back from the plane of the sprites. About the figure was a clutter of trays and jars. In the apparent distance stood a gnarled old devil that looked exactly like Palodad. He saw the second demon scratch absently at a pockmarked cheek with a hand clutching a metal sphere and he whirled to see Palodad do the same.

Astron spun back to look at the vision, took a step forward and extended his arm. The image on the wall copied his motions. He touched his forehead and bared his filed-down fangs in a grotesque grin, watching in fascination as the face staring at him responded in kind.

"How is this possible?" Astron asked. "For all of demonkind, none of us cast a reflection."

"Truly not." Palodad smiled. "Light is altered when it is scattered from our bodies. It subsequently can be adsorbed but not reflected again." He waved his arm at the wall. "What you observe here is merely what I have instructed my sprites to do. They watch how you move and then each glows in the required hue and intensity to form an image that mimics exactly. They form a precise copy so that you see yourself as you appear to others."

Astron looked back to the wall. He straightened to full height and squared his shoulders, staring intently at what he had never seen before. His head was oval and symmetrically formed, with the small knobs where the horns of his brothers would be. No tufts of hair grew from the delicate swirl of his ears, and on the supple pale flesh only a hint of scaling was visible in the glow of the sprite light. The eyes were deeply set and the nose and lips a trifle large, but as he had said, without close scrutiny he could pass for a native in the realm of men. It was for these features that he had found favor with Elezar, he knew. The prince himself was unlike most demonkind and, rather than minimize the difference, he flaunted it.

"Evidently in the grand scheme of things," Palodad said, "there was need to collect more than just superficials about you, cataloguer. That is why the image is so sharp and clear. Look to your left. There is more that can be displayed than physical form."

Astron watched a second pulsing of color next to his reflection. It quickly distilled into the image of a broodlair, with pieces of broken shell littered among the coarse grasses. Four tiny djinns, tufts of down still clinging to rapidly flapping wings, danced above the lair, while one smaller demon cowered in the straw. With a shock, Astron realized what he was witnessing. No sound accompanied the animation, but he remembered the shrieks an era ago as his brothers had swooped down upon him, claws gleaming sharp. Even worse, he recalled, was the laughter as they turned aside at the last instant, barely avoiding contact. The two more precocious of his brothers already had felt the first intuitive grasp of weaving and formed bolts of crackling pain that they sprayed upon Astron's back as they sped by.

Astron clinched his long, slender fingers as the memory of impotency flooded through him. Four brothers, all splendorous djinns, and he with no more power than a lowly sprite, able to convert the air he breathed into food and water and nothing more.

But before Astron could dwell further on the memory, the image formed by the glowsprites shimmered and shifted. He saw himself half grown, eyes wide with membranes pulled back as he examined the object he delicately cradled in his hands. The devil who stood next to him in the image had his arms folded across his chest and a face showing uncompromising pride. Astron remembered that he had not cared.

Acknowledging the magnitude of the feat that brought

condensed matter of such quality through the flame had not been in his thoughts at all. Slowly he had leafed through the delicate sheets that were stitched along one side, studying intently the rows and rows of markings and occasional drawings of other objects equally strange. Some he had recognized—coins, belt buckles, forks; a random sampling of things retrieved by other demons on their journeys through the flame. And for some of these he suddenly had understood their use and meaning from the context in which they were drawn.

Astron nodded his head as he watched. He remembered the electric thrill that had arched down his spine. Who among all of demonkind would have guessed that the cylindrical fingercap guarded a human's fingertip against pricks from the tiny sword and trailing thread that bound together two pieces of cloth.

There was more merit than mere mass in an object fetched from beyond the flame, he had realized. There was knowledge as well, knowledge that might be of use to a prince who wished to astound his peers. And with knowledge came stature and regard, even for a djinn without wings or the ability to weave.

"All the artifacts that I possess," he remembered he had said, looking up quickly at the devil at his side. "The web of the spider, the pollen of a flower, everything in exchange for this."

As the trade was made, the image dissolved. When it refocused, Astron recognized a scene of only months ago as measured in the realm of men. He stood in his hood and cloak beside a cottage hearth; only the last embers remained of the evening fire. At a table across the room, a human serving girl stared in Astron's direction, her eyes wide and unblinking, totally under his command.

"What are your instructions, master, while I wait for you to return," she had said.

Astron remembered his hesitation. He knew full well what would happen to her when she was found after his departure. Men professed to feel compassion, but they dealt with demon possession with a zeal that was hard to understand. And she was not a wizard, boldly reaching into the flame to test her will against Astron or his kin. Only by accident had she looked too long into the hypnotic dance of the fire and allowed Astron to pass through the barrier between the realms.

Elezar would be satisfied enough with what has been learned, Astron had decided. The purpose of the little orb attached to the side of the door had been perfectly explained. None of the other princes would guess that it was to be rotated before being pulled.

"Return to the way you were," Astron had said. "I release you from my control. The prince cannot care about one mind more or less. Besides us, who in the two realms would know?"

The scene began to fade. Astron turned away to face Palodad. "How did you find out?" he asked. "I have told no one of what I did. Indeed, why even bother to record my affairs, rather than the lives of the princes that rule?"

"I have the relevant information on them as well," Palodad said. "Do not prejudge your role in the scheme of things. I am, after all, the one who reckons."

The old demon squinted his good eye at Astron. "The more interesting question is not how, but why. Why did you release the human female when you had no need? Even without wings, one would not expect such behavior from the clutch brother of a splendorous djinn."

"I—I do not know," Astron said. The vividness of the memories was unsettling. The impact of all he had seen began to numb his mind. His thoughts started to go off balance. He felt his limbs tighten. Was his the madness that came with the visit to Palodad? Was his lair so overwhelming and knowledge so great that one could not hope to keep his own clear thoughts in the old devil's presence?

Astron flicked down the membranes over his eyes and concentrated on the comforts of his own den. He had not one book by now but three. Some of the strange symbology that accompanied the pictures he was beginning to understand. Of all of Elezar's cataloguers, he was held in the highest regard. He had pledged to his prince and had

34

a mission to perform, regardless of the great powers exhibited by the old demon at his side. And the results were needed quickly, before Gaspar lost his patience and it was all too late.

Astron firmed his resolve. He would not waver. Digging his shortened nails into his palms, he slowly, deliberately retracted his membranes and looked at Palodad.

"Questions concerning Astron, the cataloguer, will be for another time," he said. "I am here now by demand of Elezar, the prince."

Palodad did not immediately answer. He pointed silently at the imaging screen indicating that he could show more, his lips curved in the hint of a mocking smile.

But Astron held his determination. The urgency of his visit locked firmly in place. He willed his thoughts to calmness and waited for the devil to speak.

"Questions concerning the one who walks will be for when?" Palodad asked at last.

"For another time," Astron said.

"Yes, for another time, another time," Palodad echoed. He kicked one of the metal trays aside and again dissolved in a fit of laughter. "There is no getting away from it," he gasped. "It is always a matter of time."

The devil clutched his sides and crumpled into a ball at Astron's feet. Rolling about on the hard stone slab, he flailed his spindly legs and bellowed incoherently, giving no signs of ever stopping.

Astron waited patiently for a moment and then scowled in annoyance. Now with his focus away from his own personal safety, the pressure to obtain results felt all the greater. He looked about for the presence of a broodmother who might give aid to the stricken devil, but saw none. He hesitated a moment more. Then with a shrug copied from the humans he turned and began to walk toward the doorway behind the stacks of trays.

But Palodad stopped laughing before Astron had gone two paces. "You have not yet told me the question of your prince," the devil said calmly.

Astron paused. Now there was no hint of madness in Palodad's tone. It was as if the devil was totally unaware of his actions moments before. Astron shook his head, trying to toss off the behavior as he had all the rest. Slowly he turned back to face the devil and waited until the old one was erect.

"Gaspar's riddle is most unusual," Astron said finally after Palodad had finished smoothing his pouches and straps. "It is most unusual that the likes of a lightning djinn would even conceive of one of such difficulty."

"But nevertheless, apparently he did," Palodad said. "How unlikely the conundrums, the agreement is no less binding."

The old devil paused and a faraway look came to his eye. The corners of his mouth rounded in the beginnings of a grin. "So quickly now, state what it is that your prince wishes to know. You already have wasted enough of my precious—"

Palodad's cheeks lifted further. The hint of a giggle started in his throat.

"How does one start a fire?" Astron interrupted quickly. "On the worlds of men, in the 'hedron of the skyskirr, and in all the universes that we know, there is fire and flame."

"It is the means by which the barriers between our realms are overcome and mind is linked with mind," Palodad said. "Elezar does not need the one who reckons to tell him that."

"In every realm there is flame except for one," Astron said. "Except in the realm of daemon itself. We have pulled through the barriers artifacts that are solid and ones of liquid and gas. But never in all the epochs that any can remember has there been fire in the domain of any of the princes."

Astron stopped. He looked at Palodad intently to judge the old devil's response. For a long moment neither moved; the only sound was the background cries echoing in the confines of the sphere.

Then Palodad shuffled to the jars on the stone floor and released another swarm of mites. For many cycles of the lattices, he grabbed them from the air and affixed them to one metal sheet after another, feeding the completed trays through the slot in the wall. When he was done he turned his attention to the glowsprites, watching closely the random blink of colors and form. This time they did not shape coherent images, but Palodad nodded and smiled, mumbling to himself when he seemed to distinguish one particular pattern from another.

For how long he remained waiting, Astron could not tell; but finally, one by one, the sprite lights winked out, leaving only a surface of muted gray.

"There is the matter of the payment," Palodad said at last. He rubbed the metal ball he carried in his hand against his leg and then looked absently at the shiny surface. "Did your prince delegate to you the bargaining as well?"

"Then you do know the answer," Astron exclaimed. "You have calculated it with your strange devices even as we waited."

But Palodad held up his hand before Astron could say more. "As you have said, the riddle is most profound. It is no wonder that even the likes of Elezar could not fathom the direction in which to proceed."

The devil paused and fingered the pouch containing the hourglass at his side. "In fact, even I do not bargain with the solution to the conundrum," he said. "I can only indicate where it is the most—the most profitable for Elezar to look. As for the details of the answer, he will have to find it on his own."

The sudden buoyancy of Astron's hopes drained away. Despite all the tales of the broodmothers, the old devil knew little more than his prince. Elezar already suspected that the answer lay outside of the realm of daemon. Merely being told where to seek would be worth far less than the answer itself.

"You speak of payments," Astron said cautiously. "Surely a mere hint carries little value at all."

"Many others have found my prices reasonable enough." Palodad waved his arm out across his lair. "With each riddle I solved, I obtained a few more spars, stone for another trio of steps, cages for one or two more imps. Each exchange in itself has not amounted to much, but over the eons I have managed to build all that you have seen. And, rather than waste my wealth on trivial amusements for the senses, I have focused it on increasing my ability to compute, to collect and store even more of what happens in the realm, and to predict with greater and greater accuracy what the future will bring."

Palodad smiled and tapped Astron's chest with the ball he clutched in his fist. "Elezar chose his emissary well," he said. "I get no great amusement spending eons maneuvering through complex negotiations for the last dram of mass. Your prince merely has to fetch for me something from the realm to which I will direct him. That will be payment enough."

"If what you desire is more than base iron, then it will not be so easy for any of Elezar's retinue to wrest it back through the flame," Astron said. "The prince will not care for an agreement that carries such a complication."

"I am fully aware that the living residents of the other realms can transport objects through the flame far more easily than can any of our kind," Palodad said. "Elezar will have to enlist help from men, skyskirr, or some other beings, it is true. But I have faith in his ability to figure out a way."

"It is a complication," Astron repeated. "As Gaspar presses for an answer, my master will have less ability to comply."

Palodad scowled. He pressed the heavy orb of metal to his chest. "Tell him that I will validate his answer," he said. "Whatever he discovers, he can bring to me before he risks exposing it to Gaspar. I will weigh the plausibility of correctness with the computations that are at my disposal and no one else's in the realm. In exchange for a modicum of matter, he will know not only where to look but be certain that what he finds is correct.

"Tell him, cataloguer. Tell him what I offer. He will ponder and then finally acquiesce. It is only a question of time."

Astron grimaced, but Palodad took no heed. He slapped his arms about his waist and staggered back into the conveyer belt, howling in apparent glee. "Time,

38

time, time," he gasped. "The focus always returns to time. When will it ever end?"

Astron slumped to the stone slab in frustration. He felt the beginnings of doubt that his journey had accomplished anything at all. Perhaps all the talk of computations and hints were no more than the ravings of madness, a perverted defense against a growing presence of the great monotony.

He shrugged his shoulders. But if there were anything else to try, surely his prince would have so directed him. Palodad represented the last hope, as slim as it was. In resignation, he watched the old devil flail on the hard stone, waiting for the seizure to end.

Eventually Palodad stopped and righted himself, wiping away a mucus-filled tear as he stood. "You should now go," he said, waving to a bucket descending from a level above. "Repeat to your prince the offer I have made. Come again and tell me when he has agreed. Then I will instruct in detail where it is you are to search and what you will bring back for me in exchange."

Astron nodded and rose to meet the descending basket. The outcome of the meeting was far from satisfactory. He doubted that the duty to his prince was yet quite completed.

CHAPTER FOUR

Princes of Power

THE domes of Elezar were just as Astron had left them. He felt the talons release their grip on his shoulders and dropped the last few spans to the decorated plane on which the structures stood.

"Until the prince gives me cause to return to Palodad's lair, I will have no further need," he said to the djinn still hovering above him. "Return to your own den and await command."

The mighty demon gave no acknowledgment. With one beat of his wings he soared rapidly upward. Soon he was but a speck vanishing from sight. Astron watched him go and for a moment more followed the flights of others as they transported objects and smaller devils to and from Elezar's domain.

He was a cataloguer, Astron thought, the best in all the retinue of his prince. He understood the value of knowledge and traded it for power far beyond what one would expect for one of his size and lack of ability to weave.

He was a cataloguer and yet... He flexed his arms trying to imagine for perhaps the millionth time the sensation of darting between the uppermost spires of his prince's towers, of swooping down into the dark abysses, or even of visiting distant lairs without the assistance of a djinn dangling him from great talons and protecting him from danger.

Astron closed his eyes, wiggling his fingers in exaggerated slowness, straining for the feel of the matter about him, trying to caress its form and texture, molding it into the shapes that he commanded, and transforming even its innermost structure and bonding so that it became as he desired.

But as always, the feelings did not come. His weight pressed all too firmly on the soles of his feet. His palms and the tips of his fingers felt no more than the tenuousness of air. He was only Astron, the one who walked. Besides, there was no time for such reverie, he decided angrily. He must report to the prince.

Quickly Astron navigated through the maze of peripheral domes to the main rotunda. The slight give of the thinly stretched web of matter to each stride reminded him of the firmness of Palodad's crude steps of true stone. The outer passageways were empty; the flitter of imps and bustle of messenger devils had stopped. When he burst into the central rotunda, Astron found that every demon in the domain had gathered. In concentric circles, they hovered and squatted; all eyes were focused on the hub in which were conversing no less than two princes of the realm.

Astron felt his limbs stiffen. He might already be too late. Gaspar and his minions had arrived. Astron saw Elezar sitting on the same pillow of silk and down. Ignoring the other cushions, Gaspar stood with arms folded across his chest, his massive torso rippling with muscle that seemed just barely under control. Deep-set and cruel eyes brooded under an overhanging brow, shadowing a face that never smiled. With a wave of irritation, he brushed aside the mites that swarmed about his chin. Small bursts of unwoven energy crackled from his fingertips, arching spontaneously from joint to joint. In the dreams of men, it was demons such as Gaspar that they feared the most.

Astron hesitated. One part of his mind willed his legs forward to tell the prince what little he had learned. Another bade him to remain still; it would not be prudent for Gaspar to hear the extent of Elezar's ignorance. In nervous anticipation, Astron waited for some indication of what he should do.

"I have come to settle our wager," the lightning djinn's voice rumbled throughout the dome. "Either you know the answer to my riddle or you do not. There is nothing to be determined by delay. Submit to your doom as you have agreed."

The guard of colossal djinns behind Elezar, six in all and each identical to the tiniest scale to his brethren, tensed and bared their fangs, but the prince motioned them to remain calm.

"Your haste hints of weakness," Elezar replied. "How bored has your following become?"

"There is no trace of the great monotony in a single one." Gaspar waved at the brace of lieutenants he had brought with him, now standing off to the side. He glanced about the dome and eyed the web of vaults and spars that held the expanse of the great roof aloft. "Every one of them looks forward with anticipation to when they can reduce all of this to base iron."

41

"And even if your challenge should prevail," Elezar said, "after the few brief moments of destructive fury, what then? What new amusements will you promise? How can you hope to keep alive their will and allegiance for even an epoch more? In the end, you will lose, Gaspar. The eons and eras stretch before you farther than you dare imagine."

Elezar paused and lowered his voice to a whisper, although all present could still hear. "Are you not already weary, Gaspar? Does not the futility of it all begin to gnaw? Will one more orgy of destruction be that much different from the last? Submit, submit to me, and at least the ending will be amusing for all."

"No," Gaspar thundered. He unfurled his wings and rose a span above the floor cushions. The air around his shoulders began to crackle and hiss. Sparkles of color pulsed into existence above his head.

The guard djinns quickly interposed themselves between Elezar and the other prince. Gaspar's lieutenants vaulted over the smaller demons between and formed a rank alongside their leader, their synchronized wing strokes creating a wind that whistled through the rotunda archways.

"Are these the actions of a prince secure in his command?" Elezar continued his questioning as the djinns maneuvered. "Why do the images I propose prick at your stembrain so?"

"I will have your existence to do with what I will," Gaspar roared back. "It has been promised. Agree to the conditions of the challenge and surrender. If you do not, it will not only be the lightning djinns that you must face. All of daemon will aid my just cause."

"And if you hurl one bolt at what is mine before that surrender is made, what then of the agreement?" Elezar said. "If a single atom of my domain is disturbed before I accede you the right, on whose side will the realm render succor and aid?"

Pops of thunder exploded from Gaspar's hands. For a moment, the intensity of the arching between his fingers increased. Then the demon curled one hand into a fist and smashed it into the other, smothering the pulsating energy. He roared an incoherent bellow of frustration and waved his lieutenants back to their positions. Sullenly he drifted to the rotunda floor, again folding his arms across his chest.

Elezar's guard djinns resumed their positions behind the prince. For a long moment there was silence throughout the vast dome.

"I will illustrate my point in a less destabilizing manner," Elezar said at last. He motioned to an archway and four devils responded by carrying in a sculpture on a stand of marble.

Astron saw that it was molded in heavy bronze, a cluster of bubbles popping from a viscous broth, a copy of an artform prevalent in the realm of the fey. As the devils positioned it between Elezar and Gaspar, six more demons waddled forward, each one squat and broad, with eyes that squinted from between deep folds of flesh. They positioned themselves directly behind Elezar and gazed at the sculpture from expressionless faces.

"Now pick one of your lieutenants," Elezar said. "I give him leave. He may do with this matter as he wishes."

Almost in unison, Gaspar's djinns expanded their chests. Crackles of energy began to dance from their fingertips and eyes. Their alertness for possible battle moments before was a mere shadow of the excitement that gripped them now. Gaspar grunted irritably and motioned one near the middle forward. The selected lieutenant quickly arched across the intervening distance and landed with a heavy thud near the sculpture. His eyes widened. He wiggled his fingers, letting short arcs of piercing blue jump from one hand to the other.

"Wait a moment until the shield demons are ready and then you may begin," Elezar said. "I wish to minimize the effect of your craft upon the dome and the others who watch."

Gaspar's lieutenants nodded. Astron heard the shield demons begin to hum in a six-voice harmony. Simultaneously he saw the lightning djinn start to fade. On the top, bottom, and each side of the demon, a plane of haziness began to form, six sheets of growing opaqueness that intersected and confined him and the adjacent sculpture into a box.

As if they were filling with fog, the surfaces grew less and less transparent, finally hiding the djinn totally from view. The glow of imp light around the rotunda walls reflected diffusely from what looked like a solid cube. The shield demons had constructed a confining barrier, Astron knew. Little energy could penetrate it from either side.

But then the interior of the cube pulsed with light. In a heart beat, Astron saw a searing bolt of yellow rip from the djinn's hand and strike the sculpture with a devastating force. The power released was so immense that even the small fraction that trickled through the barrier was sufficient for all to see what was happening.

The sculpture ripped asunder where the bolt struck it at mid-height. Globules of molten metal sputtered from the point of contact. Two jagged halves ricocheted from the walls of the confining box. Before the image faded, the djinn struck a second time with two quick bolts that hit each of the tumbling pieces. Again the metal shrieked and tore; four fragments bounced about the cube.

With increasing rapidity the djinn aimed strike after strike at the fragments, ripping them into finer shards and filling the confining volume with light. Astron flicked his membranes over his eyes. The outwelling residue of the destruction was too painful to watch directly, even with the shield demons' barrier in place. Between spread fingers, he watched the djinn begin to froth and gesticulate wildly, barely in control of himself as he sought to rip the cloud of scrap into even smaller rubble.

The onslaught continued unabated until only a hazy dust filled the cube. No recognizable part of the original sculpture remained intact or any of the metal of which it was composed. Only motes of transmuted matter bathed in the glow of the careening light.

With no more targets on which to focus his power, the djinn finally stopped, slumping exhausted in one corner of the box. Elezar motioned to the shield demons. The side of the confinement nearest to Astron dissolved away as quickly as it had formed. Amidst pulses of escaping light and heat, the djinn tumbled out to lie at Gaspar's feet, limbs scattered haphazardly and with a smile on his face beneath glazed eyes.

"Such is the amusement that you offer to those who would follow you," Elezar said, "and to any who has not tasted the pleasure of total destruction, the allure might be strong indeed."

The prince looked down at the djinn slowly regaining his composure. "But I wonder, Gaspar, now that the experience has been savored, what more can you promise that will not be repetition of the same. And after the second, the dozenth, perhaps the hundredth time, what then will be your hold over this mighty djinn?"

"You speak of events that are in epochs yet to run," Gaspar said. "None of my lieutenants, nor any of the legions that they command, have tastes so jaded that they do not look forward to repeat for all your lair the small sample we have witnessed here."

"My point is not yet complete." Elezar raised one robed arm to cut off the other prince. "Let us see first the principle upon which the allegiance to my domain is founded."

As Elezar finished, a small devil came forward, barely larger than Astron himself. He entered the box from the open side and immediately sank into a deep contemplation of the still swirling dust. For a long moment nothing happened. Then a tiny spark of light blinked into existence before the devil's eyes and, following that in rapid succession, a series of others.

Gaspar rumbled with impatience but Elezar and the concentrating devil paid him no heed. For a long while more, there was no visible change in the haze, but then Astron saw a sparkling precipitate begin to fall to the bottom of the box.

"A significant fraction of the matter has been lost to light and other rays," Elezar said. "But it is of no concern. The weaver will work with what is at hand. He will first reassemble the basic particular components back into copper and tin, reversing the transmutations of your lieutenant. Then he will reconstitute the sculpture, coalescing the particles together one by one, if need be."

The prince paused and looked at Gaspar. "It took this one an era to make the first sculpture, staring from a hoard of bronze another of my minions had obtained from the realm of the skyskirr. It will take him eras more to reconstitute it and restore what he had before or perhaps craft something of greater beauty still. Eras, Gaspar, eras, not mere heart beats, and then it is done. He will be constructing, weaving, paying attention to painstaking detail to ensure that each little mote is in its proper place. It is a matter of rational control of the stembrain, not surrender to its lust.

"Eras and not heart beats, Gaspar—that is why princes such as I will endure long after djinns of lightning have long since surrendered to the great monotony."

"The stronger shall endure the longer," Gaspar said. He motioned his lieutenant to resume his position in line. "And there is little doubt between the two of us as to which it will be."

Gaspar unfolded his arms and stuck a bulbous thumb toward his chest. "My will has forever been my own," he said, "but in cold reality, Elezar, you can make no such claim." The djinn paused and looked around the assembled demons in the rotunda. "It is no less than another riddle. How can any here choose to ally themselves with one who has been enslaved by a mortal?"

"It was no common man," Elezar shot back. "No less than the archimage did I contest in wills. And I am not ashamed of the result. No prince of the realm would have fared any better than I. Certainly not a coarse djinn who has not even dared to answer a single call when it has come through the flame."

"So you assert," Gaspar said. "Such is your interpretation of the events. But if this mortal is so great that even princes bend to his will, why are there no others who also call him master somewhere in the realm?"

46

"I have spoken with accuracy," Elezar said. "The archmage knows quite well the folly of too much interaction with our domains. It is a mark of confidence in his power that he has no compulsion to exercise it wastefully."

"Spoken like a true slave of a dominating master." Gaspar laughed. "A lowly imp could not have put it better. Come, Elezar, Prince Elezar, submit to me now before my followers discover that the victory does not represent that great an accomplishment."

"I will not be distracted by your words." Elezar beat his right arm against his chest. Astron saw the agitation billow in his prince's face. He stirred uncomfortably. Against Gaspar, Elezar's strength lay in his wits, not the plasma that glowed about his fingertips.

"If dominance by a man is of such little consequence," Gaspar continued, "then why does it upset you so much that I discuss it openly in front of those who blindly follow? Perhaps there is more to the story that you have not told."

"Begone!" Elezar stood and shouted. "Flutter back to your rough stone lairs and await the answer to your riddle. I will reveal it to you when the time is proper."

"I have come for it now," Gaspar growled, unfurling his wings.

"I said begone." Elezar clapped his hands together. The air above his head hissed. Traces of blue sparked about his ears.

Gaspar flexed his fingers, letting small tendrils of light race up from the webbing near the palms to the fingertips. "You warned of the consequences that would accrue from the rest of the realm if I struck outside the bounds of our agreement," he said. "Do you not think that the other domains would judge with equal disfavor one who professes to know what in fact he does not? Admit the truth, Elezar. You might once have been a prince, but now you are nothing more than the dim-witted doll of a man."

Elezar snarled, baring fangs that he seldom showed to others. With a flick of his wrist, a bolt of ionizing blue arced between the two princes, striking Gaspar on the shoulder and spinning the djinn to the ground. Gaspar swooped into the air, a small rivulet of smoke wisping from where he had been touched. A glaze of pain clouded his eyes. Sparks showered off his knees and elbows into the air.

"The prince of lightning djinns does not submit to such insult," he yelled. "If you are so foolish as to test the strength of me and my lieutenants, then so shall you meet your doom."

With an ear-shattering roar, the djinn unleashed a huge bolt in Elezar's direction that slammed past the weaving devil and into the midst of the shield demons. One was hit directly in the chest and exploded in a spray of bone, sinew, and gore. Those on either side were hurled from their feet, colliding with Elezar's guards, who scrambled airborne to get out of the way.

Astron saw Gaspar's lieutenant rise in reply; then almost instantly the upper expanses of the rotunda filled with brilliant bursts of light painful to see. All of Elezar's followers who had surrounded the hub arose in a mass confusion, some scrambling for exit tunnels and others surging forward to aid their prince.

For a moment, Astron hesitated, shouldering aside the imps and sprites lesser than he who raced past. His stembrain said to run but he knew that his duty was to help Elezar as best he could. He heard the air implode in a great clap of thunder and then the crash of falling matter from somewhere across the rotunda. Shrieks of pain blended with the crackle of ionization; one of Elezar's guards plummeted to the floor a wingspan away, the odor of charred flesh bubbling from a smoking hole in his side.

Near the apex of the dome, two more djinns converged on one of Elezar's lesser devils who had soared forward into the fray. One methodically countered strokes of crimson with larger bolts of his own, meeting the thrusts of energy head-on and dissipating them harmlessly into the air. The other unleashed his power unimpeded, each stroke blasting asunder a limb or wing.

The prince must withdraw, Astron decided. Elezar's

48

guard demons were too few. Despite their battle lust, they would not prevail against massed lightning djinns in the confines of the rotunda. The prince must retreat to a position where he could direct all the demons at his command—draw Gaspar's minions into separate battles where superior numbers could harry each one singly.

But how to withdraw safely? Astron's thoughts raced. Even though his membranes were down, he had to squint his eyes against the fierce glare as he looked in the direction of the hub. He saw the arcs of energy, his prince, the master weaver, the scattered shield demons, and Elezar's guards trying to form into some sort of protective array.

Then, with a sudden flash, Astron realized what must be done. He whirled about, looking for a devil to carry a message to the prince but saw only chaos. There was no one to listen. He squeezed shut his eyes for an instant, picturing the smooth walls of his den in which he stored his artifacts and the comfort of leafing through his books and deciphering their meanings.

"Duty," he muttered at last. "Without duty there is no purpose—only surrender to the impulse of the stembrain and the great monotony."

Wondering if he would ever see his treasures again, he waved aside a cloud of imps winging past and headed for the hub. A blob of plasma from a fallen djinn roared by his left, hitting a small devil in the back as he ran, incinerating the tiny wings and burning its way through to the chest.

Astron ducked away from the searing rays, scrambled over the body of another fallen demon, and reached Elezar's cushion that had been hastily kicked aside. Out of the corner of his eye, he saw the figure of the prince, outlined against the fierce glow, blocking bolts of energy with his own and yelling commands to his guards above the din.

Astron scrambled around the periphery of the hub to where the shield demons sprawled in disarray. Their opaque screens had dissolved but the squat demons were too slow-witted to do more than move a few feet from where they had originally stood.

"Form your barriers," Astron shouted to the one closest. "The prince commands and needs your aid."

The nearest shield demon grunted. The space between him and Astron began to fog as it had before.

"Faster," Astron commanded, looking over his shoulder to verify that Elezar and his retinue still stood their ground. "And make it horizontal, directly on top of your head."

The forming barrier began to tip toward the ceiling and Astron scrambled aside to instruct the next in line. As he did, one of Gaspar's lieutenants saw the activity, broke off his engagement with four lesser demons, and dove to the attack. Astron saw the djinn fold his wings and dive. As pulses of energy leaped from outstretched fingers, Astron sprawled flat on the rotunda floor, feeling waves of heat roar past his head. He looked up to see the djinn swoop on by and then turn to attack a second time. Astron rose to his knees and scrambled beside the shield demon constructing his screen. The next volley spattered harmlessly from the thickening barrier as the djinn roared overhead.

Astron quickly instructed the other three shield demons that remained alive. Before the djinn could attack again, he was safely inside a box with an open bottom resting on the rotunda floor. The attacking demon released three bolts in frustrated fury, then turned his attention back to Elezar and the few remaining guards that still stood hovering over their prince.

With the attention temporarily diverted, Astron rearranged the positions of the shield demons, rotating their opaque planes until they too were inside the protective enclosure they had created.

"Now, in unison, toward the hub," he commanded. "First the left foot and then the right." The strange mechanical way that men used to move in synchronization was proving to be a most useful piece of information.

The shield demons lumbered forward, their barriers

bouncing and banging against one another as they moved. The seals between the edges did not remain perfect and backwashes of energy spilled inside to carom about the interior. Astron danced about to avoid the stray ricochets while he directed the demons forward, concentrating intently on how many steps to take before he reached the vicinity of Elezar and his guards.

After a dozen steps, he commanded a halt and then directed the demons controlling the shield nearest the hub to rotate his barrier floorward. Astron threw his arm in front of his eyes and looked out of the enclosure. He saw Elezar down on one knee, his right arm grasping the other near the elbow. The prince's face was frozen in a mask of pain as he steadied himself among the dead and dying at his feet. Two remaining guards stood on unsteady limbs between Elezar and three towering lightning djinns. Behind them all, Astron heard Gaspar's booming laugh as he urged his minions on against the other devils who flitted about the huge hall.

"Quickly, my prince, you need shelter to compose your thoughts," Astron shouted as he darted out from the protecting shields. He side-stepped a spent pulse of energy and stumbled over smoking cushions to Elezar's side.

Elezar turned slowly as he approached, released his injured arm and prepared to defend against the new attack as best he could.

"No, it is the one who walks," Astron said. "Command those that you can into the shelter."

Three more bolts of plasma screamed overhead. One of the remaining guards reeled backward, clutching his shoulder and vainly trying to stop the flow of green ichor from a gaping wound. Astron shoved away the reluctance coursing up from his stembrain and did what he had never dared before. He touched Elezar's extended hand, wincing as much from the thought of contact as from the prickles of pain created by the sparks that ran along the prince's palm.

Elezar's eyes flared momentarily at the familiarity,

but then in resignation stumbled backward with the tug. With his injured arm he somehow waved others to follow. In a rush, all of the nearby imps, sprites, devils, and demons abandoned their defenses and scrambled after the prince.

Astron heard Gaspar's roar as he realized what was happening. "After Elezar," the lightning djinn shouted. "Ignore the lesser devils; we can make game with them at our leisure. Focus your energies. Stop the one who dares to call himself prince."

Bolts of plasma lanced into the protective enclosure as Astron and the others tumbled under the upraised barrier. Shouts of agony echoed through the air. Astron felt sprays of wet stickiness on his back as he directed the shield demon to drop the open side back into place.

When the panel sealed with the others, the scene momentarily plunged into near darkness. Except for a rumble transmitted through the floor, the sounds of battle faded away. Then, just as suddenly, the top of the enclosure blazed with light, a diffuse glow that spread outward from a focus and slopped over the edges of the plane. The pulse decayed, but it was immediately followed by a pair and then a half dozen or more as Gaspar's djinns converged to attack.

The shield demons inside of the protection were undisturbed by the onslaught, however. The plane pulsed and glowed, but except for the inwelling light, they deflected the energies away.

Astron saw the bursts of energy move methodically from the top panel to the one nearest the hub and then around to the others. Gaspar was testing each one in the hopes of finding a weakness in the defense. But all the shields held, each as well as the next.

Astron felt his stembrain retreat backward from his conscious thoughts. Elezar could not hold out forever within the confines of the box. Eventually Gaspar would think to attack from underneath the thin flooring upon which there was no shield. But at least it bought some time for the prince to think and plan a counterthrust in conditions that were more favorable. In the diffuse darkness, he groped to find Elezar and tell him of what he had learned in Palodad's lair.

CHAPTER FIVE

Through the Flame

"So even Palodad did not know the answer," Elezar whispered through pain-clenched teeth when Astron had finished reporting on his trip to the old one's domain. "All that he can offer is the direction in which to look and verification of what is found in exchange for some exotic form of matter. It makes how the likes of Gaspar came upon the conundrum much more a riddle of its own."

Astron shifted uncomfortably. He had little room, sandwiched between the legs of a stonesprite and with his back pressed against the barbed wings of a messenger djinn. Elezar's ability to force aside the distractions of pain, the bursts of light, and what was happening outside of their enclosure might indeed be the necessary talent of a prince, but it was disconcerting, nevertheless.

The assault of energy against the barriers of the shield demons had continued unabated while Astron had informed the prince. In dim outlines, he caught glimpses of the destruction of the rotunda and several of the other domes beyond. Muted cries filtered through even the thickness of the woven walls as more and more of Elezar's followers were routed out of their hiding places and made the sport of the lightning djinn's lust for battle and destruction. Soon all the rest would be gone, and the attention of every demon that Gaspar commanded would be turned to the box that sat on the rotunda floor.

"How Gaspar possessed the riddle is of little enough consequence," Astron said quickly. "And since you struck the first blow, the lightning djinn will feel justified in his destructions, whether you can solve his puzzle or not."

"The key is the disposition of the other princes who rule." Elezar weakly shook his head. "If I can get word to enough of them undetected, then sufficient might can be marshalled to drive Gaspar from my domain. And once he is removed, the others will judge what he has already done to be sufficient compensation for my momentary indiscretion. He will be able to unleash his will again only if I indeed fail to present to him a satisfactory solution to the riddle."

All four sides of the enclosure flashed in unison. The flooring shook with a great spasm. Astron heard a prolonged rumble and images of falling spires filled his mind.

"All that you suggest will take time," Astron said. "The aid I have rendered is at best only temporary." Already his feeling of accomplishment was fading. The baser emotions of his stembrain had begun to reassert themselves again. "Would it not be better now to focus on Gaspar's immediate threat to your well-being?"

"I must go by stealth to another node in the realm." Elezar ignored Astron's words. "One that is dark and not the lair of any demon of power. From there, I can dispatch my messengers while Gaspar dissipates his energy with fruitless destruction here."

"But how will you journey there?" Astron asked. "Not—not all of your present retinue are winged. The few djinns here cannot carry us all."

"Do not despair, walking one," Elezar whispered. "You still possess value. I would rather you not be wasted as some lowly imp. Look at those crowded about you. You are the only one with more than a feeble bulb of pulp riding atop his stembrain." The prince paused and then reached out and squeezed Astron's wrist. "Your mission is a different one, cataloguer, and I bid you to begin it now. It is with you that I must entrust the quest for the answer to Gaspar's riddle. You are the one to bring true flame into the realm of daemon."

Astron's feelings bubbled. It had been quite enough to visit Palodad's lair once. He had returned with what he could and had saved, at least temporarily, the prince as well. What more reasonably could be asked of one such as he?

His stembrain forced him to look through the translucence of the barriers, to estimate his chances to skitter away while Gaspar and the others concentrated on more important targets. But even if he escaped safely, what if Prince Elezar then fell? What then would be the demands of duty? What reason would there be for the existence of a cataloguer? Would there be any other prince who would appreciate the value of one who only studied the puzzling details of other realms?

The shriek and tear of matter from outside the barriers pushed its way into his thoughts. Astron shook his head. The speculation was not the substance of a true riddle. There could be no other choice.

"When Gaspar finally breaks through, be sure to command a djinn to return me to Palodad's lair," Astron said at last. "I will tell him that you agree and find out in which realm the search is to be conducted."

"No, no, not Palodad," Elezar whispered hoarsely. "As the old one said, you will need the aid of a being from outside of our realm. A strong one with great will and equal to the task. You must find him first so that you will be ready."

"But where—"

"From the realm of men. You must go through the flame first to the realm of men. Dominate whomever you contact and instruct that one to carry you to Alodar, the archimage. Only he will have the wisdom to decide and choose among his minions the one best for the quest. Have the archimage contact me back through the flame so that we can agree on his succor and aid."

"The archimage," Astron said. "He is the one among men who has mastered all five of the mortal magics—indeed the only one to bring a demon such as yourself—"

"That is why you must link minds with another mortal," Elezar said, "someone with lesser strength or will whose mind you can control. Use the one you dominate to guide you to the archimage. Then you can converse with him with your own faculties intact, rather than wrestle to speak freely while under his power."

Astron started to say more, then thought better of it. The groan of twisting matter and flashes of crackling plasma had intensified rather than abated. It would not be long before Gaspar, even in his rage, deduced how to renew his attack on Elezar. His decision had been made. No time must be wasted to ponder it more. If Elezar commanded him elsewhere, then he would go. He must make contact with a mind that at that very moment was probing into the realm—make contact and hope that his will would be the stronger.

Astron twisted into a comfortable position as best he could and fought to push the light and sound out of his thoughts. He breathed deeply—a curious practice he had noticed in the realm of men—but it helped no more than it ever had before. With his membranes down, he tried to image the emptiness of his own surroundings, vast expanses of black desert sprinkled with rare oases of matter.

His thoughts soared as his body could not, past glittering lairs swarming with imps, feebly glowing fortresses of devils who no longer cared, and dark nodes unclaimed by any prince. Astron imagined himself in total darkness, undistracted by anything in his realm, his mind blank and open to the tendrils of thought that pierced through the barrier from beings on the other side.

He willed his mind to stillness, but even his stembrain knew that he must be careful, avoiding the lures that were the most tempting. As Elezar had said, he could ill afford a struggle with a wizard of great strength. The law of dichotomy admitted no middle outcome. When contact was made, one of the beings would dominate and the other must submit.

And yet it would serve no purpose for the battle to be

56

an easy one. Control of the likes of a mere serving girl did not provide the means to gain audience with the archimage of men. No, the linking of minds must be chosen to be precisely correct, a grapple with a being of some will and hence possessor of power, a being of consequence but not so great that Astron would find himself the one dominated as the final connection was made.

Astron gingerly tested one probe and then quickly flitted to another. For a mere instant, he saw a vision of dancing flame and behind it some gnarled wizard pushing with his thoughts and daring mighty djinns to accept his challenge. Astron felt his way past a dozen more, retreating from most with haste and discarding the rest as not worthy of even such a demon as he.

Finally he touched upon one different from the rest—a being of inner strength, but also with a softness that perhaps could be molded to his desire. Astron tentatively let his own mind engage the tendrils of beckoning thought. He felt the essence of his being coil like smoke and intertwine with the wisps reaching out for him. First at a single point, then rapidly with many others, the two minds meshed and flowed into one another, preparing for the struggle that was soon to come.

It was a female, he realized with a shock as the intimacy increased—a female and yet a wizard nonetheless. He felt her flow of will begin to stiffen and push back against his own thoughts as he tried to maneuver them so that they surrounded and confined. Astron increased his concentration, imagining strong sinewy vines looping through a flimsy trellis and pulling it to ground. His hands tightened into fists. The muscles in his back bunched in bulging contractions on his slight frame.

He perceived more of the universe that was joined through the flame, a pentagram of chalk, the wizard in dark robes staring into a firepit cut through a planked floor, and the strong odors of aromatic woods. Behind her was another, a dark-headed man with deep-set eyes of gray, his furrowed brow beaded with sweat as he watched the struggle unfold.

Astron felt the interlocking thoughts lose all their

pliancy, congealing first into stiff ropes and then bands of steel. At every juncture where they crossed his own, there was a sudden tugging, an urging to push through the barrier and travel from one realm to another.

Astron set his teeth and pushed out with his arms against the protecting walls of the shield demons. He wanted to vault through the flame into the other world, it was true, but only as he willed it, a master of the one who beckoned, rather than as her slave.

The floor suddenly buckled and then spattered upward sprays of molten metal. Two of the lesser imps a few feet away from where Astron struggled screamed in pain as a ball of pulsing plasma tore through from underneath and bathed them in its destruction. A gaping hole fizzed and steamed where moments before had been a plane of matter.

"Demons, surround your prince," Astron heard Elezar call out. "Guard the portal so that the lightning djinns do not pass."

"Let none escape," Gaspar answered. "We will catch and then fry them all. Pursue them no matter where they flee. I will boil Elezar and his minions, even if they vanish to another realm."

Astron was only dimly aware of the scramble among the devils and sprites who had sought the refuge with his prince. He struggled to concentrate on his own battle and strained to buckle the resistance to his thoughts.

He heard another loud crash that shook all of Elezar's domain with a shudder. The flooring split asunder, disintegrating into disconnected platelets of twisted matter. Astron felt the support of the shield demons tumble away and then a sense of falling into the emptiness of the realm.

"Yield," he shouted across the barrier as he fell, "yield to him who is the stronger." In desperation he pounded his clenched fists to his chest and strained with a final gasp to end the struggle with the wizard.

The inky blackness exploded with painful light. A stab of singeing heat rolled across his back. He heard death cries barely a span away. The panic building in his stembrain pushed against its restraints. If Elezar lost now, what could his quest matter? It would only be a question of time before Gaspar's lieutenants hunted him down for a far more ignoble death.

But just as he prepared to relax his straining will and submit to his fate, he felt a reduction of the tension and then a sudden collapse of resistance to his thoughts.

"I am yours to command, master," a voice said in his head. Astron did not bother for one final look to see how those around him fared. With single-minded dedication, he thrust himself through the barrier into the realm of men.

PART TWO

The Realms of Men and Skyskirr

CHAPTER SIX

Wizard's Wood

KESTREL shifted uneasily as the demon materialized above the flame in Phoebe's cabin. In barely a dozen heart beats, the creature stepped from the flame, apparently as solid from head to toe as the wizard he had just subjugated.

"I am Astron, the one who walks," Kestrel heard the demon say. "I command you to take me to Alodar, the archimage of all men, so that the message from my prince to him can be made known."

"I am a wizard of Brythia, the hindermost of the Southern Kingdoms," Phoebe answered in a slow monotone. "The great Alodar resides in Procolon far to the north, beyond Samirand, Laudia, and even Ethidor." She turned her hands palms upward and shrugged. "The petty squabbles of the princes have closed the border between us. Unless you are willing to wait for several months more, you will need the service of men-at-arms to cross it, not the skills of a master of the arts. Give me some other task, one for which there is some hope of success."

Astron looked around the room. "The rate of time is never quite the same among the realms," he said, "but several of your months will be far too long." The demon's eyes fell on Kestrel as he finished stepping clear of the fire that was fading into glowing embers and curls of smoke. "If not you, then perhaps your lackey. Why can not he lead me to the archimage by your command, just as you must obey my wishes as your own?"

"Ah, pause for a moment," Kestrel said. "There is a slight error in your logic." His mind was suddenly made

63

up. More anvilwood he could obtain somehow. Getting entrapped by a devil was another matter altogether. "I am but a simple woodchopper, not a hero from the sagas. I was just stopping by to show my wares. If the lady is not interested, then there is no obligation I have to her."

Kestrel stepped quickly to the side, aiming to place Phoebe between him and the demon. He glanced at the door and calculated how many more glides it would take to be safely away.

"The task is as I have stated it," Astron persisted. "My control of your mind, wizard, is not so great to smother all thought. Perform what I command and I shall set you free. Let your creativity be the key to your release."

Kestrel slid two more steps to his left. He kept his head down and avoided looking at the demon. Catching a demon in the eye was to be avoided at all costs, he remembered.

"Acting together, the wizards of my local council might successfully petition for a writ of safe passage," Phoebe said slowly. "But it is difficult to get them to agree on anything so concrete, especially if there is no gain in it for them."

"What then is the motivation that would prod them to act in haste?"

"The wizards of my kingdom are enamored of the tangible rewards from their craft," Phoebe said. "It is to the golden brandels of Procolon or the magic tokens of Pluton across the sea to which they listen the most."

"What of these things do you have?" Astron asked.

"My wealth is the greatest of any on the council, it is true," Phoebe said. "But divided and spread among them, the enticement would not be all that strong. There are ten of them and each has at least three-quarters of what you see here."

Kestrel stopped in midstride. Ten times three-quarters, he thought quickly. More than seven times the potential gain of what he had hoped for from Phoebe alone. If there were only a plausible story with which to approach the entire council, something that would appeal to their individual greed but force them to act collectively, some dealing with the realm of demons that no wizard could afford to let pass by. The allure would have to be quite spectacular, something that would withstand the scrutiny of not one but half a score.

Kestrel almost involuntarily jerked up his head and looked at Astron. The demon did not appear all that ferocious. Perhaps, with Phoebe under his command, he had no lust for another. Perhaps, in fact, the sagas were distorted and the risks far less than the babblings that had been recorded. It would be just what he expected of wizards—concocting a great peril to enchance their own importance and the magnitude of their fees.

Kestrel had hoped for ten brandels from Phoebe's purse. If he could get the devil to agree, he might leave these hills with over a hundred. And besting not one but ten so-called masters in one stroke would be all the more satisfying as well. The more he pondered it, the more the risks dissolved away and the rewards grew increasingly tempting.

"Your first instincts were correct," Kestrel called to Astron as he returned to Phoebe's side. "I am the key to getting the necessary petition from the wizards' council. Just do as I say, and we both shall be compensated as we desire from our efforts."

Astron wrinkled his nose. "As you say? It is I who have asserted the more powerful will in coming through the flame. I control the wizard who called me and, through her, any of those bound to her own command."

"This is not like that," Kestrel said quickly. "Your command of the wizard is part of the plan I have in mind, but between you and me, it is more of a mutual agreement." He stretched his face into a smile. "A contract between partners that we both swear to uphold—like the formal exchanges between alchemists and apothecaries for rare ingredients and tested formulas."

"If not the wizard, then who is your prince?" Astron asked. "And what do you mean when you speak of contracts and swearing to uphold?"

"I am a free man and have obligations to no one, neither king nor master," Kestrel said. "My will is my own." He saw the demon's face distort further and he rushed on. "The important thing is that we agree to act in each other's behalf—on our honor, not by threat of penalty but by being true to our innermost values of being."

Astron did not speak for a long while. He looked from the placid face of the one he controlled to Kestrel's sudden enthusiasm. "In my realm, one serves a single prince and no other," the demon said at last. "Breaking allegiance is such a personal shame that the will to resist the great monotony is shattered as well. Is that what you mean by contracts and honor?"

"Why, exactly so," Kestrel said. "I could not have explained it better myself."

"And if I follow your instructions, you will arrange my audience with Alodar the archmage?"

"Yes, that will be our agreement—on our honor."

Kestrel saw Astron's face relax. The demon stuck out his right hand toward Kestrel. "I do know some of the customs of the realm of men. I agree, human, to what you call a contract, working to mutual benefit upon our honor. Here, clasp my hand to seal the agreement and then let us begin."

Kestrel grasped the offered hand and shook it slowly, hardly noticing the coarse texture next to his own skin. "Listen carefully then. Here is my plan," he heard himself say, but his thoughts were elsewhere. Something about the demon was strangely disturbing. He had agreed all too quickly—too soon for Kestrel to figure out what his real motives were. An agreement on their honor—it sounded as if the devil actually meant it.

Kestrel clapped his hands for attention. Several hours had passed swiftly since he outlined his plan to Astron. Now it was nearly noon, and nine wizards had gathered in the small garden outside of Phoebe's cabin. The eldest three sat on a long wooden bench next to a small pond lined with smooth stones. Behind them stood the rest, all robed in black and wearing faces heavy with the seriousness of their craft.

66

Kestrel stood next to Phoebe on the other side of the pond, next to a tier of dove cages and neatly trimmed bushes that flashed waxy leaves at the high sun. He glanced once at the small scroll of parchment he had tossed into the pond before the wizards' arrival and smiled. As yet none of them had called attention to it; it would serve its purpose well.

To the left, Kestrel's wagon stood hitched and ready, his mare nibbling contentedly on a bed of flowering hornweed. The birch-framed canopy over his pinewood-filled sacks fluttered in a quickening breeze. The last of the doves dispatched with a summons circled overhead, apparently building up the courage to return to its roost just beyond Kestrel's reach.

Kestrel ignored the hovering bird. The message tied to its leg probably stated only that the last wizard in Phoebe's council would not come. Enough were already present to make the production worthwhile; judging from the pleasant jingle of their purses, the effort would be worthwhile indeed.

Kestrel took a moment to study the masters seated in the front. Undoubtedly they were the ones to convince; then the others would follow. The one in the middle, Maspanar, appeared the most bloated with self-importance. Any revelation of facts would have to be his; monetary aspects were of less concern.

On Maspanar's right sat Geldion, a shriveled hulk that stared back with piercing blue eyes. He seemed to dare Kestrel to speak, to commit some error that immediately could be pounced upon and exposed to the others.

The last of the three, Kestrel decided, was his primary target. Benthon's black robe was a trifle newer than all the rest. Golden rings adorned slender fingers not smudged by charred embers or sooty ash. The eyes danced about the confines of Phoebe's garden, searching for an opening, an opportunity for gain that would continue to feed his expensive habits.

"Masters, if I may have your attention," Kestrel said after he had satisfied himself that he could predict how the assembled wizards would react. "Your colleague in craft apologizes for the lack of words of greeting and sweet wine." He waved his hand in Phoebe's direction. "But her startling discovery is of such great importance that she dare not break her concentration for trivial amenities. When you have witnessed what she has to demonstrate you will understand why."

"Who is this that speaks for the wizard Phoebe?" Geldion demanded. He looked over his shoulder and spoke to the masters standing behind the bench. "He wears no robe with a logo, nor have I heard her talk of any bondsmen in her service."

"I have interrupted my studies merely as a courtesy," Maspanar said. "I doubt greatly that the youngest of our council—and a woman at that—has found anything not yet well known to most of us." He shrugged massive shoulders beneath a robe that had been patched more than once. "If the dabbler has found a means of amplifying our powers as her note indicated, then let her explain her alleged discovery and be done. There is no time for the smooth tongues and empty thoughts of others."

Kestrel forced his smile wider. Years ago when the opinions of other mattered, such rude manners would have hurt and given him pause. But now he was as hardened as the rest. He would give them what they deserved, matching their insensitivities with a disdain of his own. Kestrel looked out for himself and no one else. Let the masters beware.

"A simple flame." Kestrel pointed back through the open doorway into Phoebe's cabin, totally ignoring the challenges. It would serve no purpose to spar with Maspanar or Geldion until after Benthon was securely hooked. "You can all see it burning within the pentagram on the floor. Perhaps the keenest among you, even from the distance, can guess what fuels the blaze."

"Simple pine logs," Maspanar shot back. "The height of the yellows, smoke with little soot, and the lack of intense blues mark it as nothing else."

"Yes, dried pine it is," Kestrel said. "The tunnel between the realms for small imps and sprites and little else. For demons of true power, more exotic woods and

68

powders must be consumed to bore through the barrier that keeps them from us."

Kestrel paused, replacing his smile with a serious mask. "More exotic woods are needed for demons of true power," he repeated, "or so one would expect."

With a sudden thrust of his arm he reached into the cabin and grabbed the door by the knob. In a blur of motion he repeatedly opened the door a crack and then slammed it shut, a staccato burst of sound filling the small garden. After perhaps a dozen slams he flung the door all the way open, again permitting the wizards to view the interior.

Kestrel's smile returned as he saw Astron stride forward from the flame, exactly as he had planned. The decorum of the wizards dissolved into babble of excited voices.

"Impossible," Geldion said. "No demon of that size could come through such a simple flame."

"Some trace element, perhaps," Maspanar replied. "A substance of great power so that merely a small amount was necessary."

"But what of the control?" Benthon spoke for the first time. "That is indeed no small imp of little will. Our voices distract too much and place Phoebe in great peril."

"I am yours to command, master." Astron bowed to Phoebe as he exited from the cabin. "Give me your instructions so that I may serve."

Phoebe frowned as she heard the words, mouthing them silently for a second. Then she suddenly shook off her lethargy. "Do not concern yourselves with the risk, my colleagues," she said. "Observe, I need devote merely a fraction of my attention to control."

She turned and looked at Astron as he emerged. "Go among them, devil," she said. "Let them examine you at will. Perhaps the experience will be of interest." Then, with a flourish, she turned her back and began picking a bouquet of flowers from a bed near her feet, her features totally hidden from the others.

Kestrel saw Phoebe's face relax to a lifeless stare as

her hands mechanically groped for nearby stalks. He looked back at the wizards, but their attentions were all focused on Astron as he came forward. Things were going well. He would be far away before anyone deduced that Phoebe's words were merely the ones the demon beforehand had commanded her to say.

"Not an imp but neither a mighty djinn," the talk of the wizards continued.

"But if from simple flame and with no great struggle of will, the phenomenon does deserve some investigation."

"This is indeed most surprising, I admit. My respect for the woman must climb a notch. She may become a credit to us yet. Tell us, Phoebe, what is the name of the one you have so effortlessly summoned? How was his domination achieved?"

"I am called Astron, the one who walks," Astron said. "But that is of little matter. I have done my part. Now I wish you to perform yours with haste. Surrender to the man whatever it is that provides my audience with the archimage. It is the agreement that we have sworn on our—"

"Masters, your attention, please," Kestrel cut in. "Surely your interest is more on how Phoebe was able to perform her feat rather than its result." He frowned in the direction of Astron. He had been so busy beforehand explaining how Phoebe should be controlled that he had neglected to tell the demon to keep his own mouth shut as well. "I have been instructed by your colleague to explain her discovery while she keeps the devil under control," he said. "But be advised it might take several hours, and any attempt to rush could completely destroy what is being demonstrated."

"Several hours," Astron said. "How curious. It must be a ritual I have not witnessed before. Under any other circumstances, I would be most eager to add the details of its performance to my catalogues."

"Masters, if you please," Kestrel persisted. He flexed his shoulders trying to dislodge the tiny burr of apprehension that had suddenly made its presence felt under

70

the smooth blanket of confidence in his scheme. "The key insight that Phoebe exploited in her experiment was the willingness of the demon to come. It is true that mighty djinns, virtual kings in their own realm, are ill-disposed for the journey through the fires. Only with ex-otic woods to reduce the barriers and great struggles of will have you been able to woo them.

"But consider instead another approach—an approach in which you provide a bait, an enticement for the devil to journey on his own accord. Phoebe has shown it to be true; simpler flames are all that is needed, and the demons' spirits are more docile when they appear in our realm. One must provide in addition only the cadence of sounds that sends notice of the lure to the realm where they live."

Kestrel paused and looked at the assemblage carefully, one by one. "Think of it," he said. "Mighty djinns at your beck and call. No more costly expenditure for rare powders and woods."

"Another example," one of the wizards behind the first row called out. "Although this one before us is no simple imp, he seems to have little more value beyond his increased size."

"Little value?" Astron said. "But I am a cataloguer. I know perhaps more of your realm than any other of my kind. My prince values me highly. Because of that I am here rather than any oth—"

"Exactly so, a cataloguer." Kestrel scowled at Astron again. "He was enticed here by the scroll that Phoebe laid out before the flame. See it there in the pond. It was the lure that made possible a transition even in the fire of pine."

"That is the second time you have looked at me that way," Astron said. "What message are you trying to convey?"

"What is this that the demon is asking?" Geldion said. "Phoebe, have you given him leave to speak of his own free will?"

"No, no, pay him no heed," Kestrel said. "Focus in-stead on the second experiment. The key is to assemble a lure from your possessions that will entice another demon here. I will manipulate the door as before and you will see."

"What kind of lure; what do you mean?" Benthon asked.

"Anything," Kestrel said. He felt his apprehension lessen. Benthon speaking now could not have been more nearly perfect. "Anything at all. It seems the greater the quantity, the mightier is the demon that responds."

He paused a moment and rubbed his chin. "I guess there is one thing, however, that you of course will not attempt to employ. I have heard the jingle of your purses and could not help thinking of it. A brandel from Procolon will fetch a gold imp, a sackful, a bigger devil of the same bent. Their only interest is in hoarding. About the only useful command you could give them is to go and find it in the ground where it is not yet discovered by men."

Kestrel stopped and shrugged. "Of course I realize that you are all men of ethics and would not use your powers for such base gain of a few nuggets of metal."

"You stated that the bigger the lure, then the more powerful the demon which would respond and the more able he would be to perform his special talents?" Benthon asked.

"Yes, that is the fact of it," Kestrel said. "Why, I would imagine that a gold *djinn* would not even have to look. He would transform the metal out of baserock, as much as was commanded."

Benthon's eyes widened. He opened his purse and thrust it at Maspanar. "Then such an experiment it will be. Empty what you have into mine and we will share in whatever is gained in return."

"I think that we proceed without sufficient caution," Geldion said. "I am not yet satisfied with the explanation of what little we have seen transpire."

"Then do not participate," Benthon said. "Only those who take the risk shall benefit from the returns as well." He turned back to Kestrel. "What would it take to fetch the likes of this gold djinn to do our bidding?"

72

"From what Phoebe has instructed me, I would say about eight or nine times the amount in your purse alone. And with such a demon in your power, he should be able to produce tenfold that amount in less than a day."

"What do you say, Maspanar?" Benthon persisted. "If you decide to join, then surely the others will follow."

Maspanar grunted, looked at Astron and then back at the dying fire in Phoebe's cabin. He shrugged and reached for his belt. "What is the harm?" he said. "The worst that can happen is that the claim is not true. And with woman's work, I suspect that somehow that certainly is the case."

"But if she is correct?" one of the masters in the second row asked.

"With ten of us here, surely we can dominate whatever comes through the flames." Maspanar shrugged a second time. "If it proves to be small, we can command it into a magic bottle for study at our leisure. If something of greater size appears, we can call forth clouds of imps on our own that will harry it until it too is subdued."

For a moment no one moved. Then, in a flurry of jingles and flailing straps of leather, the six wizards who stood behind crowded around Benthon and added their contribution to a growing store. Finally Benthon himself held his bulging purse in front of Geldion, gently waving it to and fro.

Geldion scowled once and reached for his own pouch. Showing no pleasure, he emptied his coins in with the rest and then folded his arms across his chest.

Kestrel tried not to let his excitement show. The wizards had all come better prepared than he had dared hope. Now for a little more maneuvering and it would all be done.

"But, but your ethics," he said. "If you get too much gold, then even the economy can be altered—just as it was on Pluton across the sea some two decades ago."

"A wizard indeed is entrusted with a most solemn trust." Benthon stepped forward, thumping his chest with his free hand while his sack hung heavy in the other.

"Therefore, we judge the risks and take only those that are prudent." He turned and waved back at the others. "And here our judgment is unanimous. What Phoebe has apparently discovered must be verified with all expediency. Any reward that is possible for our efforts will be administered with discretion." He stopped and looked Kestrel in the eye. "There might even be a brandel or two for the lackey who made the process all the quicker rather than throw up objections that are of no real concern to one of his station."

Kestrel looked down at the sack and ran his tongue over his lips. "I guess there is only one more thing to be aware of, and then my conscience is clear," he said. "Whichever one of you actually controls the demon will have some advantage over the others. And, as Phoebe has explained it, the closer you are to the flame, the greater your chances of being the most likely to grab the demon's will. But then, of course, the closer you are, also the greater the danger. In good faith, I recommend that you all stay outside as did the woman, rather than try to crowd around the flame inside the cabin."

"One side," Benthon said. "My will is the strongest and I am not afraid."

"Wait, drop the gold here in the pond," Kestrel said as he rapidly stepped aside. "By the scroll that lured the first demon to Phoebe. You must be between the lure and the flame for the connection to work."

"Watch this for us, Phoebe," Benthon said as he gathered up speed. He tossed the sack into the water. It fell with a plunk satisfying to Kestrel's ears. "We will be back for it in a few moments, and, if you indeed are correct, for a good deal more."

Maspanar and two more wizards followed Benthon. Then, in a mass of elbows and shoves, came the others.

"The cadence of sound for a gold djinn calls for fifteen immediate slams and then a wait of some twenty minutes for the last," Kestrel said. "If the door is opened before then, the connection is broken and the entire effort wasted." He looked with satisfaction as Geldion started

74

to join the rest. Mentally he measured the strides from the pond to his waiting wagon.

"I have pondered the existence since you first mentioned it," Astron interjected suddenly, "and I cannot think of a single example. No, I am sure of it. None in Elezar's domain nor any of the princes who hang in the void near him have ever known of such. It is an extraordinary occurrence. I devote my life to cataloguing the mysteries and surprises of other realms and find that there is still much I cannot know of my own natural surroundings. Gold imps and even djinns of gold. Yes, it is extraordinary. There is no other word for it."

Geldion paused in the doorway and turned around. "What did he say?" he asked. "It sounded as if he is questioning the existence of what we are about to seek. Phoebe, make him explain what he meant."

Kestrel scowled. He ran forward and grabbed for the doorknob, blocking the wizard's exit with his body. "There is time for that later," he said smoothly. "Wouldn't you rather I get the cadence started right away? You know I won't be able to begin until you are inside and the door able to hit the jamb."

"Phoebe, answer me," Geldion persisted. "Stop denuding that flowerbed and answer me."

"Go ahead and speak, Phoebe," Astron said. "I am anxious to get things concluded as much as anyone."

Phoebe rose slowly and turned toward Astron. "What shall I reply, master?" she said. "You have not instructed me this time as to what you wish me to say."

"Wait a moment," Geldion said. "Who is the master and who the slave? Maspanar, step back here for a moment. Now that I think of it, Phoebe has been acting most strangely. She should be examined at once to verify the freedom of her thought."

"The gold djinn! Look, he comes now through the flames." Kestrel pointed back into the cabin. It was an act of desperation, but things were unraveling fast. He pressed against Geldion's side but the master did not yield.

"But if not Phoebe, then who is manipulating the

75

devil?" Geldion continued as his eyes danced about the garden. He looked from Phoebe to Astron and then to Kestrel at his side. He glanced at the wet sack of gold resting on the bottom of the pond, his eyes suddenly wide. With a strength surprising for his size, he pushed through Kestrel's restraint and staggered back into the garden. "Guardsmen," he shouted, "guardsmen, attend at once."

Kestrel heard the squeak of leather and rattle of steel in a clump of trees near a bend in the road a small distance from the cabin. He scowled at his bumbling, first with the demon and then not checking the environs to ensure a path of escape. Evidently at least one of the wizards was suspicious enough not to come by himself. The size of the treasure had been too great and he had dreamed too much on how it would be spent, rather than ensuring its capture.

Kestrel saw perhaps a half a dozen men-at-arms emerge from their hiding place and begin jogging toward the cabin, their swords drawn and shields rigidly in place. With a sudden surge, he pushed Geldion to the ground and bolted over his sprawling body. In a single fluid motion he leaped to the edge of the pond and scooped out the bulging sack of gold. He glanced a second time at the approaching warriors and back at the wizards now spilling out of the cabin. It was going to be close, he thought, but, considering his mistakes, no less than he deserved.

Kestrel ran to his wagon and started to fling the sack into its interior; but as he did, a well-aimed rock cracked painfully into his shouders, forcing him to release his grip. Like a ripe melon spewing its seeds, the wet leather pouch hit the ground and burst apart. Circles of gold flung in every direction, some rolling under the wagon and others arcing all the way back to the pond.

Kestrel bent to the ground and then hesitated. The first of the wizards was almost upon him. He would be an easy target once he crouched over. He watched the last of the coins stop their spinning and settle to the rough ground, sparkling in the sunlight. It was more than

76

he had ever seen at one time. With an almost painful regret, he pulled himself up into the wagon, empty-handed, and grabbed for the reins.

"Block his escape! Don't let him get away!" the wizards shouted to one another.

"We have the woman. They should be punished together."

"A barrier across the road. Quickly before he bolts!"

Kestrel slapped the reins against the hindquarters of the horse. The wagon jumped into motion. He grabbed his whip and increased its pace, all the while looking down the road and trying to judge on which side to try to run past the converging men-at-arms. He saw the upraised hands that were grabbing the side of the wagon wrench away as he gathered speed.

The wagon surged forward and Kestrel leaned to his left, looking back over his shoulder past the covered awning toward Phoebe's cabin. Only one wizard ran after him in labored slowness; three more were sprawled on the ground where they had fallen away. Most of the rest fluttered around the spilled sack like feasting black-birds fighting over the coins in the sand. The last two held Phoebe in tight grips on each arm, pulling her forward uncomprehendingly toward the rest. Perhaps the demon mingled among them, but in the confusion of black robes, he could not be sure.

Kestrel's eyes lingered on the woman. With him safely away, the wrath of the other wizards would all fall on her, even though she bore no responsibility for what had happened. He recalled his feelings when they stood together inside her cabin and then shook his head at the sudden impulse that welled up within him.

Madness, he thought. The only course was to be safely away before the men-at-arms could organize sufficiently to block him. But the impulse remained. He looked again at her blank face and remembered the sweet smiles it once bore, even when it carried her own caution.

"It may as well be three errors," he muttered to himself as he suddenly pulled the reins to the left, circling the wagon just before the road narrowed to a single lane. Without reducing speed he raced back toward the cabin, aiming directly toward the wizards who held Phoebe in their grasp.

Chapter Seven

The Would-be Sorcerer

KESTREL turned the wagon around well before the men-at-arms could reach him. He slapped the reins across the mare's hindquarters, urging her back toward the cabin. The master who had chased him down the road immediately scrambled to the side and let him pass. The others, busily intent on scooping coins from the ground, took no heed until he was almost on top of them. Then they too scattered in a flurry of flapping robes and tinkling coins.

Kestrel aimed his wagon directly at the wizard on Phoebe's left. As he expected, the master dropped his grip and jumped out of the way. The horse slowed and Kestrel leaned over to the side as he passed. He extended his arm around Phoebe's waist, and she flopped against the rough planking of the wagon like a rag doll as it careened by. Even though the mare was slowing, the momentum was too great for the remaining wizard. He let go of Phoebe's arm with a protesting cry.

With his free hand, Kestrel pulled the horse to a stop. Dropping the reins, he lifted Phoebe up beside him. Her eyes were glazed, totally oblivious to what was happening. He let her sag into a heap, then leaped from his seat onto the mare's back and jerked the beast's head to the left. There was too little time to back up slowly and turn.

Hoping that the front wheels had sufficient free play, Kestrel started the horse forward, pulling it to the side as much as he dared. The mare whinnied in protest and

78

started to rear, but Kestrel kept his grip firm and kicked her onward. Stepping into the flowerbed, the horse bumped the wagon wheels over the low boundary stones that separated the garden from the walk. Stomping the small bushes and spring blooms, they barely edged by the cabin on the right, the hub of the rear wheel scraping as it passed.

Just as the wagon bumped out of the garden and back onto the path that led to the road, the men-at-arms ran forward, shield and sword arms blocking the way. Kestrel did not falter. Focusing on the shield of the man on the far left, he dug his knees into the mare's sides. As the troops converged, he circled the horse's neck with both arms and swung from its back in a giant arc. With feet stiffly extended, he hit the upraised shield with a jarring blow, sending the man-at-arms sprawling before he could strike.

The impact sent Kestrel swinging backward. He raised his feet as high as he could to avoid the stomping hooves of the mare, now thoroughly frightened and running as fast as it could. He saw a sword's-length distance open between him and the men-at-arms who were nearest and then two lengths more. The warriors rallied to run after; but weighted down by shield and mail, they quickly realized that they could not keep up. In an instant, the clatter of pursuit and shouts of anger started to fade.

Kestrel clung to his precarious hold while the mare raced onward. The occasional clump of trees at the roadside grew into more frequent groves and then finally merged into the beginnings of true forest. Stately elms crowded the pathway, enfolding a canopy over Kestrel's head. From above, the sunlight alternately burst through unabated or was totally blocked from view. A gentle breeze swirled away the dust thrown up by the wagon's rapid passage.

Finally the mare spent her wind and slowed to a gentle walk. Listening between the hoof clops, Kestrel could hear no sound of the wizards or men-at-arms. He dropped to the ground and grabbed at the reins as they passed, pulling the horse to a stop.

Kestrel gave himself the luxury of a long deep breath. He was getting too old for such theatrics. And now he probably would have to move on to the next kingdom to practice his skills. He could not count on the shame of the masters in being outsmarted to keep his presence secret. Soon every wizard within the flight of doves would know to watch for a woodcutter and his wagon. He would have to change his tale altogether and probably target another of the five arts as well.

And what of Phoebe? She might not think that snatching her from the other wizards was much of a rescue. Of course, in her present state, she might not think much of anything. Kestrel looked up into the wagon. What was he going to do now?

Suddenly there was a movement from within the awning. A figure stirred. Kestrel dropped his jaw in surprise.

"Why did you turn back?" the demon Astron called down from where Phoebe still slumped. "Even more than the location of the lair of the gold djinns, that is the part I most want to understand. Why did you return to fetch the woman?"

Kestrel recovered his senses and shot back. "What are you doing here? How did you follow where no one else could?"

"I climbed in the back of this—this conveyance while you were pulling the female wizard in through the front," Astron said.

"But why?" Kestrel slowly inched back from the wagon. He looked quickly up and down the tree-darkened road. He and the demon were alone. Astron looked no more menacing than he had when he had first appeared in Phoebe's cabin with his almost human face and muted scales, but the apprehension Kestrel had felt then returned swiftly to his thoughts. And now there was no lure of gain to distract him from the risks of dealing with demonkind.

"I doubt control of my will would be that interesting," he said quickly. He brushed off some of the road dust from his arms and straightened his tunic and rucksack, trying to look as imposing as he possibly could. "Probably it would be better for you now to find some convenient fire and vanish back to whence you came," he said.

"The law of dominance or submission applies only when one of my kind transits between the realms," Astron said as he vaulted from the wagonbed to the ground. "Once I am across, there is no need to wrestle any further. I will do you no harm. Besides, there is the matter of the contract. I have yet to meet with the archimage. You have sworn on your honor to provide the means."

"That was merely half of it," Kestrel snapped back quickly. "I was to have received something to line my purse in exchange for my efforts. Thanks to you, I have nothing to show. The contract is balanced on both sides. We each entered the agreement with nothing and now neither is any the better because of it."

"That is not quite so." Astron stepped forward and opened his fist. "In the confusion that followed the bursting sack, none of the wizards seemed to mind that a demon was scurrying over the ground with them. This is perhaps not what you fully anticipated, but it is far from the nothing of which you speak."

Kestrel looked down at the offered palm. There arrayed in a neat row were more than two dozen brandels, glinting with the light that filtered through the canopy of trees shading the road. A dozen brandels—less than he had hoped but as much as he had expected from convincing Phoebe to buy his wagonload of wood in the first place.

He reached out to grab the coins as Astron slowly tipped his hand. "This is compensation for the errors you made by speaking out, is it not?" he asked. "A settlement and then we can be on our separate ways?"

"This is payment in full," Astron said. "I have honored my part of the bargain; now you must honor yours."

Kestrel shook his head in disbelief. The devil was indeed serious!

Or so he professed to be. The doubt immediately followed in Kestrel's thoughts. Honor, contracts, and trust —such things were mere abstractions. They did not really exist—not for him anyway, not since he had trusted too much and paid the price. Could it really be any different for the demon? Kestrel stared at Astron's unblinking expression, trying to fathom the true motives that lay behind it.

Astron did not speak. Kestrel looked away, noticing almost absently the foam standing on his mare's withers. He reached into the wagon for a coarse rag and began to wipe the moisture away, his mind churning with what he should say next.

Kestrel finished rubbing down one side of his mare and then started on the other. "Do you not understand?" The words burst forth at last with more bitterness than he would have liked. "Understand what it means to bargain with one such as me. I am no hero from the sagas, performing great deeds for kings and masters of the five arts.

"No, my satisfaction comes from motives much less lofty. I prey upon these so-called heroes; the masters most highly regarded give me the greatest thrill. I tempt them where they are the weakest and appeal to the baseness in their characters that is easily as great as mine.

"Was Phoebe truly interested in the properties of anvilwood or the fact that the price I seemed to offer in innocence was merely a tenth of what it would fetch from Procolon to the north? Did the wizards care about the effect of gold nuggets common as pebblestones on all those about them or merely wonder which one would end with the greater share?

"Honor, heroes, the masters—each time that I succeed, each time that they reveal the rotten core beneath their masks of righteousness, it piles proof upon proof. There are no such things as heroes, only men, and not one any better than I."

Kestrel stopped and slumped his shoulders. Why had he said so much? His values and how he acted were his business alone, certainly not the concern of a being from somewhere beyond the flame. It was best to end things

82

quickly so he could be on his way. He stared silently at Astron, waiting to see how the devil would react to what he had said.

"You speak with great passion," Astron replied after a moment. "A passion that I never before have observed." He reached into the wagon and grabbed a second cloth. Eyeing Kestrel's work critically, he dabbed at an apparent wetness on the mare's hindquarters that had been missed. The horse whinnied and backed away, but Kestrel patted her neck and calmed her back down.

"I wish that I had the time to pause and understand it more fully," Astron continued, "but for now we must continue. Tell me, what is your plan for gaining the attention of the archimage?"

"Didn't you just hear what I said?" Kestrel flung his rag to the ground. "The merging of our paths was an accident, an alignment of the random factors, as the alchemists would say. Now that the business at Phoebe's cabin is done, there is nothing more to bind us together. Here, keep the brandels. But look elsewhere for a hero with honor, if one you must have."

"I do not know as much as I must of the realm of men," Astron said. "For that, I must rely on you. But of sprites and wizards my knowledge is perhaps the deeper. For the foreseeable future that will be your greatest need."

"What do you mean?"

"Wizards are most proud. Their wills are not easily diverted, once they have set upon a goal." Astron stepped around the mare, thrusting his face into Kestrel's, his eyes glowing with intensity. "Do you really think that every master who visited the woman's cabin will forget what has happened and let you continue unimpeded on your way?

"Or will they call forth from my realm the most powerful devils that they dare and send them searching— searching until you have been found and cast in some dim dungeon as punishment for your deed?"

Kestrel felt a chill race up his spine. Maybe Astron was right. Simply disappearing and starting over might not be so easy. And years in a dark cell he could well do without.

"We are cleanly away," Kestrel said. "Once we reach the juncture, the road will be one well travelled. Demon-aided or not, I will be able to fade successfully from sight."

"It will take time." Astron shook his head. "But eventually you will be found. At first they will dispatch hundreds of small imps or perhaps even thousands if their ire is truly great. Tirelessly, these will dart throughout every corner of your world, examining the features and actions of you humans as closely as they dare. Those who match the descriptions given them will become the subject of a more intense investigation by devils with greater capacity above the stembrain. Even though, to ones of our realm, you all look very much the same, in the end all the possibilities will be eliminated except one."

Astron halted. Kestrel saw him flick transparent membranes down over his eyes. The demon's face seemed to take on a distant and preoccupied look.

"Now that I think of it," Astron continued after a moment, "our urgencies are closely intertwined. The same imps and devils called forth by the wizards could most likely have a second mission as well. If Gaspar has already triumphed, then the visitors to your realm will be instructed in addition to search for Elezar's missing cataloguer so that he can be returned to his fate.

"Yes, woodcutter, I need your help to navigate through the realm of men just as you need one such as me—one who knows the signs of the presences of my kind." Astron held up the rag in his hand and tossed it to Kestrel. "My eyes see reds that men cannot, especially when my membranes are in place to filter out the distractions of the blues. That is how I can so easily detect the areas of moisture that you missed on this creature's back. In like manner I will notice the imp glows far sooner than could the finest wizard in your realm. I can alert you of the danger while we pursue our common goal."

"What common goal?"

"Why to find the archimage, of course," Astron said. "If he stands to these wizards as a prince does to the djinns of my realm, then only he will be able to turn aside their anger and tell them to desist."

Astron paused. The hint of a smile crept onto his face. "So you see, what we seek is the same, as well as what we avoid."

Kestrel felt the dampness of the cloth that Astron had thrown him and dropped it to the ground with the other. He patted his mare and frowned.

"You can detect the presence of these imps before they can get too close?" he asked.

"Far before what you might dismiss as a fleeting spark of light or a distant buzz of an insect, I can recognize it for what it truly is."

"And once detected, you can confine them as well?"

"They would bite my fingers just as surely as yours," Astron said. "It is the bottles made by your magicians that are best to keep them in."

"Such jars cost a great deal," Kestrel said. "Far more than a dozen brandels. I have—have dealt with a guild of Procolon to the north and know full well what one might bring."

"Then too there is the matter of the gold imp and others of its kind. For those I do not know for sure that I can even detect."

"If you have not heard of such, then they most probably do not exist," Kestrel said.

"But I heard you speak of them to the wizards."

"It was a lie." Kestrel shrugged his shoulders, dismissing the thought. He looked into the demon's unblinking eyes. Not being able to snatch even a glimmer of what he really was up to made him very uncomfortable. But what Astron had said made sense. Kestrel had bruised the pride of not a single wizard but almost a dozen. The archimage probably was the only one who could get him out of his fix. Only Alodar would have enough power to turn aside the masters' wrath once he somehow was convinced it was all a simple mistake. And surely Kestrel could come up with a plausible explanation before he got to the capital of Procolon. Crossing the border would be the only problem.

Kestrel smiled. Now that he thought of it, being in the presence of the archimage might lead to other opportunities as well. The master of five magics was a man just like the rest. What satisfaction there would be in giving him the chance to outsmart a simple woodchopper. The archimage! Yes, it would be the greatest triumph of all!

"Very well," Kestrel said after a moment's more deliberation. If the demon had any ulterior motives, he would deal with them when they became more apparent. For now he would continue as he had been asked. "Our paths are still joined. I will get us to the archimage—as we, of course, have originally agreed."

"A lie," Astron said slowly, apparently ignoring what Kestrel said. "You spoke something which was not a reflection of the truth, or at least your interpretation of it."

"Of course," Kestrel said. "I explained to you already what I am about, what all men are about. Concern yourself about it no longer. The only difference is that some of us are more skilled in seeing through the words to what stands behind."

"You have this skill of observation?" Astron asked.

Kestrel sighed. The events of the past hour had already been too draining. He did not want to experience any more intense feelings. He shook his head and turned away.

Astron waved at the mare and wagon. "I understand," he said, "that you do not have the means of transporting us as swiftly as a mighty djinn. One is bound by his honor for no more than he is capable of giving." He reached out and tugged on Kestrel's sleeve. "There will be time, therefore, that can be most profitably spent with no hint of disgrace—time to tell me how you learned to discern the truth of things that are not."

Kestrel studied Astron's expression. He saw no trace of mocking judgment. The demon's words of honor and trust unlocked memories that had been suppressed for too many years. Unbidden, they bubbled up to be examined again. They would not go away until they had been acknowledged. And if only a being from another realm heard them, who would really care?

"I did not have such skills at first," Kestrel heard himself say softly. "Not at first, when perhaps they counted the most." He waved his arm up toward the wagon where Phoebe sat entranced. "In many ways the wizard reminds me of her—at least in the way she speaks and smiles."

Kestrel looked down at the brandels he clutched in his hand and ran his fingers over the bust of the old queen. "Evelyn was a wandering sorcerer, so she said, unaffiliated with those on Morgana across the great sea. The logo of the eye on her robe was plainly stitched and unadorned. A sorcerer of great beauty she was as well, as fair as Vendora, the ruler of Procolon, in her prime.

"Her love for me knew no bounds, she told me. Anything that I asked that was in her power would be mine. And who was I to believe otherwise, a lad barely out of his teens.

"The request was simple enough—to go with her among the townspeople I knew, add credence to her tale, and hold the pledges for safekeeping that each of them subscribed. When the total was sufficient she would add a matching amount of her own and then, while I waited outside the gates, negotiate with the Cycloid Guild for the sale of some properties that would aid in the enchantments. With them she would form great illusions of healing and relieve the deep-set pains that even sweet-balm could not touch. Our village would become famous for the soothing comforts the charms provided. Everyone would share in the fees that such wonders would bring. And I would learn the words of the spells and be second only to her in the eyes of the grateful.

"Three days I paced in front of the forbidding doors of the guild before some of the more suspicious townspeople came and asked to count again the contents of the sacks I so carefully guarded. When they were opened and iron disks instead of soft gold spilled out, I was as much shocked as they. Even when told how the switch must have taken place in a moment of intimacy, I would not believe. At any second, I knew, the gates would open and Evelyn would emerge with a satisfactory explanation.

"But she did not come; she left by another exit from the guild almost as soon as she had entered. No, she reappeared not then nor during any of the four years I wasted away in a dungeon in punishment for my part in the crime.

"So when I finally was set free, I started learning to look intently at the faces, to read behind the words and to serve to magicians and other masters some of the same formulas that they would brew for me."

Kestrel paused and shrugged. "It is not so difficult if you set your mind to it. Every man betrays his innermost thoughts with slight gestures and the tugs of muscles in his face, master as well as slave. You merely have to put yourself in his place and feel as your own what must be his driving desires. Each time you observe, the readings become clearer, the hidden motives behind them easier to read.

"And with that understanding comes the power to manipulate, to guide and channel according to your own desire. One can twist a master of the arts like a magic ring about his finger and show to the world, like Evelyn, how undeserving he is.

"So in the end I have become a sorcerer as much as any other. No, I know nothing of the incantations that are so hard to say but if spoken thrice bind the spells. I do not bend others to my will by force of magical art. The illusions that I spin are fabrics of the other's own thoughts, rather than my own. I merely encourage the impulses that are already there and enable them to flower for a brief moment for my own gain before they are subsequently smothered by shame."

The sadness in Kestrel's face tugged like a great weight. "Now I do have the skill of observation," he said. "I can see through men to their true worth. And unfortunately, I am among the best."

Kestrel stopped his rambling. He looked at Astron

with questioning eyes. "Now do you understand any better?" he asked.

"No," Astron said. "It is all very interesting, but in fact, I guess I do not. Why would this Evelyn say she would return and then change her mind without letting you know?"

Kestrel sighed again. At least for the moment, the bitterness was expunged. And it was far better for a demon to hear his confession than for someone who could manipulate the information against him. For a long moment there was silence; then Kestrel waved back to the wagon. "Climb inside and let us be going," he said. "I have some clothing that you should don so that you will not attract notice as we travel northward."

Astron nodded. "But you have not yet told me of the wizard. Why did you return for her at such great risk?"

"I do not know." Kestrel shrugged. "But it does not matter. Into the wagon, I say. Let us be gone."

"You had no real need," Astron persisted as he climbed aboard. "As I understand it, it could only be the act of a hero."

CHAPTER EIGHT

Talk of the Thaumaturges

THE race across the Southern Kingdoms was swift. Kestrel pushed the mare as much as he dared, barely stopping for food and sleep. Astron had no requirement for nourishment and Phoebe in her entranced state needed little. In three days' time they crossed Samirand and Laudia and entered Ethidor, which bordered Procolon on the south. During their trek, Astron saw no sign of the searching imps, but the compelling sense of urgency did not abate. At any moment, the wizards could discover where they were and subject them to their wrath. The tale of what awaited Astron back in his own realm, if he did not succeed in time, Kestrel could scarcely believe, but the demon remained steadfast in urging the wagon onward.

Toward dusk of the third day, they arrived in the port of Menthos as the onshore breeze blew thick plumes of dark smoke from foundries across the isthmus. Kestrel pulled his horse to a stop at the head of the main street of the town. He glanced back at Phoebe, who appeared to be sleeping on a rough bed under the wagon's canopy. The branches and snags meant to be foisted off as anvil-wood had long since been discarded. Astron sat at Kestrel's side, wearing a long cape and hooded like a master, although no logo was displayed. A worn tunic, leggings, boots and gloves covered most of his faintly scaled skin.

On the left side of the main street, behind a sidewalk of rough planking, stood a long row of apothecaries, wooden-faced structures mainly of one storey. Some were brightly painted and prosperous-looking, others were dull with isinglass windows scratched and hazy. "Galena and cinnabar," some of the placards over doorways proclaimed; "Fresh vacuum of all quantities, created daily," said others.

On the right, steep stairways led down a short cliff to docks and quays. Riding gently at anchor were broad-beamed galleons, all lying high in the water, though some had their decks filled with closely packed bottles, their sails unfurled, ready to weigh anchor.

At the other end of the street, behind high fences, large smokestacks towered into the sky, belching dense black clouds. Even from the distance, one could hear the roar of huge bellows feeding air into furnaces and smell the hint of metallic fumes.

The traffic on the street was the usual mixture of scurrying messengers, maids hawking fruits and material from simple carts, merchants in animated conversation, and an occasional litter bearing someone of importance. Mixed with the rest were men-at-arms in groups of twos and threes, wandering aimlessly, apparently looking for something to spark their jaded interests.

"An alchemist's town, no doubt about it," Kestrel said as he pointed to the rising smoke. He had decided it best to explain things to Astron as soon as something new was seen by the demon. It would reduce the chance of questions at inappropriate times, like those that had been asked at Phoebe's cabin.

Kestrel shook his head slightly as he spoke. He had become quite used to the physical presence of the demon. The oddity of his bizarre origin had long since faded away. A wrinkled nose, Kestrel now understood, indicated puzzlement, the flicking of the eye membranes a retreat into the deep logical thought. But beyond these simple signs, he still could not fathom any motives behind those that the devil professed. Hopefully, they would become more apparent as they drew closer to the archimage.

Despite his statements about experience as a cataloguer of the realm of men, Astron was totally ignorant about some of the simplest things. Abstract concepts beyond what one could see and touch took a good deal of explaining. But the demon was an eager and attentive pupil, asking questions until he was sure that he fully understood.

"If this is the lair of alchemists, then what formulas do they work?" Astron asked. "The chance for success must be quite high, judging from the number who are congregated all in one place."

"Vacuums," Kestrel said. "By melting metals, the alchemists of Menthos can produce the hardest vacuums on the great sea. They are in demand by magicians and thaumaturges for their own rituals and simulations."

"But a vacuum is the total absence of matter. How can that have any value at all?"

"I do not understand the details," Kestrel said, "but by connecting one of the bottles produced here to another vessel, the air can be removed far better than by any pump. Lids can be sealed with greater force than that provided by the finest waxes. Huge pistons can be made to move along long cylinders, raising bridges over navigable rivers."

"The absence of matter," Astron mumbled, "and in the realm of men great effort is put into its creation." He wrinkled his nose. "Another fascination. If only there were more time."

Kestrel started to say more, but he suddenly spotted what he was looking for on the crowded street. Half a block down from where they had stopped, three brown-robed young men were performing their services for a queue of men-at-arms standing on the sidewalk, waiting their turn. Kestrel pointed out his destination and started the mare slowly forward.

"Thaumaturges," he said, "a journeyman and two apprentices. See, one wears but a single wavy line on his sleeve; the other two are unadorned. But no matter that a master is not present. They will know what is happening by the nature of their trade better than most."

Astron leaned forward to watch the activity as the wagon approached. One of the apprentices deftly clicked short shears through the long hair of a sergeant who sat in a portable chair set up on the sidewalk in front of the line. The second scooted about on his knees sweeping up the locks as they fell and passing them on to the journeyman seated at a table a little distance away.

The last of the three carefully extracted a single strand of hair from the rest of each tress and dipped it into a pot of glue at his side. With a smooth motion, he aligned the sticky hair along the length of a piece of twine directly in front of where he sat. The men-at-arms chatted among themselves and the apprentice who wielded the shears, apparently totally oblivious of the other activities about them.

"I recognize the craft," Astron said as they approached. "The one with the doubled blades is called a barber. In exchange for a coin he removes hair from the head and face."

"In the Southern Kingdoms, there is no fee." Kestrel pulled the wagon to a halt directly in front of the line of waiting men. "The hair itself is payment enough."

"Something new for sale?" one of the men-at-arms called out, jingling the purse at his waist as Kestrel vaulted to the ground. "It has been a fortnight of staring at the fires across the marsh. This is our first day of leave."

"How much for an evening with the wench?" A second poked his head into the interior of the wagon and spied Phoebe's reclining form.

"Although she is mine to command, such base use is not—" Astron began before Kestrel reached up and laid a hand of warning on his arm.

"A fortnight without rotation." Kestrel smiled. "A long time without distraction. Tell me, how have things fared on the border for those who might wish to pass?"

The two men-at-arms turned suddenly silent and resumed their place in line. Kestrel noticed the glower of the sergeant who sat in the apprentice's chair. "My business is with the journeyman," he said. "What he has learned from all who have sat here certainly is not the fault of your own fine squad of men."

Kestrel watched the sergeant relax back into the chair as he walked down to where the journeyman worked his craft. As he approached, he noticed the hatchet-sharp nose that split the thaumaturge's elongated and melancholy face and how, with eyes furrowed with concentration, he arranged more than two dozen pieces of twine in front of him, each with a hair glued down its length from the head of a different man. The journeyman mumbled something that Kestrel could not quite catch and then began deftly to weave the strings into a stout rope the thickness of a man's thumb.

Simultaneously a second hair from each of the clippings before him disentangled from the rest. Like worms on a hot griddle, they danced toward one another and then began to intertwine. In a perfect mimicry of the weaving of the journeyman, the hairs wove into a tiny replica of the rope but with a diameter smaller than the shaft of a pin.

"What is your greatest length?" Kestrel asked as he approached.

"Over ten times the height of a man but with a carrying strength for its size greater than anything but the strands of a spider's web. You have no need for bulky ropes of hemp or cotton when you can possess such compact beauties as these braids."

"Only ten times? Oh, then it is a pity." Kestrel backed away. "I was hoping for something more the distance from here to the quay."

The journeyman looked up from his work. His eyes ran over Kestrel's rumpled tunic and he frowned. "Even with the aid of thaumaturgy which weaves the tiny strands as quickly as if they were readily handled twines," he said, "what you request would take much effort to produce. Each short length must be knotted together. You speak of something measured in golden brandels rather than the mere coppers of Ethidor. Are you sure you do not waste my time?"

Kestrel paused a moment before answering. Then he shrugged and smiled. "Perhaps you are right. There are probably others who have what I want directly on hand." He turned to go and, with what looked like an afterthought, tossed a brandel onto the table amid the braids of hair. "For your trouble," he said.

The journeyman eyed the coin as it spun to rest on the rough surface. He looked at Kestrel a second time and then apparently made up his mind. "Luthor, to the master's den," he commanded. "Fetch the other braidings with length of ten. I will knot them all together for a price that would be most fair."

As the apprentice scampered off, the journeyman called out to Kestrel, who was halfway back to the wagon. "Here, I will show you how it is done while we wait," he said. "Watch as I join together the short length I have just made with another of similar size."

Kestrel hesitated a moment but then continued toward the wagon.

"You ask of the border," the journeyman continued. "Perhaps there is something of interest I can tell you to pass the time." He waved his arm at the remaining apprentice, now working on the next who stood in line.

94

"There is much that we learn from those with whom we trade."

Kestrel turned slowly and shrugged. "I have heard that many are the numbers who mill about in the bogs."

"And for no real purpose," the journeyman answered quickly. "Our own Prince Rupert's troops are there merely because his alchemists could not abide by each other's agreements with the miners of Procolon—ambushing and waylaying each other's shipments of galena and other lead ores as they came south to the foundries. When Celibor rips his mind from lusting after some wench, he is the worst, and his rivals little better. It is no wonder old Queen Vendora dispatched a garrison to guard the way.

"Then Rupert's pride could not stand the presence of Procolon's banners on his soil. So his own legions were dispatched to ensure that none remained on this side of the border. And now they sit staring at each other, with no traffic at all going either way."

"None at all?" Kestrel asked.

"A month ago, a small wagon about the size of yours attempted to run past Procolon's lines, after bribing some squad on this side of the marsh." The thaumaturge shrugged. "Their archers gave him no chance to speak before everything was consumed in flame."

"And writs of safe passage?"

"A profitable business." The journeyman laughed. "I can point you to a dozen scribes who would gladly write the most impressive documents for a suitable fee. The trouble is that the men who walk the Procolon line are as testy as ours. They swing their swords first and then ask their sergeants if it was the proper thing to do.

"But never mind all of that. Let me show you how I will make the length of braid that you request." The journeyman positioned two lengths of woven rope in front of him, the strands in each one cemented to individual hairs. He grasped a single twine from the end of each and with nimble fingers knotted them together. Then he selected a second pair, interwove them with the first and joined them together as well. Proceeding methodically, a pair at a time, he spliced the ends in a strong bond.

Kestrel did not follow the motions of the two corresponding braids of hair but he knew what was happening. They too were becoming knotted and bound in exactly the same way as the easier to manipulate ropes in the hands of the thaumaturge. The laws of "like produces like" and "once together, always together" were being used to perform a perfect simulation.

Instead, Kestrel was looking in the direction in which the apprentice had sped away. When he saw a blur in the distance that indicated the young man's return, he suddenly reached out and tapped the journeyman on the shoulder.

"The sergeant seemed a little perturbed that his men might talk of the border," he said quickly. "What do you suppose he thinks when he hears the same words come from you?"

"What I have said will cause no harm," the journeyman answered. "He is concerned only about the regulations laid down by his captain."

"Still." Kestrel pointed at the brandel lying where it had fallen. "How would you explain that a stranger was willing to pay gold for what he has heard?"

"But you said that is for—"

"I see his frown deepen." Kestrel smiled back to the sergeant waiting for his men. "Perhaps the two of us should go over together and explain."

"No, the braided—"

Kestrel reached down and deftly scooped up the coin. "On the other hand, perhaps it is best for everybody if this transaction never took place."

Before the thaumaturge could say more, Kestrel glided back to the wagon and climbed aboard. Just as the apprentice came panting up with coils of the tiny rope about both his arms, Kestrel motioned the mare to start away. The only problem was merely getting across the border, he remembered thinking. It looked as if it was not going to be quite so easy.

* * *

96

The afternoon faded into darkness while Kestrel pondered how to proceed. He had slowly navigated the wagon up and down the streets of Menthos a dozen times, looking at all the shops and factories, but no inspiration had come. With a growing fatigue, he studied in the encroaching dimness the last of the foundry fires as they winked out for the night. Somehow, the solution to getting past two lines of armed men and into Procolon had to involve the large works of alchemists, but he could not quite put all the elements of a solution together.

Kestrel glanced at Astron, sitting patiently at his side. The demon had halted all his questions when he had been told that interruptions would not be appreciated for a while. Kestrel glanced back into the interior of the wagon at Phoebe's still slumbering form. He sighed. He was bothered about that little detail as well.

What good had it done to rescue her from the other wizards, if she remained in a semianimate state under the control of a demon? Sooner or later, someone would get suspicious about a woman in a trance, wearing the robe and logo of a wizard. Word would surely get back to her peers. Crossing the border would be difficult at best, and Phoebe in her condition was an added complication.

On the other hand, if Astron were to release Phoebe from his domination, Kestrel was not sure what would happen. She might immediately try to contact her council and aid in Kestrel's apprehension as well. How easy would it be to convince her to keep quiet about her travelling companions?

"What about the wizard?" Kestrel asked out loud after a moment's more thought. "Is it harmful to keep her in such an unnatural state?"

"Eventually, yes," Astron said. "The muscles atrophy and the thoughts turn sluggish, even after one is released. In time, she would become no more than a vacant doll with drool on her chin."

Kestrel jerked the horse to a sudden halt. "I still do not know quite why I brought her along," he said, "but certainly not for a fate such as that." He wavered for a moment in uncertainty and then thought of the warmth of her smile. "Perhaps it is better to release her now."

"By eventually, I meant a long passage of time," Astron said. "As for the present moment, do you really think it wise? I have held her to avoid more struggle of the wills, but if I were to set her free, she might not be similarly inclined. Most likely she would try to dominate me instead. The first contest was hard enough. I do not wish to undergo it again."

"No, somehow, I will take care of that," Kestrel said. His thoughts raced as he spoke. Now that he had decided, it was important that the deed be done. "She is the key element of the exchange. A countess is what we need. Yes, a countess to impress one of the alchemists with the possibility of a very large reward."

"A reward? In exchange for what?" Astron asked.

"Transport across the border in exchange for—for a mine," Kestrel said. As he spoke everything fell into place. Phoebe was the missing element that he had been searching for! By posing as a countess, she would give them the credibility that was lacking in his half-formed plans. Never mind about the risk of letting her decide for herself. He would work out something when everything could be explained. Kestrel turned the wagon into an alleyway and halted.

"Quickly," he said. "Release her now so that we can purchase some clothing appropriate for her station. At dawn tomorrow, we must be ready to start."

"Your motives regarding the female I still do not understand," Astron said. He wrinkled his nose and for a long moment nothing happened. Then abruptly his face cleared and he turned his attention to studying the tackle of Kestrel's mare.

"Awake," he said simply. "I release you, wizard, to command your own will."

Kestrel watched Phoebe's eyes flutter and then spring open. She looked up at the wagon's canopy in the darkness and then at the two figures hovering over her. Her eyes widened further and she clutched her fist to her mouth, preparing to scream.

Kestrel reached down and stroked her arm. Gently he placed an extended finger on her cheek.

Phoebe's eyes flashed in the gathering darkness. She drew a deep breath and slowly returned her hand to her side.

"Where am I?" she asked in a controlled tone after a moment. "What is it that you want?"

"Remember the anvilwood?" Kestrel tried to make his voice soothing. "I am the woodcutter who brought it to your cabin. You summoned a demon more powerful than you could control."

Phoebe's eyes shifted from Kestrel to Astron. "Yes," she said in sudden recognition. "The demon. His will was too strong. I could not resist. I am his to do with what he will." She shuddered and snapped shut her eyes. "The council was right after all. Their barbs and jeers are true." She tugged at the folds of the robe about her hips. "I wear the logo of a master only because of my father's wealth, not because of skill. Go ahead, devil, do with me what you will."

"No, you do not understand," Kestrel continued. "Test your thoughts. They are free. The contest is finished and you are dominated no more."

Phoebe cowered in silence for a long moment but then Kestrel saw the tension gradually fade away. The wrinkles vanished from her brow. Tentatively she sat up and shook her head, as if trying to toss away thoughts that did not belong.

"Free-willed I am, woodsman," she said cautiously. "Thank you for your aid." She reached down in confusion to her waist and patted a purse that was not there. "Your product is as good as you bragged it to be. You need not show me the contents of each leather sack as I originally intended. Let us go back into the cabin and I will pay you your price, though I must say that I am getting the better part of the bargain."

"Ah, things are not quite that simple," Kestrel said. "You see, we are not outside your cabin, but in Menthos, near the border to Procolon."

99

The tension in Phoebe's face returned. "Menthos! I do not understand."

"Your council of wizards has become enraged," Astron said. "As we speak, they no doubt have many imps scouring the countryside looking for—"

"You," Kestrel cut in. "Yes, you are the one they seek, a wizard in flight from what they construe as the justice that is your due."

"Yes, the council and their hidebound ways," Phoebe said. "But Menthos? I still do not understand."

"Well, this is the way of it," Kestrel said. He looked into Phoebe's questioning eyes. He should have thought things through a little more thoroughly before having Astron release her from his control.

"Yes," Phoebe said. "What indeed is the way of it?"

"The council of wizards think that—" Kestrel began but this time Astron interrupted.

"We need your help," the demon said, "to cross the border and see the archimage. Kestrel sees you as the key element of the plan. Despite what he has done to your reputation back in Brythia, we need your help here and now."

Kestrel grimaced, expecting Phoebe's face to knot into one of displeasure. Next time, he just had to get the demon to understand and follow his lead, rather than cut in on his own. Not that there would be a next time, if Phoebe decided to rectify what had happened to her good name. He shook his head, awaiting the outburst. Why had freeing the wizard been such a good idea?

But the hard words did not come. "You need my help," Phoebe repeated, "the service of a wizard, and you have come to me."

Kestrel blinked at the unexpected tone. "Wizardry, why no," he rushed to say. "It was something rather different from that." He looked into Phoebe's eyes and found the words of deception harder and harder to get out of his throat. "We must get to the archimage," he said at last, "and for that we must first cross the border. I think that I have a means of accomplishing it. We need an impersonation of a countess, one who is the seeker of thrills, one who can convince an alchemist to grant favors in exchange for profit to be received later." He hesitated and then added in a mumble, "The archimage will be able to set things straight between you and your council as well."

"Then it is true," Phoebe said. "I was indeed dominated by the demon. If it is skill in wizardry that you desire, elsewhere is where you should look."

"No, no, if wizardry is called for along the way, you are the one to whom we will turn," Kestrel said. "It is just that there are other requirements as well."

"You need me?" Phoebe questioned again.

Kestrel just nodded, trying to fathom the motivations behind the pretty smile. He was having difficulty reading the wizard, just as he did with the demon, but for a different reason. The emotions were on her face well enough; but when he looked at her, distracting thoughts warped the logical cadence of his thought.

"And it will help you with the council," he repeated weakly.

"The council." Phoebe shook her head. "I have little doubt that they have found some way to give me censure." She smoothed the folds of her robe and shrugged. "It has not been such an easy struggle. Without the largess of my father, I would never have been able to pay the triple fees the masters charged to initiate me into their art. The stocking of my larder comes less from the few payments I receive for my craft than the continued openness of his purse.

"Far better for all concerned, it has been made quite clear more than once, if Phoebe behaved more like her cousins and sisters, lounging in the dresses of brocade and attending the balls of the prince."

"What do you mean?" Astron said. "I cannot yet follow when men speak in such abstraction."

"Men, indeed," Phoebe said. "I suspect the realm of daemon is much like what you see about you here." She narrowed her eyes and looked piercingly at Astron. "Tell me how it is that only the males answer the summons through the flame and grapple with the wizard's will.

Why no females? What have you done with them?"

"Why, that is not the purpose of the broodmothers," Astron said. "They serve one function and no more. It is unthinkable for it to be any other way."

"And you, Kestrel, how many wizards of my sex have you encountered in your peddling of woods?"

"Ah, you are the only one."

"Yes, the only female wizard in Brythia, perhaps in all the kingdoms that border the great sea. Despite all the regulations thrown in the way, the unapproving stares, the whispers behind my back, I became a master—an equally accredited master in a local council, whether they liked it or not."

"Then, if your council does not look with favor on you at the moment—" Kestrel began.

"It can only be an intensification of what already was felt. I am an embarrassment to them because I am so different and do not assume their stately airs. But no matter, I have won the robe and they cannot take it away."

Phoebe paused and looked at Kestrel. "What is important to me now is not their thoughts, woodcutter, but yours. What do you think of a master who happens not to be a male? Would you use me when you could elect to choose a man instead?" She glanced over at Astron and her voice softened to a whisper. "Use one who has already proven that a demon such as that is her better in a battle of wills?"

Kestrel blinked again. "I have considered you a master, no different from the rest," he said. The question went deeper than that, but his answer was a truthful one. She had been chosen for the anvilwood because of her greater wealth, not anything else. As for the rest, he felt the old barriers sliding strongly into place. No good could come from raising the innermost feelings and trying to strip away the scarred layers of pain.

"Well said." Phoebe smiled faintly. "Perhaps my instincts in the matter were correct from the first. Stand in the light so I can see you better. No, not you, demon, only the man."

102

Kestrel climbed back down from the wagon and into the brightness of the street.

"Yes, it is all coming back now." Phoebe's smile broadened. "I remember why I invited you in. And as for now, wizardry or something else of equal value, it does not really matter. Just so I am a full partner, and not a tool to be manipulated like a sorcerer's slave."

"You will not try to continue our struggle for dominance?" Astron asked.

"No, why should I?" The smile vanished from Phoebe's face. "If you still desired to control my will, I do not see how I could resist a second time, knowing I had lost the first." She turned her eyes away from Astron and lowered her head. "I have already proven myself worthy to wear the logo of the master. Perhaps in the end, that will be sufficient."

"There is no more to it!" Astron exclaimed. "Kestrel, you are most remarkable. I apologize for my doubt. When there is more time, you must explain how you achieved such an agreement of wills."

Kestrel lightly touched Phoebe's arm again. Despite the inner warnings, it felt good to do so. "Things are not always what they seem, demon," he said slowly. "I have already told you that."

Astron wrinkled his nose and his membranes slid into place. For a moment he stared off into the distance and did not speak.

He suddenly burst out of his contemplation after a moment. "Then let us get on with your plan. The flickers of light that I now see at the end of this alley—I do not believe that they are the simple fireflies of your realm."

CHAPTER NINE

The Alchemy of Air

KESTREL hit the tapper against the brass door with authority. The gong seemed to reverberate all along the high metal-plated fencing that ran around the foundry. Even though it was barely dawn, smoke was already spilling out of the stack on the other side of the enclosing barrier. The wheeze of the bellows was quite loud, like the moan of a great djinn with nothing to destroy.

Astron had not been sure how much longer it would be before the wizards became certain of their location, but they had little time for additional delay. They had to get over the border and to the archimage soon, or it would all be too late.

Kestrel cupped his hands to his mouth and spoke directly at the demon, the noises within the foundry masking his words more than a few feet away. "Now remember, Astron," he said. "You are the consulting alchemist for the countess. You will observe the process and say nothing. Occasionally shake your head slightly in disapproval after an explanation. Under no circumstances ask any of your questions. Just be on the lookout for more of your kind."

"But an alchemist I am not," Astron said. "I cannot speak that which does not reflect reality."

"That is just the point," Kestrel said. "Do not say a thing. Let those inside draw whatever conclusions they will. For what they think, you are not responsible."

"To stand and shake my head is not very interesting, Kestrel. At least I should be able to find out something to add to my catalogues."

"I will see to it that you are suitably amused," Kestrel

said. "Just keep quiet while you are about it."

Kestrel turned his attention to Phoebe. The gown they had purchased the previous evening with eight of the dozen brandels suited her well; she carried herself as one would expect of the nobility. She returned his approving look with a smile, but he pulled his eyes away. She had enthusiastically taken on the role he had outlined to her and did not even bother to ask any more about what had happened at her cabin or even the reason he was originally there.

So long as she did not ask, Kestrel decided, there was no reason for him to explain more. He darted one more furtive glance in her direction. And yet his logic did not quite ring true. For the first time in a long while, he was somehow uncomfortable about what he was hiding from someone else.

The door suddenly opened and Kestrel turned to meet the gateman. "The grand countess of Brythia, second cousin to the king, is here to discuss terms for the shipment," he said. "Show us to the head alchemist without delay."

The gateman puckered his prunelike face into a mass of wrinkles. With studied disapproval, he looked up and down Kestrel's own plain clothing and Astron, hooded by his side. "I have received no instructions about a visitor," he said. "You will have to wait until I check with master Celibor."

"Surely we can wait inside, rather than here on the street," Kestrel said. "Perhaps even a chair so that my lady can sit. The purse she carries is most heavy. And from what I hear of master Celibor, he will be most anxious to meet her."

The gateman glanced at Phoebe, hesitated a moment, then snatched at the brandel that Kestrel waved in front of him. "You may use my stool." He waved as he headed off across the interior of the foundry yard.

Kestrel and the others stepped inside. Quickly, he surveyed the enclosure from one end to the other. The fencing formed a huge square, each side the length of a sprinter's race. In the rear corner of the left stood dumps

105

of ore, huge boulders ripped from deep running mines, glinting with crystals of gray in the morning sun. A dozen laborers swung hammers at the larger ones, reducing them to smaller chunks and dust that were shoveled onto a belt squeaking over a long row of wooden rollers. Spinning flywheels and convoluted belts moved the rock into massive grinders and then through acrid chemicals dripping from glazed retorts. At the terminus of the conveyor, a fine powder fell into a chute leading to a huge brick-lined anthanar in the center of the square. On the backside of the furnace, barely visible from where Kestrel stood, two three-man bellows alternately expanded and shot air into the burning firepit.

A tall shed spanned the opposite side of the square, covering loads of sand that fell from hoppers into a red-hot cauldron. There a dozen glassblowers dipped long hollow tubings into a transparent slag. With bursting cheeks, they blew huge flat-bottomed bottles with tiny necks. These too were conveyed to the furnace and entered on the side opposite from the processed ore.

Near the front of the anthanar stood two alchemists, each furiously writing on parchment, giving life to the formulas that formed the basis of their craft. They stood on either side of a third conveyor, this one discharging a sequence of lead-capped bottles that were collected and arrayed in designated squares throughout the yard. Behind the back of the second master, in a cast-iron trough, a river of molten metal ran into an array of molds, presses, and rollers.

A bright lead foil extruded from the last of the rotating cylinders. Intricate objects that Kestrel did not recognize dropped from the presses into a hopper. Some of the molds were simple ingots, conveniently shaped for resale elsewhere. The rest formed struts and geometric figures, evidently destined for a vast array of dull gray structures beyond the cooling area.

Among the distant sprawl were skeletons of icosohedrons in three different sizes. Nestled with solid-sided cubes, small spheres clustered like grapes on long cylindrical stems. Beyond the smaller structures, giant pylons soared twice the height of a man. Hollow balls of lead fully ten arm-lengths in diameter shone dully in the morning sun. To the left of the completed spheres stood one in midconstruction, the bottom of a mesh-covered skeleton sheathed in a foil of lead, while laborers heated and fused additional sheets above its bulging equator.

"Somehow, in the final step of the formula that the alchemists guard in their grimoires, the smelting of the metal produces the vacuum," Kestrel explained to the others. "The lead is used as a seal only because it is conveniently there. As you can see the bulk of it goes into the molds and presses for resale elsewhere as a by-product. I think the geometric shapes are used in magician's rituals, although some of the foundries make small statuary to sell to the nobility as works of art as well.

"But beyond that is where our interest lies, where the vacuum is tested to verify its quality. As you may know, not a single formula of alchemy can be guaranteed to succeed each and every time. Indeed, the more powerful have the least chance of all. Each product must be verified to ensure that the process has produced what was desired."

Astron and Phoebe turned to look where Kestrel pointed. They saw two workmen drag one of the larger bottles from a square and place it adjacent to what looked like a stitchery of cured hides lying on the ground. One connected a bellows to the collection of hides and began pumping. In a few moments it inflated into a perfect sphere. Then the second workman thrust the neck of the vacuum bottle into the bellows opening and broke the seal.

With a powerful hiss that the three could hear even from where they stood, the sphere buckled and warped, although not back to the flattened shape it had before. Like a lumpy pillow, it sagged on the ground at the workmen's feet. The first bound off the opening at the bottom and the other set it apart from the rest of the gear so that it received the full glare of the rising sun.

"Yes, what is it?" A master wearing the logo of the inverted triangle had emerged from a hut near the glass-

107

works and followed the gatekeeper back across the foundry yard. He was short and swarthy with small quick eyes that squinted in distrust. His jaws hung heavy like a bulldog's. Kestrel wondered whether, if he got his grip on something, he would ever let go.

"If it is a large order, you had better place it quickly." The alchemist waved toward the pile of rock waiting to be crushed. "When that is gone, there will be no more for vacuum for a goodly while, at least until the border to the north is once again open."

"Master Celibor, I presume," Kestrel said. "This is Countess Phoebe and she indeed is most anxious to buy." Kestrel paused and forced a smile. "Her mind as yet is not totally made up, however, between dealing with you or the establishment across the street."

"What—Iliac!" Celibor exploded. "He is no less than responsible for the blockade in the first place. You should be blaming him for the rise in prices, not giving him aid by favoring him with trade. If he had not persisted in trying to divert ore wagons rightly meant for me, then none of this confrontation at the border would have happened. Even the archimage would be visiting our fair kingdoms rather than wasting his good time entertaining the ones who call themselves skyskirr from some forsaken place or another far away."

"Nevertheless, he has the reputation for a splendid product," Kestrel said.

"Lies of the market place," Celibor spat. "He turns out great volume of glassware and at less cost, it is true. But how many prove to be nothing more than jars of clear air rather than vacuum of prime hardness, answer me that? Why, look you at the pains we take to ensure that each batch has indeed run its course, rather than randomly failed as is sometimes the case."

Celibor paused to catch his breath. The ruddiness of his cheeks began to fade. He waved in the direction of the hide sphere. The crushing indentations had vanished; the sun had warmed the air that remained until the skin was again tight and firm. As everyone watched it began gently to rise from the ground and tug at the single fetter that held it in place.

"Elsewhere along the street," Celibor said, "they merely let the balloons rise to their maximum heights and do no more. Those batches that produce the highest they label as premium grade vacuum, no matter that they might be half as good as the ones produced the day before.

"Here we do more than that. We actually calculate the degree to which the jars are empty from measuring the balloon's ascent. Nowhere else are such quantitative tests made, not in a single foundry along the street. We know the volume of our balloons; the hides have been cured so that they no longer stretch. From the height to which they rise and equilibrate with the lesser density of air outside, we can compute the mass that rides within. From these numbers we then determine precisely how well the test bottle extracted some of the original contents and thence from that how good was the vacuum it originally contained."

"That is most interesting," Astron said. "A quantitative calculation aimed at showing nothing as the result."

Celibor looked at the hooded figure and frowned. "Not every batch produces a balloon which rises so well," he explained. "Some bottles extract only half the air because only half was removed from them by the random perturbations of the creation process. Some draw no air at all: total failures the likes of which you are much more likely to find across the way."

"How high do these balloons rise?" Phoebe asked.

Celibor looked at Phoebe as if he were noticing her for the first time. With a deliberate coolness he ran his eyes over her body. "A most interesting question, my lady," he said. "We usually test only a single bottle in a batch; so, like the one you see there, they rise only perhaps as far as the top of the anthanar's stack or a little higher."

Kestrel noticed Celibor's reaction to Phoebe, but surprisingly the satisfaction of a plan going well did not come. Rather than being pleased that she had excited the alchemist's interest, he felt irritated by the degrading way in which he showed it. It would indeed be soon enough when they were well away.

"And no gondola attached for one to observe?" Phoebe asked as Kestrel tried to draw back Celibor's attention.

"Why no, not every time, my countess, it would be a great waste." Celibor did not take his eyes from Phoebe. "Although we have baskets and the necessary riggings obtained from the thaumaturges up the street, the purpose is to test, not to lift a considerable weight. And with the onshore breeze, there is risk as well. A parted tether would mean the occupants would sail right over the encamped armies and deep into Procolon itself."

"But then think also of the thrill of it," Phoebe said in a bored tone. "If only for a part of an hour, floating like a cloud and looking down on the coastline as far as one could see. So much more exciting that all those dreary teas and receptions. Yes, Kestrel, see to it. Do business with the one who will offer a balloon ride as part of the bargain."

"You are talking a considerable expense," Celibor said. He finally looked from Phoebe back to Kestrel and Astron. "And although I have been most free to point out details of my trade, I know nothing of you other than what you profess." He motioned back the way he had come. "Visit me in my chambers, my lady; I will ask more of you there." Celibor again looked up and down the length of Phoebe's gown. "Never mind the clutter along the way. It is quite safe, since we keep it well away from the flames. Just lift your hems a trifle and they will not be soiled as we walk."

"The countess and I will gladly follow," Kestrel said quickly. "But consultant Astron's time is perhaps better spent in evaluating more of what takes place here. Pair him with someone who talks well and fast. He is the best of listeners."

Astron opened his mouth to speak, but Kestrel grabbed him by the arm. "There, the man with the pen and quill—perhaps you will be amused by learning more of these calculations. Or even the sculpturing—see, look at that scaffolding going up on which they are hanging those foils of lead. Surely those will be of more interest than standing around listening to the countess and the master exchanging pleasantries."

"The calculations and the structures, why yes," Astron said. "The sculpturing is akin to what I call weaving and, for one who cannot do that, it would be interesting indeed. I need feel no guilt. While I wait I can no better serve my—"

Kestrel squeezed Astron's arm tighter and the demon stopped. He nodded and slowly started to move in the direction Kestrel had indicated. Kestrel whirled to catch up with Celibor and Phoebe as they walked to the hut. The alchemist had his arm around her waist while he pointed out other aspects of his foundry. Curse it, Kestrel thought. She permitted it just as he had instructed her to.

Kestrel watched Phoebe try to shield from her eyes the afternoon sun streaking into the hut through a low window. He shifted uncomfortably on his stool, kicked at cracked and discarded parchments that cluttered the floor, and looked out the doorway into the foundry yard. He saw Astron with some sort of sextant sighting the top of the huge lead spheres and then the pylons at their side. Throughout the yard the bustle of the activity continued as if the border blockade did not exist. The bellows whooshed. A blistering heat radiated from the openings of the anthanar.

Kestrel frowned at the lengthening shadows. Despite Celibor's other interests, his first concern turned out to be for his profits. For most of the day they had argued, and no agreement was yet in sight. Soon the sun would be setting, and they would have to come back the next day, something that Kestrel definitely did not want to do. He would have to play through the last part of his plan, whether the alchemist gave him an opening or not.

"But do you not see?" Celibor waved his hands around the confines of his hut. "This is no palace with

111

rich furnishings paid for by the profits of my trade. Iliac across the way has seen to that with his low prices and inferior products. I need the coin to pay the workers as the effort is done. I cannot afford to await until the order is complete no matter how alluring is the bounty I would receive."

The alchemist looked at Phoebe slyly. "Besides, I cannot really believe that a few moments aloft is the primary reason you are so anxious to do business with me. Why the concern, my lady, about pretending you are a bird?"

Kestrel became immediately alert. Celibor's statement was what he had been waiting for. "You drive a hard bargain." He laughed. "And this day grows long." He looked at Phoebe. "With your permission, my lady," he said.

Phoebe nodded slightly. Kestrel watched Celibor lean forward from where he sat.

"There is the matter of the new mine," Kestrel continued smoothly. "One not in the mountains of Procolon to the north, but in the very hills of Ethidor itself."

"There are no such mines," Celibor scoffed. "Our own hills have been scoured many times over."

"But not from a height, not from a vantage point no other has taken." Kestrel lowered his voice to a whisper. "And not with a sketch of what to look for drawn by a sorcerer while under a far-seeking trance." Kestrel pulled a tightly rolled parchment from his belt and waved it quickly in front of Celibor's face.

The alchemist reached for it but Kestrel pulled it away with a nod. "You understand how critical it is that word of this reach no one else. Your craft can ill-afford a repetition of what has caused the impulse to the north to occur."

Kestrel waited for Celibor to withdraw his hand and then continued. "Of course, our original plan was to find the location and then keep it from all, offering our ores to the highest bidder." His smile broadened. "But you deal with such skill that a direct share might be more in order. Enough perhaps so that you see the raising of the balloon as much in your interest as in ours."

Celibor glanced at Phoebe and then back to Kestrel. "How do I know that these are not more words, perhaps as empty as the rest?"

"You do not." Kestrel shrugged and rose. "There is a risk here that must be taken—a single balloon ride for half share in what may be the only source of ore while the blockade continues. Perhaps those across the street would indeed be more receptive."

"No, wait," Celibor said. "In good faith, I have made investments as well. Come outside and see what I have instructed the workmen to do while we talked. If we can agree on a fair price, then even today the deed can be done."

Kestrel looked over to Phoebe and she tilted her head slightly a second time. He shrugged and turns his palms upward to Celibor. "Evidently, she likes you," he said. "A few hours more she has graciously granted."

Celibor grunted and scurried past where they sat into the afternoon sun. He squinted his eyes against the harshness and motioned for them to follow over into the testing area.

Kestrel and Phoebe left the hut with regal slowness and stepped out into the daylight. They walked past the cooling lead ingots, lattices, and polyhedra and through the shadows cast by the great spheres and pylons. Astron looked up from what he was studying and motioned but Kestrel waved him away. The hook was nearly set and he could not afford to be distracted.

Kestrel noted the contents of other huts as he passed. One on the left was piled high with cured animal hides and beyond it were seamstresses lashing them together into a growing pile of balloons not yet used. On the right, knot makers tied lengths of braided hair into canopies that would fit over the balloons when they were inflated and tether them to the ground.

When they caught up with Celibor, he was pointing at a long row of bottles all connected to a hose of some rubbery fiber. Like a giant centipede the construction

113

wandered through the open area where the tests were performed.

"More than one bottle will be needed to remove enough air so that the three of you can be borne aloft," Celibor said. "My craftsmen have labored long and hard to connect all of these bottles in parallel so that the evacuation can quickly be done."

Kestrel looked down the snaking line. "Then we are almost ready," he said. "Why haggle over details when we can be at the task right away."

"It is not quite as you make it seem," Celibor said. "Two more bottles must be connected to the chain. That is no easy matter if one wishes not to lose all the vacuum in the process. Then we have to bind a valve to the balloon itself, one that will not leak once it has been removed of its air." Celibor waved to one of the leather spheres resting on the ground. It was partially inflated and tugging slightly against the beginning of a breeze. "And the heating arrangement I have not yet contemplated. Much air will be extracted for this ride, not just a little amount. Heating what remains to regain the original volume is an intriguing challenge all in itself."

Kestrel studied Celibor's expression, trying to judge the truthfulness of his words. He resisted the impulse to grab the end of the hose nearest him and hurry the process along. Then suddenly as he wrestled with what to say next, there was a loud pounding on the metal doors that led to the street.

"Open the gates," a voice sounded over the fence. "In the name of the wizards of the Brythian hills. You house the ones we seek."

Celibor glanced at his gateman in annoyance and then back in the direction of his hut toward a pile of shields and swords. Kestrel spun around to look at Astron and saw the demon pointing frantically into the air. Though it was not yet dusk, a swarm of lights could be seen dancing along the fence line in a confusing buzz. The demon had been right; the wizards had caught up with them and far sooner than Kestrel would have thought. Now there was no time left for subtle maneuvers. Every second would count.

"Defend your property rights," Kestrel shouted at the puzzled alchemist. "A direct attack from your rivals across the way. They strike in desperation to prevent the ascent of the countess into the air."

Celibor continued to hesitate and Kestrel turned his attention away. He had to get the foundry workers to act. "You, and you with the sextant," he directed. "Back to the weapons store and arm yourself against the entry. Delay them as long as you can." He waved at the apparatus directly in front of where he and Phoebe stood. "Never mind the last two bottles. Quickly affix the valve." He looked at the blank stares of the workmen and tried not to think how much more must be done.

With a sudden crash, the doors sprang inward and a squad of men-at-arms burst into the foundry yard. Behind perhaps twelve warriors, each clad in mail, came a quartet of wizards, shaking their fists and urging those in front forward.

"Benthon and Maspanar," Phoebe said, "and others of my council. What you said was true. They pursue me with great vigor."

"To the weapons." Celibor evidently shook off his indecision when he saw the men-at-arms. He picked up the hems of his master's robe and ran for his hut. "The visitors speak truly. Iliac seeks to get my share of the mine for himself."

Kestrel looked from the gates and back to the master's hut. Perhaps eight of Celibor's workers would arm and provide some resistance. He glanced at the two struggling with the valve and saw that they were now working as fast as they could.

"What of the devils?" he asked Phoebe quickly. "Where are the ones bigger than the imps on the wall?"

"Benthon is quite conservative," Phoebe said. "He will use demons of as little power as he can. Perhaps the imps are all that they have under their spell."

"Then help with the balloon," Kestrel decided. "I will aid in the defense to give us as much time as I can."

Kestrel bolted to Celibor's hut and pushed two of the slower workers aside. He reached for one of the shields and grabbed the sword that was closest of the lot. The blade felt heavy and not balanced to his liking but there was no time to choose.

Swinging his arm back and forth in what he hoped were menacing arcs he advanced with Celibor and four others to meet the first of the attacking men-at-arms. Six of the wizards' men raised their shields to meet them. With a ringing clang, steel crashed onto steel. Kestrel lunged forward, trying to get around his opponent's guard, but the man who faced him was skillful and dodged nimbly to the side. The rest of the wizards' men moved quickly behind the first and spread to outflank Kestrel and Celibor on both sides.

Kestrel retreated a step backward and darted a look back to the gate, sucking in his breath at what he saw. Another dozen men poured through the opening, lancemen and archers who fanned out across the yard. The limp balloon that was to be passage over the border made an ideal target and in a heart beat three arrows pierced the hide as if it were paper. The sphere crumpled and sagged to the ground. The lancers ran to the ore heaps and glassworks, pushing all resistance in front of them into a disorganized retreat.

"Another balloon from the storage hut," Kestrel shouted in desperation. "Start the bellows while there is still a chance." He tore his gaze away from the scrambling workmen at the shouts to his adversaries and barely ducked a swipe at his unprotected neck.

Kestrel retreated another two steps and stumbled backward over a fallen workman, trying to block out the growing sense of futility that hammered at his thoughts. He heard a crash behind him and then a clatter of metal. A hot blast of air roared from the anthanar and almost blistered the back of his head. Flames shot up from the glassworks. Globs of molten slag arced over the yard, starting small fires in the debris wherever they landed. One hit the stack of uninflated balloons, and Kestrel

116

groaned. In a moment, their remaining means of escape burned along with the rest.

Kestrel looked around for Phoebe or Astron, but acrid smoke was beginning to obstruct his view. He saw one of the pylons fall and then a second. The huge lead sphere seemed to lumber from its pedestal and lurch his way. Kestrel staggered backward and felt the wall of Celibor's hut. The alchemist had dropped his sword and was on one knee begging for mercy, a trickle of deep red running from his forehead.

The smoke thickened. Kestrel took a deep breath, plunging into where it was densest, just missing another swipe at his side. The fumes hurt his eyes. He squinted into the dirty grayness, just barely able to make out the menacing forms pursuing him and the indistinct objects toward which he ran.

Kestrel staggered a dozen steps forward and burst back into clear air. Tears clouded his vision. He shook his head in surprise, trying to understand what he saw. Almost directly in front were Phoebe and Astron, standing in the gondola Celibor had planned to couple to the balloon. Frantically the two were waving their arms and beckoning him forward.

Kestrel took one step, puzzled. The gondola was made of straw. Soon it, too, would be in flame. It was better to run as best one could. But while he pondered, the box lurched in his direction, scraping along the ground. A shadow passed over Kestrel, and he looked up, astonished. The gondola lifted from the ground and started to climb over his head.

Stunned, Kestrel watched Astron reach out over the edge of the box while Phoebe held him by the waist.

"Grab my hand, mortal," Kestrel heard Astron shout. "This is no time for your stembrain to assume command."

Kestrel nodded blankly. He raised his arm and felt a surprisingly strong grip about his wrist. Then, with a stab of pain in his shoulder, he was lifted clear of the ground, just as a man-at-arms made one last stab at his dangling feet.

Kestrel looked down at the foundry. With gathering speed, it seemed to move more and more rapidly away. He heard the ping of an arrowhead on metal and glanced skyward for a second time. There was no mistake about it. The gondola was tethered to a sphere of lead.

CHAPTER TEN

The Magic Bottle

"What wizardry is this?" Kestrel said as he climbed into the basket. "Balloons of lead cannot fly."

"There was no other choice," Astron said. "The ones of animal hide were all rendered useless by the minions of the wizards."

"It is not a matter of choice." Kestrel shook his head, still slightly dazed by what had happened. He looked over the edge of the gondola and saw the foundry yard shrink into toylike smallness. To the north, the camps of the two armies began to take shape into recognizable forms. The green wetness of the border marsh faded into the dark shadows of the setting sun. The low hills that led to the mines of Procolon grew closer with each passing moment. The onshore breeze was pushing them in exactly the direction Kestrel wished them to go.

"It is not a matter of choice," he repeated. "The metal is too heavy to be borne aloft."

"The calculations shown to me by the alchemist were most interesting," Astron said. "It seems that the force carrying a balloon aloft is proportional to its volume. The greater the size of the sphere, the more it can lift."

"One need not study one of the five arts to understand such a fact," Kestrel said. "The key point is that the weight of the balloon itself must be included in the total."

"And so it is," Astron said. "The mass of a balloon increases as the square of its radius while its volume and lifting power increase with the cube. Regardless of the density of the material, eventually there is a size large enough that it can be buoyed aloft."

Kestrel watched Astron pause, and what might be a smile of pleasure crossed the demon's face.

"I was fascinated by the concept of the vacuum," Astron continued. "And once I understood the principles, it was easy to perform the calculation for the lead sphere to which you directed my attention. Not only was it large enough to carry the skeletal structure inside which gave it shape but, as you can see, the three of us as well. I connected the gondola harness and the bottles of emptiness as soon as I saw that it was the last balloon remaining."

"It never was intended to be a balloon." Kestrel started to protest again, but then he stopped. Of course, he understood finally. For him, or any other man for that matter, connecting the vacuum bottles to the lead sphere would never have occurred as a possibility. But Astron was not blinded by the obvious. The demon merely thought it fortunate that the great ball was large enough to carry the three of them. There really was nothing of the five arts involved at all. Kestrel let out a deep breath and looked groundward. They were safely away and soon would be visiting the archimage.

But as he scanned the scene, a twinkle of light near the foundry wall caught Kestrel's eye. The feeling of relief immediately vanished. He studied the dancing pattern until he was sure, a scowl deepening on his face all the while. He pointed the light out to the others, and Astron nodded in confirmation. The cloud of imps that had tracked them to Menthos still pursued their flight. The buzzing sprites would have to be dealt with immediately, or they would have gained only a little respite from the wizards' wrath.

"Perhaps a magic bottle." Phoebe pointed at the trailing swarm. "Others of my council have spoken of them frequently. They use them to confine the imps that they summon through the flame. If we can capture them all before any returns to report where we are, then we will be cleanly away."

Kestrel stared out at the imps and pondered what Phoebe had said. His thoughts raced, pulling together the elements of another plan. "I think the wizard is right," he said after a moment. "We certainly have nothing to aid us in this empty gondola. And there are so many that we must find a way to deal with all of them at once. Let us land while there is still a bit of light and continue on the ground." He looked to the north, trying to judge their rate of motion. "If we are lucky, it will be far enough north that we quickly can reach a guild that I know of which specializes in the making of those magic jars. Perhaps, if we can intercept a single magician on the road, the odds might not be all that great."

Kestrel began constructing the details of what to do next, but stopped suddenly in midthought. The urgency of the moment was as great as ever, but somehow he still felt slightly puzzled. Despite the explanation about the balloon, something else was bothering him just under the surface of his thoughts.

Kestrel looked over at Phoebe and saw her smile. He put his arm around her waist to steady their stance as the basket began to rock in the quickening breeze. Phoebe did not protest. Instead she brought her pleasing softness to press against his side.

The full realization of what had happened thundered into focus. First the demon, and now the wizard. By his own cunning, Astron had managed to secure a means of transport over the border. Phoebe had joined him in the gondola. She alone would have been sufficient to see him the rest of the way to the archimage. There was absolutely no reason for them to pull him into the basket as it ascended. No reason at all—and yet they did.

Kestrel bargained with the baron whose crops had been damaged by the descent of the balloon and the metal sphere was traded for another horse and wagon.

Soon the trio were on the main road leading to Ambrosia, the capital of Procolon.

While Kestrel guided the steed, Phoebe and Astron held torches aloft on the moonless night. The swarm of imps that tracked their progress would not be deterred by lack of light, and the increased speed was worth the illumination.

They were on the road but for a fraction of an hour when, as Kestrel had hoped, he caught the reflecting glint from a huge bottle on the shoulder of a cloaked traveller on the crest of the hill ahead.

As the wagon grew closer to the solitary figure, bent far to the side by the weight of his load, Kestrel smiled with satisfaction. The cloak was turned inside out, but his trained eye could make out the stitching for the ring logos sewn to the other side. The man was a magician on the way back to the Cycloid Guild.

"Do you care for a ride, stranger?" Kestrel called out as the wagon drew abreast. "Your load looks heavy and you in the need of a rest."

The magician looked up with eyes dancing with suspicion. He was short and broad like a plowman, rather than shallow-shouldered like so many practitioners of the arts. "I can manage my own way," he said. "There is no assistance that I need."

"Not even if you carry an imp bottle?" Kestrel said. "I recognize the shape, straight sides of wide diameter and the narrow neck."

"What do you want?" the magician growled. He stopped and gently set the bottle on the ground. With his free hand he reached for a small dagger strapped to his belt.

"Why, to buy, of course." Kestrel pulled the wagon to a halt. He reached back under the covering and pulled out the wizard's robe Phoebe had abandoned for the dress of the countess. He pointed at the logos of flame. "We travel simply to avoid notice, just as you do. What is the price that you would set in your guild? We will pay double—double provided that it can be proven to be truly impregnable to the weaving of simple imps."

121

The magician examined Kestrel critically and then Astron at his side. His eyes widened as Kestrel pulled away Astron's hood and he saw the fine network of scales.

Kestrel reached into his pocket and pulled out the remaining brandels of the Brythian wizards. With a flourish he flung them at the magician's feet. "Double the price, and three pieces of gold more for the trouble of the demonstration." He paused and smiled. "Just think how satisfied the other masters of the guild will be when you report to them that you have sold the bottle, not for the going price, but one and a half times that amount. Twice for you but only one and a half passed on to the coffers of your guild. It would serve them right. You are the one who has had to toil in the blackness while they wined and dined in anticipation of the fruits of your labor."

The magician looked down to his feet at the gold coins sparkling in the torchlight and grunted agreement. He stooped to his knees, rapidly retrieved the brandels, and thrust them into a purse next to his knife.

"That the bottle is a true prison of imps there can be no doubt," he said. "Magic rituals lead either to perfect results or else to nothing. And I have performed the last step myself—alone in a flat field when the moon was at nadir. I completed the square of numbers precisely in the order prescribed. The cymbals were struck thrice and then buried.

"And then the glass hummed of its own volition, sucking strength from the cosmic spheres and forming unbreakable crystal. It would not have rung unless my actions were the perfect last steps to a perfect ritual, producing a jar like the imps it will surround, one that will last eternally."

Kestrel watched the magician draw the dagger from his side and flip it over in his hand. Pommel first he crashed it down onto the side of the bottle, causing it to ring the seductive harmony of the finest bell. A second time he banged on the glass and then a third but the bottle wall held firm and did not shatter.

"See," the magician said. "That is no ordinary container but one that has been transformed by the skills of my craft. You cannot break it or its stopper. More proof than that surely you do not need."

"Nevertheless, this purchase is not one of little consequence," Kestrel said smoothly. "Surely you cannot deny us the assurance of putting imps in the bottle and seeing that they cannot escape."

"Well, if I were the buyer, then perhaps I would want to know for sure that—" the magician began.

"Wait a moment," Astron said suddenly. "There is the matter of volition. Only the wizards that command the cloud that pursues can will them into what they know to be a trap."

"I have thought about that," Kestrel said. "We will just have to hope that the motives that drive your kind are not so different than those that push upon men."

"What do you mean?"

"Are not imps noted for their curiosity?" Kestrel asked.

"Except for their vanity, it is the strongest of traits," Astron said. "They are always chattering that their abilities are the equal of the mightiest of djinns. But their inclinations have nothing to do with control of their will. There is no—"

"Such is what I have heard from the writings in the sagas," Kestrel said, "and such I will use. The only other thing I need is a lure. What is it that would attract them the most?"

"In the realm of men? Why, vinegar, I suppose. At least it is said you can catch more imps with it than with honey."

"Then vinegar it is," Kestrel said. He motioned the magician into the wagon and grabbed the large bottle as it was pushed upward. "We will hasten to the next village and buy a few coppers' worth." He looked at Astron's wrinkled nose and his smile broadened. "Observe carefully, cataloguer," he said. "We will see if there might be another power that operates among the realm of demonkind, another power than what you call your weaving."

* * *

Kestrel shifted uncomfortably in the tree and pushed Astron slightly to the side. It would have been better if the demon had not come, but his curiosity could not be thwarted.

Astron looked down at the bottle directly below them in the nearly empty field and whispered in Kestrel's ear. "In the first place," he said, "this is no hiding place at all. Surely they will spot you to be here as if you were on the ground. In the second, even if one were in the bottle, you could not spring downward and insert the stopper quickly enough before he flew to safety."

"I know," Kestrel whispered back. "Those are exactly the things I am counting on. Now be quiet and watch. The sooner we settle down, the quicker they will come."

He looked back to the road in the distance where the wagon was parked. The magician leaned against one of the wheels talking to Phoebe and seemed totally distracted. Quickly Kestrel glanced out over the field. In a perimeter perhaps the span of a dozen men, small fires burned at each of the corners of a pentagram under bubbling pots of lilac water that scented the air with a sweet fragrance. Imps hated it, Phoebe had said, and oftentimes wizards used bouquets of flowers to keep them away when they probed for more powerful demons through the flame.

Kestrel sighted the distance between the fires for the last time and judged that they were properly placed, enough of a nuisance to make approaching the bottle under the tree a challenge but not so close together that the imps could not do so if they strongly wished.

For a longer time than Kestrel could judge, nothing happened. Then a single twinkle of light swept in from the distance and hovered for a moment over the open mouth of the bottle. The imp circled the glass jar twice and then darted up to within a few feet of where Kestrel and Astron hid in the branches of the tree.

The small demon hovered with his wings buzzing. Kestrel could see the tiny eyes staring into the foliage. Then abruptly it abandoned its scrutiny and plunged in a straight line to the ground. With tiny hops, each about

124

the span of a man's stride, it measured the distance to the bottle.

The imp looked back up into the tree and then along the path it had traversed on the ground. Kestrel saw it rub a bony hand along a pockmarked jaw and its eyes squint shut, apparently in thought.

A second imp appeared near the top of the tree, buzzing within inches of Kestrel's back. With a shrill cry it dropped to the ground and hopped toward the bottle as had the other. The first sprite soared skyward as soon as he heard the shriek, shouting what sounded like insults as the second laboriously jumped along the ground.

The second imp stuck out his tongue at the first. He turned his attention to the bottle at his side. Cautiously, he paced around the perimeter, extending each foot lightly and testing the firmness of the ground. He reached forward, placed a palm on the smoothness of the glass, and then immediately jumped backward as the first imp dove within a wingspan of his head, laughing raucously.

The second imp waved some gesture that Kestrel did not recognize and glared at the first until it stopped and hovered at the height of the tree. Apparently satisfied, the second vaulted up to the open mouth of the bottle and peered inside. He hesitated only a moment, extending first a finger, then an arm, and finally his entire head into the smooth walls of the mouth. All he would see, Kestrel knew, was the large cup of vinegar that had been carefully placed inside.

The sprite lowered himself to the bottom of the bottle and repeated the same slow approach to the small bowl. Squinting in the dim light to make out the detail, Kestrel saw him stick a finger into the cup and then touch it to his lips. A moment passed and then the imp abandoned his caution altogether. He plunged his head into the liquid and began loudly slurping.

The first imp apparently saw what was happening as well. He dove into the bottle, knocking the other one aside. Like two children fighting over a single toy, they began pushing each other away from the tasty prize. Al-

125

most instantly, a half dozen more sprites appeared from the distance. In a rush, they raced into the bottle one by one, bowling those that preceded into the hard glass walls and lunging for the cup of vinegar for themselves.

"Do you see any more?" Kestrel tensed.

"None at the moment," Astron said. "But—"

Kestrel did not wait to hear more. He dropped from the tree to the ground with the stopper in his hand just as the imps had decided he would. One that had been knocked the farthest from the cup of vinegar spotted his motion and shrieked a warning. In unison the imps stopped their fighting and took to flight. Like bees discharging from a shaking hive they buzzed up the height of the bottle into the neck.

Kestrel sprinted to the jar as fast as he could, but, as he had guessed, he did not have to hurry. The buzz of the imps died in the grunt of crashing bodies. In a tangled mass they wedged into the neck and could ascend no further. The ones underneath the first cursed and pushed against those above but to no avail. Kestrel dropped in the glass stopper before a single one could escape.

"Why, that is most remarkable." Astron jumped to the ground after Kestrel. "They are trapped just as surely as if you were a wizard who could command their will."

"As I told you earlier," Kestrel said, brushing his hands in satisfaction, "knowledge of the push and tugs that compel one to action can indeed be a great power. Evidently, beings are the same everywhere, whether they are men or demon."

Astron started to say more, but instead suddenly pointed at the jar. Kestrel's satisfaction evaporated. A single glow of light flittered in from the south, made two circles of the bottle, and then with a burst of speed raced away in the direction from which it had come.

"A straggler," Astron said. "One that was distracted and did not fly in formation with the rest. Imps are well known for their lack of discipline. Perhaps that is a fact that you should have utilized as well."

"Never mind that," Kestrel snapped. "He has seen what has happened. You can bet that he will streak back

126

and tell the wizards where we are without fail."

Kestrel began running back to the wagon. "Come! At least I know the thinking of my own kind better. I suspect there is very little time before some of your more powerful cousins will be visiting us on this very spot."

Kestrel waved to the magician as he passed the master running into the field. "We do not want it after all," he called out, "but you can keep the imps to demonstrate to the next buyer in exchange for your trouble."

Kestrel pushed past the openmouthed magician without bothering to offer any more explanations. He clambered onto the wagon and lent an arm to help up Phoebe. He whipped the back of the horse. In a sudden cloud of dust, the three again were on the road.

Kestrel pushed the horse recklessly, not bothering to make sure of holes and ruts before he chose his path. The more distance they put between themselves and the field, the longer they would have before rediscovery by demons who would not so easily be fooled.

"I do not deny it, mortal," Astron said, after they had bounced along for more than an hour in silence. Kestrel glanced sideways in the torchlight and saw the demon's nose relaxing into a straight line.

"You have shown me that there is more to learn in the realm of men than the things that can be described easily in my catalogues." As he continued, he looked Kestrel in the eye. "But also I wonder," he said. "I wonder if any amount of your tugging and pulling would have gotten the lead balloon off the ground."

CHAPTER ELEVEN

Archimage and Skyskirr

THE race up the coast was a blur. There was no time for
the luxury of sleep or even food for the horse. How long
it had taken, Kestrel could not recall. Through half-open
eyes, he spotted the simple sign that marked the turnoff
from the main road to the ward of the archimage. With
aching arms, he steered the wagon onto the narrow
gravel lane that wound into the low hills on his left.

After they had climbed to the pass between the nearest peaks, he could see down into the valley that lay
between him and higher buttes farther away. Birch and
aspen climbed partway up the hillsides. Tall green
grasses filled the valley floor, waving in the breeze like
ripples on a stagnant pond. One area was cleared of vegetation near the center. In it stood a dozen wooden
cabins arranged in a circle around a two-storey house of
stone. Pulsing bellows like those at the foundry spat
blasts of cold air near the closest. Curls of wizard's
smoke rose from chimneys of the next two in line. Three
spinning energy wheels of the thaumaturges whirled on
the far side of the compound. Next to them, magicians
slowly added spars to a complex latticework in step to
the intricate jingling of hundreds of tiny bells. A few of
the cottages were totally dark, sorcerers' lairs with even
the windows painted black to block out the sun. On the
grounds between the structures, knots of robed masters
argued and gestured as they walked quickly from one
experiment to another.

"I see no high walls or metal gates," Kestrel said.
"Anyone could approach the archimage with no resistance at all."

"There is a little hut at the foot of the road." Phoebe pointed. "I believe one states his reason for calling to a page therein, and he arranges an interview, if it is worthy. As for security, the power and reputation of the archimage is such that he has no need for walls and gates. If not for honorable means, it would be folly to approach."

Kestrel grunted and urged the horse onward. There was as yet no sign of imps or more powerful devils; but, even with having to reestablish the trail, they could not be far behind.

Phoebe reached out and grabbed Kestrel's arm as the wagon gathered speed down the last incline. "Before— before we meet the archimage and I am possibly questioned about my craft, Kestrel, I must understand all that has happened at my cabin." She lowered her eyes. "Perhaps it was something that would embarrass me," she said. "Yes, that is it. The demon made me do something quite unladylike in front of the other wizards. You are too much the gentleman to tell me about it."

Kestrel pulled his lips together in a grim line. He looked at Phoebe's attractiveness in the fancy dress. Despite the fatigue, he felt a great longing. Without the immediate rush, it would be easy to say the words that would result in another conquest of a master of the arts.

But the well-spun phrases would not come, not even ones that set the foundation for later. Phoebe's apparent trust was too overwhelming. How could he deceive her as he had done to all the others when what she wanted had so little value?

"The past cannot be changed," Kestrel said, "no matter how much one might wish it. If you were embarrassed, would you really want to know?"

"No, I would not," Phoebe said after a moment. "Not if it caused me to lock all that I am behind a barrier through which no one else can see."

"What do you mean?" Kestrel asked.

"You know full well," Phoebe said. "For the length of this headlong flight, I have been chattering away, telling you everything about myself that came to mind. Perhaps

129

it took my thoughts from what would happen if we are caught, but I have said much nonetheless."

"I did not wish it otherwise," Kestrel said. "If you suspect that I was bored but just being polite, put your mind at ease. I enjoy your company."

"And so about the wizard you can now recite volumes," Phoebe continued. "About the woodcutter, what can be said other than that he indeed did at one time chop some trees?"

Kestrel slumped over the reins, wishing the entry hut all the closer. Mixed with everything else, he felt an onrush of discomfort. It was not enough that he refrain from further deception. Phoebe wanted more. She was asking no less than that he reveal things that long ago he had vowed never to share again.

"I can be only one of many possibilities," he said while continuing to look straight ahead. "Why me and not some other? One more suited to your station."

Phoebe tightened her grip on Kestrel's arm and pulled herself closer to him. "It gets to be lonely in the cabin of a wizard," she said. "Lonelier than you might otherwise believe. And at first, I admit my thoughts were for a brief interlude. You appeared far better than most that I had seen in the past year.

"But there was something else," she said. "Something I saw behind the eyes of one who professed to be a simple woodcutter."

"Do not probe too deeply," Kestrel said. "You might not like what you will find."

"No, my first impression has been confirmed." Phoebe reached up and turned Kestrel's face to hers. "I saw the excitement when you explained to me how we would cross the border. I witnessed the swordsman rushing to defend when he was outnumbered two to one. There is perhaps more to Kestrel the woodcutter than he dares admit even to himself."

"Does not the ritual prescribe that the male pursues and the female demurs?" Astron poked his head out from under the wagon's canopy. "Or does the fact that the woman is the one that wears the logo of a wizard alter

130

that? It is no wonder there is so much anguish and confusion in the matter. The variations are too many for one to keep track of them all."

Phoebe pulled back her arms, like a child caught in the fruit larder. She frowned at Astron as she dropped her hands to her lap. Kestrel felt a wave of relief and then a twinge of annoyance. He could work out his feelings without any help from the demon.

He darted a glance at Phoebe. No, perhaps it was best that Astron had come forward. What he would have said if he were forced to answer at this moment he did not know. A silence descended on the three. For the rest of the distance to the entry hut no one spoke.

When they arrived, Kestrel glanced over his shoulder and then back to Astron. The demon shook his head, indicating that he detected nothing. Kestrel vaulted from the wagon and into the hut. Soon all three stood facing an ancient page, bald-pated with splotchy skin, sitting behind a high desk. His folded hands rested on a huge appointment book bound in gilded leather.

Kestrel returned the page's stare and glanced quickly about the small room, trying to seize on the story that would get them immediately to the archimage.

"Elezar," Astron said before anyone else could speak. "I have a message from Prince Elezar for the archimage that should be heard at once."

The page looked at Astron through half-closed eyes. He leafed through the pages to the very front of the book and scanned a list of names. "Elezar," the page repeated, "Elezar." Suddenly he stopped and his eyes opened wide. "Ah, exactly what is the—the nature of this prince?"

"He is a demon," Astron said. "A mighty ruler of over a hundred djinns."

The attitude of the page immediately shifted from bored indifference to obsequious concern. He climbed from his high stool and motioned the trio to follow.

"It is the foremost of the archimage's instructions," he said. "Certain visitors are to receive priority over the others who come asking no more than a boon. But above all else, master Alodar has written that he is to be interrupted on any news of Elezar the demon in the realm of men. Quickly, follow me."

In a moment's time, they were across the courtyard to the house of stone and ushered into a large library, brimming with scrolls and books of crackling parchment. A ladder was propped on each of the four walls to reach shelves that stood beyond the grasp of the tallest man. Three round tables were also covered with piles of paper. On a fourth stood a bubbling retort and convoluted paths of glass tubing. A model of a crane and small blocks occupied the fifth, next to a clump of bar magnets and needles of steel. Next to it, the light of a single candle worked its way through tiny slits and a series of lenses that alternately expanded and contracted its radiance.

Kestrel noticed Astron's membranes flick down when he saw all of the books. After the page left to find the archimage, the demon stood motionless for a long while. Then slowly, with a delicate reverence, he approached the closest table, reached out and touched the gilt letters that spelled "Practical Thaumaturgy" on the volume on top. Suddenly oblivious to the reason they had come, the demon gently opened the cover and stared at the penstrokes on the first page.

A doorway deeper into the interior of the cottage clicked softly. Kestrel turned to see who entered. His face stiffened in surprise.

"We are manipulants of the skyskirr," said the first of four thin beings who filed into the library. "We understand the astonishment that shows on your face. Many of the strange happenings of your realm affect us in a similar way. Be at peace. All that comes to pass is guided by the great right hand."

Kestrel shook his head. Astron looked almost human. The imps that had been captured in the bottle were no more than gross copies of a normally shaped child. But these four were distinctly alien, unlike anyone else he had ever seen. They were tall and slender, impossibly thin for a man. Large, puffy lips protruded from faces of bony

132

gray planes. Primitive jewelry hung from ears and noses. Each wore a simple loincloth coiled about his hips.

"You too are djinns from Astron's realm?" Kestrel asked. He backed into one of the ladders and pulled Phoebe protectively to his side.

"No, we are skyskirr," the first repeated. "On our lithons we sail through the 'hedron's sky. The wind whistles with our passage. With graceful arabesques, we circle the larger stones and from them scavenge what the great right hand provides.

"Our realm is self-contained, as distinct from that of the demons as you judge yours to be. We must use the might of a djinn and the intermediary of the flame to travel from our universe to here."

Kestrel ran his hand over his mouth. Not from the realm of demons but elsewhere beyond the flame, he thought. He glanced quickly at Astron. Yes, other realms, just as the demon had said.

"Besides those of men and demons there is a third?" Phoebe asked. "I have heard whispers of such a thing and of metalaws behind those that we know so well."

"Indeed, it is true," the first skyskirr said. "For us the laws of magic are different; we, in fact, change them all the time. Our visit here and now is to see if your thaumaturgy is a craft that will be useful besides the ones we already know."

"Of course, there are consequences in any such venture," the third suddenly said. "Perhaps it was the intent of the great right hand that such knowledge we were not meant to possess." The skyskirr pounded a shovel he was carrying against the floor and then touched the blade to the chest of the fourth, who slumped almost hidden behind the other three.

Kestrel looked at the last skyskirr for the first time. The deep-set eyes seemed not to focus but dart almost independently about the room. A thick drool ran from one corner of his mouth. With his hands, he picked at his loincloth, removing small pieces of lint that were not really there.

"Mortonzel has seen too much of gently curving hori-

133

zons," the third skyskirr continued. "He has felt for too long the oppressive pull of the great lithon that binds all of you humans. Only occasionally are there winds to caress the full length of his hair." He turned and poked with the blade of his shovel at the chest of the first. "Now even the archimage dismisses us for something he says is of greater importance. It is a sign of the great right hand, I say. Let us begone. I feel the sickness of mind beginning to bubble within me as well. Build the flame, Purdanel, and summon the djinn that will return us to whence we came."

Purdanel looked quickly at the second skyskirr and then around the room. For a moment his eyes rested on Astron, who was slowly turning the pages of the book. "You may have the volume," he said. "It was to be a gift from the archimage but I think it will provide no value in the realm where the lithons fly."

Without waiting for an answer he grunted and pounded his own shovel twice against the floor. Purposefully, he marched out of the room. The other three skyskirr followed, the last being gently led.

Kestrel shook his head again. Lithons, the great right hand, soaring through the sky—it sounded most bizarre indeed. His intuition had been confirmed. If the skyskirr reacted so badly to the realm of men, then surely he would fare as poorly if transported to where they were from.

But before he could ponder more, a second door opened as quietly as the first. Someone else entered the room.

"I am Alodar, the archimage," the newcomer said. "Tell me quickly. What is the news of the sighting of Elezar the golden? Few know even the sound of his name. What is it that you have seen?"

Kestrel jerked his thoughts back to why they had come. He watched the archimage as he approached. Streaks of white ran through fine yellow-brown hair. Furrows of concentration had become permanently etched at the bridge of the nose. The purple robe hung simply over a slight frame. On one sleeve were the logos of all five of the crafts.

Kestrel looked most intensely at the eyes. They were alive with intelligence and a driving will shone through. He felt a surge of doubt about what he hoped to accomplish. The archimage was not one to be either easily fooled or tempted.

"It has been almost thirty years," Alodar continued. "Thirty years since our one and only encounter." The furrow above his nose deepened. "And the truth of it is that one is sufficient for any man. For all this time, I have hoped there would not be the need for another."

"There is also the matter of the wizards of Brythia," Kestrel said carefully. He pointed at Phoebe and her robe that she carried over her arm. "They are ill-disposed toward this master who has travelled a great distance to seek your aid in clearing her name. Ah, hers and the ones who accompany her as well."

Alodar stopped his rush into the room and quickly looked about. "Forgive my lack of hospitality," he said. "Find a chair to your liking. It is just that dealing with the likes of Elezar is so urgent that—"

Alodar stopped and his eyes narrowed. "What demon is this?" he asked, pointing at Astron. "Which of you have him under control and why is he dressed as a man?"

Astron looked up from the book he was perusing. He threw back his hood and tilted his head slightly in Alodar's direction. "My will is bound only to the service of my prince," Astron said. "I am Elezar's messenger, bidding that you contact him at once through the flame."

Alodar frowned. "Elezar can pass through the barrier only after many lesser demons have preceded him. Since our first battle, all wizards everywhere interact with great caution so that never do too many come through to our realm at any one time."

"Contact only, not passage, is what my prince desires." Astron stepped forward. "He is in great peril from his own kind and seeks out aid from the only one he acknowledges as greater."

"Few enough know even the name of the prince," Alodar said. "But perhaps you have somehow learned. If you are truly from the golden one, then you will have knowledge that others would not."

"His eyes are green but flecked with gold," Astron said. "His stature is but fingerwidths greater than mine. Hooded, he, too, could pass unnoticed in the realm of men. His—"

Alodar waved Astron to stop. He slumped into a chair at one of the crowded tables, then looked back at Kestrel with a a weary smile. "I would much rather handle a squabble among a dozen councils of wizards," he said, "or spend more time trying to squeeze one more secret from the lore recorded in this room." He arched his back and stretched. "But three decades of running from one crisis to another eventually take their toll. The glamor of being world-saver wears thin after perhaps the dozenth time."

Kestrel did not respond. He looked out of one of the high windows, but still saw no sign of any imps or djinns. There might be time enough after all. Soon he would learn which of Astron's words were no more true than the fancies that he himself wove. Hopefully from what he discovered he would be able to spin his own scheme to turn aside the Brythian wizards. He glanced at Alodar's intense expression, deciding how much his tale should dare.

"If you would assist," Alodar said to Phoebe, his reluctance apparently shoved aside without a moment's more thought. "I will light the fire in the hearth and attempt to see if what this demon says is true." He pointed to a well just outside one of the windows. "But if he has warped his words, be ready with a full bucket. I will want the flames doused before any great harm can be done."

Phoebe stepped forward cautiously. "I—I am not sure that I am worthy, archimage," she said. "Although I won the logo of flame fairly, even the small devil who is with us I could not command."

"I am the one who will challenge Elezar." Alodar

shook his head. "Such a task I would wish upon no other. I do not need your skills as a master, just a quickness of eye and arm."

Phoebe let out her breath. She scowled, apparently annoyed at herself for the image that she presented. With a quick nod she scurried to do the archimage's bidding.

Kestrel and Astron watched the archimage deftly bring a simple flame to life in the stone-lined fireplace along the north wall. Alodar left for a moment and then returned with some powder that he flicked into the blaze. The fire immediately billowed and flashed into a rainbow of color.

As Phoebe returned with the water, Alodar pulled his chair directly in front of the growing flames. Making himself comfortable, he stared into their hypnotic dance. For a long moment, nothing more happened and Kestrel shifted his weight from one leg to another. His eyes darted around the room. He wondered about the propriety of taking a second chair for himself.

Then, just as he had about made up his mind to move, the flames flashed green and an eerie voice whispered from out of the hearth into the room.

"Ah, master, you have come." Kestrel heard a gentle sighing. "Astron has done well for his prince."

"He is so weak!" Alodar exclaimed. "This is hardly the one with whom I wrestled so long ago."

The archimage paused a moment, then immediately shook off his astonishment.

"What is it you wish?" he said. "We have decided long ago, Elezar, that the affairs of the realm of men were no longer to be your concern."

"So they are not," Elezar replied. "But I am one prince among many. I maneuver to keep the interests of the others away by your command and have succeeded because of my own great power."

The fire spit and sputtered.

"My prince has not recovered from his wound." Astron took a step toward the hearth. "And by the weakness of his voice I would deduce that he has received another."

"But consider this, archimage," Elezar continued, apparently not hearing the voice of his cataloguer. "If my own power were to wane, who then would keep the other princes from coveting the realm of men as I did myself? And unlike creatures of my kind, you age, master. Are you ready again to undergo the test of wills that you undertook in your prime?"

"What other prince?" Alodar leaned forward in his chair. "Who else in the realm of daemon focuses his thoughts in a way that should not be his concern?"

"There is Gaspar," Elezar said. "He has proven far more potent an adversary than I did first suspect. My own domain he has ripped from the void. And before his attack a full dozen other princes he had previously allied to his cause. My hiding places in the blackness he has found one by one. The dark node I now occupy is the last. There is little time left before I am overwhelmed. Do as my messenger directs; you can fight to save the realm of men now or wait till later when the outcome will be more in your disfavor."

Kestrel shook his head. He could barely believe what he was hearing. Imps and sprites or minor devils summoned with anvilwood were one thing, but warring demon princes and archimages were quite another. And evidently Astron's story was correct, just as he had stated from the first. What had he got himself into?

"These events are all very sudden," Alodar said. "I find it hard to believe that one as crafty as you, Elezar, would be reduced to such straits. I will need time to verify if what you say is true."

"Time is the luxury that you do not have, master," the flame whispered with Elezar's voice. "Gaspar hunts not only me but all who serve as well. In the last few ticks of the eon, many imps have crossed the barrier between our realms. Some have been instructed, I know, to track down my cataloguer—track him down so that mightier djinns can pluck off his limbs one by one, just as surely as Gaspar wishes the same fate for me. Each moment you hesitate brings closer the time when you must confront not one demon passing through the flame but more

138

than a score. Discover what must be done before it is too late."

The flame sputtered. Elezar's voice faded into the glow of the hot coals. Kestrel strained to hear more but the whispers of the demon dissolved into indistinctness. Alodar frowned and then turned to look at Astron. "What then is the message of your prince?" he asked. "What would he have me do that would restore him to power and protect the realm of men as well?"

"The prince needs a transporter," Astron said. "One to carry matter between the realms. One whom he trusted you to choose."

"We have little traffic with the realm of the skyskirr," Alodar said. "Ever since the metamagician Jemidon restored our laws to their natural state, the path between the two universes has been opened but rarely. It is merely by chance that you have arrived while some manipulants are also here."

"I do not think it is to the skyskirr that we must go," Astron said. "Their realm has little more diverse matter than my own. It would be somewhere else instead."

Alodar's eyes narrowed. "There are others, are there not?" he said slowly. "It was of course obvious after I learned of the existence of the 'hedron, but I dared not seek the definite proof. Contact with one other realm was disruptive enough. It would have been folly to explore too far."

"Yet, just as the number of laws number more than seven," Astron said, "so does the counting of the diverse universes that populate the void, each with its own essence and rituals, distinct from the rest."

Kestrel stirred uncomfortably. The conversation was about things he could well avoid. He would have to divert its course into matters of more direct concern.

"The wizards of Brythia are responsible for the imps of which this—this Prince Elezar speaks," he said. "Restricting the masters from such reckless action might help with your other problem as well."

Alodar nodded absently but kept his attention on Astron. "What else then, demon," he said. "Of what other

139

wonders should I know besides the multitude of realms?"

"There is the ultimate precept," Astron said. "That is what my prince seeks—the ultimate precept, a concept superior to the laws of magic, one transcendent to the metalaws behind them, the answer to the riddle that provides the greatest power of all."

"In which realm does one search for this ultimate of precepts?" Alodar asked.

"Only Palodad knows that," Astron said. "In exchange for bringing him some exotic matter from whence he directs us, he will tell us where to look."

"Palodad, additional realms, ultimate precepts." Alodar's frown deepened. "It is all too much to swallow at one sitting. Perhaps Elezar has constructed what we men call a fantasy and expects somehow to convince us that it is real."

"It is a chance for redemption," Phoebe interrupted suddenly. Kestrel saw that she had placed the bucket of water on the stone floor. Her cheeks were flushed with excitement.

"It came to me while the two of you conversed," she said. "I cannot continue through the rest of my life always blushing in apology for a single failure in my craft. I must strike out again and somehow prove a woman's worth. It is by accomplishment that I will yet show the wizards of my council the meaning of respect. By proven deed will I gain comfort, even in the presence of the archimage of all the crafts." She paused and took a deep breath. "And even though the archimage hesitates, then I will not. Tell me, Astron, is this Palodad strong-willed, like your prince?"

Kestrel bolted across the room. He put his hand on Phoebe's arm and looked over his shoulder at Alodar. "She has not quite recovered from the haste of our journey," he said quickly. "Dismiss her words as merely some nervous prattle."

He spun his head back around and looked at Phoebe intently. "This is no game with imps and sprites," he said. "Did you not hear the words from the flames and

140

see the strange beasts the skyskirr were? Be careful or you will get us into a pit deeper than we presently are."

Kestrel stopped and studied Phoebe's expression. He did not like what he saw.

"Imps and sprites," she shot back. "Is that indeed all you think me capable of? If the need arose, despite your words, would you trust me with more?" She looked away for a moment and then disengaged herself from Kestrel's grip. "I know I stated when we began the journey that the adventure was all that mattered. But how can I be other than the demon's slave, if deep inside you cannot judge me to be your equal?"

Kestrel opened his mouth to speak, but he did not know what to say. For Astron to talk of other realms was his own business. No doubt at the root of his desires was the wish to return safely home, regardless of where that really was. And the affairs of demon princes were certainly the concerns of one such as the archimage. But Phoebe was another matter altogether. He glanced quickly at her sudden determination and shook his head. He must have been right when he first explained her words. It was the fatigue of the journey. In a calmer moment she would see the folly of dealing with such immensities just as clearly as he.

But Phoebe ignored his outstretched arm. She grabbed the sack of powder still at Alodar's feet and threw another handful into the dying flame. Thrusting the pouch into her cape, she took a deep breath as the fire roared back to life. "Palodad," she said. "Palodad, come forth. I command you to submit to my will."

"Who tugs and pulls at the one who reckons?" a deep voice suddenly boomed from the hearth in response. "He is no mighty djinn who can be commanded to burst asunder great rocks or wield bolts of awesome lightning. Begone! Let him be! Wrestle with someone else, someone more worthy of your mettle."

"If you are named Palodad, then you are the one I seek," Phoebe said. "Submit now to your master so that you might answer the questions that I have about realms other than my own."

141

"It is not the one who reckons whose tendrils of thought intertwine with yours. He is my prince. I speak on his behalf for all who come asking at the doors of his domain."

Kestrel hesitated, not knowing whether to rush forward and pull Phoebe away or let her be, so her concentration would not be disturbed.

Astron released one hand from the book he still clutched to his chest and tugged on Alodar's purple sleeve. "If the one that has been touched serves old Palodad, then it is just as well," he said. "He can learn from the old one and tell us in turn in which realm we are to seek—tell us what is to be brought back in fulfillment of the bargain to the one who has him duty-bound."

Kestrel saw Astron shudder. "In fact, the intimacy of mind is probably all the better with a minion than with the old one himself," the demon said.

Alodar's expression did not change for a moment, but then he nodded. He indicated for Phoebe to continue.

"Whose mind then do I touch?" Phoebe said. "Speak your name as token of submission to my will. Tell me how it will be that you will convey Palodad's thoughts. Be swift about it. There are many assembled here and the waste of time is great."

The flame flashed hotter. Kestrel felt a blast of warmth on his cheeks.

"I am Camonel, the one who carries," the voice rumbled deeply. "Prince Palodad has instructed that indeed I do submit to what you ask. We need not exercise the ritual of struggle. Feel my thoughts. I do not resist. He can speak through me as if my mouth were his own."

There was a brief pause while the fire danced wildly and then the demon behind the flames spoke again.

"Time, did you say time?" The words rolled out from the hearth. Kestrel heard what he thought was laughter and saw Astron take a cautious step backward. "Time—there is no way either to save or waste it." The flame spat and crackled. "It flows regardless, marching past to be lost forever. Do not speak to me of what even the most powerful of wizards cannot bend to his will." The

142

laughter boomed again, this time more forceful, echoing from the stone walls and filling the room with sound.

"The riddle of the ultimate precept." Alodar forced his voice through the din. "Ask him if it is no more than a cleverly worded ruse on the part of Elezar the prince to seek again control of the realm of men?"

"Elezar, the one who is golden, is but a few time-ticks away from being but a memory," the voice answered through the flame. "His domain is gone, dissipated into a fine dust that slowly drifts in the realm. Only one dark node remains his to command and soon it too will be found. I will record in my domain his many exploits; but, except for that, he will soon be forgotten like the rest. His only hope lies in looking elsewhere—elsewhere in a realm for which I alone have calculated the identity."

"Then where is this place?" Alodar persisted.

"Will you agree to bring back to me the pollen of the giant harebell flower in exchange for what I will tell?"

"I will make no—" Alodar began.

"Yes," Phoebe interrupted. "Yes, tell us and we will go."

"No, you have no authority," Alodar cut back in. "Wait, Palodad. Only I am—"

This time the words of the archimage were put off by a second blast of radiation from the hearth. A billowing ball of orange flame rolled into the room, pushing Kestrel backward and to the side. A heavy black smoke coursed along the stone floor and an acrid smell stung Kestrel's nose. He saw a large brown djinn stoop to enter the room from the fireplace, thick scales covering limbs that pulsed with tight muscles. The tips of leathery wings scraped against the slope of the ceiling, the fire behind shining through between a network of blackened veins. A single row of coarse hair sat atop eyes deep-set in rugged and angular bone. Tiny nostrils flared with each breath above a mouth distorted to the side in a permanent sneer.

"I am Camonel." The demon's deep voice rumbled much louder than it had on the other side of the flame.

"Palodad instructs me to transport whomever you have selected into the realm of the fey."

"The fey," Alodar said. "What manner of place is that?"

Camonel's deep laugh again filled the room with sound. "You men know of it in your fantasies. Underhill kingdoms, trilling pipes with melancholy airs, creatures you think no larger than the smallest imps."

"Not the realm of the fey," Astron interrupted. "They are all wizards, every one. It is no place for a cataloguer who is merely striving to serve his prince. Why can it not be someplace gentle, as is the realm of men?"

"I am ready," Phoebe said. With her chin thrust high, she stepped forward to where the djinn stood in front of the hearth.

"Wait," Kestrel heard himself shout. "Wait, Phoebe, this is madness. Think of what you are doing. You cannot follow that monster, aided by no more than the likes of Astron."

"Why, I did not intend to." Phoebe looked back. "It is to be the three of us, just as from the beginning."

Kestrel lunged to a halt and stared. This indeed was madness. The affairs of archimage and demon prince might be of great importance to some, but they were no concern of his. Let some other so-called hero step forth for the honor and the glory. In the end, the rewards would turn to bitter ashes. The one who jumped through the hoops would find that he had been manipulated merely for the benefit of others who would not take the risks themselves. This was no role for Kestrel the wood-cutter. There was nothing whatever in the bargain for him.

Kestrel looked at Phoebe as she slowly drew closer to the waiting djinn, her nose clamped shut to hold out the pungent odor. His thoughts tumbled in confusion. He was here only to clear his name and perhaps win a few pieces of gold from the archimage so he could boast of it in the tavern.

But there was Phoebe as well. Her life probably was forfeit as soon as the leathery wings closed around her willing frame. He thought of his rescue from the foundry of the alchemist, the pleasure when she had pressed against his side, and her insistence in seeing good in him when there was none to be found.

While Kestrel hesitated, there was a sudden commotion at the door. Four wizards in sweat-dampened robes burst into the room. "There they are," the first one shouted. "The very ones who conspired to cheat the august council of Brythia. Come forward, Maspanar and the rest. We have caught them at last."

Alodar looked sharply at the intrusion, but before he could speak, the high windows along the wall above the doorway shattered in a spray of tiny shards. Two demons almost as large as the one in the hearth plunged into the room, circling overhead with crackles of blue flame pulsing from their fingertips.

One of the wizards who rushed in added his voice to the commotion. "Please forgive the interruption, master archimage. Forgive the interruption, but we come to rectify a great wrong to our craft."

"Yes, and since I have had time to ponder it," another one said, "I recognize the one bearing the rucksack from before—some five years ago in Laudia to the south." He pointed at Kestrel, his face beet-red with anger. "A swindle then of my hard-won gold, just as it was at her cabin. Do not be deceived, archimage. Their words are smooth, but carry not a word of truth, not even the ones of the demons that they command."

One of the wizards raced up to Phoebe and tugged at her robe from behind. Kestrel slapped his arm away. He looked into her eyes and saw her bold composure begin to falter in the confusion. Stepping to the side, he barely missed a searing bolt of blue that crackled from above and sputtered the hard stone at his feet into a bubbly slag.

He saw Alodar move toward Phoebe as well and made up his mind. "It is because of her and no one else," he yelled above the noise of the others. "For her alone, do you understand. Not for the sake of great princes or the well-being of mankind. Only for Phoebe am I doing this. The rest of you matter no more than you did before."

He grabbed Phoebe firmly about the waist. Desperately, he put the thoughts of what might be even worse than smacking lips and soaring lithons out of his mind. Closing his eyes, he pushed her forward toward Camonel's chest. He felt a smothering heaviness on his back as the wings closed around them and Astron's elbow pressed painfully into his side. Almost absently, he grasped the book the demon thrust at him and shoved it over his shoulder into his rucksack. He reeled from the dizziness. Reality seemed to spin. The last thing he remembered was the words of the archimage:

"If they escape, I want the word broadcast even across the sea. Apprehend them at all costs and bring them back. There is to be no place in the realm of men where safety will be theirs."

PART THREE

The Realm of the Fey

Chapter Twelve

Rings of Power

Astron watched the djinn vanish back into the flame. He glanced at Kestrel and Phoebe and saw what he more or less expected. Both stood transfixed in wide-eyed wonder. He remembered how his own stembrain had seized control on his first visit and how he had barely hid in time.

The trio stood next to one of three small fires, beside a stream that flowed between the gently rising slope of a rustic glade. The hillsides were covered with a carpet of thick grass, each blade the size of Astron's legs. Scattered here and there were huge flowers of red and gold, towering into the sky on giant stems from clumps of thick foliage. The proportions were all wrong, but in the realm of men they would be called foxglove, whitethorne, primrose, and thyme. A ring of mushrooms, each as big as a small hut, circled the hillsides in a single precise line halfway up the slopes. On the crests, the flowering bushes merged into a thick forest of glistening leaves.

No one else appeared to be present, but behind them on the bank stood a large granite-gray boulder with what looked like a wooden door in the side. The trilling of distant pipes blended with the sigh of a gentle breeze.

Astron pointed to the hillcrest. Gently, he guided the other two upward and into the shadowy cover. They moved perhaps fifty steps and then ducked beneath a low-lying leaf that was easily the size of the largest djinn. The soft sky glow that was everywhere the same winked out into inky blackness. The click of large insects in the distance blended with the crunch of lichen underfoot. Astron sniffed the fungal pungency of his surroundings and waited for his eyes to adjust to the darkness.

The canopy of leaves was not complete. After a moment, Astron could see the diffuse light from the pale blue sky trickle between jagged edges and paint the thin spots between the huge, webby veins with an iridescent glow. Behind him perhaps some ten paces, Astron knew, was a coarse and woody trunk that soared as high into the sky as the tallest structure in the realm of men. Thick emerald branches cantilevered out into a shower of leaves that hung nearly to the ground. Between the stem and the circling umbrella of foliage was the shelter in which they hid. One had to proceed cautiously in the realm of the fey, much more so than in the worlds of men.

"Where are we?" Kestrel finally found his voice. "And look at the size of this—this ragwort! What kind of giants are we among?"

"We were lucky we arrived when we did," Astron said as he retrieved the book of thaumaturgy from Kestrel's rucksack. "From the looks of things, the ring has not yet begun to form."

He wrinkled his nose, wondering what to do next. Somewhere in this realm, according to Palodad, was the answer to the riddle. But beyond that, there was no clue. And from the tone of his prince's voice, what little time had been left was almost totally gone.

Astron felt the tug of his stembrain, but wrestled it into submission. All of the imps that had pursued him in the realm of men did not help matters. And in the ward of the archimage, two colossal djinns had appeared as well. With all the traffic between the realms, Gaspar could not help but be close behind. It would be a race to see if he or Elezar would be the first to fall.

And what of the humans? At least one would be needed to wrest the harebell pollen through the barrier when the time came, but what would happen after that? Their own realm had grown increasingly inhospitable, and his was no place for any other kind.

He saw Phoebe draw near Kestrel, and the woodcutter put his arm about her waist. The crease in Astron's nose deepened. He had been with these two far longer than with any other mortals and he had learned many things. But if he were asked to explain their behavior to his prince, he would not be able to do so.

The one called Kestrel could speak of things that had no existence whatsoever in the reality of any of the realms. After the flight from the cabin of the wizard, he had seemed reluctant to continue the journey to the archimage. Then, after the terms of their agreement had been satisfied, he had continued the quest through the flame, not in response to the command of any prince, but apparently of his own volition. Despite these contradictions, Kestrel had the skill to manipulate a half-dozen imps as if he were a practiced wizard. There was much more to be learned from this mortal and new experiences to be felt and tasted before their journey together was over.

Astron looked at Phoebe, who was smiling at Kestrel in the dimness. A bonding was growing between the two —perhaps even the one that men wrote so much about in their sagas. What could be so different from the duty to couple with a broodmother whenever a prince commanded?

"I knew you would come," Phoebe said.

"Yes, and evidently now we must see it to the end." Kestrel answered. "Instead of merely weaving a story for the archimage, all we have to do is solve a demon's riddle, discover the most powerful natural law of them all, transport harebell pollen, whatever that is, across a flaming barrier, and restore a prince to power, thereby saving the entire realm of men. Then we might have a chance somehow to return to the archimage and convince him that we were right all along."

Phoebe laughed. "You left out the part about a female wizard proving her worth," she said.

Kestrel snorted. "At least it does not appear quite as bad as I had imagined. Except for the size of things, this could well be a sheltered valley in any of the the kingdoms that border the great sea. Once we understand better what goes on here, we just might survive after all."

Astron looked out onto the glade a second time. The trill of the pipes was louder, and soon there was motion on the crest across the way. A row of flute players bobbed into view. Behind them, several rows of dancers were leaping in unison to the sad melody that wafted through the air.

The leaves rustled at Astron's side and he smelled a sweet fragrance as Phoebe drew near. "We must be dreaming," she said as she squinted up at the procession. "Look, Kestrel, besides the creatures of a childhood tale, what else could they be?"

Astron looked intently at the procession. The pipers and dancers were drawing close enough that rough features could be seen. The tallest would tower two heads above Astron, but a weighing scale would tip in the demon's favor. Slender limbs protruded from tunics of deep green, and long delicate fingers arched gracefully over the shafts of the flutes. Tumbling curls of gold bounced above delicate features that gave no hint of gender. They were lithe and thin, like the skyskirr, but somehow shrouded in a delicate beauty, rather than a repulsiveness that made men want to turn away.

The step of the pipers was light, and those of the dancers lighter still. In impossibly long glides, they darted from one point of the slope to another, hovering in midleap till they barely touched the ground.

"Men know of the fey?" Astron asked. "The words of the archimage lead one to believe that this realm should be as new to your kind as was that of the skyskirr some few time-ticks ago."

"Only in legend," Kestrel whispered back. "Tales for wee ones to send them to sleep. Strange beckoning music that one must at all costs avoid. Outwelling light from deep forest mounds. Tiny enough to hide in the bowl of a flower or under a curling leaf—not the size of a man; the scale is all wrong."

Kestrel stopped and darted a quick look around at his surroundings. Cautiously he reached upward and stroked the fine hairs that lined the underside of the leaf overhead. "Legend," he muttered, "a coincidence. It can be no more than that."

Astron saw more ranks come over the crestline of the hill. He spotted the dull sheen of copper and felt the stir of his stembrain. Two more lines of pipers marched in precise step behind the dancers, their faces all grim and unsmiling, and with unsheathed blades attached to their belts. While those before them descended to the stream that transected the glade, the sentrymen fanned out to circle the shallow bowl. In a matter of a few moments, they were standing at attention, a sentry next to each of the toadstools that ringed the glade. One was barely a stone's throw from where Astron and the others hid.

The trilling of the pipes intensified. Astron saw a litter come over the crest of the hill. Surrounded by fluttering attendants, what could only be the equivalent of a prince's carriage jostled down the slope. The one inside was dressed in a tunic like the rest, but fancy embroideries of brilliant reds decorated a green deeper than that worn by the others. A garland of tiny blossoms crowned the brow where the yellow curls had faded to the color of pale straw.

Behind the first ruler came a second and a third, and then a disarray of others, some in clumps of twenty and others in twos and threes. The chatter of many voices began to be heard among the melody of the pipes. Occasionally what Astron thought might be tinkling laughter sounded with the rest. Finally, the litters came to a halt directly in front of the door into the rock. All the music faded away. The richly dressed occupant of the first rose to his feet and spread his arms to the sky. His face showed the first signs of age, and there was a cruel hardness in his eye. His melodic voice, barely deeper than that of a human woman, filled the air.

"What is happening?" Kestrel whispered. "Can you understand the tongue?"

"Yes," Astron said. "On my previous visit I learned it well from one kinder than the rest." He concentrated for a moment on the words coming from the stream side and began translating them for his companions.

153

"Come forward, high king Finvarwin, venerated judge. It is the season," Astron repeated. "Come forward, Finvarwin, and decide which creations have sufficient beauty, which will be granted the privilege of continued life. Tell us all who will receive the rewards for their efforts and who must render service as penalty for failure. I, hillsovereign Prydwin, speaking for all the others, request your presence."

The wooden door suddenly swung outward. A frail and stooped figure shuffled out into the light. The top of his head was totally bald, with a few long stringlets of bleached gold hanging to his shoulders. His face looked caved in, as if struck by a mighty blow. Squinting eyes sat atop a flattened nose. The chin jutted out from under a mouth long since vacant of teeth. Rather than a tunic of green, the newcomer wore a long robe of white, cinched at the waist with a rope made of vines.

"I am ready," Astron heard Finvarwin say. "I will judge as I have so many times in the past."

Finvarwin waved his hand out over the assemblage and then shielded his eyes. "Which one is Nimbia?" he asked. "Which one attempts to create without the aid of a mate?"

One of the fey standing somewhat apart from the rest came forward and dipped her head. "It is my creation that you have asked to inspect, venerated one. May your judgment be keen and fair."

"Look at that one!" Kestrel suddenly gasped in a voice almost loud enough for the nearest sentryman to hear. "I do not know how these creatures judge, but if she were in Procolon, men would fight for just one of her smiles."

Astron looked more closely at the one called Nimbia. She was a bit shorter than the rest, about his own height, and wore a plain tunic, with no added embroidery. Her face was slender, with soft angles, high cheeks, and a tiny upturned nose. Large eyes danced beneath a halo of gold. The way she moved was in some indescribable way different from the rest, a dancelike flow of smoothness, to be sure, but yet each step brought attention to the

154

bounce of her breasts. In the realm of men, she indeed would be judged a great beauty, Astron thought, and from what little he did know of the fey, in their underhills as well. He puzzled for a second time about the lust that went beyond the duty to couple and wondered if it affected those before him in the same way as it did Kestrel and his kin.

"You will be the last," Astron heard Finvarwin say to Nimbia. "I will judge first those more likely to prove worthy. Vastowen, prepare the ring for the use of all."

The occupant of the second litter, more heavy-set than the rest, bowed and then addressed the assemblage. "A dozen djinns," he said. "At least a dozen for I am confident that what I have started has begun to grow of its own volition."

The pipes again started their trilling. Everyone present focused their attention to the three fires burning on the streambank. Vastowen motioned to one of the females standing nearby. Shyly, she came forward and clasped his extended hand. Together they waded across the stream to the side on which Astron and the others hid.

Vastowen grabbed a handful of powder from a pouch at his waist. With a fluid motion he distributed the dust into the three fires. The flames roared skyward, each suddenly a brilliant purple of glistening heat.

"Come forward, djinns of the circle, I command you," Vastowen said. "Come forward and make the bridge so that we can see into elsewhere."

"He is a wizard!" Phoebe said. "A wizard, but evidently a foolish one at that. One djinn is sufficient a contest of wills for anyone; against a dozen no one can withstand."

"They are all wizards," Astron said. He felt his stembrain stir at the thought. "The high king, the hillsovereigns, the litter bearers, even the sentrymen formed into the ring. It is what makes a journey here so risky for one of my kind. The struggle of dominance or submission could occur with each and every one that I meet."

Astron waved at the figures before him, now all concentrating on the three fires at Vastowen's feet. "And if a single one of them has insufficient strength, he can enlist the aid of another. In twos and threes or even scores, they can meld their wills as one. A solitary devil or even a prince is no match for the scores you see before you here. They can summon and control a dozen djinns with ease. It is no wonder that none of the princes who rule cast covetous thoughts toward a realm such as this."

As Astron spoke, a transcendent djinn materialized in the first of the three purple flames. In an instant after, the other two were populated as well. Vastowen waved his arm in a great vertical circle. Astron heard the great demons grunt acquiescence, bowing their massive heads to their chests.

The djinn from the second flame beat his wings. With one great stroke he vaulted onto the shoulders of the first. Wisps of purple plasma trailed along with his jump; when the third took position on top of the second, the slender column of flame rose to an unbelievable height. The air roared with bubbling energy. Astron felt the heat penetrate even the shelter in which he hid.

More djinns appeared in the two abandoned fires. Each after his display of submission placed himself on top of those who had preceded him. In a matter of moments, a column of twelve djinns encased in a sheath of dancing flame ascended high into the pale sky.

"And now the circle, I command you," Vastowen said when the last had taken his position. "A great ring of demonic flame from the realm of the fey to the one that I direct."

A terrible groan escaped from twelve mouths in unison. For a moment, nothing seemed to happen. But imperceptibly and then moving faster, the column bowed from the vertical and arced toward Astron's right. The djinns each gripped their hands upon the legs of the one above and the topmost of all extended his arms over his head, reaching out into the empty air.

Like a supple blade of steel, the column of djinns bent more and more to the right, the one at the base leaning farther and farther in the opposite direction in response to the lateral forces which pushed on his shoulders. For a moment, the topmost demon cantilevered parallel to the horizon; then, with increasing speed, he turned head downward as the curvature of the column increased.

The tower bent into a great hook and tightened further. All around the loop, what had been the topmost djinn touched ground a span away from the fire into which were still anchored the feet of the first. Now nearly horizontal himself, the last djinn in the line pulled himself forward with his hands until he was able to grasp the legs of the first and drag them onto his shoulders. The dozen djinns had formed themselves into a fiery ring that was four times the height of a tall man.

Astron felt Phoebe stiffen next to him. The power of twelve mighty djinns bent to a single purpose probably was something that she could not easily imagine. But in the realm of the fey, Astron knew, such feats were commonplace, a single element in their own complex rituals. As he watched, the pale sky that was surrounded by the ring clouded and darkened. The groans of the djinns intensified into shrieks of true pain. The air heaved and buckled, distorting the view of the hillside beyond the ring. Bolts of lightning materialized out of nothing. Rolling thunder echoed throughout the glen.

The scene within the ring dissolved into a blur of dull colors. The hillside appeared to melt into a formless slag that oozed outward to the edges of the ring. Eventually, the entire area of the enclosed circle was nothing but an indistinct gray that occasionally pulsed and twitched.

"Is this a sorcery?" Kestrel asked. "An illusion like the ones constructed on Morgana across the great sea in my own realm?"

"Of the five arts used by men, only wizardry is employed by the fey," Astron said. "They are using that single art now to command those of my kind to open a passage into yet another realm." Astron paused and squinted at the amorphous blandness contained by the ring. "But look how they accomplish it! Not a small path that flits an imp from one universe to another. Yes, I understand now that I witness the event firsthand.

Within the ring we can all see from one realm to another."

As Astron spoke, the grayness began to take on shape. Colors deepened. Bright lights started to shine through the gloom. Muted tones appeared first, and then saturated reds and yellows. In sunbursts of color, tiny, bright, spinning balls came into sharp focus. Moving in complex yet graceful trajectories, what appeared to be intricately carved spheres spun rapidly on randomly aligned axes and darted in and out of sight within the boundaries of the ring. Occasionally two would pass close by one another and alter their velocities, revolving for a moment about a common center before dashing on.

"Ah, the music of the spheres," Vastowen said. "Look at the vibrancy of the dance, Finvarwin. I included no friction so they will orbit about one another forever. I—"

The female next to Vastowen pulled on his hand. He stooped forward to listen to what she had to say. For a moment they exchanged animated whispers, then he nodded and reached into a second pouch at his belt.

"And there is yet more, Finvarwin," he called to the high king. "My soulmate's inspiration soars beyond the richness of what has already been revealed. Look, we cast in more pollen and with our combined effort cause there to be more."

A cluster of small nodules sped from Vastowen's grasp and through the ring of djinns. The scene wavered and trembled, returning back to a muted gray. Astron saw the female fall to one knee with a gasp, although she did not release her grip on the hand of her mate. Beads of sweat popped into being on Vastowen's smooth brow. Wiping away the salty drops that streamed into his eyes, he stared at the opening, straining until his arms and legs began to tremble.

In silence, everyone around the glen watched the opaque grayness of the disk. Then, as quickly as it had formed, the indistinct fog retreated to reveal once again the whirl of the brightly colored orbs. Only this time Astron noticed there were more of them rushing among one another with trajectories tightly packed. In an instant, two collided with a burst of brilliant light. In the wake of the collision, dozens of even smaller spheres, as bright and complexly decorated as their parents, popped into being and exploded outward in wild arcs of their own.

"It is not rich enough." Finvarwin waved his arm at the display. "I need not waste time by seeing more. A multitude of such dim fuzziness soon becomes tiring. I suspect that eventually all of those tiny blobs will dissipate far from one another, devoid of interest. No one will want to watch. Everything that you have shown will all fade away."

"No!" Vastowen shouted. "The creation has volition. I know it does. I can feel the energy of its life forces pulsing inside. Suspend judgment if you must. Let the patterns intermingle and produce new variations. We can all wait and thrill in its blossoming richness, which will be all the greater when we gather the next time."

"You know the rules as well as any hillsovereign." Prydwin stepped forward to stand next to Vastowen. "Once shown to the high king, a creation cannot be withdrawn and substituted with another."

"But we added to the basic premise even as you watched. Surely that—"

"Enough," Finvarwin said. "You have presented fairly, and fairly have I judged."

Vastowen opened his mouth as if to say more, but he looked around the glade and stopped. Even the retainers that had come with him had backed away from his litter and did not return his glance. Vastowen dropped his mate's hand to his side. The scene within the ring of djinns returned to a muted gray. With hushed expectancy all of the fey awaited Finvarwin's next words.

"To Prydwin," he said. "Yes, to Prydwin. The entire underhill in its entirety. To dissipate Vastowen's holdings among the rest, rather than grant a single boon, might encourage similar exhibitions of little skill."

"Thank you, venerated one." Prydwin quickly sank to one knee and tilted his head. "I will make great use of

159

the resources that you have so generously—"

"Enough," Finvarwin said. "Who is next? What does he present?"

"But the disposition of your largesse." Prydwin rose to standing. "It is only right that everyone knows."

Finvarwin grunted. Prydwin's face broke into a smile. He turned to face Vastowen and his mate. "For you, hillsovereign, my mercy will be swift. You may choose which of my sentrymen will guide his dagger to your heart."

The expression on Vastowen's face did not flicker. "My sovereign," he mumbled. Glancing for a final time at his mate, he squeezed her hand and then pointed out randomly at the circle of mushrooms. "That one," he said. "That one will be as good as any."

"Not yet." Prydwin put up his hand to stop the sentry from leaving his post. "First there is the matter of the rest. You will probably want to hear."

Prydwin turned his attention to the litter bearers and the others of Vastowen's retinue. "For those who remained underhill and did not come, their penalty is to travel to my own domain and there begin service as I direct. You there, carry back the empty chair so that they will know that their hillsovereign is no more.

"As for the rest who were so bold as to accompany their liege." Prydwin's smile broadened. "Your yells and screams shall serve to inspire me to greater creations still. The pain may not be brief, but at least you will have the consolation of adding to the greatness of the art."

Several of the fey around Vastowen's litter suddenly started to run; but before they had travelled a dozen steps, the sentrymen cut off their escape and herded them back toward the stream.

The first two began whimpering softly as their hands and feet were bound with a vine bristling with thorns. Like slaughtered pigs, they were fastened to a beam that was placed between two pairs of crossed stakes. The oily contents of a plant bladder was spilled over their tunics. Then, without further ceremony, they were set ablaze.

The fires burned slowly, billowing up dense clouds of

pungent black smoke. Through a growing haze, Astron could see the march of the smouldering flames burning outward from where they were first lit, down each leg and arm and toward the head.

The death cries of the fey were high and piercing, so much so that even Kestrel had to release Phoebe so he could cover his ears. Astron saw the complexion of the two humans wash chalky white as they stared at what they saw.

"Let us be away," Phoebe whispered urgently. "They are so many. This is no place for us."

"We do not know where." Astron shook his head. "A moment more and perhaps something of value might be learned. See, the sounds have stopped and the hillsovereign Prydwin speaks again."

Astron translated Prydwin's words. "Those are the briefest. The rest I will save for later when there will be more time to enjoy."

He looked at Vastowen's wooden face and chuckled. "I have saved the best for last," he said. "Your mate, Thuvia, is a comely one. I think that my creations too will benefit from the experience of her pleasures."

Vastowen looked toward Thuvia, tears streaming from his eyes. "Do not be afraid," he said so that Astron could barely hear. "Perhaps he will be gentle."

"Gentle?" Prydwin suddenly barked with laughter. "To my underhill and remove her of her garments," he roared. "Prepare the pinchers and tongs. We will see if you judge me gentle."

"Enough of the unimportant," Finvarwin's reedy voice cut in. "Who is to be next in the judging?"

"I am, venerated one," Prydwin said. He turned his attention away from Vastowen's followers, their fates apparently totally dismissed from his mind.

The hillsovereign gestured to the females who stood by his litter, and one came forward to stand with him in front of the ring of demons. With an almost staged casualness, he waved his arms once, dissipating the muted gray in an instant. Splotches of color filled the disk, reds and yellows and vivid greens. Like an artist's palette left in the sun, the hues flowed into one another, creating greater blotches still of purples and orange.

To Astron, the motion appeared to be quite random. Only the greater size and amorphous shape distinguished what he was seeing from Vastowen's spheres.

"I sense the power of your creation," Finvarwin said after a moment of watching the slow movement within the ring. "The massive forms transform with purpose and dedication. Yes, the creation is worthy—not as complex as those of the chronoids and reticulates that you have seen before, but vibrant nonetheless. There is no penalty, Prydwin. Instead you fairly may receive a boon."

"You have blessed me many times already, venerated one," Prydwin said. "Of material things I have little want. I ask instead that you give me knowledge, arcane knowledge of our own realm that only you remember, knowledge so that my own worth might grow."

"Very well then, the answer to three questions shall be your prize. Think of them carefully, Prydwin. When all ceremonies have been completed, then you may ask."

Prydwin tipped his head to the high king and retreated back to his litter, satisfaction wreathing his face.

"Who next?" Finvarwin repeated. "Who next to be judged by the high king?"

Astron heard a soft murmur run through the assemblage on the other bank of the stream, but neither the owner of the third litter nor any other came forth.

Finvarwin waited a moment more and then motioned toward Nimbia. "Then the time has come," he said, "the time for the reckless one who dares to create without a mate."

Nimbia waded across the stream and addressed herself to the ring of djinns. She performed no bold display, but the gray began to dissolve slowly away. Astron saw that, rather than into a riot of color, it transformed into a field of deepest black.

Astron squinted his eyes to shield them from the glare of the sparks that danced around the circle of djinns. He drew his membranes into place, and that helped even more. In the smoothness of the deep ebony he saw the beginnings of subtle movement and then a texturing that rippled across the field of view from left to right. An occasional glint of light, reflecting from an unseen source, gave a sheen to the surface, highlighting at first regularly arranged depressions and then ribs and furrows that oscillated in sinuous patterns.

With each passing moment, the texture of the surface changed from one form to another. Astron watched fascinated, not able to predict what would happen next, but delighting in each new variation as it emerged. The effect was totally unlike the presentations of either of the other two; the slow melodic pace soothed, rather than agitated with jerks and starts. Astron glanced at the high king, wondering what his judgment would be.

"Enough," Finvarwin said. "I let us view longer in order to give you the benefit of the doubt. But there is little there to distract one from a boredom greater even than the attempt of Vastowen. The punishment can be no less. To Prydwin with your underhill, Nimbia. It is for hillsovereigns who are proficient in their art to hold sway over the fey."

"Sentrymen, to your duty." Prydwin motioned from his litter. "Arrange an escort so that her honor might not be unduly tempted. Bring her with Thuvia. It will be a pleasure deciding which will be first."

"Never," Nimbia suddenly shouted in a voice almost as deep as that of a male. "I will not meekly submit like Vastowen, just because a few wish it so. Our traditions are ancient ones, but there are times when even they must be disobeyed."

She kicked at the dagger of the first sentryman who approached, sending the blade twirling to the ground. Then scrambling in front of him, she retrieved the knife before the surprised guard could react. With a wide swipe, she spun quickly about, waving off the others who had begun to approach.

She looked quickly at those who stood near the high king and then at the sentrymen converging from across the stream. "You all saw the images," she shouted. "You

163

do not need the age of Finvarwin to search for small subtle differences. Be true to what your eyes have shown you. Mine was a true creation, a difficult balance of predator and prey. Prydwin's was no more than the bubbling flow of plasma, thick pastes swirling in convection in a heated pot."

Except for the closing sentrymen, no one moved. Finvarwin squinted at Nimbia, then shook his head.

"Your underhill is no better protected than all the rest, Nimbia," the high king said. "Against all the rest, eventually it will fall. You are dealing with the inevitable. Prydwin has offered to accept you as his mate. Go with him in peace. Perhaps together the two of you will combine to produce an imagination greater then either of its parts—just as the fourth dictum states."

"Prydwin!" Nimbia spat. "Never." She waved the dagger in the air. "Who among you has the courage to act as his heart tells him?" she called out. "The courage to aid a lady of the realm when she calls in distress?"

"The hillsovereign speaks with too much boldness for one defending herself alone," Prydwin said. "Fan out and cover all of the trails. She may have aid just beyond our view."

"That is the signal that we start to move." Kestrel tugged at Astron's arm. "I doubt it will do us any good to be mistaken for part of the losing party."

Astron shrugged off Kestrel's hand. "The one named Finvarwin is one that we need to interrogate further. Perhaps more than any other he would know of harebell pollen and even the ultimate precept."

"Yes, the old one certainly," Kestrel whispered back. "But at a time when not so many are about. Now we must be going, before it is too late. Being hunted in two realms should be enough, even for a demon."

Astron looked out at the ring closing in on Nimbia. He glanced over his shoulder in the dimness. Kestrel was right. There was a path leading through the dense underbrush and he should lead, because he was more familiar with what they would encounter.

Astron glanced a second time at Nimbia. His thoughts

took a strange turn. Kestrel also had been right about how to get the imps into a bottle. The way the human had planned to manipulate the wizards at Phoebe's cabin was something no demon would have conceived on his own. For the dozenth time he realized there was much about the mortal that Astron wished to learn.

But the words Kestrel spoke were sometimes so unexpected and peculiar that Astron could not fully comprehend the intent—duty to oneself rather than a prince, lures for gold djinns when none such existed, or travelling through the flame for Phoebe and no other.

Perhaps mere words would not be enough to unravel the mysteries of men; perhaps their experiences would have to be sampled before understanding could come. Astron looked one final time at Phoebe and Kestrel, standing close together with their arms about each other, and made up his mind.

He stripped away the hood and cape from his back. Gripping the book of thaumaturgy firmly in both hands, he suddenly sprang out from the cover of the heavy leaves. The sentryman standing nearest turned in the direction of the rustling sound, but grappled for his dagger too slowly to defend himself as Astron rushed forward. The demon swung the book high overhead and then crashed it down on the skull of the startled guard.

The fey crumpled to the ground. Astron staggered to retain his balance and somehow managed to tuck the bulky volume under his arm. He bounded down the hillock toward where Nimbia still waved a dagger of her own. A shout of alarm went up from the onlookers. Everyone seemed to freeze in their tracks. Astron felt the beginning of a compelling pressure in the depths of his thoughts.

He grimaced in resistance, pulling his face into a tight little ball, forcing the mental probes away. Through eyes half closed, he saw Nimbia dip her dagger cautiously as he ran up and extended his free hand.

"To safety, through the underbrush," Astron shouted as he closed. "If no one else will defend you, then I am the one."

Nimbia hesitated a moment, but then firmly clasped Astron's outstretched wrist. He felt a surprising tingling when the smoothness of her skin touched his, but pushed the sensation away. Almost jerking Nimbia from her feet, he reversed direction and began racing back up the hill.

The pressure against his thoughts increased. The fey dealt with a demon by force of will, not slashing blades. He felt the probes of many minds mold into one unifying whole. "Stop, desist," a voice inside his head seemed to say. "We are many and you are one. You cannot resist the combined will of us all."

Astron stumbled over a small rock, but continued his climb. His limbs began to stiffen. The panic in his stembrain stirred from its slumber. As they reached the sentryman Astron had felled, Nimbia drew even with the demon. In half a dozen more steps she was tugging on the grip between them, pulling Astron forward into the cover of the bush.

"Why did you do that?" Kestrel shouted as the pair ducked under the leaf. "Have you gone mad? Has some wizard put you under his control?"

"I do not know for certain," Astron said thickly. He waved at Phoebe and then dropped his arm heavily to his side. "But then I would not have had to, if you had explained—explained why you rescued your wizard when you could have been safely away from her cabin."

CHAPTER THIRTEEN

The Paradox of Beauty

A dagger soared into the underbrush over Astron's head, entangling in the drooping leaves. Retreat deeper into the foliage was an immediate necessity or else Nimbia would not be the only one captured by hillsovereign Prydwin.

But Astron found his thoughts becoming much more sluggish. His limbs would barely move. It was difficult enough understanding the words of both Kestrel and Nimbia as they spoke in their respective tongues.

"There are only three of you!" Astron heard Nimbia exclaim. "And none from my own underhill as I had supposed."

Another dagger crashed into the canopy. Kestrel pushed Phoebe to the ground out of its path. "Well, what is the rest of the plan, demon?" he asked. "You know this place as we do not. In what direction do we proceed?"

"Only three," Nimbia repeated, "but then effective, nonetheless. Prydwin's kind are so used to his will being obeyed without resistance that his sentrymen have little chance to do more than serve as a frame for the presentation of his creations. As I think of it now, none of my kind would have succeeded. The daggers were too many. A bold action, demon, was precisely what was needed."

Astron felt her grip tighten in his hand. "Come," she said. "If we escape safely back to my own underhill, even though you are not one of the fey, you will be rewarded."

Nimbia turned into the darkness toward the huge trunk and pulled Astron after. He clutched the book of thaumaturgy to his chest and struggled as best he could

167

not to stumble. Dimly, he was aware of Kestrel and Phoebe following behind.

The little light that filtered between the overhanging leaves vanished altogether. Astron saw Nimbia pull what looked like a gnarled root from her belt and, with her free hand, extend it overhead. The tuber glowed with a feeble yellow light that just managed to illuminate the obstacles that lay in their way.

The thick trunks that supported the overhang grew closer together. Aboveground, suckers caused more than one stumble as they ran. Grublike insects with bodies as big as the arm of a djinn scurried out of their way. Rasps and loud clicks blended with the stomp of their feet against the ground.

For how long they raced, Astron could not tell. Except for Nimbia's glowroot, the darkness was as deep as the void in his own realm. His chest began to hurt from the exertion. Sharp pains crackled through his knees. He was a demon of contemplation and not used to such stressing of his body. What little weaving he was capable of to supply his basic needs was being severely overburdened.

Then suddenly Nimbia stopped at the base of a particularly large trunk. She gestured upward and released her grip on Astron's hand. Like an acrobatic gibbon in the realm of men, she grabbed hold of a low branch and swung herself upward. Kestrel grunted in understanding. He cupped his hands to give Phoebe a boost. With Nimbia astride the limb and pulling, Kestrel pushed from below. Phoebe clawed her way onto the limb in a tumble of cape and long skirt. Kestrel followed quickly. Only Astron remained on the ground.

The pressure to submit grew in intensity. Astron found he could barely move. With agonizing slowness, he raised the book for Phoebe to grasp and then cupped the branch in his hand.

"Hurry," Kestrel whispered. "They cannot be far behind."

"It is the contest of wills," Nimbia said. "The followers of Prydwin command him to be still."

The thought that Kestrel and Nimbia had no way of understanding each other floated slowly across Astron's mind. He should serve as translator, but somehow he no longer cared. Perhaps it was hopeless to run further. Eventually they would be found anyway. Why not at least take a rest at the base of this bush, rather than exert himself any more?

Astron felt his grip on the branch loosen. With a feeling of peace, he began to slide to the ground. Slumped in a heap at the base, perhaps he would not be seen. Or even if they did see him, what really did it matter? Astron curled up into a tight ball. A crooked smile formed on his face.

But just as consciousness began to fade, a thought of piercing sharpness ricocheted through his head. Resist, it commanded. I am the closest and have the greater influence. Resist their wills because I wish it so.

Nimbia! Astron stirred from his dimness. She was a wizard like the rest. Her thoughts churned with the others. And somehow they were different—strong because of her nearness, to be sure. But the crushing drive to dominate was held in restraint. Her will was adding to his, repelling the others, giving his own consciousness room in which to function, time to construct barriers against the pressure to quit.

Astron vaguely became aware of many hands tugging on his body and of being lifted into the air. He felt the rough fiber of the stringy bark against his skin. He flailed past the first horizontal level of branches and then several tiers more. Finally he felt an embrace that held him firm. Nimbia's arms coiled around him. He smelled the exotic aroma of her closeness and heard the rustle of her tunic against his own.

"Do not fight me, demon," he heard her whisper. "Blend your will with mine. Cling to me and do not let go. When they pass below and do not find us, their command will be for you to come forth, and you must not."

Astron saw the dance of glowroots in the distance and a line of sentrymen fanning out along the crude path on which they had fled. He heard Phoebe suck in her breath and the three about him stiffen into nervous silence.

As Nimbia had predicted, the voices inside his head changed their direction. No longer was he implored to stop and freeze. Instead, he felt a growing urge for action, to bolt forth and run into the open, to flee the dismal dark cover to the gentle light of the glen.

Astron's limbs began to tremble. With all the concentration left to his command, he clutched Nimbia harder, willing his arms to stiffen. He must hold on.

Nimbia seemed to sense his struggle. Her grip tightened and her thoughts blended with his. He felt the strength of her inner being, like a vault of steel. He poured his own essence into it, molding to the contours of the container, pressing against her, like an annealing of the alchemists that could not be torn away.

Through barely open eyes, he saw the followers of Prydwin draw closer, peering cautiously into the inky darkness and listening for some sound of their flight. Some passed in the distance to either side, but three came close to the enormous bush in which they hid.

Come forward, the voices commanded. Come forward; it is the will of the fey. Astron slammed shut his eyes and crushed Nimbia to him. He heard the gasp of her breath from the force of his embrace. He felt her nails dig into his back, even through the thickness of his tunic. The trembling of his limbs shook his entire body in spasms. He ached from the effort to remain silent and still.

Mentally, he tried to keep the image of Nimbia's vault in focus, pushing against the surface of her being everywhere he could. He felt her accepting his struggle, welcoming the intertwining of what he was with her. He saw beyond the smooth strength that she projected into recesses of her existence that went beyond the immediate struggle—hints of great pride in her creations, the agony of defeat in competition with Prydwin, the frustration of the petty jealousies of her courtiers, and a deep-lying melancholy that perhaps even she did not understand.

Like the flickers of a dying flame, the images fluttered briefly in Astron's mind, then faded away. If he were struggling to dominate her across the barrier of the flame, he would have pursued them further, exposed them to view, analytically picked the one most painful, and then exploited it until her will was his own to do with as he chose.

But Nimbia was sharing his struggle. To meld the fullness of her strength to his she had to expose the foundations from which it sprang. She bared the innermost essence of her being in trust. He could do no more than accept the gift that was given.

The urge to howl in pain rose in Astron's chest. He clamped his jaws shut, feeling that his teeth would explode into fragmented shards from the pressure to remain silent. Every muscle in his body ached from the conflicting commands to remain immobile on one hand and to dance into fevered action on the other.

He felt the strong walls of Nimbia's mental vault buckle on the bottom and the band about the mouth wrench apart in a silent scream of ripping metal. Although he strained to resist, the top stretched wide and, as if pushed by giant thumbs, the bottom bulged upward toward the opening. Almost helplessly, he felt the container wrenched inside out, exposing his own being to the relentless will of the others.

But then, just when he could stand remaining silent no longer, the pressure lessened. Almost in disbelief, Astron darted a glance out of one eye to the ground below. Whistled commands sang through the leaves. The sentrymen were moving on through the brush.

As the searchers departed, so did the pressure in Astron's head. The trembling of his limbs slowed to random twitches and then stopped altogether. His own consciousness expanded to fill all of his being. Almost with a sense of reluctance, he felt Nimbia's presence within him withdraw as well.

No one moved, however. All four remained frozen, lest the smallest sound draw the attention of Prydwin's sentrymen back to where they hid. In silence, Astron heard the whistles and calls grow fainter until only the buzz and click of the insects remained.

Finally, after an immeasurable time, Nimbia shifted slightly and uncoiled her arms from around Astron's back. With muscles stiff from fatigue, he released her as well. Nimbia pulled the glowroot from her pouch and brought it up to eye level. Astron saw her look him in the eye and then quickly dart her glance aside. A hint of redness blossomed in her cheeks.

"Forgive me," she said softly. "When we struggled to resist the will of the others, I could not help but learn of things that you probably do not want to share."

"And I of you," Astron responded. "I sensed I should not but—"

"If those are thank-yous you are exchanging, they can come later," Kestrel cut in. "No doubt the others will return this way when they have convinced themselves they have lost our trail. Ask the nabob if she knows of a more permanent shelter we can reach before nightfall."

Astron shrugged and told Nimbia what Kestrel had said. Serving as the intermediary came easily now. The conversation flowed almost as swiftly as if they all spoke the same tongue.

"There is no nightfall," Nimbia said. "The soft blue that you saw in the glen remains eternally the same. Finvarwin and the old ones before him say that our realm is a globe centered inside a hollow sphere that radiates light and heat uniformly. There are no days, no seasons. It is the reason that we find such delight in our creations.

"And as to safety, we will journey to the hill under which I am the absolute ruler. Perhaps, before the other sovereigns decide on how they will combine their forces and attack, there will be enough time to create again— create before the next judging with something that even Finvarwin cannot deny is the best."

"Would not moving and staying hidden be better?" Kestrel asked. "To face again the pronouncements of your high king seems fraught with risk."

"I must," Nimbia said. "It is my duty, my duty to my people."

"Duty," Astron repeated slowly. "I know of duty— or at least I thought I did. I come to your realm in search for the answer to a riddle because my prince demands—"

"Come." Nimbia touched her finger to Astron's lips. "The human is right. We must get underhill before Prydwin's sentrymen return."

For what would be hours in the realm of men, Nimbia led Astron and the others through the darkness of the brush. They encountered no sign of Prydwin's followers and eventually emerged on the edge of a clearing similar to the glen in which they had first arrived. Rather than slope down to a stream, however, the grass-covered ground rose from where they stood. From all sides of the open space, at first gently and then with increasing slope, the soft greenness underfoot tilted upward to form a high hillock in the very center. Like a great upside-down bowl thrust against the ground, the bulge dominated the landscape; its broad, flat apex stood higher even than the crest of the bushes which edged the clearing.

As Nimbia moved out into the open, the ground underfoot began to vibrate with a great rumbling. The music of pipes and lyres filled the air. Astron saw the hillock shudder slightly and then begin to move. The ground parted with a clean horizontal slit. On dozens of stout pillars, the central portion of the hillock rose slowly into the air.

Brilliant lights, laughter, and music sweet and pure poured out of the opening. Astron saw long banquet tables groaning under piles of glistening fruit and heavy flagons coolly sparkling with a patina of dew. Scores of lithe dancers pirouetted in complex patterns. Laughing jugglers kept dozens of small objects whirling above their heads.

"Nimbia, Nimbia," dozens of joyful voices called out. "Our hillsovereign returns."

"She has triumphed at last."

"Finvarwin has been pleased. Look, he gives her three changelings as prize for her great worth."

173

"Alert the scribes and the tellers. There will be work for all."

Astron saw a throne of polished stone being pushed into a position of prominence on a dais bathed with colored lights. Two long lines of what looked like pages formed on either side. Small girls began strewing delicate flower petals from the base outward onto the grass of the clearing. Stout-cheeked pipers stuck long-stemmed pipes into bowls filled with nearly solid gels. With straining lungs, they forced upward bubbles of air that burst and sprayed all those about to their laughing delight. Fragrant odors tickled Astron's nostrils and beckoned him forward.

Nimbia said nothing. With a grim smile, she walked on the path laid for her and beckoned Astron and the others to follow. Accepting a cape richly embroidered and encrusted with jewels, she mounted the steps and sat on her throne. Nimbia looked about the gaily decorated surroundings and Astron saw her face sadden. She breathed out a deep sigh.

"I do not return in triumph," she said simply. "And those that accompany me are responsible that I return at all."

The music stopped as did the clank of flagon and flatware from those who prepared the feast. Smiles fell from the faces of those nearest. Eyes lowered. Many of the faces looked away. For a long moment, the silence filled the hilltop; even the creak of boots and rustle of tunics against one another was stilled.

Then, from the periphery of the hillock, a single piper began playing a slow, sad melody. Others caught the tone and added to it. One of the females close to Nimbia choked on a small sob. Tears began to glisten on the faces of a dozen more. In barely an instant, the infectious joy transformed into a chilling sadness.

Nimbia nodded in apparent acceptance of the changing mood. She motioned over the heads of those nearest and Astron felt the ground begin to vibrate as it had when they approached. He saw the narrow band of pale blue sky start to shrink into nothingness. Like a great

174

piston sinking into a cylinder, the surface on which he stood descended into the earth. In an instant, the hilltop again rested firmly on the ground.

The bright lights reflected by the jeweled panels and mirrors shone with undiminished intensity. Even though Nimbia had retreated underground, the area around her throne remained far brighter than the daylight outside. As the descent halted, Astron saw dimly lit passageways radiating in all directions. Great bins lined the hallways, like the walls of Phoebe's cabin. From some spilled the powders and woods that Astron recognized as essential for the summoning of great djinns. Others bulged with strange prickly spheroids, covered with sharp barbs or intricate lattices of thorns. In the distance were rows of doors and dark cross corridors radiating farther into the earth. The extent of the queen's underhill could not easily be judged.

Two of the pages, taller than the rest, pushed each other timidly from the crowd that had gathered about the throne. Each wore a tunic embroidered with the same designs as those on Nimbia's cape. Their copper daggers were sheathed on belts inlaid with gold.

"Might not what you have wrought survive despite Finvarwin's judgment?" the first one asked.

"My creation will live on unaided for a lifetime or more." Nimbia nodded her head. "Such strength am I sure that it possesses. But without the thoughts of others, it will not expand to be more than what it is now. Eventually, it will grow sluggish and decay."

Nimbia paused and looked over the heads of the assembly. She closed her eyes and seemed to absorb the mood of the piping which now swelled to a persistent resonance that could not be ignored. Tears appeared from fluttering eyelids. She slumped into the folds of her cape.

"The penalty is a severe one." She opened her eyes again at last. "Servitude to Prydwin for us all—this underhill to become one of his, rather than our own. We will be toiling to carry his baskets of pollens, blowing on the pipes as long as he commands, plucking the blossoms

175

that he decrees, whether they are part of our harmonies or not."

"You should not have attempted it without a mate," the second page said. "All of us regard your craft to be of the greatest quality, as strong as your own great beauty. But forgive me, my queen, even so, the challenge was far too great."

Nimbia looked for a long time at the second page before speaking.

"You knew of the risk as well as any other," she said softly. "You and every other page underhill. Almost any would have sufficed, provided that he had the strength of heart."

"But it could not be me." The page stepped back suddenly. He waved his arm about those who clustered around the queen. "Perhaps someone else," he muttered, "someone more worthy. Your beauty is too great. One such as I would never have a chance."

"A single page," Nimbia repeated, "and yet not one came forward. Not one chose to accompany his queen, despite what decorum demanded. I do not understand. Can the prize be of so little value?"

"A prize has greater value the less it is shared." A third voice, deeper than the first two, sounded from the rear. Astron saw a male slightly more heavy-set than the rest push his way forward, the lines of a frown etched into his forehead. Dark black ringlets of hair curled above deep-set blue eyes. He appeared slightly older than the other pages, and Astron noticed that several of the females followed him with keen interest.

"This is not the time and place to air old accusations, Lothal." Nimbia stirred slightly on her throne. "They are no less true now than they were when the two of us—"

"The rages have cooled, my sovereign." Lothal bowed deeply with an almost jeering smile on his face. "I do not come forth pressing a suit that you have more than adequately demonstrated I can never win. I speak merely as another loyal and concerned subject for the benefit of us all."

Astron saw Nimbia stiffen, but the queen said nothing. She motioned for Lothal to continue.

The courtier bowed a second time and then stood facing Nimbia with his hands on his hips. "Your wit is a sharp one. Despite everything else, I will always have admiration for that. Perhaps, from what you see happening again and again, you can finally deduce a basic truth for your conduct." He paused and turned to face the others, extending his arms slowly in great arcs.

"The queen can have anyone here she chooses." He looked at several of the females who wore bands about their waists with the same markings as those of a nearby male. "Even ones already bound can hardly resist the great persuasion of her beauty—we all know that in our hearts."

Lothal whirled abruptly and again faced Nimbia. "Any one she chooses, that is, so long as her choice is for one only." His cheeks flushed suddenly. Veins stood out in his neck. "I did not submit to share with another; and by all that lives of its own volition, neither will any other here. Amend your ways, Nimbia. Change the greed for more than one; that is all you deserve, despite the loveliness you possess. Amend your ways, and then a champion will come forward to share the tasks of creation with his lady."

"I was faithful to you from the first day to the last," Nimbia said softly. "It was your jealousies and no more, Lothal, that churned in your heart. You saw evil where there was none. Nothing I could have done would have convinced you otherwise." Nimbia threw up her hands. "And we could not create, so long as your own inner being was so troubled."

"If you were not queen, I would not let such assertions go unchallenged," Lothal shot back. "You try to use the power of your station to gain what even your beauty cannot grasp."

"Challenge whatever you will." Nimbia shook her head and pulled the edges of her cape in tightened fists, with knuckles showing white. "I give you leave as I have given you leave each time before. Try to find any proof

177

that I was ever other than loving. You cannot, because none was ever there. Come, Lothal, I would forget the pain and accept you even now, if it would spark the creation that would save our underhill."

Nimbia looked at Lothal expectantly but his jaw was firmly set. He would speak no more.

Nimbia sighed. "We waste the time of all those that have assembled here," she said finally. "And there is little time that is left." She waved her arm at the banquet rooms beyond. "Feast, my people. Make merry while you can. Prydwin's pipers will come for us all soon enough."

The mournful melody of the pipers abruptly stopped. There was a moment's pause and then they began again, this time with the lively air that Astron had first heard when he arrived. Tentatively, two of the younger females began to dance. With a sudden enthusiasm, three of the pages mimicked their steps. Nimbia began clapping her hands. A smile reappeared on her face. In what seemed like an instant, the mood transformed into the gaiety it had been before.

"I do not understand." Phoebe raised her voice above the music. "What has happened to her? The moods of the woman on the throne change faster than the purest quicksilver."

"My previous sojourns were brief," Astron said. "I witnessed the ring of djinns for the first time just as you did."

"The mysteries of the realm can wait for later," Kestrel said. "More important is the reason why we came. If this Nimbia thinks we are her savior, then ask her for a boon before she forgets. What does she know of the things we seek?"

Astron hesitated. Nimbia had saved him from the sentrymen of Prydwin—far more so than he had her. And the passions shown by the fey evidently were quite similar to those of men. He would like to have listened quietly for much longer.

"Excuse me, Queen Nimbia," he said, "but I have a request—knowledge in exchange for the small service we have performed in your behalf. If perhaps you know the location of harebell pollen or how to gain audience with a sage among you who knows the riddle of the ultimate precept..."

Nimbia stopped in mid-clap. She turned and regarded Astron for a moment with an amused smile. Then she broke into a gale of laughter, clasping her sides and poking her elbows at whomever was the closest.

"Yes, harebell pollen," she said. "That is all it would take. Who needs the logical precision of the male to temper the leaps of intuition if harebell pollen could be tossed through the ring? Even Prydwin's greatest triumphs—the realm of the chronoids, the realm of the reticulates—both could be challenged in a single judging. Yes, harebell pollen indeed."

Nimbia tried to say more but she clasped her sides again, unable to speak. Astron looked from side to side for explanation, but saw only other mirthful faces. His nose wrinkled. He turned back to face Kestrel with a shrug.

Nimbia suddenly stopped laughing. She tapped Astron on the shoulder. He saw that her face was completely sober.

"It is the way of the fey," she explained. "We cannot sip life in only half measures, but must drink deeply from the cup of emotions. It is no less than the first dictum— reality must mirror passion. How else can we create with a vividness that will live of its own volition?"

Astron started to reply but Nimbia shook her head. "For now, no more words," she said. "Do not disturb the joyousness of the feast. I owe my people no less." She reached out and gently touched his arm. "Even though you are no more than a demon, I wish that you would abide with me for a while. Abide with me, since your saving of a queen might not yet be complete."

CHAPTER FOURTEEN

Bubbles of Reality

ASTRON blew out all the candles except for the one on the far end of the oaken table. The remaining light was feeble, but he had had more than enough time to get familiar with the placing of even the tiniest obstacles in the small circular room. Fifteen marks Kestrel had gouged into the doorframe, one for each arising from his sleep. For the entire duration, Astron had been confined to the one room.

Despite the urgency, he had achieved no new progress toward his goal. The growing frustration made his stem-brain continuously active. A feeling of constant uneasiness ached just below his consciousness. He could not still the rumbling, no matter how hard he tried. With each passing tick of time, the chances of the survival of his prince and hence his own shrunk all the more. Something had to be done soon, no matter how interesting the other distractions.

They were not prisoners exactly, but Nimbia's sentry-men made clear with the force of their thoughts that wandering around underhill was highly discouraged. After the queen had dismissed them, they had not seen her again. Apparently Astron and his companions were left to their own devices until she saw fit to call them back to her presence.

Astron directed his concentration at what he had constructed. The idle time had not been a total waste, since there was much he had learned. The oaken table with the candle was straight on three sides, while the fourth was curved to meet the contour of the stone wall to which it was pressed. Square cells would have been much more efficient, Astron knew. Using stone instead of wood certainly must stress the mechanism that raised and lowered the hilltop, but he gathered that such practicalities were not the concern of the fey.

Next to the candle, hung from a cantilevered scaffolding made of twigs and branches, was a watersack from one of the large vines that grew aboveground. Astron had carefully pierced and drained the bladder and then refilled it with lamp oil obtained from another resinous herb. With bits of copper wire hooked into the surrounding leaves, the spherical globe was elongated and flattened, distorting it into a thin vertical disk.

At the other end of the table, the book of thaumaturgy that Astron had obtained from the archimage stood upright in a scaffolding similar to the first. The candle flame flickered through the orb of oil and cast a diffuse glow of light on the upright parchment, illustrating an image quite similar to the one Astron had constructed on the bench.

Astron studied the illustration for a moment more and then the arcane symbols written beneath it. The abstractions had been difficult to grasp at first, but the examples had helped a great deal. He turned to the bag of oil and moved it to a mark he had calculated before, roughly midway between the candle and book.

The diffuse halo of light on the parchment coalesced into a much sharper dot. Astron grunted in satisfaction. He cupped his hand in front of his lens so that only its very center received the candleglow and watched the focus on the book decrease to a single point of whiteness.

Astron moved the position of the book toward the candle and then adjusted the lens to regain the proper focus. He measured the distances from page to oilbag and oilbag to candle and checked the results with the predictions of the formula. After a half-dozen trials, he blew out the remaining light and sat in the darkness, contemplating what he had learned.

The ones who call themselves masters in the realm of men treated knowledge in strange ways, he thought. The basic principles of bending rays of light had no intrinsic connection to thaumaturgy or any other of the crafts known to mortals. But because these laws were used by practitioners of the magical arts, they were shrouded in secret like the rest. One went to a thaumaturge for telescopes or heating lenses, even though a glassblower could construct what was needed just as well without any recourse to the art, if he knew a few simple formulas. Unlike Prince Elezar's riddles, which extracted a price but once, knowledge in the realm of men was hoarded and reused again and again, demanding a fee each and every time.

Astron's reverie was broken by a pounding on the door. "The hillsovereign commands your presence," a voice on the other side said.

Astron scrambled out of his repose, opened the door, and burst into the hall. Perhaps at last he could continue the search for the answer to Gaspar's riddle.

He was joined shortly in the narrow curving hallway by Kestrel and Phoebe. While Astron had pondered the mysteries of thaumaturgy, they had spent much time together learning the fundamentals of the language of the fey. And the demon could not help noticing how much stronger the attraction between the two of them had become.

He had no chance to comment on the fact, however. In a short moment they were ushered into the presence of Nimbia in the central throne room. Nimbia wore a gown of iridescent pink that billowed and filled the high chair on which she sat. On either side, two pages stood at solemn attention, their copper spear points perfectly straight and aimed at the sculptured ceiling overhead. The openness that was present when Astron had first arrived had been replaced by substantial-looking panels that blocked everything behind from view. Footfalls echoed from the unadorned walls. Somewhere in the background, pipers still trilled melancholy airs.

"I apologize for my lack of attention," Nimbia said as they entered, "but the emotion had to run its course.

182

Nothing has changed, of course, but at least now I can be a more proper hostess."

"How do you seek?" Astron ignored the courtesy. He quickly reviewed the questions that he had decided to ask at the first opportunity. "I deduce from what I have seen that you command the ring of djinns to bridge between realms that you have never seen before. How do you know they are there? Would not the action be one of discovery, rather than creation?"

A weak smile appeared on Nimbia's face. "I see our control of your kind is not something you ponder lightly," she said.

"I appreciate the extent of your power," Astron answered. "The youngest hatchlings are taught to avoid the lure of the fey." He wrinkled his nose. "But even the mightiest djinn cannot respond to an order poorly formed. He cannot pass through the barrier to another realm unless you explicitly direct him there. If he knows it not and neither do you, there is no way an opening can be formed."

"But we do know the realms where the ring is commanded," Nimbia said. "We know them because they are formed by our thought. We do not discover other realms, demon; they are created by the fey exactly as you have heard us say."

Astron opened his mouth to speak again, then slammed it shut as the significance of what Nimbia had said began to sink into his stembrain. She spoke casually, as if what she said was of no great matter, but the words brought forth images as staggering as those in Palodad's lair.

"You create realms," he said slowly, trying to fight off the stunned numbness that began to tingle through his limbs. "You are the ones responsible for the realm of daemon, the realm of men, and all the others."

"No, no, not the demons," Nimbia said. "As you well know, your realm spans the space between all the others. It must have existed far before the oldest memories of our own. Somehow it is different from the rest.

"And as for the realm of men, none of my brethren

183

would admit to such an act—conceiving something so misformed. Perhaps ages ago, before our art reached its present level of perfection, it was accomplished—or maybe it was the other way around, we are all the product of the fancies of men. Otherwise still, both could be the discarded first attempts to achieve perfection by yet some other beings. If that is so, it explains why so many of the realms are similar."

"What do you mean?" Astron persisted. "What realms—"

"Of the ones you saw on the slopes of the glen," Nimbia said, "I was the author of the last. I conceived the waves of black and the forces that gave them motive power. It was my thoughts that strained against the compressive forces that push against all the realms, trying to crush them to nothingness."

"I am sorry," Astron said. "You speak too quickly. I do not understand."

Nimbia's smile broadened slightly beneath her sad eyes. She gestured to one of the sentrymen standing in a doorway at the rear of the hall. "Pipes and cooling gels," she commanded. "I must explain what to the fey is common knowledge and second nature."

Astron watched as three pages shortly appeared, each one carrying a bowl of a steaming and viscous liquid. Behind them came three more, these bearing tripods and long metal pipes under their arms. The bowls were set erect in the stands and each of the trio handed a horn.

"You saw the pipers display this art when we returned from the judging," Nimbia said. "It is a festive symbolism of what we accomplish with our thought." She pointed in Phoebe's direction. "Let the female start. The brew before her is the most fluid."

Phoebe handled the horn tentatively but Nimbia waved her on. "Insert the pipe and blow," she said. "Show the power of creativity."

Phoebe thrust the flared end of the horn into the clear broth and took a deep breath. She exhaled forcefully and Astron saw a riot of tiny bubbles cascade to the surface and burst.

"Secondly the man," Nimbia said.

Kestrel frowned but positioned the long pipe into the liquid. He tentatively puffed into the horn and then strengthened his efforts. Astron saw agitation in the broth but little else. Kestrel's frown tightened. He inhaled deeply and pressed his lips about the mouthpiece of the horn. With bulging cheeks and eyes, he forced his breath through the long passageway into the brew.

Astron saw the surface ripple and then a single tiny bubble float gently upward. Kestrel lowered the pipe from his mouth, breathing deeply from the effort.

"And now the demon," Nimbia said. "Show who is the mightier of breath."

Astron stepped forward reluctantly and placed his hands on the pipe. He had no great need for moving large quantities of air in and out of his body and doubted that his strength matched that of a man. Nevertheless, he blew as hard as he could into the resistance.

For a long moment he strained and nothing happened. He concentrated on constricting his chest as far as he could. He clamped his elbows to his sides and strained with the muscles in his back. Then, just as he was preparing to abandon the effort, he felt a sudden lessening of resistance. He looked into the broth to see the beginning of a bubble emerge from the bell of the horn. With a hatchlinglike delight, he pointed at what he had done but halted in mid-gesture as the fluid collapsed the emerging bulge back into the pipe.

Nimbia nodded. "Imagine each realm as a bubble in a great sea," she said, "resisting the surrounding pressure by outward forces of its own. If the powers of expansion are insufficient, the bubble collapses into nothingness; but so long as they are strong enough, the realm survives.

"And what is the nature of this outward-directed power? Nothing less than the belief that the realm does indeed exist. If I can formulate a consistent system that has enough clarity in my mind, a rift occurs in the great sea; a tiny bubble forms that pushes back the oppressive forces and exists where there was nothing before.

185

"The effort required is a staggering one, far far greater than what you experienced with the gels. It is not everyone that can do it. But to the extent that I give my creation a compelling richness, others will also become enamored of its beauty. They, too, will think of it often, adding to the forces that keep it alive. So long as we ponder its being, the crush of destruction can be withstood."

Astron wrinkled his nose. For a long moment he pondered what he had heard. "It sounds like the balloons in the realm of men," he said at last. He propped the mouthpiece end of the horn carefully on the floor while he watched the bell end rise slowly from the clinging viscosity in the bowl. "Are you the only ones with such a power?"

"Beings in other realms can perform these creations as well," Nimbia said. "Why, even humans with their fancies and tales for the sagas have probably created universes, even though they know not what they have done. Their passions can sometimes be as great as our own. The recording of these ideas on parchment is an analogue to what we do with our song tellers—spreading knowledge of the creation, so that others can experience the wonder and aid in its existence."

Nimbia's eyes took on a faraway look. "As for the ability of the fey, it is the nature of our very own realm —the dictums of magic that are part of it, the storm of our emotion; these are the things that make us perhaps the most proficient."

"When the tales are put away and men read them no longer?" Phoebe looked up from where she was stirring the thinnest of the three fluids with the end of her horn. She spoke in a halting voice, the unfamiliar words of a new language setting heavy on her lips.

"If the creation has by that time not achieved a sufficient vitality of its own, if it has flaws and inconsistencies like a poorly constructed watch, it will eventually run down and be compressed back into the nothingness of the sea—just as you saw with the attempt of the demon." Nimbia paused and her eyes widened. "But if

186

the construction has been a sufficiently skilled one, with sentient beings of its own that believe in themselves, in their own existence, then the realm remains. Those inside provide the outward pressure that keeps the crushing forces of the all-enveloping sea at bay—a true creation of great art.

"That is what we strive for. It is the ultimate goal to which any fey can aspire—to create a new realm equal to our own, one that exists in and of itself, with all the thought being provided from inside, rather than the continued attention of those who first brought it into life.

"You saw the vitality of my creation when viewed through the circle of djinns. It lived, lived of its own volition! There should have been no way for Finvarwin to judge it inferior to empty motions of Prydwin's—despite the fact that what I did was accomplished without a mate."

"If you think the outcome of your efforts not to be fairly determined," Astron said, "then why do you try? Surely, with all that you command, there are other amusements that would serve as well."

Nimbia shook her head slowly. "There is nothing to compare to the joy of creation," she said. "The sense of accomplishment of bringing into being an existence out of the void. To be denied that pleasure is the greatest penalty that the high king can exact."

She waved her arm about the throne room. "The melancholy is not only my own. Even though only a king or queen is able to force a realm to spring from the void, everyone who serves contributes their thoughts to make it grow. They all savor the feeling of accomplishment, the thrill and wonder when the realm takes on a sense of being of its own, the pride when other underhills view what they have wrought."

Nimbia shook her head a second time. Fresh tears glistened in the corners of her eyes. "It is the duty of a hillsovereign to provide the basis, so that all can share. Her own sadness is all the greater because she must bear the responsibility of so many in addition to her own."

"Duty," Astron said. "Is not that from the subject to

the prince? You seem to state that it is the other—"

"The other realms have witnessed this melancholy, although they do not understand." Nimbia ran on, apparently not hearing the interruption. "In times past, other underhills unable or forbidden to create on their own have been reduced to merely watching. But just to observe realms who owe none of their existence to your craft makes the restrictions all the more heartpiercing. Usually we remain underground, so as to block out even the hint of pipes from others who are more fortunate."

"Then you do look into the realm of men," Kestrel said. "It could be that our tales are not by mere luck the same after all."

"My own underhill has not viewed the affairs of humans," Nimbia said, "but that does not preclude the actions of many others. And as you probably have surmised, the ring of djinns can be seen through from either side. No doubt if you have legends of strange beings, piping music, and forced gaiety appearing out of the mists and then vanishing again, it is because of the fey."

Nimbia stopped speaking. She dabbed at one tear on her cheek and stared off into the distance, apparently consumed by her own innermost thoughts.

"We asked before about the ultimate precept," Astron said after a moment. "Could it be that it too plays a part in the construction of these creations?"

Nimbia looked back down at Astron. She slowly shook her head. "Of such I have not heard," she said. "Our realm is governed by seven dictums of magic, like all the rest. The last two are those of dichotomy and ubiquity as you well know. They are the basis for the communication with the mighty djinns of your kind."

"Then perhaps one of the others," Astron said.

Nimbia rubbed her cheek dry and flicked back a golden curl over her shoulder. She shrugged again and began reciting, as if she were a broodmother instructing her latest clutch. "Of the first I have already spoken—reality follows from passion. Our temperaments are not placid, like those of the skyskirr. Instead, they are the fuel that fires our imaginations when we attempt to wrest a new universe from the void.

"The second as simply stated—strength comes from the lattice—guides our thoughts as we try to create. It is easier to conceive of a realm with dictums of magic close to our own, rather than more exotic ones about whose existence we can only guess.

"The third is a warning—weakness comes from contradiction. As I have already explained, a realm will eventually wind down and stop, because the postulates that we use in its beginning do not mesh into a harmonious whole.

"Of the fourth, even you have probably heard enough —two is greater than one and one. Somehow, when we are paired as loving mates, the creations are more fertile, more exotic, more likely to live.

"The fifth is stated—reap what you sow. It is the pollens we toss into the rings that somehow unlock the thoughts deepest within us, that give rise to our most exciting thoughts. Each type has its own—"

"Wait. Pollen did you say?" Astron interrupted.

"Yes," Nimbia said. "We do not know for sure exactly how they play a role in the process, but none of the fey attempts to create or embellish without a large supply on hand." She motioned to one of the sentrymen standing in the entryway. He retrieved a small chest that he brought forward and placed at Nimbia's feet.

Nimbia opened the arched lid. She gingerly reached in to withdraw a prickly sphere like the one Astron had seen Vastowen toss into the ring. It was far larger than the others, however, as big as a small melon. Nimbia held it delicately with extended thumbs and forefingers.

Astron looked at the globe carefully and understood Nimbia's cautious touch. The entire surface of the orb was covered with clusters of tiny barbs. Smaller hairlike shafts radiated in all directions from each of the prickly pylons and, in a blurry haze, these were anchorage for tinier projections still. Beyond the craft of the finest weaver in his own realm, the structure of sharp piercing

189

points iterated into infinitesimals, far smaller than the eye could see.

"We toss pollens through the ring of djinns to seed our thoughts in the void," Nimbia said. "Our success seems greater the more massive they are. To create something of value before Prydwin comes, I would need to use the largest of all, but in all of my underhill I have only this one."

"Are they hard to find?" Phoebe asked. "Could a human wizard help in their retrieval?"

"The flowers that produce them abound in a glen not too far away. The problem is not in harvesting them but harvesting them now. At present, the glen is alive with the hum of its guardians, and no one dares enter until they have gone on their way. After so many did not return, wisely did Finvarwin issue the prohibition—"

"We seek a pollen as part of our quest," Astron said. "This one that you desire, what is its name?"

"This would be called harebell in the realm of men." Nimbia nodded at the sphere in front of her. "That is why your question on our arrival struck such a chord. Of course, of all that I could wish, it would be the best. But of all that there are, it is the one I cannot obtain."

"Harebell pollen—and you can create," Kestrel said excitedly. "Create for Finvarwin so that you can get answers as a boon—answers that Astron seeks." His face broke into a broad grin. "Wipe the tears, Nimbia," he said. "I have a deal for you."

Chapter Fifteen

Harebell Pollen

ASTRON adjusted the straps that ran across his chest. He had gotten quite used to the tunic and leggings of men, but now the rucksack was a totally new sensation. He looked out between the columns of the raised hilltop and saw Kestrel urging him to hurry. Beside the human stood six of Nimbia's sentrymen, each carrying a long copper-tipped spear in addition to the dagger at his side. Their faces were rigid with tension; none showed Kestrel's enthusiasm to be under way.

Astron took a step forward and then hesitated. The opening in the wall to the left led to the throne room. He poked his head through the doorway and saw that Nimbia was alone, still sitting on her throne where they had left her when the planning was complete.

Despite the short length of his training, Kestrel had been most glib. Whatever dangers lurked in the harebell glen, he had said, they well might not affect human or demon at all. With a modest escort to protect against a chance encounter with Prydwin's forces, he and Astron would fetch the pollen and share with Nimbia what they obtained.

Then, with boosted confidence from the pollen's potency, Nimbia could create something that Finvarwin certainly would approve. They would not wait for the next judging or to see if they could fend off Prydwin's attack, but go directly to the high king for a special presentation. Phoebe could even help in the control of the ring of djinns. At the very least, Finvarwin's previous judgment would be reversed and Nimbia's underhill regain its independent status.

With Finvarwin's answer to the riddle and the hare-bell pollen as payment for Palodad, the old demon would get Elezar restored to power and he in turn would explain to Alodar the innocence of Phoebe and Kestrel. With a little luck everyone would achieve exactly what was desired.

When Kestrel had finished, Astron saw Nimbia's spirits begin to lift. Now, a few hours later, as he prepared to leave, the sadness had totally vanished from her eyes; she stared off into space, presumably thinking of her new creation.

Astron scraped his pack along the doorjamb and Nimbia turned at the distraction. She smiled and beckoned him to enter.

"Any more questions, inquisitive one?" she asked as Astron drew closer.

Astron looked at the perfectly sculpted face and graceful limbs. Another unanswered puzzle leaped into his mind. "You spoke of the great melancholy that comes when those of your kind cannot create," he said softly. "I have seen your tears and I believe. But before we came, before Finvarwin's judgment, what then was the corresponding joy?"

Astron shrugged and folded his fingertips to his chest. "We shared thoughts in the forest," he said. "There I glimpsed a sadness even deeper than that which is lifting now."

For a long moment Nimbia did not reply. She sighed and beckoned Astron to sit on the steps leading to her chair. She gathered her jeweled cape about her as he squirmed to get comfortable with the pack pulling on his back.

"Yes, indeed it is a conundrum." Her voice took on a hardened tone. "As you say, I am no less than a queen of underhill. My life should be like the foolish tales that men record in their sagas, with scores of smitten pages vying with one another to do my bidding and any hinted wish their fondest desire. Eventually, from all the rest I would pick the bravest, the kindest, the one most fair.

Together we would spend our lives in a blissful happiness, about which others can only dream.

"It is not so, demon." Nimbia shook her head. "There are no hovering suitors trying to outdo one another to gain my favor. Most of the males in this underhill seem completely dumbfounded in my presence; their self-esteem seems to melt with my smile. Hardly any dare believe that they would succeed against what must be many others and so they do not try.

"And the few that do hold their own value in high regard, the ones that, in desperation, I have run to, offering to subject my will to theirs—without exception, they have proven to love themselves far more than me. To one of them, I have been no more than an object, a trophy to prove yet again his own great worth."

Nimbia paused and sighed. "Even if I were able to accept that part of it, despite how much I might try, the liaisons have never been pleasant. Underneath the bragging of conquest, my mates have been consumed with insane jealousies, irrational fears that they cannot forever hold me as their own, and that I will tire and shame them in front of another.

"It is a fantasy, demon. I do not fully understand why, but for one such as I there is no such thing as living happily ever after."

Nimbia looked at Astron with eyes once again filling with sorrow. He felt a strange stirring. The queen had shared with him some of her innermost thoughts and feelings and done so unbidden. There was no question of the domination and submission of wizardry of which he was familiar. She had trusted and given of herself freely. He knew something of another thinking being in a way that he had never experienced before.

A sense of compassion for Nimbia's plight bubbled up within him—and more importantly, an urge to show that he was worthy, that he understood, and that her trust was well-placed, with a friend rather than a stranger.

"I—I was born without wings," he heard himself blurt without thinking. "Unlike my clutch brethren, neither could I soar through the realm nor weave more than the

193

simplest of matter. I have become a cataloguer, an observer of the bizarre in other universes, and a value to my prince."

Astron lowered his voice to a whisper and continued. "But I know of what you speak, of pains deep in the stembrain that no matter of higher logic can ever completely cover. I am only a shadow of a demon, Nimbia, only a small part of what it is my birthright to be. I look at the mighty wings of the splendorous djinns as they send the air into pulsing eddies with their strokes and a rage at the unfairness of it all burns deep inside. I lower my membranes and cover my ears from the power of the great explosions that my brethren can ignite at will, and a melancholy perhaps as deep as yours stirs from its deep burial."

Astron opened his mouth to say more but the words escaped him. What was he doing? His mind recoiled in numbness. The thoughts that he struggled so hard to keep buried were whirling unabated. And he had done no less than articulate them to one who was not even in the domain of his prince. He rose on one knee to withdraw but his limbs rapidly began to stiffen.

"Forgive me," he mumbled thickly. "Those words, those thoughts, they were not meant for another. I, I have—"

Nimbia reached out and placed her hand lightly on Astron's shoulder. "Thank you," she said, seeming to ignore completely his sudden discomfort. "That is exactly what I needed. You serve your hillsovereign better than many of my own kind."

Astron managed to shake his head, straining against the tightening tendons. Then he caught Kestrel entering the throne room and felt a sudden relief at the human's presence.

"Yes, I am finally coming," Astron said. Awkwardly he rose to his feet and adjusted the pack on his back. "A final word with the queen to learn more of the dangers."

Kestrel shrugged and motioned over his shoulder. "Walk with the rest of us now or catch up later," he said.

194

Kestrel left the throne room as rapidly as he had come. Astron scrambled to follow. Another confusion had piled on top of the rest. He had not spoken to Nimbia of dangers. For the first time in his life, just like a human, he had told an untruth.

The trek to the glen of harebells proceeded uneventfully. The constant twilight did not waver. No one else was seen on the grassy trails. Shortly after Kestrel and the fey arose from their second sleep, the party began climbing a final hillock crested with giant ragwort and broad-leaved thyme. Astron inhaled deeply the aromatics which hung heavy in the air.

Behind them, the lush green carpet spread as far as the eye could see, eventually vanishing into the softness of fog and mist. Like blemishes on smooth skin, clumps of mushroom, golden cowslips, and foxglove scattered across the low-lying grasses indicated the presence of springy marshes with ground far wetter than the rest.

"What is it?" Astron heard Kestrel growl ahead of him. "We have come too far to begin slacking the pace now."

He looked up the trail and saw that the fey had stopped and Kestrel had almost closed the distance between them. Kestrel scowled and flexed his back, pulling at the straps of the rucksack he bore. Apparently the adjustment did not help; in irritation, he slipped out of the burden and let it fall heavily to the ground.

"The shrill vibrations are worse than I have ever known them before," the first of the fey said as Astron caught up with the rest.

"What vibrations?" Kestrel shook his head. "I do not hear a thing." He flexed his back again. "All I know is that we have been pushing hard for two days and the end is in sight. Now is not the time to have second thoughts."

"The irritation is part of the effect," another of the fey said. "Perhaps the sounds are too high for your ears, but they are there, nonetheless. You feel them, even if you cannot hear."

Astron strained to catch some sense of what the others were talking about, but he heard nothing. Although demon sight was keen, their hearing was inferior to that of many other beings. Nor did he feel any of Kestrel's irritation or the growing agitation of the fey.

"The risk is too great." The first shook his head. "Better to bear the burdens of Prydwin's pollensacks than not to exist at all. Your words may have been smooth enough for the queen, but she does not risk the dangers of the glen herself."

He flung off his pack and grabbed at the arm of the second. For a moment the two hesitated and then, after wide-eyed glances back up the hill, they bolted in the other direction, gathering speed as they ran. The panic was contagious. The remaining four did not even bother to lighten their loads. Fighting each other for the center of the trail, they sprinted off after the others.

Kestrel watched the fey depart and kicked at his own rucksack. Astron shrugged but said nothing. He stepped past and continued up the slope. For a long while, Kestrel stood with hands on hips scowling. Then he gathered up his equipment and scrambled to catch up with the demon. In a moment they were peering out from under the cover of a ragwort leaf into the glen of the harebells.

The hill sloped downward from the ridge under a cover of thick-leaved grasses, just as it had on the other side. But midway down the slope, a wall of skyward-pointing leaves poked out of a heavy mist and blocked the view. From what looked like a thick forest of upraised green swords, fragile stalks rose even higher, almost to the crests of the surrounding hills. Impossibly slender, the ropelike shoots wavered in gentle rhythms, as if trying by an act of delicate balance to keep from crashing to the ground. And on the end of each, looping over and hanging as a massive weight, was a deep-bowled blossom that swung back and forth. All of the flora of the realm possessed massive proportions, but the harebells seemed among the largest of all. A man or demon could easily hide within a single flower, if he climbed that high.

After a moment's observation, Kestrel stirred and started down the hillside, but Astron grabbed his arm and held him back. The demon pointed at a hint of blurry motion above the mist and then at a second and a third. One of the harebells rattled with energy. Brilliant orange-and-black stripes emerged from the petals and then hovered still.

"Bees!" Kestrel exclaimed as the recognition came to him. "Giant bees the size of the flowers." He put his hands over his ears. "And the noise—it is their wings. They buzz so fast that one can barely hear."

Astron looked at the large insect before it darted away. Knowing what to look for, he spotted several more flitting through the flowers. Large, multifaceted eyes, like great blackened shields, rode above a mouth siphon bristling with golden hairs. The wings were a blur about the bright abdomen, to which were attached legs folded in an intricate maze. From the rear protruded the sharp tip of the stinger, glistening with venom. Astron shook his head. Judging from the size, the poison would be totally unnecessary. The thrust of the lance would bore right through the chest as surely as a shaft of steel.

"If it were not for the tales of no one returning, we could risk it," Kestrel said. "Just walk out and pick a stalk that none of the bees seems interested in. Perhaps we could even shake some of the pollen to the ground."

Astron did not immediately respond. Quickly he ran over in his mind what he had learned of bees in the realm of men. "Smoke," he said after a moment. "Perhaps the ones that venture close can be subdued, if we surround ourselves with sufficient soot and ash."

"There is little here that will burn." Kestrel shook the leaf overhead to release a shower of water. "Nothing about is sufficiently dry."

"There is one thing," Astron said. He reached into his pack and pulled out the single grain of harebell pollen he had brought with him to ensure positive identification. Delicately, he placed it on the ground just beyond the cover of the ragwort, frowning in distaste at the many prickly barbs that pierced his fingertips.

He withdrew one of the oil bladders he had used when studying thaumaturgy and stretched it into a crude lens with his thumbs and forefingers. "I had wanted to try the experiment when we got above ground, anyway," he explained as he adjusted the focus. "Even with diffuse light, the energy might be converged enough if the material is sufficiently combus—"

The harebell pollen grain suddenly began to smoulder. A ringlet of dense black smoke bubbled from the surface and rose into the air. Kestrel coughed. Astron put down the lens. He saw the surface of the pollen glow into incandescence around the origin of the fire and the circle slowly begin to spread outward in a growing ring. The smoke thickened and cascaded from the pollen in billowing waves, far in excess of what one would expect from such a small amount of flame. Like a black fog, it began rolling down the hillside toward the harebells.

"Smoke subdues bees in the realm of men." Astron motioned Kestrel to follow him as he stepped forward from under cover. He stopped and picked up the smouldering grain. "Let us move quickly before it burns itself out."

Kestrel watched Astron proceed halfway down the slope and then raced to catch up. Together they reached the slender stalks of the harebell without alarming any of the bees which buzzed overhead.

"You stay here and keep the fire going," Kestrel said when they reached the base of the nearest flower. "I will climb up and shake loose what I can."

Astron nodded and watched Kestrel wrap himself around the ropelike stem that soared into the air. The demon placed the pollen grain at the base of the plant. With both hands, he fanned the dense smoke sluggishly upward, enveloping Kestrel as he slowly rose.

Kestrel reached the bowed apex of the harebell without incident. Then, letting his feet hang free, he descended hand over hand onto the bowl of the flower itself. Astron watched him tentatively test the strength of an individual petal and then pause, apparently trying to figure out the best way to get inside.

Two of the bees swooped in Astron's direction; but at the last moment, they both turned aside and buzzed off toward different flowers. Evidently the smoke was not something that they voluntarily wanted to encounter. Astron kept fanning the heavy billows outward and upward, watching warily for any signs of agitation among the darting insects.

He looked up to see Kestrel dangling in midair, one hand holding the tip of a bluish petal and the other reaching for the knobby stamen that protruded from the center of the bowl. In an instant, Kestrel vanished inside the bloom. Then a moment later, a shower of pollen grains just like the one that was burning began to cascade downward to where Astron stood.

Astron stopped his fanning and removed his pack from his back. Scampering about like a small child, he harvested the grains and stuffed them into the empty pouch. He gathered a dozen grains and then three or four more until the pack was filled. He brushed his hands with satisfaction. Nimbia would be well pleased with what they had done.

When the flap was secured and the pack returned to his back, he glanced at the burning pollen grain and saw the color of the smoke lighten into soft grays. The burning ring of fire started to sputter. Only a tiny disk remained of what once had been a sizable volume. He looked upward to call Kestrel down and his stembrain suddenly jolted in spasm by what he saw.

The bright abdomen of one of the bees protruded from the flower into which Kestrel had vanished. A second was buzzing angrily around the stem, apparently awaiting his turn. Astron reached back to untie the pack, but then he saw the wings of the first bee flutter to life in agitation. Its stinger began to extend and the entire body contort inward toward the blossom.

Astron shook his head savagely to rid himself of his stiffness. He bent forward and blew on the smouldering pollen grain, bringing the flames back to life. A wave of smoke billowed out over the ground and covered his feet in inky blackness.

Astron started to fan the coiling tendrils skyward; then thought better of it. They would be too diffuse at the height of the blossom. He grabbed the grain gingerly in one hand and cupped its prickly surface carefully against his tunic. Savagely pushing aside yet another wish for wings, he grabbed the stalk and awkwardly began to climb.

Astron heard a high-pitched whine for the first time as he struggled upward, evidently caused by the confines of the harebell petals against the insect's wings. In agonizing slowness, he proceeded, occasionally catching glimpses of Kestrel's dark silhouette through the translucent blues of the petals. The human's body was pushed up into a tight ball at the very base of the flower, trying to avoid the larger blob maneuvering itself deeper into the bowl.

Finally, Astron reached the height of the drooping calyx of the harebell. All he could see of the flower's interior was blotted by the carpet of coarse orange-and-black hairs on the back of the bee. He wrapped his legs as securely as he could about the swinging stem and stretched out his hand containing the burning pollen grain.

Only a small curved disk remained of what once was a sizable sphere. He blew down the length of his arm but the flame responded only sluggishly. A few wisps of black rose into the bowl of the flower. Astron exhaled vigorously, pushing as much life as he could into the remains of the smoke. The twitching of the bee as it twisted itself deeper into the harebell slowed but did not stop altogether.

Astron looked at the remains of the pollen grain and the progress of the bee. Something more desperate would be needed if Kestrel was to be saved. Almost without thinking, he discarded the last dying embers and coiled himself up into a ball on the wavering stem. Then kicking as best he could, he hurled himself across the distance to the dangling flower, grabbing the hairs on the bee's back with both his hands.

With a noise like ripping paper, the bee's claws tore

through the petals as the added weight pulled it downward. In an instant, the insect was dragged free; with Astron clinging to its back it hurled toward the ground.

Once free of the confines of the blossom, the huge wings exploded into a blur of action. Stinging blasts of cold air raced across Astron's body as the insect tried to right itself. The bee lurched to the right and Astron felt a stab of pain in his shoulder as he struggled to maintain a grip. With a flip that hurled Astron up over the insect's back, the bee wobbled into a horizontal position. But the ground came rushing up too fast. With a jarring thud, they crashed into the ground.

Astron felt the air rush from his lungs as he slammed into the bristly back. Stunned, he rolled to the side and fell to the ground. The bee tried to rise on its legs, but only uncoordinated spasms shook its body. Its wings fluttered out of synchronization, blowing up a scatter of dewdrops among the wide blades of grass that covered the slope.

Astron looked quickly about, trying to clear his vision. He saw motion near the base of the stem and guessed that Kestrel was scrambling to safety. A pungent odor began to fill his nostrils; he saw the stinger of the bee at his side fully extended and glistening with a foul-smelling oil. In awkward steps on three legs, the insect was gradually turning its abdomen about to where Astron swayed as he tried to regain his composure. His head still rang from the contact and, against his will, he fell to one knee.

"Come on," Kestrel shouted behind him. "Somehow they can communicate. Look, the others are coming to the aid of the one you brought down."

Astron felt a firm grip under his arm and rose reluctantly to his feet. He followed Kestrel's tug and began to place one foot in front of another. Almost mindlessly, he picked up speed and began running up the slope. The ringing in his head grew more intense and almost painful. He placed his hands over his ears, trying to concentrate on keeping up with the human as he ran.

Almost without knowing, they reached the ragwort

201

and burst over the hill crest. Astron's vision began to clear; the high buzz in his ears started to fade away. In a few moments, they had raced down onto the wet flatlands and were heading back to Nimbia's underhill.

"You did it again, Astron," Kestrel said after they had caught their breaths. "You saved me when you had no real cause. First Phoebe and then you. I'm starting to expect it. It's almost enough to restore my faith in human nat—"

Kestrel paused, looked at Astron's demonic features carefully, and then laughed. "Well, maybe that would be going just a bit too far," he said.

CHAPTER SIXTEEN

Nimbia's Challenge

ASTRON and Kestrel retraced their journey across the hills and glens as rapidly as they could. Without the fey to guide them and no directional aids in the sky, their progress was slowed. More than once, they wandered away from the faint trails and were set right only by Astron's keen eye and memory for detail. It was only after Kestrel had risen from his fifth sleep that they estimated that Nimbia's underhill was drawing near.

The last lush green hill beckoned them forward. Sparse groupings of blooming foxglove and withered cowslip past its prime dotted the hillocks. A carpet of ferns crowded close onto the muddy trail that squished in wetness with each step.

"So you knew nothing of thaumaturgy before possessing the archimage's book," Kestrel said as he paused for breath where the slope steepened. "Burning lenses and alchemical balloons. You are well on the way to becoming a master of many arts yourself."

Astron shook his head. "No, as I have tried to explain, nothing I have done involves any magical skill. I have learned only of adjuncts that can be used independent of the crafts—by you as well as any other."

"This journey has given me no more knowledge of the magical arts." Kestrel shook his head. "Indeed, if it were not for Phoebe's safety, I would not even be here." He shielded his eyes from the diffuse glare, trying to catch sight of something familiar. "Come," he said, "we have wasted too much time already."

"It is because I am a cataloguer," Astron continued as they resumed their march. "Unlike my brethren, I look beyond the facts as they are presented to the deductions that logically follow."

Despite his rush, Kestrel laughed. "If I were to judge, looking beyond what is apparent is perhaps where your faculties need mostly to be sharpened."

"What do you mean?" Astron wrinkled his nose. "As you have said, I was the one who calculated that balloons of lead could fly, that—"

"And the one who did not understand how a group of wizards would react when presented the opportunity for monetary gain." Kestrel held up his hand to stop the protest. "Nor even how to entrap the imps which you say you have known for eras.

"There is more to thought than a logical progression from one truth to another, Astron. Sometimes there is value as well in postulating alternatives, in letting ideas flow free."

Astron's puzzlement deepened. "I do not understand. How can such lack of discipline help me in my quest? Our course is clear; we merely have to follow the path to its end."

Kestrel rubbed the back of his neck and frowned. He looked up to the hilltop. For a long moment they trudged in silence.

"Well, for example, consider the matter of this Gaspar of yours," Kestrel resumed after they had climbed thrice the height of a man.

"He is not my prince," Astron said. "He would find

203

my existence not pleasing. In a tick of time, I would be given to the lowest of his djinns for sport. I serve Elezar, who finds pleasure in riddle and delicate weavings, rather than explosion and chaos."

"Exactly so." Kestrel panted. "From what little you have told me, Gaspar is a demon most unlikely to compose a riddle that would baffle your prince. Even if he could, it would not be his style. Think of it, Astron. Why has Gaspar acted as he has? From where has he obtained the plan to baffle your prince? There are inconsistencies here that cry for explanation." Kestrel shrugged and then put on a fresh burst of speed.

"That is what you should be thinking of," he said, "the deeper meaning of the riddles, not the relative weight of air and lead."

Astron adjusted his pack and hurried to keep pace. "Then what is the answer?" he asked. "Tell me what secrets this other way of thinking reveals. Do you mean to imply that Gaspar is under the control of a wizard, just as Elezar has succumbed to the archimage—that there is a being in some realm with a will great enough to subdue a prince of the lightning djinns?"

Kestrel stopped a second time at the crest of the last hill, while Astron struggled to catch up. "I do not know enough of your realm," the human said. "Perhaps there is no substance to my conjecture and everything is proceeding as it has been presented. But, as I have suggested, let your thoughts roam free. Perhaps, when you least expect it, an insight will come."

Astron wrinkled his nose. "It is hard to see the utility of such speculation," he said. "Although if that is the process by which you found a way to put imps in a bottle—"

The scene which stretched before them suddenly reached Astron's consciousness. He looked once at Kestrel and they both began to race down the slope. At the nadir of the glen, Nimbia's hillock stood elevated on the slender pillars as it had on their first arrival. But this time the underhill was ominously quiet and empty.

In silence, they ran onto the heavy stone flooring that

had been raised from below the ground. Obviously no one was about. Many of the interior walls and partitions had been removed and carted away. The dais of the throne room was bare. Empty sky showed through, where before had hung a delicate tapestry of vines. Two empty vats tipped on their sides were all that remained of the store of pollens and seeds. Several flutes and horns were scattered in a litter of leaves and copper swords on the stone floor. Here and there, spatters of blood mingled with the remains of other debris.

Kestrel and Astron raced about the empty corridors and then descended into the passageways below ground. They found almost everything ransacked there as well. They entered Astron's cubicle and saw that only the book of thaumaturgy remained, tossed into a corner, pages down. Evidently its strange script was of no interest to whoever had come. Astron turned to leave but Kestrel ran forward to the book. He flipped it over and pointed excitedly to the inside of the front cover. There in a precise script Phoebe had left a final message.

"Pipers of Prydwin have been seen in the glen," Astron read aloud. "Nimbia fears that he plans to come just before the next judging and claim the bondage that is his due. Even without the pollen, she must create for Finvarwin. It is one last desperate chance, even though Prydwin will certainly be there. I will accompany her and aid with my wizardry as best I can."

Kestrel quickly counted on his fingertips and looked at the notches carved in the doorjamb. "It is already the time of the next judging," he growled. "To the glen with the stream. If Phoebe and Nimbia escaped before the arrival of Prydwin's sentrymen that is where they will be."

Astron tapped the bulging pack on his back. "But without the pollen there is little chance they will succeed."

"Exactly," Kestrel shouted as he sprinted back up the stairs. "Somehow we must break through the ring that guards the glen and get them the help they need."

Astron felt his stembrain stir. Pulling Nimbia out of

the ring with total surprise was one thing, but breaking through to Finvarwin's rock long enough to use the harebell pollen properly was quite another. A shuddering spasm squeezed the breath from Astron's chest. He remembered all too well the crushing power of the combined wizardry of the pipers. He had expected one of Kestrel's clever deceptions as the means to allow Nimbia to compete again, not an insane dash that the humans enjoyed so much.

Astron watched Kestrel bound up the steps three at a time. Obviously the thoughts of Phoebe in peril had been too much for the human. He had surrendered to the panic of his stembrain, rather than think through what must be done. Grimly, Astron forced calm onto his own churnings. He would have to use the best of his reason to convince Kestrel to formulate a plan.

Astron laid a hand on Kestrel's shoulder to restrain him as they peered out from the cover of the ragwort. The temptation to wrestle with the human's will flitted through his mind, but he put the thought aside. There was no time for that. He would have to hope that the logic on which they had agreed would work instead.

"Look at them down there," Kestrel whispered desperately. "They are all alone, with not a single piper to guard them. At worst, Nimbia will become a slave to Prydwin; who knows what will happen to Phoebe."

"Yes, look at them," Astron answered. "Phoebe is cloaked. No one questions that she might not be one of their own kind." He touched the reassurance of the hood he had scavenged from the debris of Nimbia's underhill. "I can pass through the ring with the same pretense. Your presence will only sound an alarm."

"You are a demon and know nothing of this sort of thing," Kestrel growled. "If it were not for the fact that your command of the language is better, I would be the one wearing the cape."

"It is what we have agreed," Astron said quietly. "Propose another plan if you have one better."

Astron saw the muscles in Kestrel's face contort with

indecision. After a long moment, he sighed and slumped to the ground. "Go ahead," he whispered. "Just remember to answer any challenges the way I have indicated, quickly and with confidence—as if it is totally bizarre that there should be any suspicion."

Astron nodded and began to rise, but Kestrel caught him by the arm. "And none of those fool questions of your own. There is much at stake here, not a petty exercise in collecting data for one of your catalogues."

Astron pushed away a sudden rush of irritation. "Cataloguing is by no means petty," he muttered. "No other djinn under Elezar's command—"

He slammed his mouth shut. Kestrel was right. There were more important things to attend to now. He looked down toward the bottom of the glen, from under the cover of the ragworts. Finvarwin stood adjacent to his rock. Next to him, a circle of djinns arched into the sky as they had upon Astron's arrival. Prydwin stood in front of the flaming ring, partially blocking a view into another realm.

Within the fiery window, Astron saw what looked like two armies engaged in hand-to-hand combat, breaking limbs and spattering blood with intense dedication. The warriors on each side were thin-framed and delicate, like the fey. Their blows struck and parried in an almost stylistic dance, creating complex visual patterns that grew and decayed as the battle progressed. From the very center of the conflict, precisely straight paths of ashen white radiated out in many directions on a plane of gray and continued into the vanishing distance. Astron shook his head; he had never seen or heard the likes of such a place before.

A little farther to the right, he recognized Phoebe, despite the cloak; and next to her, similarly disguised, must be Nimbia, nervously pacing while she waited. As before, copper-daggered sentrymen ringed the slopes of the glen, adding the force of their wills to the control of the djinns who strained to bridge the gap between the realm of the fey and those that lay beyond.

Astron grimaced and concentrated for the last time to

207

push the tuggings of his stembrain far beneath his conscious thoughts. He adjusted his hood to cover as much of his face as possible and stepped out onto the grassy slopes.

He walked slowly down the hillside directly toward one of the sentrymen, looking past him toward the bottom of the glen.

"Halt," the guard said when Astron was close enough for him to hear the swish of his cape. "Prydwin defends his creations against a challenger from a far underhill. He displays no less than his realm of reticulates. There is to be no interference until the judging is done."

"I bring pollen that is plentiful in that far underhill for my queen," Astron said. "She is expecting my presence and I must pass."

A strange thrill ran through Astron as he said the words. They were filled with untruth and tasted strange on his lips. Yet he noticed that the sentryman did not immediately reach for his arms. Instead he rubbed his chin in indecision and looked closer at what had interrupted his concentration.

"Lower your hood so that I see that you indeed are not from a local glen," the sentryman said. "King Prydwin did not capture Queen Nimbia and all of her followers when he seized what had been granted to him in the last judging."

Astron's stembrain rumbled. He felt sharp impulses rip through his legs, compelling him to step backward. He clenched his fists and willed his thoughts into control. "I am disfigured," he said quietly. "A dagger such as yours severed an ear from my head and left a great scar. I wear this hood to cover my shame. Surely you can let me pass so that no one will see."

The sentryman hesitated. Astron stepped boldly forward. "In any event, I am within your ring," he said as he glided past. "You will have opportunity to challenge me again after the judging is done. For now, I must obey my queen, who bids me come forth."

The sentryman frowned, but made no attempt to follow. Through squinting eyes, he watched Astron slowly march down the slope. Astron forced air into his constricted lungs. The strange thrill blossomed into delicious triumph. He ran his tongue over his teeth, trying to savor every aspect of the feeling.

He had succeeded in getting past the guard, but not with a display of strength, as would one of his clutch brothers, or even with the knowledge of the cataloguer. He had woven an appearance of reality and it had been accepted.

He looked at Prydwin standing near the circle of djinns as he approached and then at Nimbia and Phoebe pacing nearby. Astron reached over his shoulder and grabbed the topmost of the prickly pollen grains from his rucksack. "The seeds for your planting, my queen," he said. "May your thoughts grow and prosper."

Nimbia's eyes widened in surprise and then she smiled. She said nothing, but pointed to the ground at her feet where Astron was to dump his burden. Astron removed the pack from his back and glanced again at the opening into Prydwin's realm. He saw the dancelike battle continue with an almost glacial slowness. A few spans away, the hunched figure of Finvarwin squinted at the motions with what looked like unwavering concentration.

"You see the vitality of the combat, my high king," Prydwin said. "It intensifies rather than diminishes."

"Enough," Finvarwin rumbled. "Let us see the offering of the cloaked ones who come from far away."

"Yes." Prydwin waved the demon ring to opaqueness. He stared at Nimbia's cloaked form and smiled. "I too have curiosity about this new creation—indeed, the creation and creator both."

Nimbia tugged at the corner of her hood and turned away. While everyone watched, she took a position in front of the ring. After a moment, she gestured that she was ready. Astron saw her drop to the ground, coiling into a tight ball and pulling her arms around her knees. Without speaking, she began rocking herself back and forth. For more than a hundred heart beats, nothing happened. Then a tiny spark of painfully brilliant red burst into being in the precise middle of the ring.

Nimbia screamed as if in pain and then forced a hearty laugh from deep within her chest. The amplitude of her rocking increased as more peals rang from her lips. She tossed back her head and the hood fell away to reveal her golden curls.

Astron felt a twinge in his stembrain. There could be no doubt about who she was. He saw two of Prydwin's sentrymen snap to alertness and step forward with daggers drawn. But their hillsovereign waved them to be still. With the broad smile still on his face, he struck an exaggerated pose of complete ease.

Nimbia's agitation increased. With a violent tug, she flung aside the cape and rose to her feet. Her laughter turned to tears. With violent sobs that racked her body, she raised her arms toward the ring, imploring the grayness to dissolve away.

She had known that the disguise would not long be effective, Astron realized in a flash. Her identity could not be hidden when so much passion was required for what she must do. There had not been time to create before the judging. It had to be done while all the others watched. And yet, she had come, rather than slink away to safety in the brush when her underhill was attacked. It was her duty, she had said, her duty to those over whom she was the queen. Astron shook his head. Such a thought would be completely foreign to the prince to whom he owed his fealty.

The pinpoint of light expanded sluggishly into a small disk, pushing against the gray void. The circumference seemed to tremble in a series of spasmodic expansions and contractions, oscillating in a complex rhythm, but slowly growing in diameter. When the disk had become the size of a small melon, Nimbia nodded to Astron, pointing at the pollen at his feet and then the disk.

Astron grabbed one of the harebell grains and lofted it at the vibrating circle. The aim was good, and it struck near the center, but bounced back at his feet. Of course, he thought quickly, transporting solid matter between the realms was a hard task for even the strongest of djinns.

It was the reason why Elezar had sent him to the realm of men in the first place.

He motioned to Phoebe to pick up the pollen and try where he had failed. Phoebe frowned in confusion at first, but then understood what must be done. Her lob struck the disk near the edge, but apparently close enough to what Nimbia desired, because the circle exploded into a blaze of color, expanding to banish all of the gray.

"An empty palette," Prydwin called to Finvarwin. "There is nothing there. As soon as Nimbia releases the pressure of her thoughts, the creation will collapse back into the void."

"Nimbia, here?" Finvarwin turned his attention for an instant away from the ring.

Nimbia ignored the taunt and directed Phoebe to continue tossing the pollen into the ring. The wizard hurled another grain and then, with increasing speed, began throwing more.

Astron watched the orbs as they sailed through the ring and seemed to strike the disk of red. Each seemed to transform as it flew. The prickly spines grew and bent at right angles, forming transparent squares of yellow; the bulbous central body wasted away so that only the boxes remained. Like checkerboards with some of the cells cut away, each pollen grain deposited a haphazard pattern of connected squares in the new realm, some with only two or three components, others with dozens or more.

Then, after the last grain thrown had been transformed, there was a sudden pulse of light. The plane of red shifted to a brilliant blue. But more importantly, Astron noticed, the patterns of squares had all simultaneously transformed as well. Some had vanished; new ones had appeared. The background pulsed a second time, shifting back to red and then again oscillating to blue. With each shift, the patterns of boxes transformed— some dying entirely, others growing in grotesque and complex ways, seemingly spawning children that evolved on their own.

211

Astron watched fascinated as the patterns unfolded. He concentrated on the simple ones that cycled through a series of repeating shapes and then suddenly saw the law that governed the behavior. He looked at Nimbia in admiration, struck by the clean simplicity of what she had done. Each square lived or died in the next cycle, depending on the number of its neighbors. With two, it remained from one oscillation to the next; otherwise it vanished. New squares were born according to a similar rule.

The elegance of the creation swept through him. He felt a great longing to plant a seed grouping of cells himself and see what would happen and to watch the pattern live and die. It was exactly the type of thing that would satisfy the cravings of the fey. Nimbia had created a most unique realm with a vital life force all its own. Surely Finvarwin would see the merit of what she had done.

Astron looked back at Nimbia and saw her collapse into a heap. "I call this the realm of the conways," she panted in almost total exhaustion. "It is a universe based upon—"

"I apologize for the wasting of your time with meaningless competition," Prydwin interrupted. "This is no better, Nimbia, than your offering the last time you were called forth."

"It is worse." Finvarwin squinted into the ring of djinns. "I see nothing but the dull repetition of red and blue. A well-defined realm, it is true, but one that bores after the briefest of inspections."

"But it is indeed my best!" Nimbia tried to regain her feet, but could not find the strength. "Look at what is there, Finvarwin. How can you so lightly dismiss what I have done?"

"Nimbia." Prydwin smiled. "Surely, even with the cloak, you must have known I would suspect—an unknown hillsovereign who mumbles to the high king only the minimum necessary to be granted a turn to present, an unknown hillsovereign indeed!"

Prydwin turned to Finvarwin. "You have already

granted me the boon of Nimbia's underhill, venerated one," he said. "What additional might I expect now that I have won the wager doubled?" He turned and called back up the hill. "Sentrymen, seize them. This time she will not escape."

Astron looked at Finvarwin but saw that the old one was unmoved. He swayed slightly on unsteady limbs but otherwise did nothing to explain his decision.

"No!" Nimbia cried out. "A second punishment will only add injustice to the first. It is not the fault of those who have dwelt in my underhill that these creations have failed to find your favor, Finvarwin." Slowly she extended her arms trembling from exhaustion, offering her wrists for bondage. "If any payment is to be made, it is the duty of their queen and no other."

"What, this is Nimbia?" Finvarwin said. "The hooded queen and she are one and the same?"

Astron watched Finvarwin's squint deepen as Nimbia struggled to stand. The hunched figure reminded him somewhat of Palodad, physically infirm yet continuing as he had for perhaps eons before. Age should have brought increased wisdom and the ability to judge better what his senses presented to—

Astron stopped in midthought. The explanation burst upon him. "He cannot see!" he shouted to Nimbia. "He can no longer discern detail—only large movements and general shapes. Finvarwin has judged your creations inferior because he never noticed the structures of what was really there."

Astron's thoughts raced. Just as in his experiments, sharpness of vision in a living being was a matter of lenses and bending light. He remembered the book of thaumaturgy and the many interesting diagrams it contained. Dropping to the ground, he began pawing rapidly through the contents of his pack, looking for what might give Nimbia one last chance.

With a surprising nimbleness, he fashioned some bits of copper wire into two small circles, connected them with an arc of metal and then attached longer straight segments on either side. He grabbed at one of the large

213

flat leaves near the stream bank and tore it into two disks that fit over the rings of copper, hoping the oozing sap would hold them firm. With a last segment of wire he punched a tiny hole in the center of each of the green disks.

"Here, try these." He raced up to Nimbia's side, extending his construction forward for Finvarwin. "Place them astride your nose and over your ears. The scene will be dim but a pinhole works as well as the finest correcting lens. I have tested the effect in Nimbia's underhill and seen how sharp the focus can be."

Astron's hood flew backward as he ran, but he was too excited to care. Finvarwin must see Nimbia's creation as it was meant to be viewed.

"The demon," Prydwin shouted suddenly in recognition. "The one who kept Nimbia from me, as was my due at the last competition. Challenge him, pipers, make him submit to our collective will."

Astron grimaced. The memory of his last ordeal sprang frightfully into his mind. And within their circle, there would be no way he successfully could resist.

"Like this." Astron demonstrated with the glasses and then thrust them into Finvarwin's hand. He started to say more, but felt a sudden compelling jolt. Staggering under crushing pressure, he sagged to his knees.

Through glazed eyes, he watched Finvarwin, with agonizing slowness, bring the strange object to his face. Astron pushed forward a resistance against the mental onslaught; but deep in his stembrain, he knew he would fail. His thoughts became sluggish, compressing in ways that were distasteful and bizarre. He saw the sentrymen racing closer, and among them Kestrel pounded down the hill with the rest.

"This is most amazing!" Finvarwin exclaimed. "There is more to your creation, Nimbia, than I first suspected. Yes, look at it—most clever, far more elegant that what Prydwin has offered to be compared."

"What is the ultimate precept?" Astron skrieked. "What law is supreme over all the rest? How does one start a fire in the realm of daemon? The prize for winning—the answers I must know."

"No, I am the winner." Prydwin swiped at Finvarwin's glasses, knocking them to the ground. "Do not be misled. It is some sort of demon trickery." He looked quickly about the glen. "Yes, there are four altogether. Get them all, the one still hooded and the other sprinting down the hill. Get them all while I reestablish contact with my realm of reticulates. Look again as you have before, my high king, and you will see."

Astron struggled to think what he should do, but he felt his being compressed into nothingness, all the sharp corners of his essence being smoothed away. With a dull thud, his head sagged to the wet earth. In a strange detachment, he noticed Kestrel being shoved to earth near his rucksack and Phoebe thrown beside it.

"Be careful, Prydwin," Astron dimly heard Finvarwin say. "Even a hillsovereign must abide by the decisions of the high king."

"I will accept no punishment for the likes of this," Prydwin growled.

"First, a competition that has been fairly won deserves its just reward," Finvarwin continued, "and then we will see what additional judgments are appropriate besides."

The high king paused briefly and cleared his throat. "Realities are no more than bubbles," he said. "That is the most profound truth that I know. If there is an ultimate precept, then somehow that knowledge must be a component part."

Astron tried to pull meaning from Finvarwin's statement but he could not. All he could do was focus on Prydwin's strident voice.

"There shall be no reversals of opinion, I say. If I cannot have Nimbia, then neither shall she have me. Quickly, sentrymen, I command you—all of them through the flame."

Phoebe's scream blotted out what Finvarwin said next. The last thing that Astron remembered was a sensation of being lifted and then being hurled through the air.

PART FOUR

The Two Realms Of Symmetry

Chapter Seventeen

Rotator's Move

KESTREL shook his head, trying to force his thoughts to order. The disorientation was not as great as the first time he had travelled between realms, but it was there, nonetheless. He felt Astron's pack slide from his grip and crunch into a sea of sand that surrounded him as far as he could see. Vaguely, he remembered grabbing at the pollen sack as he was hoisted from the ground by Prydwin's sentrymen and bodily tossed at the ring of djinns. When he hit the plane of the vertical circle, he had felt a tremendous deceleration, like a ball of cotton hurled into a vat of thick molasses. The pack was almost wrenched from his grasp, but somehow he had held on and burst through to the scene that lay beyond.

He sat at what looked like the edge of a desert oasis. Astron lay crumpled at his side apparently unconscious. By Kestrel's feet was a placid circle of clear water with a diameter about twice the height of a man. He felt the rough bark of a tree at his back and saw five more arranged around the periphery at the vertices of a perfect hexagon. Phoebe wallowed to alertness in front of the tree directly opposite his own, trying to get her bearings. Next to the wizard, Nimbia slumped in a disarray of tunic, leggings, and cape.

A path of crushed white stones radiated away from each of the trees into the distance, across a featureless gray plane, vanishing in an indistinct horizon that blurred the separation of ground and air. A gentle breeze bathed the left side of his face and, just as in the realm of the fey, he could see no sun, only a diffuse light that seemed to come from all directions.

Kestrel cursed himself for being so impetuous. But then what else could he have done? When Prydwin called his sentrymen down to Finvarwin's rock, there had been no option but to bolt from cover to offer what aid he could. Phoebe had been in danger, and he could not just idly stand by.

But there had been too many. Like a sack of flour, he had been hurled through the circle of djinns into the realm of Prydwin's creation. Dazed from the jarring impact, he had watched helplessly as the others followed. Before any of them could stir, the portal back to the realm of the fey clouded and then closed.

Kestrel started to rise in order to see farther from the oasis, but felt a great weight that resisted his motion pressing downward on his back and legs. He increased his effort and managed to stand, although his body twitched from side to side from the buffet of small unseen forces.

"Stop," Phoebe cried from across the pool. "Stop whatever you are doing. Somehow you are pulling me upward. I cannot move freely on my own."

Kestrel looked again at Phoebe and saw her more or less erect but hunched forward and grasping toward the ground with empty hands. He felt his own fingers suddenly start to wiggle. Then, when Phoebe flung her arm backward to clutch at the tree behind her, his own body followed in an almost perfect imitation. Kestrel frowned and released the tension in his legs. He collapsed to the ground and saw that Phoebe did the same in unison.

"Somehow we are bound together," he said in amazement. "There is great resistance when our motions do not imitate one another. What kind of strangeness is this?" He glanced quickly to his side. "Astron, wake up! Explain what is going on."

Kestrel saw the demon stir slightly and, out of the corner of his eye, Nimbia move as well.

"It is the realm of reticulates," Kestrel heard Nimbia say in an exhausted voice. "Prydwin considers it one of his two masterpieces, despite the eternal strife and

220

pain." She drew in a deep breath. "The effort to create is most exhausting. Give me a moment to regain my strength, and I will explain more."

Astron coughed and raised his head. Kestrel saw his nose wrinkle in puzzlement and then his dark eyes dart about the gray landscape. "Symmetries," he muttered, "like the hexagon of trees and the four of us at opposing vertices."

"Yes," Nimbia said. "This realm abounds in things that look the same under reflections, rotations, and other complex rearrangements. That is the way it was constructed. Actions that build symmetry are reinforced; those that break them are strongly retarded."

"Most interesting," Astron said. "I even have difficulty holding my mouth shut when I listen to you speak."

"You saw the battle before Prydwin shifted the view to this isolated node." Nimbia's voice rather than increasing in strength grew still more faint. "This realm is one of violence; we must be away."

"But the reason for our quest," Astron said. "It has not yet been completed."

Kestrel looked again at the unfamiliar desolation and felt a sense of strangeness and dread far more intense than what he had first experienced in the realm of the fey. "Let us heed Nimbia's words and begone before we encounter something we cannot handle."

"I have no answer to the riddle," Astron persisted. Struggling against Nimbia's resistance, he pulled himself to a sitting position. "As far as I can tell, the words of the high king about reality and bubbles have little to do with a flame in the realm of daemon. How can they save my prince from Gaspar's attacks?"

"Then tell it to the other, the one you call Palodad," Kestrel said. He pointed at the rucksack at this side. Phoebe's arm jerked in response. "Perhaps the one who reckons can analyze some hidden meaning, once you have paid him with the pollen."

"Palodad." Astron shuddered. He stopped speaking as membranes flicked over his eyes. "I had hoped to

221

seek out my prince directly," he said after a moment, "but your logic is correct. It is to the decrepit one that we must turn for aid and succor. Yes, Palodad first and then, with what he will hopefully add to the answer, search for the hiding place of my prince."

He looked across the oasis at Phoebe and Nimbia. "A fire, wizards," he said. "Break down the barrier between the realms and contact the one that we must."

"I do not have the strength." Nimbia rocked back and forth like a rag doll. "Certainly not the firmness of will that is needed. Let the human female try. She has been most eager to prove her worth."

Despite the difficulty in moving, Phoebe managed to smile. Fumbling with the pockets in her cape, she retrieved several matches but they tumbled out of her grasp onto the ground. She bent forward to pick them up but clutched only empty sand several handspans from where they fell.

For a moment Phoebe bent over awkwardly, deciding what to do next. "There is much resistance," she growled as she wrenched her head upward. "With what little kindling I have in my cape it is not such a small task as one might believe."

"It is the force of the symmetries," Nimbia said. "If you were broken free you could act alone."

Kestrel saw the demon look about the hexagon of trees and his nose wrinkle in thought.

"Yes, I believe it is the fact that we four are paired at opposite vertices," Astron said after a moment. "Kestrel, if you can move to another while Phoebe remains where she is, then the symmetry will be broken. All of us should then be free to act independently."

Kestrel quickly rose and turned toward the tree on his left but Phoebe's gasp of breath stopped him short. He looked in her direction and saw her body wrenched to the side, preparing to pace to the next vertex around the periphery just the same as he.

"No, not so fast," Astron said. "Relax your muscles and let Phoebe get situated first, perhaps with her arms wrapped about the tree. Nimbia can help her resist and then you can move away."

Kestrel breathed out slowly. He did not quite understand what Astron had in mind, but clearly they had to try something other than what first sprang to mind. As he let the tension out of his limbs, he felt insistent tugs that turned him back toward the tree. He let the forces wash over him and, without resisting, stepped up to the coarse bark. His arms rose from his sides and extended about the trunk. With a tight grip, his hands clasped together on the other side. Across the pond, he saw that Phoebe was also hugging her tree in the same relative position as he.

Then Astron rose and approached the trunk from the opposite direction. The demon's arms widened into a semicircle. On the other side of the oasis, Kestrel saw Nimbia extend her arms around Phoebe's tree and grasp her hands together behind the wizard's back. At the last possible moment, however, Astron brought his hands sharply downward. Rather then intertwining behind Kestrel, the demon's fingers dug into the bark at his sides.

"Now," Astron said. "Gently release your grip and step away. With Nimbia's help, Phoebe might be able to resist following."

Kestrel grunted in understanding and began to uncoil his fingers from one another. He felt the same strong resistance to his efforts and heard Phoebe gasp in exasperation as her hands also became unjoined. Kestrel stepped backward and saw Phoebe arch in response, her feet moving from the base of the tree while Nimbia struggled to hold her firm.

Kestrel took another step and then, more quickly, another. He felt as if he were walking upstream in a swift current. But each step was easier than the one before and finally, midway between the trees, the force vanished altogether; in complete freedom he turned and walked to the next vertex of the hexagon.

Kestrel saw Phoebe slide to the ground, oozing out of Nimbia's grip. Tentatively, the wizard waved her arm and then shook her entire body. The smile returned to her face for an instant, and then she sobered into a serious expression. Busily, she retrieved her scattered matches. Reaching into her cape, she brought forth some small twigs and parchment and built them into a small papered cone at her feet. She returned to the tree which Nimbia still clasped and ripped several sheets of loose bark away from the trunk.

Pulling her robe about her, Phoebe kneeled by her assemblage of materials and struck a match against one of the scraps of wood. The head of the match skittered against the rough surface but did not light. Phoebe cursed softly and tried with a second matchstick, this time bearing down harder and paying strict attention to what she was about.

Halfway through her swing, however, the match broke in two. Frowning, she gathered five of the sticks together in a tight grouping and tried again. Even from where Kestrel stood, he could see the force of her stroke. The grate of the yellow-tipped heads growled far out into the featureless expanse of the desert.

But again no sparks resulted from the swipe. Phoebe's scowl deepened. Moving quickly, she clasped the matches with both hands and ground the cluster a second time against the surface of the bark. Again nothing happened and she began stroking repeatedly, each time more intensely than before, hardly pausing between swipes and ignoring the splinters of matchwood that spewed away from where she worked. In an instant, they were all destroyed, with not even the tiniest glow to show for her effort.

Phoebe looked over at Kestrel, crestfallen. She kicked at her mound of kindling and sent it flying. "The wizards of my council," she said sourly. "They were right after all. When it came time to do my part, even make the simplest of flames, I choked like a doxy from the sagas." She reached for her cape and flung it to the ground. "Even with the mantle of the master, I must turn to another to get the simplest job done."

"My apologies but I am still too weak." Nimbia shook

her head. "The struggle at the tree took away whatever remaining reserves that I had." She looked slowly out into the desert, scanning the horizon. "It is your powers that we must use, wizard. Get us away before it is too late."

Kestrel looked up into the tree under which he stood and spied a cluster of pear-shaped fruits. "Perhaps we are proceeding a bit too hastily," he said. "We have just been through a great deal. Let us eat first. Then one of you can try again."

To Kestrel's surprise, Phoebe shook her head violently and then sagged to the ground. For a long moment, she stared at the splinters in her hand and did not try to speak. "I have failed us all," she said after the longest while, "failed us all and precisely when it was needed most. Evidently, my words in the chamber of the archimage were no more than bluster. I failed in my cabin with the anvilwood and now a second time here."

"It is not so serious, Phoebe, just the strangeness of this realm. With a bit of food—"

"Do you not understand?" Phoebe's voice strained with a hollow sharpness. She waved at the refuse strewn about her. "I cannot start a fire here, Kestrel. I know. I can feel it. Perhaps it is within the ability of one truly worthy of the logo, but I cannot, regardless of the kindling."

"Then later, after we have all had a chance to rest."

"You are not listening," Phoebe exploded. Frustration and anger shot from her eyes. She clasped her fists tightly and beat them against her arms. "It is not a matter of demon control," she said. "I did not even get that far. It is just as pompous Maspanar and the others chided. Experimentation with tiny imps in the confines of one's own cabin is one thing. The measure of a true wizard is quite another—that which is accomplished when the consequences of failure are more than the loss of a fee.

"Not a spark. Not even a single spark. It is not merely a matter of new surroundings. It goes far deeper than that. I can feel the inhibition. I am no wizard, not in this place, not anywhere in all of the realms." She stopped suddenly, then looked across the oasis at Kestrel. "I am sorry, sorry that I made you come."

Kestrel looked at Phoebe and saw her self-esteem begin to melt from her expression as he watched. It was her only real reason for the quest, he thought. She had wanted to prove herself the equal of the others above all else. He glanced at the litter of matchwood and shook his head. She alone would know the limits of her prowess. If she could not start a fire, what she said must be true. And now, despite the unknowns they were yet to face, even if he could protect her physically, what could he do to mend the way she suddenly had come to feel about herself?

Phoebe looked at Kestrel sadly. "There is more than my shame, Kestrel," she said. She lowered her eyes and sloped her shoulders, sighing deeply. "Without a flame, we cannot get passage to any other realm—to that of men, of the skyskirr, or even back to the fey. Unless Nimbia can be aroused, we are marooned here—marooned forever."

Kestrel pressed his hand against his stomach. Enough time had passed that he could be reasonably sure of no ill-effects from the fruit. Climbing the tree and tossing what he had picked across the oasis had been easy enough, although Nimbia ate little and seemed to doze in a deep lethargy when she was done.

Kestrel grimaced. The fruit had been sweet and tangy, but helped his mood little, if at all. He looked at Phoebe and frowned. Despite his most careful words, she refused to be consoled. In an almost mindless obsession, she had assembled specimens of every different type of material she could find in her proximity, blades of grass, a handful of sand, tree bark and fronds, even the skins of the fruit they had eaten. But using one of the water lenses from Astron's pack to focus the diffuse light, she had succeeded no better than with her first attempt. There was no hint of flame, not even the tiniest wisp of smoke.

And now, rather than lifting Phoebe's spirits, he felt the crushing reality of her words growing with each passing moment. The featureless plane that expanded to the horizon in all directions made the feeling of entrapment all the more intense. Perhaps there were great cities and enchanting delights just out of eyesight, but Kestrel thought it unlikely. The glimpse he had of this realm while still with the fey looked very much the same as what he saw now. Except for the presence of the fighting warriors, he recalled seeing only the same bleached straight-line paths radiating from a central point into the vast desert that was totally lacking in detail.

Kestrel kicked at the shiny metal protruding from the sand at his feet. He had not noticed at first, but at least three of the trees had some artifacts that appeared to have been hastily buried near their roots. The one where he sat was a filigree of wrought iron that terminated in a menacingly sharp point. No amount of simple tugging would free the ornate shaft from the ground. In front of where Nimbia dozed was what looked like the edge of a brass disk of substantial diameter, at least twice the height of a man. From the vacant node to Kestrel's left protruded a thin curved strip of steel that slowly oscillated in the gentle breeze.

But such things were properly only of interest to the demon, Kestrel thought. There were more important things about which to be concerned. He counted the fruit remaining in the branches of the trees and then the clear water of the pool. How long before they had eaten all that was here? he wondered. And if not great cities, would there be other oases like this one just beyond the horizon?

Kestrel stood to get a better view of a fruit cluster partially hidden by a branch. Suddenly he felt his left foot drag to the side and his entire body twist to follow. Phoebe gasped. He saw her reach suddenly to fling her arms around her tree, her legs sailing out nearly horizontal. In a flurry of sand and snapping capes, both Nimbia and Astron were tossed into heaps. Like tumbleweeds, they began to bounce out into the desert along one of the whitened paths.

"I surmise it is another symmetry," Astron shouted

backward as he tried to regain his balance. "Something acting on everyone and pulling us away."

Kestrel tried to turn and snatch the tree now at his back, but he was too late. The unseen force intensified. He was slammed earthward as if struck by a giant. He scrambled to his knees, but immediately was cast back into the ground a few feet farther from the pond. Kestrel spit out sand and clawed with his fingers, but he could tell that his efforts would be to no avail. He felt his body begin to drag across the coarse surface. The sand grated against his bare skin and then started to sting as his speed increased.

Faster and faster he flailed over the ground until even the wind whistled with his passage. A cloud of dust boiled up about him, forcing him to shut his eyes to keep out the bouncing grains of sand. The stinging on his forearms intensified from a mild irritation to a blistering pain. Kestrel raised his hands and arched his back to reduce his contact with the abrasive that surely would grind through his skin. With a gut-straining gasp, he managed to pull one leg forward under his chest and then savagely kick downward. He bounded from the desert floor and, in response to the reduction in friction, felt a rapid acceleration.

Kestrel fell back down earthward in a flat trajectory and then, like a stone hurled across a pond, skipped back into the air. This time his path straightened out parallel to the surface and he skimmed along in a straight line. As if he were a bead on an invisible wire, he hurled across the vast nothingness.

Kestrel cautiously opened one eye. When he saw that the cloud of dust had fallen away, he looked about. Phoebe and the others were also airborne on courses parallel to his own, all streaking across the plane above one of the white paths that had radiated from their oasis. He called out to Phoebe, but the whistle of the wind carried away his voice. He waved once and felt relieved when she shook her hand in reply.

Kestrel strained to look over his shoulder and saw that the oasis was already a mere speck in the distance.

As he watched, it disappeared into a haze. He turned back to squint in the direction they were travelling and detected a similar blur of detail on the horizon up ahead.

Kestrel watched the features sharpen as he approached. He recognized the tall trees and the white lines of other paths converging from different directions. He scanned their lengths as far as he could see, expecting the same emptiness on them all. But on the one that ran out across the plane to the right he noticed a hint of motion. Others were also coming to this oasis—warriors like the ones he had seen fighting within the ring of djinns.

As the two groups merged, Kestrel saw the shine of armor. He heard the clink of hard metal, even over the whistling wind. He fingered the pommel of the copper dagger from the realm of the fey, but took little comfort from it. The odds would be greater than five to one, even if Astron and the two women brandished arms as well.

Far more rapidly than Kestrel could think of what to do, he arrived at the new oasis. As abruptly as the forces had torn him from the other, they died away. He tumbled in a heap and offered only token resistance to the waning push that rolled him into the trunk of the nearest tree.

The warriors came to an abrupt halt at approximately the same time. With the precision of dismounting horse riders, they steadied themselves and remained erect. Kestrel grabbed his dagger, fearing the worst; but the warriors, after a brief inspection, paid him and the others little attention. With a few bellowed grunts that Kestrel thought he could almost understand, they quickly dispersed to each of the six trees that ringed the small pond in their center.

In an instant Kestrel was surrounded by a half-dozen tall and lean men with chalky complexions, only a few shades different from the paths that seemed to run from oasis to oasis. The first two began immediately to set up a small table from spars and hinged planks they carried on their backs, while a third uncoiled thick parchments crisscrossed with brilliant red and blue inks.

One of the men spoke and Astron immediately answered. Again Kestrel could make out most of what was being said.

"Since all of this is Prydwin's creation it is no wonder that we can converse," Astron explained. "It is merely a small change from the normal speech in the realm of the fey." The demon shrugged. "It is perhaps a detail on which Prydwin did not spend much effort."

"Your presence contributes to our freedom of movement," one of the warriors repeated, "and for that you have value. Though your appearance is different from either rotator or reflective, I do not suspect you of being chronoids, since your hands are empty of the foul artifacts they transport into our realm against the protocols."

"Share in our celebration of victory," another said. "The reflectives never suspected the richness of our symmetry until it was thrust upon them—no less than fourteen, and now they have been expulsed from every one. They did not have a chance for an exchange of bodies, not a one."

"From which did you come?" a third asked. "One of the lesser triangles of the central pentagram, or perhaps an octagonal node from the hypersphere of the great triad?"

Kestrel opened his mouth to speak but Astron was quicker. "What is the map?" the demon asked. "The lines in red and the nodes in blue with the crossed-out annotations—what do they mean?"

"It is the rendering of the great polytope, all that there is," answered the first. "See, already we make the changes that mark the victory." The warrior stopped and jabbed rapidly at the parchment. "It is all in accordance with the second protocol—all moves are simultaneous. We have occupied nodes here and here and then those over on the other side. They form the vertices of a figure with more than thirty edges. The reflectives were too concerned about this minor symmetry of three adjacent nodes here to notice what we had done.

"Look at the pattern closely, see how all thirty-seven form a beautiful pattern that is invariant if it is rotated through the small angle drawn over there." The warrior's face widened in a satisfied grin. "As the first protocol states—the greater the symmetry the greater the power. In perfect synchronization, those of us occupying the first node of the set began the journey to the second; those at the second unto the third. The reflectives who occupied part of the pattern were totally unprepared and the pressure to preserve symmetry was too much to resist. They were dragged from their fortifications into other nodes where yet more of us waited. We have won possession of more than a dozen."

Kestrel looked at the map where two of the warriors were busy erasing some sort of symbol by some of the nodes and replacing it with another. He glanced at Astron in confusion, but then relaxed when he saw that the demon had not wrinkled his nose.

"This map then is a reproduction of all that we see." Astron waved his arm outward toward the desert. "These oases are the nodes and the lattice lines the paths between them."

"It is a record of all the realm," added one of the warriors.

"And the symbol you are erasing—the nodes that are marked with it are under the control of the ones you call the reflectives." Astron stopped and studied the parchment for a moment. "You hold your territory most unlike the fashion of the realm of men," he said. "Look at how interspersed you are. How can you possibly say who has the greater advantage?"

"It is not a matter of adjacency, but of symmetry. Look at the beauty of the nodes that we possess. Of very high order are the subgroups that describe our lands."

"And that symmetry gives us power, power to strike at a dozen vertices as one, power to use the innate forces of the realm to aid us rather than fight against it in furthering of our aims."

"But why fight at all?" Astron asked. "What motivates you against these you call the reflectives?"

"Their symmetries are most foul," the first of the warriors spat. "They are invariant under reflection whereas ours remain the same when subjected to rotations instead. And as the fifth protocol states—victory is total, only one of two will be left. It is the duty of every rotator to resist reflectives wherever we can, to strive to eliminate them until none are left to poison the beauty of the true symmetries that we will build when they are gone."

"I don't understand any of this," Kestrel said. "It must be some sort of threadbare dream—scattered oases in a vast desert linked by geometrical designs, warriors engaged in mathematically obtuse campaigns. What of women and the crops that supplement these few fruits? Who weaves the clothes you wear on your backs and from where do the woolens come?"

"Most of your words make no sense whatsoever," the first warrior said. "Our lives are to fight the reflectives until either we receive mortal wounds or have totally won. The fruit of the trees provide us subsistence; our armor protects us from blows. Of these other things we have no need."

"But replacements," Kestrel persisted. "What happens when some of your number are indeed struck down?"

"Replacement?" the warrior echoed. "I do not comprehend. We fight the reflectives until one of us is victor. If some of my comrades fall, we recompute the symmetries for the numbers remaining, so that we have freedom of movement about the subnodes, as you see we have done here. There are no replacements. There never have been since the beginning of time."

Kestrel looked quickly about the oasis and noted that the warriors were deployed in what appeared to be a random fashion only at first glance. Closer examination revealed that the subgroups by each tree were different in many distinct ways from all the rest. Each had a different number, and the heights and weights were well distributed as well. The camp tasks they had undertaken were all unique and the identical weapons were stacked only where other differences outnumbered the similarities.

Kestrel glanced at Phoebe's almost vacant stare and Nimbia's listless shell hunched next to her. He looked back out onto the featureless desert. All that he could see was no more than the creation of one of the fey, he realized. It all had come into existence only by the force of thought—just like a scribe transcribing flights of fancy for the sagas, leaving out all nonessential detail. One could not really expect any more.

And they were marooned! The words boomed through his mind. Marooned in a universe in which all life apparently had to offer were the few simple rules of a game.

CHAPTER EIGHTEEN

Artifacts of the Chronoids

KESTREL looked across the new oasis at Phoebe and forced his face into a smile. He had lost track of the number of nodes to which they had been transported, but it would do her spirits no good to show how low his own had sunk. Far better it would be as well if they could share the same subnode, but the rotators, with their rigorously balanced deployments, insisted that they be kept apart.

Nimbia on occasion seemed a little more alert, but most of the time she still dozed in her stupor at the base of the tree to the right of Phoebe's. Although Astron was at Kestrel's side, the demon again was occupied with learning about some obscure detail of the realm. Kestrel was alone with his thoughts.

More than he feared, the life of a rotator was one of almost complete ritual. In a rigid sequence they would plan, eat, sleep, and then, simultaneously with everyone else in the realm, rush over the sands to a new node that looked almost exactly the same as the one they had left behind. Then, if the new node were unoccupied and there were no battle, the cycle would begin again. Plan, eat, sleep, move—they were merely playing pieces on a complex board, jockeying for position without ceasing.

Kestrel looked at the six fruit-bearing trees that ringed the small pond of water and then out over the featureless desert, trying to channel his thought in a more productive direction. He kicked at the sand at his feet, barely missing another shaft of ornately carved metal.

"Abel, what are these things?" he called out to the commander of the warriors. "Half of the oases we have visited seem to have them protruding from the ground."

One of the warriors looked up from where he had been conversing quietly with two others over the small portable table covered with the maps of the nodes. His complexion was slate gray like the rest, but streaks of black ran through his hair. His eyes were steady and unblinking in a face not creased by either smile or frown.

"They are the devices of the chronoids," Abel said with disgust in his voice, "the machines of beings of another realm—another realm just the same as yours. In our haste, we do not bury them as we might. They are a violation of the protocols."

"Another realm." Astron looked up from the scroll he had been studying intently. "We are not the only visitors you have seen?"

"Indeed not," Abel said. "Ever since the reflectives seized the origin, the visits have been most frequent. The chronoids look much as we do and they engage in some great struggle not so very different from our own. But their weapons are not similar in the least and they are difficult for us to understand."

"What kind of weapons?" Kestrel said, suddenly interested. "Something that would give you an advantage if you had them instead? Do they by chance involve the use of fire?"

"We would not use the devices of the chronoids." Abel pursed his lips. "The reflectives do so only at great peril, since they work so imperfectly in a realm different from which they were intended." The commander stopped and looked at Kestrel intently. "More importantly, they are not part of the tradition that stretches back to the memories of our creation. Only the reflectives would think of trying something so base to gain advantage."

"But where are—"

"Perhaps it is worth the effort to show you one of the foul things," Abel said. "Then you might better understand." He gestured to one of the other gray warriors. The second began to protest but Abel's stare cut short the words. The warrior spat at the ground at his feet and then began digging into the sand. Shortly he retrieved an oblong box of metal and brought it forward for the others to see.

"Why, it looks like a clock," Astron exclaimed as the object drew closer. "A device for measuring the passage of time. See the three ornate bands of metal pivoted at the center of the circular face with symbols about the rim."

"These devices do much more than merely count the swings of a pendulum," Abel said. "Just as our realm is governed by the symmetries of space, so is that of the chronoids ruled by the symmetries of time. With these clocks, as you call them, they manipulate the order of events in strange ways.

"Here, in the realm of the reticulates, the devices behave in manners even more bizarre. The manipulations of time are somehow transformed to ones of space instead. In battles where the reflectives possess them, I have seen entire moves undone against our wills, even though we held the advantage—whole squads of men exchanged with those of our enemy so that we were outnumbered, rather than the other way around."

"How did this clock come to be here?" Kestrel asked.

"Somehow the reflectives have found a way to communicate between the realms, exchanging men with the chronoids for weapons that aid their own cause. Recently the reflectives seem to have increased the frequency of their contacts. The artifacts are more and more abundant. Ten thousand moves ago, we would find them only at one node in a score; now we see them at virtually half."

"And the rotators choose not to use those clocks?" Astron asked.

"They disturb the protocols." Abel again puckered his lips. "Their very presence somehow has changed the third and fourth laws so that they no longer operate as they should. And in our realm, strange things happen with them that even the chronoids never intended. Who knows when they will affect the first, second, and fifth laws?"

Abel looked out over the sands and shuddered. "Besides the forced transport of bodies to other nodes, I have heard of things happening inside as well." He paused and seemed to chew on his tongue. "I cannot totally explain, but the transformations of the clocks in the realm of reticulates can change more than just the physical. No, despite any possible advantage, we prefer to bury what we find in the sands."

One of the warriors from another of the subnodes called to Abel. The commander abruptly turned away without another word and resumed his duties. The abruptness of the rotator did not bother Kestrel. He had come to realize that there was little need for courtesy in a realm such as this. But the information he had learned had been most interesting. Perhaps there was something in what Abel had said that would help them in their plight. Kestrel looked at Astron, trying to draw out the significance of what he had heard, but the demon was again fully occupied by the parchment in his lap.

Kestrel saw a flash of color at another of the subnodes and immediately his attention was drawn away. Something was happening that he had not seen before. A giant sling had been strung between two of the trees. While he watched, a roll of brilliant red cloth was launched in a high arc into the sky. Like a streaking comet, the material unfolded into an eye-catching arch that could be seen far over the horizon. After it had plummeted back to the ground, several of the warriors raced out onto the desert to retrieve the cloth and roll it back up into a coil.

Kestrel saw four of the warriors at one of the subnodes scanning the horizon, three looking out along paths that ran to adjacent nodes, and two others at angles in between. Almost as soon as the signal bolt was retrieved, Kestrel noticed a flash of motion down the line of sight that was farthest to the left. Another banner of red soared up into the sky in answer to the signal.

Then in a clockwise direction from the first, just barely above the horizon and far more distant, four more banners answered as well. All eyes turned to the rightmost path, the last of the six, but the sky remained calm; there was no arch of color sailing into the sky.

A sudden babble of excitement erupted from the rotators. Even though they had not yet eaten, shield straps were tightened and a dozen or more began practicing stylized jumps and feints with their swords.

"What is happening?" Kestrel asked Astron.

The demon stopped tracing his finger across a copy of the node network and listened to the rush of voices that Kestrel could not quite follow.

"The prospect for battle is high." Astron looked up from the map. "Imagine that this node is one vertex of a hexagon, just like one of the fruit trees around the oasis. The rotators also occupy the one on the left and then, on the far side of the center, three more as well." The demon pointed down the path to the right. "A contingent of reflectives just vacated this node before we arrived; they must be one adjacent move away, most probably at the last node of the six."

"So the warriors here arm for a fight against an enemy they have not even seen," Kestrel said. "The node on the right may be occupied by twice as many—or they might run before the battle can be engaged."

"That is not the way it is done in the realm of reticulates," Astron said. "After some study, I think I understand better how the moves are made." The demon stabbed at the map. "The rotators occupy five of the six

237

vertices of a hexagon; simultaneously they will all move to the node at the very center of them all. The forces of symmetry will be enormous; the reflectives at the sixth node will be drawn in as well. They will be unable to resist. And with the warriors from five nodes against those of one, the outcome of the battle should be quite favorable."

Kestrel studied the parchment on Astron's lap with the cryptic squiggles, trying to make sense of what the demon was saying.

"Besides," Astron continued, "it is a good move for us as well. It is in the right direction."

"What do you mean?" Kestrel brought his attention back to the demon.

"It places us one vertex closer to the origin," the demon said. "Look, I have been studying these maps and identified this one point as the center of all the others. All the symmetries pivot about it. Just like the center of the hexagon to which we will be moving, there is one vertex that is the origin of the entire realm."

Kestrel shook his head. He still did not understand.

"The origin is least bound by the forces of symmetries," Astron continued. "There is no other node which must have the same activities in order for things to balance. There the unusual is more likely to occur. It is the one node where we have some hope—some hope of performing wizardry and building a fire."

Kestrel felt his spirits lift. "Yes," he exclaimed, "you just might be right. How else could the reflectives communicate with the chronoids if not through the flame. And Abel said that since they have captured the origin, the contacts have become more intense." He looked at Astron's map with far keener interest.

"After the battle, we will press on to this origin?" Kestrel asked.

"Not necessarily. If the reflectives do not see such moves as part of their overall plan, they will travel elsewhere, and it will be difficult for us to resist being carried along."

"Then they will need a little convincing." Kestrel

238

smiled and rubbed his hands together. His thoughts began to jump as he looked back to Abel with calculating eyes.

"What about a trap?" he asked. "Now that I think of it, this move to the center of the hexagon seems very obvious. Suppose it is part of some greater symmetry that is being planned by the reflectives."

"I had not thought of that," Astron exclaimed. The demon looked at Kestrel and wrinkled his nose. "Another example of the kind of thinking you were talking about as we returned from the glen of the harebell, I suppose. But yes, if I can understand the strategy of the move with such little exposure, how subtle indeed can it be? Why would the reflectives move to the node that completes the hexagon, rather than choose another oasis that does not impress symmetry so strongly upon them?"

Kestrel did not bother to hear the rest of what Astron said. He sprang to his feet and walked to the subnode that was occupied by the commander. Fortunately the rotators had so carefully distributed everyone about the oasis that the resistance of maintaining symmetry could almost totally be ignored.

"Commander," he said, "how cunning have the reflectives proven to be in the past?"

Abel looked up from the map he was studying and pursed his lips. "The reflectives do not act with cunning. If they did, I would grant them a small token of respect. Instead, they employ any methods to enforce advantage —poisoning oases just as they leave or imitating our signal flares with messages of deception."

"And you?" Kestrel smiled. "The rotators do not engage in such tactics when the alternative would be a defeat?"

"Certainly not." Abel glowered. "It is the fundamental difference between the two of us. We wish to rid this realm of the reflectives, it is true; but for the rotators, the end does not justify all means."

Kestrel looked to the horizon and rubbed his chin. "Suppose I can provide you a method that will result in substantial advantage," he said, "something that might tip the struggle permanently in your favor."

"I do not know the customs of your realm," Abel said. "What you judge to be of no consequence might be totally out of concert with what we rotators believe."

"It is more a a matter of cunning than the poisoning of wells," Kestrel said.

"Speak and I shall judge," Abel said. "If what you say has merit, then I will pledge my token to your command and all of those who can be communicated with by sky-ribbon as well."

Kestrel looked into the cold gray eyes and hesitated. Among men, he had seen such an expression only in the most steadfast of wizards. "I do not seek your command," he said quickly. "I propose only to offer advice. If it is accepted, then the results will be compensation enough for those who travel with me."

"I command or I do not," Abel said. "If your plan is accepted, then you carry the burden of responsibility of our lives. That has been the way of the rotators since the beginning of time."

Kestrel looked around the oasis uncomfortably. Enough of the stone-gray warriors at other subnodes had overheard the conversation that they were looking at him intently. His goal was to get Phoebe away from another realm as well. He glanced out over the sands and felt a return of the feeling that had pulled at him until just moments before. There was no other choice. He would have to see through Astron's idea and work out the consequences later.

"I think that rather than moving to the center of the hexagon that we now occupy," Kestrel said at last, "we should strike for the origin of the realm by another route. The present maneuver is too obvious; it is most likely a trap. What do you say to surrendering responsibility if such were my first command?"

"Your scheme is one of correct moves and nothing more?" Abel asked. "No special weapons or tricks outside the custom?"

"No, none of that," Kestrel said. "But that is not the point."

240

"That is the point entirely," Abel said. "A scheme with honor is all that I ask. Sketch for me on the map the moves you propose. If they show greater merit than the plan for the moment, then we are yours to lead."

Kestrel stared back at the cold unblinking eyes and frowned. He looked for some hint of reservation in Abel's expression, some indication that the gray warrior was merely agreeing until he revealed more of what he had in mind. But the face was void of veiled tension. The commander appeared quite willing to hand everything over to Kestrel, provided that it aided in the cause of the rotators. The gray warrior took his words totally at face value and trusted him in what he said.

Kestrel's sense of discomfort grew. This was totally unlike his dealings in the realm of men. There, he always sought to find the hidden failings, the weakness that he exploited to consummate the deal. And when he was done, his conscience was not bothered; an honest man would not have been tempted by what he had to offer in the first place; in the end, just desserts were served. But this time he had no real reason, other than his own, to move in the direction of the origin. It was an out-and-out swindle, with lives at stake, besides.

"No, forget it," Kestrel said. "Your plan is perhaps best after all. Proceed to seize the center node of the hexagon. The demon says that it moves us closer to the origin as well."

"Your words cannot be so easily put aside," Abel said. "The origin has been a matter of some concern since it was seized by the reflectives some three hundred moves ago." The warrior touched the sword pommel at his side. "If you indeed have a scheme of merit, you must tell us your plan so that we can judge."

Kestrel hesitated, but Abel did not waver. With a slow deliberateness, the warrior began to withdraw his sword. Kestrel glanced at Astron waiting expectantly and over at Phoebe staring vacantly into space. He quickly pointed at the map.

"It is merely a conjecture," he said, trying to buy time with his words. "See, here is the node at the center of

241

the hexagon. And here are the five vertices occupied by your own men. The sixth here you suspect to be possessed by the reflectives, and by converging simultaneously you hope to draw them in with you."

"That is apparent to all," Abel growled. "What is your plan that has superior merit?" Several other warriors stopped whatever they were doing and drew closer to hear Kestrel's words.

"Apparent to all—as you state, that is exactly what I wish to emphasize," Kestrel said. His eyes raced over the map for an idea. "But what about—what about the ring of vertices that surround even these six, the ones that lie even farther from the center of the hexagon? Yes, that is it. When you perform your maneuver, all six of the corners of the hexagon will be vacated; if the reflectives possess all of the nodes further out, they can move in to this one and the other five totally unchallenged. You will be surrounded and outnumbered at least two to one. The reflectives might sacrifice one unit the size of yours, but the rotators will eventually lose five in return."

A murmur of surprise erupted from the warriors who were listening. Quickly they passed on what had been said to the others. Kestrel was not quite sure where his thoughts were taking him, but at least Abel's sword arm had relaxed.

"A sacrifice of one to gain five." Abel looked at the map and back to Kestrel with respect. "I would not have thought of it, nor would any other of our side. It would be just like the reflectives, though; shedding some of their own blood, so long as it produced a greater gain." He paused and puckered his lips. "Your logic has great force. What, then, is the alternative?"

"It is only conjecture," Kestrel repeated, "a thought experiment about what might be the reflectives' intent. I have no proof that it is so."

"But as you said, the convergence to the center of the hexagon is so obvious. It is rare that the reflectives would let themselves be maneuvered into such a state.

After all, they have been struggling for as long as we. Tell us the rest and then you can lead."

Kestrel frowned. Moving away from the center of the hexagon rather than toward it probably would be no worse than what Abel had originally planned. Perhaps the next node in fact would be totally unoccupied and no harm would be done. And they, in fact, would be closer to the origin. He pointed out over the horizon.

"There," he said. "We should move to that node and the other five units should move outward as well. If we encounter any of the reflectives, then the ratio will be no worse than one to one."

Abel squinted out over the desert and then nodded. He turned back to Kestrel and unclasped his sword belt. "The plan has merit," he said. "Assume the command. We will do as you say."

Kestrel looked one final time into Abel's unwavering eyes. He waited for some tiny twinge or movement, but saw none. "Signal the others," he said in a resigned voice. It was not exactly what he had had in mind. "Inform them of the plan so that there is no loss of life through misunderstanding. I will do as you say." Reluctantly he took the offered belt and put it around his waist. If felt far heavier than it should.

CHAPTER NINETEEN

Spatial Transformations

KESTREL watched impatiently as the last of the fruit was squeezed into the bowl. It was too tart to be drunk undiluted, as he knew from his first experimentation, but the elaborate method of mixing by the rotators seemed to serve no real purpose. He looked out over the unchanging desert and shrugged. They could do nothing, of course, until the time of the next move. Perhaps the purpose of the empty rituals was no more than to keep everyone occupied.

Kestrel saw Abel carefully decant oasis water into the bowl on top of the thick juice. The liquid ran down the side without mixing and formed a crystal-clear layer on top of the opaque orange sludge on which it rode. Besides the former commander, two other warriors flailed at the wrung-out pap on large flat stones, pressing it into a thin layer of sticky paste. Before the next move, the gentle breezes would have dried the pulp into a fine orange powder that was carefully packed away against the contingency of arriving at a node with nothing fresh to eat.

When the last of the water had been added, Abel opened a spout near the bottom of the bowl and let the juice slowly flow out to fill a large spoon. Then, with a practiced deftness, the rotator stopped the flow, raised the spoon back over the top edge of the bowl, plunged it into the water layer, and stirred it vigorously about. The juice sprayed into a shower of the fine droplets that quickly added a hint of orange to the transparent crispness of the water, but somehow did not disturb the darker opaqueness that rested beneath.

Using the same spoon with a hinged cover over the top, Abel next extracted some of the water and plunged it into the denser juice. He manipulated a lever that released the spoon's contents and again swirled it about, slightly lightening the deep color in the process.

Kestrel yawned, partially from the tension of waiting, but also because he had seen the ritual more than a dozen times. Abel returned the spoon to the spout near the bottom of the bowl, collected some of the lower liquid, and mixed it with the top. Again he extracted some of the result and swirled it with the bottom. With each transfer the water became more and more cloudy, the juice more and more fluid and transparent, and the horizontal line marking the boundary between the two harder and harder to detect.

Finally, after perhaps a score of transfers, the boundary line began to buckle and writhe. Fingers of liquid started to intertwine and merge. In an indefinable instant, the two liquids coalesced into one with no distinction between them. Abel grunted in satisfaction, and the warriors began lining up with their cups and gourds.

Soon everyone had their fill of juice and wind-dried bread. In a rigorous sequence, the warriors began nodding off to sleep, assuming a variety of positions, some leaning against the trees, while others curled up into tight little balls near the roots.

Kestrel watched the eyes of the last one close and then smiled across the pond at Phoebe. Now that he was commander, he should at least be able to move about as he decided, especially since Abel now dozed with the rest. He had to try again to break Phoebe out of the depression that seemed to grow with each passing moment. And, he admitted as well, the softness of her touch was something that he was beginning to miss more and more.

Kestrel glanced at Astron and saw the demon stirring the contents of one of the flour tins with his little finger. The demon wrinkled his nose as a tiny cyclone of tiny orange particles swirled up into the air. Two subnodes around the oasis from Kestrel, Nimbia sat and stretched. Finally she looked as if she were recovering from her effort of creation. It appeared that neither of them would need his attention.

With a grin of anticipation, Kestrel started to walk toward Phoebe's subnode, but then halted. Abel always seemed to sense when the next move was about to begin, he thought suddenly. The commander would shout the call to order and begin assembling the warriors in flying formation with just precisely sufficient time to start moving when the tug of the second protocol hit the oasis.

Kestrel slapped the pommel of the heavy sword. It would not do if everyone staggered awake in disarray while he was in mid-dalliance with Phoebe, despite her need for cheering. He scowled at the direction his thoughts were taking him. Such concerns were madness. What difference did it make what Abel and the others judged of his actions? They were no more than creatures of imagination. He had no real allegiance to them. They were merely the means to the end of achieving deliverance.

He ran his fingers over the smooth grooves which spiraled up the hilt of the sword. It was heavy, true, but even in the short time he had worn it, despite the undercurrent of the entrapment, there was a degree of excitement as well—something he had not felt since before he first met Evelyn. All the warriors now nodded to him with that subtle hint of respect that only Abel had received before. He was now more than just another body that broke the symmetry of the node; he was the commander in whom they trusted the course of the next move.

Kestrel looked out over the desert and sighed. His emotions began to churn in a sudden tumble. Creatures of imagination or not, they deserved better than he. There was no deceit in Abel's eyes or in any of the others' that followed him—only trust in the one who wore the sword.

Kestrel stepped back to the tree and folded his arms across his chest as he had seen Abel do at least a dozen times before. Slowly he began counting in his head, ticking off the featureless time as best he was able. After twenty thousand counts, he decided, then I will sound the alert.

Kestrel bobbed and weaved in the whistling wind. The time to the next move had passed quickly enough, and he had got the troop off in fairly decent order. Strong eddies created by the rucksack on his back rocked him about. Unlike the rotators, he was unable to keep a completely smooth trajectory over the expanse of sand. But the grace of his motion was not Kestrel's primary concern. Far sooner than he wished, the distance to the next oasis, the one that Astron said put them a step closer to the origin, was melting away.

As he squinted into the haze, he saw the tops of the ring of trees appear over the horizon and then the lower trunks. He held his breath, hoping that his wish for an unoccupied oasis would be realized, but soon he saw it was not to be. Shadowy forms of many men loomed into detail. If they were rotators, surely Abel and the others would have known. He saw the glint of arms and, at the edge of the water, a towering construction of dull metal that emitted loud clicks radiating out across the sands.

"Is there any particular formation that you use when approaching a hostile oasis?" Kestrel called out to Abel on his left. He patted the thick copper blade at his side, but received little reassurance from it. It looked as if they would be slightly outnumbered and had little hope for surprise.

"It depends on how they are deployed about the subnodes," Abel called back. "If they are evenly distributed, the force of symmetry will deposit us in a similar fashion. If they have most of their men at one of the trees, then the fewest of ours will have to face them. The bulk of our own will land at a subnode across the oasis from them."

"What is the machine by the water?" Kestrel asked.

"Something exchanged with the chronoids, you can be sure," Abel said. "I have seen nothing of that size in any of the moves that I can remember. Be on your guard; the dance of combat might be tricky the first time you engage."

Kestrel started to say more, but thought better of it. Concentrating on exactly where he would land and whom he immediately would be facing was far better than idle chatter. He glanced at Phoebe, sailing along behind him and slightly to the right. He did not like the possibility of her being separated and sent off to another of the subnodes, but there was nothing he could do about it. Astron and Nimbia would have to take care of themselves as best they could.

As they drew even closer, the details of the oasis began to crispen in the hazy sky. A lookout on top of one of the trees shouted an alarm. With a flurry of activity, the warriors at ground level started adjusting their weapons. From the distance, they looked no different from the rotators, having pale gray complexions, leather vests, leggings and boots, and blades of orange-copper at their waists.

Kestrel saw two of the reflectives run to the machine and begin straining against a large key thrust into one of its sides. From their angle of flight, Kestrel's group could see around the corner of the plate of metal into the unshielded innards of the device. Giant cogwheels with the height of a man meshed with teeth the size of interleaved fists. A

247

loosely coiled escapement banged against a long ratchet that ran the full length of the cage. Axles squeaked and gears whirled as the key brought the mechanism to life.

Kestrel did not have time to observe more. With a final whoosh, he swerved to the right as he approached. His teeth clanged with the contact with the ground. For a moment, his vision blurred from the shock.

Kestrel shook his head and reached for his blade, finding a sudden resistance to the motion of his arm. He looked quickly about and saw one of Abel's lieutenants at his side and two of the reflectives facing him an arm's length away.

He strained again for his blade, but the resistance was greater than before. One of the reflectives laughed, and the other eyed him with a satisfied grin. Kestrel looked again at the lieutenant, then back to the reflectives. With the skill of a synchronized ballet, the two warriors facing them reached in unison for their swords, and the rotator copied their motion, flowing with it, rather than trying to resist. Kestrel pushed toward the scabbard a final time, but to no avail. He had not noticed it before, but of all those who fought, he was the only one who was right-handed.

With an awkward thrust he twisted his left arm down his side, fumbling to draw his sword and pushing away the thought of the hopelessness of what he was doing. To his surprise, it did not fall from his grip as he pulled it free, but soared to a guard position in front of his body, just like the others.

The warriors yelled and swung viciously downward. Kestrel felt his arm follow through with the rest. With a grating shriek the blades slipped past one another and crashed point-first into the ground. Then as one, all four of the combatants lifted the swords and lunged forward, turning bodies to the side to avoid the duplicated thrusts by their opponents.

The motions were not totally precise copies, however. Straining as best he could, Kestrel was able to twist his blade horizontal as he drew it back. Trembling from the resistance, he turned a cutting edge slightly to the side and sliced into the leather vest of the reflective as the warrior drew back.

Kestrel darted a glance to the lieutenant and saw a trickle of blood on his right arm. Quickly he understood how the battle was waged. The forces of symmetry compelled all of the lunges to be nearly the same. The strikes were aimed to be near-misses, rather than vital thrusts. And then the extra straining effort or slightly longer reach would do the real damage while avoiding a similar wound in return. Kestrel grimaced. He gripped the pommel more tightly, but the strangeness did not go away. If anyone would be at a disadvantage, it would be he.

The four closed again, this time with backhand swipes across the body that stopped just short of the neck. Kestrel strained to push his blade forward while tipping his own head to the side. He felt his arm quiver but proceed no further, while his opponent shook his own blade back and forth in tiny arcs, trying to break it free to strike a finger-width more.

Kestrel took a deep breath and gritted his teeth. Tightening the muscles the length of his arm and twisting his torso, he slowly increased the pressure, realizing that, if all four pushed too hard simultaneously, they would all suffer the same. He saw his blade cover half the distance to the bulging artery of the reflective and then sucked in his breath as a prickly line of pain caressed his own skin. Almost instinctively, he halted his plunge and reversed direction, but the pressure did not release. The grin on his opponent's face broadened. He was trapped immobile and could not move.

Suddenly the huge clockworks at the water's edge sounded in a deep resonant gong. Kestrel heard a cry of surprise. Out of the corner of his eye, he saw a flurry of motion at the next subnode in line. The clock struck a second time. In a blur, his sword spun from his hand high into the air. Simultaneously he felt the pressure release from his neck.

Kestrel craned his head upward to see his sword and three others arch in a complex swirl and then fall back toward the earth. Spinning with precision, the pommel of one fell back into his grip, just as the first had left it. With a scrape of skin, the pressure returned to the side of his neck. The four swords had been interchanged.

The clock sounded again, and the lieutenant choked out a startled cry. Kestrel saw his thin face contort in puzzlement and then dissolve into one of the reflective's grins. Other cries sounded from all around the node, and then Kestrel felt the pressure on his neck suddenly release. He looked into the face of the warrior across from him and blinked at the sudden change. The smile was gone and the round cheeks somehow thinned into the gaunt expression of the lieutenant. At the edge of his vision, he saw the two remaining warriors in unison disengage from one another and turn to strike Kestrel and the one he now faced from the side.

Kestrel fumbled to turn and meet the new threat. Somehow, his adversary had been switched. The one who faced him fought on the same side. It was just as Abel had tried to explain. The striking of the clock mixed up things spatially in strange ways—even the inner beings between the rotators and reflectives were being transformed!

Kestrel struggled to rotate clockwise. But as he did, the warrior who faced him strained to move in the opposite direction. For what seemed like an eternity, they fought against one another, while the two reflectives smoothly pirouetted and prepared to strike.

On the third gong of the clock, Kestrel heard more cries from around the oasis. First one and then two other rotators suddenly were catapulted into the air. Their bodies were wrenched into unnatural trajectories and hurled toward the horizon with breathtaking force. Almost instantly, reflectives sailed into view and landed in the spots vacated by their foes. At several of the subnodes, the ratio of fighters was shifted to a definite disadvantage for the rotators. Through the tumult of battle, Kestrel saw Astron near the clock key, standing frozen with a blade woodenly in front, not able to fend off thrusts that were being aimed at the demon from both left and right.

The clock sounded again. This time Kestrel recognized Phoebe's shriek intermingled with the rest. He looked skyward and saw her and three reflectives from her subnode rise into the air and then vanish like the rest. Kestrel pushed against the lieutenant straining in the reflective's body and looked hastily back at the sword now being drawn back to strike at his midsection. For an instant, he hesitated, uncertain whether to stop the resistance or to assist the lieutenant's efforts instead, whirling back clockwise, hoping to rotate completely and meet the attack after a full circle.

Before Kestrel could decide, he heard the clock strike a note deeper than before. A sudden blur of nausea welled up within him. The scene before his eyes shimmered and then turned to a blurry gray. He felt a wrenching disorientation and then a sudden rush of heat as if he had a great fever. His body seemed suddenly strange and he staggered and almost fell; the resistance to his motion had been suddenly changed.

The blur dissolved. Kestrel blinked at what he saw. No longer was he at a subnode with three other warriors but near the clock itself. Reflectives on either side were drawing their swords, arms back across their bodies, preparing for deep thrusts toward his chest. He held his own sword pointed directly out in front, unable to move to one side or the other. He saw a net of tiny scales on the back of his hand and running up his forearm into his sleeve. Somehow he was conscious of a stubble of minute bristly hairs in the web of his fingers and between his toes.

Kestrel looked back across the node and saw what looked like his image still locked in synchrony with the lieutenant trying to ward off the attack coming from the side.

It could not be possible! Kestrel tried to deny the thought, but the feeling of all of his senses could not be denied.

"Astron," he called across the sand. "Somehow we have been transposed like the others. Do not fight the lieutenant. Turn clockwise with him and swing totally about."

But he need not have bothered. With the final gong of the clock, Kestrel saw his body vault up into the air and then streak away like the ones before. Grimly he forced his attention back to how he was going to ward off the two reflectives with a sword that was frozen in position in his alien left hand.

CHAPTER TWENTY

Demonlust

ASTRON cautiously felt the sand under the strange fingertips. First there had been the blurring and transformation so unlike a journey between the realms. And then the flight away from the fighting to this deserted node. He must still his stembrain before he could think further.

Astron tried to flip down his membranes and then frowned in annoyance when they would not come. He shut his eyes and tried to ignore the unsatisfying blackness. Mentally, he reached for the panic that should be upwelling and concentrated on making it still.

His eyes blinked open. He looked about, surprised. There was no panic, no rumble of the base of his skull. He felt an internal discomfort from the flight and jarring landing, and his heart seemed to throb for no apparent reason, but otherwise he was in complete control of his thoughts.

Astron looked about puzzled. He saw Phoebe stagger to standing at the subnode to the left but noticed no other occupants of the oasis. Dimly, he remembered a reflective passing him halfway in his flight, going the other way. He released the sword he still held in his left hand and absently watched it fall at his side. His nose wrinkled as he saw small curly hairs on the back of his hand and arm, providing a wiry cover to a pale, smooth skin.

Kestrel, he thought. What had the human shouted about the transpositions that the reflectives were effecting with the huge clock of the chronoids? He held both arms up and then touched the smoothness of his forehead. He ran a finger over the more or less even row of teeth in his mouth and, reaching to his back, felt no knobs where the degenerate wing stubs should have been.

He breathed deeply and marveled at the feeling of the air coursing in and out of his lungs. A growl sounded in his stomach and a pleasant longing teased at his mind. Unbidden images of meat sizzling on a spit and the smell of fresh bread flitted, real and compelling.

"Oh, Kestrel, thank the random factors that you are here," Phoebe shouted as she ran to his subnode. "The blood and fighting with all that overpowering restraint was far worse than the alchemist's foundry. We are lucky to have survived."

He was not Kestrel, Astron thought. Words of denial started to form in his throat but his tongue felt strange and he only managed a cough instead.

"What is it?" Phoebe asked as she held wide her arms and stepped forward, beckoning.

Astron motioned for her to stop and took a cautious step backward.

"What is it?" Phoebe repeated. "Tell me everything is all right. I can stand no more chaos and surprise."

Astron looked at the tension etched deeply in Phoebe's face. The events had been unsettling, perhaps more so to a human than to one of his own kind. Whatever was decided upon to do next, he would certainly need her aid. And he knew from struggles through the flame in eons past how fragile was the will to survive. It was perhaps best to explain all that had happened at a better time. He wrinkled his nose and then slowly began to speak. The tenor of the first words startled him, but he held all the tiny muscles that were alive in his face rigidly taut.

"Do not be concerned." He measured his words carefully. "For the moment, we are safe. Take a minute to bring your stembr—your feelings under control and then we can proceed."

"But we are separated from the others. What are we to do?"

"To the origin," Astron said quickly. His thoughts

seemed to rush forward without the benefit of deliberation. "There is no change in our intent. There you will summon a demon to get us home."

Phoebe pulled a folded map from a pocket in her gown and began to open it, but then shrugged. "It is kind that you still show faith in my ability, Kestrel," she said softly with eyes lowered, "but in truth, the reality of my abilities has become clearer with each passing moment. Reaching the origin may be all well and good; but without Nimbia fully recovered, there is little point for such a journey." She looked out over the sands back in the direction from which they had come. "And how can we proceed the way we want when these forces of symmetry flip us from node to node? Without Astron, how do we stand a chance? He seemed to have a knack for figuring out these mathematical things."

"Yes, the devil," Astron said grimly. He shook his head to keep his thoughts straight. "Once a djinn is under your command, you can task him to soar over this desert until he finds the others. But if the demon were here, the first thing he would do is—" Astron stopped and for the first time looked critically about the oasis.

It was very much like all the rest, a quiet circular pool of water surrounded by six trees at the vertices of a hexagon. Strewn all about, however, was the debris left by the reflectives who had occupied it before the battle and the transformations. At the adjacent subnode on the left stood a pile of branches hacked from the treetops to make soft beds. Denuded branches and an axe were tossed in a heap nearby. At the next subnode around the periphery was one of the devices of the chronoids in obvious disrepair. Stacks of gears, springs, and ticking escapements were scattered about a nearly empty framework. Directly across the pond, three or four thick leather vests stood in a heap next to a pile of eyelets, buckles, and sewing thongs. Two nicked and rusting swords rested against the tree behind. A ring of stones outlined the cooking pit at the subnode adjacent to the armory and the remains of parchment maps gently stirred at the fifth. Just like the rotators, the reflectives carefully organized their camps so as to maximize their freedom from the compelling forces of symmetry.

"From the looks of things this node served as a camp for perhaps a dozen," Phoebe said.

"And yet when the battle began, evidently it was occupied only by two," Astron replied. "Otherwise now you and I would not be the only occupants." He waved his arm out over the bleached sands. "The rest must have dispersed to yet other nodes and then converged back to where the rotators attacked. Perhaps it had something to do with the working of the devices of the chronoids."

He looked over the disarray a second time. "One thing is for sure. There is more than enough here to break up the symmetries between the subnodes for the two of us. We can move about with comparative ease."

Astron's voice trailed off. The glimmer of an idea popped into his mind. Slowly he paced off the two longest and straightest tree branches and dragged them around the periphery to the dismantled device of the chronoids. There he rummaged through the stacks of debris until he found six gear wheels of approximately the same size.

"What are you doing?" Phoebe called out.

Astron ignored the question. "Go across to the armory and start cutting the vests into leather strips. We will concern ourselves about your abilities later. For now, let us get this thing built before some part of my mind is able to convince me otherwise."

Astron unbuckled the harness from his chest with a deep sigh. His muscles ached. What had been the pleasant longing in his stomach had turned into an insistent discomfort. He looked over his shoulder in the dimming daylight and saw Phoebe unfastening the half-dozen belts that held her to the long wooden frame. She had not complained during the entire trek, and surely the strains on her body must have been the same as his.

"Go and gather some fruits." He waved at the node that was before them. "I will pull the engine the rest of the way."

Astron looked at the deserted node and then back at the horizon the way they had came. The node that he and Phoebe had been transported to was well out of sight. Even though a good portion of the time had been consumed in constructing the bizarre apparatus that fettered them, they still had managed to walk from one node to another. After a rest, they might be able to manage two moves, rather than one.

Astron ducked under the branch on his left and smiled at his handiwork. The felled tree branches had been bound by leather straps to form the irregular framework of a long box. If stood on end, it would tower three times the height of a mundane djinn. At front and rear, a row of gears from the device of the chronoids formed a framework for the smaller branches jammed between their teeth. Like giant rolling pins, they spread the weight across the sand and allowed Phoebe and him to push the contraption along the bleached path from one node to the next. Sometimes, with a burst of energy, they were able to sprint forward against their harnesses and then raise their feet and coast for a few moments before friction brought them to a halt.

Far more important than the practicalities, however, were the other additions to the craft. Five more gear wheels of odd sizes were hung along the sides at haphazard positions. Here and there, small clusters of greenery sprouted at odd angles. The rusted swords all pointed skyward from three of the four top corners and the cooking pots swung from the cross struts. Even though it gave them some difficulty in steering, the harnesses which bound them to the frame were offset from one another. Astron was near the center of the very front while Phoebe was halfway to the rear and nearly touching the left side.

At first Phoebe had protested adding all the extra weight and the number of belts that she had to wrap around her waist. But when the first tug of the symmetries had come and passed over them with barely a ripple she understood the intent. They were not two single individuals but coupled together as one. Their engine was in all probability unlike anything else in the realm. Totally unique, there was no increase in symmetry in moving it to a particular node or switching it with anything else. They could move between nodes as they chose without constraints or regard to the actions of others.

"There is ripe fruit enough that we can provision for several moves," Phoebe said as she returned to the engine. She untied several of the canisters still gently swinging from the frame and beckoned Astron to the subnode where she had laid out a cloth.

Astron finished pulling the engine to the water's edge and then sat down across from the meal that Phoebe had prepared. With a dedicated savagery that surprised himself, he began to gobble down the slices almost as fast as Phoebe could prepare them, hardly bothering to sprinkle on the flours from the canisters that balanced the meal. Only dimly was he aware of the cool pleasure of the juices that dripped over his hands or the tartness that tingled in his mouth.

When he was finally done, he leaned backward with a feeling of contentment totally unlike anything he had experienced before. He shook his head in wonder. The sensations were quite pleasurable ones, but such a weakness it must be for humans. Without food and drink, their thoughts would soon be driven to distraction; they would abandon all reason, just as if their minds were seized by the most powerful of stembrains. And unlike his own kind, there would be no hope for remaining in control.

Astron looked at Phoebe through half-closed eyes. There was much risk in this quest for his prince and yet much reward as well. He had learned things that no other cataloguer could have even suspected. Even Palodad probably had no notion of the concept of hunger or of how it truly tugged at one's will.

Phoebe smiled back at Astron and swept the remains of their meal aside. Deftly, she closed the distance between them and put her hand up to touch Astron's cheek. "I wonder about the others, Kestrel," she said, "but there is some advantage for the events as they have happened. For the first time in a very long while, we are alone."

Phoebe slid her hand behind Astron's neck and put

her lips to his. Astron choked in a moment of confusion but words would not come. He found his arms reaching around Phoebe and pulling her even closer to him. As he did, he felt a strange new feeling course through his body. He sucked in his breath at the intensity of it.

He was keenly aware of the softness of her back under the palms of his hands, even though her jerkin was in between. The press of her body tightened everywhere it touched. Without thinking, he maneuvered so that the pleasure of it would be greater. Astron felt his pulse quicken and his breath grow more shallow.

Desire swirled through his thoughts until only the tiniest ember of rationality remained. This was not like the duty for the broodmothers in any way at all. No cataloguer had dreamed of its potency, of that he was quite sure.

"You know that it does not matter," Phoebe said softly. "It does not matter what happens, Kestrel, just so long as we are together."

Kestrel. The name jarred to a halt in Astron's mind and did not go away. It was Kestrel that Phoebe was giving herself to, and not a wingless demon who could not weave. It should be the woodcutter's pleasure and not his.

Astron looked into Phoebe's expectant eyes in confusion. It would be Kestrel's body, nonetheless. Her sensations would be the same. And he would catalogue yet another experience of humankind. It was his duty to his prince. Astron licked his lips. The yearning was crisp and sharp, like the most brilliant sodium flame. Perhaps if it was not the first time, if he were more jaded to the senses of men, it would feel different, but he was feeling the rush of emotion now and must decide what to do.

"It is a compelling pleasure," Astron heard himself mumble. "In the realm of men, pleasure is regarded as a great good."

"The pleasure is because it is you," Phoebe whispered.

How much of what he was feeling was merely the construction of the bodies of men? Astron wondered. How much was some part of Kestrel that still lurked around the edges of his thoughts? What happened exactly when two awarenesses were switched, anyway? Was Kestrel, in the body of a demon, experiencing the same temptations with Nimbia? Did the woodcutter still remember his human emotions and seek to gratify them as best he could?

A sudden wash of reluctance cascaded over his desire. Kestrel and Nimbia—it would not be right. She did not deserve to be deceived in the way that the woodcutter exploited his own kind. And if she did consent, it would be because she thought it was Astron the demon, not a weak-bodied human slave given to hunger, thirst, sleep, and who knew what other tugs and emotions.

"What is the matter?" Phoebe said. "You feel so stiff, so uncertain."

Astron pulled Phoebe tight one final time and sighed. "It is not right," he said. "Now is not the time." With an ache in his loins, he then awkwardly disengaged and gently pushed her away.

"Then when?"

"After we have reached the origin. After everything has been restored to the way it should be."

Phoebe cocked her head to the side but gradually her smile returned. "All right," she said. "Perhaps the burden of our escape rests a little more firmly on your shoulders than I realized. I should be carrying more of the load, rather than be the weepy prize of the sagas. There will be time enough when we are safe."

She turned and groped for her cape. "After our rest, let me take the front position in the engine. You will need your wits, if we encounter a node that is not vacant."

Astron heard the sound of a blown kiss and then silence. He looked out into the desert and let his feelings slowly dissolve away. Getting to the origin was of the utmost urgency, he thought, but no more important than reversing the transformation between Kestrel and himself.

The next moves passed quickly. Phoebe made no further reference to the events of their first rest. As they made steady progress toward their goal, her spirits soared in proportion. Getting more accustomed to the sand engine, they were able to increase the number of nodes traversed in a single move from two to three. As with the first, each one they visited had been unoccupied; evidently the reflectives had all moved elsewhere in their struggle with the rotators. But as they drew closer to the origin, Astron knew, they must finally encounter a challenge and have an explanation that would be believed.

Toward the end of the sixth move, as they tugged to reach a node only three away from the origin, Astron saw what he had been dreading throughout the trek. The silhouettes of warriors reaching for fresh fruit stood out from the outline of the treetops. Voices mingled with the methodical ticking of rectangular shapes scattered around the oasis. A lookout sounded an alarm and a half-dozen swords were drawn in expectation of their arrival.

Astron felt his discomfort grow. Despite Kestrel's explanations, the concept of deception was still unsettling. He would have to sound convincing, using facial muscles he could barely control. And with no experience, he could not judge the inherent credibility of the tale. He knew it was totally false; why would not the others deduce the same? He felt the sweetness of the air course in and out of his lungs, and a slight taste of apprehension not unlike the stirring of the stembrain began to awaken within him.

"We bring greetings from the chronoids," Astron shouted as the engine grew close. "An example of our most powerful of devices for you to observe. If the offered price is high enough, you will be able to remove the rotators from scores of nodes."

Astron felt his chest tighten while he waited for a response. Involuntarily, his eyes darted from side to side, searching for which way to veer, if they charged, even though Kestrel had told him that one looked straightforward and smiled.

"I am Jankol, squad leader for the reflectives." One of the warriors stepped forward from the rest. He was rail-thin, with narrow eyes that pinched together in the middle of his face. "Despite the words of the doomsayers, more devices of our allies we can certainly put to good use—especially since the increase in vigor of the rotator attacks."

Jankol paused and puckered his lips. "The signal bolts cannot be wrong, yet it is still hard to believe. First, they captured a node, although substantially outnumbered. Then, with an almost obsessive passion they have massed, not scores, but hundreds to take more nodes from us still. The rumor is that they follow a new leader, but it is hard to see how that could make much of a difference."

Jankol paused a second time, looking up and down the engine that Astron and Phoebe had constructed. "A device that looks more primitive than any we previously have seen, to be sure," he said after a moment. "How can it have such power, if it is from an earlier time?"

Astron let out his breath. It was just as the human had said! The basic premise was accepted unchallenged. Now if he could only invent quickly enough to fill in the details. With a final surge, he pushed the engine into their midst and called for Phoebe to halt. While his mind raced for an answer, he slowly unbuckled the leather straps of his harness.

"This engine has the power of immunity to the forces of symmetry," he said after a moment. "How else could we travel from node to node, totally unaffected by the moves of your struggle with the rotators?"

"Immunity?" Jankol said. "How can that help? The other devices you have given intensify the force, rather than decrease it. Why, with some we can even force exchanges of body or mind." He waved his hand at the pond. "That is what we amass here—in preparation for the great battle to blunt the drive of the rotators."

Astron looked quickly around the node. The equipment of the reflectives was configured in much the same way as the first that Phoebe and he had encountered alone. This one was fully occupied with over a score of warriors, however, and not one, but three timepieces were sitting at the edge of the pond.

"Over forty nodes can you clear with what we have brought," Astron said. "Does it really matter how? The important point is the price. What have you given in exchange for the devices you have collected here?"

Jankol's lips puckered for a moment and he rubbed his chin. "Why, the price is the same for each one. It was fixed by the first. You would know that from your past, if you come afterward." He stopped and looked for a long time at the lashed-together engine. "You must be from a more primitive time indeed, but then how could the first have been the beginning of all the rest."

Astron felt the tug of muscles that were not there, but his nose wrinkled slightly, even with the human equipment. He did not understand what Jankol was saying and no one had as yet sheathed his sword. A false step would be disastrous. "Yes, a more primitive time," he said slowly. "Perhaps you had better tell us what has happened since."

Jankol shrugged. "As you know, your realm is a series of nodes, just as ours. But rather than being laid out in space, somehow they are points in time. The forces of symmetry compel each one to repeat the events that have occurred on the one downstream. The first node to establish contact explained that periodically others would follow; the transaction would be the same.

"But if you are from an earlier time and this is the first contact, what we call the first would have known of it. It would be in their history, unless—"

Jankol trailed off and his eyes took on a faraway look. "Unless the inhabitants of your node are far more successful than any that have preceded you. It would portend that your power is great indeed. Yes, yes, we will trade for your engine, the same as we have given for the rest. If it can do as you say, we will not have to consult with the other nodes. Six volunteers who will transfer to your realm and join in your own struggles."

"Six?" Astron asked cautiously. Kestrel had taught to say little while uncertain and ask questions whenever possible. There was less risk of exposure that way.

"Why yes, six," Jankol said. "As I have stated. It was the agreement of the first node with which we made contact."

"This device is more powerful," Astron said.

"Perhaps in your own realm," the leader replied. "But

262

as with the others, I expect it will work imperfectly here. After all, you build them to force the swapping of future and past in your own domain, and, when transported here, the effects are somehow warped. It is as if there were some additional outside interference that makes them behave in ways totally unexpected. There is no guarantee that it will provide any greater advantage over what we already have."

The logic in Astron's mind whirled. Kestrel probably would conclude that Jankol was pressing to close a deal. That would indicate that the transfer of six between the realms was too cheap a price. For something that could indeed influence scores of nodes, he could get more. But then this was exactly the situation that the woodcutter tried to maneuver into. Perhaps the inhabitants of the realm of reticulates were not so very different from men, after all.

"What I really desire is transport to the origin," Astron said, "but I suppose that the price for that is too dear. I understand that the rotators are the ones who occupy it and it would cost you much to seize it."

"The rotators in possession of the origin? That was some time ago and—" Jankol stopped and rubbed his chin. "Such a trip would be costly indeed," he said after a moment, "much more than the device you bring, despite its claim. There is no way we could exchange six and transport you there as well."

"The device is all that I have," Astron said. "Take us to the origin and for that I will explain its many virtues so that you can use it as well. Then I am sure you will agree to exchanging a dozen rather than six."

Jankol puckered his lips. "An explanation after the journey but before the exchange," he repeated. His eyes darted quickly to the other reflectives, as if in warning, and no one spoke. "Once we are in possession of the power, then, in good faith, we will decide what the additional payment will be. Yes, yes, I think the reflectives can agree to that. Of our good faith you can be assured."

Astron felt some of the tension dissolve, but not all. He

wished he could be more sure, but it seemed to follow the pattern that Kestrel had explained. Now if he could only get Phoebe's flame started before the reflectives discovered that their duplicity was the lesser of the two.

CHAPTER TWENTY-ONE

Coalescence of Space and Time

ASTRON had waited anxiously while the reflectives signalled from one node to the next that they were coming. Jankol could not quite believe that he could travel with Astron and Phoebe in their engine without worrying about the forces of symmetry. The time to the next move had been half spent before they finally were on their way, pushing the engine in the sand with Jankol and two of his lieutenants harnessed in the very rear.

Astron had hoped that, with the additional muscle, their rate of speed would improve, but the warriors were unused to much walking and the pace was hardly more than he and Phoebe had managed alone.

"Kestrel, I still do not understand the point of the rush," Astron heard Phoebe gasp beside him as they approached the node one away from the origin. "As I have said, without Nimbia or the services of some other wizard, it is futile to press as hard as we have done. And even if we get to where you seek, Jankol and the others will—will expect what you have promised."

"We will face the events one at a time." Astron glanced to the side between breaths. "Do not waste your energy with idle words. Concentrate only on our objective."

Astron heard the confidence in his voice as if someone else were speaking. His demon's mind knew the truth of what Phoebe said, but somehow his body would not admit it. Instead it seemed totally caught up in pushing onward toward his goal. His mouth was dry. His muscles ached from the strain. Irritating pains occasionally shot from his shoulder where the leather had begun to dig into the soft, unscaled skin. Even the weight of the rucksack containing the harebell pollen had become a heavy burden. Yet there was no other choice but to continue. To stop would be to surrender to the despair of the stembrain or whatever humans had in its place. To be marooned forever was a very long time for a demon.

"The chronoid with the long hair is correct." Jankol suddenly stopped pushing against his harness. "The next move is about to take place. We can rest here comfortably until it is over and then resume travel when we are refreshed."

"What about the rotators?" Astron said. "Had we not better circle around this oasis and continue?"

"But we are indeed fortunate," Jankol said. "Our own brethren now occupy this one and—perhaps several more as well. There is no reason why we will not be welcome."

Astron started to reply when he heard a deep vibrant gong from the direction of the oasis. He felt a tingling in his feet. The ground started to vibrate at a frequency just below his hearing. His nose wrinkled. A flick of motion from the oasis caught his eye. The trees had begun to oscillate. In slow unison, they swayed from side to side. Then the water from the pond sloshed outward to bathe the roots on one side. A great wave of sand, like a ripple in a blanket, seemed to race toward him with breath-catching speed.

The tremor passed under Astron with a mild shifting of his support. He felt his thoughts turn sluggish and difficult to understand. He heard the reflectives call out to the oasis, but their voices had become twisted, sputtering sounds that he barely recognized.

Then, just as suddenly as it had begun, the tremor in the ground stopped. The distant rumbling died away. Astron's head cleared and he was able to think.

"We should not wait until the origin," Jankol said. "My comrades at the oasis say that they prepare for a massive attack. If we are to use your device, it will be here and now. Evidently the rotators press too forcefully; we must employ everything that we can."

Astron's nose wrinkled. He tried to capture the subtle flavor of his disorientation, but with each passing heart beat it faded farther and farther away. He looked back at the oasis and the large clock that was ticking at the water's edge. He saw the warriors there testing the sharpness of their swords, some of them still stretching and arching their backs. Despite the striking clock and trembling ground, they had just barely aroused from their sleep.

Rotarians and reflectives—the two sides were not so very different, he thought. Without prior knowledge, he would be hard put to tell them apart. Images of the ritualistic regimen swept into his mind—plan, eat, sleep, and move; scanning parchment maps of the polytopes, mixing water and pulpy juice, carefully planning nonsymmetric sleeping positions around the oasis—

Astron stopped short and looked at the clock striker as it cocked for another stroke. The vision of the swirling juice and water stuck in his thoughts. "Perhaps it is not so wise," he said quickly to Jankol. "All of the interchange with the realm of the chronoids—what happens when you have shifted so much that there is little to tell their universe from yours?"

"We have a bargain." Jankol ignored the question. "Your device is to aid along with all the rest."

Astron started to say more when the gong sounded a second time. Again he saw the treetops start to sway back and forth. The water in the pond spewed from its banks in a foamy spray. A wave of sand much higher than before pulsed away from its creation.

"Brace yourself!" Astron yelled as he was suddenly thrown from his feet. With a wrenching groan, the long beams of the engine snapped their leather bindings and he tumbled to the ground. Gears ripped from their lashings; tins of flour dropped to the sands, exploding their contents in sprays of deep orange. As if he had been struck by lightning from the realm of men, Astron heard a painful clap of thunder that filled the air and reverberated into a distant rumble that left him dazed. The sky

266

seemed to shimmer for a moment with thin lines of iridescence arching from horizon to horizon.

Astron breathed the sweet taste of air deeply and
shook his head from side to side. As the sky began to
return to its former steady brightness, he saw Jankol and
his lieutenants, completely unfettered, trying to lash the
engine back to the way it had been.

"No, no more use of devices of the chronoids." Astron's tongue felt heavy in his mouth. "Stop them all. Wait
until we understand better what the consequences truly
are."

Jankol stopped his mending. He puckered his lips and
looked at Astron through squinted eyes. "What you say is
most strange. On one hand, you speak of the virtues of a
device from another realm; on the other you entreat instead that such engines not be used. It is a behavior somewhat inconsistent for one truly from beyond the flame."

Astron felt a sudden stab of panic. "No, there is no
inconsistency," he answered quickly. "You see it is
merely a matter of, a matter of—" He tried to look Jankol squarely in the eye but when the words would not
come, he turned his face aside. Scowling, he wished for
Kestrel's quickness of thought.

Jankol waited a moment more, then drew his sword.
He motioned for his lieutenants to fall in line beside him.
"I should have trusted my first instincts," he said. "What
is the truth, strange one? Tell me why you and the long
hair look so different from the rest we have seen."

Astron looked quickly to his side at Phoebe slowly
regaining her footing. Awkwardly he drew Kestrel's
heavy sword and pointed it at the three who advanced at
him with synchronized steps. He felt his chest tighten
and the air come in short gulps.

But before Jankol and the others could engage, Astron
saw one of the lieutenants falter and then fall out of step.
The eyes of the reflective widened and he waved his sword
arm in an exaggerated flourish off to the side. Jankol
stopped uncertainly and then squinted all the more in
Astron's direction. "Your device still seems to disrupt the
symmetries," he said. "We cannot engage you as one. It

feels so very uncertain which are the correct steps to take." He darted his eyes back to the oasis and then at a large blur moving in quickly over the horizon.

"First the battle." He waved his own sword in Astron's direction. "After the victory, I will return with others, dozens if need be, so that we will overwhelm you despite the tricks that you play."

Without another word, he motioned his lieutenants to follow and ran with great effort through the loose sand in the direction of the pond.

For a moment, Astron watched them go. He glanced at what appeared to be a hurling mass of men drawing closer to the oasis and made up his mind. "They will be back shortly," he said to Phoebe. "And even if they are not, I think we can little afford to wait for another stroke of the chime. You must act now. Perform your craft as never before."

"What do you mean?" Phoebe frowned. "I have told you more than once—"

"Forget what has happened." Astron reached out and shook her by the shoulders. "It is a characteristic of the realm. No one could have started a fire at the spot where we first arrived, not even the archimage himself. But now we are much closer to the center than we were before, perhaps close enough that the violation of symmetry caused by the flame will be small enough that it can be overcome. The origin itself would be better, but we cannot afford to wait."

He paused and then reached out and squeezed Phoebe's hand. The thrill of the previous move suddenly surged anew, but he managed to push it aside. "You are a wizard," he said. "A wizard as much as any other—but only if you practice your art."

"The words of symmetry have no bearing, Kestrel." Phoebe shook her head. "I can feel the failure even before I begin." She slumped her shoulders and began to sag back to the ground. "There is no point to endure the frustration, no matter whatever else might come. I can imagine the laughs of my council as clearly as if they were here."

Astron felt a sudden surge of anger and frustration

well up within him. He almost choked over the intensity of the emotion. "I do not care about your council," he yelled. "Put them from your mind." He gulped air and rushed on. "I have heard tales of the encounters with the great wizards, far more than you might guess. I know the characteristics of the ones who were successful, the ones who controlled the mightiest djinns. They did not care about the opinions of others. The practice of their craft was not for fame or good-standing with those who would be their peers.

"It was for themselves they struggled, Phoebe. The measure of success was against goals that were known by themselves alone. The reward was increased self-esteem—acceptance of their own true worth, not the fickle opinion of the lesser ones around them whom they did not choose to control. Think! Why do you want to be a wizard? So that you can be regarded as an equal—or know deep within yourself that you are unique and comparable to none?"

The oasis clock struck a third time. The sky began to shimmer as it had before and the iridescent lines stood out in a much bolder relief. Astron thought he could see faint images of gearworks at the nodes where they intersected and, with them, shadowy figures of men winding huge springs. Another wave of sand rushed at them from the oasis. This time he was more prepared and he pushed Phoebe to the ground before the wrenching jerk ripped away their footing.

As the wave passed, Astron felt a sudden blur of nausea. The trees of the oasis distorted in a blurring rush, as if one were somehow racing by them at a breakneck speed. The broken frame of the engine creaked and groaned where it had fallen. With lifelike spasms, the cracked beams and snapped leather thongs reached for one another, as if they were trying to mend. Some of the spewed flour arched upward from where it had struck the sands and cascaded back into canisters just before their lids suddenly snapped shut. Astron felt another wave of disorientation. His thoughts slowed and then started off slowly in a direction that he did not understand. They bounced around his head like fragments from a language not quite his own. He could only sit stunned and wait for the feeling to pass.

Eventually, the firmness of the sands returned. Astron started to say more to Phoebe, but saw that already she was preparing to start a fire. Clutching a match tightly in her fist, with a sweeping stroke she ran it along the length of one of the rough-barked branches at her side.

The matchhead grated with the contact and then glowed red from the friction of passage but did not light.

"Better than before." Astron shouted encouragement before she could speak. "Better than before. You must try again."

Phoebe grunted in reply. She grabbed three matches tightly together and with deliberate strength ground them against the wood. The heads sparked dully and then almost unexpectedly burst into a feebly smoky flame.

For an instant Phoebe's eyes widened in disbelief. Then she shook her head. "Some kindling—here in the pouch." She motioned with her free hand. "Make a loose pile of it, Kestrel, before the matches burn out."

Astron grabbed at the small pouch and pulled out dry needles and bits of string. He smoothed a depression in the sand and quickly constructed a fragile dome of small struts and spars. Shielding the delicate flicker of fire with her hand, Phoebe bent the matches to the kindling. She caught her breath waiting for the fire to grow.

Tendrils of smoke enveloped the needles and bits of bark. For a brief instant a small speck of tar began to glow red. But then the weak fire faltered and started to die. Helplessly, she watched each little tongue of flame grow dimmer and, in a final puff of smoke, wink out.

Phoebe fumbled for more matches. "The last three." She held out her hand. "And I see no way that they can be any better than the rest." She sighed and looked at Astron with tears forming in her eyes.

"No, wait," Astron said. "Keep your composure. It is just a matter of the kindling. We need something that more easily absorbs the heat of the matches, something with a large surface area for a given volume." Desperately he looked about trying to seize upon an idea. He heard the sound of clashing swords at the oasis and, somehow above it, the ticking of the clock. The results of each gong had been more violent than the one before. Perhaps they could not withstand the next. They had only moments left before something must be done.

Astron closed his eyes and wrenched at his memories as a cataloguer. Fires, flames, the barrier between the realms—there must be something that he had learned that could be used. What was the purpose of all of his knowledge if not—

Astron stopped with a sudden thought. He lunged at the clutter at Phoebe's feet and pawed through the debris from the engine. "Strike the last three matches," he yelled. "Just as you did before. You are indeed the wizard; without you we cannot succeed."

Phoebe hesitated but then turned back to the twisted branch. She struck the matches a first time. When they did not light, she tried again. Astron turned his eyes away, not having time to watch as she struggled. Groping in the sand he found a flour tin with weak walls and with a quick thrust jabbed a hole in the side near the bottom with the tip of his sword. He felt a sudden slice of pain in his soft hands where he had gripped the blade for control. The sudden wetness was sticky but he pushed the discomfort out of his mind. With a wrench he flung off the top of the tin, sending it sailing away.

Out of the corner of his eye, Astron saw Phoebe returning with the barely flaming matches as before. He twisted his head to the ground and placed his mouth around the indentation he had made in the tin. His shoulder felt the rumble of the ground and he had to use both hands to steady the small container in front of his face.

"Here," he shouted, "as soon as you see the spray."

Astron filled his lungs and blew into the small hole. At first the packed flour on the inside resisted the pressure. Most of his breath spilled back out onto his face; only a small portion blasted into the tin and bubbled toward the upper rim. A fine mist of flour danced from the surface into the air.

"Now," Astron gasped. "Apply the fire when I blow again."

Astron expanded his chest and exhaled even harder, sending a visible white spray skyward in a tiny geyser. Phoebe pushed forward the matches and then dropped them in the tin in surprise. An orange-red flame with tongues the length of a forearm suddenly sprang into life.

"Bring over the branches and some of the wreckage of the engine," Astron gasped between breaths. "Spark, kindling, and fuel—they are all essential for any blaze. Unless we supply the third, the fire will go out as soon as I stop." He resumed blowing into the tin, each puff sending the flames higher into the air.

Phoebe nodded and quickly twisted one of the jutting branches of the frame over the spot where Astron lay. The bright tendrils from the burning flour powder bathed the lower contour of the log and then arched around it to flicker higher in the sky. Almost instantly the peeling bark caught fire and a scant moment later began burning on its own.

Astron ceased blowing and tried to stop the rapid breathing so that he could speak again. The human body had disadvantages that appeared at the most awkward of times.

"Be careful, even in your haste," he gasped. "The first mind that you contact might be too pow—"

"Camonel." Phoebe's voice boomed out with a sudden vibrancy. From her cape she sprinkled into the fire some powder that looked the same as what Alodar had used in his keep. "I demand the presence and service of Camonel, the one who carries." She darted a quick glance at Astron and smiled. "Oh, Kestrel," she said. "You had faith in me when even my own will faltered. Perhaps I am in some way unique, as each true wizard must be, not the equal of any other but—"

"Careful!" Astron repeated. "You do not know—"

There was a sudden rush of sulphur-tinted air. The great brown djinn that had carried Astron and the others to the realm of the fey stepped from the fire. "The one who reckons instructs that I do not resist," the massive

272

demon said. "Tell me what you wish and I will obey."

"Another of your kind and an inhabitant of the realm of the fey," Phoebe said. "Quickly take us to them wherever they may be."

The djinn bowed. With one powerful swoop of its long arms he coiled Astron and Phoebe to his chest. A single beat of his wings soared them into the air. But before Astron had time to think, the oasis clock struck a fourth time. Straining to look over his shoulder, he saw the sky shimmer into a painful brightness. The network of iridescence intensified and did not fade. Massive clockworks propelled from the glowing nodes and raced earthward. Halfway to the ground, the machineries passed startled rotators and reflectives hurling skyward in return.

Astron felt another wave of disorientation stronger than before. Although he could not be sure, it seemed that even Camonel faltered, loosening his grip and fluttering to the ground.

"It all runs together in confusion," he heard the djinn mutter as he struck with a slight jolt. "Many nodes fused into one. I need not search them out for all that you seek are now here."

Astron felt the wings pull back. With dizzy steps he staggered from the larger demon's embrace. He saw that he was at the edge of a single expansive oasis surrounded by dozens of trees, rather than just six. At most of the subnodes, hundreds of warriors flailed away at each other in a massive mêlée, every one of them locked in step.

Astron quickly scanned the nearer subnodes and jerked to a halt. Three over from the nearest, he recognized his own body backed against a trunk with a bloody sword waving threateningly at a cluster of reflectives who attacked from the water's edge. Beside him were Abel and a score of rotators, each one trying to mimic their leader's stance. More than a dozen bodies were strewn from the gently sloshing surface of the central pond to the feet of those who defended against the overwhelming odds.

"Forget about their squabbles," Phoebe called from the protective cover of Camonel's wings. "Astron, Nimbia. I succeeded after all. After two failures I have succeeded when it was needed. Finally I have been able to summon a djinn and command him to carry us home."

Astron saw his own body jerk in recognition of the voice. The sword dipped in apparent salute but then returned to parry the thrust aimed at his side.

"Not now," Astron heard his own voice say. "It is too soon. They have trusted me without question. A dozen nodes we have won. Until the last, I cannot let them down."

"But something more has happened," another voice yelled. "Look about you, demon. The chances are too slim."

Astron turned to his right. There, at a virtually deserted subnode, he saw Nimbia holding a swordpoint to the throat of a reflective on the ground and waving with her free hand across the pond to Kestrel. Her tunic was in tatters, one sleeve torn free and the frontpiece ripped deeply across her chest.

Astron started to call out, but the words choked in his throat. Through Kestrel's eyes, she looked exactly as he had remembered her, but somehow it was not quite the same. Her body possessed a new sensuousness, a compelling beacon of desire that blotted out the urgency of he moment. It was just the same as with Phoebe, he thought in sudden confusion—the same as with the human, except that the exposure and the danger made the feeling much more intense.

Astron looked to either side of Nimbia's subnode to see if any reflectives were attempting to attack it. With leaping bounds, he began racing to where Nimbia stood, waving Kestrel's sword above his head.

"Kestrel, what are you doing?" Phoebe shouted behind him. "Help cut a path for Astron. He is the one that needs your help."

Astron shook his head and looked back as he ran to the subnode occupied by Abel and the others. Kestrel, laboring in his slight demon's body, would need aid soon indeed. He returned his attention to Nimbia as he approached and saw her eyes widen in confusion. Only at the last moment was he able to force himself to stop. He

274

sucked in his breath and struggled to regain control. Worse than a stembrain, he thought grimly. It is this human body with its strange desires.

He stared at Nimbia intently and slowly let out his breath. The questioning look remained on her face but she did not retreat. No, there was something more than just the impulsive lust. Astron tried to sort through his thoughts. Something was greater than the mere animal passions of the realm of men. What was it that compelled him? In his own body how then would he feel?

The ground shook with an audible rumble. Astron looked at the edge of the pond and saw dozens of clocks all ticking in synchrony and preparing to strike. He jerked his attention back to what had been their original plan. "Phoebe, the djinn," he yelled. "Instruct him to contact Palodad as he did before."

"I am already with you." Camonel's deep voice boomed out behind Astron. "I speak with the voice of Palodad, the one who reckons, the one who is awaiting what has been promised him."

Astron turned. "We did not find the answer to the riddle," he called out. "High king Finvarwin said words that do not seem to relate."

"Did you secure the harebell pollen? Have you obtained what I have asked?"

"Yes, more than a half-dozen grains." Astron felt the rucksack still on the back of Kestrel's body. "But—"

"Describe them to me."

Astron looked at the clocks' strikers reach back to their maximum extent. "There is no time," he said. "Something must—"

"What, time did you say, there is no time?" Camonel flung back his head and his laughter boomed out over the oasis. "Here there will be time eternal. Do you not see what is happening? Before there were two separate realms. Soon there will be but one. The laws have mixed so that there is nothing to distinguish one universe from another. Like two bubbles pressed together, the surface between them has dissolved away. They distort and strain, but inevitably merge into one. The single realm

275

that results will obey the symmetries of both space and time. With the next stroke of the gongs, these beings that call themselves rotators and reflectives will have their game continue forever, circling about a single oasis in pursuit of one another and playing the same move over and over and over. Yes, a beautiful symmetry that—"

"Tiny barbs and upon them smaller filaments still," Astron interrupted. "The surface of the pollen has a structure finer than that possible from the most skilled weaver. I have had no chance to study them further. But then, how can it matter? Although you might be satisfied, it does not help to answer—"

"Oh, but indeed it does." Camonel clasped his sides to control his laughter. His eyes defocused and took on a faraway look. "Barbs and filaments, you say. Yes, exactly what my calculations predicted. It is but a small reason why I am known as the one who reckons. That is why I sent you. Even without the answer, I had hoped that the pollen would still provide a piece to the puzzle."

"Then Prince Elezar," Astron said. "How does he fare?"

"Gaspar has found his dark node and driven him from it. The spark of life shines no longer in most of his followers. He is adrift, virtually alone, somewhere in the darkness of the realm, awaiting his end. I must have the pollen and the cataloguer quickly. It is the last hope that Gaspar will not be victorious in the end.

"But enough. Now, human, before the strike of the last gong that locks this realm into an eternity of repetition, clasp the pollen tightly and enfold yourself in the arms of my agent."

"There are four of us altogether," Astron said.

"No, just you and the cataloguer," the voice rumbling from Camonel said. "Of the others there is no need."

Camonel stepped forward, stretching his wings out to full span. Astron looked at Nimbia and then at Kestrel still slashing with a sword a half-dozen subnodes away. "Come." The djinn's voice boomed with authority. "Come, bring the pollen to Palodad's domain, and then we will speak of riddles and the precepts that lie beyond all others. The pollen and the cataloguer—both are essential. For no less will I continue to aid in your cause."

"No!" Phoebe's voice sounded above the demon's own. "You have stated that you have submitted. It is my commands that you must obey."

Camonel hesitated. Slowly he turned back to the wizard. "But there was no true struggle," he said slowly. "It was only because Palodad had instructed—"

"I command you to take us away," Phoebe said. "Away from here to safety for the four of us who do not belong."

"Not even a mighty djinn can find his way when the reality about him changes as he flies," Camonel said. "If we hesitate too long, I cannot be sure of even finding the lair of the one who reckons."

The clocks struck in synchrony with an ear-shattering peal. The ground began to weave and buckle, making it difficult for Astron to keep his balance. Off in the distance, he saw the sand rise in a huge wave that climbed halfway into the zenith. The sky above blinked in a kaleidoscope of rapidly changing colors.

"Away," Phoebe shouted. "To the first flame that you can find. I care not where."

Camonel grunted. "Dominance or submission," he muttered. "There can be no in between." Astron saw the mighty djinn pull Phoebe to him with one hand and then swoop to retrieve Nimbia with the other. Cradling them in his stout upper arms, he plucked Kestrel from the surrounding mêlée and then returned for Astron and the rucksack.

As the wings folded shut about him, Astron heard screams of dismay and pain, and then Abel's strong voice shouted above the rest. "We have broken the protocols and new ones come in their place. Look about you, reflectives, and see what you have done. Unwittingly, you have invoked the strongest, the ultimate of them all—coalescence follows from similarity. We are merged with the universe of the chronoids and now we are truly doomed."

With a crash of grinding reorientation the wave of sand hit the oasis. A chant of eat, sleep, cycle, eat, sleep, cycle began to ring in Astron's ears. He felt a wave of nausea far stronger than any that had gone before. Everything went blurry, and he seemed to be tumbling head over heel. The sweetness of the air suddenly lost its pleasure. His aches and pains dissolved away. In resignation, he succumbed to the protection of what was again his stembrain, only dimly aware of the closeness of Nimbia at his side.

PART FIVE

The Realm of the Aleators

Chapter Twenty-Two

A Little Bit of Luck

KESTREL looked at his outstretched hands and saw that they were his own. Evidently the last transformation in the realm of reticulates had restored him and Astron to their proper bodies. He shook his head to clear it of the last of the strange feelings. He had felt a robustness that had coursed through his veins with a pounding vigor. His basic needs for air, food, and sleep had been inherently satisfied and had not troubled his thoughts, even on the lowest level. The immortality of a demon's body he could well believe.

But to be facing an existence that stretched out forever with so little control over one's own thoughts! Kestrel frowned at the horror of it. It had been a constant struggle to keep from raising his sword stiffly over his head and plunging to certain death against any of a dozen reflective attacks. Eventually he would have succumbed. It was just too great an effort to remain on guard all the time—on guard against yourself and what your own thoughts might cause to happen.

Kestrel started to sit up and then hesitated as he became more aware of a gently rocking motion that pushed him from side to side. Looking about cautiously he saw that he was lying at the bottom of a concave wooden hull. Curved spars arched upward from under a keelboard under his back to gunwales well above his head. The last dying embers of a fire hissed in a smoky soup of bilgewater and soot. Below his feet he could see Phoebe's crumpled form and, beyond her, what probably were Nimbia and Astron stirring as well.

Kestrel looked skyward and groaned. The canopy

was pale blue and lit by a small reddish sun, far smaller than what he was used to in the realm of men. Again they were somewhere else from where they wanted to be. For a moment, he lay on the rough wooden planking, trying to put his thoughts together. The strain of the last few moves had taken its toll on his mind, as well as on Astron's poorly equipped body. Having to think consciously of every thrust and parry, rather than rely on instincts learned over many years of getting out of scrapes, was as exhausting as heavy labor.

Kestrel sighed. Yes, the effort had been exhausting, but somehow rewarding as well. If not for the gong of the clocks on the final move, the rotarians he led might have captured the node, despite the odds. They had depended on him and he had been true to their trust. He had risen to what was his duty and discharged it well. If not for the clocks, then who knew what could have happened? Perhaps there might be some way to go back, despite what the djinn had said, after Phoebe was safely home—go back and rescue those that had put their lives in his hands without questioning that he would respond in return.

"It is worse than the desert," Kestrel heard Phoebe say as she rose and came to his side. Her depressing lethargy seemed to have vanished. Even with the unsure footing of the small boat, there was confidence in her tread. "Look, Kestrel, there is nothing in sight. In the realm of reticulates, we arrived at an oasis where we could eat and drink." She looked at him intently and smiled. "It is worse than the desert and I do not care."

Kestrel looked out over the gunwale and blinked at what he saw. They were at sea with no sight of land on the horizon. Kestrel whirled to look in other directions, but there was little difference. The only feature was a thin line in the distance, separating ocean from sky.

He glanced down the length of the long boat, but, except for Nimbia and Astron, he saw that the hull was bare. They had no sails, oars, food, or water. Near his feet, the last ember of the dying fire cooled to a soggy gray. Evidently they did have at least one leak.

Kestrel put his arm around Phoebe and attempted a

brave smile. She smiled back and drew closer. "At least, this part is better than the last few moves," she said. "You hardly touched me when we were separated from the others."

Kestrel started to explain what had happened, but thought better of it. There would be time enough for that later, after they had reached safety. "How big a fire do you need to summon the djinn again?" he asked, waving at the charred splints at his feet. "Evidently in this place a blaze in a small wooden boat is not something totally bizarre."

"No, do not struggle with a demon now." Astron suddenly shook his head from where he was trying to stand near the stern. "Something is not right about the summoning. There is too much risk."

"What do you mean?" Phoebe said. "I have brought forth Camonel before and I can do it again. Do not worry, Astron. I have my full confidence now. Kestrel had faith in me and that was enough."

"I do not question the power in your craft," Astron said. "It is the words of the djinn that give me the suspicion. You have taught me, Kestrel, to look beyond the words to the meaning behind." The demon paused and wrinkled his nose. "How do we know that it was truly Palodad speaking through the mouth of Camonel? The one who reckons is a recluse, more concerned with the flipping of the imps in his own domain than delving into the working of other realms. He wants the harebell pollen grains as part of a bargain, it is true, but the insistence that I must accompany their delivery seems out of place."

"I do not know the workings of your kind." Kestrel shook his head. "So I cannot speak to how well your conjecture hits the mark. But if not this Palodad, then who else would speak through the flame?"

"Gaspar," Astron said. "He is the one who stands to lose, if we are successful in our quest. Without the pollen, we cannot expect any more of Palodad's aid. He is the one who is tracking down all those with allegiance to the prince he wishes to destroy—the one who would want my return far more than any other.

"And even though Phoebe controlled Camonel to effect our rescue, the djinn is free to act in matters that she does not explicitly proscribe."

"From what you have told me of Gaspar," Kestrel said, rising to stand, "it is unlikely he would have the skill for such complex charades. Indeed, you even said that his posing of the riddle was a surprise to your prince." Kestrel tugged at his chin and looked out over the featureless sea. "There is also the matter of the outside influence in the realm of reticulates. Given the confining nature of the protocols, what would start the barter with the chronoids in the first place? Why would even the reflectives continue when the unpredictable results from using the engines began to interfere with their plans? Who was responsible for the torrent of exchanges at the end? It is as if there were someone else behind all of this, someone far wiser than Gaspar manipulating him as well as other things."

"Prydwin!" Nimbia sat up, suddenly alert. "It all fits together when you think of it. It is his creations that have been coalesced. Although I can think of no reason why he would wish it so, because he knows the details of their creation, no one could cause the merging any better than he. Who else would be concerned about what happens to harebell pollen, if not one of the fey? Suppose that the prince of the lightning djinns did not have a free will of his own, but was under the domination of my kinsman?"

"Yes, Prydwin," Astron said. "You may very well be right. Most of my kind have little concern for the workings of other realms. Except for cataloguers such as myself, they dwell instead on instant gratifications that forestall the great monotony. Far more plausible is a being from somewhere else manipulating events for his own personal gain."

"Then what is our plan?" Phoebe asked. "Unless I can control a demon, we are marooned here as surely as we were before."

"Do not misunderstand," Astron said. "Despite appearances, we have made progress on our quest. First we learned that it was the realm of the fey in which we must look. There we successfully acquired the pollen grains that Palodad desires."

284

"And in the realms of symmetry," Nimbia cut in, "we heard Palodad say that their physical design somehow was important to the answer of the riddle."

"Only if indeed it was Palodad," Astron said. "Of that we cannot be certain." He shook his head. "No, it is the one who reckons whom we must contact directly to be safe," he said. "No intermediary agent will do."

"Then tell me of his mental signatures," Phoebe said. "When we relight the fire, he is the one I will seek."

Kestrel saw Astron's membranes flick down over his eyes and his nose wrinkle to the side.

"It is not quite that simple," the demon said after a moment. "I doubt I could accurately describe the character of Palodad's will. He is old, old even by the standards of my kind and his thoughts—" Astron trailed off and shook his head. "Mankind would probably call him mad," he continued, "and I am not so sure that I do not agree."

Kestrel saw Astron clench his fist and suppress a slight shudder. "No, I must be the agent, as we have agreed before. But in light of our suspicions, I must return unaided—return and seek out Palodad directly, rather than rely on the intermediary of any of my kind."

"Would it not be better to take the pollen with you when you go?" Kestrel reached behind his back and patted his pack. "With nothing to offer, what would be the motivation for Palodad to aid us any further?"

"I cannot carry the harebell pollen through the flame, Kestrel," Astron said, "at least not in my—my present state. Remember the reason that Elezar directed me to your realm was to secure the aid of mankind to perform the cartage. Even the most powerful of djinns has difficulty with objects that do not possess minds of their own."

"Then clasp me somehow to you," Kestrel said. He looked at Phoebe and smiled. "I have already experienced three realms other than my own in aiding in the adventures of a wizard. One more can hardly make any difference."

"I am not a mighty djinn." Astron shook his head. "Although I require the flame of anvilwood and not simple pine or fir to pass between the realms, skills in weaving or transportation I have none. We must somehow find the

285

tree most similar in this realm so that I can return alone."

Kestrel thought for a moment and then looked at Astron intently. "How can you be sure?" he asked. "With so many fetters of logic about your stembrain, how can you be sure?"

"Fetters? What do you mean?"

"And how can you know the inner thoughts of a demon." Phoebe laughed. "Even the best of wizards can only guess."

Kestrel started to answer, but then shrugged. A crooked smile came to his face. "It does not really matter," he said with a wave of his arm. "I doubt we will be able to find the proper wood surrounded by—"

Kestrel stopped and stared out over his outflung hand. Between the bobs of the waves, he thought he caught sight of a mast and sail just at the horizon. Impulsively, he began to wave his arms. "Look," he shouted. "Look to port. It is a ship, a large ship, sailing our way —what luck, what incredible luck indeed."

His feelings flipped with a suddenness that made him giddy. He pulled Phoebe close and gave her a hug. "I have sampled enough of what you are like, demon." He laughed. "Sampled enough from a fresh perspective that I have seen parts that even you are unaware of. But first let us attend to our safety in one realm before we take on the challenges of another."

"Over there on the starboard." Nimbia suddenly pointed. "There is one—no, two more, in addition to the first."

Kestrel took his eyes from the ship to port gradually drawing closer. There seemed little doubt that they had been seen. He looked to starboard and shook his head in amazement. Near the stern was another tall mast, and directly abeam was a third. There was such a thing as luck, but this was incredible. How could they have been placed in the precise center of a circle of ships in a totally featureless sea?

Kestrel looked at Phoebe, but she did not seem to care about the coincidence. She was jumping up and down as much as he. The boat rocked with each leap, and Nimbia stumbled as she tried to maintain her balance. Astron reached out and grabbed her awkwardly by the shoulder. Kestrel saw the demon's nose suddenly wrinkle with the contact. The eye membranes flicked into place, and he quickly withdrew. Nimbia smiled and reached out in return, grabbing Astron's retreating hand.

Astron held his arm out stiffly like a stick figure drawn by a child. Nimbia steadied herself and closed the distance between them.

"The retriever of harebell pollen, the swordsman leader of the rotators, and even the gentleman-in-waiting for a queen of the fey," she said. "One has difficulty remembering that you are a merely a djinn from beyond the flame."

The crook in Astron's nose sharpened. "I am a demon, you know full well," he said slowly. "But the power of my brood brethren is not mine to command. I am but a cataloguer, serving as best I can."

"And to whom is it that this service is rendered?"

"Why, to my prince, of course," Astron said. He paused and looked away from Nimbia's gaze. "And, of course, to the success of the quest of Kestrel, Phoebe, and—and Nimbia as well."

"And when the quest is over?"

"I have not thought of it," Astron said. "It is not the nature of demonkind to think of what lies beyond the present. It leads to brooding on the inevitability of the jaded senses and the ultimate despair of the great monotony."

"But as I have observed, you are no common demon," Nimbia said. "And for me, the end of the quest poses the greatest uncertainty for us four. The two humans will no doubt return to their own kind." She waved her arm in Kestrel's direction. "And you, if you so choose, will flitter back to some depressingly plain patch of mud in the void of your realm. But what of Nimbia, a queen of the fey? There is no place to which to return. Ever so much worse than before, there is no one with whom to share. Who will serve me with distinction in a manner of which I could be proud?"

Astron wrenched his hand free of Nimbia's grip. "Your

287

words prick at my stembrain," he said. "It is difficult to maintain rational control." For a long moment he stood silent; then his membranes cleared and the muscles in his face relaxed. He looked at Nimbia and spoke softly. "Do not be deceived," he said. "I am no weaver of matter; no wings of great lift sprout from my back. I am only a cataloguer whose power derives from the few facts that no other has learned. There is no special destiny for one such as I."

"In the realm of the fey and, I suspect in others as well, one is measured by his deeds, rather than his inherent potentials, whatever they might be. I remember tasting your inner doubts when you rescued me from Prydwin's sentrymen, demon. And I have seen you lead hundreds of rotators with clumsy hands and little regard for your own safety as well." Nimbia reached out and touched Astron gently on the cheek. "There is much more that you can learn, cataloguer," she said, "much more you can learn of yourself."

"Avast, you in the dory," a deep voice suddenly boomed across the waves. "Reduce your efflux so that the others will sail away."

Kestrel turned his attention from Astron and Nimbia and looked over at the ship approaching from portside. It was nearer than the others, and details of its superstructure could now be discerned. A single short mast stood in the middle of a deck that was both wide and long. A lateen sail billowed in a stiffening breeze that had not been there before the arrival of the vessel it propelled. The broad bow and even broader beam were wider than those of any barge that Kestrel had ever seen. It seemed hard to believe that the small area of cloth presented to the wind could be adequate for a hull easily the length of two score men.

Even more remarkable, Kestrel thought with a start, was the fact that he understood perfectly the words that had been spoken. Except for a slight accent, they sounded like the speech of an Arcadian from across the sea in the realm of men. This, then, was not another creation of Prydwin; but if not, how amazing that the language turned out as it did.

"Reduce your efflux," the voice repeated. "You have impressed me as much as you will. I regard you as wealthy. To spill more luck to the winds will up my assessment not a quantum more."

Kestrel looked up at the deck, puzzled. He saw a rotund man wrapped in pinkish silks and a purple sash pulled tight into an overflowing girth. Bushy black hair, as dark as night, tumbled out of a small turban down the sides of his face into a curly beard. The deep-set eyes squinted cruelly into the reddish sun. The smile wrinkles looked shallow and seldom used.

Three or four others dressed like the first huddled about their leader, each one holding high a small cage of gold that contained some small white-furred rodent contentedly munching away on greens. The neck of each man was bowed under the weight of at least a score of chains. On every chain hung small trinkets; some were mere gauze bags tied with ribbon, others intricately veined leaves pressed flat on slabs of slate.

"Why, you carry no plenuma," the black-headed one continued as the two vessels drew quite close, "no plenum chambers at all." He reached for a monocle of colored glass hanging from a chain about his own neck and quickly cocked it into his eye. "By the rush of entropy, it is in spontaneous discharge from all four of you—spontaneous discharge, as if you had been building pressure for a lifetime and using none of it until now."

He waved over his shoulder to the center of the ship. "All right, I withdraw my words. I am most certainly impressed, more certainly than I have ever been before." He paused and intertwined his fingers across his expansive girth, rocking back and forth silently as if enjoying a secret joke. "But mark you," he said after a moment, "I am not so awed as to forgo absorbing the flux for myself. And if you do not have plenum chambers, let us find out how good are your wards against the sucking chambers of Jelilac, the most fortunate."

A man much smaller than Jelilac suddenly vaulted over the gunwale of the larger ship and, with hardly a glance to see where he was going, landed firmly in the dory between Phoebe and Nimbia. He carried what looked like a bowl of soapy water in one hand and a large pipe in the other. Without spilling a drop or hesitating to catch his balance, he adroitly settled into a squatting position and submerged the pipe into the bowl.

Kestrel noticed that he had as many chains about his neck as the rest, perhaps even more. All along the arms and legs of his silken tunic were embroidered tiny leaves of clover, and each of his fingers was wrapped in bows of red ribbon.

"Luck begets luck." The newcomer noticed Kestrel's stare. "It is the third tenet." Then, without further comment, he began to blow on his pipe, causing a bubble to form in its bowl. His first few puffs on the pipe seemed easy, and the glassy surface expanded with rapid jumps. But when the bubble had reached the size of a fist, Kestrel noticed that the veins in the pipeman's neck began to stand out and his cheeks redden from the effort to force air down the stem of the pipe. It reminded him of the sport of the fey, but it was somehow different, and he suspected the effort served a practical utility.

As Kestrel watched, the surface of the bubble began to darken and take on what looked like a tough, leathery texture, far less elastic than any balloon. By the time the pipeman had finished, he had created a sphere perhaps the size of a person's head with a dark opalescent surface that light just barely shone through.

The piper dropped his grip on the pipestem. With a grunt, he removed the bubble from where it still adhered to the bowl. Then he quickly stretched out his arms and touched the orb to the hem of Phoebe's cape. There was a sudden spark of light that jumped from the draping material into the interior of the sphere. For an instant Kestrel saw what looked like a churning maelstrom of dense red smoke within the confines of the globe; but as the light vanished, the image faded away.

Phoebe immediately stumbled. Kestrel reached out just in time to break her fall on the hard planking of the small boat. "Just exactly what do you think you are doing," he shouted angrily at the piper. "What is that thing, anyway?"

The piper looked at Phoebe's sprawled form on the deck and then hefted the sphere at his side. "I suppose it does seem a bit uncivil," he said. "Certainly for this exchange, you deserve at least the most basic of talismans in return." He reached into his pocket with his free hand and offered Phoebe a necklace like one of the many he wore about his neck. What looked like the preserved foot of a small animal dangled from the lower end.

"Only good for simple accidents, I admit," he said. "But then Jelilac covets each dram. It is the way of all who wish to live more than the briefest of moments in the realm of the aleators."

Kestrel grimaced. Understanding the language was almost too good to have happened. Without it, perhaps things would have proceeded more slowly and given him time to size up better the situation they were in. He reached out to grab the offered talisman but the piper easily whisked it out of his reach. With a deft and fluid motion, he flung it over Phoebe's head, where it settled in a perfect position about her neck. "For the lady," the piper said. "And watch your manners, or Milligan might decide that you end up with nothing at all."

Kestrel reached out a second time for the piper's leg, but the little man was too swift. As Kestrel's hand closed on air, Milligan had touched the globe to Nimbia's tunic, and a brilliant arc jumped to it as before. Nimbia teetered, but Astron was slightly quicker than Kestrel had been. Not hesitating to avoid contact, he steadied the queen so that she did not fall.

"Hmmm," Milligan said. "Perhaps it would be better to give this one a chance at food and drink. If you concentrated on subsistence alone and depended on the others for protection, you might get enough to share." Again he reached into his pocket and withdrew another pendant necklace, this one an ebony lump of wood carved in intricate whirls.

Kestrel lunged out at Milligan from behind, but the little man quickly turned and held the sphere chest high to absorb the force of the rush. The spark that jumped from Kestrel's outstretched hand sent a stab of pain up his arm.

He felt a sudden tugging sensation all over his body and then a rushing away of some essence that he could not quite identify. A wave of discomfort swept over his senses; in a weakened stupor, he sagged to the bottom of the dory.

With clouded vision, Kestrel watched the sparks dance from Astron's body as it had the others. Only dimly was he aware of a leather thong that pierced a small heavy stone being placed over his slumping head. Offering only the most feeble of protests, he let himself be hoisted by a crane up to the deck of the larger ship. He clutched his hands to a growling stomach, suddenly quite aware that he had not eaten for what seemed like a very long time.

"Your contributions have mellowed Jelilac's temper," Kestrel heard Milligan say some hours later. He shook his head and willed himself to focus on the little man standing before him. He felt a second talisman being hung about his neck and then a third. Looking to both sides, he saw Phoebe and the others rousing as well. They had been piled in a tumble about the single mast of the sloop.

"Ordinarily, with ones so destitute as you, the only choices he would offer would be trials with long odds indeed," Milligan continued. "But the idiocy of such a great concentration and not even the slightest of wards has him most amused. As it is, he needs to refine a rather mundane procedure before landfall at the casino. Surely at least one of you four will survive."

Kestrel staggered to his feet and looked about quickly. Except for the helmsman and Milligan, none of the crew were above deck. The dory in which they had arrived was battened to the port gunwale and a long ladder lay at its side. The glassy calm sea looked the same, although the other ships were no longer visible. Off the port bow in the distance was a sliver of brown above the horizon that indicated the first signs of land.

"We are travellers from afar," Kestrel said, "and understand little of what you speak." He ran his tongue across the dry roof of his mouth. "But decency anywhere would demand that you offer at least some food and drink."

"Offer subsistence, offer it freely from one to another."

Milligan threw back his head and laughed. He waved his arm in a wide, flat circle out to the horizon. "Do your eyes not see the vast expanse of waste—salt water everywhere and only tiny pinpoints of land. There is no food to offer to another. Even one such as I has had occasions of hunger, despite all that I carry about my neck."

Kestrel started to respond, but the doorway leading below deck suddenly slammed open, and two seamen appeared, carrying a long table between them. "Ah, spinpins," Milligan said. "Jelilac is feeling mellow indeed. He must think that crown is certain to be his."

Kestrel looked more closely at the table as it was positioned crosswise on the deck just in front of the mast where he stood. On one end was a simple maze, a box of wooden partitions divided into compartments, each the height of a hand. Doorways were cut in many of the walls connecting the confinements together; some were empty, but in most were standing geometric arrays of tiny bowling pins. A single doorway pierced the perimeter. Near it lay an intricately carved spintop and a pile of string.

A third seaman appeared from below deck, carrying a small vertical frame on which, near the top, was hung a blade of shining metal. At the bottom were two sheets of wood paneling between which the sharp edge apparently dropped. The panels were plain and unadorned, except for a hole about the size of a finger that had been drilled through them both. The seaman positioned the apparatus near the spintop and clamped it to the table. He ran a string from a hinged release mechanism for the blade and tied it about one of the pins standing in the maze.

"The principle is quite simple," Milligan said as he moved to the ladder at the side of the dory. Struggling with its long length for a moment, he thrust it into a vertical position and twisted its orientation with a flip, so that the topmost rung fell against the mast.

"Even the simplest child knows that one's luck decreases by walking under a ladder," Milligan said. "The effect can be reversed only by quickly retracing one's steps the other way."

"We have such a tale from whence we come," Kestrel

293

said. "But it is the nonsense of ancient crones, nothing more."

Milligan frowned and was silent for a long moment. "Minions of the crazed Byron," he muttered while he clutched at the talismans about his neck. "Minions of Byron, and not one, but four." His eyes narrowed and he looked at Kestrel keenly. "No, that cannot be. You are attempting some sort of a deception to free yourselves from your plight. No fatalists could have accumulated such auras as yours. You struggle for the crown, just as does Jelilac and the rest."

Kestrel frowned in turn. Very little of what Milligan was saying made any sense. He looked down at Astron as the demon stirred and struggled to sit. Kestrel wished that he were fully alert. Some of his deductive observations would be quite useful about now.

"Anyway, the reversal raises an interesting question," Milligan continued. "It is one that Jelilac stumbled on to, the kind of insight that makes him a true contender to be archon over us all. The throne has been vacant since Sigmund's luck suddenly turned sour. Soon we will all assemble to judge which aleator now possesses the greatest power." Milligan looked down at his chest and stroked three of his talismans. "Although, under the right circumstances, who is to say what will happen in the casino where the die is cast? Yes, who is to say which is the most deserving, the most faithful to the tenets of our creed?"

For a moment, Milligan stopped speaking, his eyes burning with secret thoughts. Kestrel looked back over the bow at the land steadily growing on the horizon. He eyed the two battens that held the dory and scanned the deck for signs of any other useful gear. With so few crewmen on deck, the right circumstances were the ones he was interested in as well. He began to think more clearly. Perhaps it was best to keep Milligan engaged in conversation until the others were fully alert. Then they just might manage an escape from whatever Jelilac had in store for them.

Kestrel glanced at the ladder and then back at the table. The construction for both was rather crude and unvarnished. He could see that more than one type of wood was used in each. On the other hand, perhaps such a risk was not even necessary. A fire on deck could serve just as well. That was a possibility worth exploring before attempting the longer odds of an escape.

"What do you have carved of anvilwood?" He smiled innocently. "I am a collector and most interested in any small figurines that you have to show."

Milligan broke out of his reverie. "Anvilwood?" He laughed. "There is none here on Jelilac's barge, to be sure. You must indeed be from an islet far away. Every aleator who has stopped sucking his thumb is taught to avoid such a luck drainer whenever he chances upon it." He stopped and laughed again. "It would just be the perversity of luck that such as you would be desirous of finding some. Throughout the realm, prisoners convicted of the worst crimes are sent to uproot the trees when they are discovered and hack the branches to bits. For others, the risks in touching are just too great. The only piece that I know of is at the casino for the trials to be archon. And even that Jelilac and the others will strive to destroy, if given half the chance."

Kestrel frowned. They would have to get away after all—and then, from the sound of it, journey to one very special place. He looked up at the ladder. Perhaps it could serve another use. They would need oars, even if they managed to drop the dory over the side. He glanced back at Milligan. The little man seemed to enjoy talking. For the moment it probably was best to keep him occupied.

Kestrel fingered the three talismans hanging about his neck. "This one looks something like a match stick." He held it out to Milligan. "Where we come from, it is a mark of great honor, since only a few we call wizards have the capability to build a flame. I suppose that here such skill is also a great rarity. No one such as yourself could hope to accomplish such a feat."

Milligan cocked his head to one side. "If it were not for the aura you possessed, I would agree with Jelilac and judge you most insane," he said. "Of course I can light a fire. Why, so could any child. It is not a question of ease, but one of law. On all corners of the great sea, a flame is prohibited under penalty of death."

Kestrel frowned, but Milligan continued. "The second tenet states that the entropy of luck always increases. There is no way it can be avoided. Each transfer from one to another, even each use that dilutes it back to the ether—all such transferals reduce its potency. The last thing that anyone would want is a flame that completely disorders its fine crystalline structure and renders it useless.

"Why, even an archon could become a pauper, if he approached too close to a fire. Without his luck to guard him, all of his great displays of state on the islands would be washed away by the next giant wave that sweeps across our sea. Even if he possessed the strange book of figures that Myra is reputed to have found, his ships would start to wander aimlessly, missing all of their ports. In the time of a single sigh, he would find that he had come to possess nothing, neither food for his next meal nor even clothing to ward off the chill. And each and every one who but an instant before stooped in the deepest of bows would shun his misfortune, casting him aside and letting him wander to his death, unheralded and alone.

"No, the object of us all is to find ways to increase our luck, to concentrate it into tighter and tighter confines that enhance its potency. It is the only way to survive, to move ahead, and to strive for the mantle of the archon. The fatalists cannot be right. Things should not be left to the will of the cosmos. Outcomes are determined by men with luck; he who has the greatest will certainly emerge the winner."

"I would think that skill or wit would somehow be important as well," Kestrel said. Cautiously, he placed one hand on the ladder and looked at the rungs. Perhaps, if the sidebeams were ripped apart they would serve well enough. He smiled inwardly and looked at Astron. It was something the demon probably would have thought of, and yet it came to him first.

"In the dim past, skill and wit did determine the outcome of many events," Milligan answered. "We contested by might of arms and clever strategies of state. But then, as our legends record it, wise archon Williard with overwhelming odds was defeated by a force a tenth his size when his horse stepped into the only squirrel hole on the field of battle. An errant arrow hit his second in command in the throat, and, without a leader, the army stumbled into a mire.

"Luck triumphed over all else; and from that day to this, everyone who strives for power concentrates on increasing his own luck and dissipating that of others. Skill and talent mean little to one who can select a marked token from a bowl of thousands with but a single thrust of his hand."

"Then what need do you have of this experimentation?" Kestrel asked. He placed his hand firmly on each of the ladder's sidebeams and strained outward while smiling in Milligan's direction. "If starting a fire is of no use, then whatever else of value can we be to you?"

"The means for accumulating and dissipating luck are not written in stone monuments for all to see," Milligan said. "It is only by centuries of trial and error that the methods that we use have come to light. Doubtless many more efficient techniques yet remain to be discovered." He waved his hand in a wide circle. "Luck is all about us, albeit at very low pressure. Certain actions seem to compress it into smaller volumes and increase its potency to alter events.

"As I have said, when one walks under a ladder, a portion of whatever one possesses leaks out into the ether. Immediately reversing direction prevents the loss before it can transpire." Milligan paused and ran his tongue over his lips. "But what if one circled back and walked under the ladder again in the second direction, the one that prevented the loss. Perhaps then the vector of transaction would remained fixed in a positive direction, each circuit under the ladder increasing one's luck, rather than dissipating it away.

"That then is the test. The first of you, I care not which, will walk once under the ladder and then spin the top through the maze. He will be what we call the control. The second will walk once and then immediately reverse before taking the test. The third, after reversing direction,

297

will continue around the mast and back under the overhang a dozen times more. The last will not reverse directions at all but rotate the dozen times in the same sense as the first."

"What will the spinning top prove?" Kestrel asked while he slid his arms up the ladder to feel another rung.

"It is a test of luck, to be sure," Milligan said. "The spinning top caroms through the compartments in a manner that no one can predict, scattering pins at random. The count of how many are felled is the measure we wish to monitor. If all the pins are toppled before the one attached to the blade, then the game is stopped and you are lucky indeed."

"And if the blade topples," Kestrel said. "What does that prove?"

"The finger you place in the hole will be severed, a most unlucky outcome," Milligan said. He looked quickly back at the maze on the table and then smiled at Kestrel. "The beauty of it is that you all have ten. We will be able to run some forty trials before we are done."

Kestrel decided he had heard enough. It did not matter if the others were fully alert or not. With or without oars, they must be away. "Astron," he yelled, "unlash the dory. Get it back over the side." With a grunt he twisted the ladder from its resting place and crashed it downward on the middle of the table, hoping that the force of the blow would break it apart.

The ladder bounced harmlessly off of the horizontal surface, however, the bottom end kicking up painfully into Kestrel's thigh. He staggered a single step and then sagged to one knee, his leg refusing to give him support. As he fell, he pushed at Phoebe, propelling her forward toward the gunwale where the dory was lashed. He rolled over on his back, expecting to see Milligan spring at him with some weapon, but he saw instead the little man feverishly fingering the brightest talisman which hung from his neck.

"Jelilac, Jelilac," Milligan screamed. "They are followers of Byron. Despite the great auras they once possessed, they follow Byron, to be sure."

Kestrel rose to kneeling and grabbed Nimbia about the

shoulder. Crawling with one hand on the deck, he urged her in the direction he had pushed Phoebe. Looking forward, he saw Astron fumbling with the mooring knots, apparently not making any progress in getting them untied.

Two seamen cautiously came forward, their fingers outflexed and reaching for the thongs of leather about Nimbia's neck. Kestrel staggered erect and pointed wildly into the sky. "Look," he shouted. "Not one shooting star, but two. Not to witness it is a great misfortune."

He held his breath for an instant, but the two sailors were totally unaccustomed to such a blatant deception. As one, they turned and began searching the clouds. Kestrel limped forward a single step. As he felt his leg again give way, he staggered against the nearest of the seamen. A ring on the sailor's hand scratched his cheek as he fell. Concentrating as hard as he could, he managed to grab hold of the loops and chains about his neck and pull the man to the ground.

Kestrel gathered up as many talismans in his hands as he could manage. With a back-wrenching yank, he snapped them from the seaman's neck. The sailor screamed. With an almost animal fury, he began clawing at Kestrel's arms to get them back.

Kestrel flung them in the direction of the dory; although several went over the gunwale, two landed at Astron's feet. Almost immediately the knot on the last fetter unraveled. The demon quickly reached down and grasped the bow in the cradle of his arms and hoisted it up over the low railing. Phoebe and Nimbia reached the stern and lifted it up as well. In an instant, the small boat splashed down onto the waves.

Kestrel crawled forward to the gunwale, blocking out the seaman who scrambled on the deck with him to retrieve the two talismans that remained. Kestrel reached to scoop them up a second time but grimaced as sharp splinters from the deck dug into his palm.

Astron bent down, grasped the talismans tightly in one hand, and then grabbed Kestrel by the arm with the other. Kestrel reached out for Phoebe and Nimbia. Without thinking further, they jumped together over the side.

The salt water stung Kestrel's cheek when he hit, but he paid it no heed. Lashing out blindly, he felt the side of the dory and grasped for a hold. Through sea-spattered hair, he saw Milligan leaning over the rail, cupping his hands to his mouth.

"There is little enough gain in what you have stolen," he yelled. "Basic enhancers and navigator's fetishes are all. They are organic and soon will decay. About enough to see you safely to the island in the distance and survive a wave or two, but little more. And there, if you stay out of the clutches of doubting Myra and her arcane devices, you will learn well enough the difficulty of finding food and drink with what little auras you now possess."

Milligan looked back over his shoulder and laughed. "Followers of Byron," he said. "With the spintop, at least one of you might have had a chance."

Kestrel saw the distance between the dory and the sloop begin to widen. From somewhere, a fresh breeze had begun to blow them apart. He tried to hoist himself a little higher to see the direction they should begin to paddle. Despite the aches and pains, he felt the cold of the sea and the renewed gnawing of his hunger. Basic enhancers and navigator's fetishes, he thought. Even if they were lucky, would so little be enough?

CHAPTER TWENTY-THREE

The Darling of Destiny

ASTRON stirred with discomfort. He watched Kestrel clutch the tripstring firmly in his grasp, preparing for the moment that he would jerk away the twig that propped the splintered beam from the sandy beach. The small quail was just partway into the trap. It would be the dozenth try, and Astron doubted it would be any more successful than the rest.

He looked at Phoebe and Nimbia, huddled motionlessly near the wreckage of the dory. The heavy wave that had dashed them against the beach had destroyed their only means to travel elsewhere with any speed. The small, reddish sun was almost to the crest of the hill spine that hid the interior of the island. A heavy copse of trees covered the entire slope. Only the sandy beach that curved out of sight in both directions was devoid of the thick vegetation. Perhaps in the interior, they would find bigger game or even someone more sympathetic to their plight. But nightfall was coming too soon. For the moment, they had to hope for a single meal and find what cover they could in the wreckage of the boat.

Astron twisted his shoulders, ignoring Kestrel's sharp glance to be still. He wished he could be more sure of the path they were taking, seeking out anvilwood rather than letting Phoebe summon Camonel to their aid. But which was truly the lesser risk he could not decide. The uncertainty stirred his stembrain, forcing him to tighten his control.

He looked again at Nimbia, trying to recapture the pounding emotion that had gripped him when it was Kestrel's body he had possessed. It was not the same now, of course, but the experience had touched his rational centers as well. He remembered their closeness when hiding from Prydwin's pursuit, the piercing inner sadness that she exposed to him more than any other, the strength of duty she felt to her hill dwellers that was stronger than that of any prince. Even in abstraction, sharing more of her thoughts would bring a great pleasure, perhaps as keen as the discovery of new facts from beyond the flame. What would it be like, he wondered, if their relationship went deeper than that of a broodmother and sire?

Astron stopped the direction of his thoughts short and wrinkled his nose. He shook his head in the manner of men. She was no less than a queen and regarded him in quite a different light. At no time, he recalled, had she even bothered to call him by name. She spoke with kindness and praise, but always as she would to a servant, one perhaps to be her single loyal retainer when the quest was finally done.

If only it were finally done, he thought ruefully. He had been away from Elezar far longer than he had intended. Could there still be any hope that his prince was alive? And with Gaspar triumphant, his own grisly fate would only be a matter of time. Somehow, he must get the harebell pollen back to Palodad and trust that whatever he had learned would provide a sufficient clue to solve the riddle. Without that, then anything else did not really matter.

Astron pushed away the reverie. He turned his attention back to the immediacy of their problems. He watched the quail take another timid step under the overhang of the beam. Its tiny head twitched from side to side, looking for predators. Then, in two quick thrusts of its bill, it poked at the seeds that Nimbia had gathered along the beach. Kestrel yanked on the string unraveled from Phoebe's cape and wrenched the twig free. The beam seemed to hover for a moment in midair and then crashed to the ground, shearing away a few feathers from the quail as it ran clear.

Kestrel pounded his fist into his hand. "So close," he spat. "I should have waited a second more until the bird was more centered under the beam."

"Such is not our luck," Astron said. "And if the words of that Milligan are true, never will it be. It was only the lifetimes of unspent luck that we brought with us upon entry to the realm that ensured our rescue from the sea and a language that you and Phoebe understand as well as I. But Jelilac and Milligan evidently have drained all of that away. The ordinary trapping skills from the realm of men will do us little good here. We must approach the cause of our problem, rather than deal with its symptoms."

"That is easy enough for you to say," Phoebe growled irritably. "You do not need food and water as do the rest of us."

"I am well aware of the metabolic needs of men," Astron said. He waved his arm toward the treeline in the

302

distance. "Despite the peril, we must leave the sterile surroundings of this beach."

"Or perhaps we should all clutch these talismans and hope that a gamefowl walks out of the forest and lies down at our feet," Phoebe said.

"That is the essence of the solution," Astron agreed. "In this realm, we must strive to increase our luck and raise it to the point that the improbable happens as a matter of course. Then whatever we need will immediately follow."

"Yes, Astron is right." Nimbia pulled at the chains about her neck. "We have only survived as well as we have because of whatever minimal protection these necklaces provide."

"And how does one go about effecting this increase?" Kestrel said. "We have no masts or ladders here, and even Milligan was unsure of what would be the result."

"That is only one way," Astron said. "Surely the aleators have many other means. We must approach them again, only this time much better prepared."

"I do not care for the likes of Jelilac." Phoebe shook her head. "Perhaps others will be the same. We must instead act on our own. Despite your misgivings, Astron, contacting Camonel is our best chance."

Before Astron could reply, he heard a deep sighing noise from the direction of the water. He looked seaward and saw the foaming crestline of waves begin a rapid retreat, exposing the slope of land far beneath the extent of the lowest tide. Astron looked farther out over the ocean. Although he could not be sure, the line between the water and the sky seemed much higher than he had remembered it before.

"What is it?" Kestrel asked.

"A wall of moving water," Astron said. "Just as Milligan hinted—a tidal wave, some among your realm call it. Quickly, there is little time. Run for higher ground and climb into the trees." He raced over to where Nimbia sat and pulled her to her feet. Spinning her about, he shoved her in the direction of the slope rising from the beach.

Kestrel pounded his fist into his hands. "What rotten

luck," he growled. In apparent frustration, he reached up to pull the talismans from his neck, but then thought better of it. He lifted Phoebe from the ground. In imitation of Astron and Nimbia, they began running hillward on a slightly different path.

Astron and Nimbia sprinted up over the sandy ground into the darkness of the forest without speaking. Nimbia paused a moment at the base of the first climbable tree she found, but Astron motioned her onward. Stumbling into darkness, they picked their way farther into the dense canopy. Behind him, Astron could hear a muted roar drawing closer. Kestrel and Phoebe were nowhere to be seen.

Finally Astron stopped and pointed at a low-hanging branch. Together he and Nimbia scrambled up from limb to limb into the foliage. Despite his scales, rough branches scraped against his hands and snagged his leggings, but he did not pause to pick at the splinters. His head poked through to sunlight as he pulled himself to a slender, swaying branch that barely held his weight. Looking seaward, he saw the huge wave crest and topple over upon itself. With a booming crash, a wall of foaming water pounded onto the beach and began racing uphill.

The sandy slope was covered in an instant. Like popping embers in a fire, the trunks of the closest trees snapped from the impact and then were buried under the waterline. The dense grove of timber slowed the rush, but still it roared up the hillside. Astron flicked down his membranes, hoping that the fury of the onrush would be spent before it reached them. He saw row after row of treetops disappear beneath the churning sea and huge trunks bobbing up behind, completely stripped of foliage. The cool sea-green muted into muddy browns, and a web of debris formed on the once clear surface of the water.

The wave front surged closer, slowing as it came. Midway up the slope, the breathtaking speed seemed to be blunted. Then the wave top crashed, to rise no more. But still the water level climbed higher in a relentless swell. Astron saw the first tendrils snake about the base of the tree in which he had climbed and then the water level rise above the ground. Swiftly, the lower branches were submerged. Astron tested what remained of the trunk above his head but he already knew he could climb no more.

He looked across to Nimbia, hanging awkwardly on the branch across from his own. Before he could speak, the cold water reached his feet and then surged over his head. With an irresistible pull, he was yanked from his perch and then struck in the side by an uprooted trunk. Astron thrust his hands into the thick and deeply grooved bark and grabbed hold of the log as it passed. He scrambled around the side and thrust his head into the air, just in time to see Nimbia floating past. Releasing part of his grip, he grabbed and pulled her to the trunk. Dimly, he was aware of passing over a crest and then tipping downward to cascade into an interior valley below.

The next few moments were a blur of splashing spray and jarring caroms off of the trees on the downslope side. Somehow, Astron and Nimbia managed to hang on to the trunk that bore them and at the same time avoid being caught between it and the other trees into which it crashed.

They reached the bottom of the small valley and then hurled partway up the other side. The water slowed gradually to a halt. With a slow ponderous motion, it reversed direction and began to move back down toward the valley floor. But its momentum was nearly spent. The trunk moved sluggishly with the flow. With one final bone-jarring jolt, it crashed to the ground, letting the burbling water race ahead.

Astron held on to his grip for a few moments more, listening to the hiss and gurgle receding into silence. Slowly he dismounted and slid his feet to the ground. In a moment, Nimbia joined him, her face blanked in a daze. Oblivious to their deliverance, she looked at the wet clothing that sagged about the curve of her body.

"If you had the power of weaving, you could dry these instantly," Nimbia said. She fussed a moment at her tunic, still not mended from the battles in the realm of reticulates. "But since you do not, demon, turn your head while I disrobe."

Mixing with the dizziness of their ride, Astron felt a

subtle stirring in his stembrain, a tantalizing feeling from before, which he could not quite recognize. They should immediately begin searching for Kestrel and Phoebe, but something else tugged at him.

Astron started to answer, then halted. A flicker of movement up the interior slope above the high-water mark had caught his eye. Almost thankful for the distraction, he touched Nimbia's shoulder and pointed at what he saw. A small tendril of smoke struggled skyward from the foliage.

"Perhaps another aleator," he whispered. "One evidently with luck to burn. Keep on your clothing. This time we will be more forewarned."

Astron led Nimbia up the hillside. The ground became far more rocky and the canopy of trees gave way to scrubbier underbrush and finally an open clearing. Astron strode forward boldly, mustering as much dignity as he could in his soggy clothing. He saw a single figure sitting on a rock beside a small fire, over which was roasting some sort of pig. A horse was hobbled nearby. Next to it, a large pack was propped against a small tent of bright blue.

Upon the noise of their approach, the man looked up slowly from his contemplation, but no expression of surprise crossed his face. Cold blue eyes stared out under a head of golden blond hair, cut shoulder length and straight, with no curl. The face held the smoothness of youth, unwrinkled and without trouble—almost that of a child just aroused from sleep. Broad shoulders, heavily muscled, flexed under a thin, sleeveless shirt that sparkled with an iridescence in the last rays of sunlight filtering into the clearing. The throat of the shirt was thrown open; not a single talisman dangled about the sinewy neck.

"Whom do you seek?" A measured voice cut across the distance, each word unhurried and more of a command than a question.

"Did you not hear the crash of the wave?" Astron walked forward, motioning Nimbia to follow. "I would expect to find anyone who was able to hear its warning cautiously returning to ground from the safety of a high tree, rather than calmly fixing a meal."

306

"The wave would have reached Byron or it would not." The man shrugged. "There is no need to prepare for what is meant to be."

Astron hesitated a moment and searched about wildly for one of the spheres that Milligan had used to capture his and the others' luck. He saw no signs of one and took another step forward. After his experience with the reflectives, it seemed far easier than before. "You are one of exceedingly good fortune," he said. "I have heard that even the smallest fire dissipates what one has accumulated back into the ether."

Byron looked at Astron sharply. "Are you here to tempt me?" he said. "To test and see if I am worthy?" He stopped and darted his eyes to Nimbia as she approached. Astron watched Byron's nostrils flare and his hands suddenly coil into fists. The warrior's eyes ran slowly over her body and torn tunic. The beat of his pulse stood out strongly on his neck.

"You tempt me, indeed." Byron's voice rumbled quietly. "What is it that you would have me do?"

Astron scowled in annoyance. He recognized the reaction and understood it far better than before. Stepping in front of Nimbia, he threw wide his arms, shielding her as much as he was able.

"We might have something of great benefit," he said quickly. "It all depends on what you can offer as a fair payment in exchange."

"If it is luck of which you speak, then there is no basis for a barter," Byron said. "I have none to offer, nor do I seek any for what I must do."

Astron stirred uncomfortably. "What exactly is it that, ah, that you must do?" he asked.

"Why, travel to the grand casino to contest for the crown with all the others," Byron said. He slapped the long broadsword at his side. "But not in the same manner. If I succeed, it will be because fate wills it, not because of twists of luck."

Astron's interest immediately heightened—the grand casino, exactly where he wanted to go. Only with a firm

307

resolution did he stop himself from looking back at Nimbia with a smile. "We have experienced firsthand what happens without luck," he said carefully. "Just to survive takes more than a little amount."

"Only because some of the aleators have so distorted it," Byron spat. "They lead the realm to destruction with their tinkering, they work with fluids better left alone. Look," he said, apparently warming to the subject. "The first tenet says that luck is a gas, a perfect one that flows from high pressure to low. Without interference, it distributes itself evenly throughout the realm, favoring no one over another. The forces of fate are free to operate, to work the destinies that are intended for us all.

"But what happens when it is compressed, scooped up from everywhere into a small number of concentrations under the control of only a few? There is less left in the ambience. Without participating in the forbidden rituals, everyone else is stripped of what is his due share. To step from a hut becomes a great adventure; to fill one's stomach is a hunt of great exhaustion. Even the elements are perturbed into extremes. For the fortunate, the air is always clear and balmy. In compensation, gentle rains and waves are compressed into great disasters that prey on those who do not have the protection of the proper talismans.

"With the great accumulations come great new strains and forces," Byron went on, "distortions in the very fabric of what must happen to us all. Those who have accumulated luck must dispense some modicums to their followers, constructing all sorts of charms like those useless husks that drape about your necks. They war not with merit, but depend entirely on those who can force chance outcomes to go their way."

Byron stopped and set his lips in a grim line. "But I will stop them all," he said defiantly. "It is my calling, and to it I will be true."

"You say you have no great accumulation of luck of your own," Astron said. "How do you hope to accomplish your goal?"

"Soon my followers will return and report what they

have seen in the bay on the far coast. There Myra has dropped anchor with both her ships. We will attack on the morrow, and one of them will become mine. With it, we will cross the great sea.

"I will stride into the grand casino and win, although luck I have none. Luck favors the believer, states the fourth tenet; it is fickle and hence runs in streaks, professes the fifth. Great manipulations for enhancement and devices for reversing good to ill are built upon the two of them, but neither shall I use."

"But if you have no advantage and they—"

"I am destiny's darling," Byron thundered. "The great sagas of our past have finally been incarnated in me. I am untouched by wind or wave. I am the one to weave together the last threads of the tapestry of our fate into one final design."

Byron stopped and looked into the growing darkness. "It is true that how I will triumph is hidden. Even I do not know the means. My journey to the grand casino may be but a testing, a proof that I am worthy of being the instrument of fate. But in the moment of crisis, in the final spin of the wheel, my power will be revealed and I will be victorious, as from the beginning of time it is written that I would."

A sudden shout from up the hill cut off Astron's reply. He looked to the crest to see a line of torches in a staggered line.

"I am here," Byron called back. "I am here and the way is safe. There are no concentrations of luck with which you must contend."

With excited voices and the sound of crunching underbrush, the group on the crest began to pour down the hillside. Although the way was fairly clear and the torches gave sufficient light, Astron saw the two dozen men, women, and children pick their way carefully, holding on to one another for additional security and giving the fallen snags and large bushes a wide berth.

In the very center of the group, carefully supported on both sides, was one far older than the rest. Wisps of long white hair streamed from around a crown splotched with spatters of red and veins of purple. The eyes were nearly closed and a trickle of spittle ran from the corner of the face that sagged. Bare stick-thin arms flapped idly with the jostle of each step. The feet shuffled after one another, as if actuated by the mechanism of a child's toy.

"Centuron." Byron nodded in response to Astron's gaze. "His fame among the aleators is almost as great as—well, almost as great as mine. For over one hundred cycles of the sun, he has survived without benefit of the magical arts to shape his luck. He is the living proof that my cause is right and that I will succeed."

Astron watched the procession draw closer, noting their gaunt and sallow faces. Except for the excitement of meeting, they showed animation only slightly greater than Centuron's. With stooped shoulders and panting breath, they converged on Byron's camp, some looking with hungry eyes at the roast pig.

One separated herself from the rest. Dirt streaked her face and her hair was in tangles. Suitably cleaned, the woman would be a beauty, Astron thought, but the rigors of the trek had made her barely distinguishable from the men.

"We must move on quickly," she said. "The minions of Myra have found two others adrift in the wake of the last wave. We overheard them talk of two more whom they wanted as well. Soon there will be search parties throughout the hills."

"Kestrel and Phoebe," Astron shouted. "Were they injured?"

"They seemed to walk well enough with no assistance from their guards." The woman shrugged. "But, of course, such a condition is only temporary if Myra has experiments to run. I would guess she would use them in the games at the grand casino, if not before."

"Then we must get to that beach and—" Astron began, but Byron put up his hand to stop.

"What else, Sylvan, what else do you bring?" he said.

The woman nodded. Slowly she pulled a pack from

her back and dumped its contents at Byron's feet, a dozen ears of a black-kerneled corn, three large apples, and a scattering of small seeds.

"We saved as much as we could for your great contest, Byron, but the little ones need more than an equal share."

Byron waved at Astron and Nimbia. "It is well that you have procured what you did, Sylvan. There are two more, and I have not yet decided if they should be fed as well."

"Wait," Astron said. "By all means let the little ones eat. I for one have no need."

"No, I have spoken," Byron suddenly thundered. "I am the chosen one and my commands must be obeyed. The sacrifice of all others is of no importance. Their destiny is only to ensure that I succeed."

"We do not question." Sylvan lowered her head and stepped backward. "Even old Centuron has taken less than we might otherwise offer."

"Ah, if you do not know exactly what power you will have," Astron said, "what convinces you that you indeed are this darling of destiny?"

Byron's eyes blazed. "You are sent by the fates to tempt me!" he said. "You wish to test how firm is my resolve." He looked again at Nimbia and drew his lips into a grim line. "Very well. I will show to the overseers of our fate the extent of my mettle. You shall accompany me and yet both remain untouched." His stare locked on Nimbia and he ran his tongue over his lips. "Yes, untouched," he said, "until it is properly time."

Astron's stembrain suddenly bubbled with a fiery vexation. "Do not be overly concerned." He turned and spoke to Nimbia in the language of the fey. "Despite my size, I will serve you still. You merely need—"

Astron stopped as he noticed Nimbia's smile. She let the top of her tunic sag in disarray. "It sounds as if he invites us to join him," she said. "Accept, accept in the name of a queen of the fey."

311

CHAPTER TWENTY-FOUR

Mark of the Manipulator

KESTREL wiped the moisture from his brow and held his breath. He looked at the rope-suspended blade that slowly oscillated back and forth over Phoebe's outstretched body on the cabin deck. She was bound hand and foot, spread-eagled between four pegs anchored in the polished planking. Only by pressing herself firmly against the horizontal could she just barely avoid the swipe of the sharp edge against her neck.

Kestrel could hope for random outcomes no longer; the next click of the levers must pull the rope upward rather than let out any more slack. Desperately, he looked at the tinted windows sternward through which filtered the last rays of the setting sun and then at the sloping cabin walls, searching for some other way out of danger than the one of chance he was offered. The clutter of spinpins, glassy spheres, and instruments of small tortures he recognized from Jelilac's sloop, but nothing that would be of aid could he see.

The aleator named Myra sat in the corner behind a small table and tracked his darting eyes with a cold stare. Grabbing her chin between thumb and forefingers, she slowly brought her fingertips together, gathering up the loose flesh. Kestrel heard a raspy scrape from the contact, like that of a man testing a half-day growth of beard. A loose-fitting tunic did little to hide the angular bones underneath, and patches of splotched skin shone through beneath thin white hair pulled straight back and tied in a knot.

Myra's two ships lay at anchor side by side, far closer than the mooring one would expect in the realm of men. But with each wave that shifted them about, the two craft always avoided colliding at the last instant. The massive vessels seemed to be ably manned by very small crews, although the hold of the other ship, Kestrel had noticed when he was hustled aboard, was full of hammocks, men-at-arms, and others fettered with heavy chains.

"Just one more toss of the ball into the hoops," Myra said. "Just one more, and I will be satisfied that your words carry no true meaning. Your talk of powerful wards that shield your wealth is too implausible, too—" Myra stopped and shuddered. "No, I will not doubt," she said. "I will prepare for the games at the grand casino with the rest. Luck is the true basis of our existence. Without that, what is the purpose?"

Kestrel squeezed the rubber ball in his hand. The array of small circular openings in the slanted panel across the cabin seemed to blur in the dimming light. The gentle rocking motion of the barge did not help matters much; but even without the added complication, he knew he could not ensure that the sphere fell into one of the hoops that he wished.

Kestrel glanced at Phoebe, trying to smile encouragement, although he felt little inside. They had been apprehended after the passing of the tidal wave almost as easily as they had by Jelilac on their arrival in the realm. This time, however, since they had no real luck to be siphoned away, the glassine spheres did not become charged with the oily, amber smoke.

Kestrel reached back and touched the lumpiness of his rucksack and felt the presence of the pollen. There was no telling if the grains still had any value after the soaking, but without Astron, he had decided it probably was best to maneuver things so that Phoebe could summon Camonel. Somehow, he had to convince Myra that she could not get at his vast store of hidden luck and her only recourse was to destroy it with fire.

He glanced into her rheumy eyes and scowled. The aleator had proven to be quite stubborn. Just like Jelilac, she had insisted on subjecting them to a test that quantified the extent of their fortune.

"One more mishap will not prove what you wish." He

waved at the complicated apparatus at his side. "I have done as you instructed more than half a dozen times and my skill with the tossing ball has not changed in any noticeable way. My wealth is shielded. Not even the slightest efflux leaks from the wards."

"No one with true wealth keeps it all hidden." Myra shook her head. "At least some is contained in simple talismans to ward off the trivial misfortunes of the ambience. Why, the tosses of anyone with even a minimum of luck would find the hoops connected to the lever that raises the blade. By now it should be swinging just beneath the beams. The fact that, instead, you have sent it up and down in an almost random fashion indicates that the power of your wards is only a fantasy. You are paupers and nothing more."

She hesitated a moment and then motioned to the guards at her side. "Just in case there is an element of truth in what he says, subject him one more time to the linkage of reversal. Then have him make the final pitch."

Kestrel felt his chest tighten. One more trip of the wrong lever would prove fatal to Phoebe. Grimly, he searched through his mind for something that would give him an opening, some hidden crevice in Myra's character that he could exploit. Kestrel's thoughts tumbled while he watched the complicated mechanical linkages at his side shuffle together a thick deck of cards. He felt mild shocks from copper wires wrapped around his ankles while he watched, but by now they were no more than an annoying irritant. When the mixing stopped, he reached forward without prompting and selected one from the deck, just as he had done many times before.

He flipped the bit of stiff parchment faceup on the table and reached for the second, not even bothering to notice the ornately decorated woman with cold dark eyes staring back. "The whole deck is probably nothing other than the black queen," he grumbled. "The fact that I draw ten or so of them in a row proves little."

"Of course they are all the same," Myra said. "How else can one's luck be convinced that it is of the wrong sign? It is fickle as the fifth tenet states, and once it is

314

flipped, it will bring nothing but misfortune. If, by some chance, you do possess some wealth and I cannot have it contributing in a positive fashion to my own, then it will serve instead as a weapon against the others when we game in the grand casino."

Kestrel took a deep breath. He had to gamble on what little knowledge he had. "The book with figures," he said slowly, "the one that Milligan says you possess. It sounds to me to be no more than a navigator's almanac. Is it why he calls you Myra the doubting?"

Kestrel noticed a sudden flicker in Myra's cheeks. Her eyes widened almost imperceptibly, but then returned to their piercing stare. He waited expectantly. The signs were not much, but perhaps indeed he had chanced upon something he could twist to advantage.

"Could you be so bold," Myra said after a moment, "actually to follow the instructions as they are written, without knowing the consequences?" She waved her arms about the cabin. "None of my minions would dare attempt it, despite the apparent advantage."

Myra stroked her chin and then shrugged. "Jelilac has a great store of luck for use in the games, perhaps the greatest of all. I would rather husband each dram of mine and not waste any on getting from here to the casino, wherever that might be."

"You do not know?" Kestrel said. "A navigation almanac would be most basic on such a sea as this."

"Perhaps in dimmest memory, there were such things," Myra said. "But to use them would be counter to the basic tenets of any aleator. We sail where the winds take us, and, if we truly believe, it will be where we desire. Our luck provides. To use a calculation, no matter how reliable it might be, is a statement of distrust.

Myra leaned forward until her face was a hand span from Kestrel's own. "Luck favors the believer," she said, "just as the fourth tenet states. If you sincerely trust in it, you will weather your trials unscathed; if you doubt, then it gives the fifth tenet a chance to wreak its havoc.

"The book and the device labeled as a sextant which accompanies it," Myra continued in a hushed voice, "they must come from someone beyond the farthest extent of our realm—from someone whose wish is to do us harm, to make us doubt in our very foundations and in our reasons for existing at all."

Myra drew back and squinted at Kestrel. "No, it would do great ill for me or one of my minions to perform the calculations that would point us where we wish to go. I have often wondered if it were good luck or ill in the first place that led me to find it in the smoking ashes of a lightning-struck fire."

She reached out and tapped a long slender finger against Kestrel's chest. "But one so foolhardy as to spout of invincible wards, to him there surely could be no harm. He would not fear the misfortune that might result from following the ritual or from the weight upon his thoughts about what he has done."

Kestrel looked back into Myra's eyes, unblinking. He weighed the risks and decided that the chance was worth it. It might not be more than simple sightings, and he would be done. With just the right words, it would free Phoebe and give her a chance at Camonel as well.

"Of course, as I understand the third tenet—luck begets luck—" he said, "the ritual might not be one of misfortune, but would enhance whatever one possesses at the outset instead." He shrugged and smiled. "And since both of ours are still intact, the increase might be most significant—significant enough that even the chances of Myra the doubter will become slim in the grand casino. Yes, by all means release the woman and we will do it. I believe, I believe deeply in our triumphant success."

Myra frowned and rubbed at her chin. "Your speech is glib," she said. "Most glib for one so close to disaster. Perhaps there is some truth in what you speak after all."

Her eyes lost their focus, and for a long moment she looked past Kestrel out onto the sea. "Jelilac," she muttered. "It is he that I fear the most. Against him, I must marshal every resource. It would be folly not to take advantage of what my luck has offered."

She looked back at Kestrel and smiled. "There is also the second tenet," she said. "The entropy of luck always increases. Your wards might be a marvel of which I know not, but no matter how cleverly constructed, I doubt that they could withstand the heat of a flame."

Kestrel steeled himself from smiling in return. He forced a look of apprehension onto his face. "Just a moment." He licked his lips quickly. "We have excellent shields, it is true, but I said nothing about being so foolish as to subject them to a fire."

Myra's smile broadened. "Ah, the composure does seem to waver a bit," she said. "Perhaps you were right. Nothing in this room would provide a sufficient test."

"You know as well as I what happens when fire is applied to any container, no matter how clever its construction." Kestrel put protest into his voice. He waved his arm about the room. "Never mind what I said. You can do with us what you will with any of your devices; but like everyone else, we shun the flame." Kestrel stopped and lowered his eyes. "Please," he said softly. "We have struggled too long to build up what we have. Anything but a fire."

"Thus it shall be." Myra slapped her side. "Yes, this will be far more rewarding than any of the simple tests that the likes of Jelilac would try." She looked over her shoulder and yelled out onto the deck. "Bring the kindling and the spark. We shall set them out on a raft where the logs can be the fuel. After he has performed the ritual as the tome instructs, whatever luck they accrue will be burned entirely away."

"But—" Kestrel began.

"Silence," Myra commanded. She motioned to a sailor in the hatchway and he came forward, clutching a large leather-bound book like a servant with a tray. Balancing on its upper surface was a sextant of gleaming metal.

Kestrel forced his eyes to open wide and then slumped his shoulders. Hanging his head, he stepped aside while two more sailors pulled the swinging blade out of the way and untied Phoebe. He squeezed her hand as a signal for silence as she rose to her feet. They could be safely away, he thought. With just a little more luck— He stopped the race of his thoughts. Holding his breath, he managed to offer a token resistance to the arms that propelled him out of the cabin as the final piece of convincing.

As Kestrel watched with what he hoped was a defeated expression on his face, the entire crew seemed to come alive with a blur of activity. A small raft was lowered over the side, tethered to a long rope, and pushed by poles away from the hull. Matches and kindling were assembled and an archer was ferried across from the second of Myra's ships.

While he and Phoebe were guided by knifepoint to a small boat, the archer began donning a thick, padded vest and hood. In silence, the two of them were rowed out to the raft and unceremoniously pushed onto its rocking deck. Kestrel saw the archer place his hands in thick gloves with which he could barely grasp his bow. Bulky shields were placed behind his back. At arm's length, he gingerly struck a spark that caught some curly shavings on fire. The archer dipped a tar-soaked arrowtip into the blaze, involuntarily flinching backward as it burst into a smoky flame. Aiming awkwardly, he nocked the shaft and pointed it at the small raft.

Kestrel turned to Phoebe and smiled. "I hope that this idea is a better one than tossing the ball into the hoops," he said.

Kestrel put down the book and arched his back. Most of an hour had passed. He looked at the archer still straining at attention on Myra's barge and felt a grim satisfaction at his discomfort. It had, of course, been too much to expect that he could read as well as understand the language of the realm, especially since their initial luck had all been siphoned away by Milligan. A little more time would be a reasonable enough amount for study, he judged, and then he would go through the motions of sighting.

"When I am done and shout back the heading," he said to Phoebe, "they will undoubtedly give the instruction to fire the shaft. Let it start the raft burning and then use some of the powder you obtained from the archimage to summon Camonel to our aid."

"What about the sextant and book?" Phoebe said. "If

318

they are from beyond this realm, might not they reveal some clue about Astron's riddle as well?"

"The sextant is of some arcane design, but I think I have figured out how to use it in a convincing fashion." Kestrel shook his head. "Except for a few unusual features, the book appears much as one would expect, page after page of tables." He shrugged and again shook his head. "If Astron were here, he might make something more of the instructions, but the significance I cannot tell."

Kestrel rapidly thumbed through the bulk of the volume, grunting as the pages fell through his fingers. "It must have been constructed by more than one scribe, and certainly they did not talk to each other. See, the style changes with the entries for every few days. Initially there are four columns on each leaf, with what I guess from the accompanying logos to be the position of the sun on the upper half and the brighter stars beneath. Next, it changes to data in rows, if the headings are to be believed, and after that the solar elevations are completely separated from the rest. On and on it goes, with fancy scrollwork and then harsh starkness, changing the format every fortnight or so."

He set down the tome and laughed despite himself. "It certainly was designed to be well used. The entries run on and on for what must be hundreds and hundreds of years. I doubt that anyone would really care, unless it was passed on from one generation to the next. Surely what is here will last Myra and her crew before a twentieth is spent."

Kestrel shrugged and hefted the sextant. "But enough of that. Prepare to toss your powders into the fire." He looked in the direction of the setting sun and found the brightest of the evening stars. The slosh of the waves against the raft was definitely greater than against the massive sides of the barge. Only with difficulty was he able to keep what he looked at in the center of view.

Kestrel grunted at the heaviness of the sextant, swinging it slowly to the second sighting. The screws felt awkward to his touch and wobbled in their shafts as he tried to adjust a cursor. He ran his hand over the blistered skin of iron that framed a cloudy lens. The craftsmanship was

319

quite primitive, but he supposed it did not really matter. The heading he would shout back to Myra's barges would be the first that popped into his mind. It would depend solely upon her luck if it were accurate or not.

When he had completed the last sighting Kestrel thumbed through the book as if he were searching for corresponding entries. Phoebe tensed at his side with her hand in the pocket of her cape, ready to toss out the powder. After a moment, he stood up on the rocking platform and cupped his hands to his mouth. "A third of a circle away from the direction of the setting sun," he shouted. "The calculations have been made and there is no doubt about—"

Before he could finish, the archer released his bow. The arrow sliced through the gathering gloom of night and hit the raft squarely on the side closest to Myra's ships. Kestrel bent over and fanned the flames, no longer caring about what the aleators thought of his actions. He looked at Phoebe and saw her face flushed with confidence. With clenched fists, she waved her arms upward, seeming to add energy to the flame. The sparkling powder danced from her hand and fell squarely into the blaze.

Kestrel felt his own tension grow. Soon it really would be over. Without the rush of combining realms Camonel could head directly to wherever they wished. He could find Astron and Nimbia and send the small demon back to his own realm. Then with Palodad— Kestrel stopped. He had not fully thought through the reason they wanted to find the anvilwood and send Astron home alone in the first place. Suppose he was right and Camonel was under the control of some wizard; perhaps even Prydwin was manipulating things beyond his own realm. Kestrel touched the sextant at his side and frowned. Manipulations in another realm—a navigator's almanac and sextant served exactly the same end.

Kestrel reached out and touched Phoebe's shoulder, even though he knew he should not. "Wait a moment," he said. "Perhaps it would be better if it were some other demon that you—"

Kestrel's words were cut short. With a hiss of foul-tasting air, the massive djinn stepped from the flame and stood as a sinister, dark silhouette against the last rays of the sun.

"I, Camonel, submit to your will because my prince Palodad instructs it," the demon said. "There is no need for a struggle of wills. Speak your command and it will be mine to perform."

"Never mind about princes and allegiances in the realm of daemon," Kestrel said before Phoebe could speak. Her eyes darted to him, but he rushed on, ignoring her puzzlement. "It is your mastery which we wish to know. Yes, not princes but masters. Is the wizard here the one who dominates your will totally so that you must do all that she asks, or is there another who instructs you instead to say the words that prevent any true struggle from taking place?"

Sparkles of blue began to dance about Camonel's teeth in the twilight. In the faint glow, Kestrel saw the demon's scowl grow into one of true menace. For a long moment, the djinn was silent. Then his rumbling voice again came forth.

"Where is Astron, the one who walks? It is not only the pollen. He is needed as well."

"Your master—who is it truly?" Phoebe asked suddenly, apparently catching the drift of Kestrel's thought. "Now that I think of it, each time was too easy. I was too flushed in victory to examine closely how I felt. You merely said that I was yours to dominate, but never was there a true test."

"Prince Palodad instructs that I serve and—"

"Not him," Phoebe interrupted. "Not another demon —your master. What is his name?"

Kestrel sucked in his breath. He looked up at the glowing yellow eyes of the djinn and felt a cold numbness creeping down his spine. If Camonel was not under Phoebe's control, what would happen then?

Again Camonel was silent for a long moment. His face distorted in indecision. Finally he answered in a staccato popping of sparks that shot from his teeth and lips. "I am to do whatever I am asked by you, provided that it does not conflict with what I otherwise have been told."

321

"Then the need for Astron to accompany the pollen, Palodad's words that the grains held some clue to the answer—"

"Of that I cannot say." Camonel shook his head.

Kestrel grabbed the sextant, just as a large wave sloshed into the raft and tumbled Phoebe into his side. "Is your master the manipulator?" He waved the instrument in front of Camonel's chest. "Is it he that brought about the collapsing of the two realms of symmetry? Did he leave the sextant here so that those like Myra would doubt, so that there would be damage here in addition to the rest?"

"Yes," Camonel said. "To speak of the manipulations themselves I am not bound. But this is only one realm of the many that swim in the void. What is your command? There is much yet to be done."

"And Gaspar," Kestrel continued. "Is your master behind his riddle as well?"

"Gaspar is a demon of little brain," Camonel said. "Even though he is a prince, he could never—"

"Take us back to the realm of men," Phoebe said. "Then return and find Astron and Nimbia as—"

A sudden wave bigger than any before raced under the raft. Kestrel tipped forward, just barely managing to grab Phoebe before she fell. The water lapped over the edge of the logs and spilled into the fire. In a flash of smoke, the flame was instantly doused and Camonel was gone.

Kestrel tried staggering back to his feet, but the agitation of the sea increased. Stunned by what had happened, he looked out in the growing blackness toward Myra's ship and heard the aleator calling out over the bulwark.

"The first is spent but it has done its job. See the increased agitation of the surf. A great wave is coming and their luck does not ward it away. Pull them back aboard and we will slip offshore a league or so until the disturbance passes. Then on the morrow we will set sail as the glib one has directed. Keep them in bondage. If I can think of no new amusement during our journey, then certainly they can serve as shields on the floor of the casino."

Almost in a daze, Kestrel pulled Phoebe to him and held her tight. He looked at the last wisps of smoke from the doused fire and cursed his luck, what little there was of it. Now they would have to travel to the casino. There would be no chance that Myra would be persuaded to light a fire again. Yes, to the casino and hope that Astron would somehow be there as well. He kicked the sextant overboard and then gave the almanac a shove—devices of the manipulator, the one behind the merging realms and the riddle as well. There might indeed be something of significance to them, he thought, but it would take someone like Astron to discover what it was. Now, until they dropped anchor, he had to focus all his attention on keeping Myra's thoughts away from more testing with her swinging blade.

Chapter Twenty-Five

Broken Talismans

ASTRON peered out from the cover of the brush at the line of the crest. Leaves of deep green scattered tiny droplets of dew as he pushed them aside. Behind him, buzzing insects filled the interior slopes of the island with a blur of sound. No one had yet stirred from either of Myra's ships lying at anchor in the bay below. But in only a few moments more, Byron's force sneaking down the hillside would inevitably be discovered.

From the look of the anxious faces of those who had followed the tall swordsman, not everyone was as convinced as he about their rôle in his destiny. Armed only with blade and shield, they would be no match for aleators with necks ringed by talismans. But surely at least some would survive long enough, Astron thought. Long enough to bolt and flee back up the slope along the wide path that ran by his hiding place. And just as surely, some of Myra's aleators would follow.

Astron tightened his grip on the rope of twisted vines

that ran from his hand down onto the wide path past the bush. There was every chance that it would break or even come untied from the base of the tree across the way, but he could think of nothing better to try.

He glanced at Nimbia, kneeling at his side, a sword of steel dangling from her hip. "The words you had me say to Byron about my prowess in battle felt most uncomfortable," he said. "I am a cataloguer, not a hewer of men."

"I saw how you led the reticulates at more than a single node," Nimbia answered. "Do not be concerned about the discomfort, demon, though the modesty is becoming."

Astron wrinkled his nose. He should have felt pleasure in Nimbia's words, but he did not. Somehow the aid he offered to Byron increased her stature, rather than his own.

"Nevertheless," he growled, "too much time has been wasted in my translation of fluffs of conversation back and forth. It is better spent in observation of the realm, collecting facts that later can be used to advantage."

Nimbia smiled. "I do not consider the exchange of information a waste," she said. "You are serving me well. Without the facility of your tongue, I would know nothing of Byron beyond grunts and stares." She stopped and lowered her eyes. "And just as important, he would know as little of me."

Astron felt his annoyance grow. He did not care for the way that Byron stared at her when she was distracted elsewhere. When in Byron's presence, she behaved like a human female from the sagas. Her interest in the aleator went beyond the needs of their riddle-quest or even wresting some anvilwood from the grand casino. More than once she had laughed when he translated Byron's words and shook her head at the chastisement he suggested as a reply.

"Byron has made clear more than once that his destiny is his primary focus." Astron pulled tentatively on the rope. "Everything else is of little concern."

"A secondary position would not be so bad." Nimbia

shrugged. "I have not fared nearly so well in the realm of the fey." She flipped golden curls over her shoulder. "He is comely enough so that no one would whisper when we are seen together. Among his own, he commands a station of respect, one that fittingly links with a hillsovereign."

Nimbia stopped and looked Astron in the eye. "Besides, when all is done and you return to your own realm, what then is to happen to me?"

The wrinkle in Astron's nose deepened, but Nimbia did not seem to notice as she rushed on.

"I can tell that he is interested," she said. "Constantly he devours me with his eyes. His boldness is far better than the hesitant glances and turned-away faces that were the features of most when I was the one who held sway. Yes, he has great interest; and yet, at the same time, he shows measured restraint. Unlike the others who become victims of their own lust and interpret each gentle hesitation as a stunning rebuke or a sure indication that there is someone else, he is game for the chase."

"You have special qualities as well." Astron stumbled. "Your creations were as much for your minions as yourself. No prince have I seen display such concern. You would have earned your diadem, even if it were not given by default. And a wizard besides—only ones of that ilk can a djinn ever truly respect. You shielded me in the tree when—"

"Enough." Nimbia laughed. She reached out and touched Astron on the cheek. "You need not sing of my virtues, demon. Your place in my retinue is secure. It is rather *I* that should list the praises so that you are encouraged to even greater glories for your queen."

Astron started to reply, but then quickly snapped shut his mouth. He halted the idle flexing of his grip about the rope and froze dead still. Without moving, he looked at Nimbia expectantly.

Nimbia's face clouded in puzzlement. "Demon?" she said. "What is the matter? Did something happen in that stembrain of yours?"

325

"I am waiting," Astron said simply. "Waiting to hear the list."

Nimbia threw back her head and laughed. Her voice tinkled like a shower of golden brandels tossed against a shield. "Very well," she said after a moment. "You deserve no less."

Nimbia eyed Astron critically and then touched her index finger to the palm of her other hand. "First, there is the keenness of mind," she said. "In no other of your realm have I observed such an ability for deduction."

"Palodad and other princes that rule—" Astron blurted out, suddenly uncomfortable, as he had been before. But Nimbia put her finger to his lips for silence and then placed another beside the first.

"Secondly, there is the dedication to your quest," she said. "Despite the hindrances and dangers, you pursue the goal with an unrelenting intensity. Surely I have seen it matched in none of the mighty djinns with their easily distracted flitter of thought. And, now that I think of it, none in the realm of the fey would have persisted as long as have you."

Astron felt the beginning of a smile appear on his face, despite the discomfort. Other delicious feelings began to stir underneath. He wanted again to protest the sweep of her hyperbole, but thought better of it as Nimbia retracted her hand and began to say even more.

"Last, and perhaps most important, demon," she said, "is the comfort that you bring when we are together. I do not have to worry about somehow breaking through an impenetrable shyness or warding off a self-image that never can be satisfied. I do not have to remember that I am a woman and you are a man."

The seductive sweetness bubbling up inside Astron suddenly turned sour. Somehow Nimbia's words of praise were no longer a delight. Despite his best efforts to keep a placid composure, he felt his eye membranes quiver and his stembrain stir from its slumber with discontent.

Astron shook his head in the manner of men. Why did all of her words now affect him so? Was there a residual effect from his transposition into Kestrel's body that he somehow still retained?

Before he could begin to sort out any of the confusion of his thoughts, he saw the first of Byron's men appear on the crest. The aleator had thrown sword and shield away and was running as fast as he could. Astron scowled and pushed the feelings away. They would have to be examined later. First there was the matter of the darling of destiny and passage to the grand casino.

Three more of Byron's minions crested the hill in full rout and then six after that. Immediately behind the last, tall, well-fed swordsmen with purple surcoats over close-knit mail came racing close behind.

Astron looked out across the trail as the first of Byron's men staggered past and then back to Nimbia to see if she was ready. The rest of Byron's followers sprinted down the path into the interior of the island with the first of Myra's aleators on their heels. Astron saw a half-dozen talismans dancing about the necks of those in the foreground. Gritting his teeth, he let them pass. A score of swordsmen sped by, shouting and laughing as they ran; then behind them came a half-dozen stragglers more, not so richly endowed as the rest.

Astron waited until the last three were just beginning to rush past the hidden rope. Then he jerked it tight and held it as firmly as he was able. The first aleator unexpectedly leaped over a small boulder jutting in the way and hurled clear of the trip rope, evidently not even noticing its presence. The other two, however, were caught just above their ankles and pitched forward onto the ground. Both landed gracefully on glove-protected hands; but more importantly, just as Astron had hoped, the talismans about their necks hurled free to land a few body lengths beyond.

"Now," Astron shouted, "now, Nimbia, while we have a chance."

Nimbia sprang out onto the trail, her sword pointing the way. The two sprawled warriors rose to their feet; then their eyes widened in terror as she moved between them and their charms. Instantly they returned to their knees with hands spread wide, indicating surrender. One looked longingly at what lay a few feet away and began to sob.

Astron ran out behind Nimbia and scooped up the treasures. He flung them over his head and then turned after the third warrior who had stopped to see what was happening behind. Astron waved his sword with one hand while pointing at his own chest with the other. "Not one standard issue but two," he said. "You do not have a chance."

The third warrior froze. He unbuckled his sword and let it fall. Sagging on one knee, he bowed to the ground. Astron did not hesitate. He ran forward and, despite the small rocks that seemed to get in his way, pulled the third set of talismans away from their wearer.

"Over there." He pointed his sword back to Nimbia. "Do exactly as she says."

Astron saw the man-at-arms nod in submission. Without waiting to ensure that he fully complied, Astron began running down the trail as fast as he could manage not to stumble. So far, everything was proceeding as he had hoped. The aleators were so conditioned to depending on luck in everything they did that, without their charms, they felt completely helpless. When confronted with an opponent better endowed, they gave up rather than attempt a fight.

Astron bounded down the trail, catching up with two more warriors who ran behind the rest. He tripped over a bared root in the trail and barely kept from falling. Circling his sword over his head, he froze his face in a beserker's stare, yelling an incoherent challenge. Over a dozen talismans now bounced from his chest as he ran, and the men-at-arms' eyes immediately focused on their dance.

Just as the others before, the two warriors immediately assumed postures of surrender, letting Astron snatch their charms with a clumsy swipe before they guessed his intent. More aleators looked backward, and a shout of warning coursed through their midst. The pursuit of Byron's followers slowed and then completely halted.

Byron's warriors sensed the slacking of pursuit and

halted their own flight. With a rallying cheer, they turned and began to strike at the aleators who were looking over their shoulders at what was attacking their rear.

Astron yelled as fiendishly as he could and slashed blindly left and right. Aleators on both sides stepped backward, tumbling over one another and off the trail into the brush to get out of the way. One of Myra's captains in the vanguard caught sight of Astron's weight of treasure. He looked down at his own chest, barely ducked a swipe at the side of his head; then with a shudder, he bolted from the trail into the brush. Two more followed his lead, then a half-dozen more on the other side of the trail. In barely an instant, only five men-at-arms remained, all facedownward, offering their swords in surrender.

Astron pulled to a halt, barely believing what had happened. More than a score of well-armed warriors had been routed by a single foolhardy rush. Shaking his head, he grabbed the talismans that remained and added them to the rest. With stooping shoulders, he walked slowly back up the hill to see how Nimbia was faring in her stint at guard duty. For a moment he felt a rush of elation. He had performed as well as could have been expected of even a mighty djinn. But then, just as quickly, he put the thought aside. He was still a long way from securing any anvil-wood. There was yet the rescue of Kestrel and Phoebe to be managed. The lightning djinns that pursued might discover them at any time. And Byron? If he had survived the rush down the slope, what more could be expected from the one who seemed to covet Nimbia more and more with each passing moment.

Astron scowled at the frustration born of the inactivity. His stembrain was becoming increasingly difficult to control. He looked about the evening campfire erected just down the seaward slope from the crest of the hill and shook his head. Byron sat on the other side of the dying flame, talking quietly with two of his lieutenants and one of the captured warriors, as if the day had been the same as any other. The bloodstained rags which bound the tall warrior's leg looked blotched with black in the dimness of evening. Felled by the first man he met, Byron had been left behind when his ranks broke and began retreating up the hill.

Then, when Astron and the others returned in triumph, the aleators that remained in Myra's ships all transferred onto a single barge and sailed away, leaving the other vessel behind. Evidently, she had reasoned that she was confronting a force much more powerful than her own and did not wish to suffer the same defeat. With the next dawn, Byron had said, his own band would follow the same course and be led by her luck directly to the grand casino.

Astron ran his hand over the skin of his neck. Reluctantly, after the abandoned ship and the prisoners had been secured, he had given up the talismans to be destroyed. His arguments about the men-at-arms who had run into the forest possibly returning were ignored. The luck had to be dissipated back into the ether. Byron had insisted. To do less would not be true to his quest.

Astron looked over at Nimbia on the far side of the clearing. At least for the moment, she was occupied with other thoughts than tending to the tall warrior. Instead, the queen was watching with interest the preparations of Sylvan and Centuron for the breaking of the charms.

Astron rose and stretched, trying to remove some of the tension that froze the muscles of his back into tight knots. He supposed he should investigate the dissipation process as well. There might be something to be learned that could be used later. Besides, it probably was the last chance to talk to the hillsovereign without Byron being in the vicinity. Tomorrow they would be confined together in the barge for the final journey across the sea; then once in the grand casino, from what little Astron had gleaned, there would be little time for anything other than struggling for survival.

As Astron approached, Nimbia was peering over Sylvan's shoulder and gesturing, while the aleator slowly stirred the contents of a small cauldron over a sputtering flame. Nearby a second fire was roaring fiercely as it consumed branches of dry pinewood that Byron's followers had faithfully carried with them from the beginning of their trek.

"I think I understand what you ask," Sylvan said, "but a more intense flame makes the film too fragile. The only purpose of the heat here is to thin the liquid to the proper consistency."

"It looks like the sap of what we call the soapbark tree in the realm of fey," Nimbia said to Astron as he drew near. "Here the aleators tap the trunk and let it drip into waiting buckets."

"The same is done for syrups in the realm of men," Astron answered as he fell into the mode of automatically translating.

"This is for a greater purpose than delighting the tongue," Sylvan said. "Without its protection, the risk of contamination is far too great."

"I thought that fires destroyed the concentration of luck," Astron said. "If you must ruin the talismans, why not just toss them under the stewpot while it heats?"

"The heat would crack the shell that resists the great pressure of the gas, it is true," Sylvan said, "but when it rushes out in a burst, there is no way to tell which way it will surge. It might all lodge in a nearby tree or worse yet, in one of us who attends the fire. No, the luck must be released slowly in a way that we can control."

"Then you coat the talismans in this paste?" Astron asked.

"Watch and you will see." Sylvan shook her head. She motioned for Centuron to come forward, and the old man lumbered up, holding one of the talismans at arm's length, as if it had a foul odor.

Sylvan dipped a circle of wire into a cauldron and then drew it back. Astron saw that it emerged with a thin film of the soapbark sap stretched across its interior. She blew gently on the film, deforming it from a plane into a bulging hemisphere. Centuron continued forward until the dangling talisman met the shiny surface and then passed through it to the other side. Sylvan exhaled one more strong burst of air and a glassy bubble separated from the ring, completely enveloping the talisman.

"Now we can apply the heat." Sylvan looked back at Nimbia. She took the leather thong from Centuron's grasp and slowly moved the talisman with the encompassing bubble over toward the second fire. The bubble bounced slightly, but remained suspended, not touching the charm at all but somehow remaining hanging from the point where it was pierced by the thong.

Sylvan held the talisman bubble over the fire so that it was warmed by the rising heat, but the flames did not touch. Two or three others of Byron's followers gathered around Sylvan as she adjusted the height of the bubble, all silently waiting for what would happen.

For several hundred heart beats Astron detected no change. The fire crackled and wisps of smoke rose into the air, enveloping the bubble in a sooty haze as it floated skyward. Then, just as his interest began to sag, he noted a slight change of color on the surface of the brightly painted wood inside the glassy sphere. The yellows and reds began to fade. The blues paled into gray; the whites started to blister. In a moment, the polished surface turned to a dull, ashen indistinctness. The charm seemed to start vibrating, although Astron could not hear a hum. The sharp outlines of the intricate carving blurred. With a sharp crack like the breaking of an egg, a jagged rip appeared down one side from top to bottom.

Astron saw a sparkling iridescence suddenly shoot from the fissure and dissipate itself against the interior curve of the bubble. Like the spout of a tiny geyser seeded with reflective glitter, the essence of the talisman rushed out of its confinement and began to fill up the sphere. Sylvan waited a long while more until the exhaust from the charm had slowed to a barely discernible trickle. A slight opaqueness filled the bubble, where before it had been perfectly transparent and clear.

"Now for the controlled outgassing," Sylvan said, motioning to Centuron, who was already making his way forward with a circle of twine about one hand and a needle in the other.

"Popping the bubble would serve no better than cracking the talisman unprotected," Sylvan said. "But the strength of the soapbark film is high. It allows us to proceed with much more care." She took the circle of twine from Centuron with her free hand between extended thumb and forefinger. Very gently, she placed the ring against the surface of the bubble and quickly withdrew.

Astron saw that the band of twine did not penetrate the surface but, instead, floated on its glassy slickness, pulled into a tiny, perfect circle.

"It is the surface tension in the liquid," Astron said. "The same force that holds the bubble together in a sphere against the gasses inside deforms the string into a ring."

Sylvan ignored the comment. She carefully turned so that the floating circle was aimed away from the rest of the camp and outward toward the open sea. Reaching from the side, she quickly stabbed the needle into the small ring of film trapped by the twine.

Astron expected the bubble to pop with an explosive spray of what was contained inside, but it did not. Instead, only the small ring of film within the circle vanished, leaving the bulk of the bubble intact. Wisps of the glittering gas oozed through the opening out into the air in a gentle flow.

Astron watched, fascinated, as the bubble slowly contracted. Totally unlike a fragile sphere of film and rather like a balloon made of a cow's bladder in the realm of men, the orb grew smaller in a stately manner. As more and more of the glittering gas vented to the outside, the surface tension contracted the bubble into a tinier and tinier volume. Finally the radius became so small that the film touched the ragged edge of the rip in the talisman. With a tiny pop, the bubble flashed into nonexistence.

"Most interesting," Astron said. "I suspect that such a procedure would work with the soaps in the realms of men and the fey as well."

"But to no great practical use," Nimbia said. "There the laws are different. It would serve only to amuse the young."

"Perhaps," Astron said, wrinkling his nose.

Back near the main campfire, Byron suddenly threw

back his head and laughed at something his lieutenant had said. Nimbia quickly looked his way and then flushed as she noticed everyone watching what she had done.

"It is too bad," Centuron rumbled. He waved at the two fires as Sylvan stirred the small cauldron. "Some luck can be undone." He looked at Nimbia and shook his head. "Yes, the dabblings of men can be unmade but that which is bestowed by fate at birth is a burden forever."

"What do you mean?", Nimbia asked after Astron translated. She glanced at Sylvan and hesitated. "Are you the one until now the most in his favor? I am sorry, but if nothing yet has been decided, then surely there is no harm—"

Nimbia's words trailed off. Sylvan looked down at the cauldron and began stirring more vigorously without answering. The queen looked back to Centuron, eyeing the old man carefully. "What is your wish in the matter?" she said. "Is Sylvan here a personal favorite? If not, certainly the words of one so venerated will carry a great weight, if there is to be a decision."

The old aleator coughed and stood a little straighter. He closed one eye and studied Nimbia a long time before answering. "Can you not imagine how heavy the burden of time hangs over my head?" he croaked. "Do you not wonder what it is which drives me to rise on each new morrow, rather than curl up into nonexistence, disturbing as few as I can?"

"What does that have to do with—"

Centuron raised his hand and swept trembling fingers in a wide arc. "All of this that we see, all of the realm that lies beyond I have sampled more than once in my prime. And if Byron is cut to ribbons as soon as he enters the floor of the grand casino, there will be no more mysteries of which I long to taste."

Centuron coughed again. Astron noticed that an intense gleam came into his eye.

"But suppose he is not," the old aleator continued. "That is the chance of it that makes it all worthwhile. If somehow, without manipulating the tenets of luck, the pompous one manages to survive to the final struggles, then there is where I want to be—at the very center of the realm, when all those who have cast their lot with the vagaries of chance begin to doubt the foundation of their existence.

"Yes, I know of the futility; even Byron only guesses at it. Years ago, messengers through the flame revealed to me the workings of a distant master's plan. When the walls become dim and icy fingers of the void start to clutch at each and every heart, when I finally lie down to die, then it will all be worthwhile, knowing that I do not cease to exist alone.

"So you see, your question does not require an answer, unfortunate maid. With either outcome, your wish will be denied. Either the sands will run with Byron's blood or—"

"Do not mind his prattle," Sylvan cut in. "I suspect that it depresses him that you are so unlucky and there is nothing that he can do."

Nimbia frowned. "Without luck, yes, I understand that," she said. "It is what happened when we first arrived—but unlucky? What do you mean?"

Sylvan looked back down at the cauldron for a moment and then directly at Nimbia. "Why, your beauty, of course. How unfortunate to be saddled with such a burden."

Nimbia's frown grew deeper. She reached up and straightened a loose strand of hair. "I know that I am fair," she said. "It is what gives me an advantage when it comes to Byron's affections, I do confess, but—"

"Think, woman," Sylvan said. "Byron cannot be the only one. The souls of how many men have been warped by the closeness of your presence so that their inner worths were hidden? Whom do you know that has acted so that you could judge him as he truly is?" She glanced at Byron. "What you do is tempt him from his destiny; and if you succeed, then whom else will he blame?" Sylvan paused and shook her head. "No, I do not rue the fact that you have him smitten. I pity you instead."

Chapter Twenty-Six

The Grand Casino

KESTREL steadied himself against the gentle roll of the ship in the quickening breeze. He shielded his eyes from the emerging sun on his starboard and squinted at the smudge directly ahead of the bowsprit. The air was hazy with the remains of a clearing fog, but already he could see what must be the tall thin towers that marked the corners of the casino. Myra might not have deduced that it was her luck that brought them to the proper destination, rather than his guess at the course, but they were there, nevertheless.

They had been beset by calm for most of the first day at sea. At the dawn of the second, a lookout had spied a mast on the sternward horizon. The crew had buzzed with the speculation that they were being followed by the savages who had decimated the entire company of men-at-arms. Little that Myra had said changed the growing apprehensiveness of their disposition.

Kestrel had listened closely to the description of the one who had led the charge down to the beach and almost succeeded in boarding before they were safely away. He dared not hope too much, but perhaps there was the slimmest of chances that somehow it was Astron who followed their every move through the swirling fog and occasional gusting winds, though the description did not sound right.

Phoebe came to Kestrel's side and reached up to massage the tense muscles in his neck. He felt tight and drawn out, like an archer's bowstring before its release. For the two full days at sea he had just barely managed to convince Myra to direct her experiments elsewhere and save him and the wizard for the contest in the casino.

"It is not your burden," Phoebe said softly. "Myra

336

would have toyed with the others, regardless of what you said. Your words were not responsible. They did no more than shield me from certain harm."

Kestrel shook his head. Each time that Myra had been dissuaded, she merely turned instead to another of the unfortunate ones who were prisoners below deck. Cries of pain and pleas for a quick death echoed through his mind. A terrible weight bore down on his shoulders.

"But for what?" Kestrel said. "I have done no more than postpone the inevitable. Myra has made it quite clear that our purpose on the casino floor is to be human shields against the weapons directed at her by the other competing aleators." He grasped Phoebe's hands in his. "I am sorry," he said, "sorry that my wit has not been as strong as it needs to be."

Kestrel looked back at the cabin in the stern. He released Phoebe's hands and felt his fists clench tight. He remembered Milligan's theft of his luck without even a hint of warning and the small value Jelilac placed on their lives.

This quest had become one of mounting obligations, he thought. First, his pledge to Phoebe, then the debt he owed to rescue the rotarians who trusted him as leader, and now, if somehow he could manage it, Jelilac, Milligan, Myra, and the others like them should be made to pay for all they must have done.

Kestrel turned to look back at the shore. Drawing Phoebe close, he watched the towers of the casino become more crisp and clear. He sucked in a chestful of air slowly, then spilled it back into the salty spray. Brave words, he thought ruefully, not what one might expect from a scheming woodcutter—especially not from one who could calculate quite well the chances of surviving without luck in a casino filled with talisman-wearing aleators. He shook his head as he flexed his fingers about the sword pommel that was not there, trying to fan the flame of his conviction so that it masked the growing fear.

Kestrel pushed the bizarre thoughts away. Grimly he stood, silently watching and waiting for what would happen next. In a little more than what he judged to be an hour, Myra's ship cast anchor in a crowded harbor. Her followers and prisoners came ashore into a surging mass of aspiring aleators and their own retainers. Everyone in the realm, Myra had said, would be there—if not a possessor of enough wealth to compete, then certainly to watch to see who the next archon would be.

In the confusion of mingling bodies, one might expect someone to break for freedom, but those without talismans knew better than to try. With faces heavy with resignation, they shuffled into position as their masters directed. Kestrel kept Phoebe close, his eyes darting all about, looking for a sign of Astron or a chance to communicate through the flame.

Except for the casino itself, the island was bare of structure, low and sandy with no plants taller than bushy shrubs. The building was shaped like a huge hexagon with high walls that Myra had said enclosed a many-tiered stadium. From each vertex of the polygon, the towers soared even farther into the sky. At the apex of each, attendants stood ready near the signal beacons that would flash the results of the competition across the sea to those whose luck prevented them from arriving in time. The walls were thick, covered by many layers of fading paint that had withstood countless years of high surf and spray. Portions of old murals peeked out from behind the peeling layers of those placed on top. Faded scenes of previous victories; cornucopia brimming with talismans and devices of chance blended into the mute drabness that surrounded them.

Midway in the face of each of the casino walls, high doors thrice the height of a man stood open. Into each slowly snaked the retainers of the aleators, climbing into the high seats to cheer their lords onward.

"You two shall be in the vanguard of my contingent." Myra pointed in the direction of Kestrel and Phoebe as other aleators jostled past. "For each contender, a full dozen is allowed on the floor, but it is folly to have every minion's neck heavy with capsules of great fortune. A single reversal could spell the end of serious contention. I think it is better for at least four to be luckless as newborn babes. Let the machines of Jelilac and the others do their

338

worst. It will not be talismans of true power that feel the slings of their wrath."

Myra waited until all the aleators at the nearest door had entered. Then, with a majestic swirl of a cape she had donned for the ceremony, she walked slowly into the casino. Immediately inside the outer shell, Kestrel saw the stairways leading up into the stands on either side. Pressed against the high ceiling, globes of bioluminescent fungi bathed everything in an eerie soft light. Directly ahead, a tunnel ran onto the floor of the casino itself. The ground underfoot was bare earth, almost muddy from the humid air.

Myra motioned her followers, except for the chosen twelve, to take the stairs to the left and ascend to the highest seats, as far removed as possible from the rest of the spectators. When the last had begun to climb, she nodded to Kestrel and Phoebe to begin their entrance.

Kestrel clutched empty air at his side with a feeling of futility. He felt his pulse begin to race. On Jelilac's sloop, he had managed to escape, but here in the casino there would be too many. He started to speak when a sudden crashing boom exploded outward from the casino floor and echoed down the tunnel walls.

"Minefields," Myra grunted without losing a stride. "Evidently one of the contestants did not enter sufficiently prepared."

Another explosion ripped down the passageway. Then a third came, this one mingled with cries of pain and a roar from the crowd. Kestrel moved forward as slowly as he could with the tip of a sword planted squarely in the small of his back. He stepped in front of Phoebe just as he reached the tunnel entrance and looked out into the bright light of the contesting field, squinting to see what was happening.

From the other entrances were emerging more contingents, each with a dozen retainers surrounding a richly dressed aleator shouting commands. Nearer the center of the casino floor, still other groups surrounded their leaders, but in most cases their number had been reduced from the original dozen. Only six still protected a corpulent, well-dressed lord in their midst, and one of those limped, with his left arm hanging useless at his side. Their goal evidently was the same as the rest of the contenders, to reach one of the shallow pits dug into the ground and surrounded by chalky white boulders and low barriers of tumbled logs.

The group proceeded cautiously and then, with no apparent reason, veered sharply to the left. With a flash of angry yellow, another boom ricocheted through the stadium. Kestrel saw the retainer on the far right suddenly hurled up in the air, his body bent like a handful of broken twigs.

"Come," Myra said as she arrived at the entrance. "We will show them that my luck is sufficient to find a path to a fortress without fear or hesitation." She prodded one of her talisman-protected men-at-arms forward, and he began pacing rapidly out onto the casino floor. "Follow his footsteps, follow them exactly," Myra commanded. "Match him step for step, if you wish to survive until you are needed later."

Kestrel hesitated while he watched the man-at-arms suddenly veer sharply to the left and then just as quickly resume his course toward the protective barricades. He felt the sharp prodding in his back and sucked in his breath. Stepping out into the warrior's footprints, he reached behind to pull Phoebe's hand. He took two tentative steps and then half a dozen more, matching the zigzag path of his predecessor as best he could. Moving with increasing haste so that he would not lose the trail, he pulled Phoebe after him, only dimly aware of Myra and her other followers snaking behind.

A sudden crack sharper than the boom of the mines suddenly pierced through the din on Kestrel's right. He felt a sudden rip of pain in his hand and looked down to see a streak of blood, as if he had been neatly nicked by a blade. He looked up to see the nearest boulder of the barricade just ahead. Instinctively he snapped Phoebe forward and tumbled her over the rock, just as a second pop sounded behind him. As he jumped for cover, what sounded like a shower of pebbles skittered against the thick granite behind.

"A grenade," Myra muttered behind him as she was helped over the rock by two of her retainers. She stopped and coughed, trying to blow the dust from her lungs. "Shrapnel will find the unlucky. About that there can be no doubt."

Elsewhere in the casino, the other contesting groups were also seeking what shelter they could. Those who arrived the latest were beginning to erect makeshift barriers of shields and protruding lances on open ground as far removed from the other contingents as possible. More grenades began to soar through the air, lofted from one group to the one closest. The dull boom of the mines was replaced by the staccato pop of many tiny projectiles.

One of the less protected groups sallied from their cover and raced with swords drawn at the adversaries on their left. Kestrel expected to see a protracted and grim struggle like the carefully choreographed dances of the reticulates, but instead, in a brief mêlée, the encounter was over. Half of the attackers stumbled and fell when they engaged their opponents; the rest were dispatched by the first lucky swings of carelessly aimed swords. Kestrel shifted his focus and saw another brief flurry erupt on the opposite side of the casino floor and, far to the right, yet two more.

"The ones whose wishes exceed their stores of wealth," Myra said at Kestrel's side. "They mimic the contest of old when strength of arm and cleverness of siegecraft determined the victor. Soon they will all be gone, and those of true potential will struggle as it should be done."

Fulfilling her prophecy instantly, a strong voice suddenly rang through the din. "A challenge, a challenge of true virtue to masqueraders on our left."

Immediately the crowd fell silent and all the hostilities ceased on the casino floor. Kestrel craned around to see Milligan standing on the top of a small boulder near one of the tunnels with a megaphone to his mouth. Evidently Jelilac's had been one of the last contingents to arrive.

"We do the great practice of our art disservice by such crude measures," Milligan continued. "Avoiding mines

341

and the shrapnel of grenades takes a measure of luck, to be sure, but it in no way answers which of us has the greatest power and hence the authority to rule." Milligan paused and circled to address the stands at his back. "Remember our heritage," he said. "This very edifice is enshrined with the name of the grand casino—not the arena, not the stadium, but the casino where all is ruled by chance. The events to be decided here are to be based upon the pristine twisting of gaseous luck, not the slashing of bloodied blades."

The crowd roared in approval, but Milligan motioned them back to silence. "Yes, luck is to be the mechanism of decision—luck, pure and unsullied with irrelevant skill."

He pointed at his side to a large glass bowl with two transparent tubes snaking out of the top and filled with tiny white spheres. "Of all those who have assembled to struggle here Jelilac is the most mighty, the one with the greatest hoard of fortune. He issues a challenge to one and all. The first to have three numbers discharged will be the victor. The vanquished will cease their struggles and submit all talismans to aid in the greater cause." Milligan paused and then shut his eyes. Extending his arm, he pointed out across the casino floor and spun about three times, quickly pirouetting to a sudden halt.

"You!" He laughed as he sighted down the length of his arm toward a small fortification across the floor. "You shall be the first to test that Jelilac's luck is the most potent of all."

Kestrel turned to watch a young aleator rise from cover and shake his head. "No, that is not my plan," he protested. "My only hope is to win against others similarly endowed and capture what luck they have remaining after the battle. Only by that means would I have the chance to face the likes of Jelilac in the end."

The crowd roared in disapproval. For a long while, the high walls of the casino echoed with their lust for the confrontation. Kestrel squeezed Phoebe's hand and tried to settle into a comfortable position. At least for the moment, everyone was distracted and no grenades were hurling their way.

He watched Milligan and two other retainers set up a large wooden frame and then drape it with tapestries embroidered in intricate designs. A long hose was connected to one of the tubes protruding from the glass bowl and run back behind the panels where Kestrel could not see. In an instant, the tiny spheres began to dance in the confines of the bowl, like a boiling liquid just about to erupt. In the distance, Kestrel saw that each ball was inscribed with a few strokes of precise lettering in black ink.

"Your numbers," Milligan shouted over the fading din of the crowd. "Everyone here demands it. Remember the fourth tenet—luck favors the believer. If you have doubts and hesitate, then surely you will fail."

The aleator across the casino floor looked wildly out into the stands and then slumped his shoulders. He grasped at the handful of talismans about his neck and tightly clenched shut his eyes "Seven, nineteen, and thirty-seven," he shouted after a moment. "And by the third tenet, may these charms beget all the fortune that I will need."

Milligan laughed and marked the selected numbers on a huge slate handed to him from within the canvas framework. "Nine, forty-two, and forty-three," he called out without apparent thought and added them in a line below the first. "Now we shall contest in the manner in which it has always been intended."

Milligan removed a cover from the second tube emerging from the bowl, and the crowd again fell silent. No one moved while the white spheres churned and frothed. After a short while, one of the balls bounced into the conical orifice that fed the exit and popped out into Milligan's waiting hand. "Forty-two." He laughed as he held up the orb and waved it over his head. "Forty-two on the very first ball, even though over two hundred spin about."

Before Milligan had finished speaking, a second sphere followed the first. Another of Jelilac's retainers dashed out from the cover of the framing and caught it as it arched into the air. "And forty-three." Milligan laughed again. "I can see the marking clearly from here." He looked across the casino floor and shook his head.

"You may as well make ready. It appears that the wealth you wager against Jelilac is meager indeed."

Milligan turned his attention back to the glass bowl just in time to receive the third ball emerging from the tube. "The third is nine," he said. "Yes, after the first two so suddenly, there could be no doubt."

Most of the crowd broke into enthusiastic cheering, although Kestrel saw one small grouping high in the stands sit silently with faces pulled to their chests. Milligan waved both arms over his head to keep up the volume of sound as he tripped across the casino floor to the aleator who had been defeated. With a theatrical flourish, he accepted an armload of talismans and carried them back to Jelilac's framework.

"Who is next?" he shouted. "Who is next to challenge? Jelilac is ready to battle with one and all."

Kestrel looked at Myra out of the corner of his eye. He saw the old woman slowly shaking her head. "Not yet," she muttered. "Each contest dissipates a little of Jelilac's wealth back into the ether. And there is always the chance that he will not be able to beat them all. I will wait until the last, when my own opportunity is the best."

Kestrel scanned the casino floor and saw the wave of a banner from another of the fortifications. A new cheer went up from the crowd. "Five, thirty-nine, and fifty-two," a voice heavy with resignation sounded in the distance. "I may as well be next. It seems that at the last moment, my luck turned fickle. This fortification is made of anvilwood, not simple fir or pine like the rest."

The cheer reverberating in the stands suddenly stopped. Milligan nearly doubled over with his laughter. "Barrier logs made of anvilwood," he said. "The custodians of the casino have prepared for this contest better than most." He waved back at the glass bowl and the churning balls. "One, two, and three," he said. "Let us proceed quickly so we can get on to the next."

Anvilwood, Kestrel thought quickly, the very reason for coming to the casino in the first place! He touched the rucksack still hanging on his back. Again he scanned the rising stadium seats and the array of contestants on

344

the casino floor. "Astron, where are you?" he muttered.

He glanced down at Phoebe and shook his head. With a sigh, he settled beside her and watched the dance of tiny, white balls. With all the contingents on the casino floor, it would take some while to get to Myra. Maybe by then the demon would appear—or failing that he could figure out how to get a flame lit for Phoebe on his own.

The roar of the crowd was deafening. Of all the contingents that had swarmed onto the casino floor so many hours before, only Myra and Jelilac remained. Kestrel felt the tension grow in Myra's retainers. With each new challenger, they had hoped that Jelilac's luck would turn, but it held steady and true. Some of the opponents had taken more effort to defeat than the others. For one, over seventy spheres of no consequence popped free of the miniature maelstrom before Jelilac received his third victory. Another actually had one of his selections and for a moment trailed only two to one. But in the end, Milligan's master emerged triumphant over all, collecting the largesse of talismans and adding them to his store.

"And now Myra." Milligan pointed at the one fortification still occupied in the center of the floor. "What are your guesses, old crone? The hour grows late. We have been at this for the better part of a day."

Myra grasped the talismans about her neck and hesitated. She squinted at the bouncing spheres while the bowl was being reloaded and then around the vast interior of the casino, as if looking for a sign. "We both have warriors and shields still unspent," she called out in a hoarse voice. "It has made no sense to bring the fated twelve, if they are not to be used."

"You talk as if you had a great store of wealth, Myra," Milligan shot back. "As great as Jelilac's own. But the ruse will not shake his beliefs. Having the dozen slash at one another is only a distraction. Eventually it will come down to the spheres." He paused and waved. "If you wish to increase the stakes, then it will be done. All talismans forfeited by the loser as before—but in addition, the retainers are to be given to the victor to do with what he will."

Kestrel felt Phoebe tighten against him, but he did not know what to do. Myra or Jelilac—which one emerged the winner did not really matter; in either case, their fate was the same.

Myra scowled. She quickly counted the talismans about her neck and then looked around the now nearly deserted casino floor. She rubbed her chin and shook herself with a great sigh. Grabbing the largest stone hanging on her chest, she stared back at Milligan. For a long moment she did not waver. Then a hint of a smile formed on her lips.

"Done," she said. "Only instead of three balls let us make it two."

Two of her retainers bolted to their feet but Myra motioned them to be still. "Why not?" she muttered. "You have seen what has happened to all the rest. This way our chance is the greatest, slim though it might be."

Milligan frowned. "But only two numbers increases the variability of the outcome even more," he said. "A truly lucky stroke could win, despite where lies the preponderance of wealth."

"Precisely." Myra cackled. "Luck favors the believer and I will take what is my best chance." She stopped suddenly and then reached into the paraphernalia her retainers had lugged out onto the floor. Kestrel watched with surprise as she extracted the navigator's almanac and opened it to a random page. He had thought it at the bottom of the sea; apparently it hadn't quite gone overboard from the raft.

"Eight and twelve," Myra called out after she had stabbed her finger down onto the parchment. "If I cannot win by simple luck, then calculations shall help me instead."

She held up the volume with both hands over her head and turned slowly around so that everyone could see. The shouts of the crowd suddenly fell silent, as if their tongues had been sliced by a blade. For a long moment, no one stirred. Then a troubled murmur arose from the far end of the casino and flowed around the tiers.

"Calculations," Milligan said after a moment. "It is not our way—worse even than the slash of sword and clang of shield."

"Eight and twelve," Myra said. "Perhaps now even Jelilac is beginning to have some doubts?"

"Never!" Kestrel heard Jelilac's voice boom out from the protection of the canvas framing. "The old woman is desperate. I choose ninety-three and one hundred forty-two. Let the mixing begin."

For a moment, Milligan did not move. Kestrel saw his shoulders twitch before he motioned for the air to begin pumping into the bowl. Almost instantly, a ball popped out the second tubing and everyone waited in hushed anticipation to see what it would be. "Thirty-four." Milligan set it aside. "I admit that you will not be as easy as any of the rest, Myra, but even with calculations, Jelilac will prevail."

Myra said nothing but stared back with unblinking eyes. Kestrel could see the stringy muscles in her arms draw into tense bands. He had to try something. Anything was better than just waiting to see which would be the victor.

"Yes, thirty-four," he shouted suddenly. The prattle of numbers he had used many times before when posing as a magician came easily to his mind. "Eight and twelve— eight and twelve are twenty and thirty-four minus twenty is fourteen, which is just two numbers from twelve. Two numbers, two—two is precisely the total to be chosen— as the calculations said they would be."

Milligan frowned but said nothing. He reached for the next ball. "Ninety—" he began, but Kestrel cut him off.

"Yes, in the nineties," he said. "Eight times twelve is ninety-six. The numbers emerged according to plan."

Another ball bounced up to the exit orifice, but before it could start its journey it suddenly fell backward into the rest. The whirl of random motion died away. In an instant, all the spheres were lying quietly in the bottom of the bowl.

Jelilac emerged from the confines of his shelter. With

a waddling gait he walked out to stand at Milligan's side.

"I have stopped the blower," Jelilac said as he glanced quickly at Myra's tally on the board. "If you truly believe in the power of your calculation, I have another proposition to offer instead."

Myra tossed back her head and laughed, the tension suddenly gone. She glanced once at Kestrel and smiled. "You said that I would not cause doubt, Milligan," she wheezed, "but your master's words speak otherwise. Do not mind this old book. It does not really matter. It served to pull a lucky number from the air. It means no more than that."

"I am willing to up the stakes still further," Jelilac said, "and give you better odds."

"You heard what my minion said," Myra answered. "The flow of luck is in my direction. There is no incentive for me to change."

"If we employ instead the giant spinner, I will give you nine portions out of ten of the field," Jelilac said. "And in addition to the twelve, I propose that we become part of the prize pools ourselves."

"No, not the spinner," Milligan said. "It is not proper. We have agreed not to succumb to the temptation that was offered. Let us continue with the dancing spheres. Surely you will prevail."

Myra squinted. "Nine out of ten," she said, "and your body to probe with my pinchers as I see fit." She slapped the almanac at her side. "Why not?" she cackled. "Your luck is potent, but it cannot be that much greater than mine."

Jelilac grimaced and motioned back to his retainers. "I will be archon." He answered the question forming on their lips. "If we do not duel with the same tools, then how can we be sure?"

Milligan opened his mouth to protest, but Jelilac's stare turned him aside. He stood silent while two of the master aleator's retainers emerged from behind the tapestries carrying a large wooden frame into which a hundred pegs had been pounded in the outline of a great circle. With his head shaking, Milligan propped the panel upright. He offered no more aid as the helpers affixed a stout shaft onto an axle that protruded through the center of the frame. Kestrel saw that a flap of stiff leather was affixed to one end of the shaft and protruded just far enough to touch the circle of pegs.

"You may start the spinner into motion, Myra," Jelilac said with tension in his voice. "Then before it has completed its third spin, I will call out the ten numbers that I select as my own."

Myra stepped from the fortifications. With a flourish of her cape, she walked across the casino floor, avoiding the mines that remained. When she reached the frame, she bowed slightly toward each of the six sides of the casino. Then, with an elaborate gesture, she grasped the opposite end of the spinner from the one that held the leather flap. The few remaining murmurs of the crowd vanished in anticipation.

"A moment." Jelilac held out his hand. "Please do not begin until I am ready." Moving as quickly as he could, he joggled back into the cover of his canvas-draped box. For a moment, there was silence. Myra scowled, but waited, a smile of anticipation growing on her face.

Kestrel twisted uncomfortably. He had changed the contest slightly, but not enough to make any real difference. After one spin of the wheel, what hope did he and Phoebe have? If only there were some way to get a fire started before—

"I smell smoke." Phoebe suddenly sat up out of her slump at Kestrel's side. "There behind the tapestries, I am sure of it. Jelilac is starting a fire."

There was a sudden whoosh of wind that billowed from behind the tapestries, straining them against the hooks that held them to the frame. Kestrel felt a sudden rush of heat and then the odor of rotten carrion, like that he had detected before.

"Camonel," he said. "Phoebe, can it be? It smells just like Camonel." He shook his head, confused. "But Milligan said that the aleators avoided fire at all costs because of the second tenet."

Phoebe's answer was cut off by Jelilac's booming

command. "Now," he shouted. "Perform your best calculation, Myra, because no matter what the method, I am the one who will win."

Myra gave the bar a mighty wrench to send it whirling about. Just as she did, a burst of yellow flame shot upward above the tapestries for everyone to see. In a sudden panic, Jelilac's retainers exploded out of the box, rushing onto the casino floor. Two immediately stepped onto mines, and startled cries mingled with a spray of hurling limbs. The spectators in the stands astride the tunnel behind Jelilac's framework screamed in panic. Those in the rows nearest began climbing into the tiers above, trampling on those not fast enough to get out of their way.

"Mark." Camonel's deep voice rumbled above the din. The djinn pushed aside the canvas and stepped next to the rotating spinner. "It passed vertical, master, just as I spoke."

"Jelilac, what is this?" Myra backed away from the demon that towered over her. "I saw this monster on the raft. You deal with the manipulator far more than have I."

"You stoop to using calculation. Then do not be surprised if it is employed by others." Jelilac followed the djinn into the open. A dark curl of smoke indicated that the fire that summoned Camonel still smouldered inside. "I will be archon, woman," he said. "Soon it all will be decided."

"Mark," Camonel shouted again. "I have timed the initial rate of rotation, master. You have said that that would be enough."

Kestrel grabbed Phoebe by the arm, lifting her up to standing. They had another chance to bind Camonel to her will, and this time there would be no water to douse the flame inadvertently. He started to leap over the barrier and run to the demon, but then hesitated. He glanced at the craters and twisted bodies between his fortification and Jelilac's canvas box. Scowling, he pulled her back down to safety.

"There is too much risk of the mines," he said. "Phoebe, you must try to control him from here."

"It is too far." Phoebe shook her head. "I have al-

350

ready attempted the binding of his will, but the control of his master is too strong."

"Eighty-three through ninety-two," Camonel boomed for all to hear. "One tenth of the numbers but that is the region in which the spinner will finally reside. My master has calculated it and there can be no doubt."

"Calculation," someone shouted in the stands. "Not calculation! No!"

"Calculation," another echoed with a groan. "In the final battle, luck is pitted against calculation and skill."

Kestrel saw a wave of agitation radiate out from those nearest Jelilac's box. The aleators in the stands were mere spectators no longer. Even those scrambling to safety slowed and turned back to watch. On the side of the casino farthest away from the action, a low murmur tinged with despair began to build and grow.

"But if luck loses to some other method, then what is the purpose, what is the meaning?" Myra shrieked above all the rest.

The moaning of the crowd increased. Kestrel saw an entire section clasp hands and begin swaying back and forth to the cadence of a chant: "Calculation, calculation and skill."

Kestrel felt a twinge in his stomach. The ground under his feet suddenly felt less firm. He glanced up at one of the large windows in the far wall and saw that apparently the fog had begun to move back onshore. A subtle vibration began tickling the soles of his feet and migrating up his legs into his spine. Obviously, the use of something other than luck in the confrontation of Jelilac and Myra was deeply disturbing to all those who watched. And somehow the mood was contagious, affecting everything about them as well.

"Something is happening." Kestrel drew Phoebe close. Something, something—the thought suddenly hit him— something like two realms of symmetry starting to merge.

"Yes," Phoebe said. "I feel it, too. Only this time, there is no other realm of which the aleators speak." She glanced wildly at the dimming rays of the sun, filtering through the colored glass. She pressed herself into Kestrel's side. "And if not merging, what transformation could it possibly be?"

Kestrel looked helplessly at the distance to the fire behind the tapestries and the mighty djinn standing arms akimbo in front, watching the spinner slowing to rest. He felt the heel of his boot begin to sink into an oozy soup. Except for the burning tapestries, the high corners of the casino seemed to start fading away. Things were converging too fast. He would have to chance getting Phoebe closer to the demon, no matter what the risk.

Kestrel took in a deep breath and prepared to vault over the barrier. Perhaps if he ran ahead, she would see where it was safe to follow. But before he could move, a new voice sounded from a tunnel behind him.

"Stop," it said. "The contest has not yet run its course. There is the entry of one more who destiny decrees will win. Yes, it is I, Byron, who has come as it has been preordained."

CHAPTER TWENTY-SEVEN

The Will to Believe

ASTRON looked out over the nearly deserted casino floor. Only two contingents remained of what initially must have been many. He saw the djinn Camonel standing next to a spinner that was gradually slowing to a stop. Behind him, Jelilac was motioning the sluggish beam onward so that it would come to rest just to the left of the vertical.

Astron saw smoke curling above the canvas tapestries from the fire that had brought forth the demon and, not far away, what looked like anvilwood in another of the low barricades. Near the center of the floor, the second group of aleators stood transfixed, all watching the final sweep of the spinner. Astron's membranes flicked down over his eyes. In their midst, there could be no mistake; there was Kestrel with the pollen-filled knapsack still on his back.

Astron looked out at the scatter of small craters and mangled bodies and hesitated. Kestrel would use some clever tactic, he thought, rather than rushing pell-mell into certain danger. His stembrain strained to be free, but, despite the urgency, he had to think and plan.

Byron started out onto the casino floor. Astron tugged at his arm. "Why challenge two groups when, if you wait a moment, you will have to contend only with the victor?" the demon said. "Fate will determine which of them it is to be."

Byron grunted. He relaxed the tension in his sword arm. The blade slowly arched earthward and buried its tip into the soft ground. The aleators in the stands saw that the tall warrior had stopped his challenge and turned their attention back to the slowing spinner.

"Ninety-one," Camonel called out as it barely slid past one peg and then stopped as it touched another. "Ninety-one, just as it has been predicted."

The murmur of the crowd grew in intensity. Only a few shouted accolades pierced the indistinct rumble that coursed from tier to tier.

"Your talismans, Myra." Jelilac beamed in triumph. The aleator paid no attention to the waves of sound mounting behind him. "You were the most likely to offer serious competition. With your defeat, no other can seriously offer a challenge now."

"But you used calculation." Milligan suddenly shook off his restraint. "It is not right. Not by such a means should you become the archon."

"The most trusted advisor is a position coveted by many." Jelilac frowned in Milligan's direction. "Do not protest too much, or I will have to select another." He motioned to the retainers that remained, directing them to fan out and receive the spoils of their victory.

Astron saw Myra slump into a heap. She squinted at the spinner, resting clearly in the region that Camonel had predicted, and shook her head. "Nine chances out of ten," she muttered. "It was worth the chance." She glanced at

Jelilac's smile and then turned away. "I will offer no resistance to the removal of my charms," she said, suddenly sounding far more ancient than she looked. "Remember, I am but an old woman." She waved her arm back to the central barricade. "Come, my followers, come. Do not resist. It would be ungracious to prolong my harm."

Astron saw Kestrel and Phoebe join the procession winding its way across the casino floor to Jelilac's canvas frame. The demon looked quickly at Byron, but the warrior had not yet lifted up his sword. Moving the pollen closer to the fire could only help, but it was not yet time to act.

"No! I cannot let it happen." Milligan suddenly sprang away from the rest. He drew a short dagger from his belt and waved it over his head. "It is luck that shall triumph in the end; it must be the stronger. It must. It must."

Jelilac's frown deepened. He motioned to two of his retainers, and they drew their swords. Cautiously, they began to close in on Milligan from both sides.

A great roar of approval suddenly ripped through the stands as Milligan deftly dogged the attack. He drew his own blade and slashed at one as he passed, streaking the tunic sleeve with red. Ducking his head, he just barely missed a tumbling grenade which exploded harmlessly behind.

Short strokes of the dagger somehow darted through hastily erected guards, and two more of Jelilac's followers sagged to the ground. Jelilac's eyes widened. He quickly stepped backward and looked at the massive djinn standing by the motionless spinner.

"Help me!" he cried as he clutched at his chest. "My talismans are many, but now that I have experienced the power of your master's predictions and been close to the flame, I no longer feel so confident that they—"

Jelilac's voice trailed off. He looked in disbelief down at his stomach and then clutched his hands over a gaping wound. His face turned ashen white. With eyes staring into nothingness, he slid to the ground.

For a moment, Milligan stood silent, staring at what he had done. Then, as the realization dawned, like the doll of a thaumaturge, he jerked back into life.

"I am the victor, the archon." He danced back with his bloody blade. "As our creators must have intended —luck favors the believer."

The roar of the crowd intensified. Some started leaping up and down, shaking the tiers in violent oscillations. Milligan smiled and waved his dagger over his head with one hand while fondling the talismans about his neck with the other.

"No." Camonel's impassive expression suddenly distorted into one of malice. His voice was heard even above the chanting spectators. "Luck is not to be the victor. My master does not wish it so." With a speed surprising for his size, the djinn batted at Jelilac's framework, tumbling it aside. He reached backward and extracted a burning branch of pinewood from the still smouldering fire.

"I am a weaver of matter," he growled as he waved it menacingly in front of Milligan's face. "Here, in a realm other than my own, it is easy." Deep furrows etched into the djinn's forehead. He studied the dance of flame for a moment, and then the log seemed to burst asunder. Five globes of what looked like white-hot magma arched from his hand and landed in a pentagon around where Milligan stood.

"My master has calculated, and five will be enough," the djinn boomed out so that everyone could hear. "The heat is intense, and eventually each and every charm he carries about his neck will crack. The one you call Milligan will succumb to calculation, just as have all the rest."

Camonel tossed back his head and laughed. "Let the fogs of nothingness come forward," he yelled. "Let them come forward and dissolve all that there is. Then there will be one less. Where once there was a realm, there will be only the nothingness of the void." He stepped back suddenly into the flame. The fire roared with a burst of yellow brightness. Then he was gone.

The yells of aleators in the stands stopped just as suddenly as they had begun. The low murmur of unrest and disbelief from before instantly returned. Like a pendulum gathering energy with each swing, their emotions rocked back and forth, each time more violently than before.

355

Milligan tried to dance between two of the glowing globes of fire on the ground, but backed up and hesitated when the outermost of his talismans began to blister. Astron saw beads of sweat pop out on his forehead above eyes starting to fill with helpless panic. He bent forward and blew tentatively on the fiercely glowing globes of light, then shook his head when he saw that they were perturbed not at all. He raised his hands expectantly, as if calling for the intervention of unseen gods. For a long moment, he did not move. Then, in an almost perfect imitation of Myra, he slumped into the center of the pentagon that surrounded him. One by one he began removing his talismans and tossing them at the flames.

"Then the newcomer," Astron heard someone in the stands nearby shout. "The one on the sidelines yet to be heard. He is the chance, the final chance that luck will triumph after all."

Somehow the spectators all heard and understood. Again they stopped their keening. As one, they held their breaths.

"Luck has nothing to do with my presence here," Byron called back. "It is the decree of preordained fate. I carry no talismans, and I do not need their aid in my fight."

Shrieks of despair exploded from the crowd. Their emotions swung back to despair far deeper than before. Whole blocks of spectators suddenly rose from where they sat. With eyes suddenly brimming with tears, they began to embrace those next to them with heart-wracking sobs. Astron felt the ground tremble as it had done in the realm of the reticulates and felt the caress of a chilling wind across his cheek. It was as if a dam had finally broken. There was no hope left that would stem the outrushing tide.

"It is just as I was foretold such a long time ago," Centuron called out behind Astron in flushed excitement. "And by the fates, Byron is not even needed. The self-doubt has started even before he appeared. I have survived long enough, long enough to see it happen. Even if he does not triumph, the end will be the same."

The keening of the crowd rose to an ear-piercing crescendo. Moans of anguish became more frequent, and loud sobbing mingled with the rest. Astron wrinkled his nose. The ground under his feet definitely felt less firm than when he had first entered. The pillars and arches that held aloft the roof of the casino were somehow less distinct than before. Only a deep black painted the high window where the sun had been.

A growing uneasiness coursed up Astron's legs and into his chest. The phenomena were intereseting, but he could not force himself to consider dispassionately exactly what was taking place. He felt his stembrain writhe within the confines of his control with far greater power, straining to be free. He looked about the casino floor. All of the aleators there had fallen to their knees. With eyes focusing on nothing, they rocked back and forth and keened with the rest. Only Kestrel and Phoebe were still alert, looking apprehensively all about. Astron had waited long enough. Now was the time.

Astron looked at the beckoning anvilwood and then turned back to Centuron. "The mines of which you spoke as we entered," he said. "What is their danger? Quickly, I must know."

Centuron squinted at Astron and then threw back his head. The laughter tumbled from his lips in gasping wheezes. For several moments, he shook in spasms, unable to regain control. Astron clenched his fist in frustration, eyeing again the distance to the anvilwood, Camonel's smouldering fire, and Kestrel and the pollen, unable to decide which was to be the first objective.

"Byron and the others." Centuron ignored the question when he finally could speak. "They are all one and the same, driving down the one path to mutual destruction. Each in his own way has surrendered his free will to the ether and has given up any stake in determining events by his own volition. And with each such submission, on a level far below their conscious thought, the self-doubt has increased and the reason for existence has become less firm. We indeed are the mere puppets of some other creator, a bubble of life breathed into being by gods that have walked away."

357

"Demon," Nimbia said suddenly. "I do not like what I see. The fey can create realms out of their thoughts, but that is not what sustains them, once they are born. Only so long as the occupants believe in their own existence does what they inhabit continue to resist the pressures that push against them from the outside. All the aleators here—look at them. They slump and—"

Centuron interrupted Nimbia's words with another peal of laughter. "We are all gathered here, almost all of the occupants of our realm. We now face what we have hidden in our hearts and refused to believe. There is no purpose to existence. The triumph of predestination over luck proves it. It is the end of the universe and everyone that it contains."

"There are thousands here." Astron shook his head. "One spin of the wheel and a few words cannot affect everyone so."

"Despite your great misfortune, you are not one of us," Centuron said. "You cannot know the importance of what has transpired."

"I wish to continue living," Nimbia said fiercely as she placed her hands around Byron's arm. "Surely others do as well."

Centuron waved at the casino walls a final time. "Observe the dissolution of the fabric of existence," he said. "You and your companion are too few to keep alive an entire universe when it no longer has the will to live."

Byron looked down at Nimbia and then glanced at the fuzzy haze seeming to blur the spectators on the wall farthest away. He licked his lips and patted Nimbia's hand on his arm. "Perhaps Centuron is right," he said in a husky voice. "Perhaps afterward there will not be enough time."

Byron released the grip on his blade. He wiped the back of his hand against his lips and looked with glowing eyes at Nimbia. "There is nothing more I can do about the others." He waved back toward the center of the casino floor. "But now, at least I can succumb to the joys of my temptation." He spread his hands wide and, with a slow deliberate motion, reached to draw Nimbia to him.

"Wait, wait a moment, Byron." Nimbia hesitated and

then smiled. "I know you do not fully understand my words, but this is not what I had in mind." She waved her arm around the casino. "First we must do something about the will of the people. If you truly are a leader, then rally their beliefs to save us all." Her smile brightened. "Do your duty. Then you will deserve the reward."

Astron's stembrain boiled. He gritted his teeth, pulling it back under control. He looked at Nimbia's smile and then back at Byron, baring the fangs that were no longer there.

"No," Astron said. "The hillsovereign is not yours to do with what you will. As she states, her favor is to be for the most deserving—and not because of what emotions she excites, but the qualities she has inside. She is not yours, Byron; she is—she is mine!"

Not fully realizing what he was doing, Astron fumbled for the sword at his side. He glanced around the casino and saw the closing fog obscuring the farthest stands. The sound of the keening faded into softness and then vanished altogether. The ground underneath his feet felt like a thin sheet of linen loosely stretched over a tub of water. The wetness of the swirling fog began to glisten on his cheeks, as if he were exposed to a gentle rain.

"Do not be overly alarmed, demon," Nimbia said quickly. "I am sure that Byron has sufficient nobility to be different from the—"

She stopped as she saw the gleam in Byron's eye intensify. He spread his arms in a wide circle. Nimbia took a step backward and then halted as her foot touched the edge of the stadium wall. She looked back helplessly, her eyes growing wide with fear.

"It is your fate to be so unlucky," Byron said. "Such beauty was meant to be consumed."

"Underneath it all, I am a person like anyone else," Nimbia said, pain and disappointment putting a bitter edge to her voice. "Judge me for that and nothing else. That is all I ask."

"The allure is too great." Byron shook his head. "There is no one who can resist, no one who can look past the exterior with dispassion to see if there is any other value inside."

359

"Somewhere there must be at least one." Nimbia put out her hands to ward off his approach. She looked about frantically and then stopped when she saw Astron rushing to her.

"Dem—Astron!" she shouted. "Astron, help me. He is like all the rest. Only you are different. Please, quickly do something. There is so little time."

"The mines! What are they?" Astron yelled at Centuron as he stepped in Byron's way. "Tell me so that I may act."

"We do not know where any are buried." Centuron waved his arm. "But it does not matter. They will dissolve with the rest. Far better that—"

"Buried," Astron interrupted. "Did you say buried?"

"Why, yes—"

"That explains the blotchy appearance of the casino floor," Astron said. "With my membranes down I see far into the red, even into what is called heat in the realm of men. And turned earth is colder than that which has been in contact with the air."

He broke off and reached behind to grab Nimbia's outstretched hand. Ducking to the right, he avoided the swat of Byron's arm and started running out onto the casino floor, pulling her behind. He jogged to the right of a seemingly different-textured plot of ground and then sharply veered back to the left. Behind him, he heard Nimbia stumbling after and Byron's heavy tread in pursuit.

Astron cut to the side and felt his heel rip into the softening earth. Like a folded blanket, the ground wrinkled under the thrust. His foot dug deep into the earth and then, with a sudden lack of resistance, seemed to poke through into a chilling nothingness underneath. Frantically, he reached down and jerked his leg free, watching an inky blackness curl upward out of the hole.

From the corner of his eye, he saw that Byron had retrieved his sword and was waving it wildly over his head. "I am too swift for you," the demon called out suddenly as a glimmer of an idea darted into his mind. "And until you catch and overcome me, you will not have the hillsovereign."

Byron ran up to where Astron pulled at his leg. He

moved one step in Nimbia's direction and then hesitated. "Guard your backside," Astron said, waving his own blade as convincingly as he could.

Byron turned and looked down at Astron. The look of lust on his face distorted into one of battle rage. He gripped his sword with both hands and raised it high in the air. With an ear-piercing yell, he brought it down in a vertical swipe directly over Astron's head. The demon waited until the last possible moment and then jerked aside, just missing the slash.

Byron's sword dug deeply into the softening ground, burying itself almost to the hilt. Immediately, the warrior tightened his grip on the pommel and strained to extract his weapon. As Astron had hoped, the blade trembled, but did not bulge. He scrambled to his feet and again took Nimbia's hand. "I have decided," he said. "To Kestrel and Phoebe. It will be a moment before Byron is a menace again."

Together they zigzagged their way to the remains of Je-lilac's contingent. The swirling fog had penetrated almost to the first few rows of seats. Astron could no longer be sure that any of the aleators in the stands were still there.

"The pollen," he shouted, pointing at Kestrel's ruck-sack as he dashed up upon them.

"The anvilwood," Kestrel answered as he motioned to the abandoned fortification to the right of where Ca-monel had stood.

"And the flame." Phoebe pointed at the remains of Camonel's fire. She looked at the crumpled tapestries lying nearby. "There is wizard's work to be done."

"Wait a moment," Kestrel said to Astron as the demon dropped Nimbia's hand and started to head for the anvil-wood. "I have learned some things that might be important in the quest. Whoever merged the realms of symmetry planted the seeds of calculation in this universe as well. Look, there is the evidence of the navigator's almanac."

Astron skidded to a halt. "A book, did you say? That is most interesting and might indeed provide a clue."

"Not now," Phoebe shouted.

"I have tried to analyze the facts just as you would and extract the most important," Kestrel yelled at Astron's back when the demon resumed running to the other fortification. "Of all of the features of the almanac, it seems to be most strange that it lasts for centuries, and yet, every few days, the format is completely different."

Astron started to wrinkle his nose, but he realized he did not have the time. Reaching the anvilwood barrier, he began hewing with the sword as if it were an axe, sending splinters flying. He managed to dislodge two large logs. Abandoning his blade, he lifted them in the circle of his arms. Staggering with the load, he weaved his way back to the fire which Phoebe had fanned into a respectable blaze, despite the growing wetness of the air.

The tiers of the casino had become completely hidden in the dense black fog, and only hints of the massive support pillars were outlined where the high ceiling should be. The illuminating spheres of fungi had been reduced to dull glows. Only the fire pushed back the darkness of the encroaching gloom. It looked as if they were on an island in a fogbound sea.

Astron tossed the logs onto the fire and prepared to step into it himself, but then hesitated. "There is insufficient time." He shook his head. "You all will be gone before I can return."

"Then transport us to another realm," Phoebe said. "Like a mighty djinn, you must somehow carry us through."

"There certainly is no time for that, even if I were able," Astron said. "Piercing through one barrier to the realm of daemon is hard enough, let alone two."

"You must think of something, Astron." Nimbia touched his arm. "Look! At the very edge of the mists, I see Byron wrenching free his blade."

Astron looked at the inviting lick of the flame. The color and smell beckoned him with an almost irresistible allure. He could easily step into the warm, enfolding embrace and vanish from the peril. He watched the shrinking horizon of visibility and felt his stembrain stir in panic.

He reached out and felt the softness of Nimbia's hand still on his arm. Memories of the passion he had felt in Kestrel's body returned with a surprising sharpness. He

362

looked into her eyes and saw the confidence in his abilities that she seemed to radiate back to him.

"I will try as would my clutch brethren," he said softly as he walked into the flame. "The arc will be small, so you will have to squeeze as much as you can."

"Where will you take us?" Nimbia asked.

"If I am successful, just into the realm of daemon," Astron said. "To the darkness of my own den. Perhaps none will be waiting for us there."

He paused and studied the expression on her face. "It will be quite strange, but perhaps, after what you all have experienced, not so bizarre that you cannot act. We must get the pollen to Palodad. Remember, without that, eventually we will still fail."

Astron turned away his face and pulled his thoughts within himself, trying to shut out totally the collapse rushing inward. Groping mentally, he felt the fabric of resistance between the two realms and probed it for the flaw, the subtle discontinuity created by the burning of the anvilwood that would create the opening back to his home.

For how long he searched Astron could not tell, but finally he found it, a slight thinning in the essence of resistance that could be pierced by the strength of will. Astron concentrated on the familiar comforts of his own den—the ruggedness of the rocklike walls and the shelves that protruded from them, displaying the artifacts he had collected from the other realms. He envisioned with satisfaction the three volumes standing in a row between the shell and rock crystal that he used as bookends in the manner of men.

Astron strained against the resistance, pushing it inward, thinning it further, making it more transparent so that he could see and smell what he desired. There was a small pop and then a sudden ripping. He felt himself being drawn away, shrinking into the flame and tumbling into the comforts of his own lair.

For a moment, Astron let the feeling build within him, seeking to slip away and vanish from the dangers all about. His toes slid through the flame and dangled into the ceiling of his lair. Then his ankles followed.

Astron stopped his slide with a start. This time it had

to be different. He could not luxuriate in the narcotic sweetness of coming home. He stilled himself and stopped his transition. Instead, he concentrated on building an arc in the flame such as he had seen the mighty djinns form in the realm of the fey.

The ripping of the barrier halted, barely big enough for him alone to slip through and little else. He arched his back and placed his hands down into the fire, knotting his muscles and straining against the suddenly increased resistance. He felt the fire of the anvilwood climb up on his legs and arms and eventually meet in the small of his back. Sharp tendrils of pain accompanied their journey, somehow racing along the fibers of his being, reaching even into his fingers and toes and screaming with hurt.

Astron's jaws tightened and his vision blurred. "Quickly," he croaked. "I do not know how long I can maintain an opening this large.

"But I can hardly see anything." Kestrel peered into the arch beneath Astron's body. "It is a wall of flames and in its very center a dark disk hardly big enough for a child."

"It will have to do," Astron persisted. "First Nimbia and Phoebe, and then you can follow."

Phoebe gathered her cape about her and ducked her head between outstretched arms like a diver preparing to leap from a high cliff. She aimed her fingertips at the dark disk and slowly began to work herself through the opening.

Astron gasped as her head slipped through and he felt the widening bulge of her body. The pain intensified into an agonizing torrent. Only dimly was he aware of her passage and that of Nimbia who followed. He tried to focus on how close the swirling fogs had closed on them; but in the blur of his vision, he could not tell.

Kestrel came last, and Astron could no longer remain silent. He howled as the searing pain seemed to rip him asunder. Flashes of reds and yellow washed over him. Wave after pulsing wave dug deeply into his torso, seeking out every atom of his existence and wrenching it about.

"I cannot get through," Astron heard Kestrel call out. "It is the rucksack. The opening is too small to let it pass."

"Then take it off and try the grains one by one," Astron

heard himself answer. He ground his teeth and gasped to make his tongue do as it was commanded. He felt his last reserves of strength begin to wane. The nearest corner of his stembrain was dangerously close to breaking free.

"Kestrel," he choked hoarsely. "If, by some chance, I am unable to follow, you must act with my kind just as you have done with the imps in your own realm. Convince whatever demon passes by my lair to transport you to Palodad." He sucked in his breath in a spasm. "But do not let Phoebe wrestle with the old prince. Just get the pollen to him so that, in the end, Nimbia can be safe."

"One grain will just have to be enou—" Kestrel's answer was drowned by an increased roaring in Astron's ears. Dimly, he was aware of the prickly barbs of a pollen grain being passed through the barrier to waiting hands on the other side and then Kestrel's all too massive bulk straining to follow.

Astron felt his muscles begin to tremble and his consciousness falter. He could resist no more. The barrier closed with a sudden pop and he collapsed onto the flame, the last remnants of his tunic and leggings vanishing in smoke.

"Where have you hidden her?" He looked up to see Byron standing above him with the sword aimed at his eyes. "Quickly, tell me. There appears to be so little time."

Astron's thoughts bounced about his head. He could not control their direction. He tried to push his chest from the smouldering ashes, but his arms trembled and he collapsed back to the earth. Pools of wetness lapped at the flame. Directly in front, he saw three or four of the giant pollen grains begin to shake and bob as rivulets of water wound their way through the dense thicket of radiating spines. Beyond Byron's boots, all he could see were the dim glows of Camonel's fire spheres and, presumably, the shadow of Milligan still slumped in his confinement.

"Talk, I say," Byron persisted. "Tell me in which direction she has run."

Astron looked up at Byron through glazed eyes, but did not speak. The chaos continued to build in his mind. Lead balloons, pollen grains, ultimate precepts, bubbles of reality, symmetries, talismans, almanacs, lightning djinns, the archimage, Nimbia—they all boiled and churned, linking together in strange patterns that the ordinary discipline of his mind would not allow.

Byron scowled and pushed the tip of the sword to Astron's nose, but the demon did not move. The warrior pressed against the guard, bringing forth a drop of ichor and then abruptly pulled the blade away. "An aleator until the end I see," he growled. He looked at the sputtering remains of the anvilwood fire and quickly spun on his feet. "Let us see how loose your tongue becomes when faced with what you believe to be your bane."

Astron saw Byron move out into the dimness and thrust savagely with the sword. He returned in an instant with one of the fire spheres affixed to the tip of his blade. Despite the drenching wetness that seemed to drip from the heavy air, it still managed to sputter and glow. Byron studied the dance of flame for a moment and then thrust it at the nearest of pollen grains at his feet, plunging the two globes together into the soggy ground.

As Camonel's sphere submerged into the water, the fire sputtered out. But just as it did, the pollen grain touching it burst into a white-hot blaze of its own, suddenly glowing with a piercing intensity far more fierce even than what had ignited it.

Astron watched the burning harebell pollen float in the pool of water and burn at the same time, sending up a bubbling cloud of steam to add to the inky fog. He looked at another of the grains directly in front of his face and almost abstractly admired the beauty of the branching net of spines that bristled almost into nothingness.

"Of course." His mouth suddenly seemed to move of its own volition. "It is the same principle as the flour in the realm of reticulates. The tips of the barbs are so sharp and fine that they are perfect for the beginning of a flame. The pollen burned in the realm of the fey; even here in water, it can sustain a blaze."

Astron tried to shake his head free of the ricocheting thoughts, but the undisciplined stembrain would not be reconfined. He saw Byron free his sword from the fire sphere and stab instead at the burning pollen grain. With cruel menace in his face, the warrior brought it forward toward Astron's unprotected eyes.

"And the more difficult the environment, apparently the more intense the fire," Astron babbled on. "The grain smoked and smouldered in the realm of the fey. Here, even water cannot stop the rage of its blaze. In a realm in which it is truly diff—"

Astron stopped. Despite his fatigue he bolted up to sitting. With a savage wrench, he forced back his stem-brain, trying to regain control of his mind.

"It does no good to back away." Byron pressed forward with the burning orb. "A few more steps and you will dissolve into nothingness, as have most of the rest."

"I have solved the riddle!" Astron yelled, ignoring Byron's threat. "It is as Palodad suspected all along, but probably did not dare voice for fear that he might be wrong. The evidence we have here is proof enough. How do you start a fire in the realm of daemon? Why, with harebell pollen, of course. It is the kindling where nothing else will do. Harebell pollen, harebell pollen! It was with us all along. The quest truly is over. The ultimate precept—I have discovered the answer at last."

Byron watched Astron's apparent disregard for the burning globe and hesitated. "The ultimate precept," he said, puzzled. "Old Centuron used to speak of such a thing. Destruction is preordained, he would say. Destruction is preordained—either the sphere of existence is pierced from the outside or the will to believe decays from within."

"No, all of that speculation does not matter." Astron pushed aside Byron's blade. "The wise men of the realms guessed, but they did not know. 'Reality is a bubble,' Finvarwin said. 'Like the pipers blowing into the bowl of quickening gel, it is created by thought.' 'Coalescence follows from similarity,' Abel shouted when his relam was merged with another. Just as the juice and water were mixed for his warriors, two bubbles can be melted into one. And indeed, if the will to believe decays from within, the bubble will col—"

"Luck will be archon." A voice sounded behind Byron. The warrior spun just in time to see Milligan stagger forward out of the gloom with his dagger still in his hand. "With one vertex of the pentagon removed," the aleator said, "I was no longer confined. Luck will be archon, even if I am the only one left who believes."

Milligan began to lunge at Byron, but the ground under his feet gave way and he suddenly sank up to his waist. "The cold! My legs!" he shouted. "It feels as if they are no longer there." An expression of deep shock began to spread over his face as he sagged. With a desperate stab, he reached out with his dagger and swiped at Byron's calf. The warrior staggered to one knee and swung his sword, forcing the burning pollen grain toward Milligan's head.

"If I shall not succeed, then neither will any other," he cried as he smashed the blazing sphere against Milligan's cheek. He grunted as the other aleator's blade struck home again, this time in the warrior's chest.

"It is my destiny." Byron coughed up a spatter of blood. "My destiny just as Centuron said."

Byron's final swipe caught Milligan squarely on the jaw. With a cry of pain cut short, flesh and hair were suddenly consumed in a sickening belch of smoke. For an instant, blood spurted like a fountain from the top of Milligan's neck. Then the small aleator slumped forward to bleed over Byron's more massive form.

Astron hesitated. He watched the black mists sweep even closer. The remaining fire spheres could no longer be seen. In addition to the whirl of thoughts he could barely control, he felt the pounding panic of his stembrain increase. His limbs stiffened and he could not move. He must get the anvilwood burning again quickly—but he could not.

Despite himself, Astron wrinkled his nose. Besides the solution to the riddle, something else was bothering him. What else was it that Centuron had said about an ultimate precept? How could knowing about harebell pollen be such a powerful secret? Like mismatched elements of a magician's ritual, everything did not fit into a harmonious whole.

Astron gritted his teeth and tried to calm the rush in his mind. Wisps of fog coursed about him and he felt a prickling on his skin, as if it carried strong acids to dissolve him away. He looked at the bodies of Byron and Milligan, beginning to fade into the blackness.

He must remain in control, he thought as he struggled with the forces inside himself. He had to marshal discipline as never before. To succumb now would certainly ensure defeat. He had his duty to his prince; he must—

No, the passion thundered in his head. If only for his prince, then indeed he need not struggle more. With a stembrain running amok, to dissolve here in the realm of the aleators was as good a fate as any. But it was no longer only for his prince. The quest was for Nimbia as well.

She had called him by name, he recalled with sudden clarity—not "demon" but "Astron." "Astron, help me," she had said. It was a recognition that he served her not as subject but as equal. Yes, she was the one for whom he would continue the struggle. It was for Nimbia—Nimbia, queen of the fey.

Astron took a deep breath in the manner of men. The thought of pleasure not yet tasted flowed through his mind, bringing a small measure of calm. Yes, for Nimbia. For Nimbia and—and for himself being with her as well.

Straining against the stiffness in his limbs, Astron reached down and picked up Byron's sword. With jerky spasms, he touched the pollen grain to the remains of the anvilwood. Despite being half buried in the ooze, the logs again sputtered to life. Just as the last rush of blackness reached him, Astron struggled to merge with the flames.

PART SIX

The Ultimate Precept

Chapter Twenty-Eight

War of the Realms

"I do not like it." Kestrel frowned as Phoebe pulled away from the embrace. "What little strength we have grows weaker the more separated we become."

"The devil is hardly bigger than Astron." Phoebe waved at the demon struggling to grasp Nimbia securely around the waist. "It is clear that, at most, he can carry only two." She put a finger to the woodcutter's lips. "We only lose time by churning again through what has already been decided. Nimbia and I are to take the harebell pollen to the one called Palodad. If any sort of problem develops, it certainly makes more sense to have available the skills of two wizards, rather than one. You are to stay until Astron appears, and then he will somehow figure out a way for you to follow."

Kestrel scowled at the demon standing in the wash of light that flooded outward from the open doorway. The devil beat his leathery wings, pulling Nimbia a hand span away from the brief landing that ringed the hollow stone. Sprays of hair from the ears and nose formed long stiletto shadows that fell across a pockmarked face. The lower jaw merged into loose, hanging flesh that hung from the neck like a bulging sack.

Kestrel had found the devil cowering under the lowest shelf in what must be Astron's lair shortly after he recovered his senses from the transition. Only with difficulty was he able to interrupt a frightened babble of abject submission to explain the task that must be performed. The women's insistence had been surprising; now, in troubled resignation, Kestrel watched Phoebe surrender to the folds of the demon's free arm. In a heart beat, both

373

were gone into the deep blackness that seemed to permeate most of the realm.

Kestrel turned his attention back to the curving walls of Astron's lair. He touched the rough surface and felt the stone seem to warp and flex. Thinner than paper, he thought. It was remarkable that it was able to hold a shape with his weight pressing on a membrane of similar material that divided the hollow sphere horizontally in half.

Only the single circular opening to the outside broke the blank expanse of the walls. All available space was covered, either with shelves or pierced with hooks from which hung lamps, flower petals, spoons, key rings, thimbles, scissors, squares of printed cloth, and a lock of hair.

A single cushion sat on the rough flooring next to a pipe, a pile of small bones, and a pen and bottle of ink. The low-hanging lamp nearby illuminated a scrap of parchment on which a carefully drawn line of script had been abruptly halted in midstroke.

Kestrel stepped around the cushion and headed for the dim outline of a spiral staircase disappearing into a circular opening near the far wall. He should have explored thoroughly before Phoebe's departure, but the presence of the devil was too great of an opportunity to waste. The bottom half of the lair was probably like the top and, once Astron appeared, it would not really matter what—

A sudden wheeze of pain filled the confines of the chamber and stopped Kestrel in midstride. He looked quickly about the collection of artifacts and grabbed a long, two-pronged fork. It would be of little use in the realm of daemon, he thought ruefully, but he could find nothing more potent.

A second wheeze followed the first, and then a rustle of movement from down below. Kestrel retreated a step, gripping the fork warily. He saw the deep glow of yellow eyes emerge, and then a figure loomed into the light.

A ragged robe of deep sea-green with one sleeve torn entirely away hung over a slender body that limped with each step. A wide and angry scar ran from brow to chin on an otherwise delicate face. The remains of an upturned nose sat atop once slender lips, now swollen and red.

"I am Elezar, the one who is golden," Kestrel heard a voice rasp with difficulty between each dragging step. "I knew that my cataloguer would return, as was his duty to his prince, but I fear it is most likely far too late."

Kestrel raised the fork cautiously and held it in front of his chest. His eyes darted quickly about the confines of the lair, trying to locate just exactly where he had materialized and hence where Astron was also likely to appear.

"You speak in the tongue of men," Kestrel said softly. "I understand even though I am not the one you seek."

"I heard your petty debate and the final resolution." Elezar sagged to the cushion. "Since the outcome was the proper one, I did not interfere. Getting the harebell pollen to the one who reckons is all that is important now, despite the risk that Gaspar's minions might see the transit. It is the last hope. If it fails, then I am resigned to what will follow." Elezar waved at the fork. The edge of a smile tugged at his lips. "Put away the weapon," he said. "I do not have the strength to harm you, mortal. If you strive for the same goals as my cataloguer, then it is not my intent to do you harm."

Kestrel eyed the prince, but could read nothing in the damaged face. "We had heard that Gaspar even drove you from your hidden node," he said, "and pursued you into the very blackness of your realm."

"Gaspar does not have the wit to know where to look," Elezar spat. "To find me in the well-lighted lair of the vanished cataloguer, after he once had determined it abandoned, is entirely beyond his ken."

Kestrel could not bring himself to relax. Astron should have appeared by now. Without the demon's aid, who knew what Phoebe and Nimbia were getting themselves into? And a prince of demons, even if sorely wounded, would be more than a match for a man with no skills in wizardry.

"Then what now?" he said cautiously. "What is the will of the prince?"

"We will wait," Elezar said. "Wait and see if Palodad has sufficient time to unlock the secret to the riddle."

Kestrel did not reply. He lowered himself to the stone floor, but kept the fork at his side. Imitating the impassive resignation of the prince, he steeled himself into inaction.

Time dragged slowly by. For what seemed like eons, Elezar did not move. Occasionally a soft wheeze escaped from his lips. With each one, the glow in his eyes dimmed even further.

Finally Kestrel could be still no longer. He stirred uncomfortably from where he had slumped against the wall. The inward sloping curve pressed against the base of his head and gave no support to his back. He glanced at Elezar, sitting in regal quiet on the cushion, and scowled.

With each passing moment, his agitation had grown, but he did not know what to do about it. Hours must have passed since the prince lapsed into silence, and even though Astron had said that the flow of time was not quite the same between different realms, surely he would have appeared by now. He glanced again at Elezar's crumpled form. Even if wounded, he thought, could a prince be persuaded to carry a single man to the lair of—

"Gaspar, Gaspar, the prince of lightning djinns has observed my passage!" A sudden shriek cut into Kestrel's thoughts. He looked up to see the devil that had transported Phoebe and Nimbia twitching with spasms on the landing just outside the entrance to the lair.

"Grab control of your stembrain, or I will do it for you." Elezar suddenly sprang to life. "Speak with coherence. I, your prince, demand it."

"He observed my passage to Palodad's lair, and upon my return, forced upon me where you were. I, I am—"

"Silence," Elezar thundered. "The risk was worth taking. If you have failed, there is no point now in lamenting what might have been. Into the sky with you, assemble all that remain from their hiding places, and draw them here." The prince looked about Astron's artifacts and smiled. "Yes, here at the den of a mere cataloguer. For a final battle it is most fitting."

"If Gaspar has defeated you before, what hope do you have now?" Kestrel sprang to his feet. He felt his apprehension tighten like an alchemist's vice. Everything was crashing down, just as Astron had feared from the first. Even Elezar seemed resigned to his fate, and Kestrel and

376

his friends were in the middle of it, with little hope of escape.

"Do not give up," Kestrel said. "Get help from the other princes."

"More than half have thrown their lot in with Gaspar," Elezar said. "The rest cautiously await the outcome before they declare. No, none in the realm of daemon dare light their domains to aid the one who is golden."

Elezar stopped speaking and, for a long moment, seemed to look past Kestrel into the stone wall behind. "At least it will not be surrender to the great monotony. The few weavings of energy I have saved for the last will give Gaspar as much pain as he plans to inflict upon me."

"If not your own kind, then from the other realms," Kestrel said quickly. His thoughts spun. He would have to come up with a plan as he had never before. "From the archimage, the fey, the skyskirr, and the reticulates as well."

Elezar's eyes narrowed. He eyed Kestrel speculatively. "The denizens of other realms regard my kind either with fear or loathing. What would make them want to enter into a struggle not their own?"

"Let me handle that," Kestrel said. "First the archimage, and then we can appeal to the others. Contact any wizard in the realm of men and state that you have news of the woodcutter and female wizard. I heard Alodar ask to be informed, just as we vanished into the universe of the fey."

Elezar was silent for a moment. "Your words disturb my stembrain," he said. "I was prepared to meet Gaspar even on his own terms if there proved to be insufficient time to unravel the riddle. Now you give me one more tendril of matter to grasp. Even for a prince, there comes a moment when he must finally put aside the last of foolish hopes."

Kestrel waited without daring to speak again. Heart beats of time throbbed away. But finally a cloud seemed to lift from Elezar's face. The fading spark in his eyes glowed with a new life and he nodded.

"Tell each that you contact that they must first attempt to bridge through the flame," the prince commanded the devil just as he was about to leave. "Get the message of the woodcutter to the archimage so that he in turn will try to contact me here."

The devil shuddered a final time. Then with a trembling beat of his wings, he fluttered away. Kestrel saw pinpoints of light in the distance behind him assembling into a precise row and Elezar followed his gaze.

"Each one is a lightning djinn," the prince said. "They are forming a barrier between me and Palodad's lair. Soon they will move forward to attack us here. Your tongue must not only be glib but quick as well."

"The risk is a great one." Kestrel heard Alodar's words come from Elezar's lips. The contact had been established far quicker than he had hoped, but, as he glanced out the entrance of the lair, he wondered if even what he proposed would make any great difference. The pinpoints of light had intensified to eye-stabbing glows. Their number had increased until it looked as if a continuous arc streaked across the black sky. With each passing moment, it grew thicker and longer, arcing outward to surround Astron's lair so that there would be no escape.

"But if it is not taken," Kestrel shot back, "then the loss is certain." Somehow the archimage was able to hear because of his contact with Elezar's mind. It was as if the two were together in the confines of the hollow stone, rather than an indescribable distance apart.

"When you agreed to help send Phoebe and me through the flames before," Kestrel continued, "it was because of what would happen to the realm of men if Elezar should fall. Nothing has changed to alter the validity of your decision."

"I still am not totally sure of the truth of your words," Alodar said. "And if I and the wizards of other realms come forward and fail, there will be no defenses left to be sure."

"Would you rather wait and take on Gaspar's might one by one?" Kestrel said. "Which strategy offers you the better chance to turn aside the threat?"

For a moment, there was silence. Elezar sat on the cushion, unblinking, with his hands folded into the lap of

378

his tattered robe. "Your arguments are most persuasive," the demon mouthed Alodar's words at last. "They ring true despite whatever other doubts I might have."

Kestrel felt a slight prickle of amazement mingle with the urgency that bubbled within him. He was using no deception at all. He did not have sufficient composure to think through all the twists and turns that would be necessary for one such as the archimage. And yet it was working. He was speaking the truth and Alodar was taking him at his word.

"But perhaps most telling is the fact that you are there," Alodar said. "There and willing to take the risks along with the rest. It is the mark of a hero, rather than one looking out only for himself."

Kestrel's thoughts jerked to the side. "No, not a hero," he said. "Not me. I am not concerned about helping to save the baseness of other men. It is only for myself, only for—"

Kestrel stopped and slammed shut his mouth. Only for Phoebe, he thought—and for the reticulate warriors, for Nimbia's underhill, and even for any of the unlucky aleators who still survived—any who had to endure the tortures of their fellows who did not care.

The injustices that had befallen him were not unique; they extended through seven realms as well. And they would continue to do so until someone came forward and took the cause of many as his own, until someone like the archimage felt the duty to look beyond himself and to strive against the Prydwins, Jelilacs, and Gaspars to save the worthy and unworthy alike.

The feeling of amazement grew. Was what he had been striving for on this quest really anything less? He could not turn aside now, regardless of what escape he suddenly was offered. If that was what constituted being a hero, then perhaps it was not such a foolish rôle after all.

"Yes, I think that we will need someone to coordinate all of the contingents," Kestrel heard himself say. "Someone with experience in all the realms on which we will call for aid. I am ready to serve. Even though it might be hopeless, I will carry out what clearly is my duty and that of no one else."

"Then it is decided," Alodar said. "Send what demons through the flame that you can, Elezar. I will have the wizards ready to be ferried back for your aid."

"Next the fey," Kestrel said to Elezar as Alodar's presence faded. "And then the reticulates and perhaps the skyskirr as well."

A hint of annoyance at being ordered about washed across Elezar's twisted face, but Kestrel hardly noticed. Despite the growing terror outside, he felt far better about himself than he had in a long, long time.

"Nimbia, Nimbia are you safe?" Astron shouted as he squeezed through the vanishing opening between the realms. He felt the chill of nothingness on his legs and barely managed to pull them through with a loud pop just in time. What had been the realm of aleators was completely vanished, collapsed into nonexistence by the pressure of the void.

Astron sagged to the familiar stone flooring of his lair in a heap. The struggle against Byron had been most draining and his body cried out to rest. But his stembrain still bubbled in agitation. He knew he could not stop, not until he was sure Nimbia was safe and his alone. Immediately, he must carry the harebell pollen to—

Astron stopped. His lair was empty. They had gone on ahead without him. He rose to his feet, looking about wildly for some clue, and spotted the pen and ink next to the pile of fishbones where he had left them in what seemed like long ago. Hastily, he scooped the scrap of parchment from the ground and read the script that had been added to his own.

Almost in disbelief, Astron looked out of the open portal to his lair and saw the glowing sky that confirmed that the words were true. Phoebe and Nimbia had been transported safely to Palodad, but Gaspar now assembled all of his might to strike a final blow. Elezar had gone to direct his resistance, while Kestrel, carried by a broad-winged devil, led the wizards assembled from many realms.

As Astron slowly let the scrap fall back to the floor, a swarm of imps buzzed up from the stairwell, but he paid them no heed. The sky was almost as bright as day in the realm of men, so many djinns had Gaspar rallied to his side. With what meager forces Elezar had left, it was doubtful he would have any more need for his tiny entertainers.

Only if Palodad were swift enough to test the pollen and show it blazing in triumph would any who followed Gaspar pause and reconsider that the basis for the confrontation had indeed been won. Otherwise Elezar was lost, and, in the end, all who strove for him as well.

Astron looked at the sphere of bright lights converging on the darker knot of men and beings from other realms, now standing off in the distance and awaiting the strike. He reached out once with his empty hand, then pounded his sides in frustration. Astron, wingless Astron, the one who walked! In the end, he was reduced to being a mere spectator while others decided the fate of the realm.

Astron pushed against the tug of his stembrain. It continued to stir and boil. There was something that still bothered him, some additional conclusion that could be drawn from all that he had learned. He settled on the cushion, not bothering to bat away the imps as they swarmed about his head.

"Reality is a bubble," he muttered. "I have seen realms created, merged, and destroyed. Aleators like Centuron believe that such destruction is preordained. Either the will to believe decays the pressure within or the bubble is pierced from—"

Astron stopped. The already high state of agitation of his stembrain grew with a deep terror he had never felt before. Why the knowledge of fire in the realm of daemon held such power suddenly became clear. He knew why it was the ultimate precept, the greatest of them all.

Astron bolted to his feet and ran back to the open portal. "There is a reason why there is no fire in our realm," he shouted in panic, "a reason most profound. Fire breaks down the barrier that keeps a bubble whole; it creates an opening in the surface that protects it from the void."

Astron looked at the still brightening sky. He knew

that the distances were still far too great for his voice to carry, but he felt he had to continue on. The battle between Elezar and Gaspar suddenly was of insignificant consequence compared to what really was at stake.

"For all the other realms, the opening is to our very own," he yelled. "The pressure on both sides of the breach is the same. Except for creating a portal of transport, nothing else happens as a result.

"But a flame in the realm of daemon—think of it! When it pierces the skin of the bubble, where then will it lead? Not to another of the realms; other flames already provide those connections. No, it can only be to the void. Like the spheres of the aleators that surrounded the talismans, a small rupture lets out the essence inside. The realm of daemon would collapse into nothingness just as surely as if we had ceased to believe.

"It is not only our own universe that would wither away," Astron said. "All the other realms are connected to ours by the other flames. Like the merged realms of symmetry, they would all vanish as well, first oozing into ours and then following us into the chilling void. It would mean the end of everything, all of existence, all that there is."

Astron shook his head and tried to regain a measure of control. The battle of warring princes for supremacy in a single realm were only shadows of what confronted him. The death of a single realm or two was nothing compared to the end of them all!

"But who would wish such a fate on all of existence?" Astron wondered aloud. "Who could be so tired of living that he would succumb to the great monotony in such a fashion? Who would have the power to manipulate—"

He stopped and tried to look beyond the glare of the djinn light. "Oh, what have I done?" he shrieked. The greatest insight of all descended on him like a weight of the densest matter. "Nimbia, Nimbia," he moaned. "I have sent you to the worst possible place.

"It is Palodad." He whirled and explained to the buzzing imps. "Palodad, the one who reckons, is behind it all. I now understand it so clearly. He is the old one like Centuron whose only desire is to see the final end. He is the one who controlled events that combined two realms. He is the one that cut away the beliefs of all the aleators so that they vanished as well. Yes, who else but a demon would design an almanac with entries beyond the lifespan of a man. Who else but a demon would think it important to change the format of the entries so that the user would not get bored over such a span and succumb to the great monotony. Who else provided Jelilac with the calculation of where his spinner would come to rest.

"It is all part of his plan, the same one that he constructed to get harebell pollen to him for the final step. It is Palodad who has computed everything along the way. Gaspar's challenge, sending me on the quest, instructing Camonel merely to appear dominated by Phoebe while retaining allegiance to his prince—there was no other wizard involved at all. It is Palodad who must be stopped; Gaspar is merely a cog in his machine like the rest."

Astron looked at the converging djinns. Somehow Gaspar's rush must not only be halted but pierced as well. He had to get to Palodad's lair and stop the pollen grain from being ignited. Once it was ablaze, it would be the beginning of the end. He was the only one who knew the true peril. Not only Nimbia but all of existence was forfeit if he should fail.

He looked at the imps still swarming about him and grabbed at the thought that sprang into his head. "Servants of Elezar," he commanded. "Each of you, grab hold of my flesh where you can. Together you will transport me across the realm."

CHAPTER TWENTY-NINE

The Final Computation

KESTREL watched Gaspar's demons zoom in for their first attack and held his breath. His pulse raced. What he had chosen to do was right, but he could not keep the chilling reality of the most likely outcome from his thoughts. Even with a score of wizards from each of the realms of men, fey, and skyskirr, Elezar's forces were spread far too thin. The hastily constructed inner sphere of lesser devils that faced the lightning djinns was outnumbered at least three to one.

Kestrel pressed his foot down on the unseen blackness beneath him, still not quite believing it was there. He and the legion of reticulates stood in relative darkness on what Elezar had called an unoccupied node. Scattered throughout the realm were many such points, the prince has said, loci that remained fixed in the sky and did not fall toward whatever tugged on everything from below. On them, the djinns and lesser devils accumulated and weaved their meager treasures of matter, transforming the blank nothingness into elegant distractions that forestalled the great monotony. Kestrel pushed aside the wonder of it all. For now, although surrounded by Gaspar's forces like the rest, Abel and the others were ready to act in synchrony, and that was all that mattered.

Near the center of the spheres of converging attackers, not far from Astron's lair, Elezar blazed with a brilliant light, no longer hiding, but daring Gaspar to come forward. In the direction of Palodad's domain Kestrel had deliberately posted the fewest of the defenders in the hopes that, when the lightning djinns did swoop for the kill, their path would be directly through the middle of the two lines of waiting warriors.

The already-bright sky suddenly blossomed into splashes of intense color. Simultaneously, Gaspar's lieutenants unleashed bolts of searing energy at those who rose to fight them. Kestrel saw two devils and a smaller demon immediately enveloped in crackling tendrils of plasma, their shrieks of pain blotted by the rumble of the blow. He clenched his fists. Soon, one way or another, he would experience the fate of the hero.

More demons streaked outward, ducking past the spray of ichor and bone and launching strikes of their own. Behind them, broodmothers beat the air with heavy wings, carrying wizards in their outstretched talons. Gaspar's lesser devils swooped in behind their lieutenants, eyes wide with the choice of targets and sticky drool streaming from their chins as they contemplated the lust of battle.

Bursts of light flashed into incandescence. Kestrel had to shield his eyes with upflung arms. Three more defenders exploded in balls of boiling flesh, then a half dozen more. The deep booming laugh of Gaspar's lieutenants resonated with the rolling echoes of the explosions.

Still Elezar's defenders rose to meet the attack. The broodmothers climbed unrelentingly upward and the wizards they carried projected their wills. Kestrel saw the arm of one of Gaspar's lieutenants suddenly jerk in a spasm. A half-formed streak of energy sputtered and flew wide of its mark. The djinn scowled and turned his head to launch another bolt at the one who had interfered with his thoughts. Before he could, a brown-skinned devil soared past his outflung arm, blasting out with three sharp stabs of crackling pain. Elezar's smaller devils closed in on the mightier djinns. Even tiny imps harried them in vicious swirls, biting earlobes and cheeks when flailing hands could not keep them away.

But then a random blast ricocheted from a defensive shield and struck a wizard from the realm of the skyskirr squarely in the chest. One of Gaspar's minions shook his head at the sudden release from sluggishness. With a wild yell, he waved to the others, indicating whom they should attack.

All around the enveloping sphere, the word passed as fast as the bolts of plasma. Elezar's demons were ignored; the strikes were aimed at the broodmothers and the loads that they carried. The defending demons swooped to intercept the new focus of attack, but the first were blasted out of the way. One wizard fell, then two more. The others tried to maintain their concentration, but each misdirected bolt now did not stray as far from its intended target. The uprush of defenders halted. Gradually they began to give ground.

The warriors on the dark node stirred uncomfortably, but Kestrel indicated for them to be still. He glanced at Elezar and then back to the crumbling defense. Just as it looked as if the thin surface of protection would be pierced in a half dozen places, he saw the prince give the sign. The broodmothers and other demons along the deliberately weakened corridor suddenly turned in midflight and began to dive. With wings folded, they plunged toward Elezar, shooting directly between Kestrel and the two lines of reticulates.

For a moment Gaspar's minions hesitated. Then, with a shout of triumph, they came plunging after. The lieutenants saw the collapse. As Kestrel had hoped, they abandoned their own battles to join in the destruction of Elezar the prince. In an undisciplined riot, the mighty djinns circled to where the resistance had suddenly become nonexistent and poured down the corridor, striving to be the first to strike a blow at the one who waited below.

Elezar released two tremendous blasts of power of his own just as the first of Gaspar's devils sailed into Kestrel's midst, forcing them to stop and hastily throw up their wings to shield off the blast.

"Now," Kestrel shouted. "Demon of many heads, close your ranks just as we have planned."

The reticulates on the ends of the two rows nearest the djinns smartly heeled and rotated their lines inward. Like the lid of a box, in synchronized step they closed off the path to Elezar, presenting a perfect repetition of the lines that flanked the demons on either side.

More of Gaspar's lieutenants raced up in a flurry of wings. Crashing into one another, they looked puzzled at the silent lines of men linked together and marching in perfect step.

"And the bottom," Kestrel shouted when the last of a dozen had come. "Seal the one remaining means of escape and then they are ours. What can be the hope of a single djinn, no matter how mighty, against a foe with eight score heads and twice as many arms with which to unleash his awesome power?"

Kestrel bit his lip as he peered over Abel's shoulder. The lines of reticulates swung shut just as had the ones in front. For a precious moment, none of the djinns within the box moved or released any of their energy.

"Yes, eight score bodies all connected into one," Kestrel prattled on. "It must be so. Look at the unity in movement. Surely that would be impossible if each were somehow disjoined. One hundred and sixty torsos and hence one hundred and sixty times the strength. You have met your superior, minions of Gaspar. Surrender now so you can observe the extent of this power."

Kestrel reviewed his logic quickly. The demon mind freezes with the unusual, and it does not immediately consider the possibility of falsehood. With just a moment's more hesitation, a major part of Gaspar's strength would be neutralized.

"Inward with swords drawn," Kestrel commanded. "They will not resist one obviously mightier, one who cannot be brought down, no matter what happens to a single limb."

For a moment the lieutenants remained silent and unmoving, almost mesmerized by the cadence of the reticulates' march. Then one shook his head. What looked like a jagged bolt of blue lightning arched from his fingertips toward the warrior who was closest.

The reticulate exploded backward from the line with blood boiling from his chest, but he did not cry out. The line immediately closed and, in perfect cadence, resumed the march inward toward the puzzled djinns.

Another blast erupted and a third. Two more reticulates were hurled away, but their positions were again immediately filled, pulling the perimeter even tighter.

A fourth lieutenant raised his arm with sparks crackling between his fingertips but then hesitated. His eyes danced wildly as he tried to decide where to aim his bolt. Finally he slumped against the djinn next to him and let the plasma die away. Kestrel saw what he hoped was the beginning of despair begin to form in the devil's eyes.

"Who plays with the minds of my lieutenants?" A gruff voice behind Kestrel shot a sudden chill up his spine. He turned to see Gaspar hovering behind him, not quite touching down to land on the darkness of the node. The prince had not rushed forward with the rest.

Kestrel looked at the huge form of the djinn and shuddered. All the terror that man had for demonkind spilled over him in a crashing wave. Meeting Astron, Elezar, and even Camonel was one thing, but the presence of Gaspar was overwhelming. He saw the crackles of energy arching between the fingertips, the twitch of massive slabs of muscle barely under control, the swarm of mites about the bristly chin, and worst of all, the smouldering eyes that were focused on him alone.

"Who twists their minds?" Gaspar repeated. "Who has closed off even the suggestion that all they need do is fly upward and then they would be free?"

"It is the many-headed demon from the far reaches of the realm," Kestrel forced himself to say. "Palodad found him and instructed him in Elezar's defense. You may as well surrender as well."

"Palodad? Palodad helping Elezar, you say?" Gaspar tossed back his head and laughed. "Your words do not match the facts, mortal, and I have been warned there might be such as you." The demon looked about at the last of Elezar's defenders fighting his lesser devils. "Even without my lieutenants, the outcome is still determined—although it might take a little longer than had originally been calculated. And since you are the apparent cause of the delay, it is only fitting that you also provide my diversion until it is done."

Astron ignored the barbs of pain that stabbed his back and legs. It was better that the grips of the imps were sure, rather than comfortable. He did not like the heavy and labored sound of their buzzing wings, but what would happen if they faltered, he could not afford to dwell upon.

Astron looked back at the sphere of Gaspar's minions converging on his lair. He had half expected to be blasted out of the sky by one of them as he struggled away, but they all had rushed past in their haste to attack the prince. Evidently, one small demon in a cloud of imps was something that easily could be handled later.

The escape gave him little comfort. A few moments more of existence was all that he had gained, unless he could stop Palodad from lighting the harebell pollen. His stembrain bounced around the confines of his mind, unable to find peace with what it knew. He could no longer force it back into a quiet slumber. Only by straining with all his thoughts could he keep some degree of control on the impulses which threatened to fling his body into twitching spasms.

Inwardly focused, Astron did not note his passage through the darkness of the realm or the descent down Palodad's long entrance tunnel. Only by forcing his arm to move in clumsy jerks was he able to fling aside the barrier that opened into the interior that was blazing with light.

As the imps lowered him to the ledge that circumnavigated the huge globe, Astron froze for a moment, transfixed as he had been before by the enormous display of matter, the bizarre arrays of bound devils, the tugging fetters, and the booming cadence of whirling machines. Somewhere in the midst of it all was Nimbia— Nimbia and the pollen that had to be destroyed.

Astron ran to the first pulley-basket and climbed inside. He unwound the rope from its stay and began lowering himself hand over hand into the interior of Palodad's domain. His memories of the first visit were hard to keep in focus, but at each transit he was able to recall the direction he should take.

While he navigated the vast interior, Palodad's giant machine clanked onward, oblivious of his presence. The small, free-flying sprites darted from array to array, shuttling messages to the demons who were bound. The intricate lines of djinns who flipped from upright to standing on their heads paid him no heed when he passed.

Finally Astron spied the central platform that contained the plane of shimmering glowsprites. Huddled in front of the screen, clasping the pollen in his hands, was the ancient prince. Only hints of his raspy voice could be heard over the background, but Palodad was evidently waving his treasure about to two captives imprisoned in cages to his left.

Nimbia and Phoebe! Astron stopped his rush. They looked unharmed; but now that he was here, what exactly was he to do? Palodad could summon any of a hundred djinns to snare him like the others. How could a cataloguer, and one barely in control at that, stop a prince of demons who had plotted for eras before Astron was even hatched? What good was it to have guessed the answer to the riddle, if the final result was the same in the end?

Astron's panic grew. He felt his limbs stiffen. He knew that this time he would be unable to make them move. He strained to open his mouth and yell, knowing not what, but even his jaws grew rigid. Like a statue of inert matter, he watched Palodad cackle and preen with his prize.

The old prince seemed to babble randomly for a few moments. Then a motion on the screen caught his eye. He glanced upward and watched for a moment in silence. Finally he threw back his head and laughed raucously, his frail voice managing to be heard even over the clatter.

"It is time," Palodad burbled. "It is time for the final ingredient to come." He whirled and looked directly in Astron's direction. "Do not bother that your mobility is gone, cataloguer," he said. "Sprites are on their way to bring you to my presence." He waved his arm about the expanse of his domain. "You have come in duty to your prince, just as my calculations said that you would."

Astron should have felt shock at Palodad's awareness of his presence, but he did not. Only dimly was he aware of being lifted and brought to stand directly in front of the prince.

"It is about time," Palodad continued, a thick drool beginning to form down the side of his chin. "The ultimate precept is about time and nothing else. Time, time, time—of all the forces, it is the greatest, relentlessly pressing onward, unable to be turned aside by any of the other princes.

"But my power is by far more potent still—more so than Gaspar with his bolts of lightning or even Elezar and his keenness of mind. I will not merely harass time in its passage, but stop it altogether. The pollen at your feet, cataloguer, is the kindling, the great store of matter I have accumulated over the eons is the fuel. I will destroy this realm and all the others that connect to it. When I am done, there will be nothing left to measure the tick of time's passage. It will be gone. I will have been the one to see it finally destroyed."

Astron felt his eyes stiffly glance down at the pollen grain at Palodad's feet, a small shred of puzzlement tugging at the muscles in his face.

"You wonder why I have not already set it ablaze, do you not?" Palodad said. "Think, cataloguer! Besides the fuel and the kindling, what is the third ingredient for a flame?" Palodad's rheumy eyes widened. He pressed the metal ball in his hand against Astron's chest.

"It is the spark, the spark that ignites the kindling and sets the events on their way, a special spark that only a most unique demon can provide. That is the final ingredient, cataloguer. That is why I had to bind you to the quest, to manipulate things so carefully that in the end you would be here."

Astron tried to shake his head in protest, but Palodad ignored him and rambled on. "Yes, the spark cannot come from any demon; my calculations have shown me that just any shape and intensity of the energy will not do. It must originate from one for whose entire existence the stembrain has remained under control, a clutch brother of mighty djinns, but one who has repressed even the slightest hint of undisciplined thought."

391

Palodad pressed his face against Astron's own. "Now, cataloguer, to make the final calculation complete. Surrender, surrender at last to what has churned within you for so long."

Again Astron attempted to shake his head. He was merely a cataloguer, a stunted djinn without wings, one who could not weave. How could he provide the essence of what the mad demon sought? It could not be true, and yet— As the feelings churned within him, Astron could not deny what the prince had said.

Palodad was correct, the certainty swelled. He had been correct from the first. All the events had been calculated and there was no other outcome possible. The mad one's great machine, his incredible store of matter, and the pollen that would surely ignite—there was no logical way to resist. Not only would everything that existed vanish totally, but he, Astron, the one who walked, was to be the instrument for that destruction.

Astron tried to cry out, but he felt his final control slipping away. A ripping pain coursed through him, as if his very being were being torn apart. Thoughts exploded in all directions and bounced about his head. Through eyes wet with tears, he saw Nimbia's face contort with concern. He felt a strange tingling and then sharp nips of pain. His stembrain danced as it had never done before. Crackles of energy popped from his ears and raced down his arms. Purple and brilliant red streamers surged to his back and then onto his thighs. Helplessly, he saw Palodad kick the pollen grain between his feet, and the angry pulses of energy spurted and jumped to meet it.

Astron felt himself slipping away into a maelstrom of confusion. The lust for destruction within him grew. With the last shred of consciousness, he struggled to pull back the crackling power that radiated from him and keep it away from the prickly sphere waiting for its touch. But he could not hold back the flood. Past his knees, the sheets of plasma danced down onto his shins. White-hot sparks exploded out into the air. In a brilliant flash, globs of pulsing energy rained onto the floor.

* * *

"I have let you agonize long enough in anticipation." Gaspar stepped forward into the darkness of the node. "Now you shall experience a hint of what truly is to come." He extended his arm and pointed at Kestrel's chest. A tiny arc of energy shot from the demon's fingertip and struck the woodcutter just below the throat.

Kestrel staggered to one knee as the stab of pain exploded across his torso and ran down his arms. He gasped, then gritted his teeth, determined not to cry out. For the longest while, Gaspar had stood silently taunting him while the battles behind the two of them still raged. Now only a few cries and bursts of light illuminated the darkness of the demon realm. Elezar's last defenders swarmed about their prince, but not even the most hopeful could now dispute the final result.

"What, no pleas for mercy?" Gaspar said. "No appeal to some better part of my nature to make the ending swift?" The djinn stepped forward and grabbed Kestrel beneath the arms and lifted him effortlessly to eye level. "You will grovel before I am done, mortal, grovel like all the rest when they feel the wrath of the prince whose power is the greatest."

Gaspar's hands started to glow with pulses of energy. Kestrel felt the fabric of his tunic shrivel and part. Waves of heat radiated into his chest. His skin began to blister and flake away. He shook his head from side to side, trying to find the words that would turn Gaspar's attention away— some clever stratagem that would misdirect even a prince of demons from his fiendish pleasure. He looked into Gaspar's eyes and saw only the twisted desire that would not be denied. In despair, he realized that there was nothing that he could say that would save him now.

Gaspar saw the expression on Kestrel's face and threw back his head with a booming laugh. Short stabs of plasma arched from the demon's shoulders and elbows and smashed into Kestrel's arms, adding rips of pain to the boiling heat that already was almost too much to withstand.

As the agony intensified, visions began to swim in Kestrel's mind. He thought of Phoebe and what would be her fate after he had gone, of Abel and the warriors behind him still faithfully confining the lieutenants as he had commanded them, and of Astron, a demon most unlike all the rest, of—

Kestrel reached out and grabbed at the thought as it flitted by. He closed his eyes and concentrated on where it was leading him. Astron would not challenge Gaspar with wily words. He would use whatever solid facts he could and from them determine what must be done.

Kestrel shifted his focus as quickly as he could through the numbing haze of pain. Gaspar—what was all that had been said about the prince in the times that Astron had spoken of him during the quest? He was a most powerful djinn with his weavings of matter, indeed perhaps the most powerful of all. But in Elezar's rotunda he had been chided for his lack of wit and unwillingness to challenge any wizard who sought—

Gaspar was a powerful weaver, it was true. Kestrel churned the thought in his mind. But what was Gaspar's strength of will? How well could he fare against the archimage, or Phoebe, or even—?

"Surrender," Kestrel yelled at the top of his lungs as he seized at the last chance. "Surrender to him who will be your master. It is dominance or submission. There can be no in between."

"You are no wizard—"

"Nor need I be. It is only a matter of will," Kestrel gasped. The pain in his sides became excruciating. He thought he could smell the burning of his own flesh. But he lashed out with his mind, seeking the essence of the demon that held him, ready to twist and turn with his last dying gasp. There was nothing else to try.

Kestrel's sight dimmed into hot glowing yellows. Blindly, his thoughts exploded, not knowing exactly what it was that he sought. He felt his awareness expand in all directions, pushing everything before it. All of his essence of being, his pleasures, his hopes, his fears, and everything of consequence boiled and churned, blasting all else aside.

Then Kestrel felt a resistance, something that slowed the outswell of thought that swirled midst the pain. Impulsively, he crashed against the barrier, at first skittering against the surface, but then striking it again and again. Visualizing mental arms and legs, he tore at the covering, trying to rip it asunder so that he could plunge inside.

The images whirled in his mind, but somehow even in the delirium of his pain, he stalked like a hunter, testing the seams of Gaspar's essence one by one. He jabbed a finger into a dark crevasse; when he felt something softer than the rest, he thrust in his hand. Whatever was inside attempted to wither away, but Kestrel was quicker and grabbed and twisted as savagely as he could.

"Your minions might have victory," Kestrel shouted, "but you will not share in it, Gaspar. I have come too far and changed too much to let it be so. I cannot weave, but it does not matter. My will is the greater because I fight for what I believe, not for some idle amusement to forestall an eventual dawn."

Kestrel felt his fist rip and tear. A shudder coursed throughout all his body. He reached with his other hand and pulled at Gaspar's being, spreading it open so that it was exposed. He felt a sudden wave of pleading protest, and then a smell of self-loathing that shook him to the core. Fear and submission flooded over him, drenching him in doubt and ultimate despair.

"Desist, master, desist," Kestrel heard Gaspar say. "Stop your smiting. I am yours to command."

Kestrel paused. He opened his eyes and blinked. He was lying astride Gaspar's chest as the demon sprawled on the inky blackness of the node. Kestrel looked at his bloody hands where he had been ripping at the djinn's face; the flesh of one jowl was hanging limp and oozing green ichor.

Tears sprang into Kestrel's eyes. Mingling with the lingering pain, he felt a deep catharsis wash over him. After all these years, the burden was finally lifted. His first deceptions and every one that followed he could finally put aside.

He started to speak, but the node beneath him suddenly rumbled. There was a flash of light that lit the sky from the direction of Palodad's lair.

"Ah, even in my defeat," Gaspar slurred through the

wreckage of his face. "Even in my defeat, it sounds as if my master has still achieved his own triumph, whatever it was that caused him to direct me so."

Astron's eye membranes snapped into place, but they did not help. The harebell pollen glowed with a white-hot intensity that was greater than any normal flame. Through a series of mirrors, the blinding glare ricocheted out of Palodad's lair and across the darkness of the realm in the direction of Astron's den, evidently a signal that the deed was done. Like a boiling sun, the sphere roared in incandescence, churning the air that surrounded it into waves of convective force. The metal platform on which it rested began to pool into a slaggy liquid. Nearby spars blistered and twisted. The wings of close-flying imps burst into flame.

But worst of all was the roaring hiss. Even though the air closest to the burning pollen had greatly expanded, it did not bubble away. Instead, scraps of parchment and small loose objects tumbled toward the flame, accelerating as they grew near. Then in a final rush, they vanished into the whiteness. The surface of the realm of daemon had been ruptured. Now its very essence was leaking away to the void of nothingness on the outside.

Palodad knelt down on his haunches and watched the sucking pressure increase its power. Oblivious to everything else and cackling at the top of his lungs, he snatched imps out of the air and cast them into the flame.

"The rupture is but a beginning," Palodad cried. He waved about the expanse of his lair. "As more fuel is consumed, the opening will grow. Stronger will become the force pushing every object into its ultimate dissolution. No matter where they hide, no one will be able to resist it. Eventually, all must tumble past Palodad, the one who reckons."

Astron felt the wind pushing against his back and rushing into the orb of destruction. His entire body was alive with dancing sparks, but he no longer cared. Despite his last futile efforts, he had been unable to stop the mindless rush of his stembrain and to restrain the power that gave rise to the all-important spark. Now all he felt was the compulsive desire to flee, somehow to shake off the rigidity that gripped him, and to hide from the growing suction as long as he was able.

He looked at Nimbia desperately, a small part of his mind dimly aware of how in the end he had not saved her from Palodad's fate. He saw Phoebe standing next to her, dumbfounded, her mouth open and watching the all-consuming energy of the fire.

Phoebe, Phoebe and Kestrel, Astron thought. If only the woodcutter had been along for the final confrontation. He would not have let his stembrain get out of control. Somehow he would have used its power instead, exploiting its irrationality rather than becoming its slave. But for himself, a demon, a cataloguer, Palodad's logic had been inescapable. There was no way that—

Astron gasped despite himself. Indeed, Kestrel would not fight the vagaries of the stembrain. He would not try to keep it under restraint. He would let it roam wherever it led him, seeking out solutions rooted in emotion that mere logic could never find. Astron looked a second time at Nimbia. With a shudder, he surrendered the last vestige of control. Totally unconstrained, he let his stembrain take over his body and do with it what it would.

Astron felt the sparks that raced over his body intensify. Like Gaspar, tendrils of blue and green flame filled the spans between his fingers. Glowing plasma danced over his lips and across his cheeks. The rigidity that held him melted away. Surrendering completely, he was able to sag to the ground with his legs trembling in mighty spasms and his head jerking from side to side. His tongue poked randomly out between his teeth. A meaningless cry escaped from his lips.

And inside Astron's mind the images swirled. The safety of his den, Elezar's beautiful spires, the mysteries of the realm of men, the constructions of the fey, the lust of the human body, the merging of two realms into one, the collapse of the universe of the aleators—they all danced and swayed. Colors fused and melted, the touch of smooth surfaces transformed into pungent odors and smells. He sensed his feelings for Nimbia grow into a passion that encompassed all of him and tasted heartbreak because none of her intimate mysteries would he ever experience. She would disappear like all the rest, a pleasure never sampled, a sweetness—

For an instant the tumble of Astron's thoughts jerked to a halt. He felt himself frown and pulled at the inconsistency that suddenly hovered just outside the reach of his consciousness.

Palodad had said he had come in service of his prince just as it had been calculated. That was certainly true, but the reason had been replaced by one far more powerful. In the end, it was his feeling for Nimbia, his concern for her safety above all else, his sense of—of possessiveness that had stirred in him so, and that was the motivator of his actions, far more than anything else.

Everything was not as Palodad had calculated, Astron realized in a rush. The irrationality of feeling, the concern of one being for another, the desire for sharing—the ancient prince had not counted on such things at all.

Astron glanced down at the pollen grain raging in front of his feet, tasting all the more strongly the natural impulse of any demon to flee. He looked a final time at Nimbia, while his stembrain churned and recalled the powers possessed by the fey. He felt his thoughts explode in one last desperate inspiration. Without trying to weigh its merits, he jerked to his feet suddenly and decided to act.

Palodad frowned at the sudden motion, but did not move.

"It will do no good to resist the tug of the void," he said. "Eventually you will be swept away with the rest."

"You wanted the essence of our realm and all others vented to the outside." Astron stumbled toward him. "It is only fitting that you should experience firsthand what it is like. It is totally irrational, but I will make the sacrifice. Come, together we will make one more journey through the flame—this time to what is truly nowhere."

Astron heard Nimbia scream behind him, but he paid her no heed. He reached out with both hands and grabbed Palodad in a viselike grip. The prince leaned forcefully to the side, pulling Astron toward the raging flame, and the cataloguer did not resist. Instead, he added his own momentum to Palodad's thrust. Together they tumbled off balance. Holding the surprised prince tightly, Astron plunged headfirst into the center of the pollen grain just as if he were vanishing into a common fire.

The scene around Astron twisted and shimmered. He felt an immediate numbing cold and a total blackness, deeper than any he had ever seen before. Instinctively, he clamped shut his mouth to preserve what little breath he had in his lungs.

Astron felt Palodad twist free but he did not care. The feeling of numbing coldness began to grow. He felt his chest start to expand painfully and a sudden bubbling in his ears. His eyes bulged and he could not quite bring them into focus.

Astron whirled about and saw the feeble glow of the pollen grain sticking through from the realm of daemon into the void. The outrush of air batted against him, forcing him backward. He felt himself begin to drift away.

With a frantic swipe Astron reached out and grasped at the burning pollen, feeling a numbing pain that roared up his arms and into his chest. He was not sure that what he was going to try would work, but there was no other choice.

Palodad saw what Astron was attempting and banged the ball in his clawlike hand down on the cataloguer's elbow, trying to force him to release his grip. But Astron's senses were overloaded. The burning flesh in his hands, the numbing cold of the void, and the pressures within trying to dissipate him into the nothingness left no room for anything else. He wrenched at the pollen grain and felt it tremble slightly, like a giant root that would not quite pull free.

Tightening his grip and ignoring Palodad's rain of blows, Astron pulled himself to the surface that confined the realm. He planted his feet on its strange, spongy surface and arched his back. With a grunt that emptied his chest of any remaining air, he ripped the burning grain free and pulled it out into the void.

For an instant nothing happened. The light from Palodad's domain outwelled into the blackness. Astron could see the hem of Nimbia's tunic and behind her the rest of the prince's machine. He began to get dizzy from all of the churning impulses in his brain. He felt his thoughts begin to slow. His grip on the pollen grain loosened as Palodad scrambled to rip it free.

But as consciousness finally faded, Astron noted that the size of the hole into the realm of daemon began to shrink. He watched it close to the diameter of Palodad's metal ball, then to a coin in the realm of men. With a satisfying final rush, the rip vanished altogether and the realm was whole.

Almost absently Astron turned his attention to Palodad, frantically clawing away at what he possessed. For a second, the two demons wrestled with the sphere that no longer burned. Then with a final burst of energy Astron steadied himself against the outer surface of the realm and heaved the pollen grain as hard as he could deeper into the fathomless depths of the void.

Unable to surrender his most precious treasure, Palodad held his grip on the orb as it sailed away. He opened his mouth to scream a protest and no sounds came forth. In a spew of blood and foam, the prince arched into the nothingness and out of sight.

For a second Astron watched him go. Then he collapsed into a ball as he also began to drift away. He was ready to surrender to his fate; his job was finally done.

He had done it! Nimbia, the realm of daemon, all of existence, everything had been saved!

Only dimly was he aware of the transformation taking place around him, the formation of what looked like solid rock, shelves, a small pile of bones, pen and ink, a lock of hair, and three books and other artifacts from the realm of men.

The stembrain, he mused in misty incoherence—it was right even to the last conjecture, the slender chance that convinced him to take the risk. And she must have had deep feelings for him after all. For a mere subject, she would not have paid so much attention to the detail.

* * *

"And so Astron gambled that Nimbia would be able to construct a new realm for him in time to save his life," Kestrel explained to the wizards who had assembled in the presentation hall of the archimage. Over a dozen score were there, sitting in precise lines and following each of his words with frowning concentration. The archimage sat in the first row, with his consort Aeriel robed in the deep green of the ministry of Procolon at his side. Crowded about the periphery behind them, scribes busily squeaked their quills across thick parchments, mingling with emissaries from Arcadia across the sea and other masters of the five arts. The setting sun cast long shadows through the high windows, and serious-faced pages began to light the sconces that would continue the meeting far into the night.

Kestrel glanced at the demon next to him on the dais, shyly clasping the hillsovereign's hand, and smiled. Behind the four of them, the fire that had brought them back to the realm of men flickered silently. "If her feelings had not been sufficiently strong, she might not have succeeded," Kestrel said. "But, as you can see, Nimbia was able to create a safe haven out of the void just in the nick of time."

"Astron's mind was never besotted by my—my external attributes." Nimbia's hand squeezed the one she held. "He alone judged me for my inner worth. Once I realized that, I knew that the quest that I had pursued almost unknowingly for so long was finally over."

"Then with Palodad out of the way, it was a relatively simple matter for the hillsovereign and me to bring the demons in his lair under our control," Phoebe said. "We dispatched scores to all corners of the realm to announce the answer to the riddle and to explain that it was Elezar who had won the contest. All the other princes stopped their struggle against him and, with the prince of lightning djinns himself defeated, brought Gaspar's minions under control. Now they all defer to Elezar's leadership—in fear if nothing else, so close was there almost disaster for all."

"So the golden one is back in command and I am still his master." Alodar rose from his chair. "The realm of men is safe once again." Holding a scarlet ribbon that pierced a

401

large circle of gold, he stepped onto the dais. He cleared his throat and placed the medallion about Phoebe's neck. "The council of councils is unanimous in their vote," the archimage said. "Wear the logo of flame proudly, wizard. You have been accepted by all, the equal of any man."

"Far more important, I have accepted myself." Phoebe shook her head. "Man, woman, demon, hillsovereign of the fey—none of the opinions of the others really matter. Once a person has accepted herself, then everything else will follow."

Alodar turned to Kestrel and held out his hand. "To one who is not a true student of the five magics, the councils cannot convey any largesse," the archimage said. "But somehow I suspect that the fame of the master of lightning djinns will keep your pockets filled, nevertheless."

Kestrel shook Alodar's hand and his smile broadened. "I have gained what no amount of gold could ever buy," he said. He put his arm about Phoebe and pulled her tight. "Trust in one's fellowmen—a sense of belonging—is worth far more than even a treasure from beyond the flame."

Kestrel looked at Astron. "Of course I must admit, demon, to having learned a few other things as well. Before our journey together, lead balloons and pin-hole glasses I never would have suspected. Your use of them illustrated a powerful discipline. It was because of examining the facts of the situation that I found the way to defeat Gaspar when my glib words were sure to fail."

"Logic and calculations are indeed powerful." Astron pulled his eyes away from Nimbia. "When the quest began, it was for such knowledge of things that I hungered. Yet now that I ponder, it was knowledge of self that I gained the most.

"No logical demon would have rushed toward the burning pollen grain when every impulse was to flee. Not even the mightiest djinn willingly would travel through the fire into nothingness and then pluck away the one apparent means to return. None would think that they could pull matter through into the void if it were difficult for them to transport it between universes that are known. Without a demonstration, who could know for sure that a creature of the fey would have feelings intense enough to form a new realm in time.

"It was not logic but the freedom of the stembrain that gave me the plan, as irrational as it was. Palodad never suspected until it was all too late. We have both learned, Kestrel, from each other, you of things in the realms about you, me of the emotions that slumbered within."

Astron stood up and tugged on Nimbia's hand. "But enough of analysis after the fact. We should return to the lair that you constructed for me. We must give the tiny realm more thought and soon, so that it will grow. Together we can mold it into whatever we desire."

"After a moment, Astron." Nimbia did not rise. She pulled on the demon's hand to have him resume his seat. "I first wish to hear more of the legends that humankind have about the realm of the fey."

"But we have pledged to one another." Astron wrinkled his nose. "According to the sagas, the wishes of one are to be the other's command and—and I desire to go."

"You do not quite have it right." Nimbia smiled. "It is my desire that is the wish, your part is the command."

"But—" The wrinkle in Astron's nose deepened.

"Astron, there are still many more riddles in your future." Kestrel laughed. "And I think that you will find that Gaspar's was just one of the easy ones."

Astron looked quickly at Kestrel, saw Phoebe smiling with the rest, and then turned back to Nimbia. His stembrain told him that the words of the woodcutter were all too true.

About the Author

LYN HARDY became interested in fantasy while wandering through the fringes of fandom as an undergraduate at Caltech. In addition to reading and writing, he has sporadic bursts of enthusiasm for collecting stamps, comics, astronaut patches and playing cards. He currently lives with his wife and two daughters in Torrance, California.

TOLKIEN IS GOLDEN FROM ONE WORLD...

1938. Roosevelt is President.
Movies are a nickel. World War Two
looms ever closer. And in America,
Houghton Mifflin publishes
a book by an Oxford don named
John Ronald Reuel Tolkien,
The Hobbit.

TO ANOTHER.

1988. Ronald Reagan ends eight
years as President. Movies are
seven dollars. Treaties keep trying
to avert World War Three. And
people of all ages mark the
fiftieth anniversary of the beloved
classic, *The Hobbit.*

Now on its golden anniversary,
a *new* generation of youngsters,
teens and college students is
awaiting its turn to be entranced
by *The Hobbit...*

09

Dear Reader:

The book you a̲r̲e̲ ̲h̲o̲l̲d̲i̲n̲g̲ ̲i̲s̲ ̲p̲a̲r̲t̲ ̲o̲f̲ the St. Martin's True Crime Library, the imprint *The New York Times* calls "the leader in true crime!" Each month, we offer you a fascinating account of the latest, most sensational crime that has captured the national attention. St. Martin's is the publisher of Tina Dirmann's VANISHED AT SEA, the story of a former child actor who posed as a yacht buyer in order to lure an older couple out to sea, then robbed them and threw them overboard to their deaths. John Glatt's riveting and horrifying SECRETS IN THE CELLAR shines a light on the man who shocked the world when it was revealed that he had kept his daughter locked in his hidden basement for 24 years. In the Edgar-nominated WRITTEN IN BLOOD, Diane Fanning looks at Michael Petersen, a Marine-turned-novelist found guilty of beating his wife to death and pushing her down the stairs of their home—only to reveal another similar death from his past. In the book you now hold, ALL-AMERICAN MURDER, Amber Hunt takes an in-depth look at a controversial case that has made national headlines.

St. Martin's True Crime Library gives you the stories behind the headlines. Our authors take you right to the scene of the crime and into the minds of the most notorious murderers to show you what really makes them tick. St. Martin's True Crime Library paperbacks are better than the most terrifying thriller, because it's all true! The next time you want a crackling good read, make sure it's got the St. Martin's True Crime Library logo on the spine—you'll be up all night!

Charles E. Spicer

Charles E. Spicer, Jr.
Executive Editor, St. Martin's True Crime Library

TITLES BY AMBER HUNT

Dead but Not Forgotten

All-American Murder

from the True Crime Library of St. Martin's Paperbacks

ALL-AMERICAN MURDER

AMBER HUNT

St. Martin's Paperbacks

ALL-AMERICAN MURDER

Copyright © 2011 by Amber Hunt.

All rights reserved.

For information address St. Martin's Press, 175 Fifth Avenue, New York, NY 10010.

EAN: 978-0-312-54106-4

Printed in the United States of America

St. Martin's Paperbacks edition / September 2011

St. Martin's Paperbacks are published by St. Martin's Press, 175 Fifth Avenue, New York, NY 10010.

10 9 8 7 6 5 4 3 2 1

For those who've been silent

Acknowledgments

When a murder case touches as many lives as that of Yeardley Love, I, as a human first and journalist second, can't help but pay attention. My professional background is mostly in gritty Detroit, where enough lives end in violence each year that reporters simply can't keep up. Not every victim gets a newspaper mention, much less a book.

Some have already argued that Yeardley is no different from, nor more deserving than, the hundreds of victims who die prematurely each year in Baltimore, the big city next door to Yeardley's small-town roots in Cockeysville, Maryland. Largely, those people are right. But every now and then a crime comes along from which some good can come, and it seemed to me that Yeardley's case had that rare potential. The details in this book come from hundreds of hours spent examining police and court documents, conducting interviews, collecting first-person data, reviewing video footage, and verifying published media reports.

It has not been an easy story to tell.

The case against the suspect in this death is ongoing, as of my deadline. As such, the lawyers and law-enforcement officials connected with it were predictably unable to comment. But far beyond that, I was met with a silence I could not have anticipated. The silence in this case became part of the story. It was more than frustrating; it was frightening, and it went beyond protecting the criminal case.

My primary motivation for telling this story was to help ensure that Yeardley was known as more than a college lacrosse player who died a much-publicized death. She had hopes and dreams and flaws and family, just like everyone else. She was not merely a fleeting headline to those who knew her.

As my research unfolded, I repeatedly reminded myself of a simple journalistic truth: Not everyone wants the story told, but that doesn't mean you shouldn't tell it.

Luckily, I had a great deal of help. For starters, I owe huge thanks to Sarah MacKusick, my sister-turned-research-assistant, who helped push me along at the project's start. Toward its end, I turned to Nick DiMarco, a talented reporter and editor with the Lutherville-Timonium Patch (an online news organization). DiMarco was crucial in helping me research Yeardley's younger years in Catholic school.

I also owe thanks to Brendan Fitzgerald, reporter with *C-VILLE Weekly* in Charlottesville; Megan Pringle, anchor for WMAR's *Good Morning Maryland*; Liz Seccuro, author of *Crash Into Me*; Matthew Power, freelance writer and contributing editor for *Harper's Magazine*: and Nick Perry, *Seattle Times* reporter and coauthor of *Scoreboard, Baby!* Additionally, I send props to the *Washington Post*, the New York *Daily News*, the *New York Times*, and the other daily newspapers whose works are credited in these pages. My bias here is unapologetic and undeniable: Without newspapers, the truth would too often be lost.

On a personal front, I (once again) owe undying gratitude to Elijah Van Benschoten, my partner and backbone. (Shirley and Bryan are pretty swell, too.) For a variety of reasons, I also thank Missy, Allison, Madeleine, and Rachel, my sisters; Pat and Larry MacKusick, who treated me as family even after we technically weren't; Jane Dystel, my agent and morale booster; Allison Caplin, my editor and cheerleader; Charles Spicer, my publisher (who only had to give me one pep talk); Jim and Wendy House; and the many friends, both past and present, who helped shape me even if they don't know it: Jonathan Wallace; Alexa Capeloto; Megan Pennefather; the whole Batcher clan; Todd Bowser; Joe Swickard; and too many others to mention this time around.

Finally, I owe a great deal of sanity and self-discovery to my friends at the University of Michigan's Knight-Wallace Fellowship, where I spent 2010–2011 growing as a journalist. I got a mental boost from my extraordinary fellow Fellows, who are without question among the best journalists in the world. In addition to Matthew Power and Nick Perry, thanks go to Laura Daverio, William Foreman, Antonio Gois, Je-Seung Lee, Todd Leopold, Alec MacGillis, Ted Mellnik, Ana Laura Perez, Justin Pope, Emily Richmond, Christopher Sherman, Harry Siegel, James Thomas, Liu Tianzhao, and John Walton. Hats off as well to Charles Eisendrath, Birgit Rieck, and the amazing women behind the curtain.

PART I

"She Didn't Deserve to Die"

Chapter 1

The call for help was panicked and vague. Caitlin Whiteley, a twenty-two-year-old University of Virginia student, had returned home to her cookie-cutter apartment in Charlottesville to find her roommate unresponsive. It was early Monday morning, the end of a typically hard-drinking "Sunday Funday" on campus, and Caitlin couldn't grasp what was wrong. She'd walked home with Philippe Oudshoorn, a friend and fellow athlete, to find Yeardley Love facedown on her bed and a hole kicked through her bedroom door. Something about the way Yeardley's hair lay seemed awkward and unnatural, so Caitlin pushed it aside and gently shook her friend's shoulder. No response. Then Caitlin noticed some blood.

Oudshoorn hurriedly picked up the phone and told the nine-one-one dispatcher that something was amiss—a message that somehow was translated to "possible alcohol overdose" when patched through to nearby police cars—before lifting Yeardley's body from her bed and attempting CPR. By the time detectives arrived to the second-floor apartment on Charlottesville's narrow 14th Street Northwest, the bloody scene looked nothing like the bender gone awry they had anticipated. Medics were bent over the battered body of Yeardley, a pretty and athletic twenty-two-year-old, and were frantically trying to breathe life back into her.

They were failing.

Charlottesville police officer Lisa T. Reeves was among the first to respond, arriving at the four-bedroom apartment in an off-white building at about 2:30 a.m. May 3, 2010. The apartment was on the second floor, the entrance to which was reachable by a staircase in the middle of the building. She hunted for unit No. 9 and entered.

The front door to the apartment was open and untampered, but the door to the bedroom around which all the activity was now centered—Yeardley's bedroom, Reeves would quickly surmise—was splintered, as though someone had punched a hole straight through it. Reeves spotted Yeardley and immediately saw the blood. A pool had saturated the pillow and sheets beneath the girl's head, and smears of red discolored the bed's comforter. Even the bed skirt was stained crimson.

As the officer examined her more closely, she saw bruising on Yeardley's cheek. The young co-ed's right eye was swollen shut, and a large bruise spread down the side of her face. *Blunt-force trauma*, Reeves would soon describe in her police report, her cop voice kicking in. *There is a pool of blood on her pillow.* The girl's face was surrounded by long brown hair sopping with blood. *Probable cause exists that Yeardley Love was murdered.*

Officers arriving at the apartment quickly cordoned off the area. This was no alcohol poisoning; this was a crime scene. Reeves relayed to her superiors the grisly news: The victim, a star lacrosse player on the university's women's team, was dead, pronounced while still in her apartment, wearing nothing but the panties in which first responders had discovered her. The death was clearly violent. Officers quickly descended on the scene and began gathering evidence. They started by interviewing Whiteley, Yeardley's longtime friend, roommate and teammate, and Oudshoorn, a player on the UVA men's tennis team who was along for the gruesome discovery.

Violent crime was rare enough in Charlottesville, with fewer than 250 cases reported in 2009, but violent death was rarer still, stirring in the police force a mixture of shock and curiosity. Reeves tried to tease details from Yeardley's inconsolable roommates, one of whom had rushed to the front yard and was wailing on a cell phone to a friend. The story they weaved in between tears was like something out of a *Lifetime* movie: Yeardley had been in a rocky relationship, they said, and things had gotten progressively worse in recent days; you need to talk to her boyfriend.

Yeardley had been dating twenty-two-year-old George Huguely V, a handsome, six foot two midfielder on the men's lacrosse team, for about two years. Friends knew their relationship had foundered lately, and some felt Huguely was becoming unhinged. He texted Yeardley often, keeping tabs on her when she was out of town with teammates. Rumors circulated that he had punched a fellow lacrosse player for walking Yeardley home one night, possibly offering a goodnight kiss, and others had to break up a fight between the couple that had gotten so ugly, Yeardley had hit Huguely with her purse.

Yeardley had broken off the relationship a few weeks prior, but to some, it was hard to tell. The two hung out in the same crowd at the same bars, and when one friend asked Yeardley the night before she died how things were with George, Yeardley had replied vaguely that things were the same as always.

As Reeves set out to find Huguely, Charlottesville Police Sgt. Steve Dillon, a forensic detective, took photos of the scene, a typical bedroom in a nondescript apartment building situated about half a mile from the heart of campus. Yeardley's room largely looked like any other college student's, complete with strewn-about clothing. Dillon carefully documented each angle he could think of, taking special care to photograph the hole in the bedroom door, which Dillon noticed had little bits of hair clinging to its jagged edges. Reeves, meanwhile, learned that Huguely lived on the same street, just one building down. The roommates' story had been a little hard to follow, but what the officer gleaned was this: Yeardley had tried to call off their relationship because Huguely would sometimes drink too much and get violent. Huguely, Reeves gathered, didn't like that plan.

Officers had no trouble finding Huguely just a building away, in his apartment inside a brick building on 14th Street Northwest, near its T-junction with Sadler Street. It was still dark outside, still the middle of the night, when he agreed to answer questions at the police department. He wore a black T-shirt ironically adorned with a police logo on the front and back, his brown flip-flops and blue Nike shorts appropriate for the spring Charlottesville weather. It had reached 82 degrees the day before; even when bar hopping after sunset, the college kids often left their jackets behind and simply wore T-shirts. After reaching the police department less than two miles from his house, George waived his Miranda rights, saying he was willing to talk. Police secretly set up a video camera to record the conversation. He acknowledged that he had the right to an attorney and the right to keep silent; he invoked neither, Reeves would report. He seemed shaken and distressed, and as he began to tell his story, he admitted that he had been to see Yeardley. As he described the night's events, he used the passive language that cops so often hear from culprits—damning enough to admit some culpability, but distant enough to shirk full blame.

Yes, he'd fought with Yeardley, George told Reeves. He said the couple had ended their relationship of about two years, and the last few days they had chatted primarily over e-mail. George said he had gone to Yeardley's apartment and kicked her bedroom door in, but he had just wanted to talk. Things got out of hand. He shook her, and her head hit the wall. He noticed blood pouring from her nose. He pushed her onto the bed and left. He didn't know she was seriously hurt, he said. He had been injured himself, he said, motioning to scrapes along his right leg—the type that one would get by kicking in a door. Reeves noticed some other scrapes and bruises on George's arms and hands. He shook those off— they were from lacrosse, not the fight, he claimed. It was impossible for Reeves to know if George was being completely forthcoming. When confessing, criminals often downplay their crimes, turning intentional acts into accidents and using slippery language to minimize their involvement. George could have been doing the same. He didn't bang Yeardley's head against the wall; rather, her head "repeatedly hit the wall" as he shook her. George did, however, admit to stealing an Apple laptop from Yeardley's room and tossing it in a Dumpster. Reeves asked him where, so officers could retrieve it when the interview was over.

Huguely repeatedly asked Reeves how Yeardley was, defense lawyers told a judge months later. An hour into the interrogation, Reeves finally told him that Love was dead.

"She's dead, George," Reeves said, according to the lawyer. "You killed her."

Huguely was shocked, his attorney said, and replied, "She's dead? She's not dead . . . You guys said she had a black eye. I never did anything that would do that to her."

With his statement, Reeves knew she had plenty of probable cause to arrest George Huguely V on suspicion of murder. By the interview's end, she likely sensed, too, that the case seemed tailor made for media consumption. Reporters had already gotten word about the story, and local scribes had gathered down the street, trying to interview neighbors over the sirens and wails that shattered the early-morning calm. Yeardley's friends clutched each other and cried in disbelief.

The first news release on the death was distributed by the Charlottesville Police Department before sunrise. Its contents were sparse:

On the morning of May 3rd, 2010, at 0215 hours, City Police were called to 222 14th ST N.W. apartment number 9 for a possible alcohol overdose. Officers arrived and found a female University of Virginia Student unresponsive in the apartment. Police Officers and Rescue personnel who were called to the scene attempted to revive the victim but were unsuccessful.

   Police are treating the case as a homicide investigation at this time.

Victim identification is being withheld at this time pending notification of next of kin. Further information will be released later today. Until such time, no other information will be made available to the public or the media.

The release ended with a bolded plea for people with information to either call police or the Crime Stoppers tip line.

Local reporters with Charlottesville outlets got that initial word and headed straight to 14th Street Northwest. A reporter and photographer from the *C-VILLE Weekly*, a 24,000-circulation alternative weekly largely dedicated to arts and entertainment in the lively college town, but whose reporters kept readers abreast of breaking news online, were quickly on the scene. Reporter Brendan Fitzgerald wasn't sure what type of story the paper would want when he joined the coverage by mid-morning. The sketchy information released by police so far raised far more questions than answers.

"It's hard to predict what kind of coverage you're gearing up for, but it raises a different set of questions that inform possible stories when you hear it's a homicide rather than an alcohol overdose," Fitzgerald later recalled.

The ambiguity didn't last long. Shortly after noon, the media received an update: George Huguely V had already been questioned and was in custody. That news release had more information—including Yeardley's name and standing at the school:

Regarding the death of a University of Virginia student occurring this morning at 222 14th ST N.W. Apartment Number 9, the victim has been identified as 22 year old, Yeardley Love. Ms. Love was a fourth year University of Virginia student from Cockeysville, Maryland and is on the University's Women's Lacrosse Team.

Preliminary investigation by detectives revealed that Ms. Love is the victim of an apparent homicide. She suffered visible physical trauma, however the specific cause of her death is undetermined pending an autopsy.

George Huguely, 22, a fourth year student at the University of Virginia from Chevy Chase MD has been charged with First Degree Murder and is in custody at the Charlottesville/Albemarle jail. He is a player for the University's Men's Lacrosse Team.

According to witnesses, Huguely and Love had a past relationship.

Charlottesville Police are continuing to investigate the case and will provide more details as they become available

About 12:30 p.m., an update was posted to *C-VILLE*'s Web site, including a photo of city police vehicles surrounding the scene at 14th Street Northwest. Fitzgerald, who had been helping to weave coverage at a desk, left to join colleague Chiara Canzi at the scene soon after. The local media had long been gathered, chit-chatting as they waited for the scant updates.

"There were a few camera crews awaiting across the street from Yeardley Love's apartment building," Fitzgerald recalled, "and we all made a couple of attempts to speak with people on the street, people walking by. Not a lot of people were talking."

Fitzgerald didn't know then just how silent the campus would become.

While reporters awaited word, detectives behind the scenes were beginning to fill out the obligatory paperwork for search warrants, using the stilted language in which officers are trained to write. In a court request asking for permission to search George's black Chevrolet Tahoe, Reeves wrote: *Your affiant knows from training and experience that persons involved in crimes of domestic violence often view property that was given to a partner being forfeited back to the giver at the termination of the relationship.* Reeves wanted to check inside the SUV to see if George had any of Yeardley's belongings inside. The request was quickly granted. George's apartment was searched, as was Yeardley's bedroom. By day's end, officers had collected dozens of items as evidence, including swabs of red stains in Yeardley's bedroom, her cell phone, and her digital camera. They bagged a note on Yeardley's bureau in which Huguely apologized for an earlier fight and wrote, "You are my best friend." They also recovered her laptop from the Dumpster where Huguely said he had tossed it, and from Huguely, they took DNA samples, fingernail scrapings, his clothing, and his keys.

Charlottesville Police Chief Timothy Longo and Lieutenant Gary Pleasants tag teamed to field the dozens of media queries that flooded the police department, a small force housed in a brick building connected to the district court on Market Street. When appearing on television, their updates were brief and heartfelt. Clearly, the discovery of Yeardley's battered body was unlike anything the officers had seen before.

Asked by reporters if he had experienced a death scene like Yeardley's before, Longo somberly answered, "In the nine years that I've been privileged to serve as chief of police in this community, I have not."

The questions reporters posed were predictable: Why had Yeardley's roommate reported that she might have passed out from heavy drinking? Did alcohol play a role in the death? Why would George have attacked the young woman? Were there any warning signs that went unheeded? Longo and Pleasants answered obliquely, citing the early stages of the investigation and their desire not to screw it up.

"We're not going to go into any specifics," Pleasants told reporters. "There are too many accounts, and we have half a dozen detectives working on it." Longo, meanwhile, told a Baltimore radio station that he couldn't speculate on why Whiteley first reported alcohol overdose when she found the body. Yeardley's injuries were obvious to officers who responded, he said, but he added that by the time officers arrived, Yeardley's body had been moved. It was no longer face down in a pillow, and there was no hiding the bruises and blood on her face.

By early afternoon, the story already had reached far beyond Charlottesville. Interview requests came pouring in from national media outlets, and television personalities such as Nancy Grace and Dan Abrams were beginning to opine about the case. Charlottesville police were inundated with questions wanting to know whether Huguely could be characterized as cooperative, remorseful, or reticent.

"He was upset by the situation he found himself in but was cooperative with police," a department spokesman told reporters.

Reporters tracked down the phone number for Yeardley's family home in suburban Baltimore, where a woman identifying herself as a designated spokesman politely repeated that the family had no comment. Sharon Love, Yeardley's mother, immediately drove to Charlottesville with daughter Lexie, Yeardley's older sister. Longo told reporters that Sharon was in a state of shock.

"She was very gracious and thankful to investigators," he told one New York–based reporter. "The family wants to be left alone to grieve and mourn . . . I can only imagine what Ms. Love is going through."

Huguely's parents were also believed to be headed to Charlottesville, so reaching them by phone would be next to impossible. But the *Washington Post* managed to reach his grandfather, George Huguely III, by phone. "He was a wonderful child and he was going to graduate," the elder Huguely said. "Hopefully he will be graduating. That's all I can tell you, OK? I'm sorry."

John Casteen III, the university's president, released a heartfelt statement that described the anger welling in many at the senseless death. He described Yeardley as a student with "uncommon talent and promise."

"That she appears now to have been murdered by another student compounds this sense of loss by suggesting that Yeardley died without comfort or consolation from those closest to her," Casteen said. "We mourn her death and feel anger on reading that the investigators believe that another student caused it."

Yeardley didn't deserve it, he continued.

"However little we may know now about Yeardley Love's death, we do know that she did not have or deserve to die—that she deserved the bright future she earned growing up, studying here, and developing her talents as a lacrosse player," he said. "She deserves to be remembered for her human goodness, her capacity for future greatness, and not for the terrible way in which her young life has ended."

By Tuesday, as reporters packed a cramped courtroom to catch their first glimpse of a young man charged with first-degree murder, this much was clear: Yeardley Love's death would impact far more than her family or even just the thousands in and around Charlottesville, Virginia. Her name and her story were destined to reverberate throughout the country.

Chapter 2

At 3 a.m. Tuesday morning, when journalist Megan Pringle arrived to work at ABC affiliate WMAR in Baltimore, she knew she had a long day of broadcasting in front of her. Pringle, a petite and pretty anchor and reporter for *Good Morning Maryland*, was briefed on Yeardley's death. A one-man band—meaning a reporter equipped to do his own video work as well—had already been sent to Charlottesville and would be on hand to cover the day's anticipated arraignment, whenever that might occur. Pringle recognized the story as heartbreaking and newsworthy, but it was her co-anchor, Jamie Costello, who remarked, "This is going to be huge."

By the end of the day's broadcast, Pringle knew he was right.

"It very quickly took on a life of its own," she said.

Tuesday afternoon, reporters crammed inside Charlottesville's small district court for the arraignment police had promised would come. It seemed an impossibly tiny space. The building, situated on East Market Street near 6th Street Northeast, had long prompted complaints from county workers as being far too small for even its normal traffic. Now, with it being the first stop for one of the biggest news stories in the country, it was clear that the general district court was ill equipped for the media onslaught to come.

As has become the trend nationwide, Huguely was set to appear for a video arraignment rather than appearing in person—a move that cuts transportation costs and helps avoid unnecessary delays. As such, it was via closed-circuit television that journalists got their first look at the beefy athlete, whose team roster estimated his weight at about 205 pounds— nearly twice as much as his petite ex-girlfriend. The previous day, officials had released Huguely's official lacrosse team photo, revealing an attractive, shaggy-haired college student dressed in his team's blue and orange. Now, he wore the gray and white striped uniform assigned to him by the Albemarle-Charlottesville Regional Jail. His already bushy hair looked even more mussed than usual; his face, drawn and empty, seemed lined with exhaustion. He appeared nervous as he waited for word from the lawyers his parents had quickly retained for him. District Judge Robert Downer spoke briefly with defense attorney Francis McQ. Lawrence, then postponed a bail review hearing until June 10.

Huguely's only words during the minutes-long hearing: "Thank you, Your Honor." His parents and stepfather, who sat in the back of the courtroom, ignored reporters' requests for comment as they left.

Lawrence, looking polished in a black suit and canary tie, stepped outside the brick courthouse and approached a makeshift podium piled with media microphones and tape recorders. Most of the reporters gathered knew little about the Charlottesville lawyer. His name had appeared a few times in *C-VILLE*'s pages—once as the lawyer representing Richard Neal Willetts, a man convicted on federal sex assault charges in 2007. Another time, Lawrence made news when he helmed efforts to have an area in Darden Towe Park near the Rivanna River declared a historic site on which he hoped to build a center dedicated to Lewis and Clark. Other than that, Lawrence was to most a high-priced attorney readying to represent his biggest client to date.

After the arraignment, he looked focused and solemn as he spoke into more than a dozen recording devices. He declined to answer questions, instead reading from a prepared statement drafted on behalf of the Huguely family.

"Because this case involves an active ongoing investigation, any comment on the specific facts would be inappropriate at this time," said Lawrence, his words deliberate. "Until more information becomes available, it is our hope that no conclusion will be drawn or judgment made about George or his case. However, we are confident that Ms. Love's death was not intended, but an accident with a tragic outcome."

Reporters scribbled furiously.

George was withdrawing from UVA, Lawrence added, and would remain in jail for the foreseeable future. He concluded: "Grief has descended on this community as we attempt to understand what happened and why. Our thoughts and prayers are with those who grieve this terrible loss."

The commonwealth's attorney for the city of Charlottesville, Warner D. "Dave" Chapman, rebuffed reporters' requests for comment, saying that he planned to do all of his talking about the case in court. His graying hair matching his suit, he quietly walked past photographers as they snapped his image. Local reporters, at least, weren't surprised by his silence. Chapman, who preferred going by his middle name, Dave, rather than his given name, was known as the Limelight Dodger. In his more than fifteen years as the commonwealth's attorney, he had worked on many of the area's high-profile cases and was an active member of the local Democratic Party. He once told a *C-VILLE* reporter that he knew he was doing his job well when he managed to stay out of the public eye.

"Many times a prosecutor's office is not doing its job well when it's especially visible," Chapman said in the 2007 story. And, he added, he intended to continue his "no comment" refrain when it came to ongoing cases: "We do not try our cases on the courthouse steps."

His round face obscured by a bushy beard, Chapman was unapologetically humorless in public. In 2005, he balked at a softball question posed as he ran unopposed for his attorney post. Asked by *C-VILLE* to describe his favorite snack, Chapman responded that the question was "completely inappropriate." The newspaper replied by printing the cranky response alongside a lighthearted jab: "Man, somebody get this guy a snack!"

But the Yeardley case was far more than a fluff question in an already decided political race. A young woman was dead and a young man's fate dangled precariously. Lawrence had laid out exactly what battle Chapman would be facing. While the prosecution gathered evidence to justify the first-degree murder charge against Huguely, the defense would strive to paint the death as, at best, an accident contingent on external factors—alcohol, perhaps?—and, at worst, a crime of passion. The difference in legal terms was night and day: First-degree murder comes with a life sentence—and, in Virginia, some cases even warrant the death penalty—while second-degree could mean far less time behind bars. If the defense succeeded and secured a manslaughter conviction, Huguely could be freed by his mid-thirties. If they *really* succeeded, he could walk away altogether. In short, Chapman wanted Huguely in prison for as long as possible. The defense, meanwhile, was already underway in its job to set him free.

From the outset, the case was shaping up to be less a whodunit than a whathappened: Huguely admitted he attacked his ex-girlfriend. The question the whole country was asking was, *Why?*

Chapter 3

Yeardley Love was born July 17, 1987, to Sharon (Donnelly) Love and John Thomas Love III at the Mercy Medical Center in Baltimore, Maryland. After a brutal June, the temperatures along the East Coast had settled somewhat, making the final weeks a bit more comfortable—at least externally—for Sharon to finish up her second pregnancy. The day of Yeardley's debut, Baltimore was a breezy 71 degrees. For their second daughter's name the couple chose Yeardley, pronounced Yard-lee; of Old English origins, the name means "enclosed meadow." Yards, as her family affectionately called her, was four years younger than her older sister, Alexis, known by friends as Lexie. Yeardley was immediately in awe of her older sister, a pretty blond with an infectious smile and athletic build.

Yeardley wrote in an essay about her life in 2002, her freshman year of high school, that she liked to do whatever her older sister did. At the time Yeardley wrote the piece, Lexie had just graduated and headed off to Elon University in North Carolina. Yeardley remembered how she always wanted to tag along with her sister and her sister's friends "and not the children my age." Photographs from the girls' youth show Yeardley often at her sister's side, along with children clearly closer to Lexie's age than her own.

"She taught me a lot in life, and she has left me very good examples to follow," Yeardley wrote. "Sometimes I wonder what I could not have done in my life without her."

The Love girls predictably turned heads. They were beautiful and sweet; their parents were both charming and successful. Yeardly and Lexie's father—a man whose glasses and well-kept hair said "corporate," but whose smile had more warmth than most—had worked in finance at Morgan Stanley, according to a coworker who later recalled "Yeardley coming into the office as a young lady to see her dad." Yeardley's mother, Sharon, worked with hearing-impaired students in Baltimore city schools.

Yeardley grew up in Cockeysville, a Baltimore suburb in Baltimore County. It seemed an area of typical suburban sprawl, but in reality, the little town had sprouted up in the midst of a limestone and marble quarry. The Maryland Geological Survey boasts that Cockeysville's "white, crystalline metalimestone" was used for the upper 390 feet of the Washington Monument in Washington, D.C. By the mid-1800s, the marble was a popular accent in- and outside of the row houses built in Baltimore. The Museum of Fine Arts in Boston describes the material as white and fine grained, containing "a brownish mica that can make the stone look slightly gray."

To outsiders, the town today perhaps appears to lack cohesion—a smattering of hotels and restaurants amid industrial-looking complexes. Those who live there know better, however. Children squeal as they splash around the pools and pond at Beaver Dam, nestled, appropriately, along Beaver Dam Road, northwest of Cockeysville Road. Originally a quarry-created swimming hole, Beaver Dam morphed over time into a full-fledged recreational park, complete with picnic areas and basketball courts. Families would gather from late May through Labor Day (depending on weather) and spend entire days swimming, playing sports, relaxing, and grilling. The more adventurous could plunge into the water from a rope swing as friends cheered them on. Teenagers left on their own would engage in typical waterside teen behavior; summer romances began and ended while relaxing quarryside.

Swimmers and sunbathers had their pick between the quarry pond and two chlorinated pools (dubbed the "front pool" and "back pool" for obvious reasons). The Beaver Dam Swimming Club, as it is known, spreads over thirty acres and is a hidden, fun-filled gem that ignites nostalgia in many Cockeysville natives.

Cockeysville shares little in common with the often cash-strapped metropolis eighteen miles to the south. As of the 2010 United States Census, just over 20,000 people lived there, more than seventy-five percent of whom were white. According to a 2007 CNN Money tally, the median income was about $71,200, with an average home price of $350,000. Yeardley was clearly among the privileged. The family's home on Ivy Hill Road hugged lush parkland. According to county records, the Loves bought the 4.25-acre plot in 1986 for $170,000 and built a 4,400-square-foot home. It was a picturesque setting for John and Sharon to raise their daughters.

And the girls were as pretty as their homestead. Both had inherited their mother's high cheekbones, and by their teenage years, their already electric smiles had been perfected by braces. Sharon Love sometimes dressed the girls in matching outfits on special occasions, even pinning their neatly combed, chin-length hair with matching bows. Sharon seemed particularly fond of one outfit—a cute black dress with a cummerbund and a collar embellished with a pink rose dangling delicately at the neck. Both girls had a version of the dress, and in 1992, when Yeardley was about five, her mother took her to an Olan Mills photo studio to have her portrait taken in it. An oversized, floppy pink bow sat atop her head, pulling her hair into a half-updo.

While eulogizing her daughter, Sharon Love said Yeardley had a mischievous side, *People* magazine relayed: "Yeardley would inform her that her outfit looked horrible; Lexie would rush to change. The next day on the computer, Lexie would find pictures of Yeardley dressed in that very same outfit."

Yeardley and Lexie were undeniably sisters, sharing eyes so blue that they were virtually guaranteed to have red-eye in any amateur photograph requiring a flash. They shared, too, the same boisterous laugh, one that could carry across a lacrosse field, not to mention a room. But they had their differences, too: Lexie's look was at times more natural and clean, her blond hair often pulled away from her face and her makeup spare. As Yeardley reached college, she opted to accentuate her already noticeable eyes with mascara lining both top and bottom lashes, and when she wasn't playing sports, her light brown hair often fell loose around her shoulders.

Yeardley was an active and sporty child, and something of a daddy's girl. She began playing lacrosse with her father when she was five. Lacrosse quickly became her favorite sport, and she not only played year round, but sometimes for two teams at once.

Yeardley's first foray into private education was at St. Joseph School, which serves kindergarteners through eighth graders and costs about $5,500 per year. The parish, roughly three blocks down Church Lane off York Road in Cockeysville, is split on both sides of a narrow back road—the chapel on one side, the classrooms and offices on the other. From the school's mission statement:

> Rooted in the teachings of Jesus, our school is enriched by Catholic tradition and lived Gospel values, which are enhanced by the celebration of liturgy, sacrament and prayer. We further the children's knowledge and practice of their faith and guide them to serve others through the use of their gifts and talents. Here at St. Joseph School, we foster a safe and secure environment in which children can grow and learn.

Sister Joan Dumm, a forty-year educator at St. Joseph, taught Yeardley in the second grade. Dumm readied her for the Catholic ritual of First Holy Communion, which symbolizes a child's initiation into the church.

Dumm recalled speaking with John Love, his voice thick with an Irish accent, while he waited to pick up his then-seven-year-old daughter. He was charged with bringing his girls home from school.

"Oh, yes, every day," Dumm said. "We would bring the lines down to the crossing guard to get them across safely, if they were going to the south-side carpool."

John's affection for his daughters was obvious to everyone, she added: "He loved his girls."

Dumm recalled the simple, idle chitchat in the carpool lane that she and John shared as he waited for Yeardley to bound out of the school. The sister described Yeardley as "a happy, lively little girl" whose school life at age seven centered on the sacrament of First Holy Communion, her first reception of the Holy Eucharist—the consecrated bread and wine (or, in a youngster's case, more likely unfermented grape juice) presented as the body and blood of Jesus Christ.

"That's the big thing for the second grade," Dumm recalled.

The students tended to enjoy practicing and learning the ritual because it meant spending time away from the classroom.

"There were never any problems with getting them to go to church," Dumm said of the students. "In fact, they liked to go across the street so they didn't have to do whatever work we had to do in the classroom. So church was kind of a nice place to go."

Sister Georgia Moonis, Yeardley's homeroom teacher in the fourth grade, recalled the girl as "on the quiet side." It was around then that Yeardley played lacrosse at Sky Walkers, a program whose stated mission is to "instill in every girl the confidence that she has no limitations." Players are taught the importance of teamwork over individual performance, and the lessons are meant to carry over from the field into real life. Yeardley was quiet in the classroom, but she was tenacious on the field.

People couldn't help but be drawn to her. She was the type of young woman whose future success seemed predetermined. No one felt a need to worry about her; with her upbringing and self-assuredness, she seemed poised to map out whatever destiny she wanted. She could take care of herself, and she was from the type of family that would pick up any slack were she ever to stumble. She was the unlikeliest crime victim anyone who met her could have imagined.

Kaki Evans recalled her being "vivacious and loving" in one online post; in another, Grace Caslow marveled at the "incredible impression" the young woman made.

Friend Catherine Barthelme posted in an online memoriam that she could never find a better friend than "Yards." She missed her laugh her smile and her sense of humor "every single day."

In an online condolence posting directed at Sharon and Lexie Love, Casey Donohoe, a Jarrettsville, Maryland native, recalled first meeting Yeardley at Sky Walkers in middle school and playing lacrosse with her in high school. "I remember her with her side ponytail and bright ribbon," Donohoe described. She said she admired her kindness and generosity. Brian Frederick, a coach with the Cockeysville recreational program, recalled in a letter to the *Towson Times* that Yeardley wasn't a flashy child "except for that smile," he wrote. She was an understated go-getter, Frederick wrote, the kind of independent and beautiful young woman he hoped his son would marry someday.

Yeardley and Frederick's daughter, Meghan, were longtime friends, he wrote, having attended St. Joseph from kindergarten through the eighth grade before matriculating at separate schools. Meg and Yards played against each other throughout their four years in high school, Frederick recalled.

"God, I looked forward to those games," he wrote. "I knew I'd get a big 'hello' and that beautiful smile from Yeardley after the game—win or lose."

While some young adults need time, not to mention trial and error, to shape their paths in life, Yeardley knew hers from the time she was in elementary school: She wanted to play lacrosse throughout high school and college, and she vowed to attend the University of Virginia, the college her father had briefly enrolled in before having to leave for the military. He never got his degree; Yeardley promised herself that she would attain one for the both of them.

She decided when she was about nine years old that she would go to the University of Virginia, lacrosse stick in hand. After getting her bachelor's degree, she wanted to attend Virginia Law School for three years, she wrote in her high school essay, and after that, she wanted to become a lawyer and raise a family.

"If I had to wish for three things in my life, they would be to go to University of Virginia for college, have a happy and healthy family when I grow up, and to always keep in touch and stay close with my family," she wrote.

Yeardley competed in both field hockey and lacrosse at Notre Dame Preparatory School, a private school in nearby Towson, Maryland, which costs upward of $15,000 in yearly tuition. Lexie had graduated in 2002; Yeardley was four years behind her. In exchange for the hefty tuition, parents are promised a lower student-to-teacher ratio than Maryland's state average (comparing at about 1:9 at Notre Dame to the state's 1:16), as well as access to a slew of sports and extra-curricular activities. While area public schools struggle to keep abreast of even basic requirements, Notre Dame's students bring laptops to use wirelessly in their classes and have access to courses such as Japanese, architectural drawing, and computer graphics. The high-tech bent is balanced by decades-old traditions: The school's uniform hasn't changed since its founding in 1873.

From the time Yeardley began high school, her classes were geared toward college preparation: four credits in English, three credits in history and social studies, three credits in science (including biology and chemistry); three credits in math (including upper algebra and geometry), three credits in sequential levels of a foreign language, one credit in fine arts, two credits in religion, two credits in physical education, three and a half credits in electives, and twenty hours in social service. The latter requirement fell under the school's "service and justice" heading, which, according to the school, was meant to "address a two-fold mandate: in regards to service, to address the immediate needs of underserved populations; and, in regards to justice, to seek ways to change those systems which inherently prove unjust to individuals, societies, and the world." In short, charity work was a requirement for Yeardley to graduate, and her efforts would be rooted in the Gospel. According to the high school's mission statement, the goal was to "prepare women of moral integrity to become more loving, just, and wise."

Yeardley excelled at everything she tried, teachers and administrators at the Catholic school told reporters in the days after her death.

"Yeardley was an outstanding young lady—joyous, spirited, a wonderful person," the school's headmistress, Sister Patricia McCarron, a woman with a kind, round face, said. "I know we all enjoyed watching her on the lacrosse field and seeing her walk the hallways at NDP. We are proud to call Yeardley one of our girls."

Yeardley seemed proud in return. She regularly returned to Notre Dame when she came home on college breaks and kept in touch with Notre Dame's lacrosse coach, Mary Bartel.

"Yeardley was the core of the personality of the team—she was our laughter, a good soul," Bartel said. "She always found an appropriate way to lighten things up. I don't think there is a soul in this building who couldn't say her name without smiling. Yeardley loved NDP and NDP loved her."

If either McCarron or Bartel knew anything about George Huguely, they didn't tell reporters.

Yeardley was giving, too, said those who knew her, volunteering at a soup kitchen and counseling at a summer camp program for children living in housing projects. Neighbors in sprawling Cockeysville remembered her as an ideal mix of kind, ambitious, and intelligent. The advantages she had been given weren't lost on her, either.

Yeardley marveled at a young age at how lucky she was to have a happy, intact family that instilled values in her.

Sadly, the insulation of Yeardley's early years shattered while she was still a budding high school student. Her father,

John, with whom she had played lacrosse since she was five, died of prostate cancer three days after Christmas in 2003—Yeardley's sophomore year—in a loss that would have derailed many bright young lives. Yeardley was devastated, but her friends and family told reporters that she showed strength and grace beyond her years. She and her sister bonded, their mother told *People* magazine.

"Rather than giving in to grief, they vowed to stick together and make their father proud," Sharon told writer Jill Smolowe.

In another account, Molly Ford, a childhood friend, said Yeardley's strength had been inspiring: "She didn't fold when that happened. She was strong to her family and everyone else around her."

Added Casey Donohoe: "She handled everything so graciously and was so strong throughout."

John T. Love's obituary in the Baltimore Sun was simple, direct: "Beloved husband of Sharon Donnelly Love; dear father of Alexis D. and Yeardley R. Love." His funeral mass was held at Immaculate Conception Church in Towson; interment at Druid Ridge Cemetery.

Yeardley, then fifteen, attended the funeral wearing her Notre Dame uniform and black-and-white saddle shoes. She placed a lacrosse ball in his casket.

After her father's death, Yeardley didn't slow down, and her interest in lacrosse seemed to heighten. It's a fast-paced sport with a simple goal: to fling a ball into your opponent's net. Only the goalie can touch the ball; the rest of the players have to manipulate it using the "crosse," a stick with a net attached to its end. Growing up in Cockeysville, where even the local dollar store stocked miniature lacrosse sets, helped fuel Yeardley's passion. On the field, she was petite but fierce, manipulating the lacrosse stick with increasing ease as the years passed. She was a swift defender, making up for being shorter than some teammates with her absolute diligence. In 2004, she earned notice in the *Towson Times,* her local paper, as having netted the only goal in a game against Garrison Forest. In 2006, her senior year, Coach Bartel said that Yeardley was one in a hardworking team. "This is a good group," she said. "We have a lot of team players and hard workers." But Yeardley stood out; that year, she went All-County. After high school, she was determined to play at UVA, not only her father's would-be alma mater, but also the school at which her uncle had been an All-American lacrosse star years earlier. An archive clip from a March 2009 interview with Virginiasports.com revealed just how excited Yeardley had been to finally go to UVA; she called it a "dream come true."

"I had wanted to play lacrosse at Virginia since I was little," she told a reporter at the Web site. She praised Coach Bartel, saying she "always pushed me to work harder. She not only prepared me to play at the college level, but she taught me important life lessons. She always put a strong focus on good sportsmanship and working together as a team."

Many young people with Yeardley's popularity, talent, and looks would have an attitude to match. But she didn't, teammate Casey Donohoe told *People*. Before lacrosse games, Yeardley gave Donohoe gifts—Gatorade sometimes, a favorite snack others. The gift was anonymous, the teammate told the magazine.

"I didn't know till the end of the year it was Yeardley. She was just so thoughtful," she said. "You would think she would be cocky and conceited, but that couldn't be further from the truth. She was humble about everything."

As a senior, Yeardley was recruited by the one school on her radar. When UVA coach Julie Myers offered her a spot on the renowned team, Yeardley beamed, she told a team publication shortly before her death. "That definitely topped the happiest and proudest moment that I will probably ever experience," she said.

Yeardley spent countless hours practicing and playing at UVA's Klöckner Stadium, where soccer dominates in the fall and lacrosse in the spring. The stadium, built in 1992 for

more than $3 million, seemed a good luck charm for its ath-
letes. The men's soccer team won national championships
there, as did both the men and women's lacrosse teams. By
Yeardley's senior year, she lived less than one and a half
miles from Klöckner, an easy walk down University Avenue
and Emmet Street. Because of its proximity to both the stadium and area bars, the Corner, as locals call the area where
Yeardley lived, was a popular spot for both lacrosse and soccer players to call home. Given the tight-knit nature of her
lacrosse community, it was no surprise that Yeardley began
dating a fellow player about a year into her college career. On
the surface, the two made sense, with their overlapping interests and similar backgrounds. They were regularly spotted
hanging out with other players at area bars—the Boylan
Heights bar in particular, which was a quick walk from each
of their senior-year apartments.

As much as Yeardley loved her social college life, she was
focused on the future. Poised to major in government and
minor in Spanish, she had spent the summer before her senior year interning at a public relations and marketing firm
in New York City, and she had a job lined up for after her
May graduation—a milestone that, it turned out, she would
never reach.

As medics carried Yeardley's lifeless body from her apartment, friends doubled over in tears on the front lawn. One
young woman wailed on her cell phone, waking a neighbor
with her cries. No one working the police beat has failed to
encounter the tale of a boyfriend with a temper, the girl in
danger, the realization setting in far too late that a powder
keg had long ago been ignited. Still, this case was different
than most. Yeardley seemed to have everything, and more
than that, she seemed poised to give back to the world. On the
field, she was the type to volunteer for extra drills, playing
defense against attackers. Off the field, she was determined
but gracious, affluent but humble. She was the daughter, the
sister, and the friend that people either wanted to have or

wanted to be. Now, friends who had been preparing for the rush of finals and the relief of graduation found themselves bracing for an unfathomable funeral instead.

Amy Appelt, a former lacrosse All-America at UVA who graduated in 2005 and founded "onenine lacrosse" to train players, told *Sports Illustrated*'s SI.com that she had coached Yeardley for a season and knew her well.

"You hear that God has a plan for everyone," she mused, "but maybe He messed up this one time."

Chapter 4

As news of Yeardley's death swiftly spread across the campus, the media were given a photograph of the young woman that seemed to symbolize promise cut short. Yeardley looked as all-American as they come, her smile beaming and her face bearing a subtle tan. Blue eyes stared out from an impossibly vibrant face as she stood before a bluish backdrop and wore her lacrosse warm-up jacket. The photo had been taken by the university for the team roster. Yeardley looked perfect. By the time her identity was confirmed, media had already learned and reported the name of the ex-boyfriend fingered in her death. Now, as newspapers released his jailhouse mug shot, the juxtaposition was striking. She appeared on the cusp of greatness; he looked like a defeated criminal.

The photos underlined a heartbreaking reality: Yeardley's life was too soon snuffed out. George's, too, had been full of promise, and now it lay in ruins. They had both been set to graduate the following month. Their dreams crumbled in one fateful night.

As the media coverage continued, it became clear that if Yeardley was the story's damsel, Huguely (pronounced Hueglee) was most certainly its demon. With his pleasant looks and affluent upbringing, he was instantly characterized in media reports as the quintessential spoiled brat who couldn't handle a pretty girl's rejection. Like Yeardley, he grew up in comfort, the grandson of a previous George Huguely who co-founded a prominent building supply company in 1912 that helped build Washington, D.C. George Huguely V was born September 17, 1987, to George Huguely IV and Marta Murphy. His father was a real estate mogul; his mother, a model. The couple divorced in 1998, and George V stayed with his mother, growing up in D.C. suburb Chevy Chase, Maryland (no connection to the actor). His home on Park View Road was visibly more modest than Yeardley's, but his father also owned property on the Outer Banks of North Carolina, as well as an estate reported to be worth between $1 million and $2 million in Palm Beach County, Florida.

George finished the eighth grade at Mater Dei School in Bethesda, Maryland, a Catholic elementary school for boys from first through eighth grades. The school uniform: tan khakis, light blue button-down shirt, school tie, and tan buck shoes or rubber-soled topsiders. "Navy blue sweaters are permitted," according to Mater Dei's Web site. Catholic students historically have been given a break on tuition. The 2010–2011 academic years cost $10,225 for Catholic students, and $11,450 for non-Catholics.

Though George and Yeardley didn't meet until college, their lives until that point were strikingly similar. Both spent high school in private, high-priced institutions. Both were attractive and athletic. Both were considered high spirited and upbeat with bright futures. After eighth grade, George matriculated at Landon School, also in Bethesda, a $29,000-a-year, boys-only school for grades three through twelve. Parents scouting there are assured that their sons will get the best in academics, arts, athletics and character education. Landon, founded in 1929, is non-sectarian and initially employed many retired military men who aimed to instill ethics as well as education in the young boys who enrolled. In the 1960s, Landon students wrote an honor code to guide their actions. Forty-two years later, the school added a civility code. In 2008, after the arrests of some Landon alumni had threatened to tarnish the school's good name, the school formally adopted a code of character that encompassed both the previous codes. The emphasis was on honesty and respect. Instilled in the boys were the following sayings: "I will not lie, cheat, or steal, or tolerate those who do," and "I will treat all people with respect, civility and dignity. I will also respect my school, my surroundings and myself."

As one Landon student declared in a 2010 promotional video online, the boys enrolled at Landon have a different relationship than students in traditional high schools.

"You see the same kids in your English class, and they're in your choir class, then they're on your football team. They're on everything with you," the young man said. "They kind of just become your brothers. It's a different relationship that you have with your friends here."

That comes with the territory in single-sex schools. In a posting called "Why a Boys' School," Landon officials argue that in single-sex environments, boys have "the freedom to thrive academically and socially."

The school isn't alone in its assertions. Same-sex institutions have long argued that boys and girls learn differently from each other, and that teachers are able to cater better to those differences when the students are separated. Landon aimed to tailor its curriculum to its boys' needs based on their ever-changing stages of intellectual, social, emotional and physical development.

Teachers "tap into a boy's natural exuberance," the school claims, and encourage boys to form teams to learn cooperatively.

Proponents of same-sex schools also say that separating males from females alleviates some of the sexual tension and classroom distractions that run rampant in coed institutions. On its Web site, Landon assures parents that "scientific research" has confirmed what Landon has always known: "In a single-sex environment, boys have the freedom to thrive academically and socially."

The research is more divided than that. Some studies suggest that separating the sexes neither improves self-esteem or educational achievement. But Landon disagrees, and it insists on another benefit: family-like bonds among its students.

"Without the distraction of co-ed interactions, boys develop deep and supportive friendships with their peers," according to the school. Some boys stay lifelong friends.

George was a big gun at Landon, named starting quarterback in his senior year and leading Landon to a conference title. And he earned a reputation as a light-hearted jokester. Once he sneaked his coach Rob Bordley's car keys from an office, then drove up to the coach and chatted with him while sitting in the driver's seat until it dawned on Bordley what had happened, a prank immortalized in a 2006 article in the *Washington Post*. The story also highlighted a ballsy bet George had once made with an assistant coach: George would pick off a pass in exchange for a kiss from the coach's fiancée. As he promised, George made the play—then asked for the woman's number.

"He's always in an upbeat mood," Bordley told the *Post* at the time. "Nothing really fazes him. I've asked my assistant coaches if they've ever seen him rattled and they said no. He's just unflappable."

Keeping with Landon's teachings on giving back to the community, Huguely also joined Operation Smile, a children's charity organization founded in 1982 that aims to unite medical professionals with children born with facial deformities such as cleft lip and cleft palate. The effects of the deformities are more than aesthetic. Children are "often unable to eat, speak, socialize or smile," according to the organization's Web site. Huguely was vice president of a student branch of the organization.

Landon had seen its share of controversy, however, specifically with members of its lacrosse team. In 2006, a Landon graduate was one of three Duke University players falsely accused by a dancer of sexually assaulting her at a team party. Though the players were cleared, Bordley told the *Post* that in the scandal's aftermath, he repeatedly warned his team about the risks of alcohol abuse. Huguely was a member of the Landon team at the time.

* * *

George's star dimmed slightly at UVA, mainly because competition was fierce and he lacked the discipline of some of his teammates. As the *Post* reported, he gained weight, prompting teammates to brand him "Fuguely"—"a mashup of his name and a common vulgarity," according to the *Post*. Most of the male players were muscular and lean, conditioned through rigorous exercise to be both fast and long-winded on the field.

"You'd see him walk in . . . with other lacrosse players and you'd think, 'Oh, there goes a bunch of lacrosse players and some other guy,'" a bartender told the newspaper. "He just seemed like kind of an overgrown big kid."

As George would tell police after waiving his Miranda rights, he and Yeardley had been dating on and off for a few years. It wasn't unusual for players from the men's team to date players from the women's team. Their social circles overlapped anyway, as did their schedules. They often hung out together and drank at the same bars. Drinking, in fact, was a common pastime for many players, despite high-profile and longstanding efforts by the men's team to curtail it. In 1999, Coach Dom Starsia adopted a rule that allowed players to drink just one night a week—usually Saturdays. Players who broke the rule were to be suspended indefinitely; players who broke it again were to be dismissed entirely.

"Alcohol and lacrosse have gone hand-in-hand since my days at Brown in the 1970s," Starsia told the *Washington Post* at the time. "Whether it is post-game celebrations or just in general, there was something about the sport and alcohol, and Virginia was no different. I always thought alcohol was an issue here, and it is something we talked about before the season began."

While many applauded Starsia's efforts, others criticized the one-day-a-week green light as a permission slip to binge drink. Some said the young adults would just push their drinking habits underground, making them even harder to rein in if things got excessive. In the days after Yeardley's death, the *Washington Post* reported that eight of the forty-one lacrosse players on the UVA men's team had been charged with alcohol-related offenses during their college careers. The charges included underage alcohol possession, using a fake ID, and driving under the influence. Six of the eight were convicted; two were found not guilty.

Among the guilty, the newspaper uncovered, was George Huguely.

On November 14, 2008, Huguely had been visiting friends at a fraternity house at Lexington, Virginia's Washington and Lee University, about seventy miles from his Charlottesville apartment, when police got a nine-one-one call. Policewoman R. L. Moss and a sergeant responded and found Huguely stumbling into traffic. Moss approached the brawny athlete and asked his name.

"George," he replied.

He wasn't a student in Lexington, he told the officer. The then-twenty-one-year-old was clearly intoxicated. Moss told him she would need to place him under arrest for public drunkenness and asked if his friends at the fraternity could pick him up that night to keep him from having to sleep in a jail cell.

At that point, he became belligerent, Moss later recalled. "He became more aggressive, more physical toward me," she told reporters. He began spewing racist and sexist slurs.

"I told him to stop resisting, that he needed to comply with my orders, that he was only making matters worse," she said.

He didn't. The two tussled, and Moss said she had no choice but to zap Huguely with a Taser. The electrical current caused George to lose control of his muscles, and he went limp long enough for Moss to slap handcuffs on him—but, as the effects of the Taser waned even slightly, he reignited the fight.

"He said, 'I'll kill you. I'll kill all of y'all. I'm not going to jail,'" Moss told reporters. "He was by far the most rude, most hateful, and most combative college kid I ever dealt with."

In another interview, she said: "Am I surprised that he

was involved in another incident involving physical violence? No. Am I surprised to this extent? Yes."

Lexington Police Chief Al Thomas told reporters that Huguely was beyond combative: "He was verbally abusive; he began shouting obscenities; he would not cooperate." At a court hearing a few weeks later, Huguely said he had been so intoxicated the night of his arrest that he couldn't remember any of it—not even being dropped by a stun gun. He was charged with public intoxication, resisting arrest, and public swearing, according to a courthouse clerk.

Ross Haine, his lawyer, was hired by Huguely's family soon after the arrest. The George he met was affable and kind, completely contrary to the vulgarity-spewing drunken mess who had tangled with an officer.

"He did not remember what he did," Haine later recalled. "He was intoxicated to the point where he had some vague memories of what had happened, but he didn't remember the particulars."

Haine, who has worked as an attorney for twenty-three years—the past twenty in Lexington—had seen his share of drunken college-age antics. Huguely's case stood out. The good-looking young man was a star athlete on a lacrosse scholarship, Haine said, and his parents were clearly concerned about him.

"He was a normal college student who had a lot going for him," Haine said. "Really, I liked him."

At the time, both the defense and prosecutor were more concerned about Huguely's vile language than his tussle with Moss, Haine recalled. When the lawyer heard the racist and sexist name-calling Huguely had hurled at Moss, he realized that the young man became a completely different person when he drank. In hopes of shocking Huguely with his own language, Haine set up a meeting with the officer, George, and his parents so that Moss could repeat the words he'd used with her the night of his arrest. Haine hoped George's reaction to the filth he had spewed would both teach him a lesson and mitigate the charges against him. He wanted George's parents to hear as well. They were obviously involved in their son's life, and concerned enough to retain a lawyer and stand by his side during the court hearing.

As George listened to the vitriol, he looked embarrassed and ashamed.

"I'm so sorry, I can't believe I said that," he repeated again and again.

"He never said, 'I didn't say that,'" Haine recalled. "My goal in representing him was to keep him out of jail. I wanted the officer to see how he wasn't bullshitting, that he was sincere. I hoped it would mitigate the offense; I think it did."

Huguely's parents seemed equally shocked by the words their son had unleashed on the officer, Haine said. All of their reactions seemed genuine and sincere.

"It was clear to me he had a drinking problem," Haine said. "He could not believe he had done all that. I've only seen him sober, so what I was hearing about him did not match the person I was talking to. His actions when he was intoxicated were so far away from the person I knew, so completely out of line with his character, it just did not seem to match."

Haine stood alongside his client as George pleaded guilty to resisting arrest and public intoxication and was sentenced to sixty days in jail and ordered to pay $100 in fines. But, as he had hoped, Haine succeeded in keeping Huguely from behind bars: The sentence was suspended, meaning that if George behaved and stayed out of legal trouble, he wouldn't have to serve the jail sentence. As part of the arrangement, Huguely was ordered to perform fifty hours of community service, which he did with the Blue Ridge Area Food Bank in Charlottesville. He was also ordered to attend a twenty-hour substance-abuse assessment program. He successfully completed both, according to court records.

UVA athletes were supposed to report any legal run-ins to the university. George might not have. Athletic Director Craig Littlepage, when pressed by reporters on this point, conceded it was possible Huguely had alerted a coach or told his team-mates, but if he had, the information hadn't been passed along to administrators as required. The oversight became another item in the growing list of "what-ifs."

Journalists' uncovering of Huguely's Lexington run-in caught Police Chief Timothy Longo completely off-guard. He said Charlottesville officers had done background checks locally to investigate Huguely's legal history but came up empty. He only learned of the epithet-spewing arrest from the media reports, he told the New York *Daily News*.

Within hours of the arrest in Yeardley's death, Haine learned that a UVA lacrosse player had been identified as her killer. Seventy miles isn't a long way for such news to travel, plus Haine's wife worked in the public defender's office in Charlottesville. It flickered across his mind that he had recently defended a UVA lacrosse player, but he never imagined that the sociable young man he had represented might be the same one now accused of murder.

It wasn't until the next morning, when his phone blew up with calls from reporters across the country, that Haine learned that the young man he represented had gotten into trouble again.

"He's an entirely different person when he's drunk," Haine later said. "I've seen cases like that before, but obviously never that extreme. He's just a different person."

That day, too, reporters dug up details of another police encounter in Florida that occurred just a month after the Lexington hubbub. According to published reports, on December 29, 2008, George and some family members had been aboard the family's forty-foot yacht, named *The Reel Deal*, about a quarter-mile offshore from the glamorous Ritz-Carlton. George V announced that he wanted to go back to the beach. His father refused, saying he would take him home, but not to the beach. Furious, the younger Huguely jumped into the Atlantic Ocean and attempted to begin the quarter-mile swim back to shore. His father radioed for help, and a passing boater safely pulled his son from the salty water. Though the incident was called in as a domestic-abuse complaint, no arrests were made. Sheriff's Deputies for Palm Beach County reported that there were no blows thrown, but "lots of yelling and screaming." Because police found no evidence of violence, the incident was dismissed as a family spat aggravated by the young man's temper tantrum.

University officials said they knew nothing of that 2008 incident, either, though George wouldn't have technically been required to report it because no one was charged. Still, if the university had been properly notified about the Lexington arrest, and if they had learned of Huguely's tantrum just a month later, someone within the university might have seen fit to evaluate him more thoroughly. Instead, the administration apparently remained in the dark, and George's troubling behavior yet again slid under the radar.

And the allegations kept coming. Another report surfaced that Huguely had punched a sleeping teammate whom he learned had walked Yeardley home—possibly even kissing her—in February 2009. A bartender who later heard Huguely describe the assault told the *Post* it was "like some cheesy action movie, where he stood above the guy while he was sleeping and said, 'Sweet dreams, punk,' and then just punched him in the face."

University officials did know about that incident, they acknowledged to reporters. They said Huguely and his teammate-turned-punching-bag had approached Coach Starsia to talk about their scuffle, apparently in an effort to head off any rumors that might reach the coach first. "They said they wanted him to be aware of it, but that they had worked things out and everything was OK between them," according to a UVA statement released in the aftermath of Yeardley's death. Starsia asked Huguely and the other student if they wanted to talk about it further. Both men passed. "They told him that they shared the blame for what had happened and had apologized to one another," the university's statement said.

The final red-flags-in-hindsight that journalists uncovered were never reported to either university officials or the police. In February 2010, less than three months before Yeardley's death, Huguely reportedly jumped on her and began to choke her at a party filled with friends. Things got so heated that one former and two current University of North Carolina lacrosse players intervened to pull George off of her. Yeardley was so upset that one of the UNC players drove her home to Cockeysville to give her time away from George. A former Virginia student said that Huguely was drunk and couldn't remember the attack the next day. That led to Yeardley and George's final breakup, friends told reporters.

"He was really messed up and punched a window of a car on the way over to her apartment" the night of the fight at UNC, the friend told reporters on condition of anonymity.

Huguely tried to get her back, another friend said, but Yeardley was determined to move on.

The incident raised questions: Assuming the university was being forthcoming in denying knowledge of the attack, why hadn't fellow lacrosse players reported the incident? Why hadn't Yeardley reported it herself? Surely, if UVA administrators had learned of a physical attack between one lacrosse player and another—especially one between a dating couple—there would have been repercussions. With the lacrosse culture being so incredibly close-knit, onlookers surmised that the players perhaps didn't want to ruin George's reputation over what they assumed was a one-night, drunken lapse of judgment.

Then, the Tuesday before her death, as Yeardley visited Huguely at his apartment, she confronted him about rumors he had been seeing other girls—specifically two high school lacrosse recruits. Yeardley lost her temper and hit him with her purse, one of her sorority sisters later testified. The handbag flew open and its contents spilled out. Yeardley and Elizabeth McLean, whose boyfriend, Kevin Carroll, lived with Huguely, hurriedly gathered the scattered belongings. McLean later testified that she walked Yeardley home that night "because she was upset." But in Yeardley's haste, she had left her camera and her cell phone, and later asked a friend to go back to Huguely's apartment to retrieve them. The friend found the camera, according to police reports, but she couldn't find the cell phone. Yeardley tried to orchestrate its return several times via email, friends said.

The allegations that surfaced baffled people who knew Huguely growing up in tony Chevy Chase. Peter Preston told reporters that his children grew up playing with the Huguelys. "Georgie," as he knew Huguely, was "just a wonderful, charming, polite young man. . . . George is not a monster."

George's mother, Marta Murphy, was clearly at a loss. An attractive blond with chin-length hair, she had confidently stood by her son at his arraignment, clutching her husband's hand as they quietly passed reporters. Her relationship with George's father—George IV, who disguised a receding hairline with a subtle comb-over—had not always been easy, but now they found themselves intertwined, having to wade through legal proceedings as a united front. Neither Murphy nor Huguely IV spoke with the media at their son's arraignment, but Murphy finally broke her silence when she sent an anguished e-mail to news media calling Yeardley a "sweet, wonderful young woman with a limitless future" who had become a part of her boyfriend's family's lives. According to friends, Yeardley had spent time chatting with Murphy during a recent family's day at the university. The two sat together at a bar and grill and chatted. Huguely stopped by occasionally, but largely left the women to talk alone.

"I got to know her as George's mom," Murphy wrote in her e-mail to media. "We also know her mother, Sharon. The pain she and her family are suffering is something that no family should have to endure. No parent should have to bury a child and not a moment goes by when they are not in our thoughts and our prayers. It has been difficult to remain silent during this dark, tumultuous time. Along with my family, I am devastated and confused. We are all trying to understand and cope as best we can. As a mother, I never expected to be in a situation like this. Though my pain is great, it can never come close to the anguish felt by the Love family."

Another Huguely family friend told the *Post*, "Every time I see Yeardley's face on a magazine, I want to die. None of us can believe this actually happened. It doesn't click. It doesn't jibe. It doesn't work. The George we knew wasn't capable of that. There had to be a different George that was inside that head."

But as the details of his stormy temper emerged, it became harder for people following the case to see how Huguely was anything more than a time bomb whose history of violence had been shrugged off because of his wealth. Nationwide, the same question was posed again and again: Just how many people knew Yeardley was in danger?

Police Chief Longo fielded media questions about all the reported scenarios. Some, such as the Lexington run-in with the policewoman, he could confirm, but when it came to the reported incidents involving Yeardley, he simply shook his head.

"We're looking into what, if any, threats were made," he told reporters. "We've heard exactly what the entire community here has been hearing. The difference is that we have to prove it."

That would be an ongoing concern for law enforcement as the case slowly unfolded. Longo didn't say so at the time, but surely he knew as early as May 4 that his city, statistically homicide-free in 2009, would be mired in this new deadly scandal for many months to come.

Chapter 5

Charlottesville, Virginia, is as much Southern charm as it is college town, infused with a humidity-drenched hipness that attracts students worldwide. The city is steeped in history, the former home of founding fathers such as Thomas Jefferson and James Madison, and its origins can be spotted on the facades of its buildings, with sturdy white pillars and sprawling front porches—the trademarks of late-1700s Southern architecture.

Named after the motherland's Queen Charlotte, the settlement was formed within Albemarle County in 1762 along a trade route called Three Notch'd Road that connected Richmond to the Great Valley. Unlike many early towns, it lay slightly inland, away from the estuaries and river runoffs on which plantations of the time relied. Hugged by the Rivanna River, a tributary of the James, Charlottesville grew in a ten-mile chunk just west of the Southwest Mountains. Soon, a courthouse was built on a hillside overlooking Three Notch'd, and businesses began cropping up nearby—taverns, tailors, a gunsmith, and a jeweler. The heart of the town lay not along Charlottesville's main drag, but rather just above it, next to the 1803-built courthouse. But as the early 1800s rolled by, the development began slowly to shift from so-called Court Square back to the trade route. First, there were houses. Next came the businesses. As the decades passed, Three Notch'd Road morphed into present-day Main Street.

Thomas Jefferson, the colonial revolutionary and former United States president who by then was at the end of his accomplished career, saw the town as a perfect spot for higher-minded academics, but he envisioned the University of Virginia as having a separate identity from the rest of Charlottesville. He picked a site atop a small hill about a mile from the town center and, in 1819, founded his Academical Village, as he famously called it. There, daily life was to be infused with shared learning. Faculty would live in upstairs quarters of stately pavilions; downstairs, there would be classrooms. He envisioned ten pavilions, each assigned its own subject and serving as home to the professor who taught it. While other universities placed a chapel at its heart, Jefferson placed a library, one built with a dome reminiscent of Rome's Pantheon, which, according to the university, was symbolic of the enlightened human mind. Jefferson considered true enlightenment so unattainable that he declined to call uppermost class members "seniors." Rather, they were dubbed "fourth years"—a tradition that continues today.

Jefferson envisioned a university that adhered to a student-policed honor system, much like the one he had written in 1779 for his alma mater, the College of William & Mary. The idea was simple: Students agreed to act honorably, promising not to lie, cheat, or steal, or they would be subjected to the harshest of academic sanctions—expulsion. Jefferson believed in self-government, both on campus and off. In fact, one of UVA's main objectives was to produce leaders for a self-governing people.

In March 1825, the university officially welcomed its first batch of students, a class of sixty-eight. The institution was the first nonsectarian university in the country, and the first to allow students to choose elective courses. Jefferson, himself an architect, writer, inventor, and horticulturalist, put his many interests and talents to use by planning the curriculum and recruiting the faculty from all over the world. He designed the Village as a green space hugged by academic and residential buildings with gardens mixed throughout. The Pantheon-inspired Rotunda is regal and elegant, with perfect wood floors and ornate pillars encircling the dome room. As if its appearance weren't quieting enough, those who speak inside are greeted with a stately echo that inspires one to hush in reverence.

Jefferson got to enjoy his creation for a year, regularly hosting events at his Monticello plantation manor, located a few miles from downtown. By the time he died on July 4, 1826—the fiftieth anniversary of the Declaration of Independence signing (and, in a famous coincidence, the same day John Adams, the United States' second president, died)—he had declared the university his greatest achievement. (Monticello, too, still stands as a designated historical site just outside of city limits, and its image has appeared on the back of U.S. nickels since 1938, save for a brief hiatus between 2004 and 2005. Monticello also appeared on the reverse of the long-discontinued two-dollar bill.)

Charlottesville continued expanding, and, in 1850, welcomed the Virginia Central Railroad (first called the Louisa Railroad, and later called Chesapeake and Ohio) as its first railway. Its tracks cut through the south end of town, below Main Street. By decade's end, it connected with the Shenandoah Valley by cutting through the Blue Ridge Mountains. The new line allowed for a boom in shipping as goods and raw materials could more directly reach and pass through Charlottesville. In 1863, with the introduction of the Southern Railroad, the face of the area changed. The crossing railways divided the town into quadrants, with the university in its southwest portion, while the downtown lay northeast.

As shipping expanded, Charlottesville rooted itself as a full-fledged city, holding its first mayoral election in 1854. Its expansion briefly stalled during the Civil War, when many young men were sent into battle. The city itself fared better than many in the conflict, though canal locks were destroyed and buildings burned in Scottsville to its south. The only battle fought in Charlottesville was the Skirmish at Rio Hill, in which Brigadier General George Custer led thousands of

Union solders toward the city on February 26, 1864. It was a decoy, meant to distract Confederate soldiers from separate efforts to free prisoners of war that were being held about seventy miles to the southeast in Richmond. The skirmish did not end well for Custer: He was disoriented by an incidental artillery explosion and chased out of town by opportunistic Confederate troops. Custer got his revenge the next year, when he occupied the town for three days in March. In April 1865, the Army of Northern Virginia surrendered in the Battle of Appomattox Court House, and Charlottesville was spared the blaze that had already engulfed many of its Confederate brothers.

Today, nods to that history still stand. Statues of Generals Robert E. Lee and Stonewall Jackson are displayed in Charlottesville's public squares. Most noticeably, though, are the buildings that remain, the majestic brick-and-plaster structures that whisper reminders of the country's origins, struggles, and potential. James Monroe's Ashlawn-Highland and James Madison's Montpelier continue to draw millions of tourists each year.

But the city offers more than history lessons. In 2004, Charlottesville was ranked the best place to live in the United States by *Cities Ranked and Rated*, a book by Bert Sperling and Peter Sander. The authors weighed cost of living, climate, and quality of life. Similar honors have been bestowed by other publications for decades: *Kiplinger's Personal Finance Magazine* ranked it the fourth-best place to live in the country in 2009; the same year, *Forbes Magazine* declared it the eleventh-best town to find a job; Farmers Insurance has rated it in the top twenty safest mid-sized cities in the United States; even the AARP ranked it one of the top ten healthiest places to retire in 2008. As of 2007, the city had about 41,000 residents, according to a census update. Statistically, Charlottesville is a safe place to live. From 2007–2009, fewer than one hundred aggravated assaults were reported to the Federal Bureau of Investigation, which releases annual statistics on cities nationwide. In 2009, property crimes had crept slightly higher than the year before (from twenty-three to thirty-five), and burglaries rose from seventy-nine to eighty-eight, but the increases were modest. The city's biggest problem historically has been rape: In 2009, 247 were reported. Murders and manslaughter are exceptionally rare, with fewer than a handful a year. None reported in 2009.

Though the university continues to be a huge employer and revenue stream, the area is also drawing attention for its respectable wine industry. The Monticello Wine Trail declares itself the "birthplace of American wine," and the area's nearly yearlong humidity typically helps lock grape-pleasing moisture in the soil.

Incoming University of Virginia freshmen are routinely reminded of the university's history and prestige. It's no small feat to be accepted at UVA, especially for students coming from out-of-state high schools. In recent years, the college has accepted between twenty and twenty-five percent of its out-of-state applicants (compared to more than a forty percent acceptance rate for Virginia residents). In analyzing its incoming class of 2014, university officials said that the "middle 50 percent scored between 1300 and a 1480 on the reading and math portions of the SAT," according to the *Cavalier Daily*. "The majority of these students—93.8 percent—were also in the top 10 percent of their high school classes."

And, predictably, the academics are tough to beat: *U.S. News & World Report* ranked UVA second in "best public universities" in 2011 (tied with UCLA), and it's tied for twenty-fifth when looking at both public and private national universities. Its McIntire School of Commerce is ranked fifth in the nation; its law school, tenth; and its English department, tenth. The University of Virginia Medical Center is one of fifteen major teaching hospitals ranked in the nation's top one hundred, according to Thomson Reuters' "100 Top Hospitals: National Benchmarks" study.

In short, UVA students are expected to be among the best in the country—and they know it.

Once settled in to campus life, students ready to shed their high school personas seem to gravitate toward the city's downtown mall, a quaint pedestrian-only stretch dotted with more than 120 shops and thirty restaurants, based on a city-released count. Many eateries offer outdoor seating, making the mall both people- and pet-friendly. The stretch even has a movie theater and pavilion for outdoor concerts from spring to fall.

Yeardley had been eyeing the University of Virginia since childhood. It was the only college in her sights, and its down-home appeal differed from her small-town upbringing in the best possible ways. Teenagers in Cockeysville largely relied on the nearby Hunt Valley Towne Centre for outings. The outdoor mall boasted a slew of higher-end restaurants, a bookstore, a movie theater and a sporting goods store with a well-stocked lacrosse section. At night, the area teemed with teens—until, that is, curfew set in and youngsters were required an adult escort. In Charlottesville, the fun was spread out citywide. From her 14th Street apartment smack dab in The Corner—a seven-block cluster of restaurants, university bookstores, and bars—Yeardley could walk to grab a burger from Mellow Mushroom, some Vietnamese from Lemongrass, or a beer from Boylan Heights. Boylan Heights boasts burger fare with a twist, and is a popular place for students—athletes especially—to kick back with a beer or gather for post-class revelry.

Chaney Kent, who owned the Corner Market on University Avenue, told a reporter that Yeardley stopped by a few times each week to buy a twelve-ounce can of Diet Coke. The store was a block and a half from her apartment.

"She couldn't be nicer, more pleasant, outgoing," Kent recalled. "When a girl has a name like 'Love,' you don't forget."

George Huguely had also set his sights on Virginia. Considered one of Landon's premiere lacrosse players, he was a natural fit there, both aggressive and agile. His roots in Chevy Chase no doubt made his transition to Charlottesville different than Yeardley's. His town was more consolidated, with a downtown dotted by quirky venues such as American City Diner, a twenty-four-hour soda fountain–style joint that aired nightly film classics like *Niagara* and *Dr. Strangelove*. Huguely's hometown felt upscale but down-to-earth, as though its inhabitants were from older money that they enjoyed spending on good times. Certainly Chevy Chase was more similar to Charlottesville than Cockeysville; Chevy Chase was a mix of laid-back mom-and-pop stores that made college shopping so eclectic. Cockeysville, on the other hand, relied largely on upscale chain outlets.

Despite differences in their upbringings, on paper, Yeardley and George seemed far more alike than not. As they each wrapped up careers at single-sex private high schools, they continued their immersion in lacrosse culture—one inherently married to privilege and pedigree. The sport, of Native American origin, is today an expensive one to play. Though the sport is similar in rules to soccer, players must invest in far more than just cleats and a ball. A typical lacrosse setup calls for a stick (both shaft and head), shoulder pads, rib pads, arm guards, slash guards, gloves, mouth guard, and either eye protection or full-on helmet. Depending on the make and style, each component could easily cost upward of $200. After the gear, there is the traveling. Love and Huguely routinely traveled throughout high school and college, both to play and to watch other teams in action.

The sport required vigorous training from both. Though lacrosse isn't known as one of the country's most popular sports, it's definitely gaining ground, and lacrosse aficionados say its players must possess strength, power, speed, agility, and endurance in spades. Scientific studies indicate that the average lacrosse player must have the aerobic capacities of basketball and football players matched with hefty muscle mass—high bodyweight but low body fat—to endure aggressive physical contact. Thus, a lacrosse player might appear in size similar to a hockey or football player, but his body fat is typically lower.

When training, most lacrosse players focus on developing explosive power and endurance. Training calls for lifting lower-weight loads with more repetitions and faster movements. Unlike with other strength training, explosive power training doesn't require athletes to perform to exhaustion, but rather a typical power session would call for an athlete to lift up to forty percent of his lifting capacity, then stop his repetitions shy of exhaustion. Players are told to rest between two and five minutes between sets, with the goal of performing between three and five sets per session. Many UVA athletes hit the gym up to five times a week.

Speed and agility drills are crucial in lacrosse training as well. For speed, athletes are encouraged to work on "rolling starts," or sprints that begin as jogs, then pick up the pace about halfway through the drill. These are done on flat land, as well as up- and downhill to really push the athlete's endurance. In agility drills, players are sometimes told to weave between a series of cones, turn around, then sprint back. The exercise mirrors the dodging and darting players have to do while passing their competitors on the field in pursuit of the ball.

Because lacrosse calls for such sudden bursts of speed and power, players' muscles are flooded with lactic acid. Lactate tolerance training helps athletes tolerate higher lactate levels, allowing them to recover more quickly from those successive bursts. Shuttle runs—where an athlete springs about ten yards, then sharply turns and springs back—are typical for such training. Athletes typically rest for just thirty seconds between sprints, then cool down with a two-minute walk after wrapping up several sets.

But lacrosse—nicknamed lax—is set apart from other sports by more than how its athletes work up their sweat. It's a complicated intersection of privilege, heritage, and pride.

Journalist Jamie Stiehm for years lived among lacrosse lovers and wrote about the "close-knit, privileged lacrosse culture" in a piece published the week Yeardley died.

"As a former reporter at the Baltimore *Sun* who lived near a lacrosse field and museum, I am familiar with the intense devotion to this sport," she wrote. "Art, books, the theater: All are pretty much dead between March and May.

Believe me when I tell you that in these circles, lacrosse is very nearly the only thing—you go to a game every weekend, home or away, including some far-off place like Providence or Ithaca."

Parents are as immersed in the youth lacrosse scene as the children. Players with natural ability become town heroes. Their names are spread from one lacrosse hotbed to the next. They're scouted as youths by college coaches.

"In college lax, the spring [schedule] becomes the main event of the season, with parents travelling to home and away games, having picnics and tailgate parties—reinforcing the sense that there is nothing more important going on than lacrosse in their lives," Stiehm said in an interview.

"It's a very old-moneyed culture. It was for men for decades, and then girls got into the game . . . It almost by definition excludes people who don't have the means or the money to send their kids to private clubs or buy the expensive equipment. Usually it's a private school thing. It has gates all around it."

Stiehm, who worked for the *Sun* for ten years, mostly covering city news and general-assignment stories, found herself invested in the sport on April 18, 1998, when she was sent to the Brooklandville home of a nineteen-year-old high school lacrosse player who had committed suicide the previous night.

Alexander "Alec" Schweizer was an honor student and star player at St. Paul's School. As starting goalie on the school's team, he had been recruited to attend Syracuse University in New York. Newspapers typically don't cover suicides, but Schweizer's was a "society death," Stiehm recalled. When she arrived at his upscale home, some 300 people had gathered in mourning. They talked openly about the young man's aspirations and talents, and the *Sun* ran Stiehm's piece in its Sunday edition.

More than a decade later, as Stiehm learned of Yeardley Love's death, some of the lessons she had gleaned in her temporary immersion in the lacrosse culture came rushing back. The column she wrote for *Politics Daily* was starkly titled: "Yeardley Love Slaying: Is Lacrosse's Close Culture Complicit?" Stiehm, now a journalist in Washington D.C., offered a resounding "yes" as the answer.

"This young woman was clearly being tormented, harassed, and abused, but because he belonged to a club that protects their own, she was ultimately a victim of that," Stiehm later said. "They let her die in plain view. They ignored what was in front of them. And she didn't bring it out into the open."

As she wrote in her column: "If the entire lacrosse culture around Love had activated to protect her from a threat of violence, even if it came from someone from posh Chevy Chase, then she would be alive today."

The piece outraged some readers, who sent Stiehm angry e-mails calling her a terrible person who, as an outsider, had no right to opine about the inner workings of lacrosse.

"Some of the comments were screams of pain," Stiehm later said. "It was fury, but a little bit of guilt was at play, too."

For a lacrosse-loving college student, the University of Virginia had natural appeal. The Virginia Cavaliers, also called the Wahoos or 'Hoos for short, had won six national lacrosse titles for men and three for women. In 2006, the year Yeardley and George graduated high school and headed for Charlottesville, the men's team won its fourth NCAA Men's Lacrosse Championship, defeating the University of Massachusetts in the title game. The record audience of nearly 50,000 made it the first lacrosse crowd to surpass the attendance of the men's Final Four basketball championship. The Cavaliers were on fire, finishing the season with a perfect 17–0 record. Huguely, that year an All-American player, was expected to be a valuable midfielder, both muscular and capable of running the full length of the field many times per game. The midfielder's job is strategic at its core.

Yeardley was ecstatic when she learned she was accepted to her uncle's alma mater, her neighbors told reporters. In the fall of 2006, she packed up her belongings and drove the mountainous 172 miles to her new home—ready for her life to begin among the dogwoods and white oaks that canopied the campus. But while she was perhaps exactly the type of well-rounded and eager-to-learn student Jefferson had envisioned, surely her fate was not one he would have wished for in his academic Xanadu.

Chapter 6

The reputation Yeardley had earned in high school as bright eyed and big hearted only grew as she began college life. She was known for being quiet in big groups but lively in smaller ones, as well as for her contagious smile and quick laugh. Like about one third of the university's undergraduate females, she opted to join a sorority. Her pick was Kappa Alpha Theta, founded in 1870 as the first Greek-letter fraternity for women. Its vision statement emphasizes its core purposes—to support its members to learn and excel—while its core values are personal excellence and the development of friendship and sisterhood. The Delta Chi chapter at the University of Virginia boasts a slideshow of pictures of young, attractive girls smiling and goofing for the camera. Every year, the chapter holds a pancake breakfast to benefit the Court Appointed Special Advocate Association, or CASA, an advocacy group for abused and neglected children. For Yeardley, the sorority environment wouldn't have differed much from her experience with lacrosse: Both were close-knit and insulated. Those accepted were lifelong sisters—but acceptance was the key.

Maggie Thompson, in signing an online remembrance for Yeardley, said her husband, Nevada, was the cook for the sorority and became friends with Yeardley "during the year she lived at the house." Jayne Donohoe, Casey Donohoe's mother, said in the same online remembrance that Yeardley shined in high school and blossomed at UVA.

Courtney Schaefer, the sorority's president in Yeardley's last year, declined to describe sorority life to reporters, saying that her bylaws and pledges forbade such discussion. But one long-graduated member, who had belonged to the Duke University chapter, said that much about the Kappa Alpha Theta hasn't changed over the years. They're expected to have good grades, they tend to be pretty, and they have a secret handshake. (When one outsider posted a question in 2008 on an online blog hoping to learn the secret handshake, she got an icy response: "You find the answer . . . once you become a member of the sorority.")

Greek life at UVA, like on any campus, is viewed with nausea by some, reverence by others. In one online student review, a UVA student acknowledged that "Greek life dominates the social scene . . . Many are bitter about this and find it superficial, costly, obnoxious and over-prevalent. Those involved in Greek life, however, love the people they have met and the relationships they have formed." Outsiders find the exclusivity and secrecy of it all frustrating, the reviewer acknowledged.

This much is known: Yeardley found in her sorority a group of friends whom she considered family. As a Kappa Alpha Theta (KAO) member, Yeardley's circles would have overlapped with other sororities as well as the more than thirty fraternities on campus. The Greek events abounded: formals, semi-formals, frat parties. Between her sorority sisters and her lacrosse teammates, Yeardley never had to be alone unless she wanted to be.

As the years passed, Yeardley's lacrosse skills continued to improve. After the first season launched in spring 2007, Yeardley—proudly wearing her #1 jersey, the same number she had worn at Notre Dame Prep—nabbed her first collegiate goal in a game against Virginia Tech. She played in eight games that season, according to her team biography.

The next year, she went up to nine games, and in 2009, she played in sixteen games, starting in nine of them. Her shining moment came in a game against Richmond, when she nailed two goals. In her final year as a fleet-footed defender, she started in fewer games but was on pace to play in more. She'd seen playing time in fifteen games, as a starter in three. On the field, Yeardley was focused and toned, her hair pulled back in a ponytail or braid as she nimbly maneuvered her blue-and-orange lacrosse stick. Even while wearing awkward eye protection and a mouth guard, her pretty features shone through: delicate nose, piercing eyes, fit physique.

Academically, Yeardley zeroed in on political science, declaring government her major. Bill Quandt, a professor in the university's political science department, told the weekly Charlottesville-based newspaper *The Hook* that even in a class of 250, Yeardley stood out.

"She seemed like a very bright, dynamic, energetic young woman," Quandt told the paper of his experience with Yeardley in a Middle Eastern politics course. "She exuded self-confidence."

Meg Heubeck, a university advisor, told the *Today* show that Yeardley was "absolutely the epitome of the University of Virginia student. Thomas Jefferson would be proud of having such a young woman at the University of Virginia studying. She was just lovely in every single way."

Huguely, meanwhile, became an anthropology major and befriended many in Delta Kappa Epsilon, established in 1852 as the University of Virginia's first fraternity. Despite reports to the contrary, Huguely was not a member there, according to fraternity officials. Rather, he was friends with members, some of whom were fellow lacrosse players. On the team, he was regarded as a big, tough player with an excellent field sense, according to the profile compiled on him by the university's athletics department. When he and Yeardley began dating, they seemed a natural fit, orbiting the same social circles and coming from similar backgrounds. They made an enviable couple—both were charming, well-liked, attractive, and talented.

Yeardley was the team's smile, "the player who made everyone feel better," Coach Julie Myers said after her death.

And Yeardley was occasionally a goof, quick to stick out her tongue and contort her face to make her friends laugh.

"As genuine, kind, and gentle as she was, she was also tough as nails on the lacrosse field," Myers later eulogized. "She played with a heart of a lion."

While George was still known as a prankster, the easygoing part of his reputation began to diminish as he was introduced to the heavy-drinking element of college life. Like many college students, Huguely imbibed. But unlike many, he had taken it to such extremes that he got violent and blacked out. The Lexington incident in 2008 that landed him in a jail cell overnight was one example, but friends told reporters that it wasn't an isolated incident. Several media outlets reported that friends, speaking on condition of anonymity, had heard that Yeardley was fed up with her boyfriend's hard-drinking ways, and that she was especially shaken after he attacked her one night but couldn't recall the incident in the morning. It was one of many rumors that Police Chief Longo declined to address.

After Yeardley's death, Huguely's neighbors talked in hushed voices about the couple's drinking. Both were regularly seen with their lacrosse teammates indulging far more often than once a week, as men's coach Starsia had so publicly instructed against.

The lacrosse players were "known for partying," one fourth-year student told *People* magazine. "They have parties three times a week," said another. "The day after the murder, I saw them with a twelve-pack of beer, a cheap one—that's all they ever drank."

The New York *Daily News* quoted unnamed friends as saying Huguely "partied really hard and when he was drunk or fucked up, he could be violent. He would get out of control." He used text messages to obsessively keep tabs on his girlfriend, the sources continued, and on the night of Yeardley's death, he'd been spotted breaking bottles at a party and saying that he was going to go to her apartment to "get her back." Yeardley reportedly had been at Boylan Heights just a short walk from her apartment in an area of town dubbed the Corner. One Boylan employee said that both university lacrosse teams regularly visited the bar, with some members of the men's team stopping by several times a week.

"They usually come in about midnight," Brett Harder told the *C-VILLE Weekly*. "They're usually pretty drunk when they get here because they've been pre-gaming all afternoon. They hang out. Each of them will have a couple rounds, a couple shots. And then they usually roll out about the time we have to throw them out."

Harder said he had seen Huguely and Love at the corner joint many times.

"Occasionally, I'd see them together," he said. "Most of the time, I'd see them with their respective friends."

No one reported having seen any violence between the two, making the descriptions of Yeardley's death all the more unfathomable.

Based on police reports related to Huguely's interview with Officer Lisa Reeves, the violence he unleashed on Yeardley was tremendous. He went to her apartment and found the front door open. He walked inside and discovered the door to Yeardley's bedroom locked, so he kicked it in with his right leg, scraping his calf in a drunken rage. He had simply wanted to talk, he told Reeves, but it's unclear if anything was said before he grabbed Yeardley and shook her as her head repeatedly bashed into a wall. At some point, he noticed blood pouring from her nose, but, he claimed, he had no idea how badly she was hurt. His fury left behind crimson stains. Within hours, those stains would be swabbed by forensic investigators aiming to piece together what led to the young woman's death.

Parts of Huguely's story troubled police from the start. He told Reeves that when he left, Yeardley was clothed. However, her roommates reported that she was lying facedown and topless on her bed when they arrived. Huguely, too, said he visited just to talk, but when he left, he stole Yeardley's computer—which Reeves would soon learn contained Yeardley's response to an angry e-mail Huguely had sent.

The unavoidable imagery of Yeardley's lifeless body, her pretty face battered and bruised, was too much for many to bear.

"Just to hear that anybody in the UVA community could be suspected of that, regardless of the relationship, does give you a sense of unease," Drew Cook, a twenty-two-year-old senior, told the Associated Press. "Everybody's kind of taking a wait-and-see approach."

Yeardley's sorority sisters weren't the only ones hurting. Young men—both in overlapping fraternities, and members of the men's lacrosse team—seemed dumbstruck. They were big men on campus, both literally and figuratively, and yet they had failed to protect someone who needed help. They had lost one friend at the hands of another.

"I'm sure the boys are suffering just as much," friend Amy Appelt told a reporter. "I'm sure they loved Yards just as much as we did."

Chapter 7

After two days of stunned agony on campus, hundreds of University of Virginia students gathered on the Lawn, the heart of Jefferson's Academical Village, in a show of tearful unity Wednesday night. They sat shoulder-to-shoulder, spread out across the pasture-like setting that in just three weeks was to be the site of a joyous graduation—in which Yeardley Love was supposed to get her degree in political science. Young, tear-streaked faces were illuminated by the dull glow of votive candles. The vigil began with an a cappella version of the Pretender's "I'll Stand By You"—setting the we're-in-this-together tone for the evening.

Outside the university's amphitheater, volunteers plucked white ribbons from overflowing baskets and passed them out to people as they arrived. White ribbons have been adopted by domestic violence awareness advocates to put a spotlight on violence against women.

Ashley Twiggs, then a Charlottesville resident and freelance photographer, crouched on the lawn with her camera, scanning the crowd with her lens. She had first heard about the tragedy while getting her car's oil changed Monday. She and a few others were watching television as they waited for their cars to be returned.

"I think I live right near there," one of the nearby men uttered in surprise.

As a photojournalist regularly handed freelance news assignments, Twiggs immediately knew that she'd soon be asked to help cover the slaying. She was right; *C-VILLE Weekly* first asked her to take an image of Huguely's and Yeardley's apartments to show just how close they were. Twiggs at first tried a shot on the same side of the street so that one of the buildings sat in the foreground with the other in the background, but the angle seemed wrong. So she crossed 14th Street Northwest, attached her 17–55mm lens, and shot wide. The image illustrated perfectly that a single building separated the victim from the accused. Even more, it highlighted how carefree things had been just before the death: blue and orange balloons dangled from the FOR RENT signs outside of Yeardley's building.

Now, as mourners gathered at the evening vigil, Twiggs again pressed viewfinder to eye to capture the story. She snapped images of young adults huddled, their faces solemn and drawn, as they sat cross-legged on the grass.

"It was very somber, very heavy," Twiggs later recalled. "There were a lot of people there, and there was, at that point, a sense of just shock. No one really knew what was going on, but what they did know was bad."

Twiggs, who was then pregnant with her first child, had anticipated that hundreds would show up, so she had her husband drop her off and pick her up from the event. It was a wise move; the turnout was even bigger than she had expected. She steadied her camera as the light grew dim to capture the orange glow of the candles. From a distance, she heard someone sobbing. The sound was enveloped by the amphitheater around which the students had gathered, then echoed back into the crowd. Twiggs couldn't pinpoint the source. It sounded as though everyone, and no one, was crying at once.

As the Virginia Belles, the university's female a cappella group, sang the Pretenders' chorus—"I'll stand by you/ won't let nobody hurt you"—the song seemed both appropriate in tone and ironic in message, given that Yeardley had died alone, allegedly at the hands of a man who was supposed to care for her. Twiggs snapped more photographs as the women, all wearing black knee-high dresses, harmonized on stage.

Sarah Elaine Hart, president of the fourth-year class, approached a microphone inside the amphitheater and verbalized the anger that welled in many.

"What was done to Yeardley was the most egregious violation of trust," she said. "This is a community that is founded upon and believes in honor, but there was no honor in the violent attack that took her life."

"The way in which we have lost Yeardley has shaken us," Student Council President Colin Hood said. "We find ourselves with more questions than answers."

Casteen, the university's president, also stepped to the podium. He began to speak somberly, deliberately, his voice strained with emotion. As he looked across the packed lawn, he lamented them having to be there. It was supposed to be a time for renewal and new beginnings, he told the hushed crowd, but instead, the hundreds had gathered to grieve the ending of a life cut far too short—one "full of promise and high prospects," he said. A life that was not unlike any other student's at UVA.

University students had seen Casteen speak before—usually at press conferences about tuition rates and campus expansions. That Casteen seemed different than the one standing before them now. Before he was stoic; now, he seemed doleful.

"I want to talk tonight about Yeardley Love, and I want to talk about you, and about this community, about us. Some of what I have to say is very hard. Bear with me, and listen," he implored.

Little was yet known about Yeardley's death, he said. The prosecutor had charged a classmate with murder, and a defense lawyer had described her death as an accident. But those details were scant and piqued more questions than provided answers. Besides, Casteen said, this evening's gathering wasn't the forum to analyze evidence and weigh guilt. All that would happen in due time in the courtroom.

Instead, he said, this forum was to acknowledge "what

we do know," he said. That was that Yeardley had accomplished a lot in her short life, that she was respected by those around her—classmates, faculty mentors, coaches and sorority sisters, but most of all her family—and that she excelled in everything she strove to do in life. Yeardley did nothing to deserve being attacked and beaten, as the police reported she had been, he said. In fact, no woman—no person—deserved such cruelty.

Casteen paused, then turned his focus to the countless gathered before him.

"My hope for Yeardley, and for you, is that her dying inspires an anger, a sense of outrage . . . and wherever Yeardley's name is recognized that no woman, no person in this place, this community, this state, our nation need either fear for her safety or experience violence for any reason—not because of her sex, not because of her size, not because of an attacker's advantage or arrogance or mindless sense of right to abuse, to harm, perhaps to kill; and then that memory of Yeardley's name, her personal strengths, her successes, her human worth may survive the memory of the dying about which we ache tonight, and that you and we and all who know the story of Yeardley Love will learn the lessons of her living, of her life."

Casteen took a breath, then changed focus. He wanted to talk about the students who sat before him, he said. They'd sprawled on the Lawn, and by now, Yeardley's teammates and Coach Julie Myers couldn't hold back the tears. Their faces contorted with grief, they listened as Casteen asked each in the audience to walk away from the event empowered. He asked that they take away a determination to speak up for themselves, to act when they see or hear about others suffering from abuse or violence. He beseeched those in unhealthy relationships to seek help—to talk to a faculty member, the police, a family member, or to even seek out Casteen himself.

"If you fear for yourself or for others any form of violence, act," he said. The support belonged to them already; it was theirs inherently. They had the right to demand support, to expect it. They had an innate right to respect and assistance, and they had a duty to reach out to friends in need.

"Don't hear a scream, don't watch abuse, don't hear stories of abuse from your friends and keep quiet," he said. "Speak out."

Some huddled on the grass nodded in agreement. The air was heavy, weighed down by countless what-ifs and should've-beens. Not a week ago, the average student's biggest concern was cramming for finals. Now, all that seemed trivial. Now, they listened to a man whom most had revered and some had feared. And he was promising to take them to the police if they ever were in danger.

He asked that they leave the Lawn that night with the knowledge that the blows and abuse Yeardley had apparently endured in her final moments threatened the community as a whole. Left un-confronted, it could end more than individual lives; it could destroy a culture. The best way to honor Yeardley and her life was for the students to move forward and protect each other, to preserve the community of trust. Choose to recognize the evils in the world and confront them, he implored. Promise that in the years to come, you'll remember this loss, he told them, and "tuck away in your soul the knowledge that neither Yeardley Love nor any woman ever attacked has deserved it." No one has to die such a senseless, vicious death, he said. He asked those gathered to protect themselves and each other, not just now but for the rest of their days.

Before Casteen stepped away from the mike, he closed: "May God bless Yeardley Love."

Even journalists who sat quietly among the students found themselves moved by the event. For Brendan Fitzgerald, Casteen's words reverberated strongly. He had never seen Casteen so emotional.

"He appeared very choked up," Fitzgerald recalled, "and having been to numerous events where he offered speeches, to hear his voice waver was a novel experience for me. It was something I hadn't anticipated."

Looking around at the grief-stricken students, Fitzgerald

said he "wasn't deaf to the students who had a very difficult time remaining stoic."

Twiggs's chest weighed heavy as she looked at the sea of somber faces.

"It was profoundly sad," she recalled. "I live in the community. You can remove yourself from stuff [as a journalist], but at the same time, I live here. I could feel it."

As dusk turned to nightfall, members of the university's male a cappella group, the Virginia Gentlemen, silently filed on stage. A low, amber-hued stage light cast tall and eerie shadows on the wall behind them as they began, quietly at first, to sing. A few words in, the song was recognizable— Pink Floyd's "No More Turning Away"—as soloist Daniel Bennett (UVA '10) mustered more power behind his vocals.

In the second stanza, Bennett was joined by thirteen Gentlemen, all wearing matching khakis, sports coats and bow ties, in the somber song, and as Charles Dyer (UVA '10) stepped forward for a brief harmony, the gravity of the lyrics was undeniable.

The song's words described the "pale and downtrodden" as being speechless, uniting in a wordless alliance. Though the song doesn't specifically address violence against women, the repetition of the haunting title—"no more turning away"— seemed eerily appropriate.

As the men sang, the sky turned from deep lavender to nearly black.

"It's not enough just to stand and stare," the men sang. "Is it only a dream that there'll be no more turning away?"

When the song ended, the only audible sounds were hushed sobs from the Lawn. And with that, the men bowed their heads, and slowly left the stage.

Chapter 8

Before Yeardley's remains could return home to Maryland, doctors first needed to examine her lifeless body one last time. It would be a crucial step in evidence gathering, as medical examiner William Gormley noted not only the young woman's height, weight, ethnicity, and injuries, but also searched for clues that might shed light on her last minutes alive.

Gormley, a well-respected pathologist who graduated from the Medical College of Ohio in 1977, worked as an assistant chief medical examiner in Virginia's Richmond-based Central District. Not every death in Virginia requires an autopsy, but many do—those who die in state mental facilities or people who appeared to be in good health and die while unattended by a physician, for example. As someone who died from what appeared to be traumatic injury, Yeardley certainly qualified.

Virginia was one of the first states in the country to institute a statewide medical examiner system in 1946, abolishing its previous coroner system. The difference is significant: Coroners are politicians who win their posts by election. They often have no background in medical or forensic science. But medical examiners are licensed to practice medicine, and most are trained in forensic pathology. They're schooled specifically in determining both cause and manner of death—the former being the specific method of death, the latter being an umbrella category. In simpler terms, "gunshot to the head" is the cause of death; "homicide," the manner.

Medical examiners conduct medicolegal death investigations, which require an eye for both medical and legal detail. They typically begin with external observations, then shift to the inside of the body. In Yeardley's case, many details would have been noted, and many photographs taken, to enumerate the injuries to her face that Reeves had so quickly spotted upon entering the 14th Street bedroom. Undoubtedly there were other autopsies to conduct that day—Virginia opens about 6,000 death cases per year, the autopsies for which are spread among just four facilities—but none would have been more pressing. Statewide, there's just more than one murder a day—on par with an average year in the city of Detroit—very few of which make national headlines. Yeardley would have become the state's top priority.

Gormley no doubt checked for the types of clues that help solidify a prosecutor's case, such as using tape to lift any fibers from Yeardley's body or panties and checking under her fingernails in the hope of discovering her attacker's skin cells. He likely examined her neck for evidence of bruising, a sign of strangulation. Internally, he would have dismissed as "unremarkable" her organs, which appeared normal for someone her age, and taken notes highlighting any abnormalities he encountered. All of this would have been standard procedure for Gormley, but in Yeardley's death, he would have had to spend far more time inside her head than most, taking notes and photographs on the damage done to her brain. Surely Gormley could have predicted, even without Lawrence's "accidental death" comment, that the defense would attempt to minimize the damage George had done when he slammed Yeardley's head against a wall.

While Gormley documented his findings, Yeardley's family made arrangements for her funeral. Sharon Love planned a Saturday funeral in Towson, a few minutes' drive from their hometown of Cockeysville, close to Notre Dame Prep. The mass and preceding visitations were announced in newspaper obituaries:

> LOVE, Yeardley R. On May 3, 2010 Yeardley Reynolds Love, beloved daughter of Sharon Donnelly Love and the late John Love; devoted sister of Lexi [sic] Love . . .

The family asked that memorial contributions be made to The Yeardley Love Memorial Fund at Notre Dame Prep, or to the Yeardley Love Women's Lacrosse Scholarship Fund for the Virginia Athletic Foundation.

In today's world of online obituaries, Yeardley's, which ran on the *Baltimore Sun* Web site, reached thousands more people nationwide than it would have in pre-Internet days. And the impact was huge. More than 500 people signed her online guest book to express condolences, with posters listing their hometowns from across the country—Georgia, Florida, California, Wisconsin. One poster, from Austin, Texas, wrote: "What a tragic loss not only to your family, but even to us who did not know Yeardley." Another poster from Columbus, Georgia, wrote: "May God wrap you in his arms in this time of sorrow. Yeardley was such a beautiful young woman.

Some directed their notes to Sharon and Alexis directly. They asked that the women hold tight to their Christian faith and recognize that Yeardley was now with Jesus. Some identified themselves as belonging to the UVA community—either past graduates or current students—while others were parents of college-aged young women and men who described the ordeal as a "parent's worst nightmare." Others still had lost loved ones to the hands of a batterer—nieces and daughters taken from them too soon.

But the virtual guest book was for more than catharsis for strangers. Several people who said they knew Yeardley left heartfelt messages, clearly using the forum as a place to commiserate with others in grief.

"She was such a kind, sweet girl and her beautiful smile and eyes will live on forever," wrote Tiffany Hales, who claimed to be a former co-worker of Yeardley's father. "She is in heaven with her dad."

Brian Frederick, Yeardley's former Cockeysville rec coach, posted the same letter that was to appear in the *Towson Times*. He had to miss Yeardley's funeral, he explained, because his own daughter was graduating college, and he believed Yeardley would prefer he celebrate with her friend rather than mourn at her interment.

Sharon Donnelly Love asked that the media not attend her daughter's May 8 funeral service, but some reporters attended the visitation beforehand and described the dark wooden casket in which Yeardley was laid to rest, and the pink flowers with green stems that covered it. Visiting hours were held at the Ruck Funeral Home, and thousands arrived to pay their respects. Many had never met Yeardley, but they were touched nonetheless, brought to tears by the description of the tragedy of her final moments. Women who themselves had been battered, trapped in dangerous relationships with volatile men, wondered if they had been spared a similar fate. Despite some family members' quiet comments that Yeardley was no "shrinking violet" who would have tolerated physical abuse, the young woman's broad smile still was destined to become entwined with domestic violence.

"This isn't easy," one friend said to another as they approached Yeardley's casket at the funeral. A newspaper reporter overheard.

Photographs of Yeardley in happy times—dressed in Halloween costumes, celebrating victories with her lacrosse teammates—were strewn about the funeral home and displayed on a laptop slide show. Flowers and cards sent in sympathy came from those closest to Yeardley, as well as from complete strangers. One came from CNN's *Larry King Live*. The funeral service program passed out the next day featured a photograph of Love as a child dressed as an angel. Underneath the image was this quote: "Truly great friends are hard to find, difficult to leave, and impossible to forget"—her senior quotation from her 2006 yearbook. On the program's

back cover was the essay Yeardley had written during her
freshman year of high school. Its final line read, "So far my
life has been filled with joy and happiness, and I hope to
keep living my life that way."

Filling the pews were Yeardley's friends, family, and sorority sisters from Kappa Alpha Theta. UVA president John
Casteen attended as well. Each was handed a booklet that
included the now-haunting essay.

Though the funeral mass was private, nearly a dozen television cameramen lined up across the street, along with many
more photographers. Reporters from some outlets donned
muted outfits to quietly sit among the mourners who attended.
Some speakers told of Yeardley's goofiness and her generosity, and more than one commented on her contagious smile.

But it was UVA's lacrosse coach who led the congregation in a cheer.

The Cavaliers, she explained, took turns before each game
leading teammates in a pregame chant. "One, two, three, together, 'Hoos!" they would cry, invoking the team's nickname.
One day, as Love led the cheer, she accidentally counted to
four.

This Saturday morning, as Myers' remembrance caused
laughter to mix with mourners' tears, Myers counted to four.
On cue, the congregation responded in one voice: "Together,
'Hoos."

From then on, Cavaliers would always count to four, Myers said.

The massive Cathedral of Mary our Queen, built in 1959
and visited by Pope John Paul II some 36 years later, seated
1,400 people, which on this day was far too few. Congre-
gants spilled from the pews into the aisles. More mourners
still gathered outside, watching as a solemn sea of orange
and blue—the Cavalier colors—followed out the casket in
hushed respect. Some Notre Dame students wore their
uniforms—the same attire Yeardley herself had donned six
years earlier to her father's funeral. Others wore blue and
black ribbons and Yeardley's initials: *YL*. Yeardley's mother
and sister sat in the front. Had May 3 never happened, they

instead would have been preparing to attend Yeardley's graduation. One photographer snapped an image of Lexie, Yeardley's older sister, with a tissue pressed to her cheek, her mother's hand resting compassionately on her left shoulder.

But there were moments of levity as well. Julie Myers described Yeardley as a girl willing to ham, sometimes goofing around with propeller hats to make others laugh. She recalled when Yeardley tried to cook French bread after moving into an apartment with roommates. The attempt was a total failure, and the scorched bread filled the apartment with smoke, setting off fire alarms.

Yeardley was a rare mix of toughness and charm, she said.

"Yeardley Loves don't come around very often," she said. "She was truly remarkable, not because she tried to be, but because she just was. It came easy for her to be great, to be kind-hearted, welcoming, encouraging and engaging to all who knew her. She was legitimately awesome."

After Myers asked the congregation to hold hands and chime, "1-2-3-4, together 'Hoos!" the gathering broke into applause.

But a shadow hid behind every smile. Nuns dressed in white sweaters, navy skirts, and black habits, who had carefully arranged the delicate floral spray before mourners filed into the church, watched somberly as Father Joseph Breighner began the Mass.

"Every one of us is in a state of shock," said Breighner, known affectionately as "Father Joe" and author of a few spiritual paperbacks, including *When Life Doesn't Make Sense*. On the book's cover, Breighner looks pensive, his clerical collar peeking out from beneath a green windbreaker.

In his homily, he said Yeardley's friends and family could honor her life by living theirs the way she would have.

"She never made fun of anyone," Breighner said. "She always wanted others to feel good. . . . In memory of Yeardley, make the better choices from now on. Choose kindness instead of cruelty. Choose forgiveness instead of vengeance. Choose love instead of hate. Choose the right thing instead of the wrong thing."

Fr. Breighner, joined at Mass by Auxiliary Bishop Denis Madden, never mentioned George Huguely by name, but he reminded the congregation that Jesus preached forgiveness.

"At some point, we will have to forgive someone," he said. "Today may not be that day. It may not come for many days. But we will have to forgive, because it is the only way to heal."

He added that Yeardley's surname was apt.

"Two thousand years ago, a young Jewish rabbi named Jesus died a senseless, violent death. All he did and all he preached was love," the reverend said. "This past week, a woman has died a senseless, violent death. Her name was Love. And love is what her life is all about."

PART II

"This Guy Has Robbed Her"

Chapter 9

Within twelve hours of Yeardley's death, Charlottesville swarmed with local reporters. By the next night, Chief Longo—a broad-shouldered cop with a graying crew cut— had appeared on national talk shows hosted by television personalities such as Nancy Grace and Jane Velez-Mitchell. The interviews would be replayed often in the days that followed as more information trickled out about the case, no matter how minor.

Longo had started his career in Baltimore, graduating with a law degree from the University of Baltimore and being admitted to the Maryland Bar in 1993. For nearly twenty years, he worked on the Baltimore police force, rising through the ranks until he retired as Colonel in charge of Technical Services. After that, he accepted the top-cop post in Charlottesville. Longo was used to public speaking, regularly headlining lectures on ethics and professional standards for law-enforcement agencies. He also taught as an adjunct professor at Towson University, less than three miles from Notre Dame Prep, and served as law and business guest lecturer at the University of Virginia.

Despite his smarts and obvious speaking skills, Longo's words occasionally weighed him down as he tried to make sense of the tragedy on national television. It was a tough case even for a twenty-five-year law-enforcement veteran.

Grace repeatedly described Yeardley as "scrubbed in sunshine," a flowery turn of phrase perhaps not surprising from a prosecutor-turned-legal-commentator-turned-author, who in recent years had begun writing crime novels.

"Breaking news tonight," Grace boomed, her voice dripping with her Macon, Georgia roots. "Beautiful, talented star athlete, scrubbed in sunshine, just days before twenty-two-year-old co-ed Yeardley Love set to graduate UVA, her body found, likely still warm, battered, beaten, facedown in a pool of blood in her own bed, her life, so full of promise, cut short."

Grace called the case a "bombshell," and seemed outraged at the prospect of a bad guy with such stellar social standing.

"Oh, no, not a parolee, not a violent felon, not a drifter with a record! Suspect No. 1, another UVA athlete, a college lacrosse star turned killer."

Grace's overly animated vexation—and her quickness to convict—mirrored the country's. The George Huguelys of the world weren't supposed to turn into murder suspects. Even as reporters dug into his background looking for the dark triggers that might have precipitated such an evil turn, the most they uncovered was an idyllic childhood marred slightly by divorce. His legal run-ins had begun just two years prior, and while they were troublesome, they had never foreshadowed murder.

Courtney Stuart, the senior editor of the weekly newspaper *The Hook*, explained how the heartbreaking tale spread across the campus:

"We got word yesterday that there was a student that had passed away," said Stuart, who paused her own coverage of the case to appear on Grace's show via Skype. "At first, it was presented . . . as a possible alcohol overdose, but by the middle of the day yesterday, they had announced her name and also the arrest of George Huguely, both, of course, lacrosse players. Then over the course of the next twenty-four hours, details have been coming out . . . They've been pretty horrific."

Longo elaborated little on what he had already said publicly to reporters.

"Suffice it to say that investigators very quickly began looking at Mr. Huguely in this particular case, perhaps because of his relationship with Ms. Love and information that they began to gather from potential witnesses," he said. "They contacted him initially at his apartment."

By then, search warrant affidavits had been obtained by some media outlets. In them, Huguely was described as having made incriminating statements after waiving his Miranda rights. As he referenced the beating Yeardley endured, Longo's measured façade seemed to waver.

"The facts are horrific," said Longo, who was interviewed by phone. "They're shocking. They're incomprehensible. They're unthinkable. And to witness that, and particularly as a parent, to look at the body of a young girl who, as you said, you know, had so much to look forward to—it's just a terrible situation. And to have to sit here tonight and to hear the graphic description of how her body was discovered and to think, at home in a hotel room somewhere here tonight in Charlottesville, her mom is hearing that, is just completely troubling. And this is a very sad, sad set of circumstances for an entire community."

Longo declined to speculate on a cause of death, saying the autopsy was still pending, though some reporters had incorrectly begun reporting that Yeardley was strangled.

Grace, having invited a forensic pathologist, defense attorney, and prosecutor on the show, hammered Huguely's lawyer for his statement outside of the courthouse. "I couldn't believe my ears, so I got a printout to make sure 20/20 and 20/18 got it right," she said, referring in folksy manner to each of her eyes. She read Lawrence's statement declaring the death an "accident with a tragic outcome."

Grace cried bull.

"She was beaten to death. That is not an accident," she said, exasperated. "That is one blow, another blow, another blow, another blow until she bled through her nose, ears, and mouth."

Grace wasn't alone in her disbelief: Velez-Mitchell, also on CNN, declared it impossible for Yeardley's death to have been accidental. She called the slaying another incident in the "war on women," and invited law-enforcement analyst Mike Brooks to weigh in on the case.

"There's no way there's an accident here," Brooks said.

Velez-Mitchell incredulously asked Stacey Honowitz, a sex crimes prosecutor, how Huguely's lawyer could try to claim the death was accidental when the beating was apparently so vicious.

"Well, listen, he's not going to stand up and tell you that he intentionally killed her," Honowitz replied. "Then he'd be confessing, basically, on behalf of his client. So what he's trying to do is probably ease, you know, into people the notion that it was just a tragic accident in the hopes, maybe, that the prosecutors will re-look at this case and think about the relationship that they had, and maybe try to downfile it from a first-degree murder."

Predictably, the speculation had begun. And not just on the national stage.

Back in Charlottesville, defense lawyers who knew Francis McQ. Lawrence quietly dissected his first public statements about the case. Some thought it was too soon to declare anything accidental. After all, by saying Huguely didn't mean to kill her, Lawrence was implying that she indeed died at his client's hands. Perhaps that point wouldn't matter in trial, where comments made to reporters weren't likely to be repeated. But Lawrence's peers wondered if he had already dealt his client a fatal blow in the court of public opinion.

For Brendan Fitzgerald, the *C-VILLE Weekly* reporter, Yeardley's death wasn't the isolated incident that it had been portrayed to be by some national reporters. In fact, Yeardley was the seventh UVA student to die that academic year—making it an unusually tragic year.

"There wasn't similar national presence for previous instances," he said.

The deaths were all different. One student, twenty-two-year-old Stephanie Jean-Charles, had returned to her home in Haiti and was killed in the catastrophic January 12, 2010, earthquake that killed an estimated 230,000 people. Another student, twenty-six-year-old John Jones, was spelunking in November 2009 when he became stuck upside-down in Nutty Putty Cave about eighty miles south of Salt Lake City. Twenty-eight hours after he got stuck, he died, becoming the first known fatality at the cave. On December 14, Justin Key, a first-year business student, succumbed to the flu, according to his friends' Facebook memorial page. In January 2010, Scott May—a nontraditional student who enrolled in the university in his forties—died of natural causes after several long-term health problems. Matthew King, a graduate arts & sciences student, died April 19, 2010, in a cycling accident away from campus. Also in April, fourth-year student Joseph Arwood passed away at the University Medical Center after a fraternity brother found him unconscious one morning at their shared Sigma Phi Society house. Arwood's official cause of death has still not been publicly released.

In late April, the university's Student Council voted in favor of a bill to honor the six students who had passed away so far. On a Friday afternoon just weeks before graduation, about 200 students gathered to honor the six. Relatives of each student were invited. The bill, sponsored by Council President Colin Hood, while in reality inconsequential, was symbolically meant to "attempt to improve the rights, opportunities, and quality of life of every student in their honor."

Every college endures heartache and loss. A microcosm of outside society, campuses are just as likely as the non-campus world to have freak accidents, disease, and suicide. In a typical year, UVA might have lost three or four students, university officials said. But seven was unusual, and one being a homicide, allegedly at the hands of another student, was devastating and rare.

And yet, it wasn't the only homicide the Student Council

paused to remember. The remains of Morgan Harrington, a pretty Virginia Tech student, had been discovered in January in Charlottesville. Her case was the only one in the spate of recent tragedies to garner even a fraction of the national attention that Yeardley would receive just months later. She wasn't enrolled at UVA, but her disappearance had haunted many of the young adults on the Charlottesville campus.

Chapter 10

Twenty-year-old Morgan Harrington, a striking blond education major, had traveled to Charlottesville's John Paul Jones Arena for a Metallica concert October 17, 2009. She got separated from her friends when she wandered outside the arena hoping to find a bathroom. Without a ticket to get back inside, she called from her cell phone and told them not to worry about her, that she would find a way home. Witnesses described seeing a woman hitchhiking a few miles from the stadium, but Morgan never made it home. She was last seen walking across a bridge near busy Ivy Road wearing a black mini-skirt, black tights, knee-high black boots, and a Pantera T-shirt.

A few days passed before officials were satisfied that Morgan hadn't simply stayed over with a friend. The search frenzy began. Morgan's purse and cell phone were discovered in a parking lot near the university's track and baseball fields, but there were no signs of a struggle, and certainly no Morgan. Ominously, the battery in her cell phone was missing, a possible attempt by an attacker to keep authorities from tracking her down via pings off cell phone towers.

The search stretched into a nearby valley. Students not only from UVA and Virginia Tech, but also from Shenandoah Valley's James Madison University, combed the targeted areas and passed out flyers alongside law-enforcement agents. Police painstakingly pieced together her movements from the time she left the arena, at about 8:30 p.m., until about an hour later when she was last spotted on the Copeley Road bridge.

Virginia State Police Lt. Joe Rader used the media to issue a plea for information.

"Perhaps you saw someone stop a vehicle," Rader said. "Perhaps you saw this young lady get into a vehicle. Somewhere out there lie the answers or lies the vital link."

The disappearance ate away at the area's college students. How many times had they walked alone in Charlottesville at 9:30 p.m.? Whatever happened to Morgan could have happened to anyone.

While the arena was criticized for refusing Morgan re-entry, many who attended the concert were shocked that anything had gone awry. Despite heavy metal's harsh reputation, this particular concert was remarkably placid.

"The thing that surprised me the most of all about this concert was how calm it was and how safe and in control the security was in the venue," one concertgoer said. "There were policemen inside and out."

After Morgan had been missing about a month, police released a description of a Swarovski crystal necklace she had been wearing in hopes of drumming up any new leads. The chunky piece was made up of large crystal chain links, an edgy addition for a planned night of head banging.

The case generated national attention. Morgan was, after all, gorgeous and white, two prerequisites for widespread coverage. And her parents' appeals were too dolorous to ignore.

"Please come home," Dan Harrington, her father, said while fighting back tears. "If someone has Morgan, please let her come home safely."

"She has her Halloween costume picked out, and we'd love to see her walking around in it," said Gil Harrington, Morgan's mother. "She's got a dog that's missing her. Let's bring her back, and she can address all these things, so she can be back with her family."

The anguish was amplified with dozens of Morgan sightings nationwide, not only locally in Virginia, but from as far away as New Mexico. Police couldn't discount the reports, especially considering that in recent years several college students had faked their own kidnappings to get attention. But Morgan's family and friends knew this wasn't in her makeup. She would never intentionally cause her family so much grief. Besides, she did what she was told, her father told reporters: "I called her two weeks ago and told her to get her flu shots. She got it the next day."

As the search dragged on, Gil Harrington took to a blog to regularly post updates in hopes of generating tips for police. Christmas was unbearable, she had written on the blog (www.findmorgan.com) on December 29, 2009:

"Our pain was sharpened by expectations for this holiday season. I found Christmas compromises that were acceptable to me. It was challenging to have a new, different tradition that acknowledges Christmas and still honors our missing Morgan. Our décor was pretty muted, but what has been done is genuine and celebratory of love and caring. It's tricky, though, to find that path. Every time I go into our closet, Morgan's Christmas gifts reproach me from the top shelf. And then despair almost takes me out."

As the weeks continued, Gil Harrington's words alternated between heartrending and hopeful. She balked at the police's characterization of Morgan's disappearance as an "abduction."

"It is soft language," she wrote. "Abduction means to move away from—that is a passive euphemism for what has occurred here. Morgan was not 'moved away' from us—she was *ripped* away, *severed* from us! She was *amputated* from her life. The person who did this *robbed* her from us. I think even the posters could better reflect what has been inflicted on our family—Morgan is not missing—like my frequently misplaced reading glasses—SHE was stolen!!"

That was written January 12, 2010. Three weeks later, Morgan's parents got the nightmarish phone call: A farmer had spotted a skeleton on his rural Albemarle County land about an hour's drive northwest of Richmond. The Harringtons rushed to the area. All that remained were bones, but they were sure it was their daughter. DNA testing eventually proved they were right. (Though authorities determined that she actually died in 2009, near the time of her abduction, the remains' January discovery placed the homicide statistically in 2010 for record-keeping purposes.)

In February, Morgan's death was officially ruled a homicide.

Because crime is so rare in the area, and because Morgan, like Yeardley, had been slain in her prime, the case seemed tailor-made for crime-hungry media. The experience left many in Charlottesville disenchanted. It seemed reporters only swooped into town for horrific news, splashing images of the picturesque city alongside gruesome descriptions of tragedy. Morgan's parents seemed to recognize that public attention was a necessary evil in drumming up leads in the case. It was at their prompting that police released a sketch of a possible suspect after DNA testing connected Morgan's remains with the sexual assault of a Fairfax City woman in 2005. Dan Harrington, Morgan's father, said that based on the location of his daughter's makeshift burial spot—farmland that is difficult to reach by car—he was certain the killer was someone local. "Someone has to be comfortable with knowing the area, knowing where to go," he told the *Today Show*. The Harringtons also were vocal in their disappointment at what they perceived as foot-dragging by the Charlottesville police. On January 23, Gil Harrington took to the blog:

"I am concerned about the complacency in Charlottesville. I am feeling a tendency to downplay Morgan's abduction, to protect the idyllic reputation of the city. I bought into that idyllic image until my daughter was stolen there. I understand the reluctance to be associated with this crime. I myself would prefer not to be known as the Mom of a missing girl. Charlottesville would prefer not to be recognized as the location of abduction. But there is no going back."

Despite the offering of $150,000 in reward money—
$100,000 from Morgan's family and $50,000 from the band
Metallica—Morgan's murder remains unsolved.

Five months after Morgan's bones surfaced, as TV cameras
choked the usually peaceful street on which Yeardley and
Huguely lived, it seemed like déjà-vu for Charlottesville
residents. Frustrated with the negative attention, many passersby ignored reporters' questions and looked perturbed
when caught on film for B-roll, or supplemental footage to
be interspersed with interviews and talking-head experts
opining about the case. One Boylan Heights employee told a
reporter she was tired of talking about the case. She had
been interviewed three times already that day, she said.

Journalists tried to gobble up whatever morsels of detail
they could, talking to people on the street and interviewing
area business employees. Those wanting to dig deeper, to
find out if Yeardley had any clue she was in danger or to
learn if there was a broader lesson to be gleaned from the
tragedy, were shut down. Unlike in Morgan's case, where
the missing girl's parents invited journalists into her bedroom to ensure she was seen as person and not merely a
statistic, Yeardley's loved ones were mum. Surely they were
blindsided and overwhelmed by the massive national attention. And unfed journalists become all the more ravenous. It
seemed everyone remotely connected to the Loves and Huguelys were contacted in one way or another—by phone, by
e-mail, through social networking sites. The less information reporters get on a high-profile, competitive story, the
more desperate they become for any tidbit of information.
Sometimes the perseverance pays off with someone landing
a scoop; other times, it backfires, causing people to clam up.
The handful of friends who had been willing to talk to the
media were quickly asked by Yeardley's family to quit responding, and they complied. Calls to Sharon and Lexie
Love were met with "no comments" and assurances that
other people close to Yeardley would decline to comment as

well. The only family member to speak, albeit briefly, was Granville Swope, Yeardley's uncle—the UVA alumnus who had once been a star lacrosse player. Known to Yeardley as "Uncle Granny," he called his niece a "delightful lady in every respect."

"She had a great future," Swope told a reporter. He accused Huguely of robbing her of it.

Yeardley's sorority sisters were clearly floored by the loss. They huddled on the front porch of their three-story brick Kappa Alpha Theta home and embraced in tears. Nevada Thompson, identifying himself as the sorority's cook, answered reporters' knock on the front door and somberly said they weren't ready to comment.

"We're in mourning," he said.

A pall hung over the entire university. Normally early May buzzes with end-of-year activities, eleventh-hour cram sessions for finals, and graduation parties galore. For Yeardley's sorority sisters especially, the joy had been sucked out of their final month on campus. Outwardly, they said little, posting a one-sentence mention of the tragedy on their blog that Yeardley was a wonderful person and that her "sisters" were praying for her family. The posting prompted responses from "other Theta sisters" that echoed the sentiment. One woman wrote: "I hope your warm memories of Yeardley carry you through this difficult time."

Courtney Schaefer, the chapter's president, issued a statement: "We are in a state of mourning, and for the respect and privacy of Yeardley and her family are not ready to comment further on the situation." Schaefer and other sorority sisters declined to speak with reporters even months later, saying they had promised Yeardley's family that they would remain silent until after the case went to trial.

Though the public sentiment was in their favor, Yeardley's family didn't want conclusions reached before trial for fear that a potential jury would be tainted. In declining one interview, Sharon Love, Yeardley's mother, said that her primary concern was "doing right" by her daughters, and assured one reporter that answers would come in time.

Chapter 11

Just as Love's death seemed to eclipse all other news in Charlottesville, reporters back in Baltimore saw a community reaction like few others. By the end of May 4's broadcast of *Good Morning Maryland*, reporter and anchor Megan Pringle knew the station would stay on top of the story at every turn—for better or worse.

If someone ever sat down to map the characteristics required for a case to infiltrate the American consciousness, many of its bullet points would coincide with the Yeardley Love homicide. Attractive victim, check. Life full of potential, check. Loving upbringing, check. Unlikely suspect, check. Nothing in Yeardley's background remotely hinted that her life could someday end in such brutal fashion—and that made her a perfect victim for Americans to rally behind.

People immediately began calling WMAR with stories. They knew the Loves, some said, and remembered how devastated Sharon Love had been when her husband passed away a few years prior. Even at gas stations, people talked about the case. They were sickened by the news, and many asked whether funds had been raised to help pay for funeral costs or start a scholarship in Yeardley's name. (There were.) For Pringle, a Michigan native turned Maryland transplant, it was the first time she fully fathomed just how small a town the big city of Baltimore really was.

"Baltimore and the surrounding communities are very close knit," explained Pringle, who moved to Baltimore in 2007. "When people ask, 'Where did you go to school?' they don't mean what college. They mean where you went to high school. It's been a very tough place to meet people. People who grew up here and went away to college come back, and they're still friends with people they went to high school with."

The Baltimore area is specked with private Catholic high schools. Even Pringle's co-anchor sent his daughters to institutions similar to Notre Dame Prep, where Yeardley graduated. Jamie Costello, who has worked for WMAR for twenty-four years, said some parents send their children to private religious schools for the theology. Just as many are looking for the best mix of academics and sports. Increasingly, the private schools' lacrosse programs have become big draws, Costello said, because talented players can secure hefty scholarships for top-rated universities.

Baltimore City Public Schools long ago earned itself a lackluster reputation. In the 1990s, the city and the state of Maryland swapped barbs, each blaming the other for failing students. In 1995, the city even sued the state, saying it had violated the Maryland constitution by failing to give students an efficient education. The state fought back, saying the city had mismanaged the district. After an all-out public brawl, a resolution was finally reached that called for the state to give the district more money and, in exchange, Maryland would have more control in running the city's schools. The plan, as intended, only lasted a few years, but the criticisms lobbed at the district never seemed to stop. Newspaper editorials regularly called on the politicians in power to strengthen the schools. In 2006, for example, the Maryland State Board of Education aimed to revamp the whole system, from instruction to leadership to school management. State Board members said too many schools weren't making the grade.

The public district's mediocre reputation prompted many

in Baltimore and surrounding areas to seek out private institutions. Schools such as the Institute of Notre Dame (pronounced "dahm"), which came before Notre Dame Prep, were deeply rooted in their communities and had stellar reputations. IND, as the all-girl Baltimore institute is called, boasts alumnae such as former U.S. Speaker of the House Nancy Pelosi and barrier-breaking NBC news anchor Catherine "Cassie" Mackin. IND opened in 1847; when it became overcrowded, the School Sisters of Notre Dame opened the Notre Dame of Maryland Collegiate Institute for Young Ladies in 1873. Notre Dame's Towson campus continued to turn out noteworthy graduates, including Susan Aumann, a Republican member of the Maryland House of Delegates representing the 42nd District in Baltimore County.

Students at the various Baltimore-area private schools invariably know each other, either from overlapping during elementary or middle schools, or from competing against each other in high school sports. Many still hang out at the same summer swimming holes and play at the same recreation centers. Jamie Costello said most grow up with lacrosse sticks in their hands. Those who didn't know Yeardley personally felt as though they did, and the sense that the community had lost one of its own was overwhelming. Even more telling, many Baltimore residents knew of the Huguely family because they followed high school lacrosse—never mind that Bethesda-based Landon was nearly an hour's drive from Baltimore.

"When you're here, everybody knows everybody," said Costello, an Overlea High School graduate. "They all play one another—the DC schools play the Baltimore schools. Everyone overlaps."

The outpouring after Yeardley's death was immense, Pringle said, and the station's coverage reflected it. In the first days, *Good Morning Maryland* ran multiple stories. Reporters kept tabs on both the legal turns in Charlottesville and the community reaction back in Cockeysville and nearby Towson. Notre Dame Prep officials spoke briefly and solemnly about the loss, describing it as profound and unimaginable.

Pringle and Costello continued to field phone calls from heartbroken residents, some of whom called more to share their grief than assist with stories. There was a communal sense of loss beyond anything Pringle had experienced in Baltimore before.

Violent death is by no means rare in the big city, which reported 238 murders and non-negligent homicides to the FBI in 2009. Baltimore often ranks alongside Detroit, St. Louis, and New Orleans as having the highest per-capita murder and manslaughter rates in the country. Many of the slayings don't make the news at all simply because the media outlets don't have the staffing to keep up.

"Some people said there are lots of women the same age in Baltimore City who are murdered perhaps at the hands of domestic violence and it doesn't get the same kind of attention," Pringle said. "They said, 'You guys are just doing this story because it's a pretty, rich, white girl.'"

That prompted debate in the newsroom. Did Yeardley's case warrant more coverage than average? It was a tough discussion, Pringle said, in part because the station—like dozens of other media outlets nationwide—could not ignore the community's response to Yeardley's death. It was all anyone talked about. On the other hand, Pringle struggled with thoughts of the many other nameless women whose deaths were going unreported. She couldn't help but wonder whether the outcry would have been as deafening had Yeardley been black or poor.

The newsroom divide reminded Pringle of a similar debate in 2007, when the body of twenty-five-year-old Sintia Mesa was discovered in the trunk of her own car. Mesa, a former Morgan State University student, had been reported missing just days prior. Police found her cell phone and other personal items near a Dumpster. Then came her body. The other big news of the day was the death of racehorse Barbaro, notable in Baltimore especially because of the area's huge horseracing following. Barbaro won the 2006 Kentucky Derby, then shattered a leg two weeks later after a false start in the Preakness Stakes. Six operations failed to properly heal the horse, and it was euthanized January 29, 2007. WMAR producers planned to lead the evening news with the horse, followed by coverage of the gruesome discovery of Mesa's body. Some balked, arguing that a woman's life was worth more than a horse's. In the end, Pringle said it was a split decision: Barbaro led the 5 p.m. newscast, Mesa the 6 p.m.

Pringle's newsroom wasn't the only one contemplating its coverage of the case. The *Washington Post's* Daniel de Vise penned a column titled "Yeardley Love slaying: overplayed?" on the newspaper site's College Inc. blog. De Vise, responding to dozens of reader comments posted beneath the previous days' news stories, defended the case as being worthy of the *Post's* newsprint: It took place where homicides are rare, and the suspect was from an affluent Chevy Chase family. So while Yeardley being a Baltimore resident would perhaps not have elevated the story to warrant eight bylines in the Sunday edition, de Vise reasoned, Huguely's status as a local boy would have.

"What if Huguely were from Baltimore?" de Vise pondered. "I am sure we would still cover the story. But perhaps not on the front page, and perhaps not with seven or eight reporters."

He pointed to the Morgan Harrington homicide as proof that it takes more than a young, white female victim to land on the *Post's* coveted section fronts. Harrington's case had gotten ink, but never section-front ink, he wrote, "because Morgan wasn't local."

In the weeks surrounding Yeardley's death, there were dozens of fatal and nonfatal shootings plaguing both Washington, D.C. and Baltimore. Many weren't reported. In one, a nineteen-year-old pregnant woman was shot March 21. Three months later, a second young pregnant woman survived two bullets to her abdomen. Neither woman was white. Pringle said it was telling that the local news barely followed up on either story, while even the smallest developments in Yeardley's case often led the newscast.

* * *

Historically, stories about young adults slain in college settings have made substantial headlines. Eight months before Yeardley's death, the country was transfixed by another East Coast campus murder—that of twenty-four-year-old Annie Le, a doctoral student at Yale University who disappeared just days before she was to be married. While officials at first wondered if she fled in fear of the lifetime commitment she was facing, her friends and family knew that Annie had been happier than ever and was thrilled to be getting married. The days of worrying came to an end on September 13, 2009, the day she was supposed to walk down the aisle. Le's body was discovered crammed into a wall panel of a research building. She had been beaten and strangled.

Like Yeardley, Annie seemed on the cusp of greatness. She was attractive and intelligent, working in the medicine school's Department of Pharmacology. She wanted to cure cancer.

The media attention was so great that one TV producer ended up crushed in a bum rush at a news conference. *NBC News* producer Alycia Savvides reported that she "saw stars" after a cameraman—one in a throng gathered around a police spokesman—bashed into her with his camera, knocking her to the ground. Afterward, a police sergeant admonished the journalists.

"We don't want anyone getting hurt, all right? . . . Those cameras are heavy," Sgt. Anthony Zona said.

Spokesman Joe Avery reportedly slowly shook his head.

"I've never seen a bunch of people so out of control in my life," he said.

Two days later, the media mob reassembled for word that a suspect had been arrested: Raymond Clark III, a lab technician who worked in the building. On March 17, 2011, Clark pleaded guilty to murder and attempted sexual assault in a deal that called for a 44-year prison sentence. For the first time, prosecutors revealed that he had left behind evidence of a sexual assault and related DNA evidence. Until then, they had not publicly suggested a motive for the killing.

The arrangement, made under Connecticut's Alford Doctrine, allowed him to agree that the state had enough evidence to convict him without admitting he committed the crime.

In reporting Yeardley's death eight months after Annie's, some national outlets drew parallels. But there were other, seemingly long-forgotten cases that more closely mirrored the UVA student's death than that of Annie Le. One such case is that of Kathleen Roskot.

Roskot was a sophomore and star lacrosse player at New York's Columbia University in the fall of 1999 when she met Thomas Nelford Jr. Though Nelford, a struggling artist, had dropped out of school out of fear that academics would interfere with his artwork, he was bright and kind, and the two had much in common—including sports.

Nelford was a wrestler, making a big enough splash his freshman year to be named "one of the top" freshman wrestlers in the Ivy League by the Columbia sports media guide. Roskot, meanwhile, was known as an upbeat, go-get-'em type who often took to the field and told teammates, "It's a great day to get better," a high school teammate recalled at her funeral. Like Yeardley, she was all drive and discipline, and a powerful on-field competitor. With green eyes and dark hair, Roskot, too, had been raised in insularity by still-married parents in an affluent suburb—in her case, Long Island.

Over their six-month relationship, Roskot and Nelford spent a lot of time together, as college paramours tend to do. For Nelford, whose parents had dragged out a nasty divorce, Kathleen was his first real girlfriend. To her friends, Nelford perhaps seemed a little weird—more reclusive and arty than her previous boyfriends—but he never seemed violent.

Still, like Huguely, Nelford provided plenty of red flags in hindsight. Nelford's cartoons, published in the student newspaper, sometimes turned lugubrious. As the *New York Times* described:

> In one cartoon, a man and woman trade a series of insults and ugly confessions, culminating with the man saying, "The voices told me to kill you in your sleep."

The woman then screams, "April Fool's!"
The man replies, "That's today?"

Another strip, called *Sid, the Ugly Kid*, described a smart but troubled teenager who fantasized about slaughtering those who ridiculed him for being ugly, according to a New York *Daily News* account. In one panel that later haunted classmates, Sid finds a rope and hangs himself because "that fucking bitch broke my heart."

Roskot was discovered February 5, 2000, in her dorm room with her throat slashed. The security guards who found her naked body had been asked by her lacrosse coach to check on her after she failed to show up to a morning meeting at the school gym. An hour later, Nelford was found dead beneath a subway car uptown. He had his girlfriend's college ID and her wallet. Though the couple had been seen holding hands just hours before Roskot's death, friends said she was trying to end their relationship. It's the only motivation for the murder-suicide that police could offer. Busloads of classmates and lacrosse teammates attended her funeral.

Kathleen Roskot's death was basically in another media era, however, before twenty-four-hour news cycles and lightning-fast Internet communication. There were no Twitter or Facebook updates about her death, and today, only a handful of stories are accessible online. Occasionally, for a few years after her death, Roskot's name and a brief paragraph describing her untimely death appeared alongside a fresher crime for comparison's sake.

At the time, however, the impact was comparable to Love's death. The New York newspapers posed similar questions: What warning signs were missed? Were colleges doing enough to head off potentially deadly problems? *Time* magazine mentioned the case in 2001 in a story about a spate of recent campus suicides—at least two of which began with murders. Those accounts focused on whether campuses were ill equipped to deal with the mental-health issues buried deep inside some students.

But another issue was raised, too. Erica Goode, a *New York Times* writer, penned a piece called "When Women Find Love is Fatal," highlighting three separate domestic attacks that all occurred within the span of a weekend.

Roskot's case was the first. The next day, thirty-nine-year-old Marie Jean-Paul's husband cut her throat with a machete, then set her body ablaze. Soon after, eighteen-year-old Joy Thomas was shot in the head by her ex-boyfriend. Somehow, she survived. Goode's piece highlighted frightening domestic-violence statistics that were true in 1998: 32 percent of nearly 3,500 women killed in the country died at the hands of husband or boyfriend, either past or present. "In comparison, 4 percent of 10,666 male homicide victims in 1998 were killed by current or former intimate partners," she wrote.

"We haven't come close to affecting intimate partner violence and homicide the way we have other kinds of violence and assault," Dr. Susan Wilt, a representative with the New York City Department of Health, told Goode. "It remains a shocking issue that this is the main reason that women end up dead and that it occurs within the context of their home and family, where they are supposed to be safe.

"Women worry when they go out," Dr. Wilt added. "They should worry when they stay in."

Wilt had been tracking homicides by intimate partners in New York since 1990. She found, and other studies had borne out, that many of the deaths occurred either while or soon after the woman tried to leave the man.

"It's absolutely a crime of rage," she said in 2000. "There is a sense of 'How dare you think you can live without me?' "

It's a question resurrected at least once a year with a high-profile domestic violence slaying. Entire true crime libraries are dedicated to cases in which one half of a once-happily married couple kills the other. Domestic violence experts say the statistics can't possibly tell the whole story, either: There are many murders that likely were committed by one's partner that have gone unsolved for lack of evidence. Many of those cases eventually are forgotten by everyone but the victim's family, perhaps a reflection of a "she should have known better" mentality.

But in cases where the killer is known and the victim is a young college student, it seems more likely that people will pay attention. Such was the case with Kristin Mitchell's murder in 2005. And when Mitchell's father learned of Yeardley's death five years later, he felt an immediate connection—and a sinking in his stomach.

Kristin was a pretty, blond twenty-one-year-old studying food marketing at St. Joseph's University in Philadelphia. Like Yeardley, she had attended Notre Dame Prep, though after two years, she felt she didn't relate well with the privileged girls in Towson. She ultimately graduated from Mount de Sales Academy in Catonsville, Maryland, which was still a private institution, but was slightly less expensive. Also like Yeardley, Kristin had been devoted to helping the less fortunate, volunteering for Project Appalachia, which helped build homes for the poor, and spending time in other career-service programs at St. Joe's.

And like Yeardley, she met a guy who, police said, would cut her life short.

Bill Mitchell, Kristin's father, said there were red flags, but her circle of friends didn't know how to recognize them—least of all Kristin. At twenty-eight, Brian Landau, her boyfriend, was several years older, and he seemed to crave control. The text messages were constant. He'd ask her to skip her night classes at school to spend more time with him, then sulk if she said she needed to keep up on her schoolwork. He harped on her to lose weight, then accused her of cheating on him when she shed a few pounds. Brian seemed generous at first, buying Kristin gifts for no reason—but then used the gifts to argue that she owed him her loyalty.

"We learned these things after the tragedy," Bill Mitchell said. "We lived near Baltimore; she lived near Philadelphia. She was almost twenty-two, so you hope she's safe on her own."

She wasn't. Aside from an occasional comment about her

relationship with Landau not being "perfect," Kristin's life seemed more or less normal, and she focused on graduating. She began the joyless task of pursuing job interviews when potential employers set up shop at her college's job fairs in the fall of 2004. She seemed to do well making the rounds, talking with companies such as Hormel and Rubbermaid, but the big job, the one everyone wanted, was with General Mills, her father recalled.

Bill Mitchell coached her through her through several interviews, but they concentrated mostly on the big job interview with General Mills. He helped her prepare for the dreaded "where do you see yourself in five years" types of questions. Bill told his daughter to study the company and its competition. "Go in and win it," he encouraged her. "She had nothing to lose and I wanted her to be as confident as could be," Bill later recalled. "She was always good in an interview setting."

She dressed in power clothes—likely her favorite dark gray business suit—and nailed the interview, landing a job as a sales associate. She was to start her new career on July 8, 2005. Part of Kristin's new beginning, however, included ending things with Landau. She told some friends things just weren't working out. Then, on June 3, police discovered Kristin's bloodied body inside her apartment in Conshohocken, Pennsylvania. Her life had drained out from dozens of stab wounds.

Though the discovery was made in the morning, Bill Mitchell said he didn't learn about his daughter's death until that evening. Police, apparently busy collecting evidence, had trouble finding Bill's cell phone number and called the local police in Baltimore for help. Bill was in the car, driving, when his phone rang. He didn't understand why police would be calling, he recalled, and, suspicious when the officer insisted they talk in person, Bill agreed to meet at a public supermarket, just in case the person on the other end of the line was an imposter. He met the officer near the front doors of a Giant supermarket. The detective asked him to come into her police car, but Bill refused.

"This situation was just so out of place. I wanted to hear whatever the detective had to say right there at the doors of the supermarket," Mitchell later recalled.

The officer hesitated, then told him that Kristin had been killed.

"I walked to her car and sat in the passenger seat and called a detective in the Philadelphia area as I busily wrote notes on a legal pad," Mitchell recalled.

Mitchell had already told his wife that he was meeting with the police. Now he headed home to tell her and their son that Kristin was dead.

Landau, in a dramatic display of what hardened cops call overkill, stabbed his girlfriend more than fifty times. Her throat had been slashed six times; her back stabbed eleven.

He told police that the couple had been fighting, and each had stabbed the other, according to news reports in the days that followed. Though Landau went to a hospital for treatment of his own wounds, the medical examiner determined they were actually self-inflicted. Landau backtracked and said that some of the wounds were from an aborted attempt to kill himself. When the news stories came out, Bill Mitchell was mortified. The media had reported what Landau told police—including a claim that Kristin had slashed him when he rebuffed a sexual advance.

"Talk about insult to injury!" Mitchell said. "Imagine: Your daughter's been murdered and our newspaper sends up the tabloid version of what happened."

Kristin simply would not have grabbed a knife in anger, her father said.

"My daughter would have been panicky if she had a tiny splinter in her finger," he said. "She had no tolerance for pain, whether it be hers or someone else's."

District Attorney Bruce Castor Jr. opted not to seek the death penalty in the case but still charged Landau with first-degree murder, meaning life behind bars without parole. The court proceedings dragged. The trial, originally set for early December 2005, was postponed, leaving the Mitchells to endure their first Christmas without Kristin with no idea when the case would reach court.

"The wait," Bill recalled, "was numbing."

Eventually, a new date was set: June 5, 2006. But before the jury was selected, Landau hedged, pleading guilty to third-degree murder against the advice of his counsel. Facing life imprisonment, he opted instead to plead to the lesser charge and was sentenced to thirty years in prison, making him eligible for parole beginning in 2020.

The Mitchells considered it a victory. Though they wanted Kristin's killer locked behind bars and away from society forever, there was always the possibility of things going terribly wrong in the courtroom.

"A trial would have been devastating," Bill said. His family had already endured what he considered Kristin's character assassination in the days after her death. He never believed her fight with Landau was mutual; it wasn't in Kristin's character to grab a kitchen knife and stab another human being.

"We knew from advice we were given that in the courtroom, first they kill the person, then they kill the person's reputation," Bill said. "Kristin would not be there to defend whatever this man or his attorney would say about her. We would also be at the mercy of the judge."

And then there were the crime scene photographs. Kristin's body, mutilated and bloodied, looking nothing like the sweet-smiled cat lover her family knew and loved.

"It's as if she would have been murdered all over again," Bill said.

Mitchell and his wife, Michele, collaborated with two of Kristin's friends and created the Kristin Mitchell Foundation (www.kristinskrusade.org), a non-profit educational organization meant to raise awareness among young adults about the potential dangers of unhealthy dating relationships. Each year, it sponsors Kristin's Krusade, a 5K run/walk on St. Joseph's campus. The goal, her family said, is to warn young adults about the dangers they face in the hope that another family might be spared their pain.

It was a lofty aspiration, one reinvigorated with the death of Yeardley Love five years after Kristin's murder.

Bill learned about Yeardley through an e-mail from a friend who had attended UVA years earlier. The details released by police rang painfully familiar: A young Baltimore-area woman, well educated and immersed in volunteer work, killed by a boyfriend near graduation time at college. The Mitchells were drawn to the case; they attended Yeardley's wake and extended condolences to family members. It wasn't the first death since their daughters that struck a chord.

Somehow, though, Yeardley's death seemed different than the others. It seemed that this time, the whole world was paying attention.

Chapter 12

Yeardley Love's Death a Wake-Up Call About Domestic Violence

> *Domestic Violence While Dating: The Yeardley Love Case*

> *Yeardley Love's Murder Shines Light on Domestic Violence*

So read the headlines in the days after Yeardley's death. The newspapers and Web sites presented them with such fervor that someone who didn't know better would think that the death actually *did* serve as a wake-up call to society. In truth, such headlines have appeared time and again with little impact. Like the batterers they describe, the stories themselves are mired in a cycle, telling readers that this time, things really will get better. But they rarely do.

Even UVA's immediate response implied to some that the administration was viewing Yeardley's death as yet another "she should have known better" situation. Mike Gibson, chief of the university police, sent out an e-mail at 9:18 a.m. May 3 advising students that "the best defense is to be prepared and take responsibility for your own safety and for that of your friends and fellow students."

Among the "reminders" he laid out: Trust your instincts

and call nine-one-one if you're uncomfortable; avoid isolated areas and walking alone at night; keep your doors and windows locked; don't allow strangers to follow you into a locked building; never prop open card-reader doors; alert the police if you spot someone peeping into a residence or see someone watching, photographing, or filming an area.

None of the suggestions would have helped Yeardley the night she died. One student complained to a reporter that the advice consisted entirely of strategies to avoid stranger danger. "Locking doors and walking home with a friend will do little if that friend is the one who will later beat or rape you," the third-year student said.

In 2008, the Violence Policy Center, a nonprofit violence educational foundation, released a report titled *When Men Murder Women: An Analysis of 2008 Homicide Data.* Among the findings:

- For homicides in which the victim-to-offender relationship could be identified, 92 percent (or 1,564) of female victims were killed by someone they knew.
- Of those, 64 percent (or 997 women) were wives or otherwise intimately involved with the killers.
- "Women face the greatest threat from someone they know."

The only upside to the statistics was that the number of homicides across the board had been declining for years; however, the likelihood appeared even greater in 2008 than a decade earlier that a murdered woman had died at the hands of someone who had professed to love her. (Of course, the domestic crimes weren't limited to homicide. According to the National Institute of Crime Prevention, intimate partners commit more than one-quarter of rapes and sexual assaults, while strangers are responsible for about one in five sexual assaults. Most of the others are committed by acquaintances.)

Love and Huguely's case was considered more shocking than many, not only because both victim and accused were rich, popular, and successful, but because in hindsight, Huguely seemed wrapped in warning signs. Bob McDonnell, Virginia's governor, released a statement sending his "thoughts and prayers" to the Love family.

"Yeardley Love was a young woman of terrific talent and promise; her innocent young life was taken far too soon," the governor said. "While there are no words that can properly convey the sadness and pain that so many are going through, it is heartening to witness the positive way in which the student body of UVA has come together to remember Yeardley Love, mourn her passing, and help each other through this difficult time."

McDonnell closed the statement by saying he had asked UVA president John Casteen to meet with him "to study and fully consider every possible idea that could help prevent such a senseless crime from taking place in the future." The governor also took to *Good Morning America* to call for changes to how criminal records were reported. Yeardley's death could have been prevented if someone had spoken up, he said.

"There's ways to get information to administrators obviously from police, from court records, but it brings the larger question of the obligation to all of us in our society [that] if we see things that look wrong or strange behavior or violent behavior, to really be more involved," he said. "Particularly in domestic-related situations, can other people intervene because they see things going on . . . Maybe this could have been prevented."

By the time of the May 12 interview, McDonnell had already met with Casteen to talk about what legal steps could be taken to ensure that administrators learn of a student's violent history—either on or off campus. The governor said he wanted to avoid what he called a repeat of an "unprecedented tragedy."

"There's reviews going on now," he said. "We're conducting our own look at the facts after all the investigation is done. When the general assembly comes back next year, we can make those changes."

The case even grabbed the attention of Phil McGraw, better known to TV audiences as Dr. Phil. Three women a day die from domestic violence, he said, and women between twenty and twenty-four years old are in the highest risk group.

"This is a serious problem. These intimate relationships . . . are fueled by so much jealousy," he told *Good Morning America.* "It gets a lot of attention when it's a star athlete, but this is something that permeates every area of our society."

While Huguely's history of violence should have been noticed by school officials and coaches, McGraw didn't blame either for missing the warning signs. He did, however, call on schools to start teaching girls how to spot the risks and warning signs of an abusive relationship.

"This type of violence is preceded by emotional control, threats," he said. "If you're in a relationship like this, the last thing you want to do is confront your abuser. . . . Talk to somebody that you trust, somebody responsible that can help you find an exit strategy."

Ironically, that message had been delivered to UVA students just three weeks before Yeardley's death. Liz Seccuro, the founder of STARS—Sisters Together Assisting Rape Survivors—had been invited to the campus to talk about sexual assault at her alma mater. In 1984, as a freshman at UVA, Seccuro, still a virgin, was drugged and gang raped by three members of the Phi Kappa Psi fraternity. She didn't know any of her attackers, and, because of the drugs coursing through her system, could only remember one of the rapes graphically. The next day, she awoke on a sofa wrapped in a bloody sheet. Determined to learn her rapist's name, she foggily sifted through his mail before fleeing his apartment. Armed with his identity, she reported him to the then-Dean of Students. The dean's callous response still causes her to shudder: "Are you sure you didn't have sex with this man and you don't want to admit that you aren't a 'good girl'?"

Seccuro went to the hospital for treatment, then to the university police and to student health. She said she made dozens of reports, none of which went anywhere. The dean told her that the Charlottesville police had no jurisdiction over Phi Kappa Psi, and he said he spoke with her attacker, who claimed the sex was consensual. "I was told, in so many words and actions, to go away," Seccuro wrote in a column published online in the wake of Yeardley's death. "I did not, but my life was diminished. I felt that I did not matter."

Nothing happened in Seccuro's case for twenty years. It was then that she got a letter from her attacker, William Beebe, who wrote to her as part of his Twelve-Step recovery program. He said he got her home address by calling the university's alumni office, and that he had been following her whereabouts for nine years. He was sorry he raped her, he said. Seccuro took the letter to the Charlottesville police, which, as it turned out, did indeed have jurisdiction over the frat house where she was raped. Luckily for her, there was no statute of limitations on filing a rape charge.

It was during the lead-up to trial that Seccuro learned of Francis McQ. Lawrence and Rhonda Quagliana. The duo—known locally as Fran and Rhonda—represented Beebe. In March 2006, she faced her attacker in person and gave two hours of testimony at a preliminary hearing. The judge ruled there was enough probable cause for the case to go to trial.

Instead, Beebe pleaded guilty to the lesser charge of aggravated sexual battery. He had struck a deal with prosecutors: He would provide them with information leading to the arrests of the two other fraternity brothers who had raped Liz before his attack, and in exchange, he would be sentenced to ten years with all but eighteen months of the sentence suspended. Beebe began serving his prison time in March 2007; he was released less than six months later. The other two suspects have not been charged in the assault.

The experience turned Seccuro into a victims' rights activist. She founded STARS in 2006 in hopes of helping rape survivors and secondary victims (friends and family) through education and Web-based resources. One major facet of the organization's mission is to help colleges and universities revamp their responses to rape and sexual assault. Twenty years may have passed, Seccuro said, but much has stayed the same on campuses nationwide.

In April 2010, just three weeks before Yeardley's death, Seccuro returned to UVA. She was invited to speak at the annual Take Back the Night Rally, which highlights violence against women. The twenty-one-year-old event, peppered with local bands, speakers, and free food, was designed to give a voice to survivors and encourage people to take steps to prevent sex crimes. It would begin with a rally, followed by a march across campus, and wrap up with a "speak-out" at the university's amphitheater on McCormick Road.

Seccuro stood alongside Dan Harrington, the father of homicide victim Morgan Harrington, and spoke at the rally of blame and responsibility.

"Blame for sweeping crimes against women under the rug," Seccuro later wrote. "Blaming victims for going to concerts or parties or dating a fellow student. We are, I said, collateral damage, acceptable losses in the University's now-failed PR campaign that they are one of the best, most elite schools in the United States."

Though a lot of her speech was about sexual assault, she preached pointedly about violence between intimates and "the whole 'if you see something, say something' bit," she later recalled. When she learned of the death so soon after her speech, she was both heartsick and angry. She had been told that local law enforcement had created a series of videos for students that addressed an array of problems plaguing the campus: Assault, dating violence, substance abuse, and eating disorders were among the issues. But the videos never made their way to UVA's students because they were deemed inappropriate to show at a student-governed school. Seccuro wanted to scream.

"I had a friend who had been raped her First Year there near the new dorms in total darkness," Seccuro recalled. "When she approached the administration about better lighting, she was told that 'Mr. Jefferson would not have wanted the ugly aesthetic of such lights on the grounds of his Academical Village.' Point blank."

Seccuro was incredulous: "Really? Really??"

Eventually, the lights were installed after both women and men complained that they felt unsafe walking home from the library.

Seccuro, who wrote a book about her ordeal (*Crash Into Me: A Survivor's Search for Justice*), considers UVA's approach to campus violence downright deadly. Violence exists at every college, she said, but UVA, by standing by its status as a student-governed university, has been particularly steadfast in refusing to require that its students have to attend orientation, much less education in sexual assault or dating violence.

The criticism has been leveled before at the university. In 2004, *The Hook* wrote a daring cover article titled "How UVA Turns Its Back on Rape," in which reporter Courteney Stuart described the clandestine Sexual Assault Board that meets, takes testimony in secret and issues rulings in response to rape allegations among students. The story questioned exactly whom the policy was designed to protect, and highlighted the case of twenty-one-year-old rape victim Annie Hylton. Even though the young woman's attacker had been found guilty by the secret committee, his punishment was laughable: He was banned from the first-year dining hall and from the aquatic and fitness center, and he was ordered to attend counseling. He was never booted from campus, and remained at UVA until he graduated in 2003.

"One of the most bitter ironies for UVA rape victims is that the school seems to reserve its harshest penalties not for sexual predators, but for students who violate the Honor Code, an antebellum proscription against lying, cheating and stealing," Stuart wrote. "Honor offenses can include such things as copying a classmate's French homework or stealing a bicycle. Honor violators draw just one penalty: immediate and permanent expulsion."

UVA's honor system is entirely student-policed, meaning that a panel of students is convened to hear allegations against their peers. The panel weighs guilt and innocence, and just one sentence comes with a guilty plea: permanent dismissal.

The first student-run honor system cropped up in the late 1700s at the College of William & Mary. Jefferson envisioned something similar at his academical utopia, though it wasn't introduced until after a student shot a law professor on campus in 1840. Professor John A. G. Davis died of a pistol wound while trying to calm a disturbance between students on the university's lawn, according to UVA's history of its honor system. "This incident resulted in the adoption of the Honor Code in 1842," according to UVA's Web site, and is "one of the school's most venerated traditions. Administered solely by students, the Honor System requires that an individual act honorably in all relations and phases of student life."

However, as the years passed, UVA's system narrowed to highlight just three mandates: no lying, no cheating, and no stealing. Any of those violations meant immediate dismissal. Committing murder, meanwhile, wasn't included on the automatic expulsion list. While UVA's system is unique, it is mirrored in a few other institutions. Princeton University, for example, has boasted an entirely student-run honor code since 1893. On the Ivy League university's Web site, Princeton claims: "Entirely student-run, the honor code has been successful because generations of undergraduates have respected it, and by common agreement they afford it the highest place among their obligations as Princeton students."

UVA's system has made its own slew of headlines over the years. In early May 2001, the university was wracked by controversy after professor of physics Louis A. Bloomfield leveled academic dishonesty charges against 122 students. That was nearly twice as many charges as had been filed against all UVA students during the previous two years combined. Bloomfield, who taught "How Things Work"—a popular introductory physics class—was alerted to possible cheating after a student complained that the grade he had given her was low while others with higher marks had cheated.

Bloomfield created a software program to help him ferret out cheaters. The software would detect similarities of six consecutive words or more between papers submitted to him over the last five semesters. According to an account in the

New York Times, it took the program fifty hours to run through the more than 1,800 papers. It worked. Some of the papers were virtual replicas.

"I expected to see a couple of matches," Bloomfield told the Times. "I was a bit shocked to find sixty."

Bloomfield's experiment turned into a scandal, one that served as the apex for students' increasing complaints about the university's disciplinary unfairness. Some filed lawsuits, including a student whose degree was revoked eight years after he graduated. The trial leading to that revocation was held without the (former) alumnus present.

Thomas Hall, who headed UVA's Honor Committee during the Bloomfield scandal, said at the time that an investigative panel was going through the 122 cases, and that some students were expelled. Others, however, were found to have shared work to help each other out but didn't know the work would be plagiarized. In those instances, the students were allowed to stay.

One student likened the honor system to the "death penalty" because of its black-and-white severity. But despite the growing complaints, UVA students chose to stand by the system, flaws or not. The student body voted in a referendum to reject proposed changes to the code.

Meanwhile, students accused of rape and assault weren't treated with nearly the same obduracy. A student alleging rape could go to the police, but prosecutors have publicly acknowledged that some cases are too he-said/she-said to generate enough evidence for criminal charges. In many campus rape cases, both parties had been drinking, and there weren't any witnesses. Prosecutors can prove there was sex, but proving it was forced is too great a legal hurdle. Accusers in those cases have a university-provided recourse: They can bring their allegations to the University Judiciary Committee and hope for a guilty verdict by a panel of students. But unlike with cheating allegations, there is no set-in-stone punishment.

That discrepancy led to the creation of www.uvavictims ofrape.com, a group created by Susan Russell, the mother of a UVA student who claimed to be sexually assaulted in her dorm room by a man she was not dating or interested in. "The University mandated that she use a weak administrative process to handle this crime of sexual assault," Russell says on the site. "No other type of crime committed on grounds is trivialized in this manner."

Russell launched the site in 2004 and plays off Thomas Jefferson's emphasis on honor. "Is it Honorable for a University to support Zero Tolerance for Cheating but not for Rape?" Russell asks. "Is it Honorable for campus police to refuse to transfer jurisdiction for felony crime to the local police? Is it Honorable to do nothing when you're told by a young woman that she's been sexually assaulted?"

The site, sharp as a knife in its allegations, accuses the university police of mishandling the case and posts photos of various UVA administrators whom Russell deemed complicit in the case. It immediately made headlines, as did Annie Hylton's subsequent civil suit against her alleged rapist.

Hylton, a member of the varsity volleyball team, had been on campus just five months when she went on a date that ended in rape. She went to the hospital and reported the attack to university authorities, then pressed to have her case heard by the secretive Sexual Assault Board, a subcommittee of the University Judiciary Committee. The experience was nauseating, she told a CBS reporter in 2006. The six-hour hearing was in a small conference room, where she sat just feet away from her alleged attacker.

"Even thinking about it now makes my chest get tight," she told a reporter.

The assault board sided with Hylton, agreeing that the man had violated the school's code of conduct, despite his insistence that the sex was consensual. But if Hylton expected to feel vindicated by the ruling, the hope was short-lived. The board didn't even suspend him. Outraged, Hylton went public in hopes of drawing attention to UVA's ludicrous double standard. Cheat on your final? Immediate expulsion. Rape someone? You're banned from the fitness center.

Even worse, Hylton was told that if she spoke about the case, she could face charges of her own from the University Judiciary Committee. But she spoke out anyway, and UVA's mind-boggling disparities became public: In three years, from 2000–2003, thirty-eight students had been booted for cheating—in the same time span that sixty UVA students had reported they'd been sexually assaulted. No one had been suspended or expelled for sexual assault, *The Hook* reported.

Charlottesville prosecutors never brought criminal charges against Hylton's attacker, but she was eventually awarded $150,000 by a jury in her civil suit. More than that, her decision to speak out about the case was rewarded as well: The college safety nonprofit Security on Campus, Inc.—formed in the aftermath of the grisly 1986 murder of Jeanne Ann Clery at Lehigh University—filed a complaint against UVA in late 2008 for mishandling sexual assault cases. The Department of Education ruled that the university had repeatedly violated federal law by threatening victims of sexual assault with punishment if they spoke about their cases. Victims were free to speak—in theory, anyway.

More than seven years after her daughter's attack, Russell still maintains the UVA Victims of Rape site and said she continues to hear from young women looking for support.

"Do I think that anything has changed? Perhaps the school is more clever in how they hide assaults on their campus," Russell said. "The Commonwealth of Virginia is a state of 'good old boys.' There is great opposition to change, and crimes that involve women are treated as though 'she' brought it upon herself."

UVA alums like Seccuro agree the university still has a long way to go. The policies have changed, but the mentality and culture haven't. And it extends beyond rape allegations. Students on campus are implicitly taught to keep quiet, mind your own business, don't sully a classmate's reputation with even a cheating allegation.

For Russell, one of the biggest frustrations was the university police. She wanted to turn her daughter's case over to

Charlottesville police and was surprised to learn that the university department had jurisdiction.

"Many people living in the commonwealth, to include most lawmakers, are under the assumption that local law enforcement has the jurisdiction to investigate any crime that occurs on a college campus," she said. "Unfortunately, that assumption is wrong. Campus police have jurisdictional rights for dormitories and classroom buildings. Local law enforcement may be called in to assist, but unless the University or college transfers jurisdiction to them, campus police retain jurisdiction."

Russell wanted to change that. She sought a sponsor for legislation that would change how felonies would be investigated. The bill, eventually titled Virginia House Bill 2490, was sponsored by Delegate Paula J. Miller and called for university police to be required to contact local law enforcement when a felony occurred on the campus.

Specifically, the bill directs the chief law-enforcement officer of "a public or private institution of higher education" to immediately notify the local law enforcement agency when someone died on the campus or a rape had been reported. "Upon notification, the local law-enforcement agency shall assume responsibility for leading the investigation. The campus police department and all other employees of the institution of higher education shall cooperate."

"Why this bill? Because campus police tend to turn a blind eye to campus rape crimes. They treat them as administrative matters," Russell said. "This bill is not meant to demean the hardworking campus police, but to aid them. It allows the crime to be investigated by the local police, who are highly trained and staffed to handle crimes of this magnitude."

After Yeardley's death, questions swirled about how much university officials knew of Huguely's legal run-ins. Athletic Director Craig Littlepage said neither he nor UVA president John Casteen had been alerted, but Littlepage stopped short of saying that none of Huguely's coaches had been told. Had Coach Dom Starsia been told? Huguely had confessed to him the late-night beating he unleashed on a teammate for allegedly kissing Yeardley. Starsia chose not to report the incident to the school's Judiciary Committee because both young men supposedly had assured him that they shared the blame and had worked things out. But surely someone had noticed after Huguely's 2008 conviction in Lexington that he began fulfilling his community service sentence. Were coaches in the dark, or did they look the other way?

Huguely was supposed to report the run-ins himself. The university's policy required that students self-report any arrests. But those who do face expulsion or probation, making it unlikely that an average student, much less an athlete with everything going for him, would willingly step forward and put a bull's eye on his chest.

As Stetson University law professor Peter Lake told the *Washington Examiner*: "The pressure to win and compete and maintain eligibility is so strong that it actually plays against safety."

Huguely, like seven of his teammates who had also been entangled in alcohol-related charges, opted to overlook the self-reporting rule in favor of saving his own skin. As the media scrutiny mounted, Casteen turned to Governor McDonnell to push legislation that would require police agencies statewide to report student arrests to the university.

So much for the honor code.

In another cruel twist of timing, one week after the Take Back the Night rally, Claire Kaplan, director of Sexual and Domestic Violence Services at UVA's Women's Center, had scheduled a nearly three-hour session for some athletic department staff members to discuss creating a support network to help student athletes deal with domestic abuse.

"I was very excited to have the athletic department involved," Kaplan told a *USA Today* columnist, who wrote that Kaplan was unable to shake the "heartbreaking irony of the timing" of her requested meeting.

"There's not much that shocks me, so I don't know if I was shocked, but I was horrified," said Kaplan, who didn't know Yeardley or Huguely. "It's a hideous wake-up call here. If there was a pattern of violence, did she reach out to anyone at all, did she reach out to friends who didn't know what to do? Or was she stuck in her silence?"

The answers were proving difficult to uncover. Yeardley never reported Huguely to police or campus authorities as someone she feared. Based on police documents, some friends knew there had been spats and discord, but no one was speaking publicly about what warnings should have perhaps been better heeded. If there were lessons to glean from the case, Yeardley's family made it clear they'd have to come out in the courtroom.

"I feel like this whole thing was so preventable," Kaplan told columnist Christine Brennan. "Somebody knew something that they thought wasn't important. Did anyone speak out? Did people say to her, 'Yeardley, you are not safe with this person?'"

Kaplan hoped Yeardley's death would ignite outrage and trigger state-mandated change.

"People can't close their eyes anymore," she said. "They can't pretend it's not happening. I hope there will be more support on a state level and more specifically on each campus for mandatory, thorough education on gender-based violence. In the meantime, if students have friends who are in questionable relationships, they can't stay silent anymore."

Russell isn't convinced that Yeardley would have been saved even if she'd reached out to UVA for help.

"They may say that Yeardley Love should have reported her concerns, but I know firsthand that when those concerns are reported, nothing happens," she said.

By now, it's been so often repeated that domestic violence is about power and control that it sounds more like the moral of an after-school special than a real-life lesson. But, experts say, it's true. And dating violence doesn't always manifest in telltale "I walked into a door" types of bruises, according to Break the Cycle, an organization whose mission is "empowering youth to end domestic violence."

Sometimes there's physical violence, while other times

there's emotional abuse—verbal put-downs, name-calling, mind games. Abusers could use social status to make their partners feel subservient, or they could make threats—anything from threatening to leave or swearing they'll commit suicide.

A week after the Love slaying, Marjorie Gilberg, Break the Cycle's executive director, lambasted Virginia for its shoddy civil protection laws in cases of dating violence. The organization had been tracking states' laws for three years, and for the third year in a row, Virginia received a failing grade because its laws limit the types of behaviors that qualify for a protection order. Even if Yeardley had sought an order, she couldn't have been granted one because she and Huguely had separate apartments.

Journalist Jamie Stiehm, who herself had once been mired in a violent relationship, wasn't entirely surprised that Yeardley hadn't reached out to the university or local police for help.

"She was a very accomplished athlete and student," Stiehm said. "On the outside, she had everything going for her. The encoded message is, something like that doesn't happen to people like us. The elite class sort of comes with the expectation that everything in your life is peachy keen."

By asking for help, Yeardley would have been forced to admit to herself that everything wasn't as perfect as it seemed.

"You're confronting your own sorts of flaws in an otherwise perfect façade," Stiehm said. "These girls are very resilient . . . They're used to cultivating this air of hardiness and great enthusiasm and capability. Yeardley was the girl who had everything."

Dr. Barrie Levy, a psychotherapist and expert in dating violence, said young women in abusive relationships are in too much denial to recognize that they're mired in the type of relationship they've been warned to avoid.

"It's not just the thinking, 'This doesn't happen to people like me,' but it's the denial that it's even happening," said Levy, author of several books, including *Women and Violence*. "You don't call it violence. You just think he gets upset now and then."

Levy, a member of the Women's Studies Department at the University of California at Los Angeles, has heard countless stories of teenagers and young adults who initially mistake controlling behavior as unbridled passion. Levy began researching violence against women in the 1970s, and she worked in prevention education in high schools and middle schools. That's when she first began hearing stories of teenagers whose puppy-love romances had turned tragic.

"That was an eye opener," she recalled. "Some of my colleagues were having the same experience. You think nobody would get trapped in a relationship at that age."

But they do.

While the gender roles are sometimes reversed, the situation typically is this: At first, the young suitor seems romantic and impossibly attentive, wanting the girl all to himself. He calls and sends text messages, shows up at her door unexpectedly, meets her outside of her classrooms. She's flattered and floored by the attention—and far too love-struck to notice as he slowly begins usurping her free time, edging out her friends and family.

"Among girls who haven't been exposed to violence earlier in their lives, they think maybe he's had a troubled past and that she can make it better," Levy said. "They think, 'He'll have a good, healthy relationship with me, he'll learn to trust me and he'll change.'"

Most never see their partner as abusive, especially if he doesn't outright hit. The controlling moments are explained away: "This is the exception, I understand him so well, he doesn't mean to hurt me, he cares about me so much."

The common refrain is that he will change, Levy said.

"But what happens is that she begins to change, he doesn't, and he begins to have an even more powerful effect on her," Levy said. "She becomes more traumatized, more ashamed, more isolated. She's less confident, less certain of her own strength. He may be critical all the time. She starts to avoid doing anything that will get him upset. She thinks, 'I'm just really going to focus on being in this relationship.'"

And if she does decide to leave, she puts herself in great

danger. Domestic violence experts have coined the term "separation violence" to mark the perilous phase in an abusive relationship when one party tries to leave the other. That is when the abused partner is at greatest risk of being killed by his or her abuser.

"Many girls try to break up and the reactions are so much worse than staying together and trying to fix things," Levy said. "He might promise to go into counseling, and she's ever hopeful that he will change. That's what rules these relationships: hope and fear."

To the people who balk at the idea of someone like Yeardley Love—by all accounts a strong, smart, independent woman—stumbling into the role of victim, Levy has a message: "Any one of us could fall in love with someone who crossed that line. It could happen to anyone, no matter how strong or how weak you are."

Yeardley Love's strength perhaps made her a powerhouse on the lacrosse field, but it did nothing to save her life.

Chapter 13

The image of domestic violence is coated in stigma, the woman often assumed to be meek and weak-willed. While women are assured in books and on Web sites that domestic violence crosses all socioeconomic boundaries and is nothing for the victim to be ashamed of, they're rarely provided with testimonials from women professionals—lawyers, doctors, highly educated go-getters—who have suffered at the hands of their partners. The message is clear: Maybe it *does* happen in affluent society, but you sure as hell don't talk about it.

No doubt, Yeardley Love was taught never to tolerate domestic abuse. Notre Dame Prep, her high school, prides itself on instilling strength in its students, and Yeardley's own academic and athletic achievements indicated that she intended to bust through any obstacle that cluttered her path. By all accounts, she was tough both on and off the lacrosse field.

Maybe too tough for her own good.

Strong, educated women sometimes lull themselves into a false sense of security, domestic violence experts say. These women believe abuse simply doesn't happen to people like them, so those who do experience violence in their relationships shroud themselves in silence. They trick themselves into thinking that the relationship isn't even abusive, much less that it's the type to escalate into one of those grisly stories covered on the nighttime news.

Yeardley seemed to be growing increasingly concerned, according to details in police reports and her friends' accounts in the days after her death. A week before she died, she reportedly shared with a teammate a disturbing e-mail Huguely had written her. She had also gone home for a weekend to get away from George after a particularly heinous fight. To journalist Jamie Stiehm, the red flags were there, but everyone seemed to ignore them.

"They couldn't imagine something so vicious could happen in their circle," Stiehm said of Yeardley's friends and teammates. "It's a lack of imagination and profound elitism as well. That willful oblivion really cost her her life because they didn't protect her."

Affluence and education can work against the victim of an abusive relationship. People shrug off her concerns because they assume she has the means to leave the situation.

Add to that a privileged abuser, and things get even more complicated. The picture of Huguely painted in the wake of Yeardley's death was that of a young man who had been given too many breaks for behavior that would have likely landed most people in jail. Somehow, he had evaded real consequences for all of it.

"George exemplifies the Cavalier culture with a capital C," Stiehm said. "The privilege, the breeding, the sense of entitlement, the thinking that the rules don't really apply to me . . . His teammates, if they weren't protecting him, they were ignoring him."

Women trapped in abusive dating relationships are sometimes hesitant to seek help, experts said. They tend to focus on their partner's better attributes rather than examining the put-downs and the violence they're secretly enduring.

"She sees a good side of him. You don't fall in love with someone who's horrible all the time," Dr. Barrie Levy said. "You see him when he's not being abusive. Maybe he's really loving or has a lot of other qualities you really like."

Yeardley didn't have children or a lifestyle to support, so

she had no solid reason to stay with Huguely—except, perhaps, that she didn't want to put her lacrosse friends in a tricky situation by breaking up and having to air the couple's dirty laundry, a development that undoubtedly would have made the final months of their college careers much less pleasant.

Maybe that's why some of her friends didn't even know she had broken up with George.

Court records show that police began investigating whether Huguely had threatened Yeardley immediately after her body was found. At the same time, they were gathering other information—specifically about Huguely's constant text messaging.

In today's society, cell phones and smart phones mean people can stay in constant communication. For an emotionally unstable partner, this can provide yet another tool aimed to tether a couple together. Friends told reporters soon after Yeardley's death that Huguely was texting her constantly after their break-up. While the contents of the texts weren't immediately released, dating violence experts said they needn't have been threatening to constitute what's been dubbed as "textual harassment."

"It's gotten astonishingly worse in the last two years," Jill Murray, an author of dating violence books, told the *Washington Post* for a 2010 story on the high-tech stalking method. "It's part and parcel of every abusive dating relationship now."

The messages perhaps seem benign at first glance: *Call me. Where r u? Who r u with?* But they arrive at the sender's will, never mind if it's during class or dinner or a family vacation. Kristin Mitchell's family said she seemed to get text messages constantly from her then-boyfriend and killer-to-be. After her death, detectives discovered an ominous message on her phone that she had sent to Landau just hours before he stabbed her to death: *You are being ridiculous. Why can't I do something with my friends?*

Victim advocates say technology, yet again, is proving a

double-edged sword: With all the convenience attached to being easily found, there's the potential danger of being easily found.

"The advances in technology are assisting the perpetrators in harassing and stalking and threatening their victims," Kacey Kirkland, a victim services specialist with the Fairfax County Police Department, told one reporter.

Charlottesville police were granted a search warrant to examine Huguely's Blackberry smart phone in December to see how many, and what types, of text messages he may have sent Yeardley. Even if the messages had been deleted, a forensic examination of the phone could potentially turn up saved screen shots of the notes. Police would also subpoena cell phone records in hopes of learning just how many of those notes Huguely tended to send out. If the messages themselves were benign, perhaps the quantity would be telling.

As a public service, Break the Cycle posts "ten warning signs of abuse" right on its Web site: checking your cell phone or e-mail without permission; constant put-downs; extreme jealousy or insecurity; explosive temper; financial control; isolating you from family or friends; mood swings; physically hurting you in any way; possessiveness; telling you what to do.

Bill Mitchell is convinced that nothing will change without education. Years after his daughter's death, he hears regularly from people trying to save loved ones from dangerous relationships. The Kristin Mitchell Foundation's Web site spells out ways to get help and highlights the common theme that seems to run through most cases of dating abuse: control.

"I think every time a young woman dies like this, it's the opportunity for everyone to wake up and find out what this is all about. Dating violence is *real*. It happens a lot! It's just that you don't hear about it much."

In the months that followed Yeardley's death, that began to change—much to the apparent discomfort of the university and the slain woman's family.

Chapter 14

As it became clear to local reporters that Yeardley's case would surpass any other they had covered in recent memory, reporter Brendan Fitzgerald said the *C-VILLE Weekly* began to devote more and more resources, because the case raised a slew of questions that authorities did not seem ready—or willing—to answer. One of the biggest questions was that of entitlement.

As word of Huguely's earlier outbursts surfaced, some wondered if the good-looking Landon graduate had been given a pass for behavior that would have landed others behind bars. And others questioned how many of Yeardley's own friends had ignored signs that her boyfriend was unstable—possibly even dangerous. Looking for answers, Fitzgerald knocked on doors lining a half-mile stretch of 14th Street Northwest. Few people answered, and those who did declined to talk. He headed to the lawn outside of the university's rotunda, where students lounged between classes. They sprawled on the grass in T-shirts and shorts, the early May days creeping above eighty degrees.

None talked.

In a world where there's no shortage of people to opine on anything and everything, Fitzgerald was shocked to meet only silence. It was one thing when Huguely's advisor in the anthropology department declined to comment—that was to be expected—but never had Fitzgerald encountered so many tight lips among students.

"It was a surprise to me as a reporter and as a former UVA student to approach a group of half-dozen students to ask for any comment on any respect and have them all decline, and not for lack of words," Fitzgerald said. "It's rare in any of my experiences in UVA that students were hesitant to share their opinions. They are a very bright lot reliably year after year. I expected no shortage of nuanced takes or ideas."

When pondering why this case seemed to trigger silence at UVA when so many others encouraged an outpouring of thoughts and emotions, Fitzgerald came up empty. Finding students to talk about Morgan Harrington's disappearance had never been difficult. But there was something about Yeardley Love's death that left students guarded and speechless. Was it the case itself, the blinding media coverage, or the last straw in a deadly year that left the whole campus emotionally drained? Fitzgerald didn't know.

"To find nothing was startling," he said.

Still, reporters toiled away. Sensationalized or not, Yeardley's case had touched thousands upon thousands of people worldwide. It eventually would grace the cover of *People* magazine, whose average single-copy sales in the first half of 2010 were nearly 1.3 million. Though Sharon Love gave a brief comment to *People,* its coverage, like most other publications, relied heavily on early newspaper accounts, quotes, and information gathered immediately after Yeardley's death. And none of the accounts shed any light on Yeardley's relationship with George.

University officials, in fact, instructed those who knew the couple to keep quiet. One student athlete told a reporter that members of the university's sports teams—not just lacrosse—had been told not only to refrain from making public comments, but to refuse new friend requests on social networking sites such as Facebook in hopes of filtering out anecdote-seeking reporters. Indeed, dozens of UVA students contacted via Facebook and LinkedIn (another social site but with a more professional slant) simply ignored incoming messages asking about Yeardley and George.

Faced with few live sources, reporters turned to paper ones, filing a slew of requests under federal and state Freedom of Information Act laws. Journalists wanted the details: What evidence had been collected at the crime scene? What exactly had Caitlin Whiteley and Philippe Oudshoorn described in the nine-one-one call to police? What crucial information had Huguely tried to trash when he stole Yeardley's laptop and tossed it in a Dumpster? The day after the death, news media were given what they were accustomed to receiving: limited access, but some access nonetheless. In an ongoing investigation, journalists don't expect to be given information that might jeopardize a case, but they do expect to have access to police and court documents that have historically been deemed public by legal precedent. It's a checks-and-balances system, after all: The media can't keep tabs on the government and governmental procedures if the government completely closes its books. Reporters were allowed to review three search warrants linked to the crime, and the contents of those warrants were instantaneously reported in print, on television, and online.

But suddenly and without explanation, the records were sealed in a move that baffled the news outlets. On May 6, three days after Yeardley's death, Judge Cheryl Higgins with the 16th Judicial Court granted prosecution motions asking that warrants for several searches be sealed—specifically, the searches of Yeardley's apartment, of Huguely's apartment, of Huguely's car, and of Huguely himself. Higgins filed four separate orders, each of which was, like the warrants themselves, sealed.

The *Washington Post*, no stranger to waging battles over the public's right to know, joined the *Daily Progress* and *Richmond Times-Dispatch*, as well as the Associated Press, in challenging the Commonwealth of Virginia for sealing the documents.

It wasn't just that some documents weren't available, the media consortium argued, but that Higgins's order failed to say which records were sealed and why—nor did the judge specify for how long they would remain out of view. Attorney Craig T. Merritt argued that Virginia Supreme Court guidelines require that the public be given such specifics so that they have the chance to oppose the action. Higgins's filings were unfairly vague, Merritt argued, and offered no timeline—saying only that the documents would be sealed "temporarily."

Predictably, George's family said little to the media—not an uncommon position for people whose loved one has been charged with a vicious crime and could face life imprisonment. Yeardley's family also remained cloistered, as did her friends. The day-after pleadings for time and space turned into a widespread vow of silence at the request of Yeardley's family. Her likes and dislikes, her goals and dreams, the details that turn a tragic story into a human one, were kept under wraps.

Mary Bartel, Yeardley's lacrosse coach at Notre Dame Prep, told one reporter via e-mail that Yeardley's mother had originally granted her permission to speak to Yeardley's character and history at the school. "Beyond that, we continue to respect the family request that our response to questions be 'no comment.' Thanks for your understanding," she wrote. Others similarly shied from talking, saying that they had promised Yeardley's family their silence.

Somehow, despite the disconnect, Yeardley's story wasn't lost. Within days of her death, several groups on Facebook had been dedicated to her. One online memorial had more than 100,000 members by week's end. Six months later, "In Memory of Yeardley Love: UVA Lacrosse Player" still had 75,960 members.

Another Facebook memorial page, titled "R.I.P. Yeardley Love, May 3, 2010" drew more than 24,000 members.

"Did not know Yeardley personally, but feel free to post on the wall . . ." wrote the page's creator, twenty-four-year-old Benjamin Edmonds of Cooperstown, New York.

"I had no idea that it would get so big," he said later. "I

just happened to be the first person to create it. It started out one by one and soon I was getting thousands of members an hour."

The outpouring on the Internet provided a forum for both friends and strangers. It was a sign of the high-tech times: Just as young adults had begun turning to the Web to create and maintain friendships, they turned there, too, to share stories of grief, to express their outrage and to post poems and songs they had written in Yeardley's honor. Social networking proved it's about more than connecting people in life; it could connect in death as well.

"I never knew Yeardley but this story has really stuck with me," one woman wrote. "A young life taken too soon and so tragically."

Wrote another: "It is critically important that women protect their friends. NEVER allow anyone who is being threatened to remain silent. . . . Yeardley lost her life because of silent acceptance of violent behavior."

Some who posted online were angry, calling on the Commonwealth to pursue the death penalty against Huguely. Others were more tempered. "He deserves a trial," one man wrote. "Get your stuff together before you speak." Thousands reached out to Yeardley's family, offering support and prayers.

Tiffany Danielle, a lacrosse player from Cincinnati, Ohio, put her thoughts to music, publicly posting a dedication video with a nearly three-minute song written for Yeardley. Through a mixture of rap and R&B, she sang that though she didn't know Love, the young woman's death had brought her to tears.

The two shared a mutual love of lacrosse, she sang—"a lax family that we were both part of"—and that commonality made them family. "And when we step on the field, you're the one we think of," she sang, before promising to root for orange and blue.

Phyllis Botti of Los Angeles was one of the countless people who had no connection to the case but found herself drawn to it anyway. Months later, she could recall exactly

Yeardley (left) immediately looked up to her older sister, Lexie. "When I was little, I liked to do whatever my sister did," Yeardley wrote in an essay about her life in 2002, her freshman year of high school. *Photo courtesy of One Love Foundation/joinonelove.org*

After her death, Yeardley was described by many as an angel. As a little girl, she once dressed as one.

Photo courtesy of One Love Foundation/joinonelove.org

Yeardley and Lexie turned heads growing up. Both were athletic, slim, pretty and quick to smile.

Photo courtesy of One Love Foundation/joinonelove.org

In the days after her death, friends told reporters that Yeardley had a goofy side. *Photo courtesy of One Love Foundation/joinonelove.org*

After the death of John Love III, Sharon (Donnelly) Love (far right) grew even closer with her two girls.

Photo courtesy of One Love Foundation/joinonelove.org

Images of a broad-smiling Yeardley, affectionately known as Yards to her friends, helped catapult her story to international news.

Photo courtesy of One Love Foundation/joinonelove.org

The Boylan Heights bar, located just down the street from both Yeardley and George's apartments, was a popular hangout for UVA lacrosse players.

Photo by Amber Hunt

George Huguely V was recruited as a valuable midfielder, both muscular and capable of running the full length of the field many times per game.

Photo by Andrew Shurtleff

In 2008, Huguely was arrested for public intoxication after spewing racist and sexist slurs at a police officer who ultimately used a Taser to control him.

Rockbridge Regional Jail photo

Both George and Yeardley spent countless hours practicing and playing at UVA's Klöckner Stadium, located less than two miles from their separate apartments. *Photo by April Barney*

Charlottesville Police Chief Timothy Longo, formerly a Baltimore cop, speaks to the crush of media who began swarming the city in the hours after Yeardley's death first made headlines.

Photo by Andrew Shurtleff

Police were called in the early morning hours of May 3, 2010, to discover Yeardley's bloodied body in her second-floor apartment. *Photo by Amber Hunt*

George lived just two buildings away from his girlfriend in this brick building. *Photo by April Barney*

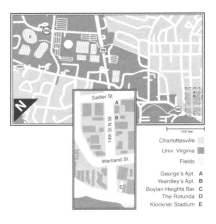

Illustration by John James Anderson

Thousands of distraught students, faculty and community members flooded the campus for a candlelit vigil two days after Yeardley's death.   *Photo by Eric Kelley*

Members of the UVA women's lacrosse team sob at the vigil.
                          AP photo by Steve Helber

George looked defeated and drawn in the first mugshot released of him after his May 4 arraignment.

Albemarle-Charlottesville Regional Jail photo

Since his arrest, George Huguely V has been housed at the Albemarle-Charlottesville Regional Jail in a pastoral part of town.

Photo by Amber Hunt

how she first learned of Yeardley's death and admitted that her friends accused her of being obsessed with the case.

"I'll never forget it. It was May 4, I was at work and I see this blurb from AOL saying that this young man was arrested for supposedly killing this young lady," she recalled. "It was odd. I live in Los Angeles and we hear of people getting killed all the time, or kids being kidnapped. I read about those and get sad, but I move on, but this one really got to me. There was something about this case. My friends said, 'Phyllis, you're like obsessed with this story. You act like this is someone from your family.'

"I just think it's her face and her eyes," she continued. "She just looked like an angel on earth to me. Her eyes completely haunted me. It's interesting because before I saw the photo, it still got to me, but when I saw her face . . . She was full of life and promise, and that smile."

It wasn't that Botti identified with the violent ending Yeardley had met, either. The fifty-three-year-old divorced animal rights activist said she's never been abused either verbally or physically. (With a name like Botti and a six foot four father named Bruno, no one would dare, she joked.) It was more that Yeardley's death seemed so pointless and avoidable. She takes to heart the famous Albert Einstein quote: "The world is a dangerous place, not because of those who do evil, but because of those who look on and do nothing."

"It's so tragic that no one did anything and there were all of those signs," she said.

Botti has followed every development. She regularly posts links to updates on her Facebook profile page. She can rattle off the case's twists and turns with ease—the campus vigil, the details of Huguely's past arrest, his reportedly heavy-drinking hours leading up to the death. She found herself in tears talking about the case with friends. She even got in arguments with some who didn't like how the media had focused so much on Yeardley and Huguely's wealthy upbringings.

"I would say that I know it could happen anywhere, but you don't expect it to happen in a place like that," she said.

Yeardley had no shortage of friends through her profile page on Facebook. (It's unclear if George ever had one, or if it was swiftly deleted after his arrest.) In her public photo, she wore a strappy dark top and white pants draped alongside a friend on top of what appeared to be a barroom pool table. The girls, facing opposite directions with their heads propped, were fresh-faced and beaming; Yeardley's arms looked toned and tan.

Friends posted and tagged hundreds of photographs of Yeardley. Some of the pictures, later shared with reporters or posted in video montages elsewhere online, showed her smiling and laughing alongside her friends. Her clothes were flattering and fresh, appropriate for Charlottesville's humid summers. She seemed to favor tops either strappy or strapless, sometimes accented with bold, chunky necklaces. She was known to dress up both for Halloween and New Year's Eve, and while many of her photos were posed and smiley, she wasn't afraid to ham it up for the camera. In one, she looked appropriately goofball, dressed with two friends in rainbow propeller hats and nerdy glasses, complete with thick tape at the bridge. In another, she wore an expression of mock seriousness while dressed in camouflage overalls and a hunter orange vest.

She had more than 1,000 Facebook "friends," though several who responded to journalists' interview requests said they had only peripherally met the young woman. The hefty friend count isn't surprising for a girl Yeardley's age, on the cusp of graduating college, with so many interests. Nowadays, Facebook is used as much to catch up with high school classmates as it is to discover new people with overlapping interests, said Dave Awl, author of *Facebook Me!* which is in its second edition. In his book, Awl describes how people Yeardley's age and younger have different concepts of what friendship is than previous generations. They meet someone either in real life or online whom they deem interesting enough to warrant "friending," and from there, they recalibrate, he said.

Plus, he said, a college student set to graduate is wise to have a huge network (allowing some "friends" more access to personal info than others, he cautioned), as you never know where information about a job might surface. Many of Yeardley's friends were fellow lacrosse players, both male and female, from universities across the country. Many, too, were from the Baltimore area, some of whom she had met just once or twice before they became part of her entrusted online circle.

"If you're outgoing, if you're gregarious, if you have diverse interests and an intellectual curiosity, it's normal to have 1,000 friends online," Awl said.

By all accounts, Yeardley was each of those things.

Within six months of Yeardley's death, her Facebook profile had been deleted. All that remained were the pages created in her memory.

Chapter 15

Immediately after Yeardley's body was discovered and Huguely's arrest had been made public, the fate of the UVA lacrosse season for both men and women was unclear. Both teams had lived up to their stellar reputations in the regular season. The men had dominated in every game, save one conference match against Duke in April. As the quarterfinals neared, the team bounced between first and second ranking nationally. Though the women's season had been peppered with a few losses, they still ranked a more-than-respectable fourth place by April's end, even after coming off of two painful losses to Maryland and Northwestern during the Atlantic Coast Conference Tournament.

About 3 p.m. the day Yeardley died, ESPN's Quint Kessenich turned to social networking site Twitter to drop a lacrosse bombshell: Virginia had canceled the remainder of both the men's and women's seasons, he announced.

Sports Illustrated rushed to confirm, but UVA denied the development, prompting Kessenich to hastily issue a correction. Within hours, Kessenich's entire Twitter account disappeared. ESPN issued a statement on the sportscaster's behalf: "I am sorry for this mistake. While I had heard from two reliable sources that the seasons were canceled, I should've discussed it with my news editors and checked with University of Virginia officials before reporting it. When I discovered it was inaccurate I immediately issued a correction."

To some lacrosse players and fans, the rush to report a rumor was a bad sign that the tragedy unfolding would cast a pall over not just the university and the academic year, but over lacrosse as a whole. Some newspaper columnists and bloggers pointed fingers at the close-knit culture as being complicit in Yeardley's death. The warning signs had been there, some argued, and Huguely's violent tendencies should have been spotted long before he had the opportunity to kill.

On May 7, the *Baltimore Sun* ran an editorial with the headline: "A Shadow on Men's Lacrosse: Sport must deal with persistent reports of violence and sexual abuse." Penned by Peter G. Prowitt, the Sunday piece declared that "if ever there was a wake-up call that the culture of sex and alcohol abuse surrounding the sport of men's lacrosse has spun out of control, the case of Yeardley Love is it."

Lacrosse had seen this type of backlash before. In March 2006, a female student at North Carolina Central University accused three Duke University students of raping her at a party in Durham, North Carolina. The accusation dripped with scandal: The accuser, Crystal Mangum, was a stripper and escort, and she was black. The men she accused were white, and they were privileged lacrosse players. The allegations rocked the collegiate world in general, and that of lacrosse—a sport largely comprising privileged, white players—in particular. Not only were the three Blue Devils players accused of a crime, but of one that was racially motivated. Mangum said the men had called her a nigger, and, in leveling the charges, Durham County Prosecutor Mike Nifong suggested the assault might be a hate crime. The picture painted was of rich white boys feeling so entitled and superior to their black escort that they could justify forcing themselves on her.

The accused men declared their innocence, but the public's perception of them wasn't helped by an e-mail sent by one of the lacrosse players just hours after the party ended. Ryan McFadyen wrote to other players that he planned to have some more strippers over. The e-mail, rife with punctuation and grammatical errors, read:

> To whom it may concern
>   tomorrow night, after tonights show, ive decided to have some strippers over to edens 2c. all are welcome.. however there will be no nudity. i plan on killing the bitches as soon as the [sic] walk in and proceeding to cut their skin off while cumming in my duke issue spandex.. all in besides arch and tack please respond
>   41

Forty-one was the jersey number for McFadyen. The e-mail, quoted in a probable cause affidavit, was used by law enforcement to secure search warrants related to the alleged attack and bolstered the prosecutor's belief that the men accused were guilty as sin.

The media latched onto the outrage-invoking story. Pundits opined about such a crime keeping in step with lacrosse's culture of entitlement. Some went so far as to say they were shocked not at the alleged behavior of the players, but rather at the authorities' insistence that these ne'er-do-well rich kids finally be held accountable. In her show immediately following the indictment of two of the lacrosse players, Nancy Grace roasted a guest who suggested that the athletes might be innocent. "That's your first concern?!" Grace interrupted. "Do you have a sister? I assume you have a mother." Fewer than eight percent of reported rapes are proven to be false accusations, she added, so the possibility that the young men were innocent meant "not a hill of beans in my assessment of this case."

The lacrosse world was rattled—even the Huguelys. George V and his father were both interviewed for their reactions to the scandal by the *Washington Post*. Huguely's father told the paper that he'd used the incident as an opportunity to counsel his son about avoiding potentially dangerous situations.

"Regardless of what winds up happening, you have to

learn from this experience and take what you can from it," the elder Huguely said. "You always have to remember and can't let yourself be in a situation where something like this could happen."

Huguely V said he couldn't help but sympathize with the team.

"They've been scrutinized so hard and no one knows what has happened yet," he told the paper. "In this country, you're supposed to be innocent until proven guilty. I think that's the way it should be."

Duke wasn't as cautious in its reaction. The university suspended the lacrosse team for two games in late March, then canceled the remainder of the 2006 season, because of the allegations. Lacrosse coach Mike Pressler, who had helmed the team for sixteen seasons, was forced out. (Though his departure was outwardly presented as a resignation, he was awarded a settlement of an undisclosed amount from Duke in October 2007 for wrongful termination.) As it turned out, the university had perhaps reacted too hastily. In April 2007, thirteen months after the supposed off-campus gang-bang, North Carolina Attorney General Roy Cooper dropped all charges against the three accused players. More than that, he declared the three innocent, which was an unusual move; most prosecutors dismiss charges with prejudice, allowing law enforcement to save face by saying there maybe isn't enough evidence *now*, but we might levy the charges again if we find more evidence. Instead, Cooper said Nifong, the county prosecutor, had gone "rogue," and the North Carolina State Bar filed ethics charges against Nifong that ultimately got him disbarred for "dishonesty, fraud, deceit, and misrepresentation."

Not every word in Mangum's story was a lie: She and another woman had indeed been hired as escorts for a party hosted by several members of the lacrosse team, but she had never been assaulted there. DNA swabs taken from her body did not match up with any of the white Duke lacrosse players. Her motivation to lie was tough to gauge. She might have been under the influence of prescription drugs and possibly alcohol, and she seemed to believe the tales she told, police said. But the damage to the Duke players' reputations had already been done. They would forever be linked to a violent assault that never actually happened.

Though the charges were dropped, the story wasn't over. Pressler moved on, becoming coach of Bryant University's Bulldogs, finally telling his story in 2008 as a contributor to a book written by author Don Yaeger. Mangum's outrageous legal run-ins continued; in February 2010, she was arrested and charged with attempted first-degree murder and arson for allegedly trying to stab her boyfriend and set his clothes on fire in their bathtub. Though a 12-member jury found Mangum guilty of child abuse the following December, they couldn't agree on the arson charge, resulting in a hung jury and mistrial in the case. Some of Mangum's supporters told reporters that she was targeted as punishment for the Duke allegations four years prior.

On April 3, 2011, Mangum was arrested for another fight with a different boyfriend. This time, she was accused of repeatedly stabbing Reginald Daye in the abdomen; the 46-year-old died eleven days later, prompting prosecutors in Durham, North Carolina, to charge her with first-degree murder. As of this writing, she remains in jail awaiting trial.

The details of the Duke case were resurrected every time a new allegation even peripherally linked with alcohol or sex was publicly leveled at a men's lacrosse player—like in 2009, when three players at Sacred Heart University in Connecticut were charged with conspiracy to commit first-degree sexual assault. The charges apparently stemmed from a drunken encounter in which two of the players inappropriately touched an eighteen-year-old girl while she had sex with the third player. Charges were dismissed in 2010 for lack of evidence, but the incident reopened an old wound.

As the case against Huguely unfolded, the wound was more than reopened; it was picked at and salted until it festered and oozed. Some wondered if lacrosse would ever regain its footing as an all-American sport played by clean-cut kids.

"I don't want to repeat the Duke debacle of self-inflicted flagellation, but the [alleged] murder of Yeardley Love by a Virginia lacrosse player . . . brings to mind another dimension that the Duke mess revealed," one blogger wrote. "The culture of lacrosse epitomizes privileged swaggering wealth and elite violence comfortable with its own superiority and confident in its ability to act with impunity."

After Yeardley's death and Huguely's arrest, the divide between those who believed the allegations and those who didn't wasn't an issue, as had been the case in the Duke scandal. There was no denying that Yeardley was dead, and no one questioned—publicly, at least—whether her death was at George Huguely's hands. Even his defense lawyer didn't deny that—yet, anyway. But what hadn't changed between the Duke scandal and this new heartache were the criticisms lobbed against lacrosse.

An opinion piece posted on Opposing Views (www.opposingviews.com) declared that "lacrosse presents a different form of entitlement" than other scandal-ridden sports, such as football and basketball.

"It's a niche sport protected and supported by serious East Coast wealth," the piece said. The sport may be "slumming" now by entering community centers and trying to recruit the middle class, it continued, but it traditionally flourished at posh finishing schools.

For those born and raised in the sport's East Coast hotbeds, lacrosse, with its Native American roots, is considered the most American of sports. Often said to be the "fastest-growing sport on two feet," lacrosse programs have popped up in Florida, California, Texas, and Colorado, as well as some Midwest states. In an article about preventing lacrosse injuries, the Cleveland Clinic, regarded as one of the country's top hospitals, approximated that lacrosse had more than 130,000 high school players in 2010. "It is estimated to have grown faster than any other sport at the high school level over the last ten years, and is also the fastest-growing sport over the last five years in the NCAA," the hospital stated.

It's a sport steeped in history. When played by Native Americans, it was considered stellar military training. Sometimes entire villages or tribes would play against each other, and the goals were separated by miles rather than yards. The players used sticks that looked like a bishop's crosier, and because the ball (then made of hair-stuffed deerskin) was often nowhere near each player, their attacks against each other were strategic and violent. French explorers spotted the game in action in the 1800s and immediately adopted it. It spread quickly in Europe and Canada, and took root in cities dotting the United States' East Coast. The Montreal Lacrosse Club is largely credited with organizing and modernizing the sport, creating the first written rules in 1856. A rewrite followed eleven years later, and the new rules called for twelve players per team (a rule that would later change for men), as well as a hard rubber ball. William George Beers of the Montreal club designed a stick better suited to catching the ball and throwing it with accuracy.

Ice hockey and lacrosse have long been considered siblings. Johns Hopkins University in Baltimore was a major hockey-playing college in the late 1800s. When lacrosse was introduced toward the turn of the century, it caught fire throughout Maryland, prompting the creation of programs for all age groups. Johns Hopkins remains the heart from which the lacrosse lifeblood pulsates: It's home to the Lacrosse Museum and National Hall of Fame, and its men's team has won more than forty national titles.

The rules for men's and women's lacrosse differ in a lot of ways: In the men's game, ten players take the field; in women's, there are twelve. The size of their sticks are different. Even their field sizes can differ. But they deviate most in the physicality allowed: In women's lacrosse, body contact is forbidden. So-called "rough checks"—or swinging your stick at an attacker's stick—are also banned. Both types of contact are fine by men's standards. The differences, which slowly evolved over the past 100-plus years, have inspired criticism: Some say that the differences between the men's rules and women's rules are so great that they should be classified as two different sports altogether. As one player said, plenty of female athletes would prefer the rougher incarnation, while plenty of men would like the challenge of using skill and endurance over size and aggression.

Because of the physical contact allowed, the genders differ in equipment as well. Men must wear helmets with facemasks and four-point chin straps, as well as padded gloves. Women don't have to wear gloves or helmets as they aren't expected to endure as much physical punishment. (The exception is the goalkeeper, who has to wear a facemask, chest protector, and throat protector.) The women are mostly concerned with protecting themselves from the dense rubber ball zipping by, so they tend to wear mouth guards and either goggles or eye masks.

The sport has slowly spread from its New England roots into other parts of the country, fueled largely by people who grew up with it in their hometowns only to be heartbroken when they moved as adults to lacrosse-less parts of the country. The introduction of the sport to some Western states can be directly traced to East Coast transplants. It helps, too, that beginner lacrosse gear has gotten a bit more affordable in recent decades, beginning with the introduction of plastic stick heads in the 1970s. Some athletic companies have begun marketing low-cost starter sets, too, so that parents don't have to drop more than $100 to let their children at least test out the sport.

"The game is the mix of the best attributes of all sports," Matt Cone, president of the Washington Lacrosse Foundation, told the *New York Times* for a 2005 story about lacrosse's booming popularity. "It has grace, finesse, contact, and is a lot of fun to play and watch. People become addicted to it."

Some insist the sport would grow even faster if there were more coaches: "There have been several teams that wanted to start, but weren't able to find a coach, so they didn't happen," Alexis Longinotti, the Northern California chapter president of U.S. Lacrosse, told the *Times*. U.S. Lacrosse oversees both men and women's lacrosse in the United States.

Lacrosse magazine, published by U.S. Lacrosse, boasts a circulation of more than 300,000.

No matter its growing popularity, the sport still draws its share of (sometimes envy-driven) ridicule. In a 2007 episode of the NBC sitcom *30 Rock,* black comedian Tracy Morgan quipped to Tina Fey's character: "I'm gonna have so much money, my great-grandkids are gonna play lacrosse. Lacrosse, Liz Lemon!"

Players gather in online forums to tout lacrosse's superiority over other U.S. sports (baseball seems a particular foe) and to joke about balls, shafts, and heads. But lighthearted though some of the jokes and jabs are, lacrosse's reputation seems to fall under fire every few years—a fact not helped by the dark, anonymous underbelly of the World Wide Web. Separate from the sex and alcohol scandals, some lax players—or those purporting to be as they type behind a cloak of untraceable online handles—seem determined to paint the sport as one played by racist, entitled members of society's upper crust—most of them harboring a "boys will be boys" mentality.

"As my old lacrosse coach used to say, 'They invented soccer because they had to come up with something for the girls to play,'" one online poster wrote in early 2010 beneath video footage of a lacrosse interview. Even that comment was light-hearted compared to countless others.

One far-from-unique example: A young black player posted a video review of his lacrosse shaft and head on YouTube, prompting a slew of racist responses: "Your [sic] black, go play basket ball [sic] with the rest of your people, cause lacrosse does not want you!" wrote one commenter with "lax" in his or her profile name. The comment was mirrored by dozens of others. On other sites, writers said that while sports in general seemed to harbor a "mind your own business" mentality when it came to violence against women— "pro bowl quarterback Ben Roethlisberger receives a slap on the wrist for violence against women while Michael Vick loses his career for violence against dogs," one blogger wrote on OpposingViews.com, referring to the two NFL players—lacrosse presents a deeper-seated sense of entitlement. It's not the type of sport that, say, a poor, urban kid can discover and infiltrate, but rather a niche sport of seemingly impenetrable environs. In short, collegiate sports offer one layer of insulation from the real world, and cloistered deeper still is lacrosse.

Just three days after Yeardley's death, Andrew Sharp, an editor with SBNation.com, wrote a piece anticipating the lacrosse debate in which he provided unique insight into the lacrosse culture and the possible role it played. The case was more personal than most, he wrote, because he'd once met Huguely and shared friends with Yeardley.

"George Huguely went to Landon, my high school's biggest rival," he wrote. "He partied with some of my best friends. In high school he was known as a lacrosse prodigy, and eventually, as the starting quarterback for Landon's football team. His life may not have been 'charmed' on the inside, but from afar, it looked like he had it pretty good. Girls loved him, and guys respected him."

Sharp had braced himself for the lacrosse discussion, then decided to delve in and head it off with a piece of his own. He knew the discussion would come, just as it did in the Duke scandal. For outsiders, the lacrosse culture is as bizarre as it is impregnable. Its male players more often than not fit the stereotype—their hair shaggy, their clothes preppy, their attitudes cocky. They're the top echelon in a sport for the elite, and those who are gifted are treated like celebrities first in high school, and then in college. The excesses start early, too, with adults and community members sometimes looking the other way when a player is caught breaking curfew or drinking underage. With college, it seems the excesses only heighten: more booze, more power, more prestige.

Sharp attended a private and costly boys' school much like Landon, he wrote, and many of his closest friends played lacrosse. Because of that, Sharp grew up alongside a lot of guys who partied hard and "treated a lot of people like crap." Women, non-athletes, and authority figures were all dismissed as lowly creatures.

"Pretty much anyone that wasn't *one of them* either didn't exist, or existed solely as an object of ridicule," Sharp said.

That of course didn't apply to all players or all teams, according to Sharp, but enough to make a real concern of the sense of entitlement some say goes hand-in-hand with lacrosse.

Perhaps George Huguely didn't feel entitled to date Yeardley Love over her objections, Sharp concluded, but it was possible that being immersed in the lacrosse culture helped lead him down a dangerous path where he used alcohol as a coping mechanism and his enviable social status to shrug off any real repercussions for his behavior.

Peter Prowitt, the *Sun* columnist and a Virginia native, said he would "readily defend the virtues" of lacrosse, but he saw a danger in pretending that Yeardley's death was "a freak occurrence."

"Closer study of the culture of sexual misconduct and off-the-field troubles in men's lacrosse reveals a disturbing trend up to Ms. Love's case and suggests that there exists an ugly side to lacrosse, as is often claimed regarding basketball and football."

The editorial indictments kept coming. Author and columnist Michael Kimmel wrote a story called "Lacrosse and the Entitled Elite Male Athlete" two weeks after Yeardley's death. In it, he described Huguely as a "rich preppy jock at one of America's richest and preppiest schools."

"To some, Huguely was simply a monster, a deviant psychopath," Kimmel wrote, then dismissed that as a minimizing assessment leveled by "us 'normal' folk . . . Others, though, pointed out how unbearably common and 'normal' such attacks actually are: In the United States alone, three women are murdered every single day by their intimate partners and more than a million are physically assaulted every single year."

The pundits pointed out how violent lacrosse is, questioning whether Huguely was drawn to it because of his own violent tendencies, or if the sport actually created the violence. While women's lacrosse is no-contact, it's common in men's lacrosse for one player to hack at another with his stick. Pretty much all forms of attack are green-lighted, short of from-behind shoves and head shots.

But some in the lax world said too much was made of Yeardley and Huguely's lacrosse ties. On one lacrosse forum, one poster—identified as "3rdPersonPlural"—said the media coverage of the case seemed hyper-focused on the students' athletic prowess. Some news outlets used the word "lacrosse" more than "murder or tragedy," the poster wrote. Why was the couple's lacrosse connection any more relevant than, say, their majors?

Megan Pringle, the *Good Morning Maryland* anchor, found herself agreeing. Months after Yeardley's death, she said she never saw Yeardley as a lacrosse player first and a young woman second. Yeardley's impending graduation and strong ties to her family and friends were as much a part of her as her love of lacrosse, Pringle noted.

"It's not like lacrosse was all she was," Pringle said. "She led a very nice life and was a beautiful woman. It was more than that. And it was profoundly sad."

In the days after Yeardley's death, the fate of the UVA lacrosse season was quietly weighed. The postseason was nearing, but Athletic Director Craig Littlepage said everyone was in too much shock by the loss of Love, who he said was "described as an angel by teammates and friends." The players yearned for normalcy, and wanted desperately to get back into the rhythm of their grueling practices and adrenaline-pumping games—but they didn't want to return to the field if it would upset Yeardley's family. It was only after Sharon Love gave her blessing that the university officially announced the continuation of both the men's and women's seasons. There was no doubt in anyone's mind that Yeardley would have wanted them to continue, women's

coach Julie Myers told reporters. Players returned to Klöckner Stadium for stretching and practice. Media reporters
were kept away to give the still-mourning athletes their privacy as they readied for NCAA battle.

Chapter 16

The UVA men's lacrosse team was the first to step on the field after Yeardley's death. It was a somber homecoming. The team was down one player, as George Huguely continued to sit in the Albemarle-Charlottesville Regional Jail, but his teammates weren't outwardly mourning the murder suspect. Rather, it was Yeardley's name on their warm-up shirts. Printed in a cursive font, set in orange type against blue fabric, it read ONE LOVE.

The combination of Yeardley's jersey number and last name had come to symbolize the way she had vowed to live her life in the wake of her father's death. "One Love" had quickly been adopted by everyone who knew her, and many who didn't. Her name and number seemed too perfect: It was inclusive, hopeful, even elegant. The men also wore orange and blue ribbons, adorned with a simple white emblem that read LOVE.

"She's out there with us when we're playing," sophomore attackman Steele Stanwick told a *USA Today* reporter.

Before game day, sportswriters had questioned how the team would hold up. Sure, their record was 14–1 before Yeardley's death, but it was impossible to predict how such a blow would affect the team psychologically. And it wasn't the first tragic loss the team had endured: In November 2008, just shy of Thanksgiving Day, word spread that teammate Will Barrow had committed suicide. Barrow, twenty-two, had completed his four years of lacrosse eligibility but still lived in Charlottesville as he wrapped up his sociology degree. He'd burst from the high school scene having been named the best athlete at Baldwin Senior High School in New York, and his reputation had only improved in college as he helped lead his team to its 2006 national championship. His senior year, he finished with a career-high twenty-eight ground balls, scoring seven goals and assisting in three. Considered one of the top defensive midfielders in the country, he already had been drafted eleventh overall by the Chicago Machine, a Major League Lacrosse team, and had scored three goals in the five games he had played. He aimed to shatter stereotypes, reaching out to other young black men in hopes of teaching them lacrosse.

Coach Starsia called Barrow a leader, and his death a shock to his teammates.

"I can only begin to describe adequately the agony within the Virginia lacrosse community," Starsia told reporters. "Will is a dear friend, respected and admired universally by his peers and the staff. He was a leader in our program, on and off the lacrosse field."

Though few talked in-depth about Barrow's death, it had a profound impact on his teammates and the lax community as a whole. Just as news of Yeardley's death filled the forums, so too did questions about Barrow's. "When one of us passes away, we get affected by it," one poster wrote. "Most of the members here didn't know him personally, but because he was on . . . the greatest stage within the sport of lacrosse, we feel it." Some questioned whether Barrow had really killed himself; the university had kept the cause of death so quiet that some circulated rumors online that the broad-smiled athlete must have died at someone else's hands. Though small in comparison to the outcry that would follow Yeardley's death, online memorials popped up for Barrow as well, including a Facebook page that two years later would still have more than 2,000 members. Most of the recent posts on the page, however, were obscene spam messages; the last real message that was posted came in October 2010 to promote the second annual Will Barrow Memorial Flag Football Tournament.

Despite the university's silence about Barrow's death, fourth-year players on the 2008–2009 lacrosse team, who had played alongside Barrow the previous year, took turns talking in private about him and the impact his life and death had on them.

"Will is someone who we think about every day and night," Max Pomper, one of Barrow's closest friends, told a reporter. "Before the game, we talk about Will. We talk about how we want to play like he did—play hard, play fast, play strong. He was an incredible leader and we'll never forget him. We want to honor him by playing well and playing hard."

Barrow's death had been mourned publicly, but in subtle ways. Many players wore special T-shirts during pregame warm-ups with "Will" embroidered on the sleeve.

Eighteen months later, they'd be donning remembrance T-shirts again, this time bearing Yeardley's initials. And they'd be joined by thousands. One CBS affiliate reported that tickets and T-shirt sales surged in the wake of Yeardley's death for both men's and women's teams.

"I think now, especially, they're going to show their support and their love for the teams and all the players and support what they're going through right now," UVA student Michael Parente told a television reporter.

Ken Clausen, a team captain, painted "Y.L." in eye black under one eye and "W.B." under the other. This game was in honor of both the fallen lax players.

It was Saturday, May 15, twelve days after life stopped for Yeardley and changed for everyone else. The Cavaliers were pitted against unranked Mount St. Mary's University, an 1805-founded private university in Emmitsburg, Maryland. Players from both teams bowed heads while Yeardley's picture appeared on the scoreboard for a moment of silence before the first-round NCAA tournament game began.

For Coach Starsia, the official return to Klöckner Stadium was his first following two gut-wrenching emotional blows: The same week Yeardley died, the coach's father succumbed to cancer. In the weeks that followed, he had to serve as a pillar to his dazed team, while at the same time nursing his own psychological wounds. For men like Starsia, and for the team that revered him, the best way to cope with pain was to unleash it on the field.

The Cavaliers exploded from the gate. Shamel Bratton, who wore No. 1 for the men, was fittingly the first to score. Seven more goals followed before Mount St. Mary's had a chance to respond. The 'Hoos were electric, seeming to exhale after nearly two weeks of bated breath. They were raw from mourning. Their sport had been scrutinized, their characters assassinated by association. They came ready to pummel.

"We wanted to play with a whole lot of heart and passion," Ken Clausen said after the game, "and I think we did a great job of doing that."

No. 1 Bratton scored two more goals for three total, tying for a game high with Brian Carroll and Chris Bocklet.

The 18–4 blowout had been cathartic, players said. Lacrosse had been both the team's bond and its sanctuary.

"By escaping and releasing some emotions and getting back to something we all love, I think that definitely helped us heal," said Clausen, who just a week earlier had been among Love's pallbearers and considered her one of his best friends. "But by no means has it healed. I don't think anything is going to go away anytime soon."

"Emotionally, it's been a tough ride for us," said junior goalie Adam Ghitelman, who added that "the best thing we've got going is the community of our teammates. . . . It's been a roller coaster. We've had to step up and kind of have iron hearts this past week. I think our team has come together, as well as the girls, helping each other out."

The men had won their comeback game. Next, it was the women's turn to take the field.

Chapter 17

Pressure ran high for the women as they geared up to battle Towson University on Sunday, May 16. The men had already come back to slaughter their first opponent. Now, everyone's eyes were on their female counterparts. News outlets that never before paid attention to lacrosse—much less women's lacrosse—sent reporters and photographers. Fans brought signs bearing heartfelt messages and Love's name.

It was a home game, again at Klöckner Stadium, meaning the women 'Hoos had the same home field advantage that the men had just a day prior. They made it no secret that they wanted to win this one for "Yards."

And there were reminders everywhere. Colorful flowers lay in memoriam by the game sign. Beneath the players' jerseys were shirts that read ONE TEAM. ONE HEART. ONE LOVE. The women, too, wore black patches on the front of their jerseys with the word LOVE in white letters.

Even Towson, the competition, paid their respects, honoring Yeardley with orange wristbands with Y.L. written in dark blue. Just as the community had united in mourning after Barrow's death, they were united now. The Towson players wished the 'Hoos well for the rest of the season, and gave each of their opponents a pin of an angel carrying a lacrosse stick.

A season-high crowd of more than 2,200 people filled Klöckner's stands.

"I just felt like I needed to take time out and show some support," Bob Mattie, a local lacrosse coach and UVA fan, told a reporter. Added Cricket Capucci, a Towson fan: "We're all parents and it could happen to any one of our kids. You feel helpless when you see something like this happen."

Fans and players alike acknowledged a moment of silence for Yeardley and her family. Several wiped away tears.

Cavalier player Whitaker Hagerman, a pretty but fierce blond who started in eighteen contests in the 2009–10 season, dropped her head and spoke to Yeardley in the stillness.

"Be out here with us," Hagerman quietly pleaded.

The silence was shattered by a Cavaliers fan in the grandstand, whose raucous "Let's go UVA!" seemed to energize both sides.

"We had to go out there, we had to play a game, we had to play lacrosse, and we had to play well," Hagerman later told reporters.

Like the men, the women seemed to explode with ferocity, scoring three goals in the first three minutes. But unlike the men's game, the fervor wasn't unmatched. Towson quickly responded to every goal. By the fifty-minute mark, the game was tied at eleven goals apiece. The crowd had erupted with every Cavalier goal—especially two netted by Caitlin Whiteley, the roommate who had discovered Yeardley's body in their shared apartment—and Towson's perseverance seemed as much in honor of Yeardley's competitive spirit as her own team's.

Megan Pringle, the *Good Morning Maryland* anchor, walked downstairs in her Baltimore home to find her husband, a sports reporter, watching the match at home. Tears streamed down his face. Rob Carlin, who had covered a few Yeardley-related stories as a freelancer for Comcast, was leveled not only by the players' tenacity, but also by the obvious outpouring of support by the fans. They wore ribbons and held signs. The camera regularly returned to shots of

Sharon and Lexie Love in the stands. Lexie, her eyes hidden behind dark sunglasses, was clearly in tears.

The camera seemed to focus in on one player, No. 14, more than others, Pringle recalled. When she asked why, her husband told her the player's name: It was Whiteley. Pringle suddenly understood.

As the game remained tied with ten minutes remaining, Coach Julie Myers noticed two pink-clad women in dark sunglasses making their way to the Cavaliers' bench. The younger of the women had Yeardley's beaming smile and, one teammate said later, even Yeardley's laugh. After a moment, the players on the field spotted the women, too. Yeardley's mother, Sharon, and sister, Lexie, had stepped forward to show the team their support in the game's waning minutes.

"When they came down, and I saw them kind of walking up behind our team, I felt like we were going to suddenly be OK," Myers later told reporters. "I felt like they were going to kind of be our extra emotion on the side."

The boost worked: Cavalier Brittany Kalkstein scored, giving her team a 12–11 lead. Next came Whiteley, whose third goal of the contest seemed the most powerful, pushing the team to a two-goal lead. Each team scored once more, and as the buzzer sounded on the 14–12 Cavaliers win, the team players stood together and held into the air white cards bearing Love's No. 1.

Lexie Love's head dropped as she cried.

After the game, the players spoke publicly for the first time since Yeardley's death. While they were careful not to discuss the case or their feelings about George Huguely, they described their friend and teammate—and the horror they had experienced over the previous two weeks.

"For me, it's been really hard, but I don't know where I'd be without my team and all my close friends," Whiteley said. "Playing today meant a lot, and it's obviously not normal, but I feel like each day we're getting stronger, finding out what we need from each other."

Though their season ended with the loss, Towson's players seemed satisfied.

"It was hard coming here knowing everyone was rooting against us a little bit," Towson senior Jackie Kendell told reporters after the game. "I think in respect to the Virginia team, it was our duty to play as hard as we could against them. I think that's what everyone would have wanted. On the field, that's where all that drama goes away, and it was our job to give them a really good game—and we definitely did that."

Yeardley was "an absolutely unforgettable person," UVA player Marye Kellermann told reporters. "When you met her, you just loved her, she was great. My very best friend . . . I am going to try my best to make sure the world doesn't forget what a good person she was."

Brittany Kalkstein, who scored the all-important, tie-breaking twelfth goal for the Cavs, said the previous two weeks had been "unbelievable."

"Our team is going through it together—and, no, I can't compare this to anything," she said, responding to a reporter's question. "It was just a crazy last two weeks, and I think being together and trying to stay focused and coming out to practice is the strength we needed to be with each other and get through it."

Kaitlin Duff, another fourth-year player who also roomed with Yeardley, said the community outpouring had been invaluable.

"Seeing everyone being so positive and so nice just really helps our team and helps our team get stronger," she said at a post-game news conference.

"We are one team," added Lauren Benner, the team's goalie. "We have one heart, and we're doing it for one purpose. And it's for Yeardley."

For Coach Myers, the Sunday afternoon victory was more than a simple lacrosse win. It was life affirming.

"I know I wasn't ready to be done," she said. "I don't think the girls were close to being ready, either. Partly because we're really competitive, and we really love playing lacrosse, and we feel like we're a good enough team to still be alive, but also because we still need to be together as we take these next steps.

"This was obviously much more than just a game today," she continued. "An NCAA game with obvious consequence of not being able to move forward if you don't win. Just a huge hurdle for our team to clear through. You hear that you always want to try to find some kind of normal, and to be back on a game field, I think is something that's normal at this point in the season. I'm very proud of the way they were able to play, especially during the circumstances we've been in."

The win marked the first in the NCAA Tournament for the 'Hoos since 2007, and it advanced them to the quarterfinal round the following weekend.

"Emotionally, we've been through an awful lot," Myers said. "I think the girls really were phenomenally inspiring this week. I felt like they played really hard with lots of attention and just emotion—positive emotion."

As the team celebrated its win, a song began to blast over the Klöckner's sound system. It was Cher, belting her 1998 hit "Believe."

"Do you believe in life after love?" began the chorus. The team exploded in excitement.

They believed indeed.

Chapter 18

Six days later, the fourth-seeded UVA women's lacrosse team faced third-seeded University of North Carolina. Some of the remembrances that had graced Klöckner Stadium carried over to Chapel Hill's Fetzer Field: wristbands worn in Yeardley's honor, a pregame moment of silence, Love's name adorning the UVA team's jerseys. The intervening days had been a whirlwind of grueling practice hours, commencement rehearsals, and mourning. The women tried to reignite the fire sparked during the game against Towson, but the vibe was different. Sharon and Lexie Love didn't attend this game. Instead, they sent players text messages, including one to Kaitlin Duff that read *1-2-3-4, Go Hoos*. Love's uncle, the former UVA lacrosse player in whose footsteps Yeardley had followed, told the women that their team was "everyone's team, the country's team right now." Heading into the contest, it was clear the Cavaliers were the sentimental favorites.

UNC Coach Jenny Levy sought out Coach Myers before the game to offer condolences. The two were lacrosse teammates at UVA years before and had stayed good friends as they moved on to teach competing teams. Levy's team had a game the day of Yeardley's funeral; her players wore wristbands with YL1 embroidered on them, and Levy sent Myers a text message and photograph of her captains wearing the bands before the game.

Myers told reporters that, aside from giving players a day off after the previous win to recuperate, they prepped for their Chapel Hill appearance as hard as ever.

"We're making sure our game is sharp and taking breaks when we need to," she told a reporter. "We're still in the healing process, but still trying to get ready for the game. We're trying to make sure we're doing enough to be ready but not too much to overwhelm."

But as the match began, it became quickly clear that some of the electricity had dulled. This time, as the Cavs gave up the first goal, it appeared to onlookers that the roller coaster of the past three weeks had finally caught up with the team. Instead of attacking, the players limped. They seemed drained, unfocused. Even the crowd had lost its fervor. Instead of a packed stadium with thousands of spectators, fewer than 700 people had gathered at Fetzer Field.

The Cavs found the scoreboard three minutes into the game, but UNC responded with eight more goals, jumping to a 9–1 lead. By halftime, the score was a painfully lopsided 11–2. In the end, the Tar Heels doled out a 17–7 loss—the biggest deficit the 'Hoos had endured all year—ending the mourning team's season.

After the buzzer sounded to end the sixty minutes, the Cavaliers stayed on the field. Some slumped onto the grass, breaking into tears. Several clutched each other in hugs. They simply weren't ready to walk away, to have the season end. They had survived so much together; the close of the season seemed to symbolize that they would now have to face things alone.

"The end of any season is a really hard, sudden ending," Coach Myers told reporters after the game. "I think that the end to this season, given all that we've been through, makes it especially hard."

Myers said she knew it wasn't an easy victory for North Carolina, either.

"Emotionally, it was hard for them to play a hand in the

ending of our season. I give them credit. I think they did a nice job with a lot of poise and a lot of competitiveness in making sure they won this game today."

After the 'Hoos finally left the field, the coach gathered with the young women and told them she was proud of them.

"The message was that I love them," Myers said. "And I couldn't have asked them to do anything more—not on the field, and not off the field. They've been really outstanding. Our first few days we literally took it hour by hour and, eventually, we were able to think as big as two days away. I don't think I ever thought where we would be three weeks down the road."

Kaitlin Duff again was a stellar scorer, securing three of the Cavaliers' goals. Caitlin Whiteley, whose three-goal performance less than a week prior had galvanized the crowd, was scoreless.

"I think we had a great season, and we had a lot of ups and downs, but we really stuck together," Duff told reporters. "It shows there's a lot more to the game of lacrosse than winning. We didn't play our best today, but I think we feel great about the season."

Reporters asked the inevitable question: *What next?*

Brittany Kalkstein answered thoughtfully.

"I don't think that there is any way you can really move on from this," she said. "Obviously, it's going to be in our thoughts forever. We will try and stick in town for a few days and be with each other . . . It's been a huge learning experience these past few weeks, and I think it taught us about life."

The women's season had ended, but the curtain hadn't fallen on UVA lacrosse entirely. Up next: the men.

Coming off the women's loss in North Carolina, the first-seeded men's team faced eighth-seeded Stony Brook University. The Seawolves, as the Cavaliers' counterparts were named, got home field advantage at the 1,000-acre campus on Long Island's North Shore in New York, about 500 miles north of Charlottesville.

By then, the intense media attention had shifted. The

women's run was over. While news photographers and cameras still lined the field at LaValle Stadium, the outlets were mostly familiar again—ones that normally would have paid attention to an NCAA quarterfinal match.

Shamel Bratton and Chris Bocklet again scored three goals apiece, helping the team eke past the Seawolves with a 10–9 win. While the women's team had halted, the men headed to another round.

"Watching the scores yesterday, finding out the girls didn't get the win they wanted, you really want to get to the end for them," Adam Ghitelman told reporters afterward. "For me personally and for the team, those girls deserve everything. We're going to play the rest of the season for them; they deserve it."

Captain Ken Clausen echoed the sentiment.

"With everything that's been going on, and lacrosse aside, we want to be able to stick together as a team and going out there and playing for the girls and playing for Yeardley," he said. "That's been in our minds and it's been some motivation for us. We're ready to keep playing hard and stick together for another week."

The men, like the women, had "been through a lot," Clausen added.

"Kind of our motto has been that we don't want this thing to end."

Six days later, it did end.

The Cavaliers faced fifth-seeded Duke in another away game—this time in front of 44,238 fans at M&T Bank Stadium in Baltimore. The turnout made the game the sixth-largest attended semifinal game in NCAA men's lacrosse tournament history, according to VirginiaSports.com.

Bocklet again led in team scoring, netting four goals, but the effort fell short. Thanks to Duke's stellar third quarter, during which they outscored UVA 4–1, the Blue Devils snuck past Virginia with a 14–13 win.

Coach Dom Starsia, wearing a patch that read Y.L. 1. on his shirt, somberly told reporters that the team had played hard and showed courage both on the field and off.

"The final score is probably the least important part of what has transpired here," he said.

Bocklet wiped away tears as Starsia spoke. Several players couldn't stomach the season-ending press conference and instead sought solace in the locker room. They were "upset the final result wasn't what they hoped for."

"Emotionally, it was hard. Emotionally, I think it's a lot to handle," sophomore Steele Stanwick, who tallied three goals and two assists in the game, said. "The season may be over, but we're still a team. We're going to stick together through this thing and make sure everyone's OK."

Again, George Huguely's teammates never mentioned his name, which by then had even been deleted from the team's official 2009–10 roster online.

It was as though he hadn't existed all season.

PART III

"You'll Get Nothing From Me, Pal"

Chapter 19

Students on the university's campus tried to get their lives back to normal, but it wasn't easy. The media scrutiny, while perhaps waning, was still pervasive. With every university milestone came another round of reporters looking to cover it from the "Yeardley Love" angle. On May 13, *People* magazine hit newsstands and mailboxes with Love on the cover. In bold letters, layered over the team photo that had run in newspapers nationwide, the cover text asked: "COULD SHE HAVE BEEN SAVED?" An inset photo of Huguely in jail garb hovered over the ominous title: "Virginia Lacrosse Killing." It was heavy fare, juxtaposed alongside a photo of actress Sandra Bullock with her new adopted child and an announcement that country music artists Blake Shelton and Miranda Lambert had gotten engaged.

By the time freelance writer Matthew Power showed up to cover the university's graduation, the whole town of Charlottesville seemed exhausted by what he described as a "shark frenzy" of media attention.

Power, a contributor editor to *Harper's Magazine* whose works have been published in dozens of high-profile magazines, including *Men's Journal*, *Mother Jones*, *Slate,* and *Maxim*, got a surprise phone call from *Rolling Stone* magazine. Editors there had been slow to pick up on the Love slaying, but following the cover story in *People*, they seemed interested in providing readers with a more detailed takeout than they'd seen to date. Power hadn't paid much attention to the case until he was asked to cover it. But his mother knew all about it.

"It had been an oversaturated media circus since" her death, Power later recalled. "I knew I was going into a tough situation, and *Rolling Stone* knew it, too. I was so far behind the curve of the rest of the media coverage."

Power wasn't thrilled with the assignment, but he accepted it anyway—largely, he acknowledged, because he didn't want to pass up a gig with *Rolling Stone*. Plus, despite his distaste for the way Americans eat up grisly murder tales, he had been assured that the magazine would allow him the time and space he would need to tell Yeardley's story in a respectful, insightful way. Perhaps some good could come from telling the story thoughtfully, he reasoned.

"With *Rolling Stone*, you have the great fortune of space and time and context and nuance," he said. "It didn't have to be boiled down to 'dead, cute girl.' You do have the potential of doing it right without it being as sensational a story."

Armed with as many story clips and contact phone numbers as he could quickly gather, Power rented a car and drove from his home in New York City to Charlottesville, crashing at the home of a journalist friend. He tracked down Brendan Fitzgerald, the reporter with *C-VILLE Weekly* who had covered the death from the very first hours. Power tried to reach Yeardley's family, but to no avail. Sharon apparently had spoken briefly to *People* but was declining further requests. Attorneys from both sides weren't speaking, either. Power then reached out to Yeardley's friends, most of whom were polite but clearly unwilling to assist with the piece.

None of that shocked Power, but what did surprise him was the reluctance of people who didn't know Yeardley but who could have nonetheless helped tell the tale of her life at UVA. It was as if the whole city was on lockdown, as though some directive had been passed out community-wide instructing people to shrug off all media inquiries. It didn't

matter what outlet the reporter was from or how earnest he
or she was about telling the story properly. Yeardley's death
had united the city in silence.

The Sunday after Power arrived in town—about three
days into his trip—an attempt at a profile piece on Huguely
was published in the *Washington Post*. The story largely was
based on public court records, some of which already had
been made public, and unnamed sources—a noticeable lack
of substance in a story that boasted three reporters in its byline and several more as contributors. One unnamed source
was a bartender at Boylan Heights, the bar down the street
from Yeardley and George's apartments, an establishment
that reportedly had been busy on the night of the slaying.
Even though the source wasn't identified, Power learned that
the bartender who blabbed had been fired after the piece ran.
And when Power himself reached out to the bar, a different
bartender snarled, "You'll get nothing from me, pal."

Power half-smiled, handed over his business card, finished his subpar $3 drink of well vodka and soda, and left.

"The fact was, there was no upside for anyone to talk,"
Power said. "They had been completely swarmed over by
the media. Most of them were young kids about to graduate,
and they suddenly found themselves in the deep end of a media pool. Every kid on both of the teams had been swamped
with calls and calls and calls from reporters. Imagine your
whole life is ahead of you, and you're suddenly thrust into a
sordid murder investigation."

Power paused, then mused the university's colors.

"There was an orange wall of silence," he said.

Power reached his contact at *Rolling Stone* and told him the
story might be tough to deliver. Somehow, the case was the
talk of the town—but no one was actually saying anything.
Still, Power decided to stay on through the university's graduation ceremonies in hopes that he might find two or three
people to help him tell an appropriate story. The story he felt
he was uncovering, even in people's silence, was one about
wealth and connections in an insular high society. In fact, he
said, it was an "insular culture within an insular culture within

an insular culture"—a group of wealthy young adults admitted to the prestigious University of Virginia who belonged to the cloistered lacrosse culture. The story made headlines not just because Yeardley was young, beautiful, and white, Power said. It garnered international attention in part because of the "shock that trailer park behavior would occur" within that society.

Behind the scenes, Yeardley's family was hard at work trying to distance the young woman from the image of a domestic violence victim. While John Casteen's heartfelt words at Yeardley's on-campus vigil had garnered national praise, the family, by many accounts, was not happy with her being depicted as a victim—or, as in the lyrics of the haunting Pink Floyd song, among the "weak and the weary." As the family's displeasure became known, university employees were cautioned not only to avoid media questions, but to particularly shy away from any phrasing that might depict Yeardley as the victim of intimate partner violence.

One employee felt this was a mistake. Frances Godfrey*, whose name has been changed because she fears she will lose her job by speaking publicly, said the university missed an opportunity to reach out to young adults by acquiescing to the family's request to stay silent.

"It might seem honorable within the university to honor the family's wishes, but I can't help but wonder if it's the right way to go. There are ways to talk about the incident that don't make Yeardley look like this was somehow her fault," Godfrey said.

Others at the university agreed. Some wanted to use the case to reach out to young women in unhealthy relationships, but they were forbidden. Publicly, only Casteen had been granted permission to speak about the case, and even he fell silent within a week of Yeardley's death.

"He was considered by many to have made very eloquent statements," Godfrey recalled. "Everyone at the university was consoled by that. But then even he stopped talking. Everything got quiet."

Asked via phone message and e-mail about the university's response to the tragedies, UVA spokeswoman Carol Wood refused to reply. To some, it seemed reflective of the university's decision to fall mute. The pall cast over the university was palpable, employees said. The academic year had been so difficult. People felt sucker punched and drained, and now they felt they had to walk on eggshells around campus when so many were ready to scream out.

This had been a year when students kept hopeful vigil on the bridge where Morgan Harrington was last seen, only to be devastated with the discovery of her body three months later. A year when the peak of lacrosse season was marred by the brutal slaying of one student, and the unfathomable arrest of another. A year when six other students—three of them seniors, on the cusp of graduating and entering the so-called real world—died suddenly. For many, these instances marked their first introductions to death, serving as a wake-up call that the world they were entering could be unthinkably sinister and heartlessly random.

"It had been a terrible, terrible year. Just god-awful," Godfrey said. "This genuinely isn't a place that we think of as being violent. It was so shocking—profoundly, profoundly shocking."

Outside of Yeardley's vigil, students involved in the White Ribbon Campaign—meant to raise awareness for violence against women—passed out the looped material, but Godfrey said she later learned that they had already been asked not to directly link Yeardley with domestic violence. Instead, the volunteers—mostly young women—passed the ribbons out quietly to people approaching the campus lawn.

Sharon Love acknowledged to one reporter that she was tired of the media portraying Yeardley as a domestic violence victim. The reporter, a woman, said that she was personally familiar with such violence and saw Yeardley's story as a chance to illustrate how even smart, strong women could be victimized. Maybe some good could come from the story, the reporter suggested.

"Yeardley was no shrinking violet," Love interjected.

The reporter was taken aback. "Neither was I," she answered.

"The family did not want it to be called domestic violence because that meant particular things about Yeardley, and that was the end of that," Godfrey said. "It could no longer be called that. We were not to link these two things."

Liz Seccuro, the UVA alumna and victims' rights activist, noticed that people shied away when she called it domestic violence as well.

"That is what it is: Domestic violence," she said. "People don't like that moniker because it doesn't speak to 'nice kids' who go to 'nice schools.'"

The family's decree colored how—and whether—Casteen and others would discuss Yeardley from then on.

Though Yeardley wouldn't be there to cross the stage, she was still set to graduate from the University of Virginia. The school announced that she would receive her degree posthumously, allowing her to achieve in death what she'd set her sights on years prior: the UVA degree her father never got.

The first graduation was on May 23, and it was the one most university students attended. Yeardley would not have crossed the stage in that ceremony had she lived because she would have been traveling with her teammates 180 miles away in Chapel Hill, North Carolina, after playing in the final lacrosse match of the year. Still, her absence seemed to weigh down the crowd, recalled Matthew Power, who, like Brendan Fitzgerald, attended the ceremony.

Tens of thousands of people gathered to watch the sea of graduates, garbed in black gowns and colored hoods, make the hour-long trek across the stately lawn to their seats. As they walked, the heartache of the past few weeks lifted slightly and gave way to high-fives, hugs, and laughter. Students snapped photos of themselves on their cell phones and texted them to friends. Images from the ceremony were posted to Facebook profiles before the commencement even began.

As soon as the class was seated, however, the crowd quieted for a moment of silence to honor the four members of the graduating class who did not live to see graduation. Though Yeardley was just one of four, her death seemed to overshadow the others. Perhaps it was just timing as hers had been the most recent, or maybe it was the lingering what-ifs, the senselessness of it—and the feeling that it could have, and should have, been avoided.

As Charlottesville's streets clogged with commencement-goers, volunteers again quietly passed out their white ribbons—reportedly 25,000 of them—in hopes of raising awareness. Caitlin Donaghy, a UVA student, was one of only a few to agree to speak to reporters.

"The reality is, domestic abuse is prevalent everywhere, and people really need to talk about it and know that there are resources out there," she told CBS's *Early Show*.

But the reality was, no one was talking about what killed Yeardley Love. As the commencement speeches began, there would be some allusions to, and a few direct mentions of, Yeardley, but there would be no discussion of what caused her death. Nor would there be any mention of Huguely, who had also been set to graduate that day.

John Casteen, looking even more like an academic than usual, approached the podium, wearing a traditional black robe. He "appeared both timeless and unshakeable before a crowd of thousands," Fitzgerald wrote in the May 25 edition of *C-VILLE Weekly*. For the university president, the day weighed heavy for more reasons than Yeardley's death. He had announced prior to the academic year that 2010 would mark his final commencement before an August 1 retirement, bringing to an end a twenty-year legacy at the school. He had arrived amid a budget crisis, navigating through complicated changes to how the state would fund the university. In 1990, the university had been smaller; Casteen helped it grow, both in terms of its facilities and in student enrollment. In his two decades as president, the university had built or bought 134 new buildings, increased female undergraduate enrollment from 50 to 56 percent, increased minority enrollment by nearly 7 percent, and increased overall enrollment from about 18,000 to nearly 21,000. Casteen had been lauded for creating the Office of Diversity and Equity at the university in the wake of racial incidents between 2003 and 2005, during which black students reported experiencing racial epithets scrawled in bathrooms and screamed at them as they walked down the street. Largely, Casteen was praised as a university president. Some said he would likely go down in history as its best.

But his last year on campus had been remarkably dark. Seven of his students had died, four of whom were on the cusp of graduating and beginning new lives, and the murder of Morgan Harrington had also disquieted the town.

"This is, in a sense, a daunting moment for me," Casteen began as he faced some 6,000 graduates. "Just as the University has not been perfect in your time here, the world to which you go is flawed and, in some senses, corrupt."

Casteen admitted that he was more accustomed to watching commencements rather than speaking at them, and he struggled to find the right words and advice. Jokingly, he passed along his wife's tip—"don't sweat the small stuff." But his real message was wrapped in references to John Keats, the nineteenth-century poet whose life was cut short at age twenty-five by tuberculosis. For Casteen, it was Keats's theory of "negative capability"—or the capacity to accept the uncertain and unresolved—that resonated most.

"Here we must decide for ourselves whether or not to act—whether we will step out courageously to explore those dark passages," Casteen said.

Though he didn't say Yeardley's name at that point, those attending were sure he was referencing her.

Casteen mused about the things he would miss hearing most when he left the campus: "The sounds of children on the lawn during Halloween. The chapel's bells. Cheers at games, no matter what the sport. And the name of Yeardley Love."

It was the only time he uttered her name, and they were the final two words Casteen spoke. His message seemed clear: Yeardley must not be forgotten.

For those familiar with Keats's life and death, that message was especially poignant. The young man, whose poems and letters were only appreciated after his death, was both afraid and certain that his existence on earth would be forgotten. The epitaph he wrote for his tombstone reads: "Here lies one whose name was writ in water."

Casteen seemed to be urging the campus to make sure Yeardley's name was written in stone.

Department chair Jeffrey Legro presided over the ceremony for Yeardley's 250 political science classmates. It seemed a bittersweet day for those crossing the lawn to receive their diplomas. The death was too fresh—just three weeks had passed—for students to feel ready to selfishly celebrate their own accomplishments. A sense of survivor's guilt hung thick in the air.

After what seemed to be the last name was read and the final diploma received, Legro said he had one remaining.

"As you know, Yeardley Love was killed just weeks short of this ceremony," he told the crowd. "Today, we are not mourning Yeardley. We are celebrating her achievement as a member of the class of 2010 at this University of Virginia."

Several members of Yeardley's family sat in the audience, including an aunt and uncle and some cousins, Legro said. He called on Lawren McChesney, Yeardley's cousin and a 2006 UVA graduate, to accept the diploma on Love's behalf.

"It is a privilege to recognize all that Yeardley achieved as a student at UVA and all the potential she had in life by awarding a posthumous degree of bachelor of arts in government," Legro said.

He paused, then called her name the same fashion as everyone else who had received a degree: "Yeardley. Reynolds. Love."

The crowd erupted in applause. It lasted a raucous forty-five seconds, tempered only by Legro's prompting.

"You are now officially alumni," Legro told the graduating class. "You will be missed."

* * *

On Monday, the university held a special graduation for the men's lacrosse and softball players who had missed the previous day's ceremonies. The athletes filed into Old Cabell Hall, one of three buildings designed by Stanford White for the south end of the Lawn in 1898. Originally known as the Academical Building, it was stately and grand, with an auditorium stage lined with giant organ pipes and adorned on the north wall with a copy of *The School of Athens* by Raphael.

Several members of the men's team wore buttons bearing Yeardley's name and the date of her death on their robes. Ken Clausen, the men's captain who had worn both Yeardley's and Will Barrow's initials on his cheeks, was introduced as a stellar athlete, one of the men's lacrosse team captains. He took the microphone to uproarious applause and thanked the university, its faculty, his coaches, his teammates, and all the lacrosse parents. He shared in the university softball team's solid 2010 showing, and said that they gathered this day not only to celebrate the athletes' accomplishments in the classroom, but also their accomplishments on the field.

The weeks leading up to graduation had tested everyone, he added.

"The untimely death of Yeardley Love sent shockwaves through our program, the university, and the country," he said, reading from a speech. "This tragic event forced our teams and the university to stick together to come out stronger rather than fragment and fade away.

"Well, I can assure you the latter has not occurred, and that our university has come together like no one could have imagined."

The coaches, staff, students and parents had all supported the team immensely, he added. He thanked them on behalf of his whole team.

After his speech, as the applause began to quiet, Clausen stepped down. Matthew Power, who had already e-mailed and called Clausen before the graduation, tried to sidle up to him in hopes he would elaborate. Power's approach was respectful and a bit laid-back—more "please consider calling me" than the stereotypical microphone-in-the-face approach that some attach to journalists. He knew the kids were hurting. He knew, too, that they already seemed banded together in silence. Clausen had come across as a stand-up guy, and it seemed he had a lot more to say on the matter than what he presented in his seven-minute speech. But Clausen declined, as did Caitlin Whiteley and the other members of both the men and women's teams. No one was willing or able to shed light on either Yeardley's or George's personalities or their relationship.

Power had repeatedly run into the same refrain. After about a week of in-person and phone research, he gave up and alerted *Rolling Stone* that the story had stalled. It was the first time in his professional career that he had ditched a story because no one would cooperate. He assured *Rolling Stone* that the failure wasn't caused by any personal shortcoming.

"I said they could be comforted in the knowledge that no one else would have the story, either," he said.

A few months later, as he recalled the experience, Power said he couldn't blame anyone for refusing to cooperate. He suspected that many felt complicit in Yeardley's death—and he didn't disagree. There had been several public run-ins between Yeardley and Huguely, and for whatever reason, apparently not one of those instances had been reported to the authorities.

"Everyone should have known it was a huge problem," Power said. "I'd be surprised if many weren't aware, which makes them complicit in some way."

Chapter 20

If the people involved refused to talk, perhaps the documents could speak for them. Reporters had already started filing requests under state and federal Freedom of Information Act laws, which ensure that public documents are actually made available to the public. The laws perhaps seem like no-brainers, but they were enacted for a reason: Government agencies had a long history of refusing to release information that they thought might make them look bad.

The federal Act was signed into law by President Lyndon B. Johnson on July 4, 1966. While the president said flowery things at the time—"this legislation springs from one of our most essential principles," and "a democracy works best when the people have all the information"—he actually had fought against the bill, which was pioneered largely by a group of journalists, a Democrat creator (congressman John Moss), and a Republican co-signer (then-congressman Donald Rumsfeld—yes, the same one). The goal was to make the paper trail behind democracy accessible to the people. Built in were three paragraphs of cautionary language about military secrets, personnel files, confidential advice, executive privilege, and investigative files.

As with any high-profile case, reporters on the Yeardley Love case sought as many documents as the law allowed them to have: police reports, court records, and search warrant requests. All could help flesh out a story that otherwise would be told only by opposing sides with decidedly biased outlooks. Reporters filed, too, for copies of the nine-one-one call in hopes of learning why the death at first was flagged as a possible alcohol overdose, and they asked for the autopsy reports that would indicate exactly what caused Yeardley's heart to stop pumping.

Sometimes, journalists need do nothing more than ask. That depends on the source, the state, and certainly the reputation of the reporter. With criminal cases, of course, things can get tricky: What the public wants to know can pit one constitutional guarantee (freedom of the press) against another (innocent until proven guilty). Circulating details about a crime could compromise inquiries, undercut cases, or hamstring investigations. Thus, many documents are redacted or even sealed, citing "ongoing investigation" as the exemption from FOIA.

Within days of Yeardley's death, it was clear that access to police reports and court documents would be contested. Some of the initial search warrants had been released, and then, within days, suddenly sealed by court order even after they had been posted on the Internet. No doubt the sealing was meant to set a precedent in the case, establishing that most, if not all, of the records pertaining to the commonwealth's case against George Huguely V were exempt because of the ongoing investigation.

The *Washington Post* balked. Joined by Media General (publishers of the *Charlottesville Daily Progress* and *Richmond Times-Dispatch*) and the Associated Press, the *Post* filed a petition on May 11 asking that the search warrants and other documents in the case be unsealed.

Circuit Court Judge Cheryl Higgins presided over a hearing Tuesday, May 18, during which the media outlets' lawyer acknowledged that the judge might have "a very valid reason for closing the search warrants." Higgins had previously worked as a partner at Huguely's lawyer, Francis McQ. Lawrence's, Charlottesville law firm. The two focused on litigating divorce cases with St. John, Bowling & Lawrence, LLP (which later added Quagliana to its name). Perhaps sensing that the media might ask Higgins to recuse herself because of her past relationship with the defense, Lawrence and his new partner, Rhonda Quagliana, preemptively released a statement insisting they had not been part of any hearings regarding the order to seal the documents, nor had they sought materials related to the search warrants sealed by the court. In fact, they said, they hadn't taken a position yet as to whether the documents should be sealed or open.

Not so the prosecution. Warner "Dave" Chapman said in court that the widespread media attention was potentially damaging to the case and could make it difficult come jury-selection time to find people who hadn't formed an opinion on Huguely's guilt or innocence. He had long been known as a prosecutor who refused to talk about open investigations, and this case would not break his resolve.

"We have a duty that this is a proceeding that can take place in the city of Charlottesville," Chapman said. "We have a duty that this is a trial that can take place in front of unbiased jurors."

According to the media's petition, the *Daily Progress* obtained a search warrant inventory from the court clerk's office two days after Yeardley's death. When a *Washington Post* reporter went to the same office to view the same records, the reporter was told that it and all other records had been sealed. Even the order sealing the documents had been sealed.

The media groups' lawyer was flabbergasted. How could they argue against the judge's reason for sealing the documents if they weren't allowed to at least know the reason?

Higgins wasn't ready to rule. She wanted to review the briefs submitted by both sides, she said, and she would share her decision on May 26.

And she did. Higgins ruled that the news groups hadn't filed their petition in the proper format. She kept the documents sealed, as well as the order sealing the documents, and dismissed the petition.

The media outlets weren't ready to admit defeat. They

protested again, re-filing the petition in the manner that the court clerk had deemed proper. In early June, Higgins released partially redacted orders explaining why the search warrants and affidavits had been sealed. But the records themselves were still hidden.

The orders, boasting thick black marker over many words, stated that "public dissemination at this time of highly detailed information such as contained in the affidavit, the search warrant, and any return made thereon may prejudice the ability of law enforcement authorities to continue their investigation."

Additionally, they said, the release of the information "may prejudice the ability in any subsequent trial to select an impartial jury."

David Lacy, one of the lawyers representing the media consortium, told reporters that it wasn't enough to say that potential jurors *might* be tainted. The judge had to show that there is a "real possibility" of harm to a jury pool, he said.

Chapman declined to comment on the documents battle. He made it clear in court that he wanted them sealed to protect his case—which, in fact, was "the people's" case. He and the media were at odds over whether the release of details would derail justice.

Leonard Niehoff, a law professor at the University of Michigan and a media law expert, said the sealing of search warrants isn't unusual. Niehoff, who isn't connected with the Huguely case, said such warrants pose a peculiar set of problems.

"In one sense, they're related to a specific event—a search—and in another sense, they're related to what may be an ongoing criminal investigation, and they could contain evidence that might be admitted against a defendant if the case goes to trial," he said.

Once the search is over, some argue that the documents connected to the search should be released. The event has passed, so there no longer is a worry that releasing the information might tip off the parties and prompt them to destroy potential evidence. But law-enforcement officials have sound reason to hesitate, Niehoff said.

"The full disclosure of a search warrant might tell more information than the police are willing to disclose at that particular time," he said.

Some of the items that had been sought might still be pursued in later search warrants at different addresses, he said. And some of the sought items that weren't found could taint the defendant unfairly if the details were released publicly before a trial. Take, for example, a warrant seeking bomb-making materials or child pornography. Even if police don't find the items, they could stick in potential jurors' minds and forever paint an innocent person as a terrorist or pedophile, Niehoff said. In trial, judges have a ruling for keeping that kind of impossible-to-ignore information away from jurors' ears: "more prejudicial than probative." But when such information has already been released, it's sometimes tough damage to undo.

The argument of jury tainting is a battle fought time and again in high-profile cases. One side or the other worries that releasing information about a case will make it impossible to find jurors who can set aside their previously formed opinions and listen only to the evidence presented at trial. But, Niehoff said, jurors have repeatedly proven that they're willing and able to dismiss what they've heard or read and weigh only what the judge deems admissible. Take, for instance, the Charles Manson case: It was beyond question one of the most-publicized mass murders in U.S. history, and a paperback book containing confessions from one of Manson's so-called "girls" had hit bookstores long before the trial began. Then-President Richard Nixon declared Manson and his cohorts guilty of murder before a verdict was rendered. Still, lawyers from both sides signed off on a jury they felt would be fair, and Manson's conviction has withstood the obligatory onslaught of appeals. Then there was the case of O. J. Simpson, who some people believe got away with murder. He had been declared a killer by some news outlets before charges were even filed, and his attempt to flee police had been broadcast live on television. Despite all that seemingly damning publicity, his jury acquitted him based on the evidence presented in his trial.

"I'm very rarely persuaded by the argument that it's impossible to seat an impartial jury," Niehoff said. "Most judges aren't moved by it, either. When judges do things" in the name of protecting the jury, "they're usually being extraordinarily careful in how the case is handled pretrial so as not to give the defendant a good grounds for appeal."

No matter how pervasive the pretrial publicity is, Niehoff said, there are plenty of people who neither read the news nor watch news on television.

"It is much easier than people think to find jurors who have not heard about pending controversies," he said. "People are not all that well informed. You find jurors often who don't read newspapers or watch television, or if they watch television, they don't watch television news."

And that doesn't mean they're not intelligent, jury-worthy people, he added, describing a college-educated and successful friend of his who proudly boasts that he has neither watched TV news nor read a newspaper in twenty years. The friend finds it too depressing. And he's not alone, Niehoff remarked.

"It actually turns out that tainting a jury pool through pretrial publicity is harder than you might imagine," Niehoff said.

The threshold isn't whether a potential juror has heard of the case, but rather if she can set aside what she'd heard or read before and weigh only the evidence presented in the courtroom. A lot of jurors take those instructions to heart, and not simply because they're supposed to by law.

Still, the Yeardley Love case had stirred deep emotions in Charlottesville and Albemarle County. It seemed likely to legal onlookers that the defense would request a change of venue.

For most cases garnering even moderate publicity, the request is more or less pro forma, and it's more often than not denied. There are exceptions, however, when a judge feels a defendant simply has no chance of getting a fair trial in his or her backyard. In 1992, the case against four white Los Angeles police officers accused of beating Rodney King, a black man, was moved from Los Angeles County to neighboring Ventura County. The defense argued that the enormous pretrial publicity, matched with the defendants being police officers, had outraged Los Angeles residents so much that they weren't likely to be fair. (The riots that ensued when the officers were acquitted perhaps bolster that theory.)

Convicted terrorist Timothy McVeigh also was granted a change of venue in his trial on charges he shattered the Alfred P. Murrah Building, a federal office, in 1995. One hundred and sixty-eight people were killed, another 450 injured, making it the deadliest act of terrorism on U.S. soil until September 11, 2001. In McVeigh's case, it seemed a no-brainer that the trial should be moved: The United States District Court for the Western District of Oklahoma, where the case was to be heard, was located directly across the street from the Murrah building. Jurors would have to pass by the demolished building each day as they geared up to decide McVeigh's fate. More than that, the courthouse itself had been damaged, and people inside the courthouse were injured. The case was transferred to U.S. District Court in Denver instead. McVeigh ultimately was convicted of eleven federal crimes, including use of a weapon of mass destruction.

Virginia defense lawyer John Zwerling, who has handled many cases in Charlottesville, thinks that jurors within the college town are among the most open-minded and fair in the country.

"The jury pool there is excellent," said Zwerling, who is not connected with the Huguely case. "You can wind up with a bright, highly educated jury—or at least predominantly one—and there's always going to be a cross-section who understands the case, understands the importance of the law, and follows the law."

Zwerling speaks from experience. Not only did he represent Andrew Alston, the college student convicted of manslaughter rather than second-degree murder by a Charlottesville jury, but he also represented Valentina Djelebova, a self-described Bulgarian countess who had been charged as an accomplice in the 1997 murder of Charlottesville jewelry dealer George Moody. Though her lover had been convicted in the high-profile case, Djelebova was acquitted of all but an after-the-fact accessory charge.

"There was tremendous hatred for her in the press," Zwerling recalled. "The jurors were able to separate that out."

But it's easy for onlookers to dismiss fears of tainted juries when they're not in the hot seat. To people whose lives hang in the balance—in their hope for either a conviction or an acquittal—it seems too great a risk to have potentially prejudicial information released before a case reaches trial. As Sharon Love told reporters seeking comment, her only remaining concern in life was to make sure that Yeardley got a fair chance in court.

The media continued to fight, and finally, on July 1, they won.

Sort of.

Judge Higgins released documents that shed some new light on what happened inside 222 14th Street NW in the early-morning hours of May 3, but the documents were heavily redacted. In her ruling to grant the media's "motion to unseal search warrant records," Higgins vacated three of her previous four orders sealing the records based on "consideration of the pleadings filed, the exhibits and evidence received" and "the argument of counsel." The slew of blacked-out information would include witness names and Huguely's Social Security number. Also, the inventory list itemizing what had been taken off Huguely's person would not be released.

In one search warrant affidavit, dated May 5, Detective Lisa Reeves requested the following:

Any paper, cloth, clothing, shoes or other item that may contain blood or other bodily fluid; trace evidence such as, but not limited to, biological fluids and fingerprints; photographs, writings and documents related to Yeardly *[sic]* Love; computers and electronic storeage *[sic]* devices

In another warrant request filed the same day, Reeves also requested "cell phones, digital cameras, financial records, and any other electronic devices; any weapon that may have been used to include firearms, firearms components, firearm documents or manuals, and ammunition; any other evidence associated with the death of Yeardley Love at 222 14th Street NW, apartment number 9."

Both requests included a page titled "search inventory and return," which, between the two, spelled out thirty-nine seized items. Based on the array of items gathered into evidence, it was clear that investigators were combing through both Huguely's and Yeardley's apartments carefully.

Still, they would miss one important item, for which they would need to return later with an additional search warrant.

Among the items gathered inside Yeardley's apartment:

Swabs of red stain
Hair and fibers
A golf tee
The door to her bedroom
A mobile phone
A digital camera
A backpack containing miscellaneous books and papers
A purse
Towels with red stains
A Natural Light beer can
A pink laptop case
A comforter with red stains
Sheets and pillow (including the pillowcase), all with
    red stains
A note in a desk drawer
A possible fingerprint lift
A bedskirt, also with red stains

Just one item of the fifteen removed from Huguely's apartment was described as having a "red stain"—a white UVA lacrosse T-shirt. The rest of the items—two white Apple laptop computers, blue cargo shorts, a green spiral notebook, two socks, a letter addressed to Yeardley Love—seemed to indicate that officers were trying to narrow down what Huguely had been wearing during the confrontation, and what communication he had had with Yeardley before he walked into her apartment's unlocked front door. Additionally, officers grabbed items from his bathroom—a rug, the shower curtain, swabs from the bathtub—which suggested, at least to case watchers, that officers hoped to trap any potential evidence before it, quite literally, went down the drain.

Among the most detailed information released was contained in a May 6 search warrant affidavit that requested access to a black 2002 Chevrolet Tahoe. Reeves wrote that she hoped to find "any paper, cloth, clothing, shoes or other item that may contain blood or other bodily fluid; trace evidence such as, but not limited to, biological fluids and fingerprints; any property identifiable as that of Yeardley Love."

In trying to sway Judge Higgins to grant the request, Reeves described some of the scene she and her investigative cohorts had come upon when they entered Yeardley's bedroom three days prior. The witnesses at the scene (their names redacted) "described finding Yeardley Love face down on her pillow in her bedroom. There was a pool of blood on her pillow. Love had a large bruise on the right side of her face which appears to have been caused by blunt force trauma. Love's right eye was swollen shut and there were bruises and scrapes to her chin."

Reeves described the battered door—the one that had been bashed in, and from which hairs had been pulled as evidence. The detective also detailed her conversation with Huguely at the Charlottesville Police Department, how he admitted he had been in a fight with Yeardley, and that as they fought "he shook Love and her head repeatedly hit the wall."

The standard search warrant affidavit form sets aside enough space for a lengthy paragraph in which to describe probable cause. Reeves needed much more than that. On an additional sheet titled "Continuation of Paragraph #4," Reeves, referring to herself as "your affiant," laid out even more.

> Huguely told your affiant that he had communicated with Love by email. Huguely admitted that he took Love's computer from the residence and disposed of it. Huguely provided the location of Love's computer and it was recovered. Huguely stated that he and Love had been in a relationship and that the relationship had ended.
>
> Your affiant was told by (name redacted) that George Huguely operated a black Suburban. Your affiant walked the parking lot of 230 14th Street NW and observed a black Chevrolet Tahoe with Maryland registration. Your affiant ran the registration through the Maryland Department of Motor Vehicles. The registration returned to George Huguely IV. The parking space of the Chevrolet Tahoe is in close proximity to the apartment of George Huguely.

After describing some of the items already seized from Huguely's apartment, Reeves continued in her stilted police talk to say that she knew from investigative experience that sometimes trace evidence and bodily fluids can be transferred from a victim to a suspect's car and, in short, she wanted permission to search Huguely's vehicle. Also, she wanted to see if anywhere inside the vehicle were items that Huguely had once given to Yeardley but then reclaimed.

The request was granted by the judge the following day. From the vehicle, police seized some handwritten notes, a Canon digital camera, and a Verizon flip phone. It was unclear what, if any, evidentiary value the items had.

Within the documents was also a description of an item that police had missed. When medics arrived at Yeardley's apartment, she had been topless. Huguely, however, insisted she was clothed, and even described the T-shirt she had been wearing. The shirt hadn't been collected by crime scene investigators, but when detectives scoured the crime-scene photographs, they spotted it on the floor. The warrants released showed that police had searched her apartment again in a vain attempt to find it.

News stories across the country included the oversight in the reports: Could Charlottesville police have jeopardized the case with shoddy evidence gathering? Before the question could gain ground, Charlottesville Police spokesman Ric Barrick allayed the concerns. Love's family had turned in the T-shirt a few days after the police's unsuccessful search for it, he said. Hopefully, whatever trace evidence it might have had embedded in its fibers was still intact.

Just because Higgins had acquiesced and released some of the public documents didn't mean the media could now smooth their hackles. In August, more heavily redacted affidavits were released. This time, the judge gave a reason for the omissions: The investigation was ongoing, the affidavits identified by name people who had been cooperating with police, some information had not yet been made public and may or may not be admissible at trial, and the public dissemination of some of the information could hinder authorities' efforts to find a prejudice-free jury come trial time.

What was released of the request, however, was this:

Apple laptop computer, white in color. This laptop has a sticker located on the corner with the following inscription "University of Virginia-2006 Desktop Computing Initiative ITC Helpdesk: (434) 924-3731." There is also a barcode under this inscription with the number 600431 underneath. This laptop is currently being stored [at] The Charlottesville Police Department in The Forensics Department under evidence tag #245472. This computer is one of two computers siezed [sic] by police during a search warrant executed at 230 14 Street NW, Charlottesville Virginia.

In short, police already had the computer in storage. What Reeves wanted now was permission to look inside. The affidavit also sought:

Any emails sent, received, stored or deleted referencing the email addresses (redacted). Any emails sent, received stored or deleted referring to Yeardley Love between the dates of April 3, 2010 and May 3, 2010.

Any stored or deleted documents referring to Yeardley Love or referring to past events involving George Huguely and Yeardley Love.

In her two-and-a-half page probable cause summary, Reeves wrote that one of Love's friends had seen an e-mail the week before Yeardley died that seemed to show the two had been fighting. Detective Jim Mooney interviewed the friend, who had shared a hotel room with Yeardley in Chicago. Yeardley told her friend that Huguely had sent an e-mail to her, and she read it out loud. The next day, she read it aloud again.

Reeves wanted to find that e-mail. Judge Higgins granted her request, and both laptops—first Yeardley's, then George's—were sent to Fairfax, Virginia, for a forensic examination.

Chapter 21

Detectives suspected that some of the most important evidence would be discovered not in the bloodstains on Yeardley's floor, but in the e-mails stored on her computer. They figured that something housed in the hard drive struck Huguely as potentially damaging enough that he went to the trouble of stealing the laptop and tossing it in the trash, where two detectives discovered it just before his arraignment.

Reeves got permission from Yeardley's grieving mother to forensically inspect the computer's contents. With Sharon Love's permission, the white Apple laptop was shipped to Fairfax, about 100 miles northeast of Charlottesville.

Detective Albert Leightley, a computer investigative specialist who was also involved with the U.S. Secret Service Electronic Crimes Task Force, was tasked with searching both Yeardley's and George's computers. He declined to be interviewed while the investigation was ongoing. According to several experts not connected with the case, but with extensive backgrounds in recovering evidence from computers, the process typically used is both complex and precise, designed to protect the computer's hard drive from tampering while giving investigators a mirror copy to search.

Casey Hiser, a forensic consultant at a litigation support firm and a graduate in computer and digital forensics from

Burlington, Vermont's Champlain College, said there are several processes that investigators can use. ("It is actually one of the problems with our field, lack of standardization," she said.) But the identification and seizure phase is fairly universal.

The computer system is collected using an anti-static bag for safe transport of its electronic components. The bag protects the hard drive from static electricity, which can discharge enough voltage to sufficiently destroy internal microchips. A person walking across a rug can produce up to 12,000 volts of static electricity; as little as 10 volts can damage the delicate innards of a computer system. (Humans can't even feel a static electricity zap until it reaches about 1,500 volts.) Once the item is bagged, the investigator is charged with recording its chain of custody, meaning that the components' whereabouts have to be catalogued with every move to show a judge and jury that the evidence found within is reliable.

To actually peruse the computer's contents, a mirror copy must be made. Most computer users know how to back up their hard drives, but making a forensically sound copy is much more complicated. The investigator has to use a write blocker, which ensures that he's only reading information from the drive and not writing information to it. (Writing onto the hard drive would be akin to scribbling across an incriminating note found at a crime scene; it would be deemed tampering with evidence and tossed from the trial.) Most forensic investigators use software such as EnCase or Forensic Toolkit (FTK), which create a bit stream image—or mirror-image backup—of the hard drive.

"It convinces the computer locally that the drive is accessible, but in effect it's read-only," explained Doug White, a computer forensics expert based in Rhode Island. "It protects it from modification by us."

White, who has testified in both criminal and civil trials—but is not connected with the Huguely case—is a professor at Roger Williams University, where he's considered an expert in security, computer technology, electronic crimes, and computer forensics. He also works for the International Society of Forensics Computer Examiners.

He explained that when he creates a copy of a hard drive, he starts "at byte zero, and I go to the last byte on the hard drive and duplicate the whole thing."

To prove that the copied drive is identical to the original, the investigator uses a hash, which is a mathematical algorithm that serves as something of a fingerprint for a hard drive. If even the tiniest bit of information—right down to a deleted period or an added space in a document—is tweaked from the original compared with the copy, those algorithms won't match, and the analysis of the copy won't hold up in court.

And that's paramount. Evidence gathered from computers hasn't always been welcome in trials. Just as DNA evidence was scrutinized when it was first introduced, computer technology has just in recent years been consistently deemed admissible—but only when the examiners can prove that the data they found is from an untainted, mirror copy of the original.

John B. Minor, a Texas-based communications expert and member of the International Society of Forensic Computer Examiners, said that creating a mirror image does more than capture information that's easily accessible to laymen on the hard drive, such as one's documents folder. It also captures random bits of data, or flotsam, floating around the free space of a hard drive. Named after the debris left behind a shipwreck, that data can prove to be invaluable to an investigation.

"It's an area littered with bits and pieces of files," Minor, who is not connected to the case, explained. "It's often where we find the gems of evidence. It can be part of a chat stream, part of an e-mail or an instant messenger chat exchange."

Take, for example, an average e-mail: The recipient opens it, reads it, and perhaps deletes it. Even though the message has been deleted, it's stored on a free area of the hard drive. If a computer user doesn't regularly use specialized software to clean out the flotsam—and few people do—the information stays until it's eventually written over by other information stored in similar fashion. The free space becomes a hodge-podge of bits and pieces of random data—flotsam—that an investigator can collect, organize, and then carefully search.

White also described discovering information in cache files: "Say you're looking at the weather. The information is old, so you hit the refresh button. When you hit refresh, the Web browsers want to speed things up, so they write copies of stuff to the hard drive. Things you're looking at may be stored physically on the hard drive. When you hit refresh, your browser dumps that cache and gets a new one."

Modern computers tend to update more often than older computers, he added, but investigators still find tons of information hidden inside the hard drive.

"We've grabbed screen shots of e-mails, texts, chats, child pornography you were looking at yesterday or last year or who knows when," White said. "It might just be fragments of it, too. We might just see an e-mail address."

Another gold mine of information can be found in what's called file slack, or the unallocated space between the end of a file and the end of the disk cluster it's stored in. It occurs when a computer gets a new file that overwrites a previous file. Rarely are the two files exactly the same size, so there often is a smidgeon of space leftover where residual data can collect. Investigators sometimes find meaningful data hidden inside.

"Sometimes the information is intelligible, sometimes not," Minor said. "It could be an entire e-mail. In some cases, it's an entire PDF file. There might be bits and pieces of a live text chat."

And then there are the partitions that some crafty computer users try to delete entirely. White translated it as such: Let's say a bookshelf contains an entire set of encyclopedias, but you as the owner want to hide one of the books. You take its cover off, and someone viewing the shelf will likely notice that your collection is missing one volume. With a computer, a user can delete an entire drive, and it will look as though it's missing—but forensics investigators know how to find it. That information usually is a jackpot, White said, because investigators not only discover what the user was trying to hide, but they also can prove in court that he took great pains in trying to keep it hidden—providing prosecutors with circumstantial evidence of a guilty conscience.

According to the search warrants initially released by the Charlottesville Police Department, law enforcement wanted to search Yeardley's computer for e-mails between her and Huguely. Leightley, the examiner, likely would have first looked through Yeardley's available e-mail account, and then carefully sifted through the data in hopes of finding more about her doomed relationship. After that, experts said, he probably would have started the daunting task of sorting through all of the gathered information. It's no easy job, Minor said: An e-mail account showing perhaps just 400 messages might actually turn up 14,000 when the hard drive is thoroughly examined.

"There's not a practical way to look through all of those, though sometimes we do," said Minor, who regularly works with law-enforcement agencies and testifies in criminal and civil trials. He has not been asked to work on the Yeardley Love case.

To more easily track down specific information, investigators organize the data into a searchable database, then run keyword searches. They might look for nicknames or monikers to find all the e-mails sent from a particular person—sometimes this points investigators to additional e-mail accounts used by the same person—while other times they might look for words that seem likely to turn up threatening messages ("kill" or "hurt," for example). When looking up browser history, they might stumble upon some incriminating searches. Hiser said that's "a great source of info if your killer happened to look up 'how to hide a body' . . . Don't laugh; it has happened."

In the Love case, detectives curtailed their hunt by searching through just one month's worth of e-mails—from April 3, 2010 to May 3, the morning Yeardley was killed. The search warrant request on Huguely's laptop asked for "any stored or deleted documents referring to Yeardley Love or referring to past events involving George Huguely and Yeardley Love."

During his search of Yeardley's computer, Leightley discovered fragments of an e-mail that Reeves said appeared to be "in response to an e-mail sent by George Huguely," according to a court document dated Aug. 17. The media filed requests hoping the e-mail fragment would be released. They received a document that included a chunk of text, measuring about a dozen lines long, completely blacked out with dark marker. But Reeves's words surrounding the mystery text were telling: "Further examination of the fragmented e-mail . . . is evidence of a prior incident between Huguely and Love," she wrote. That incident, she said, was the one in which Yeardley had hit George with her purse, causing her belongings to spill out, including her cell phone, which she believed Huguely held on to.

But while detectives suspected the fragmented e-mail found on Yeardley's computer was in response to an upsetting one from George, they couldn't find the original e-mail on her hard drive. Leightley set off to search George's laptop in hopes of finding it.

He came up empty.

Reeves tried another tack: After talking with Leightley, she learned that sometimes, when an e-mail is written on a person's smart phone rather than on a computer, the messages could be retrieved from the phone long after the message was written. She asked Judge Higgins for permission to search Huguely's phone to see if any additional messages could be recovered.

Minor said such a request isn't unusual, especially these days when few people use their phones simply for making calls. With smart phones, it's difficult to completely erase data. Forensics experts can extract the memory of the entire cell phone, then go into that information and carve out pertinent data.

"Smart phone evidence can be corroborating evidence, or it can be key evidence," Minor said. "Smart phones can be sometimes be dead giveaways" that a crime has been committed.

Higgins granted Reeves's request. The search for more e-mails was under way.

Chapter 22

Every bit of evidence collected, and everything still being sought, seemed directed at helping authorities understand Huguely's state of mind when he made that fatal visit to Yeardley's apartment. Had he threatened her beforehand? Did he say he meant to hurt her? Was there any hint she might be in peril?

With the first public denial by Huguely's lawyer, it was clear that at least one prong of the defense would be that George never meant to hurt Yeardley, that he went over to talk and things got out of hand (an accident, as Lawrence had described it). As more search warrants became public, it seemed clear that police were looking for evidence to obliterate that defense or create a new one altogether.

The search for evidence of intent came as no surprise to Gregory Mitchell, a self-described "evidence guy" and professor at the University of Virginia's law school, who found himself questioned by reporters about the case even though he had no direct involvement in it.

"The dispute here is about state of mind, how much harm he inflicted on her at the time, and whether it was foreseeable that this"—her death—"was the kind of result that would happen," Mitchell said. "Everything I saw about the case through the media indicated the prosecution was trying to make the case that this was an intentional killing, that he could have stopped but he didn't."

In movies and on television shows, much is made about motive: Why did the killer do it? In real life, prosecutors don't have to establish motive. It's not their job to get inside the heads of the accused and figure out why they do the things they do. They just have to prove *that* they did it. Sure, painting the "why" picture is helpful, and it often can sway a jury to convict when evidence is otherwise so-so—even if lawyers and the jurors themselves don't admit it. But establishing motive is not legally necessary.

In Yeardley's case, according to her friends, the motive could have been that George Huguely was the jealous type, and far too controlling to let the relationship end. But even having the motive question out of the way wouldn't keep prosecutors from having to climb inside his head to anticipate the defense they would likely face at trial.

The questions they had to answer: What was his intent? Did he mean to kill her? Could he have stopped?

The Hook, a weekly newsmagazine, ran a story titled "Playing defense: Legal eagles prognosticate on Huguely strategy." Fifty-cent headline aside, the piece drew comparisons between Huguely's case and that of another UVA student who had been charged with murder, Andrew Alston.

Alston was a twenty-one-year-old third-year student in 2003 when he headed out for drinks with some friends and his older brother, who was in town visiting. During a night of bar hopping and booze, his path intersected with twenty-two-year-old Walker Sisk, a volunteer firefighter, near the Corner—the same area Yeardley and George lived near and where they regularly bar hopped. What happened next became hotly debated during trial a year later: Alston, who regularly carried a pocket knife, testified that Sisk grabbed the knife and lunged, and in the struggle, Alston wrestled back the weapon and stabbed Sisk twenty times in self-defense. He claimed he learned his knife-redirecting skills in an eight-week martial arts course he had taken. Police arriving at the scene followed a trail of blood to, ironically, 222 14th Street

Northwest, Yeardley's apartment complex, where they arrested Alston. He stood trial on a second-degree murder charge in November 2004.

Sisk's family balked at Alston's explanation of the fight, and the only possible defense wound Alston suffered was a cut that the testifying medical examiner said could have come from his hand slipping on the blood-slicked knife. Still, the jury weighed both his testimony and the evidence of substantial drinking—Sisk's blood-alcohol content was at least .19% when he died, more than twice the amount needed to be considered legally intoxicated—and came back with a surprising verdict: voluntary manslaughter. Their agreed-upon sentence: three years in prison.

"I looked at all the evidence, and didn't think it was malice—just tragic on both sides," one juror told *The Hook*.

Alston, dubbed the Corner Killer by some media, was released from prison in 2006 after serving two-thirds of his sentence, as is typical if the prisoner has behaved behind bars. Sisk's family filed a wrongful death suit against Alston upon his release and was awarded $600,000—of which Alston paid just $3,600 after filing for bankruptcy.

The Hook, which had run a series of prosecution-favored stories during and after the trial, pointed to Alston's light conviction when presenting the "legal eagles" story forecasting Huguely's likely defense.

"So what can a shocked community expect when Huguely eventually comes to trial?" the paper asked, then turned to area defense lawyers for some predictions. The consensus: that Francis Lawrence, Huguely's attorney, was well respected and highly skilled and wouldn't have stated that Yeardley's death was a tragic accident unless he felt certain of it.

"I won't second guess him," said defense lawyer John Zwerling, who had represented Alston seven years earlier. "I would think he has information that the intent of the client was not to kill her, and that it was accidental."

Perhaps Huguely meant to slap, punch, or shake, but that doesn't mean he meant to kill, Zwerling continued.

Unlike Alston, Huguely wasn't charged with second-degree murder. He faced first-degree murder. And that hinged on him having intended to kill his victim, or at least having had ample opportunity to slow down and halt his actions. Second-degree murder is more a crime of passion—not unintentional enough to be an accident (and downgraded even further to perhaps a manslaughter charge), but, typically, quick and rage-fueled. Perhaps the killer walked in on her husband with another woman, and she snapped. That scenario is more likely to fall into the second-degree category, while the woman who leaves her apartment, buys a gun, and returns the next day to kill her husband is far more likely to be charged with first-degree murder in most U.S. states.

Of course, there are many gray areas, and outcomes vary not only state by state, but jury by jury and judge by judge. One jury might rule that a strangulation, which takes on average at least three and a half minutes to complete, is a snap, impulsive action, and perhaps that jury would only convict a suspect of second-degree murder. A jury in the same courthouse might determine that those final minutes dripped like molasses, giving the assailant plenty of time to stop himself and reassess whether his anger warranted taking another human life. That jury, perhaps, would convict him of first-degree murder. Same circumstances, same courthouse, but different verdicts.

In Virginia, there's the added complexity of capital murder—or a murder that qualifies for death-penalty consideration. The Commonwealth of Virginia, in fact, has a storied history with hangings, electric chairs, and lethal injection. The colonies' first formal execution occurred in 1608, when Captain George Kendall, living in Virginia's Jamestown colony, was hanged for spying for the Spanish government. According to Espy, a database that tracks executions, Virginia to date outranks relative U.S. newcomer Texas as having executed the most people since 1608 (though its numbers have dropped significantly since 1976, after the federal government lifted a four-year ban on state executions).

Not every murder qualifies for capital consideration. Second-degree murder is out entirely, and only certain premeditated murders qualify. For example, a premeditated murder committed while in the commission of an abduction, a robbery, a rape, or an attempted rape would qualify. So would the premeditated murder of someone under age fourteen by a person over the age of twenty-one, and the premeditated murder of more than one person within a three-year span of time. Also, premeditated murder of certain types of people could land a culprit on death row—such as a pregnant woman, a law-enforcement officer, a judge, a juror, or a witness.

Whether Huguely qualified was debated not by prosecutors and the defense, but by the media. On *Good Morning America*, Robin Sax, a former Los Angeles County district attorney, pointed to Huguely's theft of his ex-girlfriend's computer as a possible nail in his capital-punishment coffin.

"This is Law School 101," Sax said. "This is a felony murder that happened in the course of a burglary."

Mark Geragos, a defense attorney also not connected with the case, said he doubted prosecutors would seek death.

"This is not the type of case that generally prosecutors will seek the death penalty in," he told *Good Morning America*. "He's going to argue, 'Well, I had no intent to kill and I didn't have malice. I never wanted to kill her. I loved her.'"

If District Attorney Chapman was weighing the death penalty, he wasn't saying so publicly. But his actions in court at least indicated that he had no plan to heed the defense's claim that Yeardley's death was nothing more than a tragic accident. That proclamation by Francis Lawrence, which came while he addressed reporters after his client's arraignment the day after Yeardley's death, seemed to lay the foundation for Huguely's defense.

In short, it's the "I didn't mean to" argument.

Lawyers weren't the only ones struggling to get inside George Huguely's head. The case sparked interest among domestic abuse experts nationwide, some of whom used it and its notoriety to highlight the dangers of dating violence.

On paper, Huguely was the antithesis of the stereotypical abuser. He was charming, educated, talented, and wealthy. And Yeardley seemed one of the unlikeliest victims imaginable. She was smart, strong, ambitious, and, by all accounts, emotionally well adjusted. On top of that, she had no reason to stay—she wasn't bound by marriage vows or forever tied to Huguely through children.

But while the case left many perplexed, Huguely appeared to some to fit a mold: that of a man with narcissistic personality disorder. On talk and television programs, as well as on mental health blogs, domestic violence experts and psychiatrists posited that Huguely's behavior could be attributed to the disorder. The condition is hotly debated among psychiatrists, and its future as an official personality disorder is gray: The *Diagnostic and Statistical Manual of Mental Disorders,* published by the American Psychiatric Association, has targeted NPD as one of several personality disorders to be axed when its fifth edition is released in 2013—not because people don't have it, but because some scientists are looking to revamp the labels psychiatrists and psychologists use. (One Harvard psychologist described the potential elimination as "draconian" and "unenlightened" to a *New York Times* reporter.)

Narcissistic personality disorder is a clinical diagnosis, one that can't be made by reading police and court documents alone. Named for Narcissus, the handsome hunter in Greek mythology who fell in love with his own reflection in a pool, narcissists are preoccupied with their own self-importance. They believe that they're special and should associate only with other special people, and they harbor disdain for people they feel are inferior. They have a sense of entitlement and expect nothing short of adulation and admiration from others. They exploit other people to further themselves, their arrogance is undeniable, and their fragile egos make them quick to become jealous of others.

When breaking down the red flags reported in the wake of Huguely's arrest, the definition could fit, some experts said.

He lashed out at a police officer, threatening to kill her.

He beat a fellow teammate for walking Yeardley home and supposedly trying to kiss her.

In a fit of self-indulgent rage, he jumped into the ocean to swim to shore because his father refused his request to turn the family's yacht around.

He attacked Yeardley at least once in public, choking her until he was pulled off by fellow lacrosse players.

And even his high school behavior, as reported by the *Washington Post* in 2006, pointed to potentially unhealthy self-aggrandizement that at the time was laughed off as Huguely being a jokester: He stole his coach's car keys, then drove the vehicle to the coach to show off behind the wheel. He bet another coach he'd make a play in exchange for a kiss from the coach's girlfriend. When he indeed made the play, he went a step further, asking for the woman's phone number.

But Levy said there's a difference between being narcissistic and having a diagnosable disorder.

"Certainly someone who is so wrapped up in himself that he could hurt someone he loves is only focusing on himself," Levy said. "He's not seeing the consequences of his own behavior, and he's not empathizing with how she might feel. But that's during the abuse. He may go back and forth. He may be attentive at other times.

"You do see narcissism often in people who are abusive," she continued. "But whether they all fit a clear diagnosis for narcissistic personality disorder, that's a stretch."

Even if Huguely had NPD, a jury likely would never be told. Occasionally defense lawyers try to use the diagnosis to trim time off a client's sentence post-conviction, but NPD is not grounds for an insanity defense. For the insanity claim to stick, the culprit must be unable to tell the difference between what society deems is right and wrong. Narcissists know the rules; they simply don't want to abide by them.

And if Huguely's drinking was nearly as heavy as his neighbors told police and reporters, it could have made it tough for Yeardley to see his eruptions as something more sinister than booze-fueled outbursts.

Domestic violence studies have shown that women are more easily able to blame drugs or alcohol for their partner's moody behavior. According to statistics compiled by the Marin Institute, a self-described "alcohol industry watchdog," two-thirds of victims of intimate partner violence reported that alcohol was involved in the incident, and women whose partners abused alcohol were more than three times as likely than other women to be assaulted by their partners. In 2002, more than 70,000 students between the ages of eighteen and twenty-four were victims of alcohol-related sexual assault in the United States, according to a study published in the *Journal of Studies on Alcohol*. In Huguely's case, most of his legal run-ins reportedly came during booze fests. Friends and relatives seemed to have trouble understanding how a young man who appeared so likeable and charismatic one minute could be accused of such outrageous behavior the next. Some apparently blamed the alcohol and reportedly asked him to curb his drinking.

But according to some substance abuse experts, that would have been a naïve—if well-intentioned—request. Levy has for years dealt with the misconception that alcohol is the sole cause of violent behavior.

"With men who batter and also drink, they were violent before the drinking and they're violent after the drinking," Levy said. "It's just an excuse."

Rather, alcohol abuse is considered a complication of narcissistic personality disorder, according to the Mayo Clinic. The disorder is rare, affecting more men than women, and its cause is unknown. According to the clinic, some evidence links the disorder to excessive pampering and extremely high expectations in childhood. Other evidence indicates it's prewired in the brain.

For a young man like Huguely, whose upbringing was posh and whose athletic prowess was routinely praised, it might have been difficult for those around him to recognize his behavior as possibly indicative of a personality disorder. After all, he wasn't the only lacrosse player known to occasionally act superior or cocky. It was only in hindsight that people seemed to string together the series of outbursts and wonder if they should have recognized Huguely as a lit powder keg.

By friends' accounts, Yeardley was growing tired of it all. It's not clear if Huguely had physically abused her before he choked her in public—she can't speak out, and he so far has refused interview requests—but research indicates that it's unlikely for someone to escalate from zero to murder in just a few weeks. Perhaps there were put-downs or verbal threats. Maybe he had grabbed an arm or pushed her. It might be that he showed some signs of troubling behavior that Yeardley initially dismissed as being out of character or forgivable.

Whatever happened, one thing seems clear: Yeardley couldn't have known that the young man she had let into her heart and introduced to her family would one day be arrested in her violent death. Had she any clue, she certainly would have summoned the strength to ask for help.

Yeardley was nothing if not strong.

Chapter 23

Months after Huguely's lawyer declared Yeardley's death an accident, John Zwerling, an onlooker, acknowledged he had been taken aback by the lawyer's first public comments. He suspected that Francis Lawrence had been asked by Huguely's family to give the statement; Zwerling felt it was premature.

"I wasn't expecting that comment," he said. "He was in a time and place where he didn't know what his defense was going to be. He still might not know for sure."

The word "accident" drew Lawrence a lot of criticism. At the same time he described Yeardley's death as such, the media were just beginning to report details of Huguely's alleged statements to police. Nancy Grace wasn't the only analyst who scoffed at the notion of someone "accidentally" bashing a woman's head against the wall until blood poured from her nose.

Zwerling said Lawrence likely meant that Huguely perhaps intended to hurt his ex-girlfriend, but had no intention of killing her. "Which is different," Zwerling said. "It's subtle, but wording it that way is a way to avoid some of the criticism."

For Gregory Mitchell, another legal onlooker, Lawrence's "accident" statement was not a surprising declaration. Nor was Mitchell shocked when, months after the slaying, defense lawyers asked for access to years of medical records in order to explore whether Yeardley's death was caused by more than her fight with Huguely.

"From the defense's perspective, you're basically trying to do the mirror image thing" with the prosecution, Mitchell said. As prosecutors tried to pin blame for Yeardley's death solely on the brutal head trauma, the defense would try to spread the blame. Was Yeardley drunk? On drugs? Did she provoke Huguely somehow? Mitchell expected all of those questions to be posed to jurors. No doubt, the defense would counter any prosecution expert witnesses with experts of their own. Like so many cases in the American court system, it would likely become a showdown between specialists on the stand.

For outsiders, however, the specifics of that battle remained a mystery even months after Yeardley died. While autopsy reports can be released under Freedom of Information Act laws in some states, Virginia law considers them part of a person's medical records even after death, according to Stephen Murman, an administrator with the Medical Examiner's Office. Thus, requests to see the pathology reports detailing what injuries Yeardley had suffered were denied. Police had announced her cause of death as "blunt force trauma" after her autopsy, but, according to outside pathologists, that definition was far too vague to shed light on exactly how Yeardley Love was killed.

Though court documents pointed to blunt force trauma as Yeardley's cause of death, Police Chief Timothy Longo was cautious when it came to officially releasing the cause. Early media reports had suggested she might have been both beaten and strangled, and though Longo certainly knew there were no obvious signs of the latter—none of the telltale bruising around her neck or tiny hemorrhage spots (called petechiae) in her eyes or mouth—he declined to set reporters straight in the days immediately after the death.

Even when the commonwealth's medical examiner released a preliminary cause of death to police in mid-May,

Longo delayed announcing it until he and detectives had a chance to read the final report, which was still weeks from being completed.

Finally, in early July, police announced the cause. It indeed had been blunt force trauma to the head.

Though no other details were released, the two months that had passed had given authorities enough time to get toxicology reports back from state labs. It would be months before a defense motion released some of those findings: a blood-alcohol content of 0.14%, meaning Yeardley was drunk when she was attacked, as well as the prescription drug Adderall, designed to treat people suffering from attention deficit hyperactivity disorder. Dr. Bill Gormley, the medical examiner who performed Yeardley's autopsy, determined that the alcohol/Adderall combination did not cause her death. Rather, he decided, it was the repeated beating of her head against a wall.

The brain is a delicate organ, a soft, mushroom-shaped bundle of arteries and veins, nerves and fluids. Kindly, evolution provided vertebrates with not one, but two layers of protection for the brain: the skull, of course, and in between that and the brain itself, a system of connective tissue membranes to serve as a sort of cushion between soft tissue and tough bone.

Despite those protective encasings, about one million people a year visit doctors because of blows to the head. Of those, upwards of 50,000 (with some estimates being closer to twice that) suffer prolonged problems. News reports in recent years have placed great emphasis on head injuries sustained in sports—especially those affecting kids and young adults—but in reality, the bulk of head injuries are from car wrecks. Even a seemingly minor fender bender can cause the head to whip to and fro, bruising both the front and back sides of the brain. With bruising can come swelling, and that's when the unforgiving skull can turn from ally to enemy.

While the medical examiners involved in the case declined

to elaborate on their findings while the trial was still loom-
ing, Dr. Daniel Spitz, a Michigan-based pathologist not connected with the case, offered some insight. Yeardley's skull
wouldn't have to have been fractured for the beating to be
fatal, he said.

When someone sustains a head impact, there's an acceleration and a deceleration: the movement of the brain inside
the skull (acceleration), and then its abrupt halt when it hits the
skull (deceleration). Because the brain is made of a different
substance than is bone—similar in consistency to gelatin—it
moves at a different rate than its encasing. So as the head
is slammed, the brain moves within the cranial cavity and
strikes the skull.

And that, Spitz explained, causes what's known as traumatic axonal injury (also known as diffuse axonal injury). In
layman's terms, the brain gets compressed and stretched as
it slams around inside the skull. Axons, which conduct nerve
signals, can get disrupted or even torn, and thus the brain
can't continue to send out those all-important instructions to
the rest of the body: keep breathing, keep pumping blood,
keep living.

"Basically, you have disruption of the brain at a cellular
level," said Spitz, co-author of *Differential Diagnosis in
Surgical Pathology*. (Spitz also contributed as an author and
editor of the 4th edition of the so-called Bible of forensic
pathology, *Spitz and Fisher's Medicolegal Investigation of
Death: Guidelines for the Application of Pathology to Crime
Investigation*—though the Spitz in the title refers to his father, world-renowned pathologist Werner Spitz, who is now
retired.)

"If the brain doesn't function, you have disruption of heart
rate, breathing, and everything else," said the younger Spitz.

Multiple impacts are "of greater concern than a single
impact," he added. George Huguely had described Yeardley's head hitting the wall repeatedly, meaning that she potentially endured the axonal shearing several times. Imagine
taking a hammer to a melon. Hit it once and you cause *some*
damage. Hit it repeatedly in the same spot and you're guar-

anteed to destroy it. Unlike a melon, the brain can heal—but only if given the chance.

"That's why so many are concerned about kids in sports and pro-athletes who suffer concussions," Spitz explained. "You don't want to put them back in the game right away because if they sustain another impact such as the first one, it could be really detrimental. . . . *Any* impact could be potentially serious or even fatal, but when you have repeated blows, the effects are exaggerated."

Upon finding Yeardley's body, Detective Reeves had immediately noticed external injuries: the facial bruising, the right eye swollen shut. Neither of those injuries would help determine exactly when in the beating Yeardley likely fell unconscious, said Spitz. Yeardley perhaps could have been knocked unconscious immediately, or she could have remained alert until the final throes.

Huguely told police that at some point, he noticed blood pouring from his ex-girlfriend's nose. It was soon after, he said, that he finally pushed her back onto her bed, stole her laptop, and fled.

He claimed he didn't know how badly she was hurt, and that he certainly didn't know she was dead. According to Spitz, with the viciousness of the described attack, immediate efforts to save Yeardley might have been in vain—and even if she had lived, the damage done to her delicate brain could have impaired her forever.

Chapter 24

Dr. Daniel Spitz has testified in hundreds of court cases, many of them involving homicides. As a medical examiner in suburban Detroit and a former pathologist in homicide-heavy Miami-Dade County, he has sat on both sides of the courtroom, often testifying for the prosecution, but occasionally, usually when he has been hired privately, for the defense.

Without doubt, he said, the defense in the case against George Huguely V would aim to minimize the damage the repeated head bashing had caused the twenty-two-year-old athlete. One way, predicted Spitz, would be to minimize the number of impacts. If the prosecutors say she banged her head seven times, the defense would likely look for evidence that it could have been as few times as two or three.

"Of course, I'm sure they'd try to get it down to one," he said.

But to Spitz, "it doesn't really help. You don't accidentally hit your head against the wall to the point of causing [the] kinds of injuries [that police had described in the case]."

UVA Professor Gregory Mitchell said he expected the defense to attack Yeardley's behavior with whatever information they could gather.

"From the defense's perspective, they're going to try to

say that he was intoxicated and that impaired his view of things—or that she provoked him," Mitchell said. "Whatever the prosecution says, they're going to try to show the flipside of that."

If Yeardley had been drinking, that would open the door for defense lawyers to argue that the depressing effects of alcohol were the real reason her life ended.

And that's where Yeardley's supposed "Sunday Funday" would likely come into play.

Sunday night was usually a social one for both the men and women's UVA lacrosse teams. Game days typically fell on Saturdays, Sundays, and Tuesdays, meaning that Sundays offered the one night in a weekend in which players were usually guaranteed not to have a game the next day.

Like many college students, the lacrosse players were known to mix alcohol with their "fun," according to neighbors and area bartenders.

On May 2, as on so many other nights during the academic year, the beers were tossed back at Boylan Heights, just down the street from Yeardley's apartment. It was the perfect kind of establishment for a gathering of sports-minded college students: a bit dingy, with a worn concrete floor inside and the type of battered stuffed chairs you often spot on front porches in college towns. But the place had a hint of chic as well, with loft-style exposed brick and ambient lighting.

The beer-and-burger joint thrived off its college patrons. Even its signage was written in the same heavily outlined block font so often associated with universities. Instead of standard menus, customers were given checklists with which to create their burgers (patty options: beef, turkey, veggie or chicken). Fries were of course a mainstay, though Boylan Heights offered an option with a twist: sweet potato fries.

A deck area surrounded by blue railing provided outdoor seating—ideal for people watching—while inside, patrons could gather around a massive projection television screen usually tuned in to one sports competition or another. As one online reviewer wrote, Boylan Heights's pros were its thick burgers, pool tables, and happy-hour specials. Among its cons? Being packed with college students during the school year.

Indeed, it was a regular hangout for the lacrosse teams. The players often arrived late and stayed until closing, sometimes watching sports on the TVs inside. (Yeardley was said to have insisted on complete isolation during Baltimore Ravens games, but on this Sunday in early May, the Ravens were still months away from taking the field.) Caitlin Whiteley, Yeardley's friend since the sixth grade and UVA roommate, later testified that the gathering May 2 was altogether ordinary. A group had gathered in the early evening for a friend's birthday party, but Yeardley didn't feel like staying long. Caitlin walked her friend home, then went back to Boylan Heights about 11 p.m.—without Yeardley.

"She was tired," testified Whiteley, who added that Yeardley drank beer at the bar but didn't seem drunk.

Caitlin testified that her roommate and Huguely's relationship had been on and off for years, but, according to other friends who spoke to reporters in the days after the death, not everyone knew. The *Washington Post* quoted one unnamed friend who said, "I still didn't know they had broken up. Everything seemed fine." And another friend said she approached Yeardley at the Boylan Heights birthday gathering and asked, "What's going on with you and George?" Yeardley replied, "Same old stuff. Everything is good."

As it turned out, Huguely was headed to Yeardley's apartment soon after. Friends testified that he had spent the day at a father-son golf tournament at the Wintergreen Resort, a mountainous retreat about forty-five minutes southwest of Charlottesville. After spending the day golfing and drinking, Huguely was "definitely drunk," his roommate, Kevin Carroll, would testify months later. At 11:40 p.m.—not long after Whiteley left Yeardley alone in their apartment—Carroll said he left to buy more beer before the stores closed at midnight. Huguely stayed behind. When Carroll got back, Huguely was gone.

About ten minutes later, Anna Lehman, who lived downstairs from Yeardley, heard "very loud" banging noises coming from upstairs, according to testimony she gave months later. Next, she heard footsteps come down the stairs and spotted a man wearing a blue shirt leaving the building. Soon after, Huguely returned to his apartment and told Carroll that he had gone downstairs with two friends for a few minutes. Carroll called one of the friends, Will Bolton, to suggest he join the upstairs crew for a few beers, but Bolton said he wasn't there, immediately disputing where Huguely said he'd been.

The other downstairs friend also said he hadn't hung out with Huguely that night. In fact, he testified, he was so busy studying that when Huguely knocked on his door earlier in the evening, he told Huguely to go away and locked his door.

Caitlin got back to the apartment she shared with Yeardley about 2 a.m., she testified, and spotted the hole in the door to Love's bedroom. She peeked in the room and noticed her hair, which had earlier been pulled up, splayed in that unnatural fashion.

"I saw Yeardley in bed facedown with a comforter over her," Whiteley testified. "I shook her shoulder. I moved her hair to the side and touched her shoulder."

That was when, she said, she saw blood on Yeardley's neck and face. She and Oudshoorn called police, and as Oudshoorn lifted Love out of the bed to attempt CPR, he saw more blood on Yeardley's face and eye. Soon, the apartment filled with police and medics and the once-calm home was transformed into a crime scene.

Yeardley's body, found around 2:15 a.m., offered investigators something they were less likely to be able to obtain from Huguely: a relatively accurate reading of her blood-alcohol content. While police wouldn't tell reporters whether Huguely voluntarily submitted to any Breathalyzer or blood tests to determine whether he was intoxicated—and if he was, how much—Detective Reeves's search warrants seeking bodily fluids and DNA samples wasn't signed until 11:52 a.m., presumably more than eight hours after Huguely would have last had a chance to drink. And even if the sample had been taken earlier, he might have had more to drink after Yeardley's death, thus raising his BAC, or perhaps he had stopped drinking, which would have given his body time to process the alcohol and lower his reading by the time Reeves caught up with him.

Yeardley, however, would likely have been tested soon after her death.

If police had a BAC for Huguely, they didn't release it to the public, leaving many to speculate. A high BAC could work in favor of his defense, bolstering Lawrence's assertion that the death was an accident. If Huguely had been significantly impaired, his ability to form intent was questionable, his lawyers could argue. *He's a generally good man with an unfortunate illness*: It was a sometimes-successful argument to jurors. It worked in Andrew Alston's case, after all. As far as the jury in that case knew, Alston had no significant criminal history. (In reality, he had been previously charged and acquitted of assaulting his girlfriend. The judge ruled that to be inadmissible in the murder trial.) He was the son of a well-respected lawyer, and he'd just two years earlier suffered the tragic loss of a brother to suicide.

On the other hand, Huguely was well aware of his ongoing alcohol issues—the blackouts he reportedly told friends about, and the public service sentence he got after threatening to kill an officer trying to arrest him. If jurors were told about those incidents, they could lose sympathy for someone who should have known better, even if he was too drunk to at the precise moment of his crime.

Yeardley's drinking could theoretically have played a role in her death, Spitz said ("Anything's possible," he regularly testified in trials), but the issue would likely become a contentious one between the prosecution and defense. Spitz had seen it before.

PART IV

"It's the Elephant in the Room"

Chapter 25

After George Huguely V appeared via closed circuit television on May 4 for his arraignment, he was entitled to a speedy preliminary hearing. Apparently, he didn't want one.

By law, the preliminary hearing—basically a baby version of the trial, meant for prosecutors to lay out just enough of their case to convince the judge that there is sufficient probable cause for the case to move forward—is supposed to be set soon after arraignment. Very often, however, suspects agree to postpone the date to give their lawyers enough time to collect and digest the evidence and prepare themselves for a defense. After the preliminary hearing, the judge decides whether the case should be forwarded to a grand jury, which then determines whether the defendant should face trial. With a case like the one against Huguely, there was no reason for defense lawyers to rush.

Huguely had admitted a fight with Yeardley, and his lawyer had stopped short of denying any culpability, instead calling it a tragic accident. If Lawrence was preparing to fight for a lesser charge, as legal onlookers expected, he faced the difficult task of convincing a judge that the prosecution didn't have enough evidence to justify the first-degree murder charge. At the preliminary hearing stage, the judge doesn't need to be convinced beyond a reasonable doubt. Rather, she must be swayed only enough to believe there is probable cause that a crime was committed. And that standard is far lower. Most states define probable cause as a "reasonable belief" the person committed the crime. Thus, the standard from preliminary hearing to trial shifts from "he might have done it" to "it's unreasonable to think anyone else did."

Huguely's defense would be significantly helped if his lawyers were able to nix the first-degree murder charge before it ever reached a jury. And that's typically why a defendant in a high-profile murder case might waive his right to a speedy preliminary hearing—to give his lawyers as much time as possible to gather evidence before both sides begin presenting their cases in court. The defense's job, while not easy, was simple: undermine the prosecution's case at every turn. If Chapman planned to argue that Huguely had murder on his mind, Lawrence needed to be ready to prove that his client had just meant to sit down for a chat.

Predictably, Huguely waived his right to speediness, and his preliminary hearing was scheduled for Thursday, June 10.

Less predictable was his lawyer's decision to not request bond. In many cases, it's perfunctory, even if it's unusual that a judge would grant someone charged with first-degree murder the freedom to roam the streets while murder charges loomed. Many lawyers at least request that their clients be allowed to go home under house arrest, monitored by Global Positioning Satellite technology to track their whereabouts. Lawrence skipped the request.

Some speculated that in May, so soon after the slaying, the vitriol was too intense. Perhaps Lawrence would try to secure Huguely's release after his scheduled June preliminary hearing.

John Zwerling, for one, didn't question Lawrence's decisions. He knew his colleague as a fine attorney with a stellar reputation.

"He has developed a reputation over the years as being very competent," Zwerling said. "So is his partner."

Liz Seccuro, the UVA alumna whose rapist had been defended by Lawrence and Quagliana, had a different take.

"They are paid to plant a tiny seed of reasonable doubt into the mind of just one juror," she said. "It's business. That's all."

Francis Lawrence had been selected as one of Virginia's so-called "Super Lawyers" by the magazine of the same name every year since 2006. *Super Lawyers* is a rating service for lawyers; those chosen are selected based on peer nominations, peer evaluations, and independent research, according to its mission statement. Lawyers aren't able to buy themselves onto the list, the organization insists, and the final list may represent no more than five percent of the lawyers in the state.

Lawrence graduated from Washington & Lee University in Lexington, Virginia, first for his bachelor's degree, which he obtained in 1971, and then for his juris doctorate, which he got in 1975. He lectured at the University of Virginia School of Law from 1989 to 1999, according to several online profiles, and once served as president of the Thomas Jefferson Inn of Court, an organization of attorneys, professors, and law students "who have an interest in litigation," and judges who hear cases in Albemarle County. Rhonda Quagliana, nearly sixteen years Lawrence's junior and a later addition to the 1974-established law firm on Charlottesville's Park Street, had graduated from the University of Virginia School of law with her juris doctorate in 1995; she'd previously earned a PhD from the college in 1992. She worked as president of the Charlottesville Albemarle Bar Association, a not-for-profit professional association meant to improve the Charlottesville area's legal profession.

The duo's firm claims to offer "individualized and courteous attention essential to effective legal representation," according to its online profile (www.stlawva.net). "Our attorneys have the experience and resources to handle complex cases."

As word of Yeardley Love's death spread through Virginia, the legal community began to speculate which lawyer would be tapped by Huguely's wealthy family. That they chose Lawrence and Quagliana was no surprise, Zwerling said.

* * *

Journalists from throughout the East Coast, as well as those with national operations such as ESPN and TruTV (formerly CourtTV), began gearing up for the planned June preliminary hearing. So did Brendan Fitzgerald, the *C-VILLE Weekly* reporter, who had followed the case from its onset. When perusing the court docket, Fitzgerald noticed that on the same day in the same courthouse, another young man charged with murder was also set to have a preliminary hearing. He couldn't help but be intrigued: The courthouse would teem with reporters covering Huguely's case, while the other went unannounced and uncovered in a courtroom just down the hall. Fitzgerald decided to write about it.

"It was characterized by an entirely different dynamic, a different economic dynamic, a different racial dynamic," he recalled. "And, because it involved a person involved in a completely different walk of life than George Huguely, we thought it an interesting project to put those two things side by side."

Unlike Huguely, whose name and face had flashed across television screens and in newspapers nationwide, relatively few people had heard of nineteen-year-old Demonte Burgess. Physically, he and Huguely both stood six foot two and weighed about 200 pounds. Both had been charged with ending another human's life. Both would see their cases begin in Charlottesville General District Court.

That's where the similarities ended.

Burgess was black; his listed address, "homeless;" his income, "zero." Huguely, meanwhile, came from a family owning second and third homes in the Outer Banks and Palm Beach.

Burgess's alleged victim, thirty-two-year-old Miguel Salazar, was shot in the head on January 22 in a trailer park after what police described as an "altercation" between four Hispanic men and two black men. Salazar's name is likely still unknown to many in the Charlottesville area; he certainly never graced the cover of *People* magazine after his death.

Huguely and Burgess lived just three miles apart, Fitzgerald noted in a June 8 story comparing and contrasting the men's predicaments, but "during the four years since Huguely moved to Burgess' hometown of Charlottesville to go to school, it seems unlikely the two would have crossed paths."

Fitzgerald wrote the piece, he said, because as the national media swarmed Charlottesville to cover Huguely's court hearings, he grew increasingly bemused at the picture they painted of the city. Writers used flowery words like "pastoral" and "bucolic." Meanwhile, the area in which Burgess lived was far from pastoral. It was, basically, a rundown slum literally on the other side of the tracks from UVA's well-to-do college kids. If ever there was a concrete example of town versus gown, this was it.

Fitzgerald compared the upbringings of Huguely and Burgess, and *C-VILLE* ran photos comparing the crime scene locations and the defendants' original homesteads. While Huguely attended an expensive private school for boys, Charlottesville High School had no record Burgess ever attended. Questions about Huguely's case were directed to, then ignored by, high-priced lawyers. When Fitzgerald approached the dilapidated duplex where Burgess had reportedly once lived, a man answering the door told him that Burgess "didn't do that shit," and threatened that he would "lump up" the next reporter to knock on his door.

Fitzgerald's point was that Charlottesville couldn't be summed up with pretty adjectives, and that while the whole nation might envision it as far removed from drugs and violence, people who really lived there knew the city had an underbelly that wasn't reflected in the crime statistics. (Burgess's case was forwarded to a grand jury, which determined in October 2010 there was enough evidence to send it to trial. As of now, Burgess is still awaiting trial.)

Fitzgerald's story, posted on *C-VILLE*'s Web site and featured on the front page of the weekly print publication, sparked some heated debate. Some applauded him for pointing out the disparities; others accused him of "stirring the pot." Readers of his story began commenting online just past midnight the morning it went to press. "I'm offended by your thinly veiled, baseless, and at this point quite cliché criticism of the UVA community just because of its privilege," one commenter wrote. "Please stop indicting all of UVA in this terrible tragedy."

It was telling, perhaps, that, despite Fitzgerald describing two separate slayings, the commenter referred to a "tragedy"—singular rather than plural.

As it turned out, neither Burgess nor Huguely actually had their hearings on June 10 as planned. While Burgess's was postponed until mid-August, Huguely's was delayed even longer, until October 7. Neither the defense nor the prosecution commented to reporters when asked why, though such delays aren't uncommon. The wheels of justice can sometimes turn agonizingly slowly.

Huguely reportedly awaited his court dates in isolation inside a 4-foot-by-8-foot cell inside the Albemarle-Charlottesville Regional Jail. Officials said he was segregated from the rest of the jail population and released about an hour a day for exercise, phone calls, or bathing. The jail, set off I-64 east of the 5th Street exit, is sprawled on a rural chunk of land away from the bustling UVA campus. Its locale, perhaps ironically, is among the most bucolic in Charlottesville. The jail was built in 1974 so that Albemarle County could shutter its outdated city and county jails. The staffs from those facilities were combined, and the Albemarle-Charlottesville Joint Security Complex was born. Its name was changed to the Albemarle-Charlottesville Regional Jail twenty-two years later, in 1996.

Aside from lawyer visits, Huguely was allowed a maximum of two visits per month, as per jailhouse rules. His family could send money to his "canteen fund"—an account from which he could buy commissary items such as shampoo, body wash, cough drops, or candy bars. Because he was segregated, he couldn't take part in some of the jail's inmate activities, dubbed "Beyond the Bars," such as its art show in

January 2011. Nor could he enroll in the jail's many classes, which ranged from culinary arts to crocheting.

Jail officials declined to say why Huguely was segregated from the others. Asked by Fitzgerald, Major Adam Rodriguez vaguely replied that "it could be either for disciplinary" reasons "or for his own protection—the safety and security of him." Despite early reports to the contrary, officials insisted Huguely had never been on suicide watch.

By mid-August, the October 7 court date had already been changed. Anticipating a mass of media, Charlottesville officials decided to push the date by one day and move it to the Charlottesville Circuit Court, which contained a larger courtroom than would be available in the district court.

Police Spokesman Ric Barrick told reporters that Charlottesville had turned to other cities that had handled high-profile cases for advice on how to handle the crush of journalists who surely would descend on the city come trial time. For example, they had contacted Chesapeake and Virginia Beach to find out how those cities handled the hundreds of reporters who arrived to cover the 2003 sniper trial. (In that case, John Allen Muhammad and Lee Boyd Malvo were linked to twenty shootings, resulting in thirteen deaths in Virginia, Maryland, Alabama, Georgia, Louisiana, and Washington, D.C. Both men were ultimately convicted.)

"We're not exactly sure what's going to happen through the trial, or how much interest we're going to have, but the interest has remained since the beginning of this incident," Barrick told one reporter. "We're going to need more space, and we're going to need to coordinate things a little bit more carefully and strategically than we currently do in Charlottesville."

While reporters waited to cover the preliminary hearing, bits of details in the case slowly trickled out thanks to the media consortiums' constant pressure to have public documents released. Every few weeks, some of those details would appear under headlines such as "New info released in

Huguely-Love case." The stories would invariably be short and direct, with no quotes from family members, lawyers, or even friends of the victim or suspect.

Josh Bowers, a UVA associate law professor, said that with each new story came reinvigorated interest in the case around Charlottesville. The lulls in between developments were so lengthy that it gave people who might otherwise have grown tired of the story time to regroup and get re-invested.

"Even if they were getting sick of the massive coverage, by the time a new development occurred, the story was somewhat fresh again because the last development had occurred some months ago."

Summer brought the first sustained breather. Aside from a smattering of quarter-turn updates, the case parties fell quiet, as did Charlottesville as a whole. The TV trucks and spotlights had been packed up and hauled away. About one-fourth of the student population had graduated, and a new crop of freshmen were enjoying that contemplative recess between high school graduation and college matriculation.

Bowers was impressed that so little leaked out.

"The parties have been somewhat admirably tight-lipped," he said. "We want our justice system to be transparent, but we want it to be transparent during the trial process. We don't want our cases litigated in the courts of public opinion, and by newspapers and other media. That kind of public judgment has the tendency to flip the presumption of innocence on its head. We see an exacerbation of reputational harm simply from the levying of charges itself. Ideally, you want at least to let the process play out in court without too much in the way of guilt and innocence arguments being made through media outlets. I'd rather see those arguments made in an open court."

Plenty of journalists would have agreed with Bowers, but in August came the realization that Huguely's first day in court might not come by year's end.

Chapter 26

The summer break wafted through Charlottesville like a lazy afternoon, and by Saturday, August 21, thousands of students crowded the streets as they moved into their homes away from home both on and off campus. While orientation wasn't required, it was offered from Saturday through Monday, with courses beginning that Tuesday. The town's temporary serenity gave way to the all-too-familiar horn-honking SUVs and parking-garage nightmares of another academic year.

Huguely's constantly changing court date loomed overhead, and though the summer had offered a reprieve, the case cast an ominous shadow across the again-bustling campus. Students filled the bookstores stocking up on academic supplies—notebooks, textbooks, and, of course, UVA sweatshirts and hoodies. Parents helped their youngsters move in to residence halls and apartments during the day, then flooded the city's family-friendly restaurants at night. Some young adults dragged their folks to the bars, bracing for their months-long separation over some beers.

The university had scheduled a weekend's worth of orientation events, including a so-called "move-in day 'oasis' fair" at the Aquatic & Fitness Center. Complimentary drinks were served while parents and students toured the recreational facilities and programs, enjoying some air-conditioned relief from the ninety-degree scorcher outside. Inside O-Hill Dining Hall, it seemed easy to pick out the fresh faces from the returning students—one group looking wide-eyed and slightly lost, the other a bit more comfortable with the routine—as hundreds flocked to have their photographs taken for their all-important student identification cards. Minority students were invited to a bevy of events, from ethnic-targeted meet-and-greets to a gathering for lesbian, gay, bisexual, and transgender students. One evening wrapped up with a Welcome Back Concert at John Paul Jones Arena.

Teresa Sullivan, UVA's newly minted president, welcomed the students in an hour-long speech. Though Sullivan had just three weeks prior moved into her new home at Carr's Hill—which had housed every UVA president since its completion in 1909—she already had made plans to address Yeardley's death in what she dubbed a "Day of Dialogue" on September 24.

In public speeches, Sullivan addressed Yeardley's death, even if she didn't always mention the young woman by name. In one speech to the Student Council on the first day of classes, she tasked the student representatives with empowering their classmates.

"You will help change the patterns of bystander behavior," Sullivan said. "Of course, we are each responsible for our own actions, but as members of this community, we also have responsibilities for one another. We are responsible for being aware, for recognizing threatening situations and behaviors, for reacting appropriately, and for respecting each other."

Mostly, however, Yeardley wasn't mentioned at all that first weekend back on campus.

"We really haven't heard anything," said the mother of one Baltimore-born first-year student. "It's the elephant in the room. Everyone is thinking about it, but no one is saying anything."

They weren't yet, anyway.

* * *

Sullivan had left her job as a provost at the University of Michigan to become UVA's first woman president. Round and cheerful, she came to campus with her husband, Douglas Laycock, and brought a different vibe to the post than the men who preceded her. It was no doubt a daunting legacy to continue. Casteen had the helm for two decades, and despite the many successes he boasted, his last year without question was shadowed by sorrow. Sullivan's efforts to bring people together to talk about the previous year's tragedies were applauded by some who had worried the administration had so far fumbled the human side of the tragedies.

Sullivan touted her Day of Dialogue as a "first step in building the caring community we all want to have." She began the day with a speech, taking the stage after the Virginia Belles and Virginia Gentlemen student groups sang the same songs they had performed at Yeardley's vigil more than four months earlier.

"In a very real sense, we are picking up from where we left off last May," Sullivan said.

The university and its community were different now than they had been the previous May, she told the crowd. The fourth-year students had moved on, and 25 percent of the undergraduate student body—the incoming first-year class—was new. Some faculty hadn't been there the spring before, and neither had Sullivan, she acknowledged.

"Some faculty weren't here last spring; I was not here last spring," Sullivan said. "Those of us who weren't in Charlottesville last May experienced Yeardley's death from a distance. Even from a distance, it was heartbreaking," Sullivan said.

But this day was to be about more than Yeardley, she added. The year prior was unusually tragic, marked by the deaths of seven students, as well as the slaying of Morgan Harrington. While some of the deaths happened elsewhere and seemed unpreventable, others haunted the university grounds.

"We are left to wonder if we might have done something differently to change what happened," Sullivan told the somber crowd. The question was especially impossible to ignore in Yeardley's case, when a young life was, by police accounts, ended by repeated and vicious blows to the head. Sullivan said that those who knew Yeardley even peripherally had to be wondering if they could have done or said something to change the trajectory of tragedy. To save a life.

Not everyone wanted Sullivan to go through with her planned day of discussion. The new president's staff had fielded angry phone calls from concerned parents who wanted her to call it off.

"Some expressed the opinion that we should not talk about these issues, that these issues are depressing or upsetting, and that young people should not have to consider things that are depressing or upsetting," Sullivan said. She understood the hesitancy. They were difficult matters to discuss and ponder, and she was as uncomfortable as anyone having to talk about them in her first weeks as university president. It would be easier to ignore the subjects, and certainly more palatable for parents sending their beloved children away from home to think they'd be inherently safe.

The Victorians, Sullivan said, had no qualms talking about death, but they wouldn't dare to talk about sex. Though the word "sex" triggered laughter in the crowd and allowed Sullivan a brief moment of levity, her point was this: "In our society, we talk constantly about sex but don't dare talk about death."

People have unique perspectives on violence and death, their standpoints painted by life experiences. Some in the crowd had experienced abuse only from a distance, Sullivan said. Some had never experienced death. Others had witnessed both first-hand, and perhaps even been the victims of violence or abuse themselves.

"We need to understand and respect reality, that these are intensely personal matters for some of us," she said.

Unlike Yeardley, whose face and story were splashed across newspaper and magazine covers, most victims suffer in silence and anonymity, Sullivan added.

"We gather today for those people, too," she said. "Although we have seen horrible events right here in Charlottesville, we acknowledge that violence, bias and abuse are national and global problems. All over the world, victims of hate and abuse are suffering, many of them with no recourse for help or even for making their suffering known."

She encouraged those who gathered to speak openly with each other about Yeardley's and Morgan's deaths, as well as Huguely's arrest. With Sullivan's arrival came a new student-led program called the Let's Get Grounded Coalition that focused on so-called bystander behavior. The group united representatives from thirty-five student organizations across the campus to work with the university administration on creating a safer community. Will Bane, a University Judiciary Committee member and member of Let's Get Grounded, told the *Cavalier Daily* that the initiative encourages students to seek help when needed.

Let's Get Grounded played a big role in Sullivan's Day of Dialogue, during which faculty members led small group discussions in rooms across campus. The talks had lofty titles like "Am I my sister's/brother's keeper?" and "Are we a caring community?" Student groups such as the Minority Rights Coalition set up booths on the campus grounds and chatted with passersby. Fewer students showed up for the discussions than expected, and male students were particularly underrepresented, according to reports, but organizers considered the event a success.

"It's not so much a day for solutions as a day for questions to keep the conversation going," Sullivan had said. "The solutions will come later. Today is the first step in building the caring community we all want to have."

Sullivan promised to follow up the daylong discussions so that the ideas and concerns presented wouldn't end up as wasted words. Let's Get Grounded went a step further and began developing training programs to combat the so-called bystander effect. As of late September 2010, more than 500 students and faculty members had been trained, and the group was creating pledge cards to pass out to students who promised to "recognize, react and respect" problems that they might otherwise have seen and ignored.

The same day as Sullivan's dialogue, Judge Downer decided to again postpone Huguely's court date. Instead of appearing in October, Huguely was to have his preliminary hearing January 21, 2011. Again, there was no explanation for the decision, though it wasn't a particularly surprising one. No one in the Huguely camp appeared to be in a rush. Even if Huguely ultimately was convicted of a lesser crime than first-degree murder, as his lawyers clearly wanted, he still could face a hefty amount of time behind bars, and he would be credited for time he had already served. It was more important that his lawyers be completely prepared rather than rush to trial. And at this point, Huguely remained in solitary confinement, apparently safely removed from other prisoners who might want to make a name for themselves by harming the high-profile suspect.

Downer made it clear, however, that despite the intense media scrutiny of the case, there would be no cameras allowed inside the courtroom once the preliminary hearing got underway. Ric Barrick, the police spokesman, said reporters would be given room to write and record their stories in a space near the Charlottesville General District Courthouse.

To John Zwerling, the Charlottesville-area defense lawyer, this was good news. Downer had made it clear he would ban the gavel-to-gavel coverage that some news outlets undoubtedly had requested.

"Putting a trial on television changes the dynamics," said Zwerling, whose firm handled the CourtTV extravaganza that was the Lorena Bobbitt trial. ("That put CourtTV on the map for a while," the lawyer mused.)

"First of all, the judge becomes extremely cautious and puts his or her instincts away, which is usually bad," he said. It's tough on attorneys, too, he added, because even the best, most experienced lawyers can start doubting themselves when they know people will be commenting every day on every little thing that occurred in the courtroom.

And, with an audience watching, sometimes lawyers feel pressured to perform—even when the best move for their client is to sit down and shut up.

"Some of the best cross-examinations are 'No questions, your honor,'" he said. "I've seen famous lawyers destroy a witness who had actually helped them. They destroyed the value of all the good stuff they gave. The lawyers may want to shine and sometimes that's consistent with effectiveness, but sometimes it is not. It makes you shake your head."

Even the jury feels pressured with cameras in the courtroom, Zwerling said. People outside of the trial pass judgment on the verdicts handed out inside because they feel they have real insight into the case thanks to the TV coverage. In reality, however, TV viewers of a trial are able to see and hear arguments for which the jury isn't present.

Despite the repeated delays in the preliminary hearing, the case itself still appeared before Downer for occasional motions. It was during one such motion in December 2010 that Huguely's lawyers dropped a bombshell—one that cast aside the "tragic accident" defense and instead attempted to exonerate Huguely altogether.

Chapter 27

The newspaper headlines on December 16 were sensational:

"Yeardley Love died from drugs, not assault, defense says."

Some even nixed the attribution, so the headline read as fact rather than conjecture.

The day prior, Dr. Jack Daniel, a pathologist from Richmond, Virginia, in private practice and hired by the defense, shocked the courtroom when he testified that he disagreed with the commonwealth's medical examiner and believed that Yeardley Love didn't die from blunt force trauma to her head. Rather, he said, the young woman died of cardiac arrhythmia caused by her consumption of alcohol and the prescription drug Adderall. The arrhythmia in turn caused insufficient blood flow to her head, Daniel said.

The doctor said the lack of oxygen caused "ongoing damage" that proved fatal.

Toxicology tests revealed that Yeardley had .05 milligrams of Adderall per liter of blood in her system—considered a therapeutic amount—as well as a blood-alcohol content of .14%—nearly twice the legal limit to drive in most states. In searching the coed's room after her body was discovered, police recovered a prescription bottle in her name for Adderall, which contains amphetamine.

Daniel said he examined Yeardley's brain and found that she suffered no lethal injuries. Any damage that did exist, he said, could have been caused while emergency responders administered CPR in their efforts to save the young woman's life. This was counter to the opinion of Dr. Bill Gormely, who had conducted the initial autopsy. Gormely told the court that the Adderall and alcohol "were not enough to have contributed to her death."

Yeardley's skull was not fractured, Gormley acknowledged for the first time in open court, but he noted a two-to-three-inch hemorrhage on Yeardley's scalp.

"It wouldn't necessarily cause death, but it could in conjunction with other injuries," Gormley told the court.

Add that to bleeding deep inside her brain, and Gormley said his findings pointed to "some sort of force."

Daniel disagreed, insisting that the patterns Gormley said were caused by a beating were "unusual for blunt force."

"Vigorous CPR caused these injuries interpreted by Dr. Gormley as primary traumatic injuries," Daniel said.

The battle of experts had begun earlier than expected.

Adderall is the brand name for a stimulant marketed largely to people with attention deficit hyperactivity disorder and narcolepsy. Designated a psychostimulant, it's thought by scientists to work by increasing dopamine and norepinephrine in the brain to make the taker feel more alert and better able to concentrate. It is also supposed to increase libido and reduce fatigue. Many psychiatrists prescribe the medication and find it a godsend for certain patients.

"There are people with [attention-deficit disorder] who can be on big doses and function just fine, and in fact need it to function well," one psychiatrist said. "I don't think of it as a drug with a very narrow window of dosage, like Lithium. Lithium has a narrow window between what's therapeutic and what would be toxic. Adderall isn't that way."

Generally, ADHD drugs aren't considered very dangerous when taken as prescribed. Some doctors even prescribe the medications to elderly people suffering from acute depression.

Seniors who previously refused to get out of bed have been known to rally back from the blues when given Adderall, Ritalin, or other ADHD drugs.

"They're not the beastly drugs that some people make them out to be," according to one psychiatrist.

Still, since its introduction in the 1990s, Adderall has caused controversy. Some people have complained that their heart seems to race after a dose, and the drug's advertised risks—glossed over in both print and TV ads with fine print and rushed voice-overs—include sudden death among people with heart abnormalities, stroke, heart attack, hypertension, psychosis, seizures, and aggressive behavior.

Adderall is abused plenty, too. People who take it when it hasn't been prescribed to them—or who take more than is recommended for them—can get a speed-like rush, one that can prove to be as addictive as cocaine.

At universities, it's sometimes dubbed a performance-enhancing drug, and not necessarily for athletes. Some misuse it as a study drug as users claim it keeps them awake and focused much longer than usual, providing much-needed fuel for their all-night cram sessions. Entire Web sites are devoted to young adults praising the drug's effectiveness.

"I love Adderall," one poster, identifying himself as Andrew, wrote on www.squidoo.com. "If I need to pull an all nighter, all I have to do is pop more pills and I'll be good to go, concentration and everything. Regular people can go for up to seven days without sleep if they take Adderall two to three times a day because it eliminates fatigue." Wrote another: "It has helped me through some of my darkest days. I wouldn't come down so hard on college students or anyone who uses it to enhance their performance. Most professionals and athletes all use some kind of enhancer."

In February 2005, Health Canada, the government department responsible for national public health in Canada, suspended sales of Adderall after twenty reported deaths. Of the deaths, twelve were from strokes, two of which were in children. In a letter to Shire Pharmaceuticals, which manufactures Adderall, Health Canada wrote that the "identified risk of sudden death following recommended doses cannot be managed by label changes." Shire shot back that the suspension came as a complete surprise. The U.S. Food and Drug Administration didn't follow Canada's lead, finding that the data wasn't definitive enough to merit a change in either Adderall's labeling or marketing in the United States. Six months after the ban, Health Canada agreed to allow Shire to resume its Adderall XR sales, provided it agree to some conditions: The company had to revise its patient information to reinforce that using the medicine could cause sudden cardiac death; it had to send letters to healthcare professionals explaining the risks associated with the product, and it had to commit to improving its post-market surveillance of the drug and update safety information to Health Canada.

But that hardly quieted the debate surrounding Adderall. Director for the Center of Alcohol Studies Robert Pandina conducted a study in 2007 that focused on Adderall use among Rutgers University students who did not have a prescription for the drug. The study found that nearly twelve percent of the 122 students surveyed said they used Adderall, while nearly 90 percent said they used alcohol. When asked why they used the ADHD drug, most said it was to beef up their academic performance. The study also found that more than three-quarters of the students found the use of Adderall without a prescription was socially acceptable.

According to Sober Living By the Sea, a treatment community based in Newport Beach, California, up to 25 percent of students enrolled at competitive universities have taken Adderall as a study aid. Another study, administered by the federal National Survey on Drug Use and Health, found that while just 6.4 percent of students said they had used the drug in 2008, college students between the ages of eighteen and twenty-two were twice as likely to abuse Adderall as nonstudents.

By all accounts, Yeardley did not fall into that category. According to court documents, her prescription for Adderall was valid. But her doctor likely would have warned her about another potential Adderall pitfall: the way it interacts with alcohol.

Studying aside, there's another use of Adderall rampant among college students: to keep the party going. Users report that they take Adderall before drinking to stave off the effects of alcohol, allowing them to drink longer without feeling drunk. Plenty of online forums discuss this effect, complete with descriptions of crushing the pill and snorting it to get even speedier results. Mixing alcohol and Adderall can even lead to alcohol poisoning, according to the Office of Alcohol and Drug Education at the University of Notre Dame:

"The stimulant effect can cause students to prolong use resulting in consuming unhealthy amounts of alcohol, which has lead [sic] to cases of alcohol poisoning. Stimulants in the system can block the depressant effect, shutting off the warning signs to a person's body that they may be drinking too much."

Instead of feeling drunk and drowsy, someone mixing alcohol and Adderall might well end their night by passing out, having been able to fend off the typical symptoms of drunkenness for longer than is healthy.

The complaints are similar to the ones circulating around drinks that mix caffeine and alcohol. Take the Four Loko controversy: The caffeinated drink had a 6% or 12% alcohol by volume content, depending on which state it was sold in. After a series of college students landed in hospitals because of Four Loko benders, the federal Food and Drug Administration put pressure on the drink's makers, finally forcing them to remove the caffeine from the product.

Francis Lawrence and Rhonda Quagliana, Huguely's lawyers, seemed prepared to argue that mixing Adderall and alcohol could have been the sole cause of Yeardley's death. During a December court hearing, they asked to see all of Yeardley's medical records from her time at the University of Virginia. They argued it could prove crucial to their defense strategy.

"This is an important time to have available to us very important information," Lawrence told the court.

Judge Downer, however, declined the request. It took him a week to make his ruling, during which time he said he reviewed all of the medical records Huguely's lawyers had sought.

"I find nothing even remotely material to his case in there, with the exception of what has already been described previously," the judge said from the bench on December 22, referring to the Adderall/alcohol levels the night Yeardley died.

"I'm not going to permit a fishing expedition," Downer said.

Lawrence pressed further. He wanted to know if Yeardley had any "diet or weight" issues—both of which could also weaken her heart and perhaps make her more susceptible to an Adderall-sparked cardiac arrhythmia. The judge said she didn't.

"There is nothing remotely embarrassing or unusual for a woman who is a student-athlete," he said.

The new Adderall defense caught many off guard. Death is rare even among those who abuse the drug; onlookers wondered how Huguely's lawyers planned to convince a jury that an appropriate dose killed her.

"It's not likely that the alcohol and therapeutic Adderall played a role in the death," speculated Daniel Spitz, the Michigan forensic pathologist not connected with the case. "Repeated head impacts are the real issue and seem to be what caused her death. The etoh [ethanol in alcohol] and Adderall are of course helpful to the defense because it gives them something to put in front of the jury as a potential cause. Also, it will help cloud the real issue and allow them to try and minimize the severity of the head trauma."

John Zwerling saw the Adderall hearing as possible insight into Lawrence and Quagliana's defense strategy. They had seemingly shown their cards early on when they described the death as a tragic accident—a move that left many assuming they wouldn't deny Huguely's role in the death, but would do their best to argue the charges down. But with this latest turn, it seemed possible that they had an ace up the sleeve.

"It could be that it's a two-prong approach," Zwerling said.

He likened it to the strategy his firm had laid out for Lorena Bobbitt, who infamously maimed her husband in 1989 by cutting off his penis and tossing it in a field.

"The defense there was 'self-defense, and in any event, I was temporarily insane,'" the lawyer recalled. The jury bought one of the two defenses, and found Bobbitt not guilty by reason of insanity.

Megan Pringle, the *Good Morning Maryland* anchor, said the newsroom was aflutter with the Adderall development.

"It's crazy what's happening now," she said shortly after the defense's revelation. "Every intern at our station said, 'Oh, everyone takes Adderall.'"

Liz Seccuro, the UVA student whose 1984 rape on campus finally resulted in a conviction twenty-two years later, was especially outraged by the turn of events. She called the "Adderall defense" disgusting, and characterized the defense's attempt to peruse all of Yeardley's medical records as particularly disturbing.

"They'd want to find anything—birth control, antidepressants, suicide attempts, abortions, eating disorders, cutting, alcohol abuse," she said. Luckily, she added, "the judge said 'no.'" He'd allow the inclusion of Adderall, which was found in her backpack and was allegedly being taken for the right reason (ADHD) and in the correct dosage.

"But it's their job to defend Huguely, not to make the dead girl look good," Seccuro said. "That said, I do think there is a broader issue of 'blaming the victim' at stake and it's become more permissive in courts, even when we speak of a deceased victim. Even when we have a defendant who admits to shaking her around the neck violently, causing her head to repeatedly strike a wall. So, yes, I do think that there's a fine line between defending a client and making a victim out to be the one who somehow caused her own death by associating with such an alleged perpetrator. She broke up with him. He bashed in her door with his foot. She had every right to feel safe in her own home with a locked door. That is domestic violence."

Seccuro took to the Huffington Post, considered by many to be among the most powerful news Web sites in the world, to write an opinion piece about the case. To her, she wrote, the defense "might as well be saying [Yeardley] is a speed junkie."

"It's unorthodox, even shocking, but not surprising," she wrote. "They must go after the cause of death and try to remove their client, who allegedly confessed to hitting Love, from the full responsibility for his actions."

Chapter 28

In mid-December, the Washington *Examiner* posted a story headlined "No death penalty for Huguely, cops say." The lead paragraph said exactly that: "Prosecutors have no plans to seek the death penalty for George Huguely V. . . ." But it was the second paragraph that was picked up by the Huffington Post Web site and reprinted around the world:

"And there is a growing consensus that the case will be settled in a plea deal before trial, said persons close to both the prosecution and the Huguely family."

The story, written by journalist Hayley Peterson, wasn't unexpected. Anytime a case drags out in court, there obviously exists the possibility that the defense and the prosecution could be negotiating behind closed doors. After all, the vast majority of convictions aren't the result of trials, but of plea deals, Bowers said.

"Ninety-five percent of convictions are the result of guilty pleas, and the overwhelming majority of those guilty pleas were the result of some explicit or implicit plea bargains," he said. "Very few—five percent or fewer—end up being litigated at trial."

With murder cases, the figure drops a bit for a few reasons. For starters, there is more at stake. Defense lawyers are fighting for more than a few years of their clients' lives;

they're sometimes fighting for life itself. And prosecutors aren't as willing to let a murderer plead to a lesser crime as they are, say, a first-time dope dealer or a robber. Then you add in the wishes of the accused, and things get even more complicated.

"Criminal defendants are sometimes quite present-focused and don't always take the long-range view," Bowers said. "If you have a twenty-five-year-old confronting the possibility of fifty years in prison or life, he or she might go ahead and try to get an acquittal because the results of a conviction by either trial or plea seem intolerable."

Still, he added, about two-thirds of murder convictions are historically the result of guilty pleas.

"Trials are a relative rarity even with murder charges," he said.

It wasn't a surprise then that Peterson found sources willing to say that a plea deal was likely in the Huguely case. What *was* shocking, however, was that one of the sources was a Charlottesville police spokesman.

Lieutenant Gary Pleasants had helped field the early media onslaught in the Huguely case, appearing by phone on Velez-Mitchell's CNN show two days after Yeardley's body was discovered. It was an unusual step into the limelight for a man who typically was interviewed about Charlottesville's petty crimes: Not two months before the murder, he was the prime police source for a story about a rash of motor scooter thefts throughout Albemarle County. As the immediate crush calmed, however, most media calls were shipped to spokesman Ric Barrick, who declined to say much on the record.

So it was a surprise to most when Pleasants was the *Examiner* story's main source on the plea-deal discussion.

Peterson wrote that prosecutors would lay out just enough evidence at Huguely's preliminary hearing to convince a Charlottesville judge to send the case to trial: "But Pleasants says it is unlikely the case will make it to opening arguments. . . . He said he believed it is likely that [District Attorney] Chapman and Huguely's defense will instead negotiate a settlement."

Charlottesville defense lawyer David Heilberg chimed in, telling the paper that he believed prosecutors would want to settle if the commonwealth's case was strong enough. "[Prosecutors] are getting what they want out of the case by agreement: Angling for Huguely to plead to something, whatever it might be, [for a sentence] not less than forty years, and then let a judge decide," said Heilberg, who was not connected with the Huguely case.

To some, a plea deal seemed the best option for both sides—especially the Loves. Bill Mitchell, who buried his daughter Kristin in 2005, couldn't have fathomed having to sit through weeks of gut-searing testimony at trial.

"I feel terrible for what the Love family is going through," he said. "Unless Huguely pleads and goes away, the Love family will be dragged through hell all over again. Unfortunately, the legal system is not about getting to the truth and then administering a sentence. It's about either 'sending him to a life sentence' or 'making it seem as if he wasn't the responsible party'—as if he were the victim."

Mitchell wanted to see his daughter's killer spend as much time behind bars as possible. But he also believed that families traumatized once by heart-breaking loss could face even more trauma once mired in the judicial system.

"[P]eople who kill people don't belong around innocent women. Ever. You can quote me," Mitchell said. "That life of freedom should be forfeited. I don't believe in 'serving time and paying a debt to society' any more than my daughter will come back to life after she serves a term as a dead person in fifteen to thirty years. His life isn't worth more than hers. If anything, for what he did, it's worth so much less."

But the news of a possible plea sparked outcry from some, especially victims' rights activists. Liz Seccuro again wrote an outraged piece that ran on Huffington Post. She couldn't help but connect the recent unveiling of the Adderall defense with the heightened talk of a plea arrangement. Were Huguely's lawyers providing a sampling of the character assassination to come?

"What Huguely and his team are doing is trying to allow a frisson of reasonable doubt to creep into the mind of just one sympathetic and uninformed juror in order to set him free, hang the jury or have a mistrial," Seccuro wrote. She found it insidious and disgusting, she wrote, as well as a red herring. Instead of focusing on Huguely's behavior, they instead were aiming to sully the reputation of a young woman "who, by all accounts, was extraordinary in every way."

In a later interview, Seccuro said she wrote the piece to rail "against any sort of plea deal that blamed the victim."

"In this case, Rhonda and Fran [the defense lawyers] are trying to say that Yeardley's perfectly safe and prescribed use of Adderall caused her death," Seccuro said. "Um, yeah, I'd have a heart attack too if my 200-plus pound . . . ex-boyfriend kicked in my door. She died of blunt force trauma," she said, echoing the autopsy.

Seccuro compared it to the defense Lawrence and Quagliana provided her own attacker: They had argued that Beebe's attack was a "thoughtless college sex encounter" during which Beebe behaved in an "ungentlemanly manner."

"Yes, the 'Twinkie Defense' for the ages," Seccuro said. "So, nothing new for these two. They are just doing their jobs."

The Charlottesville Police Department tried to repair the damage.

"As for talk of a plea deal, I believe that officer spoke out of turn," Barrick said in an e-mail. He assured reporters that the January 21st preliminary hearing was going ahead as planned and "I anticipate the upcoming court date to be important to attend."

From then on, getting answers to even the most mundane what's-next questions in the case became all but impossible.

Chapter 29

Yeardley's family kept quiet in public about the young woman they had lost, declining interviews from Oprah Winfrey and Piers Morgan, according to some close to the case. While Sharon Love said she worried that any pretrial publicity might hurt the case against Huguely, she also said that her sister—Yeardley's aunt—planned to write a book about the ordeal and that she preferred to let the book speak for the family. But while she and Yeardley's sister said nothing to the media, they and other loved ones toiled tirelessly behind the scenes creating an organization designed to both honor Yeardley's memory and help other young adults, regardless of the outcome of the criminal trial.

In mid-September, Yeardley's family and friends unveiled the One Love Foundation, a nonprofit organization created as "a tribute to Yeardley Reynolds Love, who wore #1 as a lacrosse player at both Notre Dame Prep and the University of Virginia. Yeardley lived her life with one purpose: to make her world a better place." The foundation, online at www.joinonelove.org, includes heart-adorned messages such as "inspire others." It is a registered 501(c)(3) organization, meaning it is a tax-exempt charity.

One Love's creation made headlines across the country, including on ABC's *Good Morning America*. By the time of its unveiling, the foundation already had several fundraisers in the works, including a Baltimore Orioles game, a golf tournament, and a marathon. Notre Dame Prep, Yeardley's high school, announced it wanted to build a turf field in honor of their slain alumna, and funds raised by One Love would help offset the costs. The school also aimed to create a scholarship in Love's name. The Texas-based Charles T. Bauer Foundation offered a challenge match to donate, dollar-for-dollar, all gifts up to $500,000. The exchange would support a scholarship fund to provide a full, four-year scholarship every fourth year for a Notre Dame student.

Sharon Love released a short statement to the media about the foundation:

"The mission of the foundation is to encourage and develop in children and young adults four qualities of character that Yeardley exemplified—service, kindness, humility, and sportsmanship—that together add up to One Love. The foundation would like to 'bring out the Yeardley' in everyone. . . . It is our turn to make Yeardley proud, and we will do our very best."

The foundation's Web site spells out its lofty goals, which include encouraging young adults to "choose a path of goodness." Among its other aims: to help children and young adults participate in service programs, to draw attention to society's "unsung heroes," and to create a character-based program to bring sports, specifically lacrosse, into underprivileged communities. "In turn, the beneficiaries of such programs would be encouraged to 'pay it forward' and volunteer in their own communities." The site includes a brief biography, describing Yeardley's upbringing and ambitions, as well as a copy of the high school essay she wrote about herself that had been handed out to mourners at her funeral. The family also posted photographs of Yeardley from happier times— swimming with friends, at the beach with her family, dressed in her Sunday best with her sister, smiling broadly with friends. In one picture, she mugs to the camera in her lacrosse gear, jokingly jutting out her bright green mouth guard. In another, she stands alongside roommate and teammate

Caitlin "Caity" Whiteley, who would later discover her battered body. In the photograph, the girls are beaming; both are wearing #1 jerseys.

The foundation's site includes ways to donate, as well as links to One Love merchandise, from T-shirts to wristbands to bumper stickers. Donors are encouraged to leave messages, which the foundation posts online:

"Yeards, the girls play with your sticks and we feel you right here with us. Keeping you close . . ."

"For our children, may they always love and honor life like this young woman did."

"I keep a little bit of Yeardley with me every day, and I miss her so much! This is just a small tribute to the impact she had on me as a friend and mentor at UVA, and I just feel so lucky to have met someone as beautiful, caring and kind-spirited as her. I will always remember her."

The last message was signed by Boyd Vicars, a member of UVA's field hockey team.

The site closes with a quote from Mother Teresa: "So let us always meet each other with a smile, for the smile is the beginning of love."

Hoping to raise money for the foundation, the Timonium, Maryland–based Baltimore Coffee and Tea Company released a special blend in Yeardley's honor. The coffee mixed two beans—Costa Rican and Brazilian Santos—to create something "a little sweeter and a little softer, to emulate her," Norman Loverde, the company's executive vice president, told journalist Nick DiMarco. "It's a make-everybody-happy kind of coffee. That's what she was about."

For each $9.50 bag of "Yeardley's Blend" that it sold, the company said it would donate $5 to the One Love Foundation.

Loverde said his motivation was simple: He had sent his daughters to Notre Dame Prep, and his family had always placed importance on giving back to the community and the school. The company had been roasting and cultivating coffees at its 9 West Aylesbury Road location for fourteen years,

DiMarco reported, and had regularly developed private-label coffees for local businesses and fundraisers.

"This is our niche," he told DiMarco. "It's a part of our culture and philosophy. We've always done this."

But Yeardley's Blend hit closer to home, Loverde admitted. One of his daughters had been friends with Yeardley, and the slain girl had been to his home and played with his children.

"I don't think you need much motivation for this. I'm a parent," Loverde said. "My daughter being friends with her, obviously we're affected by it. It's tragic. . . . We're just trying to make something good out of something bad."

Catherine Barthelme, one of Love's best friends involved with the One Love Foundation, told DiMarco that the coffee was a "great personalized way to keep Yeardley's memory alive.

"It's one of the positive things that has come out of this tragedy, that everyone has come together to keep Yeardley's memory alive," Barthelme said. "I think that every single girl in my class could say this, but she had the most contagious laugh and smile."

Yeardley's Blend became a popular gift at Christmastime, allowing people to both buy coffee for loved ones and donate to the One Love charity. The foundation also planned a New Year's celebration marking January 1, 2011—or 1/1/11, an appropriate date for a young woman who had worn a #1 jersey. Tickets to the $75-a-person event sold out in late December and, just days later, the foundation announced that it had reached its first fundraising goal.

"Notre Dame Preparatory School is pleased to announce that a $500,000 challenge grant from the Charles T. Bauer Foundation has been met," read a news release from the high school. "With the funds, the school may begin two projects honoring deceased alumna Yeardley Reynolds Love: The Yeardley Reynolds Love Field, and a scholarship in Ms. Love's name."

Of the $500,000 raised, One Love donated $220,000 in gifts and pledges, the school reported.

"This challenge grant received tremendous support from the NDP community and beyond, locally and nationally, demonstrating the regard people hold for Yeardley and her family," said headmistress Sister Patricia McCarron in a released statement.

School spokeswoman Cami Colarossi told Patch reporters that school officials were taking "sheer delight in the fact that this one grant is really launching two projects. We are thrilled with that."

Sharon Love again spoke to the media through a released statement: "We are so grateful for the support of the community. We are thrilled that . . . future generations of need-based students will have the opportunity for a NDP education. We all know how special NDP was to Yeardley, and think this is an amazing tribute to her."

As the weather grew bitter, many of Yeardley's friends sent messages to the Love family offering support and prayers. Even strangers sent their version of comfort online—one such message, sent via the social networking site Twitter, called on people to pause and remember the Loves on Christmas Day. Their grief must have been crippling.

Outwardly at least, the One Love Foundation kept its messages upbeat and succinct. Through its own Twitter account, it posted thank-yous to followers as it promoted the foundation. As the holidays neared, its Twitter account, @JoinOneLove, posted photographs of college-age girls wearing One Love T-shirts and bustling crowds at events such as one held in a Baltimore bar called Pickles Pub. Notre Dame Prep hosted the Yard for Yeardley event Oct. 1, inviting supporters to watch the Baltimore Orioles take on the Detroit Tigers at Camden Yards. Tickets cost $15, and proceeds went to the Love fund. In another play on words, the "Every Yard for Yeardley" racing team formed, raising money through donations for a November run in Richmond. The team ultimately raised more than $60,000, according to the foundation, and as of late January, the team had re-launched in hopes of raising $10,000 more for the Charlottesville 8K, Half-Marathon, and Marathon to be run April 9.

On Christmas Day, One Love sent out a simple message: "Merry Christmas and Happy Holidays from the One Love foundation! Thanks for all your support!" Barely a week later, it sent an emphatic thanks to the 800 people who took part in the "1.1.11" fundraising event: "You are all amazing!!"

The benign comments and fundraising efforts highlighted how the Loves chose to outwardly mourn: by turning to activism. It was a method that Morgan Harrington's parents had used as well as they grappled with their daughter's recent murder. REMEMBER MORGAN T-shirts for sale at www.findmorgan.com helped support both a memorial scholarship at Virginia Tech, and the construction of an educational wing in an African village. But while the families were similar in their attempts at advocacy, they deviated when it came to sharing their grief. Gil Harrington, Morgan's mother, continued to turn to the Web to vent, to post poems, to describe how life was like a minefield around the holidays.

"There is a lot of pain in discarding family traditions that are fractured for us without Morgan taking her part in them," she wrote in January.

The Loves had endured two horrific losses in less than a decade: first John Love, then Yeardley. How many broken family traditions were they being forced to endure?

Nick DiMarco, editor of the Lutherville-Timonium Patch (an online news organization backed by AOL), had by then written several stories about Yeardley, particularly about the outpouring of community support in the months after her death. Out of respect for the still-pending trial, he refrained from asking questions about the criminal case but asked to learn more about Yeardley as a person. The most he had learned about her personality was that she was a "sweet, sweet girl," as Loverde had described. DiMarco was employed as a research assistant for this book.

He contacted officials with Notre Dame Prep, Yeardley's high school, and at first was greeted kindly by a public relations representative. Soon after, however, he received a terse e-mail from the school's headmistress, which stated that "no one affiliated with Notre Dame Preparatory School will participate in the research in any way." She demanded that DiMarco "cease" his research "regarding this project or any other information about Miss Love or her family."

While taken aback, DiMarco complied and reached out next to Karen McGagh, a Love family friend and self-described spokeswoman for the One Love Foundation. The two spoke amicably on the phone about DiMarco's intended research and agreed to communicate via e-mail. During one e-mail thread, McGagh abruptly replied, "Hi nick! (sic) I will not be speaking with you on this issue." The signature line on the email read, "Sent from my iPhone."

Then DiMarco received an e-mail from a woman with whom he had spoken for Patch's story about "Yeardley's Blend," the coffee whose sales had benefited the One Love Foundation. The woman thanked DiMarco for his story, then continued:

"I understand that you now have a new assignment. I would ask you not to use my name as a frame of reference for that or any other assignments. . . . Again, I appreciate your coverage of Yeardley's Blend."

DiMarco finally made headway with St. Joseph Parish, home of Yeardley's elementary school. Sister Anne O'Donnell, the school's principal, agreed to organize a gathering of Yeardley's former teachers to talk about the young woman behind the headlines. On Friday, January 14, she led Di-Marco to a work area of the school where about twenty-five teachers were sitting at tables after a work session. The students had been given the day off for an extra long weekend, thanks to the following Monday being Martin Luther King Jr. Day, a national holiday.

DiMarco again explained his intentions—that he wanted to assist in a manuscript meant to humanize Yeardley and describe what kind of person the world had lost with her untimely death. The teachers agreed and began to talk about Yeardley's younger years—her bright smile and blue eyes, her loving relationship with her father.

Four and a half minutes into his interviews, DiMarco was interrupted. O'Donnell pulled him out of the room, saying she had been contacted just then by someone with the One Love Foundation.

"It was like going to the principal's office," DiMarco described. "O'Donnell said that I could no longer be there and asked that all information I had collected be given back to her. I said I could not do that."

DiMarco collected his things and was escorted from the building.

It was a frustrating experience. DiMarco considered himself a sensitive reporter who had clearly spelled out his intentions both in writing and in person. Weeks later, one of the sources would reach out to him again to ask for help publicizing another fundraising event, and while she apologized for her earlier snubbing, she still declined to describe the young woman for whom the money was being raised.

Chapter 30

As January got under way, people began gearing up for the anticipated preliminary hearing set for the 21st. But the month had barely started before the prosecution made an announcement that would change everything:

Huguely faced new charges.

On Friday, January 7, District Attorney Warner "Dave" Chapman issued a memo on city letterhead announcing that five additional warrants were requested and issued against Huguely. Now he faced charges of felony murder, robbery, burglary, statutory burglary, and grand larceny. Until this point, Huguely had faced one charge: first-degree murder. George was to be arraigned via video feed the following Monday in the Charlottesville General District Court.

The memo reminded reporters—and the public—that the new warrants were still nothing more than allegations. "Every person is presumed to be innocent unless and until proof beyond a reasonable doubt is established before a judge or jury." And it suggested that Chapman expected the defense to ask that the preliminary hearing be delayed yet again.

Late in the day, Lawrence and Quagliana released a statement saying the new charges were not a surprise.

"These additional charges were not unexpected and we have been fully prepared to defend against them. We think it is significant that the amended charges acknowledge that there was no premeditation."

Word of the new charges piqued curiosity among the gadflies. Did this imply that prosecutors no longer felt they had enough evidence to prove Huguely had intended to kill Yeardley—a necessity for a first-degree murder conviction? Or were these new charges meant to offer the defense some wiggle room in which to reach a plea deal, possibly sparing Huguely from having to face trial?

John Zwerling guessed neither. Upon hearing of the additional charges, he said they seemed as though they would be more beneficial to Huguely's defense lawyers than to the commonwealth.

"There's plenty of punishment attached to murder," he said. "I imagine it would have zero effect on negotiations."

Felony murder is a form of first-degree murder that looks quite similar on paper. Both mean you're charged with killing someone, and if you're convicted, you'll likely spend life behind bars. But they differ when it comes to intent. While first-degree murder requires premeditation, felony murder means that someone died while you were committing a felony that generally is considered dangerous. For example, if a gunman robs a store and kills the resisting storeowner, he maybe didn't go to the store to kill anyone, making it tough to prove premeditation. But because he caused the victim's death while he was committing a robbery, he could more easily be convicted of felony murder.

Before January 7, Huguely hadn't faced other felonies. Now, he faced several, robbery among them. According to the search warrants, the only item taken from Yeardley's apartment during the attack was her laptop. That perhaps constituted burglary, but it raised another question of intent: Did Huguely go to the apartment to steal the laptop, or was that an afterthought? Unless prosecutors could prove that Huguely went to his ex-girlfriend's apartment intending to bash in her door and steal her laptop, they could risk handing a jury reason to reduce the charge significantly.

Josh Bowers, the UVA associate law professor, saw the

charges as a chance for the prosecution to come at the murder theory from multiple angles.

"It's advantageous for a prosecutor to pursue a felony murder theory where such a theory is available," Bowers said. "It provides an additional opportunity to make out the top charge—the charge of murder—without having to actually demonstrate that the defendant had a guilty, culpable mindset as to the death itself. All the prosecutor needs to do is prove that the elements of an underlying felony were met, and a death resulted."

In short: felony plus death equals murder.

"It's better for a prosecutor to have two theories than one," Bowers continued. "You don't want to have so many theories that you leave the jury confused, but having two ways to make the case is probably reasonable."

Bowers laid out an example he teaches to students in his substantive criminal law class, a required course for first-year law students at UVA: Let's say a man steals a car. He wants to avoid drawing the police's attention, so he drives exceptionally carefully. He obeys speed limits, signals when he turns, and yields to passing ambulances. Despite all these precautions, a child jumps into traffic and is mowed down by the stolen car. The child dies, and the car thief is arrested. Bowers said that it would be difficult for the prosecutor to win a first- or second-degree murder case against the car thief, and it might even prove impossible to sway a jury to convict him of manslaughter because the thief was neither reckless nor grossly negligent. But it could be possible for the prosecutor to charge the thief with felony murder—because felony plus death equals murder.

"There are limitations, of course, and it varies from one state to another what felonies will serve as a predicate, as a trigger, for a felony murder charge, and there are also questions of causation," Bowers said. But in nearly all states that have felony murder on the books, burglary and robbery charges would qualify—and now Huguely was faced with both.

* * *

Though many inmates would have happily left the confines of their jail cell for a daytrip to the courthouse, Huguely waived his right to appear at the next Monday's arraignment in Charlottesville General District Court. Instead, his lawyers appeared alone—and indeed asked for more time to review the newly added charges.

"Judge, I can say that both sides have been moving with diligence, and the commonwealth certainly has been cooperative, but there is a bunch of stuff still out there," Lawrence said in court.

He and Quagliana still needed to analyze about twenty of the more than 100 pieces of evidence collected against their client in the case, Lawrence added. Judge Downer agreed to the continuance, saying that justice would be better served if the case weren't rushed to a preliminary hearing. The latest rescheduling marked the third time the defense won a delay, first from June to October, then from October to January, and now until April. No one ever accused the wheels of justice of spinning too quickly.

The sides couldn't immediately agree on a date that worked for everyone, but within a week, they had settled on April 11—three weeks shy of the one-year anniversary of Yeardley's death.

Chapter 31

With the rescheduling came a jolting realization: Both the men's and women's lacrosse teams would be immersed in their new seasons by the time the horror of the previous year even began to unfold in a courtroom.

The new academic year was well under way. Christmas break had come and gone. The twinkling strands of multi-colored lights had forced some festivity on the tragedy-weary town, and then were packed away for another season. Yeardley's jersey number was retired, and the roster for the women's lineup began with #2—freshman Lauren Goerz of California. She was one of eleven freshman players. It was a young team, featuring just four seniors. The previous year, the team had had seven freshmen and six seniors.

In contrast, Huguely's jersey number had seemingly been resurrected. In the days after the slaying, the official UVA men's Web site at www.virginiasports.com dropped him from the lineup. Suddenly, the online roster jumped from #10 Chris Bocklet to #12 John Haldy. Huguely's number, position, statistics, and photograph were outright deleted from each of the four years he had played on the team. For the 2010–2011 team, however, #11 reappeared, having been handed over to Pat Harbeson, a freshman from Annapolis,

Maryland, who undoubtedly knew well the history behind the number he now bore.

The women's team had played in a series of fall and winter scrimmages, but as late January approached, it was time to focus on the regular season. Their first game was set to be on February 19 at Loyola College in Baltimore, Maryland; the men's would be the same day against Drexel at home.

Together, both teams issued a statement acknowledging how difficult the time off had been:

With both of our seasons about to unfold, the players and staffs of the University of Virginia's men's and women's lacrosse teams would like to take a moment to express our thanks and gratitude to all our families, friends, fans and alums for their support since the tragic event of last May. Yeardley Love and her family remain constantly in our thoughts and prayers.

It is difficult to describe the emotions and feelings we have all experienced since losing a friend, teammate and fellow student. We are dealing with this loss as teams and individuals while also searching for ways to move forward. We are grateful for the support and counseling made available by the University and so many wonderful staff members.

Some members of the media have expressed a desire to interview us about what we have experienced during the last nine months. We understand the interest in wanting to explore our healing process, our thoughts and our feelings in greater detail. As we move forward and out of respect for the ongoing legal process, we do not feel it is appropriate for us to answer those kinds of questions. We will instead focus on our continued healing, our teams and the upcoming seasons. We appreciate your understanding.

Clearly, the death still hung over both teams. There would still be the occasional public remembrances—a moment of silence before some games and the counting to four before the women took the field—but for the most part, it would remain the elephant in the room.

Outside of the locker rooms, as the case against Huguely slowly crept through the court system, Yeardley's death continued to make headlines. Governor McDonnell's talk of proposing a state law that would require police departments to notify universities when a student was arrested collapsed under what he called "logistical issues." But different legislation aimed to make it easier to get protective orders.

Love's death also sparked proposed legislation to change Virginia's protective order laws. As it stood, Virginia didn't allow couples in relationships to get protective orders unless the pair was living together or had a child—meaning that the laws didn't help people embroiled in what experts call dating violence. Virginia Delegate Joe Morrissey, a Democrat from Henrico County, introduced legislation that would nix the cohabitation requirement. A similar bill had been proposed the previous year by Republican Delegate Robert Bell, but it was debated by police officers, domestic violence advocates, and attorney general representatives, and ultimately failed to win approval.

Morrissey said Love's death "has brought this to a head."

"Everyone in law enforcement is concerned with providing protection without swamping the system to the point where they can't provide protection to those who need it," Bell told reporters.

Morrissey hoped his bill would strike that balance.

UVA kept its promise to revise its seven-year-old self-reporting policy. New president Teresa Sullivan announced that all students would be required to disclose in writing their criminal records before they'd be allowed to access course material information and school e-mail services. The question would be posed as each student accessed the university's computer system, followed by a prompt that reminded them of their obligation to report new incidents within seventy-two hours of the occurrence. The change greeted students as they gathered in late August for the 2010–2011 academic year.

Sullivan, gathered with reporters for a news conference about the policy change inside the campus's Madison Hall, said the background check requirement "has been changed from a passive notification system to a more active notification system," and that students caught lying about their criminal histories would be found in violation of the school's honor code. In short, like hundreds of test cheaters and thieves before them, they would be expelled.

Student athletes were required to inform their coaches of an arrest within twenty-four hours. If coaches found out that a player conveniently forgot, as Huguely apparently did, he or she would face sanctions from the athletic department.

"The one place where there is a difference is student athletes have additional obligations to the athletic program and their coaches," Dean of Students Allen Groves told reporters.

UVA's Division of Student Affairs also began reaching out to other colleges and universities in the commonwealth in hopes of devising a system that would enable them to alert one another if a student was arrested at another school.

Sullivan said she planned to walk the fine line between making the campus a sanctuary and forcing students to face a sometimes ugly reality.

"We cannot build a bubble around the Grounds," she said. "Things that happen, bad things that happen in everyday life, also happen on the Grounds."

Life moved on throughout the campus. The football season kicked off in early September with the team winning 34–13 over Richmond. The following month, as the leaves across campus turned vibrant shades of scarlet, thousands of alumni flooded the city and watched as the 'Hoos fell to their North Carolina rivals. Winter came and coated the city with snow just as students wrapped up the first semester of the academic year.

But there were signs, too, of Yeardley's impact. The

Women's Center on campus worked with university police to promote the Red Flag Campaign in October, also known as Domestic Violence Awareness Month. The campaign's goal—encouraging people to speak up when they saw signs of unhealthy relationships—fit perfectly with the "bystander behavior" training that Sullivan had been promoting. The Dean of Students also spoke to the school's daily newspaper to spread word that female students needing help could turn to his office for residence relocation assistance, no-contact orders, and no-trespass orders.

Yeardley's now-infamous apartment #9 no longer sits empty on 14th Street Northwest. One hundred days after the slaying, as a new crop of students crowded the Charlottesville campus, the apartment was rented out to four students who had signed the lease before the fateful day in May.

Katelyn Krause, a neighbor, told reporters that she helped the young women move into the apartment.

"It was just weird knowing what happened in that room, to be inside it," she said. "There's no way I could ever be so inclined as to take that lease . . . It's something that's going to be on your mind every night when you go to sleep. Just the thoughts of what happened in that room would keep me awake."

The battered door leading into Yeardley's bedroom, long ago removed by police as evidence, had been replaced. The blood stains and signs of struggle had long been cleaned away.

Huguely, too, was gone. He had celebrated his twenty-third birthday in a jail cell three miles away from the room where his ex-girlfriend's lifeless body had been discovered. New tenants had moved into his apartment two buildings away. The turnover would have happened regardless of the tragedy; both young adults would have left Charlottesville for their new lives as full-fledged adults. But standing at the Sadler Street T-junction, looking past the brick-and-cream apartment complexes toward the Corner businesses that bustled with students, it felt even months later as though something had irrevocably changed. Yeardley Love's death wasn't the first tragedy to bring the city to its knees, nor would it be the last. But for tens of thousands of students who had endured the heartache of May 2010, and for thousands more who would attend UVA in its aftermath, it would be the tragedy that defined their coming-of-age on a campus forced to acknowledge that its ideals didn't always match its reality.

Even if no one said so.

Epilogue

When it comes to criminal cases, time can change form, morphing from predictable metronome to mercurial ooze. Such is the case with the murder trial against George Huguely V.

Though the grand jury handed down its indictments in April 2011, Huguely's trial date was pushed off nearly a year to February 2012. The delay was prompted by many factors, including scheduling conflicts for the defense team. As of this writing, Huguely's lawyers have never asked that their client be released on bond. He remains in the Albemarle-Charlottesville Regional Jail awaiting his day in court. In a newly released mugshot, he bears the hallmarks of a prisoner: His once-shaggy hair—the en vogue look for a male college lacrosse player—is shorn off, his blue-and-orange jersey traded in for black-and-white jail garb. His face appears more angular, slightly hardened, but there's something still doe-like in his eyes, something that seems to ask, *How did I get here?*

One year after Yeardley Love's death, as spring slowly crept across the University of Virginia campus, the excitement of a graduating class was again tempered by bleak reminders of life's frangibility. The campus marked the May 3, 2011, anniversary quietly, but Yeardley's name again was forefront in the media, both mainstream and social. Thousands of Twitter users marked the day with the hashtag "#onelove" and asked that Yeardley's family be in their thoughts. At Notre Dame Prep, Yeardley's high school, family and friends gathered that day to remember her and to ask each other to "bring out the Yeardley."

"That's what we've encouraged people to do—a kindness for someone, make their day," Cami Colarossi, the school's spokeswoman, told a reporter.

Some of Yeardley's friends and family members spoke exclusively to *Good Morning America* to describe the friend they said saw the world through "sunshine-colored glasses" and to promote the One Love Foundation. Sharon and Lexie Love also broke their silence, speaking most in-depth to *Sports Illustrated*. Though they still refused to talk about the man accused of murder, they described the grief that threatened to level them—until they paused to ask themselves, "What would Yards do?"

"Nothing good comes from not being positive," Sharon Love told journalist L. Jon Wertheim.

It wasn't easy, she said. Sharon had grown accustomed to nightly phone calls with her youngest daughter, chats that always ended with "I love you." Lexie recalled sharing a bed with Yeardley in the days after their father died in 2003, just as the two had done growing up. The two felt like—and were often mistaken for—twins, despite their three-year age difference.

In some ways, life had moved on. Sharon returned to her job as a Baltimore schools teacher; Lexie worked as an IT specialist. But those were just day jobs compared to what had now become their mission—to do right by Yeardley.

The One Love Foundation had generated hundreds of thousands of dollars in donations. Its goal to build a lacrosse field bearing Yeardley's name at her high school alma mater was well under way, and in May, one male and one female Atlantic Coast Conference lacrosse player was to each receive the inaugural Yeardley Reynolds Love Unsung Hero Award. The foundation's Web site had grown and become more polished with each passing month, announcing new events in Yeardley's honor and new goals aimed to keep her memory alive.

The foundation and its success kept the women focused and motivated, providing them with their "good days." So, too, did the letters and emails that poured in from strangers worldwide.

"I'm not sure people realize how much little things help, how much of a difference it's made in our lives," Sharon told Wertheim.

The bad days could be triggered by a holiday, a birthday, or nothing at all, Lexie said.

"There are days when we're devastated," she said. "The emotions come out of nowhere . . . and it hits you: *This is real.*"

On May 3rd, UVA posted on its Web site an article that served both as homage to Yeardley and description of what steps the university had taken since her death. It recapped the Day of Dialogue organized in the fall by University President Teresa Sullivan and outlined other projects under way, including the creation of five new groups to discuss issues such as violence and socioeconomic class. The Let's Get Grounded movement continued its "Recognize, React, Respect" campaign to supposedly provide bystander intervention training, though its calendar of events was nearly empty.

The university said other measures had been taken as well: Patricia Lampkin, vice president and chief student affairs officer, sent a memo in the fall of 2010 to faculty to help them identify students who might be in abusive relationships. Lampkin also reached out to 70 other colleges and universities in Virginia requesting courtesy calls when a UVA student behaved inappropriately while in their area. (Thirteen institutions agreed to make those calls, and UVA reported that it had received one notification in December 2010.) Student conduct records were revamped in October 2010 to give officials room to store more data and documents and share that information with outside agencies "when appropriate."

Most importantly, students seemed more determined to intervene when they saw something amiss with a classmate.

"We are fairly certain that students are calling us more often and reporting incidents more frequently—something we want and encourage them to do," UVA Police Chief Michael Gibson said in the article.

"Students took the lead and have made important progress this year," Lampkin said. "I foresee that progress continuing as new leaders fill their shoes."

University officials still declined to discuss Yeardley or her case, however. One official told a journalist that workers had been warned not to talk with reporters near the anniversary of the death because the university had recently been alerted that Yeardley's family was considering filing a wrongful death lawsuit against the institution. As of this writing, no suit had been filed.

But Yeardley's memory is still honored at the university, most notably in the women's lacrosse locker room. There, long after Yeardley's #1 jersey was retired, her locker and nameplate remained.

"We all take a glance and very privately think for a few minutes when we see it," Coach Julie Myers told *Good Morning America*. "She still has a way of making us reflect back, but making us feel good about reflecting."

And Yeardley's story continued to reach strangers. Female lacrosse players at Perry Hall High School in Baltimore had never met the girl with the piercing blue eyes, but when their coach suggested a charity game, they immediately knew which charity they wanted to benefit. The girls sold bracelets, bumper stickers, and heart-adorned T-shirts that read "Lax for Love," raising hundreds of dollars for the One Love Foundation. During the game, the players lifted their lacrosse sticks and chanted, "One, two, three, Love!" each time they broke from a sideline huddle. The Perry Hall Gators won the game handily.

An overwhelmed Sharon Love attended the game. "We really didn't know anybody here before tonight, but they reached out to us to support a cause that we think is pretty important," she told a reporter. "It's just so nice of the girls."

No matter the trial's outcome, Yeardley's family and

friends said they would remain dedicated to preserving and promoting her legacy. It seemed to be the only way that anyone touched by Yeardley could assign meaning to the tragedy.

"The entire university still mourns her loss," Myers told *GMA*. "I think every month we try to get a little stronger, but what's happened in that time is she's gotten deeper and deeper into our hearts."

It's a legacy those who knew her say they want—and need—to live on.

The legacy of Love.